ART & CREATIVE DEVELOPMENT

FOR YOUNG CHILDREN

Aesthetic

EIGHTH EDITION

ART & CREATIVE DEVELOPMENT

FOR YOUNG CHILDREN

Jill Englebright Fox

University of Houston—Victoria

Robert Schirrmacher

CENGAGE
Learning

Australia • Brazil • Mexico • Singapore • United Kingdom • United States

CENGAGE Learning

Art and Creative Development for Young Children, Eighth Edition
Jill Englebright Fox
Robert Schirrmacher

Senior Product Manager: Mark Kerr

Content Developer: Kassi Radomski

Content Coordinator: Margaux Cameron

Product Assistant: Coco Bator

Media Developer: Renee Schaaf

Senior Marketing Development Manager:
Kara Kindstrom

Associate Market Development Manager:
Molly Felz

Content Project Manager: Rita Jaramillo

Senior Art Director: Jennifer Wahi

Manufacturing Planner: Doug Bertke

Rights Acquisitions Specialist: Tom McDonough

Production Service: Lynn Lustberg, MPS Limited

Photo Researcher: Scott Rosen, QBS

Text Researcher: Kristine Janssens, PMG

Copy Editor: Christine Sabooni

Text & Cover Designer: Lisa Buckley

Cover Image: © iStockphoto.com/rzdeb

Compositor: MPS Limited

For product information and technology assistance, contact us at
Cengage Learning Customer & Sales Support, 1-800-354-9706

For permission to use material from this text or product,
submit all requests online at **www.cengage.com/permissions**
Further permissions questions can be e-mailed to
permissionrequest@cengage.com

Library of Congress Control Number: 2013938463

Student Edition:

ISBN-13: 978-1-285-43238-0

ISBN-10: 1-285-43238-X

Loose-leaf Edition:

ISBN-13: 978-1-305-49545-6

ISBN-10: 1-305-49545-4

Cengage Learning
5191 Natorp Boulevard
Mason, OH 45040
USA

Cengage Learning is a leading provider of customized learning solutions with office locations around the globe, including Singapore, the United Kingdom, Australia, Mexico, Brazil, and Japan. Locate your local office at **www.cengage.com/global**

Cengage Learning products are represented in Canada by Nelson Education, Ltd.

To learn more about Cengage Learning, visit **www.cengage.com**

Purchase any of our products at your local college store or at our preferred online store **www.cengagebrain.com**

Printed in the United States of America
2 3 4 5 6 7 18 17 16 15 14

Brief Contents

Contents

SECTION ONE

Creativity

SECTION TWO

Young Children As Artists: A Developmental View

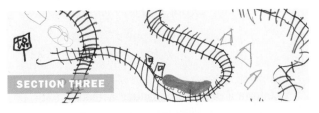

SECTION THREE

Art and Aesthetics

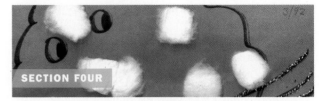

SECTION FOUR

Providing Art Experiences

SECTION FIVE

Roles and Strategies

Preface

Art education and artistic processing help children understand their world. When children look at art, they learn to make meaning of symbols that communicate ideas, experiences, and feelings that can be shared. Of course art is fun, but it is also mentally engaging. The art of young children may not resemble anything in the real world. With older children, art begins to approximate reality more closely. Young children, art, and creativity are very compatible. Young children can be noisy, active, and messy. Art too can be noisy, active, and messy. Art can also be quiet and meticulous, like a child who sits motionless while small fingers try to glue together pieces of paper, yarn, and ribbon. Art allows children to experiment and explore, to see what they can create. Their creative self-expression enhances their self-esteem.

The eighth edition of *Art & Creative Development for Young Children* is written for early childhood educators and those preparing to work with children in a public or private preschool, child care, and pre-kindergarten

through third-grade settings. Sound principles and basic art media are appropriate regardless of the age of the artist. The book will take you back to your own childhood to help you move toward your future as a professional early childhood educator who will help young children reach their creative and artistic potential.

Based on developmentally appropriate practices, this new edition continues to reflect an art focus, emphasizing child-directed (opposed to teacher-directed) activities and outlining an art studio approach for your classroom. It is full of ideas and activities for all children to enjoy integrating creative experiences in visual art, music, dance, drama, and literature into the early childhood curriculum.

Conceptual Approach

The book is written from three different perspectives attempting to synthesize the authors' training and experiences as artists, teachers of young children, and teacher educators. It is neither a cookbook of activities nor a review of theory and research; it blends theory and research with practical application. It is based on the developmental perspective that knowing what and how to provide for an art activity is as important as knowing why. The early childhood teacher plays a key role as facilitator within the recommended art studio approach, maximizing creative expression, responsible freedom, decision making, and discovery.

Organization

There are 16 chapters organized into five organizational sections: Creativity; Young Children as Artists: A Developmental View; Art and Aesthetics; Providing Art Experiences; and Roles and Strategies. Each section contains two or more chapters using photographs and questions to introduce the chapters that follow. The organization of the sections and chapters was carefully planned to introduce readers to key topics, build their understanding of the ideas, and then consider their application with children in classroom settings. Each section also includes a suggested "Letter to Families" that may be used within the college classroom to stimulate discussion on sharing key concepts from the section with families of children in the early childhood classroom.

New to the Eighth Edition

While the conceptual approach and organization of this book have stayed the same, this edition includes several exciting new features.

- **Learning Outcomes** at the beginning of each chapter correlate with main headings within the chapter and the Summary at the end of the chapter. The outcomes highlight what students need to know to process and understand the information in the chapter. After completing the chapter, students should be able to demonstrate how they can use and apply their new knowledge and skills.
- **naea naeyc DAP Standards Addressed in This Chapter** at the beginning of each chapter provides a list of the National Arts Education Association (NAEA) Standards, NAEYC Program Standards, and Developmentally Appropriate (DAP) criteria covered in each chapter. **Standards icons** throughout the chapter indicate where standards-related content is found within each chapter. In addition, a Standards Correlation Chart on the inside front and back covers provides a complete list of the standards throughout the book. Each one of these features helps students make connections between what they are learning in the text and professional standards.
- **TeachSource Video** boxes within the chapters feature footage from the classroom to help students relate key chapter content to real-life scenarios. Critical-thinking questions boxes provide opportunities for in-class or online discussion and reflection.
- **Did You Get It?** quizzes at the end of each major heading help students measure their performance against the learning objectives in each chapter. One question for each learning objective is featured in the textbook. Students are encouraged to go to CengageBrain.com to take the full quiz and check their understanding of each chapter.
- **Digital Downloads of Lesson Plans** at the end of each chapter provide grade-specific ideas for putting content into practice. The lesson plans in the text—and additional lesson plans not found in the text—can be downloaded from CourseMate and used in the classroom. (CourseMate can be bundled with the student text. Instructors, please contact your Cengage sales representative for information on accessing CourseMate.)
- **Up-to-date content** throughout includes a historical discussion of the Froebelian roots of art in early childhood programs; thoughts about the benefits and logistics of displaying children's artwork; an overview of responsive teaching and teachable moments as they relate to art for young children;

and a synopsis of play therapy, as it is used with young children.
- **Brain Connection** boxes highlight current topics in brain research.
- **Additional Resources** are now listed at the end of each chapter.

Standard Features

Abundant classroom-tested activities are the hallmark of this book and are provided in Chapters 2–16. Age ranges are provided for many activities; however, these should be regarded as guidelines only. A teacher's knowledge of a particular child's developmental level must be the main guide in determining the appropriateness of any activity.

While all of the suggested activities in this book encourage young children's development in producing and appreciating art, many support children's sensory exploration of various media and materials rather than their personal expression of emotions, ideas, and experiences. To help students and teachers distinguish between sensory exploration activities and personally expressive art activities, like activities are grouped together at the end of each chapter.

In *addition* to activities and the new features mentioned earlier, you will find many other features within the text:

- A photo and introduction for each section-opener.
- A **"Letter to Families"** at the beginning of each section-opener, which is also available for digital download.
- A **vignette** and related photo at the beginning of each chapter.
- **Hints** boxes within the chapters provide helpful time-saving suggestions for teachers by providing easy-to-use ideas and shortcuts like using chalk for art activities (Ch. 3), using glue (Ch. 4), how to prevent paint from spoiling and how to make your own finger paints (Ch. 5), working with clay (Ch. 11), and more.
- **Something Extra** boxes highlight additional information related to the main ideas of the chapter. Topics include "Tailoring Art for Children with Special Needs" (Ch. 4), "The Reggio Emilia Experience" (Ch. 7), "How Would You Approach This Art Activity?" (Ch. 10), and "Fact or Inference?" (Ch. 16).
- **An Opportunity for Teacher Reflection** boxes allow students to step back, reflect upon their own experiences, and apply them to the content at hand.
- Issues related to children with special needs are addressed throughout each chapter.

- A **multicultural icon** honors children's different cultural art experiences.
- A **Summary** correlated to the main chapter headings, **Key Terms** list, **Suggested Activities**, and **Review** at the end of each chapter.
- **Appendices** include Artistic Junk (Appendix A), Where to Go in Your Local Community for Artistic Junk (Appendix B), Art-Related Books (Appendix C), National Standards for Arts Education (Appendix D), and Multicultural Picture Books (Appendix E).
- **Glossary of Key Terms** includes precise definitions of the key vocabulary presented throughout the text.

Supplements

Creative Arts for Young Children Professional Enhancement Text

A supplement to accompany this text is the *Creative Arts for Young Children Professional Enhancement Handbook* for students. This resource, which is part of Cengage Learning's Early Childhood Education Professional Enhancement series, focuses on key topics of interest for future early childhood directors, teachers, and caregivers. Becoming a teacher is a process of continuing to grow, learn, reflect, and discover through experience. The *Professional Enhancement* text helps tomorrow's teachers along their way. Students will keep this informational supplement and use it for years to come in their early childhood practices.

Online Instructor's Manual with Test Bank

The *Instructor's Manual* to accompany *Art & Creative Development for Young Children* contains information to assist the instructor in designing the course, including sample syllabi, discussion questions, teaching and learning activities, field experiences, learning objectives, and additional online resources. For assessment support, the updated test bank includes true/false, multiple-choice, matching, short-answer, and essay questions for each chapter.

PowerPoint® Lecture Slides

These vibrant Microsoft® PowerPoint lecture slides for each chapter assist you with your lecture by providing concept coverage using images, figures, and tables directly from the textbook!

Education CourseMate

Cengage Learning's Education CourseMate brings course concepts to life with interactive learning, study, and exam preparation tools that support the printed textbook. Access the eBook, Did You Get It? quizzes, Digital Downloads, TeachSource Videos, flashcards, and more in your Education CourseMate. Go to CengageBrain.com to register or purchase access.

For instructors, CourseMate includes EngagementTracker, a first-of-its-kind tool that monitors student engagement in the course. The accompanying instructor Website, available through login.cengage.com, offers access to password-protected resources such as PowerPoint® lecture slides and the online Instructor's Manual with Test Bank. CourseMate can be bundled with the student text. Contact your Cengage sales representative for information on getting access to CourseMate.

About the Authors

Jill Englebright Fox is a professor of early childhood education and the Director of Assessment at the University of Houston–Victoria. After teaching kindergarten and first grade in the Texas public schools for eight years, Fox received her Ph.D. in Early Childhood Education from the University of North Texas. She continues to be active in early childhood classrooms as a volunteer, a professional consultant, a researcher, and a teacher educator.

Robert Schirrmacher was an instructor with the San Jose/Evergreen Community College District. He received his Ph.D. in Early Childhood Education from the University of Illinois. His experience includes teaching preschool, kindergarten, and first grade and teaching at undergraduate and graduate levels. He has assisted in Montessori schools and directed programs for young children. Schirrmacher has served as a consultant to parent groups and public and private early childhood programs. As an advocate for developmentally appropriate education and quality care for young children, the author has been involved in professional organizations at the local, state, and national levels.

Acknowledgments

We would like to thank children and parents with whom we have worked in Michigan, Illinois, Florida, Alabama, Virginia, Texas, and California, including all former and present students of child development and early childhood education who have helped us refine our thinking on children's art.

We extend our thanks to the faculty, staff, parents, and children at two child-development centers: San Jose City College and Evergreen Valley College. In addition, we thank the Children's Discovery Museum of the Golden Crescent in Victoria, Texas for allowing us to photograph the beautiful environments and activities they provide for children.

A special thanks to the staff and children of PS27 c/o Schuyler Elementary School, Schenectady Country Community College, Astor Services, Community Family Development, and Battery Park City Day Nursery in making this book special and unique.

Finally, our thanks to the following reviewers who provided us with feedback and ideas that helped us shape this eighth edition:

Jacqueline Batey, University of North Florida

Michelle Bauml, Texas Christian University

Debra Brodowski, Aiken Technical College

Johnny Castro, Brookhaven College

Patricia Clark, University of Maine at Augusta

Janice Glunk, Point Park College

April Grace, Madisonville Community College

Rea Gubler, Southern Utah University

Ann Renee Guy, Lawson State Community College

Jamie Harmount, Ohio University

Dan Keast, University of Texas of the Permian Basin

Cindi Nicotera, Harrisburg Area Community College

Julie Orgel, Lorain County Community College

Laine Rieger, Minnesota West Community & Technical College

Cindy Salfer, Ridgewater College-Willmar

Mary Sciaraffa, University Of Louisiana at Lafayette

Lorraine Weatherspoon, Sacramento City College

Lisa White, Athens Technical College

Pamela Wood, Humphreys College

Creativity

Because creativity peaks during the early years, it seems fitting that Chapter 1, Understanding Creativity, should contain an extensive discussion on the nature of creativity.

Look at the preschoolers in the photo. What are they doing? Is anything creative happening? The teacher has carefully planned the classroom block center around the theme of skyscrapers. This was prompted by an informal discussion in which a child shared her visit to a large city with "lots of tall, tall buildings that went way up high." Other children picked up the theme of "tall, tall buildings" and began to plan their own city of skyscrapers and busy streets. The teacher encouraged their interest by reading aloud from books about cities and skyscrapers and providing photos of

cityscapes. Based on these sources of information and their own experiences, the children began to explore what a city might look like. Their play is rich with language and social interaction. It is also open-ended in that there is no single right way to build the city.

Chapter 2, Creative Thinking, identifies components of creative thinking (also called divergent production) and activities that can be incorporated into small or large group times.

Art is an obvious way for children to express creativity, but it is only one of many ways. Chapter 3, "Creative Experiences," explores areas of play, language, music, and movement that incorporate creative expression.

Dear Families,

For children, creativity is a way of interacting with people and things in their environment. When children pretend a block is a cell phone or a bandana is a cape, they are demonstrating creativity. As children mature and begin to take different roles in their play, their creativity is evident in the language and actions of their characters. Play, particularly dramatic play, is important in helping children develop creativity because it allows them to move beyond the concrete and into a world where imagination is in control.

Helping children develop creativity is a primary goal of our program. Because children need time, space, and materials to realize creative potential, our classroom and our curriculum are designed to support exploration and problem solving. Our day is organized into blocks of time during which children can explore without rushing to the next activity. Our classroom is organized in learning centers. Each learning center offers children the opportunity to interact with a topic, use related materials in different ways, and act on information.

The materials in our learning centers are open-ended, encouraging multiple uses. In the block center, unit blocks can be used to build an airport, as food for a picnic, or even as tools for measuring.

Time, space, and materials are important for supporting creativity at home, too. Your child needs opportunities to choose activities and to play alone and with friends. Your child also needs inside and outside places in which to play without worrying about too much mess or noise. As a parent, you can support your child's creativity by being nurturing and responsive but also by enforcing expectations for your child's behavior. Creativity flourishes in environments where children feel safe to explore and experiment.

Sincerely,

Your Child's Teacher

1 Understanding Creativity

© Cengage Learning

Children can be creative with just about anything.

What do you see happening in this photo? The teacher has planned an art activity that will allow children to be creative.

The teacher provided different colors and weights of paper, as well as scissors and tape. It is best when children use colors that they themselves select and that they cut into the shapes they want. Some children cut large shapes and taped them together. Other children cut small shapes and taped them to make a design on a large sheet of paper. Some used markers to add details or texture. The child in the picture appears to be actively engaged and focused. How simple, and yet how creative!

Learning Outcomes

After reading this chapter, you should be able to:

1-1 Provide definitions of creativity.

1-2 Describe creativity as a process or a product.

1-3 Discuss the different explanations of creativity.

1-4 Identify obstacles to creativity.

1-5 Describe ways adults can facilitate children's creative expression.

1-6 Compare and contrast creativity with conformity and convergent thinking.

1-7 Discuss the relationship between creativity and intelligence.

1-8 Discuss the implications of brain research.

1-9 Explain the relationship between creativity and child development.

Standards addressed in this chapter

DAP Criteria
  1 Creating a caring community of learners
  2 Teaching to enhance development and learning
  3 Planning curriculum to achieve important goals
  4 Assessing children's development and learning
  5 Establishing reciprocal relationships with families

NAEYC Standards
  1 Relationships
  2 Curriculum
  3 Teaching
  4 Assessment
  7 Families
  9 Physical Environment

1-1 Definitions of Creativity

With whom or what do you associate **creativity**? Do you think of architecture by Frank Lloyd Wright, a painting by Georgia O'Keeffe, or Henry Ford's Model T? These are classic examples of the creative works of some very creative individuals. You may have other examples. Children were not included in the preceding list. Were they included in yours? Let's explore creativity and see how it relates to young children. Creative expression begins early in life (see Figure 1–1). Babies manipulate toys, explore space, discover their body parts, test hunches about their world, and even solve problems. For example, Lea wants a rattle she has accidentally kicked to the foot of her crib. Through trial-and-error, she discovers that she can get the toy by tugging at the blanket underneath it.

There are many ways to define creativity. Perhaps this has added to the confusion and misunderstanding surrounding it. People have different definitions for the same term. How would you define creativity? Some accepted definitions are:

- the ability to see things in new ways
- boundary breaking and going beyond the information given
- thinking unconventionally
- making something unique
- combining unrelated things into something new

How does your definition compare with these? Torrance (1963a), a pioneer in creativity research, chose to define creativity as the process of sensing problems or gaps in information, forming ideas or hypotheses, and communicating the results. For example, two 5-year-olds, Missy and Eric, want to build a school, but they have no blocks or pieces of wood. They decide to use shoe boxes, which are durable and stackable.

People who think creatively often have the ability to find connections between things that don't seem to be related. Their thinking may be described as **synergistic**, combining existing elements in new ways. **Serendipity**, making unexpected discoveries while looking for something else, may also be a key component of creative thinking (Gelineau, 2004).

Gardner (1993b) offers a four-part definition of creativity. He sees the creative individual as a person who regularly solves problems, fashions products, or defines new questions in ways that are initially considered novel but that ultimately become accepted in a particular cultural setting. First, Gardner believes that a person can be creative in a particular developmental domain, rather than across all domains. This directly challenges the concept of an all-purpose creative trait that underlies tests of creativity. Second, Gardner believes that creative individuals regularly exhibit creativity as opposed to having a once-in-a-lifetime burst of creativity. Third, he insists that creativity can involve fashioning products or devising new questions as well as solving problems. This greatly expands more traditional definitions that emphasize the making of products. Fourth, he believes that creative activities are only known as such when they have been accepted in a particular culture. Creativity depends on cultural judgment.

Although attempts to define creativity may provide a general feel for the concept, there are other ways to understand and explain creativity.

Photo Courtesy of Jill Englebright Fox

Figure 1–1 Creative expression begins early in life.

Did You Get It?

According to experts on creativity, creative individuals are incredibly and uniquely adept at finding _____ between different things.
  a. differences
  b. similarities
  c. connections
  d. uniqueness

Take the full quiz on CourseMate.

1-2 Creativity: Process or Product?

In viewing young children's creative activities, early childhood teachers have long pondered this question: Which is more important—the process or the product? The question remains the same whether the activity is play, music and movement, or art. Both sides of the **process versus product** debate should be explored. Is the process, or the "how," more important than the "what," the finished product that results?

Young children play for the sake of playing. They stack blocks for the fun of stacking. They make up words to songs and dance creatively just for the joy of it. For art, process involves active, hands-on doing, exploring, experimenting, trying out, and manipulating of artistic tools and sensory-rich media. Processing is serious work and a means to an end in itself. Processing honors the unexpected and provides opportunities for problem solving. These small twists in perception and thinking are what push children into creativity (Matlock & Hornstein, 2004). The focus and engagement in processing replaces a need to "make something." The reward and pleasure are in the doing—whether singing, dancing, playing, or engaging in art. It is not necessary to make something that is recognizable or rewarded by compliments. With the processing approach, there may not be anything to display on the wall or to post on Mom's refrigerator. Processing does not need to culminate in a finished product to validate its importance. The value of the activity is in the doing. Edwards (2006) calls this process approach *experiential*, in that children engage in the process of art without knowing what the steps will be along the way or what will result. Process-oriented children do not know or care what the outcome will look like, or if indeed there even is an outcome or product.

The process of doing art could be called "arting." According to Edwards (2006) and Isbell (2007), in the early years "arting" is more important than creating finished art products. Cherry and Nielsen (1999) state that the important goals of early childhood art are the involvement, the movement, and the discovery of self-accomplishment.

A focus on product rather than process argues the importance of making a final product and emphasizes that processing is secondary to that final product. Adult artists sell finished products, not the processes required to make them. According to Isbell (2007), some children become interested in products as they develop skill in using art materials and techniques. For them, the art product is important, but this importance should be self-imposed and not demanded by adults. Often, these children have an idea of what they want to make. This idea drives their artistic processing. They get excited when they execute their plans and something turns out the way they wanted. Often, they repeat the process to make more than one of the same artistic product. They enjoy others' recognition of their products as what they set out to make.

DAP **naeyc** A concern about the product approach should be discussed. Children may be tempted to bypass creative processing for the sake of making a product, especially if they expect adult recognition, approval, and reward. For example, a child may hastily draw a flower to hear a teacher say, "Oh, how beautiful. I love flowers." This is not the nature of art. Art requires children and adults to express themselves and leave a mark that is personally meaningful.

Artistic processing and product making go hand in hand (see Figure 1–2). A product is created out of processing, but even adult artists engage in endless processing before achieving an acceptable finished product. Still, artistic processing should be at the heart of early childhood art activities. Teachers should value children's processing without expecting a finished product. In turn, accept the interest of some children

Figure 1–2 Creative processing at the easel.

© Cengage Learning

(often older) in making finished products. Isbell (2007) proposes an interdependent progression in the process versus product discussion. She believes the creative process begins during exploration and play with tools and materials. After many experiences, children move to the next step by focusing on a particular approach. Once an approach is chosen, children use this method in the production level. The last step involves evaluating, or even reworking. It is difficult to pinpoint when one step ends and another begins in the visual arts. The very young child often spends more time in the exploratory stage, whereas the more experienced child may spend more time at the production level. Each step, however, is important.

Did You Get It?

In dissecting the process versus product debate of creativity, the "process" is considered the "_____."

a. why
b. what
c. where and when
d. how

Take the full quiz on CourseMate.

1-3 Art Explaining Creativity

Although there is no single definition of creativity, there are different ways to explain it. Creativity can be explained as:

- an attitude
- a process
- a product
- a skill
- a set of personality traits
- a set of environmental conditions

1-3a Creativity: An Attitude, Not an Aptitude

For young children, it may be helpful to view creativity as a way of identifying and solving problems. Creativity is a different way of viewing the world in which there are no right or wrong answers, only possibilities. Think of creativity as an attitude rather than an aptitude. Children demonstrate a creative attitude when they:

- try out new ideas and different ways of doing things
- push boundaries and explore possibilities

- manipulate and transform ideas and materials
- take things apart and put them back together in different ways
- physically play with objects
- imagine, engage in fantasy, or just daydream
- solve problems or try to figure things out
- ask questions or challenge accepted ways of thinking or acting

1-3b Creativity as a Skill

Although all children are creative, the potential to create remains dormant without practice. With practice, the potential to create becomes a reality. For example, the skill of playing tennis is quickly lost without practice. The skill of creativity also requires exercise to grow. Without practice, the abilities to write, make music, sing, dance, and paint would be lost. Creativity as a potential and a skill requires exercise. Sternberg and Lubart (1995) believe that creativity, like intelligence, is something that everyone possesses in some amount. Moreover, creativity is not a fixed attribute. It is something almost anyone can develop to varying degrees. In a discussion of creativity, many adults will state, "I'm just not creative." Everyone knows someone who is creative, but not all people believe themselves to be creative. Still, all people show some degree of creativity, whether in writing, sewing, cooking, making crafts, decorating, or even teaching! It is important to find a creative outlet and practice skills involved.

Still, why do some adults feel themselves uncreative when by contrast young children are considered highly creative? What has happened between early childhood and adulthood? Research suggests that the child reaches a peak of creative functioning during the early childhood years. Torrance (1965) plots the degree of creative functioning versus age. Creativity often peaks during the fourth year of life and is followed by a sharp drop upon entrance into elementary school. Only in a few adults do levels of creativity ever reapproach what they were in early childhood. Perhaps the push for conformity and academics in elementary school explains this drop. Yet this drop is not inevitable. Environmental conditions and practice will keep creativity alive.

1-3c Creativity as a Set of Personality Traits

The personality approach attempts to identify the personality profile of highly creative individuals. Researchers have identified personality traits that highly creative individuals share. Some of these include:

- an openness to the new and unexpected
- a tolerance for ambiguity

- a willingness to experiment and take risks
- impulsivity and curiosity
- a preference for complexity
- being highly intuitive and sensitive
- flexibility
- individualism, independence, and introversion
- nonconformity
- playfulness and a sense of humor
- a strong sensory awareness (Gelineau, 2004)

This list is extensive, and not every highly creative individual will possess all of these traits. Also, the list varies depending on the researcher. Torrance (1962) identified the following seven indicators of creativity that may be useful in identifying and explaining the behavior of the highly creative young child.

Curiosity. The child's questioning is persistent and purposeful. Curiosity can be either verbal ("What is that?" "Why?") or nonverbal (manipulation and active exploration).

Flexibility. If one approach fails, the creative child will try a variety of different approaches.

Sensitivity to Problems. The child is quick to see gaps in information, exceptions to rules, and contradictions in what is seen and heard.

Redefinition. The child sees hidden meaning in statements that others accept at face value. New uses are found for familiar objects. The child sees connections between things that appear unrelated.

Self-Feeling. The child has a feeling of self-importance and individuality. Self-direction permits the child to work alone.

Originality. The child has surprising, uncommon, interesting ideas.

Insight. The child spends much time toying with ideas and possibilities.

This set of global traits may provide assistance in identifying these individuals and understanding the nature of creativity.

1-3d Creativity as a Set of Environmental Conditions

If creativity is an inherent potential, there must be conditions or experiences that enhance or retard its development. Environmental conditions include people, places, objects, and experiences. Children do not create out of a vacuum. They need a source of inspiration or an experiential background from which to draw. For example, a child who has never visited an airport or been aboard a plane will have difficulty incorporating these concepts into play, movement, art, and other creative activities. By contrast, a child who has visited an airport and flown on a plane will be able to use them as pivots for creative expression. The greater one's background of experiences with people, places, and objects, the greater the range of possibilities to draw from in creative activity. Children's creative acts will incorporate what was previously learned and experienced, as well as new ways of expressing those experiences (Matlock & Hornstein, 2004).

DAP **naeyc** **Optimal Home Environment.** Obviously, the home environment is a critical factor in a child's creative development. Is there a home environment that optimizes creative development?

According to Healy (1994), parents who produce creative children share these characteristics:

- They show children how to be problem finders as well as problem solvers.
- They have full lives themselves and do not depend on their children to meet their emotional or achievement needs.
- They are not in awe of their child and do not defer to his or her demands or feel compelled to entertain him or her.
- They tolerate divergent ideas and mistakes made "in the service of learning."
- They provide discipline and structure to give children security to explore.
- They set realistic standards and encourage pride in achievement.
- They show active interest in the child's thoughts and creative efforts.
- They encourage a close, nurturing relationship as well as freedom of physical expression.
- They give children early responsibility for making choices and taking the consequences for their own decisions.
- They permit children to have solitude and develop imaginative thinking by daydreaming.
- They show children how to be curious and observant.
- They allow honest expression of emotions.
- They encourage children to feel intuitively as well as think logically.
- They do not put pressure on school for "competency" that excludes intellectual creativity.
- They expose children to a broad range of artistic and intellectual pursuits.

An Opportunity for Teacher Reflection

Ms. Berry's Kindergarten Class has been studying communities. The children are now creating a bulletin board display of their own community. Jermika is making a hospital. She has cut a large, gray rectangle from construction paper and carefully drawn in windows and doors. Now she is trying to cut the outline of a red cross to be pasted over the door. Twice she reaches in frustration for a new piece of red paper, as she decides the shape she has cut does not look like a cross. Suddenly, as she stares at the paper scraps around her, an idea occurs! "Look!" Jermika says excitedly to Ms. Berry. "If I put two rectangles across like this I can make a cross!" *How should Ms. Berry respond to Jermika? Should she reinforce Jermika's problem-solving skills or celebrate Jermika's creativity?*

Because sensory awareness is an important component of creativity, Gelineau (2004) encourages adults to provide multisensory opportunities for children's learning.

Did You Get It?

Which of the following is not a trait of parents who either willingly or by default present a child with an environment in which to flourish creatively?

a. They are highly tolerant of "mistakes."
b. They model curious and exploratory behavior.
c. They set realistic goals and standards.
d. They encourage social interaction and actively discourage solitude.

Take the full quiz on CourseMate.

1-4 Obstacles to Creativity

Just as a stimulating environment and family factors can enhance creativity, negative conditions can restrict it. Potential obstacles to creativity can come from:

- home
- school
- gender roles
- society, culture, and tradition

1-4a Home

Families often have expectations for behavior that creative children are challenged to meet. Highly creative children often question authority, limits, adult logic, and explanations. Families may view this as misbehavior. They may perceive and treat their creative child as odd, immature, abnormal, or naughty. Families may

need to be educated about the nature of creativity through classroom observation, readings, and informal sessions in which they discuss creativity and engage in creative processing themselves. Teachers who value and support creativity in the classroom find that young children are most successful when their families collaborate with the teacher to support creativity at home (Kemple & Nissenberg, 2000).

1-4b School

Too often, the creative child must operate in a classroom based entirely on conformity and convergent thinking. With the current emphasis on academics in early childhood education, little time may be spent on creative activities. It is also possible that some children feel confined in noncreative classrooms and shut down or rebel to protect their creative integrity. It is important for teachers to understand, value, and encourage creativity by providing curricular activities that foster it.

1-4c Gender Roles

Gender roles limit boys and girls to certain behaviors. Creative functioning, however, transcends gender role barriers. Forcing children to conform to stereotypical gender roles denies them their optimal development as individuals. We do children a disservice when we expect boys to be active, independent, and rugged and girls to be passive, dependent, and gentle. If gender roles were to dictate, boys would be denied access to quieter expressive activities, and girls would be denied access to reactive manipulative experiences. Either way, children lose, because both types of experience are vital to creative processing.

1-4d Society, Culture, and Tradition

Society, culture, and tradition are distinct concepts, but each dictates a certain set of behaviors, values, and attitudes that are transmitted to children in the form

SOMETHING EXTRA......

Profile of a Gifted/Talented/Highly Creative Child

All young children demonstrate creativity. Those who demonstrate high levels of creativity may be considered gifted and talented. Think of a child with whom you have worked and would call highly creative. What words would you use to describe this child? Although the following traits describe creative children, no one child will perfectly match this profile. Highly creative children tend to be:

- original, imaginative, spontaneous, resourceful, and uninhibited.
- sensitive to sensory stimuli and have heightened awareness. They are open to new ideas, see things afresh, and are intuitive.
- curious, alert, impulsive, willing to take risks, adventurous, and into everything.
- independent in thinking and social behavior. They can appear aloof and may prefer older friends and adults to their peers.

- developmentally advanced, precocious, fast learners with good memories and extensive vocabularies. They are interested in books and may teach themselves to read at an early age.
- perfectionists with a good sense of humor; they ask "why" questions.
- persistent, with a long attention span; they can stick with a plan or idea.
- nonconforming and unconventional; they question the status quo.
- Inventive, innovative, and good at solving problems.
- not overly concerned with being neat or prompt; they may be easily bored with routine and mundane tasks.

---

of expectations. Unfortunately, creative children may operate with a different agenda. Problems arise for highly creative children in a milieu where adults have all the answers and children are expected to fit a rigid behavioral mold or pattern. It is important to respect, reinforce, and uphold the expectations of society, tradition, and one's culture without sacrificing individuality in the process.

Did You Get It?

When operating under the expectations of the pressures of society, culture, tradition, morals, and mores, a creative thinker should _____ these expectations without sacrificing self.

   a. respect and uphold
   b. shun and reject
   c. bend and twist
   d. run from and escape

Take the full quiz on CourseMate.

DAP naeyc 1-5 Facilitating Creative Expression

Children need adults who facilitate creative expression. The following strategies send messages to children that their creative expression is valued.

1-5a Celebrate Creativity

Help children identify with creative heroes. For example, bring in telescopes on Galileo's birthday. Read books about creative individuals. Discuss their accomplishments. Ask questions to help children think creatively about these accomplishments: "What if we didn't have lights?" Turn off the lights and light candles. Discuss the importance of the lightbulb. Point out creativity when you see it: "A Velcro lunch box, now that's a creative idea." It's important for children to understand that creativity isn't limited to those who show special talents; creativity can flourish wherever it is supported and appreciated (Gelineau, 2004).

1-5b Value Children's Creativity

View creative development as a vital component of the whole child. Allow children the freedom to think and act differently. Accept attempts at creative processing that do not result in finished products. Discuss the importance of creativity with children, parents, staff, and administrators. Speak up against budget cuts for the arts or attempts to replace play-based learning with academic instruction and recess with structured physical education.

1-5c Be a Creative Partner

Empower children by making yourself available to enter their creative worlds. Be a play partner who follows the lead of children rather than imposing your own plot, sequence, and script (see Figure 1–3).

© Cengage Learning 2015

Figure 1–3 Follow the child's lead in creative activities.

🆔 1-5d **Provide Time and Space for Creative Expression**

Children need plenty of space to lay out materials and work alone or together to give form to ideas. Time and space should be fluid and flexible. Tables, chairs, and movable units may need to be rearranged for creative activities. Creativity often involves social interaction (Matlock & Hornstein, 2004) and may entail noise, movement, and clutter. An excessive concern for constant cleanliness or neatness inhibits creative "messing about."

1-5e **Provide Toys and Materials Conducive to Creativity**

Let children creatively use and transform toys and materials. Accept the fact that small blocks from one center will be transported to another for play. Clean smocks from the art center may find their way to the dress-up area to be used as capes or aprons. In choosing and providing toys and materials, open-ended items are more conducive to creative expression than closed-ended ones. Open-ended materials are loosely structured and do not require one specific use.

They have multiple rather than single outcomes. For example, water, sand, blocks, play dough, and building pieces are open-ended because they empower children to use them in different ways. By contrast, a puzzle is an example of a closed-ended material because it is designed with a single outcome or correct use: to fit the pieces together in a predetermined pattern. Although one can use puzzle pieces creatively—for example, as food or money—that is not their intended use.

Toys and play materials can also be categorized as simple and complex. Simple toys and materials foster a degree of creative expression, whereas complex toys and materials extend the potential for creativity. Toys and play materials that offer some degree of creativity can be made complex. For example, blocks alone are considered simple in that they can be creatively combined. Block play can be made more complex by adding props, including small containers, vehicles, and animals. The same is true for water and sand play. Adding kitchen containers to water and sand play expands the creative possibilities.

🆔 🆔 1-5f **Provide a Psychological Climate Conducive to Creativity**

Children flourish in a psychologically safe setting that respects, trusts, and empowers them to act autonomously without fear of criticism, rejection, failure, or pressure to conform. Children need to make choices and decisions and to do things on their own in their own ways. By providing an array of materials and activities from which to choose, the environment can be set up to foster autonomy. An overly structured day revolving around teacher-directed activities impairs children's creative development. Children quickly learn to override their drive for creativity and autonomy and instead become dependent on others for answers or solutions. If all the children in the classroom are made to feel that their contributions are worthwhile, then the classroom climate will support creative thinking (Gelineau, 2004).

🆔 🆔 1-5g **Weave Creativity and Creative Expression Throughout Your Curriculum**

Creativity should not be approached as an isolated skill scheduled into an already overcrowded day. Children cannot magically turn on their creativity to fill a half-hour time slot on Friday. The curricular areas (mathematics, social studies, science, language arts) provide ample opportunities for children to use both sides of the brain. For example, children may need to learn about the food groups and making healthy choices, but they can be creative in planning menus and making posters for healthy eating. A resourceful teacher finds ways to integrate creativity into the curriculum.

1-6 Comparing and Contrasting Creativity

Another way of attempting to understand and explain creativity is through comparison and contrast. Comparing and contrasting a concept with others that are similar or different is a way of understanding that concept.

1-6a Creativity versus Conformity and Convergent Thinking

Convergent thinking (noncreative) and behavior based on conformity are built into our educational system and reflected in school goals. There are facts and bodies of knowledge that we want all children to possess. For example, children need to know that up is the opposite of down, that STOP on the traffic sign does not mean to run, and that there are five pennies in a nickel. This type of knowledge involves memory and convergent thinking because all children are expected to produce one right answer. Beyond this, conformity in school often entails behaving in a certain way, with an emphasis on sitting still, speaking only when spoken to, obeying, not challenging authority, not questioning, complying, and doing what is generally expected. Obviously, conformity is important if groups of people are to get along. When it is carried to extremes, however, an emphasis on conformity and convergent thinking can kill the creative spirit.

1-6b Creativity vs. Intelligence

Creativity can also be compared and contrasted with intelligence. It has sometimes been erroneously assumed that a high IQ is needed to be creative. Research, however, indicates that high scores on tests of creativity are not correlated with high scores on IQ tests. A high IQ says something about intelligence, but it cannot guarantee high creativity. This is easy to understand because answering items on an IQ test

requires remembering bits and pieces of factual information and involves convergent or noncreative thinking. Thus, it is possible for a child with a high IQ to be quite uncreative compared with other children of average intelligence. It does seem, however, that some basic level of intellectual functioning and an average IQ near 100 is required for creativity. For example, a child must have some basic knowledge of the properties of a shoe box and transportation before he or she can creatively transform an empty shoe box into a moving van. Therefore, using tests of intelligence to screen highly creative children must be done judiciously. Such tests are merely one of many tools, including teacher observation and parental reports, which can be used. According to Torrance (1962), if we were to identify children as gifted solely on the basis of IQ tests, we would eliminate approximately 70 percent of the most creative. In summary, intelligence is merely one factor influencing creativity.

Because children's thinking is a concern of early childhood educators, it may be interesting to explore the relationship between intelligence and creativity. It appears that profiles for the highly intelligent child and the highly creative child do not match. Nor does the profile for the child of low intelligence match the profile for the child of low creativity. Wallach and Kogan (1965) studied the interplay of intelligence and creativity in school-age children. Four patterns emerged:

1. High intelligence and high creativity—These children were flexible and could be serious at one time and playful at another. They could easily adapt to different learning environments. They were very self-confident and displayed high attention and concentration for school tasks. They also engaged in attention-getting and disruptive behavior.

2. Low intelligence and high creativity—These children were frustrated and had a difficult time in traditional schools. This probably tended to make them feel unworthy and inadequate. They were cautious, lacked self-confidence, and engaged in disruptive behavior.

3. Low intelligence and low creativity—These children did not appear to understand what school was all about. They spent their time in intense physical activity or passive retreat.

4. High intelligence and low creativity—These children were devoted to achieving in school. They had high attention spans and high self-confidence. They were unlikely to act up in school and were well liked by their teachers.

Teachers were later asked to identify their ideal pupil from these four profiles. Which one would you select? Teachers overwhelmingly selected children characterized as highly intelligent but low on creativity. The behavior problems that could arise from creativity (or its stifling), as in the first pattern, appear to outweigh any advantages. It is understandable that the teachers favored high intelligence over high creativity. Highly intelligent children follow directions, work independently, listen, pay attention, obey, and conform. On the other hand, the highly creative child often causes problems requiring individual attention. According to the general personality profile, highly creative children tend to be daydreamers, independent, nonconforming, impulsive, outspoken, challenging, and questioning individuals who test limits.

DAP naeyc Gardner (2006) cautions against the use of creativity tests to measure and/or predict creativity because their validity has not been adequately established. A valid test is one that contains items that reflect the nature of the concept or skills being tested. Some creativity tests contain items that are not directly related to the construct being tested, creativity. Instead of using tests of creativity, Gardner favors assessing creativity in real life (as opposed to artificial testing situations) where children are engaged in creative pursuits, and their creative processes and products are documented. This line of thinking provides the rationale for using portfolio assessment as discussed in Chapter 16.

Did You Get It?

A high level of creativity is almost always correlated with a high level of general intelligence.

a. According to experts, this statement is true.

b. There is a correlation in about half of children.

c. Experts disagree whether there is a correlation.

d. No correlation has been demonstrated.

Take the full quiz on CourseMate.

1-7 Gifted and Talented Children

Creativity may or may not be a characteristic of children identified as **gifted and talented**. Children who are considered gifted and/or talented show high performance in one or more of the following areas: general intellectual ability, academic aptitude, creative thinking or production, leadership ability, talent in visual and performing arts, and physical ability, such as athletics. Educational programs may provide enhanced opportunities for gifted and talented children in any of these areas. According to Gordon and Browne (2008),

educators are increasingly concerned about the underrepresentation of children from low-income populations, children who are ethnically and culturally in the minority, children who have disabilities, and children who are bilingual. Characterizing gifted and talented children can be challenging because their development across domains may be uneven. Generally, young gifted and talented children may:

- be curious and inquisitive
- have a good sense of humor
- be unusually aware of their surroundings
- be able to think quickly and at higher, abstract levels
- have an extensive and mature vocabulary
- ask thought-provoking questions
- have a long attention span
- be able to sustain concentration
- have a developmental lag between their physical and intellectual domains, with fine motor skills lagging behind their cognitive skills
- have a developmental lag between their social and intellectual domains that may lead them to be intolerant of less-advanced peers

Gifted and talented young children are most often found in mainstream early childhood classrooms (Gordon & Browne, 2008). Because of their unique needs and characteristics, they present special challenges and opportunities for their teachers. Programs and approaches that provide challenges, nurture diversity and divergent thinking, and enable children to learn at their own pace and in multiple ways provide a good match for gifted and talented children. Enrichment activities to supplement their mastery of core curriculum will challenge their gifts and talents. Mixed-age grouping is recommended, because a child who exhibits one or more gifts may not excel socially. Open-ended art activities (see Chapter 10) and the art center approach (see Chapter 13) provide creative challenges for gifted and talented children.

1-7a Multiple Intelligences

According to Gardner (2006), there are many ways of demonstrating intelligence. Gardner defines intelligence as the capacity to solve problems or make things valued by one's culture. Gardner believes there are eight criteria for identifying intelligence. Wilkens (1996) explains these as:

1. Each of the intelligences can potentially be isolated by brain damage or degenerative disease. A true intelligence will have its function identified in a specific location in the human brain. This means it is possible to destroy the ability in one sector while leaving the others intact.

2. Each of the intelligences exists in exceptional people, including idiot savants and prodigies. Mozart, for example, who performed at the piano at the age of four, was a musical prodigy. Difficulty in interpersonal or daily living skills may also be involved. There is no guarantee of competence across all the intelligences.

3. Each of the intelligences has a process of development during childhood and has a peak end-state performance. For example, verbal-linguistic intelligence presents itself in early childhood whereas logical-mathematical peaks in adolescence and early adulthood.

4. Each of the intelligences is evident in species other than human beings. For example, birds make music and rhythm while whales use a linguistic intelligence to communicate with each other.

5. Each of the intelligences has been tested using various measures not necessarily associated with intelligence. Although IQ tests may be used, they are by no means the only measure.

6. Each of the intelligences can work without the others being present.

7. Each of the intelligences has a set of identifiable operations. Gardner compares this to a computer needing a set of operations in order to function.

8. Each of the intelligences can be symbolized or has its own unique symbol or set of symbols. For example, interpersonal intelligence uses gestures and facial expressions.

The multiple intelligences, related "smarts," and corresponding strengths and interests are depicted in Table 1–1.

Gardner asserts that we all have some of each intelligence as well as particular strengths. Everyone can be characterized as smart in one or more of the intelligences.

How do art skills and process match up with the eight intelligences? How are multiple intelligences strengthened through art? Refer to Table 1–2.

Gardner has provided a wider view of intelligence. What are the implications? The theory of multiple intelligences offers implications for both instruction and assessment to include the following:

1. We must broaden our views of intelligence to incorporate multiple examples. All intelligences are important, and children come to us with different sets of developed intelligences. Not all children are verbally or mathematically inclined. This does not mean they are not smart. They are just smart in other ways. Traditionally, schooling has focused on verbal-linguistic and logical-mathematical intelligences. Children who excelled in language arts, math, and logical thinking flourished. They were "smart" in the areas the school valued. Unfortunately, children who did not excel in these areas had no outlets to express their different intelligences.

2. The different ways to be smart must be respected. It is crucial to plan experiences that include the different intelligences. Gardner (1999) refers to

Table 1–1 Gardner's Multiple Intelligences (1993b)

Intelligence	"Smart"	Strengths and Interests
bodily-kinesthetic	Body	sports, movement, dance, acting, dramatics, large motor and playground activities
musical-rhythmic	Music	singing, dancing, playing a musical instrument, listening to music
interpersonal	People	making friends, socializing, cooperative projects, being a leader, resolving peer conflicts
visual-spatial	Pictures	art, looking at pictures, daydreaming, puzzles, maps, charts
verbal-linguistic	Words	speaking, reading, writing, listening, telling stories, thinking in words, discussions, memorizing, word puzzles, word games
logical-mathematical	Math	math, reasoning, logical and abstract thinking, problem solving, patterns, working with numbers, computers
intrapersonal	Self	understands self, knows strengths and accepts limits, works alone, pursues own interests, reflective, self-paced learner
naturalist	Nature	recognizes plants, minerals, animals, clouds, rocks, flora, fauna, other natural phenomena

Based on Gardner H. (2006) Multiple Intelligences: New horizons in theory and practice New York: Basic Books.

Table 1–2 Relationship of Multiple Intelligences to Children's Art

Multiple Intelligences	Relationship to Art
bodily-kinesthetic	• manipulation of art tools enhances use of large muscles, sensory-motor integration, fine motor skills, and eye-hand coordination • involves bodily and kinesthetic movements and multisensory stimulation • different media require different types of processing, involving different physical movements and skills
musical-rhythmic	• children can make musical instruments or sound makers • art can be produced in response to music • background music can trigger artistic processing
interpersonal	• children talk about and share their art with others • children work together and practice social skills at the art center • children use peers as resources while doing art • children elect to engage in group art projects • as part of the project approach, art involves collaboration • children comply with rules and limits of the art center
visual-spatial	• art involves symbolic representation • provide materials for two- and three-dimensional processing • use art books, art posters, and illustrated children's books that are visually aesthetic and stimulating • display children's artwork at their eye level
verbal-linguistic	• encourage children to talk about their art • encourage art sharing as part of show-and-tell • read art books to children • engage in art dialogue with children • take art dictation, encouraging children to tell and write their own art-related words and stories • teach art vocabulary, including the artistic elements • label art materials and supplies • conduct art critique using artistic elements for children to discuss works of art
logical-mathematical	• involves patterning, color mixing, quantifying, and problem solving • set up an organized art center in which similar materials are grouped together or classified • children make choices, decisions, and carry out plans
intrapersonal	• children work alone and reflect on their processing and results • personal emotions, thoughts, and ideas are expressed • provide multicultural art supplies • plan art activities focusing on the child's sense of self; art replies to "Who am I?"
Naturalist	• take nature walks to collect nature specimens for art • provide natural materials for painting, printing, collage, sculpture, and weaving • children use personally meaningful symbols to represent nature and their surrounding natural environment

this as "multiple key entry points" to content. Not every activity involves all the intelligences, but the more intelligences involved, the greater the chance that all children will excel.

3. Using an integrated approach to curriculum development will increase the likelihood that many intelligences will be involved in a course of study.

4. Target the development of specific intelligences by setting up stations throughout the classroom with resources related to each intelligence. For instance, a verbal-linguistic center could include books, a word processor, and writing tools.

5. Provide students with choices of activities t talize on their learning styles and brai

Dominant intelligences can be reinforced, whereas weaker intelligences are strengthened. Students have opportunities to improve weaknesses by tapping their strengths.

6. **DAP** Because all children do not learn in the same ways, they cannot be assessed in the same ways. Consider creating an intelligence profile for each student. A good approach to assessment is to allow students to explain or document what they know or have learned in their own ways using their different intelligences.

Chapter 16 will offer additional guidelines for appropriate assessment of young children. After observing children in a variety of activities, you, as the teacher, will soon have a good picture of each child's strengths and weaknesses. Sharing this information with the children, however, may provide them with a rationale for avoiding activities that do not come naturally. Be careful not to label a child as having a "visual spatial intelligence" or being a "naturalistic learner." Instead, encourage children to use their strengths to support learning in all areas.

Brain Connection

Each region of the brain is made of a very sophisticated neurological network of cells, dendrites, and nerves that interconnect one part of the brain to another. Good early childhood curriculum will reinforce these connections by engaging many of the five senses and activating more than one of Gardener's eight intelligences at the same time (Rushton & Larkin, 2001).

Did You Get It?

Gifted children have _____ awareness of their surroundings.
- **a.** almost no
- **b.** a lowered
- **c.** a heightened
- **d.** an almost obsessive

Take the full quiz on CourseMate.

▶❚❚ **TeachSource** Video

Infants and Toddlers: Creative Development

In this chapter, teachers are encouraged to be play-partners with children and join in their creative activities ~~while~~ still letting children be the leaders and ~~...~~ Compare and contrast this idea with ~~the~~ teacher in the video. Is she being a ~~...~~er?

~~...~~'s multiple intelligences do you see ~~...~~? How might the teacher scaffold ~~...~~ other intelligences?

© 2015 Cengage Learning.

1-8 Creativity and Brain Growth

Early childhood educators have long believed that rich, early experiences and quality time with a caring and loving family are critical to a child's development. These beliefs are supported by the discoveries neuroscientists have made about brain growth in the early years. **Brain research** is a line of study documenting the impact of early experiences on the architecture of the brain and on the nature and extent of adult capacities. During the early years, the brain has the greatest capacity for change. How the brain develops hinges on a complex interplay between a young child's genes (heredity) and life experiences (environment). The developing brain is malleable and flexible and has the ability to virtually explode with new synapses or connections. The brain's neural plasticity allows it to constantly change structure and function in response to external experiences.

The environment affects not only the number of brain cells and number of connections among them but also the way those connections are wired. On the positive side, brain growth can be positively stimulated. The brain develops in an integrated fashion over time, so an enriched environment addresses multiple aspects of development simultaneously. The brain thrives on taking in unexpected information, as long as the unpredictability isn't accompanied by insecurity or perceived threat (Heath & Wolf, 2004a). On the negative side, however, neglect or abuse can impede the child's developing brain functions. If a child receives little stimulation early on, synapses will not sprout, and the brain will make few connections. The harmful impact of stress on early brain development damages overall growth and development, placing the child at much greater risk of developing a wide range of cognitive, behavioral, and physical problems. In some cases, these effects may be irreversible. While traumatic events may significantly influence adult behavior, they actually change the *organizational framework* for a young child's brain. Life experiences are now believed to control both how the infant's brain is architecturally structured and how intricate brain circuitry is wired. Early experiences have a decisive impact on the architecture and wiring of the brain and on the nature and extent of adult capacities.

Early in a child's life, the brain has many more cells (neurons) than the child will need (Allen & Marotz, 2010). Connections among neurons are formed as children explore their environment, play, and develop attachments to others. Connectivity is a crucial feature of brain development because the neural pathways formed during the early years carry signals and allow information processing throughout life. Timing is also crucial. Even though learning continues throughout life, there are critical periods during which the brain is particularly efficient at creating neural pathways that facilitate specific kinds of learning. Experiences children have during these sensitive periods stabilize neural pathways and lay the foundation for optimal development. For example, the window of opportunity for vision and language development appears quite early and is lost by about age 10. If a child is born deaf, the neural pathways remain silent and atrophy. This is not to say that an adult cannot learn a second language. However, it is much more difficult to learn a foreign language after age 10 or so, and the language will probably be spoken with an accent. Lack of experiences during critical periods will result in underdeveloped neural pathways. Thus, the architecture of the brain reflects the presence or absence of a wide range of physical, cognitive, and socio-emotional experiences during the early years.

Play is a critical element in early childhood because it provides the context for experiences that are vital to the development of neural pathways. Children must have time to practice and master the skills they learn before moving on to learning new ones, and learning must take place in a meaningful, supportive environment. A developing brain does not know the difference between an inexpensive set of plastic measuring cups and an expensive toy with exaggerated claims by the manufacturer. Rushton and Larkin (2001) found that children engaged with play in active learning environments score higher on measures of creativity. The key is for adults to be responsive to children, engaging in subtle give-and-take in which the child leads and the adult follows.

And what about art? In the past, art was viewed as an affective process. We now know that art is both a cognitive and an affective process. Children think and feel when engaged in art. Because making art requires that children think and feel about experiences or ideas and find symbols to express them, art is a highly symbolic and meaning-making activity. We also know that the brain functions in very different ways during various phases of the creative process. The brain's plasticity influences creative outcomes (Heath & Wolf, 2004a).

Did You Get It?

A rich environment has been shown to increase the number of cells and connections in a young child's brain. The connections between cells are called

- **a.** grey matter.
- **b.** synapses.
- **c.** dendrites.
- **d.** neural bridges.

Take the full quiz on CourseMate.

1-9 Creativity and Child Development

What is the relationship between creativity and a child's development? Are there developmental benefits to a child's creative functioning? Whatever the form that creativity may take, the child develops large and small muscles by manipulating the appropriate tools or apparatus. Musical instruments are played, paint is mixed and spread, clay is pounded, and the body moves to music and song. Creative expression enhances physical development. Socially, it also helps children interact with others. At times, creativity involves solitary thinking or problem solving. At other times, social skills, including sharing, taking turns, and considering other points of view, are practiced. Creative expression fosters emotional development and positive mental health by validating individual uniqueness. Juan, age three, made a clay dinosaur with two legs and an oversized head. He was proud of his accomplishment, and it did not matter that dinosaurs have four legs. Philosopher Mihaly Csikszenthmihalyi (1997) believes there is a strong connection between creativity and happiness based on research showing that being creative stimulates the brain's pleasure

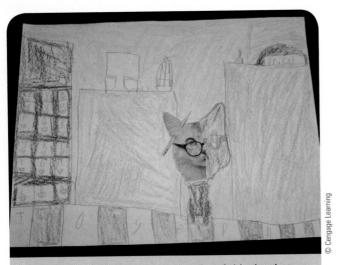

© Cengage Learning

Figure 1–4 The eight-year-old artist of this drawing imagined and created a doctor's office as he interpreted a magazine photo.

centers. Creativity fosters cognitive development. It involves many higher-level thinking skills, including problem solving, discovery, analysis, hypothesizing, predicting, testing, and communicating (see Figure 1–4). In the classroom, creativity can enhance and reinforce learning in the traditional curricular areas of math, science, social studies, listening, speaking, pre-reading, pre-writing, and other expressive arts.

Did You Get It?

Given that solitude can spawn creativity, experts state that creativity _____ social interaction with others.

a. aids
b. hinders
c. stalls
d. stops

Take the full quiz on CourseMate.

Summary

(1-1) Creativity has many definitions, including seeing things in new ways, combining unrelated things into something new, breaking boundaries, and thinking unconventionally. (1-2) Children often focus on the creative process rather than a final product. (1-3) Creativity may be explained as an attitude, a skill requiring practice, or a set of personality characteristics. (1-4) Environmental conditions can either foster or hinder creativity. (1-5) Adult attitudes have a significant influence on children's creativity.

(1-6) Convergent thinking seeks to find the right answer, but creativity is divergent, seeking many possible solutions to a problem. (1-7) Creativity and intelligence are assessed in different ways, and a child with a high IQ may not have a high degree of creativity. (1-8) Brain research documents the impact of early experiences on the structure of the brain and their influences on children's creativity outcomes. (1-9) Children's creativity can enhance their learning and development across all areas of the curriculum.

Key Terms

brain research, 16
closed-ended, 11
convergent thinking
   (noncreative), 12

creativity, 5
gifted and talented, 13
open-ended, 11

process versus product, 6
serendipity, 5
synergistic, 5

✔ Suggested Activities

1. Identify at least one thing you do creatively. Practice and continue to refine it. Document your own creative development, including setbacks, frustrations, and successes, with a journal.

2. Make a resource list of local businesses and contacts that are good sources of free (or

inexpensive) recyclable materials. Include the name, address, e-mail address, and contact person for each resource.

3. Spend one morning observing a teacher's use of time, space, and curriculum, as well as his or her teaching behaviors. List specific recommendations

for how each could be modified to enhance creativity.

4. With your peers, brainstorm a list of creative individuals. Identify their names and claims to creativity. Use gender to examine your list. Do you have an equal number of female and male creative individuals? Keep brainstorming until you have five of each.

5. Examine Healy's (1994) portrayal of what families can do to raise creative children (see the section "Optimal Home Environment," earlier in the chapter). Do these characteristics match your own upbringing? Discuss your answer.

6. Consider the letter to families included at the beginning of this section. How will you define creativity for the families of children in your classroom? Write your definition, and share it with others who have done the same. Note similarities and differences. Discuss elements of creativity that are most important for families to understand and the roles teachers play in building this understanding.

7. What creative processing activities might you provide to help families understand the nature of creativity? Work with a partner to develop a list of five.

8. Working with a partner, review the eight intelligences outlined in Gardner's theory. Identify those in which you feel you have strengths and those in which you do not. Discuss which intelligences might be most important for a teacher of young children.

Review

1. What is the relationship among creativity, convergent thinking, and intelligence?

2. Name three different ways of understanding creativity.

3. Pretend you are speaking to a group of parents about creativity. The parents ask you for important things that they can do at home to enhance their children's creativity. Specifically, what three suggestions do you share?

4. List and discuss four obstacles to creativity.

5. Are young children more process-oriented or product-oriented in their creative expression? Explain your position.

6. List the characteristics of families that nurture creativity in young children.

7. Is intelligence a single concept confined to thinking? Include a discussion of multiple intelligences to justify your position.

8. Creativity may be one characteristic of children who are gifted and talented. What other characteristics may gifted and talented children exhibit? Discuss strategies you could use in your classroom to meet the needs of gifted and talented children. Explain why these strategies would be successful.

9. Explain what the research on brain development means for early development. What are two key implications?

Additional Resources

Read more about the work of E. P. Torrance, noted researcher on creativity (www.gifted.uconn.edu).

Go to Artella (www.artellawordsandart.com), a Website that allows you to explore aspects of your own creativity.

Go to YouTube to view Sir Ken Robinson's video, "Do Schools Kill Creativity?"

 Visit CourseMate for this textbook to access the eBook, Did You Get It? quizzes, Digital Downloads, TeachSource Videos, flashcards, and more. Go to CengageBrain.com to log in, register, or purchase access.

First/Second Grade Lesson Plan

The Big Orange Splot

GOAL

Students will express their thoughts and ideas creatively, while challenging their imaginations, fostering reflective thinking, and developing disciplined effort and progressive problem-solving skills.

OUTCOMES

Upon completion of this lesson, students will be able to:

a. explain the importance of individual expression
b. give examples of idioms and explain their meanings

MATERIALS

a. *The Big Orange Splot* by Daniel Manus Pinkwater
b. Dry erase board and markers
c. Coffee can and lid
d. Manila paper, scissors, markers or crayons for each child

INTRODUCTION

Begin with the following: *Boys and girls, today we're going to read a book titled* **The Big Orange Splot:** *This story is about people who decide to be different and to express their ideas so that everyone can see. The main character is Mr. Plumbean. During the story, Mr. Plumbean has a talk with each of his neighbors. At the end of the story, I'm going to ask you what you think Mr. Plumbean said to each of his neighbors when they talked.*

DEVELOPMENT

Read the story to the children. As you end the story, use the following questions to begin a discussion:

a. *When the orange paint splatted on his house, what did Mr. Plumbean do? Why on earth would he do that?*
b. *How did his neighbors react? Why do you think they felt that way?*
c. *But then Mr. Plumbean talked to each of his neighbors. What do you think he said to them?*
d. *And then what did the neighbors do?*

Help the children to understand that just as we draw pictures to tell about things that are important to us, Mr. Plumbean wanted to paint his house to show things he liked and that were important to him. When he talked to his neighbors, he was able to convince them that it is better to show what is important to you than to be just like everyone else.

Go back to page 13 in the book and read to the children the sentence: *Plumbean has popped his cork, flipped his lid, blown his stack, and dropped his stopper.* Ask the children what the neighbors meant by saying this. Use the coffee can and lid to demonstrate "flipping a lid." Ask the children, "Do you think this is how Mr. Plumbean flipped his lid?" Explain that this phrase is an *idiom*. Write the word on the white board. Define an idiom as a phrase that has a completely different meaning than each of the words by themselves. For example, the word *flipping* means turning something over and *lid* means a cover or a top to something. But altogether, this idiom means doing something totally different from what you would usually do.

Go back through the book and identify other idioms used to describe Mr. Plumbean. Share with the children that they will be reading more books with idioms in the next few days.

Distribute Manila paper, markers, and scissors. State that each child now has a sheet of paper exactly like everyone else's. They each have a job, however, to design a house on their sheet of paper that tells about the things that they like. Allow the children to cut outlines of their houses and decorate them as they choose. As they finish, ask each child to share with you or with a peer how they decorated their houses and what those decorations tell about them.

ASSESSMENT

a. Were the children able to explain how they decorated their houses and how those decorations were significant?

b. Were the children able to identify idioms in the story *The Big Orange Splot?*

2 Creative Thinking

© Cengage Learning

What do you see happening in this picture?

Is this something you would do with children?

Ms. Willows and her class of four-year-olds are playing with rhythm band instruments. The children are engaged in an informal music activity. The teacher asks open-ended questions to stimulate their language and thinking: "What are you hearing?" "How else can you play your instruments?" "What other sounds can your instruments make?"

Learning Outcomes

After reading this chapter, you should be able to:

2-1 Give examples of creative thinking.

2-2 Discuss creativity as a function of the brain.

2-3 Describe the environmental conditions which support young children's creative thinking.

2-4 Identify strategies for facilitating young children's creative thinking in the curriculum.

2-5 Plan and implement activities to facilitate young children's creative thinking.

Standards addressed in this chapter

DAP Criteria

2 Teaching to enhance development and learning

3 Planning curriculum to achieve important goals

4 Assessing children's development and learning

NAEYC Standards

2 Curriculum

3 Teaching

4 Assessment

9 Physical Environment

2-1 **What Is Creative Thinking?**

All people have the capacity to be creative in some area, provided conditions are right and they have acquired the needed knowledge and skills (Robinson, 1999). Some outlets or modes of creativity include play; the expressive arts: art, music, movement, dance, drama, and mime; and thought and language. Play, for example, is an excellent opportunity for creative expression. A young child building with blocks relies on past experiences in transforming pieces of wood into a train or castle. Putting on an oversized coat helps four-year-old Beth become a business executive or pilot. Children use their bodies to creatively move like animals, robots, or astronauts. They also use paint, markers, and clay to give form to their thoughts and experiences. Young children also creatively transform Standard English. Darrell, age three, felt that "carage" made more sense than garage. Swiss made no sense to five-year-old Kyle. He insisted on "hole cheese" in his sandwiches. Young children also engage in creative thinking, although this particular mode is often given less emphasis in the early childhood curriculum.

Many believe creative thinking is abstract and reserved for adult authors, artists, scientists, and inventors. Young children can and should engage in creative thinking. Creative thinking is a skill that helps children solve problems in their daily lives and prepares them for life in the twenty-first century. If we are to solve social, economic, political, and environmental problems, it will be through creative problem solving. Children who grow up valued as creative and original thinkers will have the necessary skills to confront and solve problems in the twenty-first century.

Just what is creative thinking? Creativity has been identified as a cognitive process or way of thinking. DeBono (1970) identified two types of thinking: vertical and lateral. Vertical thinking involves learning more about something or arriving at an accepted, convergent answer. For example, when Ms. Bell asked her preschoolers, "When do we eat breakfast?" Lin answered, "In the morning." But if the object is to find unusual, divergent, creative solutions for problems, lateral thinking is appropriate. Lateral thinking is a way of using one's mind that leads to creative thinking

or products. For example, Katie, who was playing alone at the sandbox, decided to use sticks and twigs to represent pretend playmates in the sandbox who would keep her company.

2-2 **Creativity and the Brain**

Creativity can also be discussed as a function of the brain. Creative thinking stimulates the brain, making reasoning skills stronger and improving mood, behavior, and concentration (Aramowicz, 2008). The human brain houses two separate but interacting thinking hemispheres. The right and left hemispheres are joined by the corpus callosum, a thick branch of nerves that serves as a communication system between them. Each hemisphere has specialized functions. The left hemisphere reacts to input in an analytical way. Left-brain processing is organized and logical, specializing in learning logical ideas and skills such as the rules of reading and math. The right hemisphere controls creative abilities, body awareness, spatial orientation, and recognition of faces. The right hemisphere recognizes negative emotions faster, and the left side recognizes positive emotions faster (Charlesworth, 2004). Research indicates that this differential functioning of the brain is present at birth and that infants require good communication between the hemispheres for efficient brain functioning. However, the activities of each brain hemisphere may change as the individual engages in new activities and develops skills.

It is imperative that children have experiences that capitalize on and integrate the functioning of both sides of the brain. Although most schools are set up to emphasize convergent thinking, or left-brain functioning, Gardner (1991) reminds us of the importance of the years between ages two and seven: "artistry and creativity in general are unleashed—or blocked—at this time" (p. 82). Teachers of young children are in a key position to plan experiences that engage both left- and right-brain functioning.

2-2a **Left- and Right-Brain Functions**

Seen from above, the human brain resembles a walnut. The two hemispheres, right and left, are connected at the center by the corpus callosum, which provides communication between the two hemispheres. The nervous system is connected to the brain in a crossed-over fashion. The left hemisphere controls the right side of the body; the left side of the body is controlled by the right hemisphere. The two hemispheres are specialized and process information differently. Each side possesses capacities for certain mental processes that are independent of the other. The right hemisphere operates in a mode that is nonverbal, subjective, intuitive, and global. The left hemisphere operates in a mode that analyzes, abstracts, verbalizes, and uses logic.

Did You Get It?

_____ thinking is a means and a method for using one's mind in a way that leads to creative outcomes.

   a. Horizontal

   b. Vertical

   c. Lateral

   d. Dimensional

Take the full quiz on CourseMate.

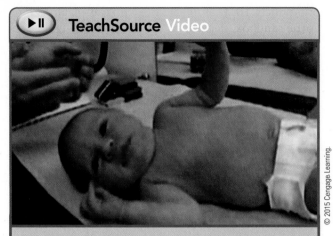

TeachSource Video

Infancy: Brain Development

Consider your art curriculum in light of the video's description of left- and right-brain thinking. Identify activities and experiences that will utilize each side of the brain.

Watch on CourseMate.

© 2015 Cengage Learning.

Table 2–1 Brain Specialties

Left Brain Specializes In	Right Brain Specializes In
Language functions	Intuition
Analysis	Synthesis
Counting	Drawing
Marking time	Dreams

(Edwards, 1999)

According to Edwards (1999), the two hemispheres work together in a number of ways. Sometimes they cooperate and divide the task, with each half contributing its abilities in doing what it does best. The hemispheres can also work singly; one hemisphere dominates and is "on" while the other is "off." The hemispheres may also compete, and one may try to do what it knows the other can do better. For example, Zena is at the easel, trying to paint her family. How does her brain approach this task? The left side of her brain reacts logically, telling Zena she needs four figures, two male and two female. If the left side dominates, her father would be painted with his beard and depicted taller than her mother. Zena would plan to paint herself smaller than her older brother. If the right side of her brain dominates, Zena reacts emotionally rather than logically. She becomes engrossed in mixing colors and making designs to highlight clothing. Or, her mother could be painted larger than life and wearing a crown while her older brother appears in the background, lacking facial features.

DAP naeyc Schools that pay only lip service to creativity are organized according to left-brain functioning. Curricular implications based on brain specializations are listed in Table 2–1. In left-brain-oriented schools, teaching is sequenced, and time schedules are rigidly followed. Children sit in straight rows of desks. Teachers reward convergent thinking with letter grades. Language arts and math form the core of the curriculum. Right-brain pursuits including art, music, and movement do not receive equal time, attention,

or funding and may be the first areas eliminated when the budget is cut.

What are the implications for teachers and students with matching or opposing brain preferences? Teachers with left-brain strengths generally prefer to teach using lecture and discussion. To incorporate sequence, they put outlines on the board or overhead, and they adhere to time schedules. They give problems to students to solve independently. Teachers with left-brain preferences assign more research and writing and prefer a tidy, quiet, and structured classroom. A left-brain teacher is a good match for left-brain students who prefer to work alone, without a lot of distraction. By contrast, teachers with right-brain strengths prefer to use hands-on activities. With the right-brain preference of seeing the whole picture, these teachers incorporate more art, manipulatives, visuals, and music into their lessons. They embrace the concept of multiple intelligences. They like to assign group projects and activities and prefer an interactive environment. Right-brain students prefer to work in groups. They like to do art projects and would, for example, prefer to design and make a representative collage than write a term paper.

The information on brain functioning provides teaching challenges and opportunities. Students with strong left- or right-brain tendencies much prefer to be taught to their neurological strengths. If you are a left-brain teacher, try adding at least one right-brain method such as role playing or group projects into your teaching. If you are a right-brain teacher try adding at least one left-brain method such as direct teaching or individual projects. Give your students a variety of assignments from which to choose, and watch children gravitate to their neurological strengths.

2-2b Characteristics of Divergent or Creative Thinking

Creative or divergent thinkers share the following mental qualities. They are

1. *fluent* thinkers who have many ideas and solutions.
2. *flexible* thinkers who have different ideas that cross categories or break boundaries.

3. *original* thinkers who have unique and unusual ideas.

4. *elaborate* thinkers who add details to the ideas.

The **divergent thinking** of creative children is fluent, flexible, original, and elaborate, although not all four qualities appear in each thought or action. When confronted with a problem, creative or divergent thinkers are able to come up with a long list of possibilities or options. This characterizes **fluency**. For example, ask children for their ideas on celebrating Earth Day. Their fluent replies might include cleaning up the playground, creating posters about protecting the environment, making a web on ecosystems, planting a tree or a garden, starting a recycling program in the neighborhood, making green gifts for their families, or taking a nature walk in a park. The sheer quantity of responses indicates fluency. They are the result of brainstorming for many ideas. All ideas should be accepted and respected.

The preceding responses indicate **flexibility**. Flexibility is the ability to mentally push boundaries, shift categories, and take mental detours. It results in varied and diverse responses. Thinking can be fluent without being flexible. The children's thinking was fluent in that it generated several suggestions related to the school grounds. It was flexible in that their options went beyond these ideas for themselves to include families and the neighborhood. Creating a web on ecosystems is one original idea, especially for a young child. **Originality** refers to uniqueness. Original ideas are uncommon, unusual, different, and unexpected. By contrast, the other party-type suggestions are obvious and common.

Creative individuals have elaborate ideas and express themselves in complex ways. **Elaboration** involves a lot of detail and rich expression. For example, in her poster on protecting the environment, Arden merely drew herself putting litter in a trash can and did not elaborate. By contrast, Beau was elaborate by drawing a detailed picture of a trash-covered park and a second picture of the same park without trash

Figure 2–1 Working with clay supports fluency between the medium, the child's body, and the child's idea.

and dictating the phrases, "Where do you want to play? Keep our environment clean." Beau was able to stretch and expand his thought. Creative children embellish both their artwork and their language (Figure 2–1).

DAP naeyc 2-2c Whole Brain, Whole Learning

Few would argue that schools should not stress conformity and convergent thinking. Still, a better balance is needed between creativity and individuality versus conformity and convergent thinking. We need to balance left- and right-brain learning. Our educational goals, curriculum, and practices should exercise many modes of learning and different styles of processing information. Certainly, we do not want children to creatively read the word "shoe" as anything other than what it is. Nor would we want children to creatively add 2 + 3 and come up with 32. Still, children should not be spoon-fed knowledge, nor have their left brain overworked and their right brain left to atrophy. Author Robert Schirrmacher observed a kindergartner being corrected for stating that the color of the sun was "white hot." It appeared that the teacher was looking for convergent thinking to produce the acceptable answer of "yellow." Conformity and convergent thinking can be taken to extremes. Over time, children come to reject divergent thinking as incorrect or useless. (And as an aside, the child's right brain was correct; the sun is not yellow.)

Not all creative-thinking activities provide opportunity to assess all four components of divergent production. The following item from a test of creativity will help us informally evaluate children's thinking for originality and elaboration. In the following example, children are asked to complete an open-ended drawing

---

Brain Connection 🧠

The human brain is continually growing and adapting to its environment. A child's intelligence is not determined at birth; it fluctuates throughout life, depending on the stimulation of the child's surroundings and the chemical reactions happening in the body. Teachers see the changes that take place in children daily. These changes are unique to each child. Teachers have the responsibility to notice and accept the changes and then adjust curriculum accordingly (Rushton, 2011).

similar to the one in Figure 2–2. Obviously, there is no one right way to complete this picture, and many possibilities exist. Examine the finished product in Figure 2–3. What can you say about this six-year-old's originality and elaboration? The authors would rate this low on both originality and elaboration. The completed picture is rather stereotyped, unimaginative, and mundane. Details are minimal and the picture lacks elaboration. From this one sample, the authors are not in a position to make a statement about this child's creativity, but it suggests that this child needs practice and encouragement in divergent production. On the other hand, consider a drawing completed by a different six-year-old (see Figure 2–4). What can you say about this child's originality and elaboration? The authors believe that this completed drawing evidences a high degree of originality and elaboration.

Not every creative activity will or should lend itself to evaluation for fluency, flexibility, originality, and

Table 2–2 Rating Scale

Low	Fluency	High
• few different		• many different
	FLEXIBILITY	
• lacks variety		• wide variety
• rigid		• flexible
• limited range		• wide range
	ORIGINALITY	
• stereotyped		• unique
• unimaginative		• imaginative
• common		• unusual
	ELABORATION	
• lacks detail		• very detailed
• unelaborated		• elaborate
• simple		• complex

Source: Guilford, J. P. (1977). Way beyond the IQ. Buffalo, NY: The Creative Education Foundation.

Figure 2–2 Open-ended drawing.

Figure 2–3 Completed drawing by a six-year-old.

Figure 2–4 Completed drawing by a six-year-old.

elaboration. Fluency and flexibility may be more appropriate to games of creative thinking. Originality and elaboration can be applied to children's art. The informal rating scale in Table 2–2, adapted from Guilford's 1977 work, can be used to assess divergent production. Again, the intent is not to grade or label creativity, or to include it on a child's report card. Discretionary use of the following instrument will help keep track of progress as young children work toward the goal of demonstrating fluency, flexibility, originality, and elaboration in their creative processing and production.

2-2d **Children Need to Engage in Convergent and Divergent Thinking**

What is creative thinking? When is thinking creative, and what makes creative thinking different from uncreative thinking? Lasky and Mukerji-Bergeson (2003) assert that in children younger than four years of age, the creative process begins and ends with exploration. For older children and adults, creative thinking can be equated with divergent thinking. Thinking is divergent when many possibilities or options result. Divergent thinking is open-ended, allowing for an array of possibilities. For example, you can engage in divergent thinking when planning a creative curriculum. Ask yourself, "What can I provide that will enhance children's creativity?" There is no one artifact or activity, but rather endless possibilities, including experiences in art, play, language, music, and movement, among others. By contrast, convergent thinking results in one correct answer. Much of what is learned in school requires convergent thinking. Convergent thinking is

© Cengage Learning

required to produce the one right answer to the following questions:

- What is the name of the largest dinosaur?
- What comes out at night, the sun or the moon?
- Name the months of the year in proper order.
- What is the opposite of hot?
- What is the sum of three plus five?

Both modes of thinking, convergent and divergent, are very important. Children who lack opportunities for convergent thinking will lack access to a core body of knowledge needed for academic success and achievement. Acquiring a body of factual information is not enough, however. Children also need opportunities to engage in creative thinking. Children denied access to creative processing and divergent thinking will become conforming individuals who do not realize their creative potential. A problem arises when conformity and convergent thinking dominate the curriculum at the expense of individual and divergent thinking.

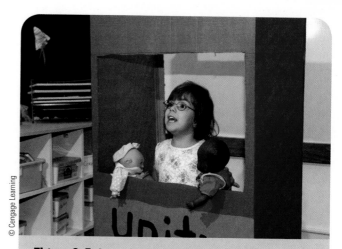
Figure 2–5 A psychologically safe environment will help creativity flourish.

© Cengage Learning

> ### Did You Get It?
>
> A typical thinker might see simply what is on the surface. _____ thinkers are skillful at taking a particular object, thought, or concept and adding details to it.
> **a.** Fluent
> **b.** Archetypal
> **c.** Unorthodox
> **d.** Elaborate
>
> Take the full quiz on CourseMate.

2-3 Setting the Stage for Creative Thinking

Although children will act and think in creative ways without prompting, adults can facilitate creativity by providing time, space, and resources, as well as setting the stage.

DAP naeyc 2-3a Provide a Psychological Climate Conducive to Creativity

Children flourish in a psychologically safe setting that trusts and empowers them to act autonomously without fear of criticism, rejection, or failure (see Figure 2–5). Expectations for children's behavior are high yet appropriate. Autonomy involves acting freely but in responsible ways. Children need to act autonomously by making choices and decisions, solving problems, and making things happen on their own. By providing an array of materials and activities from which to choose,

the environment can be set up to foster children's autonomy. An overly structured day, in which choices regarding activities are made for the children, impairs their creative ability. They learn to override creative impulses and autonomous drive while becoming overly dependent on others for answers and solutions.

naeyc 2-3b Creative Thinking Takes Time

Children need large blocks of time to engage in activities that involve thinking. Exploring and exhausting possibilities take time. Time should be viewed as fluid and flexible. The daily schedule should be divided into a few large blocks of time rather than several short blocks. Larger blocks provide enough time to think, plan, and try possibilities and then to leave, return, and begin again. Children who are rushed are not only denied adequate time to think and do but may also resist by misbehaving. Children need time to daydream and reflect, to sit and think. Let creativity and creative thinking permeate the day. Use individual and small-group times, snack, and transition to play creative thinking games. Sometimes creativity is unpredictable and will require additional time. The intentional teacher is flexible and able to flow with "teachable moments" as well as to bring closure when warranted.

DAP naeyc 2-3c Children Need Space in Which to Be Creative

Children need plenty of space to lay out materials and to work alone or together to complete their plans. Like time, space should be fluid and flexible. Creative thinking may require enclosed, solitary space for private thinking and daydreaming. Other creative activities may require larger open spaces for group involvement. Tables, chairs, and movable units may need to be arranged to meet the needs of each activity. Creativity may entail excitement, movement, and clutter. An excessive concern for constant neatness inhibits creative "messing about." Perhaps this is why creative expression and young children are so compatible.

> ### Did You Get It?
>
> Children who are to be encouraged to explore and come up with creative solutions should be presented with _____ periods of time to do so.
>
> **a.** long
> **b.** short but intense
> **c.** moderate
> **d.** unlimited
>
> Take the full quiz on CourseMate.

DAP naeyc 2-4 Creativity and the Early Childhood Curriculum

A misunderstanding pervades the concept of creativity and its role in the curriculum. With the present emphasis on accountability, academics, testing, reform, and budget cuts, creativity may be eyed suspiciously by taxpayers and teachers, who often report that they believe creativity to be important and yet find little time to encourage it.

The elusive nature of creativity merely complicates the issue. Reporting to parents that their child is reading at a specific level may convey more information than saying their child is highly creative. Some believe that doing well in math is more important than being creative. At a parent meeting, one father asked, "If creativity is so important, why doesn't it appear on report cards and school records?" He went on to state that he did not recall creativity being part of his academic studies and felt he was a success in spite of it. His point may reflect wider public opinion. This is another reason why parent education, teacher education, and arts advocacy are critical.

DAP naeyc 2-4a Strategies to Facilitate Creative Thinking

The following strategies will help children feel that their attempts at creative thinking are valued. They can easily be integrated into traditional content areas in the early childhood curriculum.

Build Creative Thinking into Your Program. Integrate your curriculum. Avoid overemphasis on conformity and convergent thinking. Children who are led to believe that there is only one right way or correct answer will have their creativity stifled. Expect that creative children will challenge your ideas and ways

of doing things. Provide opportunities for children to explore creative options, to play with their ideas.

Model Creative Thinking. According to Sternberg and Lubart (1995), the best way to foster creativity is to provide creative role models. If you want children to be creative, no set of activities will help them more than being a role model of creativity yourself (see Figure 2–6).

Children learn to take sensible risks and to fight obstacles by watching others doing these things. Share your creative solutions to problems. For example, you promised the children that they will be able to finger-paint in the morning. You promised, however, before discovering that there is no more paint. You announce the problem and describe how you came up with a solution: "We ran out of paint so I thought of what else we could use. I'll put shaving cream into each of these trays and we can use that for finger-painting." Also share your frustration and setbacks. Let children know it took you several tries to find a way to keep the door closed so the classroom pet would not escape at night. Try new ways of doing things. Let children know that if one way does not work, you simply think again and try another.

Figure 2–6 Be a model of creativity for the children in your class.

© Cengage Learning

Recognize, Encourage, and Value Creative Thinking and Problem Solving. Reward the process of thinking creatively rather than the idea itself. In the previous classroom pet example, the teacher should also recognize her accomplishments by saying, "I like my idea of an open padlock, and it seems to be working. It took some creative thinking." This is not the same as bragging. Encourage children to be creative thinkers. In the former shaving cream example, Carlos gets the liquid watercolor and says, "Let's make colors." Reply, "Carlos wants to add coloring to our shaving cream. Good thinking."

Help Children Value Their Own Creative Thinking. Help children stand up for their ideas in the face of criticism and peer pressure. Say, "That was your idea and it's OK if your friend doesn't agree." For example, what if the children do not like Carlos's idea? The teacher could say, "I think Carlos has a good idea. If you don't want color, just say so. Carlos, it's OK if some friends don't want color in their shaving cream." In turn, help children respect the ideas of others. Help them see that it is OK to be different and to have different ideas.

Pose Problems Requiring Creative Solutions. For example, to a group of school-age children who want to go on a field trip, say, "How can we raise money to go?" Look for many and different ideas. Help children build on each other's ideas. Provide ample think time, during which you remain silent and wait for them to reply. Keep in mind that creativity can be found in the approaches that individual children bring to solving problems (Di Leo, 2003). Defer judgment and evaluation. Resist the temptation to step in too soon and shield children from manageable amounts of frustration or even failure at times. Help children test their hunches and rethink possibilities. Encourage **critical thinking**. Discuss the pros and cons of their ideas.

Engage Children in Critical Thinking. For example, once again Miss Tina finds herself reading the story of *Goldilocks and the Three Bears* to a group of preschoolers. It is a favorite, and she always provides puppets, stuffed animals, costumes, character headbands, and a set of felt pieces for children to retell the story in their own words. She approaches today's reading with a different goal in mind—critical thinking. Before reading, she asks the children to listen carefully and decide who is nice as opposed to who is naughty. Devlin says the bears are bad, especially Papa Bear, because he scares the little girl and she runs away. Afi thinks that Mama Bear is good because she cooks for her family and will not let them eat the food if it is too hot. Rosa thinks that Baby Bear is bad because he woke up Goldilocks. She adds that she gets into trouble if she wakes up her baby sister. Kalmir disagrees. He believes Goldilocks is naughty because

she broke Baby Bear's chair. Nan adds that Goldilocks ate the porridge and that was not right because she did not ask first. Sergio says that Goldilocks is the "baddest" because she walked right into the house; the bears could call the police and take her to jail. The children are thinking critically about the characters in simple terms such as good versus bad and naughty versus nice that they easily understand. Miss Tina was able to help the children look beyond the labeling and see the bigger issue of safety and intent. She agreed that Goldilocks did something that could be called bad because it was unsafe and rude. She asked the children if it is okay to go into a stranger's house. Fay said it would be okay if she knocked first. Miss Tina asked the other children what they thought. And so the critical thinking continued.

Ask Open-Ended Questions. Open-ended questions are worded in such a way that there is not one correct answer. They invite an array of possible responses. They require children to engage in divergent or creative thinking and to operate at a higher mental level in formulating answers.

For example, Miss Tina might ask the following open-ended questions after reading *The Three Bears*:

- Let's give the bears first names. What could we call them?
- Let's change the story. Who can share a different ending?
- What do you think about going into a stranger's house?

These questions will engage children in higher-level thinking as they actively construct answers. By contrast, **closed-ended questions** aim for one right answer and are based on recall. Either you know it or you do not. Answers to closed-ended questions are stored in memory as pieces of unrelated information.

If Miss Tina wanted children to engage in low-level thinking and give back factual information, she could ask the following closed-ended questions:

- How many bears were there in our story?
- What was the name of the little girl?
- Why was she called Goldilocks?

She knows that these questions and others like them will be easy for her children and will not engage them mentally. For both open- and closed-ended questions, it is important to allow think time. Children need time to reflect on questions while mentally and verbally formulating one or more answers. Do not become impatient and answer your own question. This disrespectful practice sends a negative message to children. It tells them you will not invest the time in waiting to hear what they have to say. They may interpret this to mean that you really do not care about their ideas.

Did You Get It?

Robert Sternberg and Todd Lubart (1995) believe the most effective means for fostering creativity among students is providing creative

- **a.** tools.
- **b.** space.
- **c.** role models.
- **d.** reward systems.

Take the full quiz on CourseMate.

DAP naeyc 2-5 Facilitating Activities for Creative Thinking

Sample items taken from tests of creativity (Torrance, 1966) and modified for use with young children provide suggestions for activities to foster creative thinking. Some general guidelines are in order. You may want to try out these activities yourself first. Record and evaluate your responses. Allow yourself and your children plenty of think time to grapple with the problem posed. The activities can be conducted with individual children or with small or large groups. Creative-thinking games can be played at any time and can easily become part of classroom routines. Explain the nature of the games. You are looking for unusual responses, and there will not be one right answer. Because the games are so open-ended, they may create some initial discomfort, especially to children who have been told that all questions have one right answer. Participation should be voluntary, and some children will feel more comfortable with these activities than others. Some children may get silly, and their answers may have no relation to the question asked. These children may simply be testing your commitment to creativity. Initially, the games should be kept short. Stop when the children show signs of restlessness.

2-5a Activities for Creative Thinking

Because children vary in their levels of creative thinking and verbal ability, it is difficult to recommend specific age ranges for the following activities. Consider carefully your children's abilities in language, drawing, and writing as you choose activities for your classroom.

Kindergarten and School-Age Activity: Finish My Picture. Ask the children to complete one of the pictures in Figure 2–7. The pattern could be drawn on the board at child level or run off as a photocopy. The advantages of using a photocopy are that children may be less prone to copy other children and that later they can share their products with one another. In this way, they see that there are many, many possible responses.

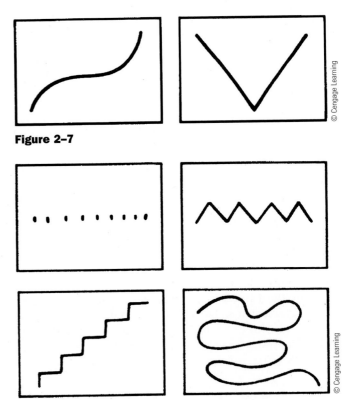

Figure 2–7

Figure 2–8

Kindergarten and School-Age Activity: Picture Possibilities. Draw one of the line or pattern pictures in Figure 2–8 on the board. Allow the children time to think about possible meanings. Ask them to give you a possible title or interpretation: "What do you see in this picture?" "What else could it be?"

Preschool, Kindergarten, and School-Age Activity: Tell Me about My Picture. Seat a small group of children in a close circle. Hold up an interesting picture you have clipped from a magazine or printed from the Internet. Try to find pictures that are vague and have a variety of possible meanings. Ask the children to examine the picture carefully and

- give different names or titles for the picture. What else could we call it? What else could this story be about? What happened to cause this? What could happen next?
- tell their own stories about this picture. Beginning writers can be encouraged to dictate or print their own story lines. Individual children may enjoy recording their stories at a learning center.

Preschool, Kindergarten, and School-Age Activity: Picture Guess. The open-ended designs in Figure 2–9 can be sketched on the board one at a time. Ask the children to study the shapes carefully. Allow think time, and do not encourage quick shouting out. Have the children brainstorm different things each picture could be.

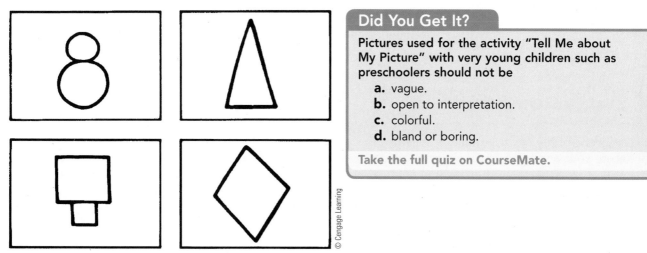

Figure 2–9

Did You Get It?

Pictures used for the activity "Tell Me about My Picture" with very young children such as preschoolers should not be

   a. vague.
   b. open to interpretation.
   c. colorful.
   d. bland or boring.

Take the full quiz on CourseMate.

An Opportunity for Teacher Reflection

Lisa Teaches Four-Year-Olds in a public school pre-kindergarten. Lisa works hard to promote and support the creativity of the children in her class. Her curriculum features activities to encourage divergent thinking. She includes time for children to explore and experiment and provides open-ended materials in learning centers to support imagination. Because her children are accustomed to pretending with open-ended materials, they frequently bring materials from other centers to the dramatic play center to use as props: paper from the art center, counters from the math center, and small blocks from the construction center. Lisa allows, even encourages, this creative use of materials across centers, as long as the children return the materials during clean-up. During the last few days, however, this borrowing of materials between centers has led to conflicts among the children. Builders in the block center have been upset when children from the dramatic play center wanted to borrow blocks. Loud voices, angry words, and tears have resulted as the children argued over who could use the blocks. Lisa is concerned and wondering how she can avoid conflict while still encouraging the use of open-ended materials across learning centers. *How could Lisa use this conflict as an opportunity to engage her children in creative problem-solving? What language might Lisa use to present the problem to the children? What open-ended questions might she ask the children?*

Summary

(2-1) There are many ways to engage in creative thinking. Play, the expressive arts (art, music, movement, dance, dramatics, and mime), language, and thought are just a few relevant to early childhood. (2-2) Both hemispheres of the brain make their own and complementary contributions to the creative process. Creative thought and production are characterized by fluency, flexibility, originality, and elaboration. (2-3) A positive classroom climate, large blocks of time during the day, and adequate space for moving, building, and interacting must be considered in a curriculum that supports creativity. (2-4) Further, there are many strategies that teachers can incorporate throughout the curriculum to support creativity. For example, posing problems that require creative solutions can be part of a math lesson or part of daily clean-up activities. (2-5) Teachers should consider children's abilities in language, drawing and writing when planning activites to support creative thinking.

Key Terms

✔ Suggested Activities

1. Do several of the creative-thinking activities. Record your responses. Use the rating scale to evaluate your divergent thinking and production. Record your strengths and weaknesses in fluency, flexibility, originality, and elaboration.

2. Do one of the creative-thinking activities with a small group of young children. Record their responses. Practice using the rating scale to evaluate their creative thinking.

3. Check out tests of creative thinking from the library or on the Internet and review them. Begin a file of creative-thinking activities. Be creative and modify test items rather than merely copying them.

4. Observe in a kindergarten or primary grade classroom. Select a time when the teacher is engaged in direct teaching. Record the questions the teacher asks. Are they closed/convergent or open/divergent? Do the teacher's questions accomplish the purpose of the activity? Explain.

5. Review the **Letter to Families** from the beginning of this section. Talk to a parent of a young child. Ask the parent to relate incidents of his or her child's creative thinking. Compare those incidents to your own ideas and definitions of creativity. How are they similar? How are they different?

Review

1. List components of divergent thinking and production.

2. Match each term with its description.

   – coming up with many possibilities
   – the uniqueness of an idea
   – making an idea rich
   – coming up with very different responses

   a. elaboration
   b. originality
   c. flexibility
   d. fleuncy
   e. complex

3. Name five specializations for each hemisphere of the brain.

4. List five ways adults can facilitate children's creative thinking.

5. Identify the two types of questions. Compare and contrast them. Which type of question is reflected in the following: "Children, I want each of you to think of what it means to be a friend." Justify your answer.

Additional Resources

Read about critical and creative thinking in Bloom's Taxonomy at Eduscapes.

This website provides an overview of educational resources and tips for teachers. (http://www.asa3.org/ASA /education/areas.htm).

Go to the Scholastic Website and look for the article, "Left Brain, Right Brain: Pathways to Reach Every Learner" by Diane Connell, Ed.D.

Go to the Creativeteacher.org Channel on YouTube for a series of videos in which teachers explore "Creative Teaching for Creative Learning."

 Visit CourseMate for this textbook to access the eBook, Did You Get It? quizzes, Digital Downloads, TeachSource Videos, flashcards, and more. Go to CengageBrain.com to log in, register, or purchase access.

First/Second Grade Lesson Plan

Thirty-six Views of Mount Fuji

GOAL

Each student will observe and record changes in the appearance of objects in the sky such as clouds, the moon, and stars, including the Sun.

OBJECTIVES

Upon completion of this lesson, each child will:

a. define "perspective" as it applies to art.
b. record changes of celestial objects in before and after paintings.

MATERIALS

a. Examples from Katsushiki Hokusai's series *Thirty-six Views of Mount Fuji* are available on-line
b. Manila paper and tempera paints for each child
c. Teddy bear

INTRODUCTION

Introduce Katsushiki Hokusai as a Japanese artist in the eighteenth and nineteenth centuries. Share paintings from the series "Thirty-six Views of Mount Fuji." Ask them to identify similarities and differences in the paintings, helping them to see Mount Fuji in each painting. Explain that Hokusai painted Mount Fuji multiple times, sometimes up close and sometimes far away, sometimes in the day, sometimes at night, in every different season, and in many different kinds of weather. He changed his *perspective* by painting it from different viewpoints. Write the word perspective on the board.

DEVELOPMENT

Place a teddy bear in the center of the room. Ask one child to stand behind the teddy bear and describe what he sees. Ask another child to stand in front of the bear and describe what she sees. Help the children to see that both observers are describing the same teddy bear, but what they see is different because they each have a different perspective, in the same way that Hokusai changed his perspective in different paintings of Mount Fuji.

Remind the children that over the last few days we have been studying the moon. We have learned that what we see of the moon changes as the Earth rotates and revolves, making it look different each week of the month. Review the phases of the moon. Share with the children that today they will be drawing two pictures of the same landscape, each showing a different perspective and each showing a different phase of the moon. Remind them that the different phases of the moon give different amounts of light, and that should be reflected in their paintings.

Distribute materials.

CONCLUSION

As the children finish their paintings, ask them to pair-share their paintings, explaining to their partners which phases of the moon they chose to portray.

ASSESSMENT

a. Did the children show two different perspectives in their drawings?
b. Did the children accurately portray two different phases of the moon?

A full-size version of this lesson plan and two other lesson plans for this chapter are available for digital download.

TeachSource Digital Download Download from CourseMate.

© Cengage Learning

What do you see in this picture?

Is Tanesha at work or is she "just playing"? Are art and play the same? Why or why not?

The teacher has provided easels that extend the art center. She believes in organization and plans so children have a defined work space when doing art. Individual pieces of chalk are provided in the cells of an ice cube tray. Tanesha uses the chalk and draws as she pleases. Drawing when seated provides a different physical experience than drawing while standing at the easel. Although Tanesha seems quite wrapped up in her drawing, double-sided easels could allow for social interaction. Rather than drawing a picture, Tanesha enjoys using linear vertical and horizontal chalk marks on her paper. This chapter will introduce the reader to a variety of mark-making activities.

Learning Outcomes

After reading this chapter, you should be able to:

3-1 Identify modes of creative expression within the arts.

3-2 Discuss the characteristics of play.

3-3 Describe how children use language creatively.

3-4 Develop creative experiences in music and movement for young children.

3-5 Explain how adults can facilitate children's creative expression.

3-6 Engage children in mark-making activities.

Standards addressed in this chapter

DAP Criteria

1 Creating a caring community of learners

2 Teaching to enhance development and learning

3 Planning curriculum to achieve important goals

NAEYC Standards

2 Curriculum

3 Teaching

8 Community

9 Physical environment

3-1 Modes of Creative Expression

Chapter 1 introduced the reader to creativity in its widest sense. Chapter 2 focused on creative thinking. This chapter begins a discussion of various art media by examining the process of mark making, as well as activities to help children make creative marks. It also outlines other ways that children express their creativity. These include play, language, and music and movement.

Creativity and creative expression—whether demonstrated through art, thinking, play, language, music, or movement—foster development of the whole child, including the physical, social-emotional, cognitive, and creative domains. For example, Tearra wants to use the unit blocks to make a doll house. Physically, she must lift, carry, manipulate, and position the blocks. Her eyes and hands work together as her fingers stack and straighten the blocks. Initially, Tearra works alone. Creativity respects the child's right to privacy. Later, she invites Portia to help. Socially, they work together practicing cooperative skills, including turn taking and sharing. They practice language skills as they talk and listen to each other.

Building a house to accommodate four dolls takes much thinking and planning. First they make a wall around their dolls but become dissatisfied, saying it looks too much like a cage. They want separate rooms for each doll. The problem is posed and they brainstorm different solutions—they are problem solving. Looking at their finished product, the girls are proud of their joint accomplishment, which enhances their self-esteem. Their structure is their own creative idea. They show their teacher, who takes photographs to add to their portfolios.

Our exploration of creativity in the first two chapters sets the stage for creative expression discussed in this chapter. Creativity requires the courage to think and act upon one's own thoughts. Nurturing adults must begin to encourage creative expression early in young children's lives (Di Leo, 2003). It is important to remember that art or visual art is merely one aspect of the arts. What is included in the term "the arts"? According to Edwards (2006) "the arts" include literature, drama, music, dance, and the visual arts. Edwards (2006) provides subcategories for each of the five arts as follows:

- Literature: poetry, illustrations, writing, books, story-telling, reading, and speaking
- Drama: creative dramatics, pantomime, improvisation, play production
- Music: sound, pitch, rhythm, singing, playing musical instruments, musical games, listening, and creative movement
- Dance: body awareness, movement, and creative expression
- Visual Arts: self-expression, visual and tactile art, print and craft media, artistic analysis, and interpretation; both two-dimensional (drawing, painting, printing) and three-dimensional (modeling, sculpting, construction)

For young children a comprehensive arts program is most effective, including opportunities for them to respond to art through conversation, storytelling, play, drama, movement, music, and making art (Mulcahey, 2009). This chapter will discuss the modes of creative expression for young children found in play, literature and drama, and music and movement. The visual arts will be addressed in the chapters that follow.

Why are the arts important? According to Wright (2003), the arts involve a unique form of knowing—thinking that fuses thought, emotion, and action. Through the arts, children are involved in a special kind of literacy in which they turn action into representation. Because artistic thinking involves meaning and understanding, Wright (2003) recommends ample time in the curriculum for young children to experience the arts, their modes of expression, and related processes. This helps develop an understanding of the artistic components: processes, discipline-based forms of expression, elements, and concepts. What are the goals of art education for young children? The National Standards for Arts Education provides recommended skills and abilities for children from kindergarten through fourth grade. (See Appendix D.)

Did You Get It?

What is not a component of the art subfield of music?
- **a.** rhythm
- **b.** movement
- **c.** listening
- **d.** pantomime

Take the full quiz on CourseMate.

3-2 Children Express Their Creativity Through Play

Balke (1997) sees similarities in children's play and art. She believes that play's expressive elements are what make it similar to the work of the artist. Children play with toys just as artists play with media. Although neither art nor play is necessary to survival, she questions what life would be like without art. She asks, "How could we have culture without art?" Similarly, "What would childhood be like without play?"

What is **play**? Play is a difficult concept to understand because it lacks a precise definition. A variety of behaviors can be labeled play, ranging from what infants do with their bodies and toys, to games, hobbies, sports, recreational pursuits, and creative activities such as art, music, and dance. Although play cannot be precisely defined, perhaps it can be contrasted with work. Historically, play has been viewed as the opposite of work. It was the Puritan work ethic that gave impetus to this work-play dichotomy. Adult work was considered earnest, serious, worthwhile, productive activity. By contrast, children's play was viewed as idle, frivolous fun bordering on evil. The present impact of this thinking is evident when a child is said to be "just" playing. The qualifying *just* connotes a lack of purpose. Rarely does one complain about a child who "just" reads, because this behavior is valued. This negative attitude toward play is reflected by parents and educators who feel that children must work rather than play if they are to learn.

Generally speaking, play is process-oriented while work is product-oriented. One plays for the sake of playing; one works for the outcome of one's endeavors. Examples of creative processing through play include:

- building with blocks, stacking or fitting them together
- filling and emptying containers with water
- using kitchen tools and containers to scoop, sift, and mold sand
- pounding and hammering nails into soft wood; sawing and gluing wood pieces together
- making up a new version of tag, hide-and-seek, hopscotch, or jump rope

So, what is play? Garvey (1990) identifies five criteria that define play:

1. Play is pleasurable and enjoyable.
2. Play has no extrinsic goals. Children are intrinsically motivated to play. They play because they want to.
3. Play is spontaneous and voluntary. Play empowers children to make decisions about what to play, who to play with, and how to carry it out, as well as when to start and finish.
4. Play involves active engagement from the player. Young children are active learners, and play is an active process.
5. Play is linked to nonplay in children's thinking and development. Play fosters development of the whole child and supports learning in all curricular areas.

During play, children are physically and mentally active, socializing with their peers, and feeling good about what they have playfully made happen. Because there is no right or wrong way to play, children are creative and successful at play, and their self-esteem is enhanced. Play also allows children to express and master feelings and emotions. They think and form concepts while playing.

According to Elkind (2003), play is as fundamental a human disposition as loving and working. Play is characteristic of children at all times and places. We play because we are programmed to play. It is part of human nature.

In reviewing the literature on the benefits of play, Berk (1994) found:

1. Make-believe play strengthens a variety of specific mental abilities.
2. Language is greatly enriched by play experiences.
3. Make-believe also fosters young children's ability to reason about impossible or absurd situations—a finding highly consistent with Vygotsky's (1986) position that fantasy play assists children in separating meanings from the objects for which they stand.
4. Young children who especially enjoy pretending or who are encouraged to engage in fantasy play score higher on tests of imagination and creativity.

In sum, fantasy play contributes to social maturity and knowledge construction. For people who question whether play activities, so natural and absorbing to children, must be curbed in favor of more *productive* activities or whether play constitutes a powerful zone of proximal development, the findings reviewed clearly grant play a legitimate place in children's lives.

DAP naeyc 3-2a **The Teacher's Role in Children's Play**

According to Balke (1997), the younger the child, the more important the adult's involvement in the play. Yet what exactly should the adult role be? Jones (1993) says the teacher's role in children's play should be nondirective. She believes that adults who take over or monopolize play are denying children their need to invent or construct it for themselves. Because children do benefit from adult input into their play, Jones recommends the following five strategies:

1. setting the stage
2. adding props and dramatic ideas
3. helping with problem solving
4. observing and talking with children about their plans and ideas
5. helping children invent new plans or rework old ones based on their observations of children at play

She suggests that adults share and model their own playfulness without overwhelming children or performing for them.

3-2b Creative Play with Boxes, Cartons, and Accessories

Merritt (1967) said that every child who achieves some kind of concrete representation of his or her ideas is demonstrating creativity. Children can be creative with just about anything they find. Play materials need to be safe, clean, and sturdy to foster creativity, but not expensive. Costly commercial toys may not enhance creativity, despite their labeling. Empty cardboard boxes and containers are great props for fostering creative play because they are safe, sturdy, durable, recycled, versatile, and can be used indoors or outdoors. Large appliance cartons can easily become structures or vehicles. They can also be personalized using tape, paint, crayons, or markers. Cut doors and windows for the children, but do not suggest what the box should become. Let the children impart their own meaning. Providing more than one large appliance carton fosters small-group cooperative play in which individual children have space and a role in the activity.

Play with boxes requires supervision. Some children do not like being enclosed in a small area. Adding props or accessories such as old sheets and a steering wheel increases the range of creative possibilities. Use cartons to enhance your language and literacy program. A carton decorated like a house sets the stage for dramatizing classic books such as *Goldilocks and the Three Bears*. A carton-turned-bridge facilitates the dramatization of *The Three Billy Goats Gruff*.

3-2c Types of Play

Play takes many shapes and forms. These overlapping categories include physical play, constructive play, dramatic play, play with natural materials, and games.

naeyc Physical Play. Physical play involves motor activity and movement, entailing both gross motor (large muscle) and fine motor (involving the small muscles and eye-hand coordination) activity.

Outdoor play activities such as running, climbing up and going down a slide, riding tricycles, and jumping involve gross motor or large muscle activity. Large muscle play can occur indoors, but limited space may restrict it. Still, indoor climbing structures do provide for gross motor activity, especially on days when the weather keeps children inside.

Activities with manipulatives such as stringing beads, pegs and peg boards, parquetry and design blocks, puzzles, small blocks, sewing and lacing cards, and table toys that lead to sorting or being taken apart and put back together involve fine motor or small muscle activity as well as eye-hand coordination. Because young children are physical beings, physical play is a high priority. Infants grasp and release soft toys and shake rattles. For a toddler, physical play means repeatedly filling and dumping toys into a plastic bucket while wandering about the room. Preschoolers enjoy fitting Lego® blocks and bristle blocks together. Whether they actually make something is secondary to the process of fitting together and taking apart. Kindergartners have mastered puzzles with many pieces and may build complex structures with connecting blocks while dramatizing with small people and vehicles.

School-age children who have mastered running, catching, throwing, and skipping may progress to competitive games involving races and tests of physical prowess.

PHYSICAL PLAY ON THE OUTDOOR PLAYGROUND Rarely does an early childhood program have enough outdoor space or equipment for outdoor play. Space is often at a premium, and some sites have only a blacktop or small yard with which to work. Others must share space with different age groups or have inherited outdated equipment. Quality playground equipment is expensive. If children were to have their say, however, they would probably allocate most of the annual budget and daily schedule to outdoor play (see Figure 3–1). The following areas and materials are recommended for well-equipped outdoor play environments:

- water table, dishpans or tubs, kitchen gadgets, and containers.
- sandbox or sand table, dishpans or tubs, kitchen gadgets, and containers.
- carpentry or woodworking table with sturdy tools, goggles, lightweight woods.
- flexible, multipurpose, multilevel equipment for large muscle activities like climbing, jumping, and sliding.

Photo Courtesy of Jill Englebright Fox

Figure 3–1 Physical play outdoors is an important large muscle activity.

- riding vehicles (simple and complex, one—and two-passenger) and a clearly defined one-way path, traffic cones, and signs.
- art materials on an art cart and easels that are freestanding or attached to a fence.
- music and movement materials, including dance props, rhythm instruments, recorded music and player.
- pets or small animals and cages.
- garden and gardening tools.
- playhouse, dress-up clothes, bridge, stage, elevated platform or other structure for dramatic play.
- shady area for looking at books or listening to and telling stories.

- obstacle course stations to jump on and off, crawl through, and so on.
- construction materials: large and small blocks, barrels, boards, planks, lumber, old sheets, crates, cardboard boxes, appliance cartons, large sheets of cardboard, tires, tree stump, and so on.
- assorted props: balance beam, balls in a variety of sizes, jump ropes, bean bags, hoops, ring toss, parachute, flat wooden ladder, cargo net, low basketball hoop and net, and so on.

DAP **naeyc** **Constructive Play.** Children play constructively when they manipulate materials with the goal of creating something new or something representing a real object (Kieff & Casbergue, 2000). **Constructive play**

SOMETHING EXTRA.....

Play Therapy

Play is an intense sensory experience which provides physical stimulation. It is a developmentally appropriate means for building adult-child relationships, developing cause-effect thinking critical to impulse control, processing stressful experiences, and learning social skills. Through play therapy, the child gains a sense of power and control which can be used to solve problems and to master new experiences, ideas, and concerns. This in turn builds feelings of confidence and accomplishment (Drewes & Schaefer, 2010).

Play is a natural language for children and provides a medium for working out problems and communicating with others as well an appropriate modality for therapy. **Play therapy** is a dynamic interpersonal relationship between a child and a counselor or therapist trained in this procedure, which provides selected play materials and facilitates the development of a safe relationship for the child to fully express and explore self through play (Landreth, 2012). Here, a counselor uses toys and play as the primary vehicle to communicate with children (Kottman, 2009). Landreth (2012) explains that play is children's symbolic language, which offers a way to express experiences and emotions in a natural, self-healing process. The manipulation of toys allows children to show how they feel about themselves, people, and events in their lives more adequately than talking (Ginott, as cited in Henderson & Thompson, 2011).

Although play therapy works with all ages, including adults, most play therapy is done with children between the ages of 3 to 12. It is effective with children experiencing a wide variety of social, emotional, behavioral, and learning problems. As well, play therapy can be helpful with children struggling with various life situations:

abuse and/or neglect, adoption, divorce of parents, family violence, grief, hospitalization, chronic or terminal illness, parental deployment, severe trauma, and post-traumatic stress disorder brought on by such events as war, earthquakes, car accidents, and kidnapping (Vernon, 2009). It has been identified as the treatment of choice in school, mental health, agency, developmental, hospital, residential, and recreational settings (Carmichael, 2006; Reddy, Files-Hall, & Schaefer, 2005). The Association for Play Therapy purports that play therapy helps children:

- Become more responsible for behaviors and develop more successful strategies
- Develop new and creative solutions to problems
- Develop respect and acceptance of self and others
- Learn to experience and express emotion
- Cultivate empathy and respect for thoughts and feelings of others
- Learn new social skills and relational skills with family
- Develop self-efficacy and thus a better assuredness about their abilities Reprinted with the expressed consent of the Association for Play Therapy.

Children must be approached and understood from a developmentally appropriate perspective. It is the counselor's responsibility to know how to communicate effectively at all levels. Children often are inaccessible at a verbal level and developmentally unprepared to express their feelings. Play therapy offers children the opportunity to respond and to bridge gaps between their experiences and abstract thinking. It allows children to express their inner world in concrete form.

Written by Elsa Soto Leggett, PhD, LPC-S, RPT

is organized and goal-oriented (Johnson, Christie, & Wardle, 2005). Although constructive play is most often associated with woodworking and blocks, children also play constructively when they are engaged with art media and other manipulatives to create something that will remain, even after the play is over. Constructive play is probably the most common activity of young children (Christie & Johnson, 1987), and it occurs in both indoor and outdoor settings. The process of physically constructing new connections between objects and their own thoughts makes constructive play a valuable opportunity for creative expression and innovation (Drew, et al., 2008).

Building with blocks is one example of constructive play. Dramatization, as well as physical activity, may be a part of block play. In Figure 3–2 children are using blocks to build a farm and dramatizing with related props. Blocks serve all facets of development, as seen earlier in the play of Tearra and Portia. Physically, blocks are lifted and carried, enhancing development and coordination of small and large muscles. Socially, children may interact and talk with others as they build. This involves cooperative group effort and social give and take. Emotionally, children feel good about what they have successfully created. Destruction of the creation may bring emotional release and as much joy as the construction. Cognitively, children think, plan, and learn about balance, height, shape, space, cause and effect, architectural forms, and even gravity when tall towers give way to an unsturdy base. Because block play is open-ended, it fosters creative development.

TYPES OF BLOCKS There are several types of blocks: unit, large hollow, cardboard bricks, and miscellaneous, including smaller table blocks and those made of soft foam. Wooden blocks, including unit and large hollow, are an expensive but sound investment. If properly cared for, they will last many years. Wooden unit blocks

are built to scale—square or half unit, unit, double unit, and quadruple unit—so children encounter mathematical concepts as they compare blocks by length. There is also an array of block shapes, including curve, ellipse, switch, triangle, ramp, column, buttress, arch, and pillar that supplement the lengths of unit blocks. Older block builders may rely on some of the additional shapes but do not feel obligated to purchase multiples of each and every shape, especially for beginning block builders.

BLOCK CENTER Block play requires ample space and protection from foot traffic. Building on a carpet reduces noise levels. Blocks should never be randomly placed in a box or storage bin. This damages the finish, edges, and corners. Instead, blocks should be arranged on low, open shelves according to size, length, and shape so they are easily found and put away. Reserve a bottom shelf for the heavier pieces with lightweight props on the higher shelves. Providing an outline of the block shape helps in matching and cleanup. Trace the shape of the block onto colored contact paper, cut it out, and attach it to the back of the appropriate shelf. Provide props such as small animals, people, vehicles, and traffic signs to enrich block play, as well as small sheets for roofs, boards for ramps, blue construction paper for water, Plexiglas®, and masking tape for streets or sidewalks. Similar props such as cars and trucks can be kept together in clear tubs. Rotate props and include items connected to the curriculum. For example, include toy fish and blue fabric when studying sea life.

There is nothing more frustrating to young builders than having their construction "accidentally" knocked down. This can be avoided by reminding children not to build too close to each other or too close to classroom walk ways. To make cleanup less chaotic, remind children to only take a few blocks out at a time and then use them before going for more. Also, dismantling buildings from the top down eliminates unnecessary noise and accidents.

Whereas unit blocks stress fine motor and eye-hand coordination, large, hollow blocks provide a gross motor and large muscle challenge. They also allow children to build larger, child-proportioned structures. Include steering wheels for children who make child-sized vehicles with large blocks. Smaller unit blocks encourage children to build in miniature, which is why small props are provided.

Blocks foster active play, and you will need to set guidelines regarding safety issues like how high children can build. Children may also need this reminder: "Blocks are for building, not throwing. They are heavy and can hurt." These printed words can appear as signs in the block center. Keep a camera ready to photograph block constructions. Take dictation or encourage children to write the words that accompany their

© Cengage Learning

Figure 3–2 Constructive play with blocks.

buildings. The dated photos can be included in their portfolios. Children may need assistance in making signs such as "Please do not knock down" or "Keep up." Reserve a shelf in the block area for books on construction and building, along with paper and writing instruments. This will connect block play with literacy. Along with labeled shelves, include photographs of multicultural homes and neighborhoods, as well as males and females involved in related pursuits like construction, farming, and transportation.

Cardboard bricks are a third type of block. They are inexpensive and not sturdy. They are large but lightweight, which inhibits complex building such as making high towers and may frustrate the skilled builder. On the positive side, they make less noise when they tumble. On the negative side, children enjoy walking on them, which quickly destroys them. Cardboard bricks are a good choice for the very young, who can later graduate to heavier wooden blocks. Make your own blocks by covering shoe boxes or milk cartons with contact paper.

Other types of blocks include rubber, foam, and small table blocks. Rubber and foam blocks are lightweight, inexpensive, and recommended for young and beginning block builders. Table blocks, which are smaller than unit blocks, involve small muscle control and eye-hand coordination and result in construction on a smaller scale. Different types of blocks can also supplement each other during constructive play.

DAP **naeyc** **Dramatic Play.** Dramatic play is also referred to as play that involves fantasy, imagination, or make-believe. Children engage in dramatic play alone or with others and usually with props. When children play, they build in their minds a scenario in which they see themselves in control of the themes and details of their pretend play (Heath & Wolf, 2004a). A child who is dressing a baby doll is engaging in dramatic or symbolic play. Toddlers learn that the doll symbolically represents a real baby. A preschooler may use a box as a table. Children who engage in dramatic play have attained representational ability. They are able to re-create and represent what they know.

Dramatic play encourages children's social and emotional development. When children feel safe and protected, they can act out scenarios or events that are troubling to them. As children negotiate all the situations inherent in group dramatic play, they feel a sense of competence and satisfaction in their own abilities (Miller, 2008).

Children practice language and social skills, as well as planning and decision-making skills, in dramatic play. Because dramatic play is open-ended, children cannot fail. Instead, children grow and learn at their own pace, according to where they are in their own development (Miller, 2008).

Smilansky (1968, 1971) views socio-dramatic play as an advanced form of dramatic play. Socio-dramatic play revolves around a theme with children engaging in behaviors that support the theme. For example, Figures 3–3, 3–4, 3–5, and 3–6 document socio-dramatic play around a medical theme.

What are the characteristics that qualify make-believe as socio-dramatic play? According to Smilansky these include:

Role playing—Children assume make-believe or pretend roles involving talk and action. What are the roles that you see played out in Figures 3–3a–d?

Make-believe with objects—Children use make-believe objects to represent real ones. What make-believe objects are visible in Figures 3–3a–d

Make-believe with actions or events—Socio-dramatic play incorporates situations or events related to the theme. What actions or events are happening in Figures 3–3a–d?

Verbalizations—Verbal expressions are related to the play theme. What could the children be saying in Figures 3–3a–d?

Social interaction—At least two players are engaged in socio-dramatic play. Is this criterion met in Figures 3–3a–d?

Persistence—The play episode engages children for more than five minutes. Although it may not be evident from examining Figures 3–3a–d, this particular socio-dramatic play episode lasted much longer than five minutes, with children leaving and returning periodically.

Socio-dramatic play is a more organized, cooperative type of fantasy play engaged in by older preschoolers, kindergartners, and young school-age children in which roles are divided and players have different parts. For example, in playing house, there may be a mommy, a daddy, twin babies, and a pet dog. Each child has a role, function, and speaking part to play.

In Vygotsky's (1978) sociocultural theory (see Chapter 4) play serves at least four major purposes:

1. Play, and representational play in particular, creates a zone of proximal development within which children advance to higher levels of psychological functioning. Through play, children not only repeat concepts and skills already learned but also challenge themselves to learn new, higher level ones.

2. Representational play helps children learn roles and rules, for it is driven by rules for behavior that children must follow to successfully act out a play scenario. Make-believe play not only

supports development in the preschool years but also evolves into games with rules during middle childhood.

3. In representational play, young children create an imaginary situation that permits them to cope with unrealizable desires and develop the capacity to renounce impulsive action in favor of deliberate, self-regulatory activity.

4. Fantasy play helps children in separating meaning from the objects for which they stand. Play is vital preparation for the later development of abstract thinking.

DRAMATIC PLAY CENTER An indoor dramatic play center can be located next to the block area because both invite loud, active, imaginative play. Similar items should be organized, grouped together, and labeled. Providing furniture that resembles a home, including a table and chairs, cooking and eating equipment, kitchen appliances, food, multiethnic dolls and clothing, stuffed animals, mirrors, and telephones sets a familiar and comfortable stage. Props enhance dramatic play by expanding the realm of creative

possibilities. Children are learning about their social world, so expect boys to try on skirts and jewelry and girls to play being the daddy. Providing open-ended props like a sheet or one-inch wooden cubes will challenge older preschoolers.

Connecting Dramatic Play to the Curriculum. Connect dramatic play to your curriculum. Providing "money," such as poker chips or strips of green construction paper, facilitates counting; grouping food in the grocery store builds classification skills. Include books on multiethnic families and the occupations currently being studied. Children can only re-create what they know, so they will have difficulty dramatizing being a banker or a farmer unless they have directly experienced what you want them to act out. Invite a parent who is a dentist to set the stage for dental play in your dramatic play corner. Encourage socio-dramatic play by building prop boxes for dramatic play around a theme (see Figures 3–3a–d). For example, collect clothing and props related to a veterinary hospital and place them in a large box labeled with symbols (e.g., pictures of animals and the word *Veterinarian*). The following items might be included: stuffed animals, lab coats, surgical

© Cengage Learning

Figure 3–3 Socio-dramatic play involves pretend play and social interaction.

gowns and masks, and Red Cross armbands for doctors and nurses; lab coats for office workers and dress-up clothes for pet owners; doctor tools and medical bag, Band-Aids, and length of gauze; boxes, baskets, bowls, and brushes for sick pets. Introduce your prop box with a book, or better yet a field trip or class visit by a vet. Connect your prop box and dramatic play area to literacy. Include writing instruments, clipboards, stamps, papers, envelopes, cookbooks, and magazines. Specific literacy props for dramatizing a veterinary hospital include an appointment book, old X-rays, a doctor's In/Out sign, magazines for the waiting room, and books on animals, first aid, or veterinarians. Including paper and writing tools will encourage children to write letters, lists, receipts, and to send and receive mail.

Favorite stories can be acted out in the dramatic play area. This will work better with children who have interacted in socio-dramatic play. Start with a simple nursery rhyme such as "Humpty Dumpty," moving on to short stories with a few characters, simple plots, and manageable speaking lines. Provide simple costumes and props to ease children into the roles. For example, Humpty Dumpty may wear a simple crown, and horses may hold simple masks. Girls and boys can play the king's men and take creative liberty to change the rhyme to include "all the king's people."

CELEBRATING DIVERSITY THROUGH DRAMATIC PLAY To make the dramatic play area diverse, incorporate the following strategies, tools, props, and clothing for children to explore race and ethnicity, culture, gender, and special needs. Always begin with the diversity represented in your classroom and expand from there to other groups in your community.

- Stage rooms of the house other than the kitchen. Include male and female clothing, pictures of both boys and girls, men and women, and pictures and books that show diverse family compositions.
- Include tools and equipment for people with special needs. Examples include wheelchairs, walkers, braces, ramps, eyeglasses (without lenses), books written in Braille, crutches, canes, and magnifiers.
- Include food containers, boxes, and tins representing items from different cultures and with labels in different languages.
- Include clothing, shoes, hats, scarves, and belts that represent both everyday wear and holiday attire from a variety of cultures.
- Supply multiracial dolls and dolls with adaptive equipment for a range of disabilities.
- Include eating utensils from different cultures such as Chinese soup spoons; chopsticks; and wooden, tin, and plastic bowls, dishes, cups, and ladles.

- Have cooking utensils from different countries on hand, including saucepans, kettles, steamers, strainers, wok, garlic press, tortilla press, grater, tea balls, fry pans, whisks, and so on.
- Supply cushions, pillows, mats, small area rugs, and placemats from traditional cultures decorated with representative colors, patterns, and designs.
- Include a variety of infant carriers such as baskets, strollers, infant slings, and Native American cradle boards.
- Have a variety of beds and bedding for dolls including blankets, cradles, hammocks, and futons.

DAP **naeyc** **Play with Natural Materials.** Adults who appreciate a walk on the beach, splashing in the waves, or smelling and feeling sawed wood will understand how play with water, sand, and wood appeal to young children. Play with natural materials is sensory-rich and soothing. Although water is wet and sand is dry, both hold great sensory appeal and lead children to similar discoveries; for example, both can be poured and measured. Children can also discover that water, sand, and wood have unique properties. Unlike sand, water can freeze and melt. Wood can be sawed into small pieces and attached with either glue or a hammer and nails. Natural materials are open-ended and provide unlimited creative possibilities while also supporting physical, social, emotional, cognitive, and language development. Along with the obvious physical challenge, carpentry and woodworking foster children's verbal and social interaction. They develop skills in observation, problem solving, measurement, and hypothesizing.

WATER/SAND PLAY Water and sand need large containers that will provide ample room for small group play. Tables for water/sand play with lids are commercially available and a sound investment. They tend to be large enough to accommodate four children and come with a drain plug. Alternatives might include a baby bathtub or a shallow wading pool.

Place your table near the sink and cover the surrounding floor area with a vinyl shower curtain or old towels that can be thrown in the dryer when wet. Cleanup equipment for mopping up water or sweeping up spills should be kept on an adjacent storage shelf. Provide waterproof smocks and remind children to roll up their sleeves. Children should also keep a change of clothing in their cubbies. Limit the number of children on the basis of the size of your water or sand table. Discuss guidelines and limits and set them in positive terms: "We play with sand and water and keep it in the table. Splashing water gets our friends wet." "Throwing sand is dangerous and can hurt the eyes." Give

Figure 3–4 Many children prefer to rotate sensory materials in an outdoor table.

children a choice of either upholding the guidelines or playing somewhere else. Remind children that part of the cycle of playing with water and sand is cleaning up.

Water/sand play can occur both indoors and outdoors. Some teachers prefer to have an indoor sensory table that rotates contents between water (with and without soap bubbles); sand; shaving cream; nature specimens such as shells, pebbles, stone, or flower petals; snow; shaved ice; aquarium gravel; marbles; sawdust; birdseed; or cornstarch and water (see Figure 3–4). It is of foremost importance that children experience the tactile quality of the contents. Later, add props and accessories to supplement tactile exploration. Choose those that are appropriate for contents. Check the book's Website for a list of materials and a list of activities for play in the water/sand table.

CARPENTRY OR WOODWORKING The thought of carpentry or woodworking and young children concerns some educators. It may be a safety issue or one's own discomfort level based on a lack of knowledge and skills in using tools. Tools empower boys and girls as well as provide opportunities in refining large muscle and fine motor skills and eye-hand coordination. Carpentry and woodworking also allow for emotional release. An angry child who has difficulty verbalizing his or her feelings can hammer or saw them out. This does not address the heart of the problem but it does relieve pent-up anger. Tools must be individually introduced through modeling, with children practicing the correct way to hold and use a tool. Safety is a foremost consideration. Carpentry or woodworking takes very close supervision with a maximum of four children participating at a time, one per corner. Children should wear aprons and safety goggles. Provide real tools in smaller sizes as opposed to toy tools which can easily bend and snap. Tools can be displayed on the peg-board with

the outlines of each drawn around it. Tables can be commercially purchased, but a handyperson could easily make one to your specifications, or simply cut the legs off a wooden kitchen table. Sawhorses with a sturdy plank or old door that has been securely attached can also be used. Height is important—the bench should be waist-high to the children, neither too high nor too low. Provide a sturdy workbench in the center, along with materials listed on the book's Website. Young children will approach carpentry or woodworking activities with a process orientation. They want to see what they can do with tools, wood, and fasteners. Sawing wood and hammering nails are pleasurable in and of themselves. Older children will be more interested in making something and may even plan their finished product in advance. Encourage them to make blueprints or simple sketches of what they plan to make. Invite children to:

- hammer nails into layers of cardboard that have been glued together, a tree stump, Styrofoam™, or a block of plasticine
- hammer golf tees into Styrofoam
- tighten screws on toys, tricycles, and furniture
- use sandpaper on rough edges of blocks of wood or on old wooden toys and blocks
- use tools to make block props
- glue wood scraps into a wood collage

DAP **naeyc** **Games.** Have you ever observed a teacher trying to play duck, duck, goose with a group of young children? They play out of turn and do their own thing. Young children have difficulty playing games. Their egocentricity keeps them from waiting, taking turns, and playing by the rules. They change and break the rules at whim to make it work for them. This is not cheating, but rather reflects an inability to hold to rules that protect others and may keep them from winning. With years of social interaction, older children see how rules protect the rights of all individuals and may ostracize a child whom they believe is cheating.

Games are competitive, usually resulting in a winner and loser. This may be difficult for children to face. Depending on your group it may be wise to modify games. For example, musical chairs can be modified so that the play is ongoing but no chairs are removed so there are no losers; everyone gets to play every round of the game. School-age children, however, become socially competitive as they test their mental prowess with card and board games. They compare physical abilities such as aiming, racing, chasing, or hiding, and in sports such as baseball, soccer, basketball, and kickball. You may want to introduce them to cooperative games that foster team building and cooperation rather than winning at the expense of others.

DAP naeyc 3-3 Children Express Their Creativity Through Language

The profile of the creative child reminds the authors of two famous characters in children's literature. First, like the little boy in *The Emperor's New Clothes*, creative children are able to see what others do not. They are also able to stand up for their beliefs and not yield to social pressure, whereas others may change their opinions to conform and not appear different. Second, like the ugly duckling who becomes the beautiful swan, children can trust their creativity to help them become the unique individuals they are destined to be. Help children acknowledge and accept their creative uniqueness by identifying with characters in literature.

The early years are a time of rapid language development. Language is acquired through meaningful interactions rather than learned in formal lessons. Children learn an extensive collection of words or vocabulary, which helps them communicate with others. The infant who says "bobba" will be given a bottle by an adult who knows the infant is asking for a bottle. Saying "bobba" will not get a ride in the car although saying "go" may. Much of language development entails learning that words refer to specific objects and actions. Children also creatively invent their own words as evidenced in the following examples:

- Sahid calls his brother's convertible a "top-down car."
- When served pancakes for breakfast, Jocelyn exclaims, "Oh good, flat cakes; my favorite."
- Gabrielle asks her teacher for "cutters" as she points to the empty scissors rack.
- Daryl asks his mother if he can talk to his grandma on the "hello phone."
- Amira walks with a doll in the stroller as she announces, "I'm getting a baby pusher like this for my birthday."

- During lunch Cory argues that they are drinking "cow juice," not milk.
- Mrs. Lo is doing a food activity with her small group. She passes an uncut pineapple to Orin who remarks, "Oh, Christmas tree fruit."
- McKenzie's parents pack a slice of pepperoni pizza in her lunch box. Her friends look on with envy as she exclaims, "Oh, cold meatzza for lunch!"
- Vui is proud of her new umbrella. She says, "See my new rain-brella."
- Mother asks, "Did you get in trouble today at school?" Skeet answers, "Nunce. Not even once!"
- Emily reminds her grandma to take the God book (Bible) to church with her.
- While at the beach, Carmen ran to get her parents to come see the "walking shells" (hermit crabs).

Language is actively constructed. Children invent words and creatively err when forming plurals or verb

Hints

- Demonstrate for children how to hold a hammer. Young children tend to grasp the hammer near the head. Holding the handle farther back, however, provides greater leverage and pressure. You may want to tap a nail to help children begin hammering. Or push the nail through an index card with the child holding the end of the card as he or she strikes the nail. This way, fingers and thumbs stay clear of the hammer. When the nail is adequately pounded, the index card can be pulled away.

- Provide nails that are short with broad heads, such as roofing nails. Longer nails take too long to hammer in and often bend in the process.

- To help children use a saw, secure wood in a vise or C-clamp. Help the child hold the saw at a 45-degree angle and use light pressure to rhythmically move the saw downward in a back and forth motion.

- Reserve the hand drill for use with school-age children. It is difficult to operate since one hand applies downward pressure while the other makes it go around. Also, young children tend to turn the handle backward, which loosens the drill bit.

- Make cleanup fun. Provide brooms and dustpans for sweeping up sawdust and magnets for picking up fallen nails, nuts, bolts, and screws. Always match up tools to their outline on the peg-board. Tools left lying around pose potential safety problems.

tenses. They are constructing the rules of language and may over-generalize in the process. Knowing that you add an *s* to the end of words to form plurals leads children to talk about "geeses" and "fishes." Because *ed* is added to the end of a word to signify past tense, children proudly announce, "I wented home," or "I goed to school." Adults who have learned English as a second language will testify that English is a complex language with more exceptions than regularities. Express interest as children creatively construct and invent words that work and make sense to them. There is no need to correct. Instead say, "Meatzza—that's a clever name for meat pizza." In this way, McKenzie learns that her creative expression through language is valued but that conventional alternatives also exist.

3-3a **Informal Creative Language Activities**

A child's waking day offers a wealth of opportunities for fostering language development (see Figure 3–5). Children in school learn language while interacting with peers and adults. In considering the structure of a program for young children, adults should recognize that children who are vertically grouped with a range of ages are exposed to a wider array of vocabulary and language patterns than children who are grouped by identical chronological age. Regardless of the grouping, teachers must model and provide opportunities for speaking, listening, reading, and writing. Try some of the following informal creative language activities.

- Provide oral language props, including puppets, telephones, and walkie-talkies. These props help shy children and those beginning to learn English.

- Tell stories in novel ways using unusual props. Invite children to tell you stories or "read" the pictures in books.

- Make storytelling props like felt or Pellon® (interfacing) pieces available to children. Tell them how much you enjoy being at the receiving end of a good story.

- Take creative liberty with traditional and contemporary literature. Add, change, or delete characters. For example, invent new adventures for Dazzle the Dinosaur and his friend Maia.

- Take dictation. Ask children if there are words or a story to go along with their artwork. Carefully listen, write, and read it back. Encourage the child to read along with you (see Figures 3–6, 3–7, and 3–8).

- Observe opportune times to get involved and facilitate children's play. For example, children who are simply sitting in the dramatic play area may be waiting for a good idea. Facilitate play by suggesting that the babies appear hungry and may want to go out to eat before their afternoon nap. Stay involved as long as necessary but without imposing your way of doing things.

Photo Courtesy of Jill Englebright Fox

Figure 3–5 Gisele shares her art with her teacher.

Photo Courtesy of Robert Schirrmacher

Figure 3–6 Keara learned about the first letter of her name.

Figure 3–7 Curtis dictated his story to his teacher.

Figure 3–8 Joseph wrote the caption for his picture: "I like lightning."

3-3b Literacy and Multiple Literacies

The term literacy means knowing how to read and write. Emergent literacy explains the spontaneous and early unfolding of reading and writing in the early years. Children are meaning makers. They construct meaning from spoken and printed words. As with intelligence, the single definition of literacy is being questioned. There are many ways to be literate. Broadly speaking, being literate means being well educated. As with multiple intelligences, there are **multiple literacies**. The concept of multiliteracy acknowledges multimodal ways of thinking. According to Wright (2003), a multiliteracy approach to education views children as transformers and reshapers of knowledge who use a range of representational resources and multiple modes of thinking. The early experience of young children with the computer gives credence to the concept of technologic literacy, including computers, the Internet, and digital media as well as hypertext, Web pages, and e-mail messages. The same holds true for

mathematical and scientific literacies. A case can also be made for the development of artistic literacy, because art is a complex form of object and imagery. Constructing insightful meaning from art requires time, focus, reflection, effort, and analysis. In summary, there are many ways to be competent and literate in our postmodern, rapidly changing, technologic world. Visual and **media literacy** will be discussed in the next section.

DAP naeyc 3-3c Visual Literacy

From an early age, children are immersed in a visual culture composed of visual images that bombard their senses at an alarming rate, given their hours of screen time. Children are surrounded with visual images, whether it be pictures of new toys in a catalog or the logo on a cereal box. Based on the idea that visual images are a language, **visual literacy** can be defined as the ability to understand and produce visual messages. Children become visually literate by the practice of visual encoding and decoding. Visual encoding involves expressing one's thoughts and ideas in visual form. Visual decoding involves translating and understanding the meaning of visual imagery. The importance of visual literacy is increasing because of the ever-expanding proliferation of mass media in society. Children live in an information environment saturated with visual images. As more and more information and entertainment are acquired though nonprint media, such as television, videos, movies, video and computer games, and the Internet, the ability to think critically about the images presented becomes crucial.

3-3d Picture Books and Visual Literacy

Picture books develop children's visual literacy. A picture book is any book in which the message depends upon pictures as much as, if not more than, the text. The pictures must be accurate and synchronized with the text to give the reader key information regarding the written text. A storyline, however, is not required as is the case with ABC, counting, and single concept books. Wordless picture books usually do tell a story, though they have no text. A picture book conveys its message through a series of sequential images. What is the relationship of picture books to literacy?

Because of early exposure to picture books as first reading experiences, children do not think only in written language but in visual images as well. It is the pictures young children see along with the words they hear that help them develop a sense of story. Pictures are the story. They give meaning to words. The child must decode visual messages in pictures and encode them into oral language. When children begin to retell stories from books, their words are guided by their individual "reading" of the illustrations. Beautifully illustrated picture books provide a context for the development of reading, writing, and oral language.

3-3e Media Literacy

Older children need to become not only educated producers but also critical consumers in a wide variety of media. The goal of media literacy education is to help children read, analyze, evaluate, and communicate in a variety of media. According to Hesse and Lane (2003), media literacy extends the traditional concept of literacy, defined as the ability to read and write, to electronic media.

Positive aspects of the media can be identified, such as prosocial behavior, whereas media messages of hate, violence, prejudice, discrimination, consumerism, rejection, or intolerance must be discussed to help develop critical awareness. The study of visual literacy is approached from a range of disciplines, including a study of the physical processes involved in visual perception, use of technology to represent visual imagery, and the intellectual strategies used to interpret and understand what is seen. For example, the swastika is a visually encoded symbol made up of a series of lines—at a purely visual level nothing more than a simple, visually encoded form that resembles the convergence of four "Ls." What does it mean to you? Through visual decoding, its underlying meaning can be perceived as disturbing and emotionally charged in that it represents the hateful terror of Nazi Germany's Third Reich and horrific images of torture and concentration camps.

Figure 3–9 Children love listening to music and moving to it.

Did You Get It?

What is the most essential component in acquiring linguistic skills, knowledge, and fluency?
  a. formal lessons
  b. freedom to err followed by constant critique and correction
  c. meaningful interactions
  d. hearing and integrating concepts and rules before speaking

Take the full quiz on CourseMate.

DAP naeyc 3-4 Children Express Their Creativity Through Music and Movement

Music and movement begin early in life when parents and grandparents sing lullabies and dance with infants in their arms. Children learn that people use music and movement to communicate. They sing while at play, in the bathtub, or when falling asleep, often repeating TV jingles and familiar songs. They creatively make up their own words to familiar tunes. See for Pica's (2013) Developmental Stages of Musical Experiences.

Music and movement complement the developing child who is naturally talkative and constantly in motion. A child's singing and body movement indicate mood. A happy child will sing and actively move his or her body. An overly quiet, sullen child with halting, limited movements may signify a different mood. As with art, there is a human need to make music and move to it (see Figure 3–9). This need crosses time and culture. People have been making music and dancing since the days they lived in caves. Music and movement are lifelong pursuits. Adolescents appear addicted to music and dance, while adults are known to hum, whistle, sing in the shower or while driving, play an instrument, and dance. The interest and love for music and movement compensate for any perceived lack of innate talent or ability.

3-4a Why Music and Movement Are Important

Why is music important? According to the position paper by the National Association for Music Education (MENC) (1994), music is a natural and important part of young children's growth and development. Early interaction with music positively affects the quality of children's lives. Successful experiences in music help children bond socially, emotionally, and cognitively

Table 3–1 Developmental Stages of Musical Experiences

As with motor development, every child progresses through the stages of musical development at his or her own pace. Although the sequence of developmental stages remains the same for all children, the ages at which they reach and pass through each stage can vary from child to child.

MUSIC EXPERIENCES FOR INFANTS AND TODDLERS

According to the National Association for Music Education (MENC) (1991), infants and toddlers experience music by hearing it, feeling it, and experimenting with musical sounds and vocalizations. Very young children should experience music daily while receiving caring, physical contact. Strategies for enhancing the musical development of infants and toddlers include:

- singing and chanting to them; using a diverse selection of songs and rhymes
- imitating the sounds infants make
- exposing the very young to a wide variety of vocal, body, instrumental, and environmental sounds
- providing exposure to selected live and recorded music
- rocking, patting, touching, and moving with the children to the beat, rhythm, patterns, and melody of the music they hear
- providing safe toys that make musical sounds that the children control
- talking about music and its relationship to feelings and emotions

MUSIC EXPERIENCES FOR TWO-, THREE-, AND FOUR-YEAR-OLDS

According to MENC (1991), preschoolers need an environment that includes a variety of sound sources, selected recorded music, and opportunities for free improvised singing and the building of a repertoire of songs. An exploratory approach, using a wide range of appropriate materials, provides a rich base from which conceptual understanding is gradually constructed. A variety of individual musical experiences is important for preschoolers, with little emphasis on activities that require children to perform together as a unit. As a result of their experiences with music, four-year-olds should initiate both independent and collaborative play with musical materials. They should also demonstrate curiosity about music. For children in kindergarten through fourth grade, National Standards for the Creative Arts are contained in Appendix D.

TWO-YEAR-OLDS

- Can learn short, simple songs
- Show increasing ability to follow directions in songs
- Respond enthusiastically to favorite songs, often asking to hear them repeatedly
- May sing parts of songs (often not on pitch), but seldom sing with a group
- Enjoy experimenting with sounds from everyday objects and musical instruments
- Can discriminate among songs

THREE-YEAR-OLDS

- Have greater rhythmic ability
- Can recognize and sing parts of familiar tunes, though usually not on pitch
- Make up songs
- Walk, run, and jump to music
- Enjoy dramatizing songs

FOUR-YEAR-OLDS

- Can grasp basic musical concepts like tempo, volume, and pitch
- Show a dramatic increase in vocal range and rhythmic ability
- Create new lyrics for songs
- Enjoy more complex songs
- Love silly songs
- Prefer "active" listening (singing, moving, doing finger plays, accompanying music with instruments)

FIVE- TO SIX-YEAR-OLDS

- Can reproduce a melody
- Begin to synchronize movements with the music's rhythm
- Enjoy singing and moving with a group
- Enjoy call-and-response songs
- Have fairly established musical preferences
- Can perform two movements simultaneously (e.g., marching and playing a rhythm instrument)

SEVEN- TO EIGHT-YEAR-OLDS

- Are learning to read lyrics
- Can learn simple folk dances taught by adults
- Enjoy musical duets with friends
- May display a desire to study dance or play an instrument
- Can synchronize movements to the beat of the music
- Can compare three or more sounds

From PICA, Experiences in Movement, 3E. © 2004 Cengage Learning

with others through creative expression in song, rhythmic movement, and listening experiences. Music in early childhood builds a foundation upon which future music learning is built. Encourage children to become active music makers rather than passively watching others perform or entertain with their music. Music empowers young children. They can make their own music and construct their own meaning from musical experiences. Both music educators and early childhood educators agree strongly that music should be a valued and ongoing part of children's experience and learning.

Music facilitates brain growth and development. Multisensory musical behaviors that involve oral,

▶❚❚ TeachSource Video

© 2015 Cengage Learning.

Preschool: Creative Development

Visit the public library to identify other books that might be used in activities with rhythm band instruments. In the video, children use their rhythm band instruments to provide sound effects for a story. Consider how you might use these same instruments to teach a lesson on sound patterns and rhythm.

Watch on CourseMate.

visual, and tactile movements are concurrent with critical growth spurts in the brain. Multisensory behaviors of singing, moving, playing musical instruments, and listening activate both hemispheres of the young child's brain and optimize learning.

If music is vital to brain growth and development, is the force so powerful as to increase intelligence? This is the question surrounding the so-called "Mozart effect." The media have given much attention to the notion of increasing intelligence by playing classical music such as the works of Mozart. Although lacking in supporting research, claims suggest that listening to Mozart for even a few minutes on a regular basis can increase intelligence and subsequent performance on tests of intelligence. The claim appears simplistic and too good to be true. In reality, music may simply serve as a tool for warming up or getting the brain ready to engage with and process information.

What should an early childhood music program entail? According to the position paper by MENC (1991), music education for young children involves a developmentally appropriate program of singing, moving, listening, creating, playing instruments, and responding to visual and verbal representations of sound. The content of such a program should represent music of various cultures in time and place. Music is an inclusive activity in that everyone joins in at his or her level of comfort and competence. Musical activities can include all children in meaningful ways when

they are designed to offer varied levels of participation. According to Humpal and Wolf (2003), music offers varying levels of engagement ranging from listening or observing to joining in as an active participant. For example, a child with autistic-like behaviors may be comfortable listening to and sitting near other children who are singing but not directly participating.

Creative experiences in music and movement serve two major purposes. First, they meet the needs of the whole child: physically, socially, emotionally, cognitively, creatively, and in the area of language. Second, they help integrate and enrich the early childhood curriculum. When moving to music, children are involved in physical activities—stretching, bending, reaching, hopping, crawling, and leaping, to name a few (see Figure 3–12). Small muscle and fine motor control as well as eye-hand coordination are needed to play musical instruments. Socially, young children may sing and dance with others. This involves taking turns, cooperating, and sharing musical instruments—all important social skills. Multicultural songs and dances extend children's social horizons and help them see the universality among people—all people everywhere sing and dance. An acceptance of how children sing and move fosters their self-acceptance and promotes positive self-esteem. Emotionally, they are also able to express their feelings. Music can have a calming effect on an upset child or provide an outlet for feelings of frustration or anger. For example, children can sing in mad voices or use their bodies to show the anger they are feeling. Cognitively, music helps children develop concepts of fast-slow, high-low, colors, animals, shapes, the alphabet, and numbers, as in counting songs. The patterns heard in music prepare the child for the patterning that underlies math and reading. Learning about themselves and their world can be done in developmentally appropriate ways through the use of music and movement, as opposed to a didactic academic approach. Adults who accept children's attempts at singing and dancing send a message that there is no right or wrong way, thereby nurturing children's creative development. The language arts, speaking, listening, reading, and writing, are also enhanced through music and movement. Because singing is speech set to music, children's oral language development can also be supported. Children practice listening and auditory skills like discrimination and memory when learning the words to new songs or attending to music's repetition, rhythm, and rhyme. Music is intimately connected to a young child's emerging literacy. Children can compose and even draw-write their own songs or dance steps. They may also want to write their own books about a favorite song. Song charts based on simple repetitive favorites such as "There Were Ten in the Bed" can facilitate word recognition, reading, and math.

TeachSource Video

School Age: Creative Development

The video shows the children following puppets in a structured series of movement activities. If you were the teacher in this classroom, how might you integrate opportunities for creative movement?

Watch on CourseMate.

© 2015 Cengage Learning.

3-4b Components of Music and Movement

There are four vital components to a comprehensive music and movement program. These include listening to music, singing, playing instruments, and moving to music.

Listening to Music. Although most children are able to hear, not all listen. Hearing is physical in that it involves receiving auditory input. Listening involves the brain's perception of musical input and making sense out of what was heard. Listening is a learned skill. Music contributes to its development and enhancement. Listening involves three related auditory skills: awareness, discrimination, and sequencing. An example of each skill follows. Children demonstrate auditory awareness when they attend to quiet background music played during naptime. Discriminating between sounds made by a drum and a bell reflects auditory discrimination. Children can identify which musical instrument made which particular sound. Children practice auditory sequencing when they repeat a pattern or rhythm clapped out or played by the teacher.

Teachers should discuss music just as they discuss books and art prints. Teachers can ask children to describe what they hear; for example, is it fast or slow? How does it make them feel? Which instruments were used? Do you like this piece of music? As with art and language, music can lead into other activities. For example, children may want to make their own guitars after listening to a guitar solo. They can also extend their musical experience by representing it through art by forming a clay model or painting a picture that captures the musical mood. They can perform their own dance or dramatic rendition of a musical piece such as "The Nutcracker." Listening to a song is a good preparation for singing. It allows children to learn the words and rhythm. Provide a variety of music for children to listen to. Play music throughout the day. Music with an upbeat tempo will facilitate cleanup. Lullabies by Brahms will set a quiet, relaxed tone for rest. Provide more than just children's songs. Introduce children to folk music, jazz, classical music, and music from different cultures. Provide a CD player with a jack and multiple headsets for more than one child to use at a time. Color-code instructions (e.g., green dot on play and red dot on stop) to foster children's independent use. Record children's songbooks on CDs or download them to an MP3 player.

Children will enjoy having their individual or small-group singing recorded for future playbacks. By listening to a variety of music, children come to learn that music

- can be fast or slow, just like when they walk, march, or run
- has tempo, as they compare a lullaby with a march
- can be loud or soft (they can also sing in a loud or soft voice)
- has a beat, like a clock or their hearts

STAGES OF MUSICAL DEVELOPMENT MENC (1994) identifies four stages of children's musical skills development that parallel those of language development. Music and language have similar roots. First vocalizations such as cries, coos, and babbles are the precursors of song and musical understanding, just as they are the precursors of speech and language. The musical stages include awareness, exploration and inquiry, and utilization. First, at the musical awareness stage, children use their senses to touch, manipulate, and gain an initial awareness of musical sound. They do this by playing with a variety of sound sources, including musical toys and objects that make noise. Second, the musical exploration stage, children's musical play behaviors include moving, listening, playing rhythm instruments, and singing. This includes singing isolated song fragments and "chime in" phrases. Children perform rhythm patterns and a steady beat. They begin to discriminate basic musical ideas including same/different, loud/soft, fast/slow, and high/low. Third, at the musical inquiry and utilization stages, children begin to translate musical understandings through singing, moving, and playing rhythm instruments. They also

Brain Connection

The parts of the brain that process music, rhyme, and rhythm are deeply integrated with the brain functions of perception, memory, and language (Sorgen, 1994). Rhyme and rhythm are powerful memory aids (Rushton & Larkin, 2001).

© Cengage Learning

can follow song pictures and puzzles and begin to verbalize elements or characteristics of music such as melody and rhythm. They engage in more complex problem-solving processes involving music and music making as well as translating familiar musical ideas to unfamiliar context.

Singing. Wolf (1994) believes that children progress from listening to tagging on, which is followed by joining in, and culminates in independent singing. According to this framework, children learn to sing by first listening to songs sung to them. Toddlers soon start to "tag on" to songs that they hear and like. They may echo bits and catchy parts while at play. Preschoolers join in singing as part of a group. Eventually most young children not only enjoy singing with a group but also are equally comfortable singing alone. This usually occurs by kindergarten. Children can sing alone, with others, or while listening to a record or tape. Because music and movement are closely related, choose songs that are accompanied by activity. For example, children enjoy hammering with their fists while singing "Johnny Works with One Hammer" and the finger and hand motions that accompany the "Itsy Bitsy Spider" or "The Wheels on the Bus." It is not required that the teacher be a gifted singer. Children are more interested in an enthusiastic model who loves to sing. Children are not critical if you cannot sing well because they have a very limited singing range (a few notes above and below middle C) and often sing off-key when notes are too high or too low. Begin by learning the song well before presenting it to the children. When introducing a new song, sing slowly and clearly, repeating the song. Then invite the children to sing along. Young children enjoy songs that are silly and involve body actions or their names. Select short, simple, active songs with a limited musical range, repetition, and simple rhythms. Examples include "Do You Know the Muffin Man?" and "If You're Happy and You Know It." Each of these allows for creative improvisation. Have parents teach you songs in other languages, and help translate songs learned in English into a second language. For four-, five-, and six-year-olds, write the lyrics to songs on chart paper, and point to the words as the children sing. Later, as the children come to know the words, you might invite individual children to point to the words as the group sings. This will reinforce literacy skills like left-to-right and top-to-bottom orientation. You can also ask children to point out the rhyming words, proper nouns, or action words in the lyrics.

Sing throughout the day during transitions and routines like arrival time, group time, play time, cleanup time, and departure time. Continue singing when outdoors. Plan for music but also allow for spontaneity. Break into a song when it begins raining or when welcoming back a child who has been hospitalized. Sing familiar songs but encourage children to creatively invent their own. Work with small groups in creatively changing the words to familiar songs just for fun or to fit a routine or transition. For example, to the tune of "Are You Sleeping, Brother John?" try singing "Are you cleaning, are you cleaning, Jay and Kate, Leslie and Don?" Or, "This is the way we clean up our room, clean up our room, clean up our room. This is the way we clean up our room on Monday morning." Become familiar with a host of child-oriented popular recordings but do not restrict children's musical diet to pop music, simple finger plays, and rhymes. Certainly it is a good, familiar start, but definitely not enough. Children need a well-balanced and diverse musical menu. Young children will respond to the music of great composers including Mozart, Bach, Chopin, Beethoven, Strauss, Grieg, Ravel, Tschaikovsky, and Prokofiev. Why classical music? It is soothing and may also support brain development.

Find your favorite composers and identify selections for your children. Visit a children's bookstore or Website where CDs and songs feature classical selections that have been specifically chosen for use with young children. Edwards (2002) recommends playing classical music along with traditional favorites that include:

- Hap Palmer
- Ella Jenkins
- Greg and Steve
- Pete Seeger
- Lisa Atkinson
- Sharon, Lois, and
- Bram
- Bob McGrath
- Jose Luis Orozco
- Raffi
- Thomas Moore
- Woody Guthrie
- David Jack
- Peter Alsop
- Linda Arnold
- Burl Ives
- *Sesame Street*
- Barney
- Wee Sing
- Disney
- Rosenshontz

Categories for selecting children's music include traditional and folk songs, nursery rhymes, lullabies, and finger play and body action songs. You may remember some of the traditional and folk songs from your own childhood. The same holds true for nursery rhymes and lullabies. You may have used lullabies to soothe or help a baby fall asleep. When participating in finger plays, children make finger motions to accompany a rhyme. They use other parts of their bodies to make actions for the rhymes. Given the context of traditional nursery rhymes, the words may be abstract and/or controversial. A teacher has the option to change the objectionable wording, avoid using the selection, or use the selection as written along with an explanation and critique. How to choose songs for your classroom? According to Wolf (1994), look for in-tune singing, children's voices, easy-listening adult vocals, and simple instrumentation. Songs can integrate and extend into other curriculum areas. Singing "Old MacDonald Had a Farm" can tie in with a discussion of animals or life on a farm. "The Wheels on the Bus" can introduce a unit on transportation or vehicle safety. "Mary Had a Little Lamb" can lead to a discussion of rough and soft, with children decorating their own lambs with cotton balls. This activity extends a music-based book into the realm of art. A book-based curriculum connects literacy with the creative arts.

STORY SONGS Rhythm is important to story songs because it provides structure. Creative teachers can take familiar songs and change words or ideas to match their curriculum. Singing is also paired with movement or visual aids that can foster multisensory learning and the use of multiple intelligences. Begin by modifying or borrowing elements such as the tune from an existing song. For example, sing the words of the book *Polar Bear, Polar Bear* by Bill Martin Jr. to the tune of "Twinkle, Twinkle, Little Star." What is the advantage of this strategy? When a teacher sings with children, as opposed to playing recorded music, she or he can adjust the speed and volume to suit the group. This is an effective strategy for use with children with language delays, hearing loss, cognitive deficits, or for those learning English as a second language.

Making Music with Rhythm Instruments. Children love to make music, as evidenced by the popularity of banging on pots and pans. Do not overlook the body as a musical instrument. Children enjoy clapping hands, shaking body parts, stamping feet, slapping thighs, and snapping fingers to music. There are different types of musical instruments that are commercially available. Include both rhythm and melodic instruments in your selection. Drums, tambourines, sticks, triangles, maracas, cymbals, and sandpaper blocks are examples

of percussion instruments that make a single sound and can be used to make and keep a beat. Children can play a tune on melodic instruments including a xylophone, a piano, a keyboard, and tone bells. Be sure to include other items that make sounds, including kitchen gadgets, keys, musical toys, music boxes, a metronome, or sound containers. Although commercially available, rhythm instruments can be inexpensively made. Music is integrated with art when instruments are creatively decorated.

Children need experience with rhythm if they are to use rhythm instruments successfully. Having young children listen to music and clap out the beat with their hands or tap it out with their feet is a good introduction to rhythm instruments. Provide ample experiences in clapping rhythm patterns to their names, simple poems, and nursery rhymes. For example, Ida's name involves two claps: I (clap) *da* (clap). When introducing a rhythm instrument, first listen to the music for its rhythmic patterns and then match the beat with the instrument. It is wise to have multiples of rhythm instruments and introduce them one at a time—for example, four tambourines in a small group. This prevents children from just creating noise by playing a group of unrelated instruments with no regard for rhythm. Before distributing rhythm band instruments to children, establish a visual signal, like flashing the lights or holding up your hand to use when children need to stop playing their instruments to listen for directions. When children have their instruments, give them a few minutes to freely explore the sounds they can make. Know that for those few minutes the noise will be intensive, but later, when you ask the children to play the instruments loudly or softly or to make a sound pattern, they are more likely to be attentive if they have had the opportunity for free exploration. Children also enjoy having a parade or playing in a band. They can take turns using the baton to lead the orchestra. Sing "Old MacDonald had a band, ee-i-eei-o. And in that band he had a (add instrument)." Or sing "The Farmer in the Dell" with the instruments choosing each other, or "This is the way we play our bells," and so on.

Moving to Music. What are movement skills? According to Pica (2004), movement involves three major skill categories: locomotor, nonlocomotor, and manipulative. Locomotor skills involve moving the whole body from one point to another. Walking, running, skipping, galloping, sliding, crawling, and climbing are examples of locomotor skills.

Nonlocomotor or stability skills are executed in place as the axis of the body rotates around a fixed point. Twirling, spinning, stretching, turning, twisting, bending, and stooping are examples of nonlocomotor skills in which children work on balance.

Manipulative skills involve either the large or small muscle groups as well as a combination of both. Bouncing a ball, throwing, catching or kicking a ball and striking with a bat involve the large muscles. Manipulative skills are usually associated with playing games. Manipulative skills are more difficult than locomotor or nonlocomotor. Because of this, Sanders (2002) recommends frequency and repetition in an early childhood movement program.

Children need movement experiences on a daily basis. According to Carmichael (2007), research indicates that regular physical activity improves blood flow and releases chemicals that make the brain more receptive to learning. So including movement activities in the curriculum will support children's learning of content and the development of their bodies. Children will need to periodically revisit and practice core skills to attain mastery. Knowledge of one's body and body parts is also a necessary component to movement exploration. Children need to be aware of their body and what they can make it do along with understanding their relationships to objects and others in their immediate space. As with art, movement also has its own set of concepts or musical elements. These include space, time, and energy or force. Simply put, children move through space with varying degrees of speed and with different levels of force. Children can travel through space both indoors and outdoors. They can also move by remaining fixed in their own personal space. They wiggle their bodies fast or move them slowly (time). They can tiptoe about lightly or stomp their feet (energy or force).

Large motor actions like walking, hopping, swaying, marching, and galloping can be paired with music. Children enjoy moving like animals, vehicles, or story characters. Model movement and dance. You need not be a gifted dancer. It is more important to share your enjoyment of music and the way your body moves to music. Props help the unsure or shy child. Include hoops, crepe paper streamers, scarves, hats, crowns, fancy costumes, ribbons, magic wands, grass skirts, fans, soft batons for leading the band, pom-poms, and lengths of sheer fabric. Streamers taped to outstretched arms make dancing wings. Creative movement gives children an outlet for their physical energy, encouraging them to express their feelings and creativity in nonverbal ways. Creative movement activities can be either totally open-ended or teacher-guided. In open-ended activities, children move in ways that are individually meaningful. For example, a teacher can play a tape of *Swan Lake* and watch the children dance as the music moves them (see Figure 3–10). In teacher-guided activities, the adult provides the stimulus or frame which subtly structures

Figure 3–10 Creative movement provides both a physical and emotional outlet for children.

the movement activity. Examples include asking children to move

- creatively, like a flying car
- in ways that enact a nursery rhyme like "Jack Be Nimble" in pantomime to waking up, getting dressed, eating, or falling asleep
- in ways that are angry, sad, happy, scared, or surprised
- as if they were trees swaying in the wind, clothes in a dryer, water going down the drain, or food in a blender
- with imaginary wings and fly away
- by making their body grow very tall or shrink very small
- by using their hands and arms to make rainbows in the sky
- by becoming very crooked or very soft and squishy

Solicit children's input on other ways to move. In planning movement activities, keep developmental appropriateness in mind. It will be impossible for a child to move like a helicopter or an elevator if he or she has never directly experienced one. Remember that images in books or on TV are symbolic images. The symbolic images of cows in books are small, flat, mute animals who do not smell. As such, these vicarious experiences do not advance a child's knowledge of cows. You will be more successful if you structure movement experiences around things children know and have experienced. Children living in rural areas may have well-developed concepts of farm animals, whereas city children may not.

Children also need ample space, including their own personal space, in which to move. By extending their arms out around them, children can define their personal space, which others must respect. Remember to move with the children without telling or showing them how to move. There is more than one way to move like a snake. Above all else, remember to provide a psychologically safe environment in which children feel comfortable to trust their creative impulses and move in ways that make sense to them. As with singing, respect the right of children to refrain from participation, especially for those who are shy or unsure.

MOVING WITH A PARACHUTE IN CREATIVE WAYS A parachute is a good investment and a piece of movement apparatus that has many uses. A small parachute is best, but if unavailable, use a tablecloth or sheet. Tie knots at the corners and midpoints to signify places and something to hold. Use with a small group of children to reinforce spatial, directional, and temporal concepts. Some parachute activities include having the children

- hold the parachute high (above their heads) or low (down on the ground).
- lift their arms and parachute as high as possible, release, and then watch as it floats to the ground.
- move the parachute slowly and then very fast.
- bounce lightweight objects like balloons or balls on top of the parachute (either try to keep them on or try to have them bounce off).
- make the parachute get small by walking to the middle and then get big by walking back to their places.
- walk to the right and then to the left while holding the parachute waist high.
- run under the parachute without getting caught.
- extend arms upward and while still holding on, turn around and sit on the ground while the parachute covers them up.

naeyc MUSIC AND MOVEMENT CENTER Provide a soft, comfortable place for children to listen to and make beautiful music as well as move and dance. (See Figure 3–11.) Location is crucial. Select an area where children making noise will not disturb those involved in quiet activities. If inside space is very limited you may want to think about an outdoor music and movement center. A music cart allows you to take your music program outdoors on good weather days.

Include:

- CD players designed for children, that are easy to operate, along with a jack box and several headphones.
- CDs labeled with title and picture.
- rhythm instruments: both percussion and melodic. Percussion includes maracas, tambourines, castanets, finger cymbals, and rhythm sticks. Melodic includes

Figure 3–11 A creative place for music.

© Cengage Learning

bells, small keyboards, tone bars, xylophones, and piano (if available). Hang your rhythm instruments on a peg-board. Draw an outline around each to show children where to store them. Cup hooks under a shelf are good for hanging small items like castanets and triangles. Include homemade rhythm instruments.

- materials for making their own instruments.
- a small selection of papers and writing tools for children to make their own songbooks or sheet music. Blank staff paper, pencils, and markers will encourage older children to write their own music.
- books on music, musicians, and musical performances. Include other visuals such as songs on charts.
- multicultural picture books of the countries from where the music and instruments come.
- Plexiglas® mirrors so children can watch themselves move and dance.
- scarves, streamers, and lengths of fabric.
- a prop box of fancy dress-up clothes that facilitate movement and dance.
- a small selection of mark-making materials to encourage children to combine drawing with music.
- pictures of children and adults singing, dancing, playing instruments, and listening to music. Include male and female dancers and musicians from many cultures.

Provide ample time for children to discover and make music. To round out your music and movement program, take children on field trips where they can hear music and see dance performed. If this is not possible, invite family members and community volunteers who sing, dance, or play musical instruments. This is a good way to have family members share their cultures' music and dance.

To make your music and movement program culturally responsive be sure to

- integrate music from other cultures into your daily program
- learn and sing songs from different cultural groups
- play and display musical instruments used by various cultural groups
- learn the dances and rhythmic movements of cultural groups represented in the wider community

DAP **naeyc** **TEACHER'S ROLE** What follows is a list of recommended strategies and aspects of the teacher's role in music exploration.

- Set up a physically and psychologically safe environment in which children can be free to express themselves creatively through music and movement.
- Value music and recognize that an early introduction to music is important. All children have the potential to be music makers and music appreciators.
- Model an interest in and use of music in daily life.
- Be an active participant not a passive spectator. Your positive attitude and enthusiasm will be contagious. Interest and enthusiasm are key attributes.
- Recapture your own "musical child" and sing, move, play, and dance without inhibition. Children will follow your lead.
- Accept and validate children's creative musical expression by smiling, nodding, and joining in.
- Be confident in one's own level of musical ability. Children are looking for a music partner, not a trained singer, dancer, or musician.
- Be willing to improve your musical skill and stretch your musical tastes.
- Seek assistance in acquiring and using appropriate music resources. Invite parents to share aspects of their musical heritage.
- Use developmentally appropriate songs, rhymes, chants, singing games, and musical books, and rhythm instruments.
- Encourage spontaneous music by singing, dancing, and making music with the children in your class.
- Use developmentally appropriate musical materials and teaching techniques.
- Find, create, and/or seek assistance in acquiring and using appropriate music resources.
- Create a musical learning environment. Structure the indoor and outdoor learning environment to include music/movement.

- Be sensitive and flexible when children's interests are diverted from your original plan.
- Sing with the children, do finger plays, and take an active music part during transitions, center time, and group/circle time.
- Expose children to a variety of musical forms and compositions including folk, classical, jazz, and alternative.
- Base activities on children's interests. Empower them. Let children choose their own partners, select the songs to be played, and change the way to use props or play a game.
- Weave music throughout your day and curriculum. Extend children's ongoing projects by adding music and movement to their theme.
- Provide opportunities for different levels of participation to include all children.
- Provide adequate time for sustained practice and repetition of key skills while slowly introducing new ones.

Neely (2002) recommends the use of musical conversations in which teachers speak musically to children. They sing, speak rhythmically, move expressively, and play instruments throughout the day. They also comment, foster decision making, provide choices, suggest options, and facilitate problem solving. These scaffolding strategies help children construct meaning from their musical experiences.

Examples of these music-based teachable moments include:

- modeling expressive and rhythmic speech with children during transitions, group or circle time, and choice time.
- encouraging children to sing, move, dramatize stories, or add instruments as they bring to life words in a story or poem.
- improvising or making up new songs or changing familiar ones. Sing high, then low; soft, then loud. Change the words of a familiar song and/or change the melody.

Did You Get It?

Generally, children around three years old find particular enjoyment in which song-related activity?

   a. dramatizing songs
   b. altering songs
   c. making up songs from scratch
   d. memorizing songs

Take the full quiz on CourseMate.

DAP naeyc 3-5 Facilitating Children's Creative Expression

Teachers can build on children's creative drive by implementing the following strategies:

1. Provide ample blocks of time for creative expression. Children need large blocks of time to create and re-create. Being pressured to begin or finish works against the creative impulse. Children also need time to start, change, and return to their creative processing.

2. Provide ample space indoors and outdoors for children to express their creativity. Space should be fluid and flexible, allowing for spontaneous activity which may extend across learning centers. For example, block building may extend into dramatic play.

3. Provide resources including open-ended toys, props, materials, and creative junk. Children cannot create from workbook pages.

4. Set the stage for creative expression by providing a psychologically safe environment. Be accepting of children's processing. Give them permission to be different and to do things their way, as long as their health and safety are not at risk.

5. Play a variety of roles. Observe and record individual children as they create. Be a player and participant in children's play, without taking over.

6. Comment on and interpret the content and processes of children's play. Provide emotional support and facilitate negotiation and problem solving. Expand play activities by offering suggestions and questions. Extend play into all curriculum areas. Scaffold children's play to foster growth and development. Match your

Did You Get It?

Should you provide a "psychologically safe" environment in which children can be free and open to express themselves creatively and artistically?

a. The sky is the limit as long as it is not dangerous or harmful and it stays within rules.

b. Yes, but within limits. The outside world is not as tolerant of differences as your classroom might be.

c. There should be distinct and delineated times for freedom and openness and for being conformist.

d. Providing such an environment often leads to classroowms that are chaotic, tumultuous, and unruly.

Take the full quiz on CourseMate.

observations with well-timed interventions that skillfully combine children's present level of functioning with an optimal challenge or next step.

DAP naeyc 3-6 Mark Making

Mark making is a term used to refer to the variety of artistic marks that young children make. Young children begin by making scribbles or unrecognizable marks and progress to recognizable shapes and forms.

Scribbling is important both in itself and as practice for later printing, writing, and drawing. Scribbling is to drawing and printing or writing as babbling is to talking and crawling is to walking. Most young children will have some experience with using crayons, pencils, markers, or pens at home.

Young children need large sheets of paper to make movements with the entire arm. Later, with practice, they will develop hand coordination and fine motor control. Crayons are recommended for the beginning mark maker. Colored pencils are too long and thin and have a soft point. They are hard to control, and the points break easily. The advanced mark maker can be given colored pencils for making precise drawings. Scribblers need crayons, but not a wide array of colors. Often, one dark color is enough. Their interest will be in making marks and strokes rather than using a variety of colors. Crayons will be peeled and broken. Actually, scribblers need peeled crayons so that they can use both the tips and the sides to make a variety of marks.

There is no one best position for mark making. Older infants and toddlers enjoy sprawling on the floor on their tummies and marking with crayons on a large piece of paper. This setup can accommodate four mark makers at any one time, one at each side of the paper. Others may enjoy kneeling on the floor while marking. Easels are not just for painting. Some children may be most comfortable standing while making marks. Others will prefer to stand or sit at a table (see Figures 3–12 and 3–13). The seated position is most appropriate for the older, experienced mark maker, since it requires more-restricted small muscle movement. Standing, reclining, and kneeling permit greater whole body involvement and movement while marking.

Children can make marks with a variety of tools:

- pencils
- chalk
- crayons
- markers

3-6a Pencils

colored—for advanced mark makers

drawing—#2 for making marks

erasers—to be used sparingly, not in striving for perfection

Figure 3–12 Being creative while sitting at the art table.

Figure 3–13 A mural by standing mark makers.

grips—three-sided pencil holders, more important for printing than for artistic mark making

lead—#2 for making marks

primary—thick for younger children

3-6b Chalk

chalkboard—good for marking with long, sweeping strokes

colored—for marking on chalkboard and on black, white, and colored construction paper

pastels—leave a soft, smooth, velvety line; not recommended for beginners. Use to draw on cloth or paper but not chalkboard. Pastels provide the best of chalk and crayons. They are powdery but do not rub off like chalk. They are not as hard as crayons but are just as colorful and brilliant.

white—for marking on chalkboard and on black and colored construction paper

3-6c Crayons and Accessories

Chunk-o-Crayon—a small, square stick of heavily pigmented color; comes in primary colors, black, and a rainbow of colored specks; good for wide strokes and rubbings

Cray Away—washable crayons, water-soluble. Or dip in water for watercolor effects.

crayon sharpener—save the colored shavings!

Easy-Grip or Chubbi Stump—look like small ice cream cones and fit tiny hands

Easy-Off—can be removed from washable surfaces, such as walls; good for use at home

fabric—for marking directly on cloth, or use on paper and then transfer to fabric with a hot iron

fluorescent—bright, vibrant colors

grater—for shaving crayons

hexagonal—six-sided crayons; will not roll and are a good size for little hands

jumbo or extra large crayons—may be too big and heavy for the youngest

nonroll—for children working on slanted surfaces or who find the major use of crayons is for rolling

So Big—first crayons for older infants and toddlers

standard size—thin and prone to break with pressure

An Opportunity for Teacher Reflection

Patrick is a Child in Your Class of three-year-olds. Although Patrick uses language appropriately and effectively to communicate with you and with other children, you are concerned because he never joins the rest of the class in singing or movement activities. Instead of participating, Patrick just watches the children around him silently. When you take his hand to encourage him in movement activities, Patrick does not resist, but he will return to watching the group as soon as possible. You discuss your concern with Patrick's father, and he is very surprised. He tells you that every afternoon as they drive home, Patrick sings to him all the songs the class has sung during the school day. *What is happening with Patrick? If he knows the songs, why isn't he participating in class? Is he intimidated by the group? Is he too self-conscious? Or is he just caught up in watching his friends?*

thick or large—sturdier than standard

triangular—long, three-sided; good for wide, sweeping strokes

3-6d Markers

Markers are popular mark-making tools for young children because they can make bright strokes with little pressure. They come in a variety of colors and tip styles and are indispensable to any early childhood art program. Some drawbacks are their relative expense compared with crayons and the fact that they dry out and must be replaced.

Items to accompany mark-making tools include:

* ruler
* stencils
* protractors
* lids and tops (to trace)

Here are some **Personally Expressive Art** activities for mark making.

Infant, Toddler, and Preschool-Age Activity: Scribbling. Older infants, toddlers, and preschoolers scribble. They make marks for the joy of moving a tool across paper and seeing what happens. They need a variety of mark-making tools and large sheets of paper.

CRAYONS Crayons are a preferred medium (see Figure 3–14). They are colorful, responsive to children's movements, and fairly inexpensive. They are always ready for use and do not require mixing or special preparation. Most young children will have experience with them and will automatically be drawn to them. Young children will have color preferences. Vibrant colors, such as silver, gold, and hot pink, will quickly lose their pointed tips. Young scribblers do well with only the basic primary colors. (But note that yellow is difficult to see when used on white paper.)

Crayons are composed of pigmented wax. Dark crayons contain more wax, are softer, and will leave an opaque mark. Light crayons contain less wax, are harder, and will leave a transparent mark. The older mark maker discovers that if you color dark over light, that is, brown over yellow, the lighter color will not show. The younger mark maker, however, will not be that concerned with color mixing and planning.

Marking or scribbling with crayons will progress in stages. Young scribblers push, pull, and drag their crayons across the paper, resulting in horizontal, vertical, diagonal, and circular marks. The crayons will not be lifted off the paper, and the resulting marks will be continuous, with little or no variation. Beginning scribblers will often look away while marking, being more interested in the muscular activity itself than in the finished product. Details and small marks will be

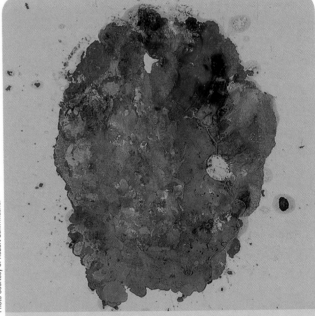

Photo Courtesy of Robert Schirrmacher

Figure 3–14 Coffee filter art and print.

largely absent because of limited fine muscle development and control. With time, practice, and control, shapes and symbols begin to be included.

There is no one best way to store crayons. While many children prefer to keep their own basic set of eight crayons, teachers often feel that it is important to provide a container of crayons with a broad assortment of colors and encourage children to share. Maria Montessori could have advocated grouping a mass of crayons by color and sorting each in its own container—for example, all the reds together. She would most likely have provided only the primary colors and encouraged children to mix these basic three to get all others.

Children will inevitably break crayons to hear the pleasurable popping noise and peel the paper off. It is a way for them to exhibit power over objects. They can break a crayon in two with their own bare hands! Thicker crayons are harder to break but are also more difficult to manage. Removing the paper allows children to use the sides in wide, sweeping strokes. Many parts of a crayon other than the pointed tip can be used. Children may also quickly discard the box, because fitting the crayons back in once they have been removed is difficult and frustrating. Never throw away a broken crayon. They can be melted down and made into new ones. Try one of these "recipes" for recycling crayons (note that these activities are for the teacher and are not appropriate for children):

- Melt several small, peeled, broken crayon pieces into a nonstick muffin tin resting in a skillet of boiling water. Or line metal muffin tin openings with tinfoil to eliminate sticking. Colors can be kept separate or creatively combined in the muffin tins. Let cool. Carefully remove and use as fat crayons. Remember, never melt crayons directly over heat; they are highly flammable.

- An alternative method is to place the muffin tin in the oven at 250° F until the crayons have melted. Turn off the oven when crayons are completely melted. Remove the muffin tin when the oven is cold. Remove crayon cookies by pushing on the bottom of the muffin tin. Remind children that these tempting cookie-type creations are made of wax and are not to be eaten.

- Layers of different melted colors can also be poured into a film container or pill bottle. Carefully pour from a muffin tin or use an old pot, making sure to wipe it clean between color meltings. Let harden between layers of color. Put it in the refrigerator to hasten hardening. Gently tap the bottom to remove, or quickly dip in hot water to loosen. The result will be a lipstick-shaped crayon that produces stripes and rainbow colors when used on its side.

- Broken crayons can be slowly melted together in a plastic egg carton placed on a cookie sheet in the hot sun.

- Pour melted crayon wax into a sturdy paper cone. Wrap several layers of sturdy paper into an ice-cream cone shape. Tape securely. Pour in layers of colored wax. Carefully unwrap the paper when the cone hardens Small colored cones fit nicely into small hands. Remind children that these are special crayons and not for eating.

- To make a crayon egg, carefully poke a pin through both ends of an egg. Blow out the yolk and white of the egg. Place in the egg carton. Enlarge the opening on the top of the egg so you can pour melted crayon wax into the empty egg. To melt wax, place unwrapped, broken crayons or stubs in an empty coffee can. Place the can in a pan of boiling water. When melted, pour into the egg mold. (Do not do this part with children.) When crayon wax has hardened, peel off the eggshell.

- Peeled, broken crayon stubs can be recycled into crayon creatures. Cover the bottom of one to six cookie cutters with two layers of heavy-duty tinfoil to prevent leaking of melted crayon. Place on a cookie sheet. Fill each cookie cutter with peeled, broken crayon bits and pieces. Mixing colors is an option. Place the cookie sheet in a warm oven for about 10 minutes or until crayons melt and float but are not totally liquid. Place the entire cookie sheet with cookie cutters into the freezer for about 30 minutes. Carefully remove crayon creatures from cookie cutters. Use like crayons. Wash cookie cutters with hot, soapy water.

- Soap crayons can be made using mild, powdered laundry soap, food coloring or liquid watercolor, and water. Add one cup of laundry soap to a bowl. Add several drops of color. Slowly add water by the teaspoon until the soap is liquid. Stir well. Pour into ice cube trays. Set in a sunny, dry spot for a few days. Allow crayons to harden. Great for writing on sinks or bathtubs.

Some variations on children's use of crayons include:

- scribbling with a crayon in each hand

- marking with a crayon in the nondominant hand—for example, a righty uses crayons with the left hand

- using two or more crayons that are tied together with a rubber band

- making notches or grooves in a peeled crayon and using it in a sideways, swirling, or up-and-down motion

- mixing colors by blending or overlaying crayons on white paper

- using crayons on colored construction paper

- varying the pressure on crayons, coloring heavily or lightly, and noticing the effects of pressure on the types of marks

- polishing crayon marks by rubbing them with a tissue to make a shiny surface

- using all sides of the crayon: the point for small dots; the flat end for larger, round circles; the side for sweeping, wide strokes; and holding the crayon in the middle and rotating it to make bows or large circles

- using only dots made with a crayon to form a picture, outline, or design

Infant, Toddler, Preschool, and Kindergarten-Age Activity: Musical Scribbling. Children also enjoy scribbling or mark making to music.

Make a mark or stroke that shows how the music makes you feel. Most of the previous suggestions also apply to musical scribbling. Make a simple doodle to music. Stop and turn the paper in a different direction. Attempt to continue the design or to complete a picture that the doodle suggests. For example, a mass of looping lines might suggest a snake. A tail and head could be added. Or it could be spaghetti, with the child drawing a fork and plate.

Kindergarten and School-Age Activity: Drawing or Sketching. Older children develop from random scribbling to more purposeful drawing or sketching that is often systematically planned in advance. Some children may enjoy drawing or sketching

- each other.
- objects in the room.
- a very simple display, such as two stuffed animals.
- school or center experiences, such as a field trip or outdoor play.
- people, places, and things at home.
- numbers, letters, and words.
- using only geometric shapes.
- a new animal made up of two very different ones, for example, a "turtlephant" with a turtle's head and an elephant's body.
- items brought for show-and-tell.

Kindergarten and School-Age Activity: Chalk and Pastels. Older children will enjoy marking with chalk. It is messy, but the colors produced are beautiful, and the possibilities for blending are endless. Children can mark

- with light chalk on dark paper, such as white on black for a snow scene.
- with colored chalk on white paper.
- with dry chalk on wet paper.
- with wet chalk on dry paper.
- with the tip and/or side of the chalk.
- by rubbing or blending chalk dust on a cotton ball (scrape with a dull knife or popsicle stick).
- on rough, textured paper that responds to chalk.
- by dipping the chalk in liquid starch before marking.
- with chalk sticks soaked in a solution of 1/3 cup sugar to 1 cup water for five to 10 minutes before use. The colors will appear more brilliant and tend to resist smudging.
- on paper wet with buttermilk or a combination of canned milk and liquid starch, to add sparkle.

- outdoors on sidewalk and blacktop (it washes away with rain).
- with pastels, which provide a compromise between crayon and chalk. They are fairly solid and come in brilliant colors, but are slightly expensive.

Toddler, Preschool, and Kindergarten-Age Activity: Sidewalk Mark Making. Older infants and toddlers will enjoy making marks with chalk on the sidewalk. Provide large chunks of colored chalk that are easy for young children to grip. Select a section of the sidewalk out of the regular traffic patterns. Sit down on the sidewalk with a container of chalk and begin to draw by yourself, in order to draw the children's attention. As the children join you in mark making on the sidewalk, describe their actions: "Ramsey, you're making a long line with the red chalk." Respond to the children's vocalizations with positive and nonverbal reinforcement.

Preschool, Kindergarten, and School-Age Activity: Mural. Making a mural involves many social skills and collaborative decision making. How will we share the entire mural space? Who will make what, and where? Murals can revolve around a theme, such as outer space, but young children will likely include elements from outside the theme. There may be three planet Earths in the mural or animals floating about in space. Often, there will be a second bottom baseline at the top of the mural. This is to be expected. Murals can be the focus of a group story or dictation. Provide a long strip of paper. Place it on the floor in an out-of-the-way spot and encourage each child to make his or her unique contribution. Letters, names, numbers, and words can also be added to the art picture story.

Preschool, Kindergarten, School-Age Activity: Fence Mural. A fence mural is a good outdoor art activity when weather permits. Several child artists can make their marks at the same time on the same piece of paper. Begin by securing a long, wide, heavy length of paper to a fence. Use lots of strong tape so the paper will not tear, blow away, or fall down. Place containers of markers at intervals on the ground along the base of the fence. Free end-rolls of heavy paper are often available from newspaper printers.

Preschool, Kindergarten, and School-Age Activity: "Me" Marks. Most young children are interested in talking and learning about themselves. This can be part of social studies or a unit on "me." Some related mark making activities include:

- a self-portrait.
- drawing, making marks, or making self-sketches that show being happy, angry, sad, scared, hurt, lonely, or silly.

- a "me" book that shows things that make me feel one of the previous ways—for example, a separate page with happy on it.

A wall mirror will help children notice details, including eye and hair color, clothing, and the presence or absence of freckles and front teeth. Still, even though young children can visually see, they will not necessarily represent realistically.

Kindergarten and School-Age Activity: Crayon Etching. Probably everyone has done at least one crayon etching. Older children can fill up a piece of manila paper with a crayon design. Leave no space empty. Polish with a paper towel to help the layer of color adhere. Next, using black crayon, color darkly over the entire surface. Polish again. Last, use a craft stick to etch out a design. A fairly thick etched line will reveal a rainbow of colors beneath. This activity is recommended only for older children who have the patience and muscular strength to color dark over an entire sheet of paper and stay with this activity through its several steps.

School-Age Activity: Pass-It-On Picture. Fold a piece of white paper into quarters with the top fourth folded down and the bottom fourth folded up. One child uses the top to draw a head. The paper is turned over and passed to a second child, who draws the middle. The third child uses the unused portion to draw legs. When the paper is opened, a creative

Hints

- Chalk can be used wet or dry. Chalk is messy, and older children will enjoy blending colors made with chalk. Chalk needs a fixative.

- Brushing liquid starch or buttermilk on the paper first will help the chalk adhere. Chalk can also be dipped into either of these fixatives and then applied. Children tend to dislike the smell of buttermilk. Spraying with hair spray will also help the chalk adhere. Use hair spray outdoors and sparingly.

- Chalkboard paint is available at hardware stores. You can paint on your own chalkboard surface on the side of a cabinet or on a wall.

- Like crayons, chalk will quickly break, especially if loosely thrown into a box. A piece of foam rubber can make a chalk holder. Use a scissors point to carefully bore small holes or openings into the foam rubber. Insert one piece of chalk into each hole. Make sure that the chalk fits tightly in an upright position.

combination of head-middle-bottom appears. Children may need to practice this activity a few times to understand the process.

Tile Marking. Children can make marks with permanent felt markers on a piece of ceramic tile. In turn, these can become holiday gifts. The tiles can be used as paperweights or trivets. Building contractors might be willing to contribute leftover tiles. You can also contact home improvement stores for tile samples or surplus. Choose white or a light, solid color. Begin by covering your work surface and have children wear a smock, since permanent felt markers will stain. Children should be encouraged to carefully and quickly make their design because the ink in permanent markers dries quickly.

Here are some **Sensory Exploration** activities for mark-making:

Polished Drawings. Children who use vigorous, hard strokes when coloring with crayons can have their colorful marks "polished." Use a paper towel over a pointer finger and polish the crayon marks until they smear together, blend, and sparkle.

Kindergarten and School-Age Activity: Object Trace-Over. Much of the artistic junk (see Appendix A) will have a characteristic shape and outline, often geometric in nature. Lids, tops, caps, boxes, and containers can be traced over. The shapes can be creatively combined. Some can be repeated in a sequence or pattern. Some children may prefer to make something out of their traced objects. For example, a series of traced-over circular lids could suggest a caterpillar or wheels on a bulldozer.

Kindergarten and School-Age Activity: Graph Paper Cube Design. Buy graph paper with large squares or make a series of 1-inch squares on a sheet of paper and photocopy it. Children can be encouraged to think of an object that has a square or rectangular shape or is composed of small boxes. For example, it would be more difficult to make a round swimming pool than a rectangular skyscraper. Sketch out the exterior outline. Fill in the individual squares to complete the picture.

Kindergarten and School-Age Activity: Run, Mark, Run. Children will enjoy using markers on paper towels or thin fabric on which they will blend and run. Place newspaper or cardboard underneath.

Preschool, Kindergarten, and School-Age Activity: Sandpaper Art. Children can use crayons to make heavy marks or a design on a small 4- to 6-inch square of sandpaper. Use fine or medium grade rather than coarse. Press hard, and make solid-colored forms.

When the sandpaper is fairly well covered with crayon marks, it can be heated in a warm oven at 250° F for 10 to 15 seconds until the crayon melts. The crayon wax will harden and produce an interesting effect. Also, this activity can be a good tie-in to discussing the effects of heat and temperature change. What happens if we leave crayons in the sun or on the heater? Will the same thing happen to pencils? Who knows why?

Kindergarten and School-Age Activity: Crayon Shavings. Old, broken crayons can be recycled for this activity. Carefully scrape a dull plastic knife or Popsicle stick along the crayon and catch the shavings. Place them on a piece of wax paper and arrange them into a design. Add glitter, ribbon, tissue paper, and a piece of string if a hanging is desired. Place another piece of wax paper on top. An adult can press with a warm iron to melt the wax and seal it. Cut the excess wax paper off or snip it into an interesting shape. Use black construction paper for the outer frame. Hang it over the window and let the light shine through.

Kindergarten and School-Age Activity: Coffee Filter Art. Crayon shavings can also be placed on a flattened paper coffee filter. Place a sheet of construction paper on top. An adult can press with a warm iron. You will get two pieces of art. The heat will melt the crayon wax, and you will have a colored design on a round, white background. You will also get a print of that design on your piece of construction paper.

Kindergarten and School-Age Activity: Iron Art. Fold a sheet of drawing paper in half. Mark or color dark and solid on one half. Refold the paper with the colored design inside. An adult can press with a warm iron to make a print. Open. A colored image or print will appear on the other half.

Fabric crayons can be used in a similar way. Mark with fabric crayons on white paper. Color heavily. Place the paper face down over fabric. An adult can transfer the picture onto the fabric by ironing the paper with a warm iron. The wax will melt, and the heat will set the colors into the fabric.

Fabric crayons are designed to be used with fabric. Locate some material scraps—prewashed muslin, an old T-shirt, or a white sheet. Staple a small square of old sheet or muslin to cardboard to keep the fabric from slipping. Use the fabric crayons to make heavy marks or a design. Place paper on top and press with a warm iron. The heat will melt the colored wax and set the design. Individual squares could be sewn together into a quilt.

Kindergarten and School-Age Activity: Rub-a-Dub-Rub. Rubbing a marking tool over a textured surface produces an interesting rubbed effect. Some people do this over gravestones while studying family or local history. Visitors to Washington, D.C. make rubbings of family and friends whose names are listed on the Vietnam Memorial.

Crayons are recommended for children, although chalk could also be used. Hold a piece of paper in place while rubbing. Possible textured surfaces include:

- wood grain tree bark
- fabric
- cement and concrete
- flocked wallpaper leaves and other flat nature specimens
- screens and grills brick

- signs with raised letters
- comb
- sandpaper
- mosaic tile
- leather
- buttons
- paper clips

School-Age Activity: Glue Design. Make a design using a bottle of liquid white glue on wax paper. Make thick masses, shapes, or forms. Let dry until it's hard and clear. Decorate the dried glue with thin- or fine-line felt-tip pens. The dried and decorated shapes can be carefully peeled off, laced with thread, and hung overhead or worn as jewelry.

Preschool, Kindergarten, and School-Age Activity: Lazy Susan Art. Find a base that revolves. Place a round sheet of paper on the turntable or base. Gently spin the base while holding a marker on the paper. Children will discover that too much pressure will stop the turntable. This is recommended for older children with good coordination because it involves doing two things at the same time. Children can also work in

Hints

- Markers and their tops or caps get easily separated. A marker cap keeper will also help young children or those with physical disabilities who may have trouble pulling off the caps. To make a marker cap keeper, collect deep Styrofoam trays and fill them with plaster of paris (inexpensively purchased from hardware and craft stores). While it is wet, press in about eight markers, caps down. If the caps are smooth, try wrapping rubber bands around them first. Let dry. This creates a keeper for the markers, makes it easier for children to use them, and avoids the problem of lost tops.

pairs with one spinning and the other marking, and then change jobs.

School-Age Activity: Record Player Art. An old record player can be used with close adult supervision. Place a paper plate on the turntable and turn on the record player. Have the child hold a marker on the plate as it turns around. The marker can be moved about to create interesting line designs. The child may want to change colors or use more than one marker at a time, perhaps one in each hand.

School-Age Activity: Kaleidoscope Art. Accordion-fold any white absorbent paper such as coffee filters, white tissue paper, or one-ply paper towels. Then fold in half. Use markers to color along the edges and then dip in water. Squeeze out excess moisture. Let dry before attempting to unfold and open.

School-Age Activity: Magnet Marker. You will need a marker, a hardware nut, 1.2-inch washer, duct tape, clear Plexiglas®, magnet, and blocks for elevation. Place an uncapped marker through a nut. Place the nut and marker on top of the washer so that the tip

of the marker is exposed. Secure marker, washer, and nut together with duct tape. Place Plexiglas® on top of blocks to make a bridge. Plexiglas® needs to be elevated high enough for a child's hands to move easily underneath. Tape a piece of paper to Plexiglas®. Stand the marker up on paper. Make sure the washer lies flat against the Plexiglas®. Slowly and carefully move the magnet underneath the Plexiglas® to begin mark making on paper.

> **Did You Get It?**
>
> Your students are engaged in "mark making," and one of your students has nerve damage in his dominant hand, limiting his ability to apply pressure or squeeze tightly. Which "mark making" would you recommend?
> **a.** colored pencils
> **b.** glue
> **c.** magic markers
> **d.** a computer keyboard
>
> Take the full quiz on CourseMate.

Summary

This chapter continued our discussion of creativity and introduced the reader to three major modes of creative expression other than art. (3-1) These included play, language, and music and movement. (3-2) Play was examined as an elusive term; it was not conclusively defined. Nor could it be simply contrasted with work, for children work very hard at their play. Instead, criteria for characterizing play were identified. A discussion of play in its many forms covered physical play, constructive play, dramatic play, play with natural materials, and games. Ideas for creative play using cardboard boxes,

cartons, and accessories were suggested. (3-3) As with play, information on centers, materials, and activities in language and literacy were provided. (3-4) Music was identified as an essential experience for children and the four components of an early childhood music program—listening to music, singing, making music with instruments, and moving to music—were discussed. (3-5) Providing space, time, and resources were identified as ways adults can facilitate and enhance children's creative expression. (3-6) The chapter ended with a discussion of mark making and sample activities for children.

Key Terms

constructive play, 38

creative movement, 36

dramatic play, 40

games, 43

literacy, 35

mark making, 35

media literacy, 46

modes of creative expression, 35

multiple literacies, 46

physical play, 37

play, 36

play with natural materials, 37

socio-dramatic play, 40

story songs, 52

the arts, 35

visual literacy, 46

✓ Suggested Activities

1. Observe children at play. Capture a creative episode by writing down what transpired. Record children's language and actions objectively. Analyze your observation and justify why this episode was creative.

2. Work with a small group of children in implementing one of the following creative activities discussed in this chapter:

   a. boxes, cartons, and accessories

   b. parachute

3. Implement one of the water play activities discussed in this chapter with a small group of children.

4. Work with a partner and implement one of the movement activities discussed in this chapter. This can be done informally during play time or large group time.

5. In small groups, discuss your early childhood memories. Think back to the types of play you engaged in and play materials used. Were your play experiences similar or different from others in your group? Now, think about what children play today. Has play changed since you were a child? How so?

6. Review the *Letter to Families* included at the beginning of this section. Interview the parent of a young child about that child's dramatic play. What characters does the child like to be during dramatic play? Does the child pretend while playing alone or with others? What props does the child like to use during dramatic play?

7. Refer to the mark-making activities in this chapter. Select one and provide the necessary materials for a small group of children to engage in a mark-making art activity.

Review

1. List three modes of creative expression other than art.

2. Identify at least three criteria that characterize play.

3. Name five different categories or types of play.

4. List the four components of music and movement.

5. Discuss three different ways adults can facilitate children's creative expression.

6. Stone (1995) identifies three things teachers need to know or be able to do to become play advocates. Identify and briefly explain each.

7. Play was given a major role in children's development according to Vygotsky's (1986) sociocultural theory. Explain four major purposes that play serves.

8. Discuss the concept of multiple literacies. Include a discussion of picture books and visual literacy.

Additional Resources

"Trackers Kids: Woodworking for Kids," Winter 2010, a YouTube video on children and woodworking.

"Dramatic Play: You Be the Mommy and I'll be the Dog" is a Web-based learning unit for pre-service teachers by the Better Kid Care Program at Penn State (www.betterkidcare.psu.edu).

Experiences in Movement and Music, 5th edition by Rae Pica, ©2013, Cengage Learning.

International Reading Association (IRA), a guide to resources in the teaching of literacy for teachers of all ages (www.reading.org).

Go to the Education.com Website for the article, "The Value of Music in Early Childhood Education," by Carol Seefeldt and B. A. Wasik.

 Visit CourseMate for this textbook to access the eBook, Did You Get It? quizzes, Digital Downloads, TeachSource Videos, flashcards, and more. Go to CengageBrain.com to log in, register, or purchase access.

Pre-Kindergarten—Kindergarten Lesson Plan

Introduction to "My Body: Inside and Out"

GOAL

The student knows the basic structures and functions of the human body and how they relate to personal health. The student is expected to name major body parts and their functions.

OBJECTIVES

Through participation in this lesson, the children will:

a. identify visible body parts and explore how those body parts move.
b. move their bodies in rhythm to music.
c. trace and cut body outlines.

MATERIALS

a. Hap Palmer's "Shake Something"
b. Reproduction of full-length masterpiece portrait
c. Paper for body cut-outs
d. Markers and scissors for children

INTRODUCTION

Play Hap Palmer's "Shake Something" and invite the children to move and groove with you. After the song, seat children on the carpet and ask individuals the following questions:

a. Show me the part of your body that you moved back and forth. What is that body part called?
b. Show me the part of your body that you moved side to side. What is that body part called?
c. Show me the part of your body that you moved round and round. What is that body part called?

DEVELOPMENT

Show children a large reproduction of a masterpiece full-length portrait. Tell the children the title of the painting and the name of the artist. Ask the children to identify body parts on the portrait.

Tell the children that over the next two weeks the class will be studying our bodies, how to take care of them, and the people who help us take care of our bodies. Today we have talked about parts of our bodies that we can see. Tomorrow we will begin to learn about parts of our body that we can't see—parts that are on the inside.

Ask children to choose partners and demonstrate how each child will lay down on the butcher paper while the partner traces around him or her. Each child can cut his or her own outline and add facial features.

CLOSURE

Help children to label body parts as they finish cutting.

ASSESSMENT

a. Were the children able to identify body parts throughout the activities?
b. Did the children move in rhythm to the music?
c. Did the children trace and cut out their body outlines?

Go to cengagebrain.com for a full-size version of this lesson plan.

Young Children As Artists:

A Developmental View

© Cengage Learning

What do you see happening in the photograph?

These children are painting a mural as their teacher watches. The teacher had planned the mural painting to encourage verbal and social interaction among the children. Each child is free to paint whatever he or she wants, but, after some discussion, the children have decided to work together to paint an outdoor scene. They've chosen to use green to paint the ground at the bottom of the mural. Then, each will paint a zoo animal in the foreground, and they will all paint the sky overhead. The children have made decisions about the structure and content of their mural. They have chosen their work space, the colors, and the perspectives they will use. These decisions are the essence of creativity.

Why is art important for young children? Is there more to art than just enjoyment? Pretend you are teaching, and a parent complains that there is too much emphasis on art in your program. You show the parent your schedule, reflecting an array and balance of activities, but she is still not satisfied. Although her daughter loves art, the

mother asks, "Why is art so important?" How would you respond?

Let's review what we know about the developing child and connect this to art. What is the relationship between art and child development? Does art foster the development of the young child physically, socially, emotionally, cognitively, and creatively?

Chapter 4, "Art and the Developing Child," addresses these questions. Although the development is divided into domains for individual analysis, the focus is on an interactive model of the whole child. Always remember that each child is unique, and our job is to recognize, accept, value, and nurture each child's uniqueness.

Chapter 5, "Children's Artistic Development," examines different theories and stage sequences in children's art. Theories provide explanations for the how, what, and why of children's art. Stages provide a sequence in children's artistic development. Over time, beginning scribbles become more controlled, shapes are combined and detailed, and pictures become recognizable.

A LETTER TO FAMILIES

Dear Families,

Along with this letter you will find a self-portrait drawn by your child. After looking at self-portraits by Romare Bearden and Mary Cassatt, your child examined his or her face in a mirror and drew a self-portrait. We will repeat this activity in June. A comparison of today's drawing and the later drawing will show your child's growth and development.

Just as your child will grow and learn new academic skills this year, he or she will also develop artistically. As your child grows physically, he will strengthen small muscles in his hands and fingers, gaining control over art tools. As your child learns social skills, she will share materials and collaborate with others. As your child discovers information and new ways to investigate the environment, he will add details, record experiences in different media, and show varying perspectives and viewpoints through art.

As a toddler, your child experimented with art materials to see the effects that could be achieved. Now, when your child begins a project, she usually has a specific subject in mind. As this year progresses, you will see recognizable subjects in your child's art: scenes from the classroom and playground, as well as imaginary characters and events. Whenever we introduce new materials, however, your child will revert to exploring what the materials can do, just as when she was younger. It takes time to learn to use new materials, and this exploration will ultimately support your child's learning and development.

Sincerely,

Your Child's Teacher

4 Art and the Developing Child

© Cengage Learning

What do you see happening in this photograph?

What activity has the teacher prepared? This young painter is mixing colors and using a variety of brush strokes: vertical, horizontal, straight, and curved. There is no right or wrong way to paint, and this boy has been creative in exploring the many possibilities. The boy is developing creatively, just as he is growing and developing physically, socially, emotionally, and cognitively.

Learning Outcomes

After reading this chapter, you should be able to:

4-1 Identify the domains of child development.

4-2 Explain the importance of considering individual differences in planning an art curriculum.

4-3 Describe how the environment provides an interactive context for child development.

4-4 Provide opportunities for children to process with art materials and tools.

Standards addressed in this chapter

DAP Criteria
1 Creating a caring community of learners
2 Teaching to enhance development and learning
3 Planning curriculum to achieve important goals
5 Establishing reciprocal relationships with families

NAEYC Standards
1 Relationships
2 Curriculum
3 Teaching
5 Health

NAEA Visual Arts Standards
1 Students use art materials and tools in a safe and responsible manner

DAP naeyc 4-1 Domains of Child Development

This chapter provides a developmental overview of the young child: physically, socially, emotionally, cognitively, and creatively. According to our holistic model of child development, these aspects influence and are influenced by one another. Ideally, we use this knowledge in planning art activities. Our present analysis attempts to answer the question: How does art foster development of the whole child? Our purpose is twofold: first, to help understand how art can support and enhance a child's development, and second, to use what we know about art and child development in planning our art program and explaining it to others. Providing a justification is more than being defensive: "Art is important, and that's why we spend a lot of time doing it!" If art is important (and it is), we must provide a rationale for including it. Relating art to child development provides one rationale.

One way to get a working knowledge of young children is to build a model for studying development in the following areas:

physical—including large muscle, or gross motor, skills; small muscle, or fine motor, skills; perceptual-motor skills or eye-hand coordination; sensory development; good health; and self-care

social—including development of self and relations with others (see Figure 4–1)

emotional—including feelings about self and emotional expression as well as personality and temperament

cognitive—including thinking, problem solving, discovery, language, curiosity, reasoning, and learning

creative—including original thinking, imagination, and verbal and nonverbal expression

This model of development is depicted in Figure 4–2. Still, this neat division is too simplistic. A pizza might be neatly cut into five pieces, but a child's development cannot. Domains of development interact; they are interdependent and interrelated. It is impossible to study a child's physical development in isolation. Physical development is influenced by—and also directly influences—social, emotional, cognitive, and creative development. For example, five-year-old Joey has been included midyear in a regular kindergarten classroom. Muscular dystrophy has left him confined to a wheelchair. This influences what he can and cannot do physically, but it is not the only influence on his overall development. Joey's physical state affects, and is also affected by, his social, emotional, cognitive, and creative functioning. Initially,

Figure 4–1 Art can be a social experience.

© Cengage Learning

Joey was ignored by his peers and misunderstood by his teacher. Slowly, he withdrew. Emotionally, Joey began feeling sorry for himself, wishing he were like his peers. His self-concept suffered. Cognitively, he began to avoid school tasks, shunned class discussions, and refused to work. Creatively, however, Joey channeled his energies into making original pictures of outer space. Interestingly, Joey always drew himself as a space captain, with powerful legs and strong arms. As in Joey's case, child development is uneven, reflecting developmental spurts and lags. Fortunately, Joey's teacher recognized the problem and her lack of knowledge and enrolled in a course on inclusion. She worked closely with Joey, his parents, his peers, and his resource teacher. The students openly discussed special needs and how all people have strengths and weaknesses, assets and limitations. Over time, the children accepted Joey and welcomed him into their activities. In fact, they became overprotective, and Joey regressed to an earlier stage of helplessness. Continual support and encouragement helped Joey become more independent. He began to show improvement in his schoolwork and eagerly reported to his mother what he was learning. Joey became very well liked by his peers, and his self-concept improved.

Providing a detailed description of child development is beyond the scope of this chapter. Instead, a general overview of a young child's physical, social, emotional, cognitive, and creative development is presented.

4-1a Physical Development

Young children are physical beings characterized by much activity and energy. Physical development depends on adequate rest, exercise, sleep, and good nutrition.

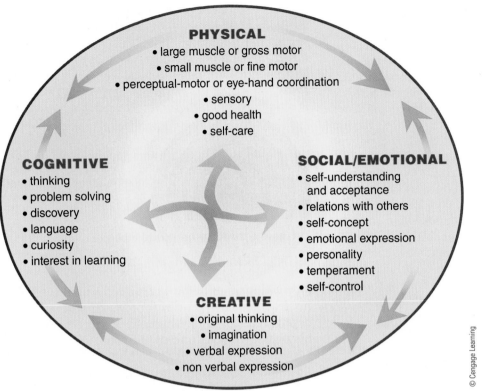

Figure 4–2 Holistic model of child development.

Young children are intrinsically motivated to affect their environment. They do this primarily through motor activity and sensory exploration.

Infants develop prehension, or grasping, and a pincer grasp that allows them to hold objects between their fingers and opposing thumb. Older infants can hold a stubby crayon and be guided into making marks on paper. Young children are more adept with large muscle (gross motor) skills than with small muscle (fine motor) skills. They master easel painting with large brushes before they can use a small brush with watercolors. By age three, most preschoolers can hold a crayon with their fingers, as opposed to the earlier clenched-fist grip. Young children are good doers, talkers, and movers. They have difficulty sitting still, listening, and remaining silent.

naea **naeyc** **Art and Physical Development.** Art activities provide experience and practice in developing and refining gross motor, or large muscle, skills. Art involves physical and manipulative activity. While easel painting, children use their entire arms and upper torsos in making large, sweeping motions with paintbrushes. Large, long-handled, wide-bristle brushes facilitate this movement. Muscles in the hands are developed while working with clay—tearing, rolling, twisting, coiling, pounding, pinching, and flattening it. Whole hand and arm motions are involved in hand painting. Children can spread and work paint with their fingers, their whole hands, their fingernails, knuckles,

fists, and the backs of their hands.

Gross motor, or large muscle, skills are perfected before fine motor, or small muscle, skills. Cutting with scissors, painting with a smaller watercolor brush, and modeling with clay require children to use smaller muscle groups in the wrists, hands, and fingers. As muscle strength increases, so does the child's control of tools in many other activities, particularly writing (Fox and Diffily, 2001). Although making children into early printers or writers is not the purpose of art, art does facilitate the development of this skill.

SCISSORING Scissoring is a physical activity that involves a patterned *open-close* rhythmical movement. Cutting with scissors on a line fosters eye-hand coordination and visual acuity, with the eyes and scissoring hand working together. Children do not develop this important skill without some guidance and practice (see Figure 4–3). Using scissors gives children a feeling of power and mastery. Guidelines for helping children cut and for selecting proper equipment follow.

1. Tearing paper is a good starting point for young children. Torn pieces can be pasted on paper to make a collage, as seen in Figure 4–4. Tearing paper is itself an important skill that need not be eliminated when a child learns to cut.

Figure 4–3 Cutting with scissors can be a physical challenge for young children.

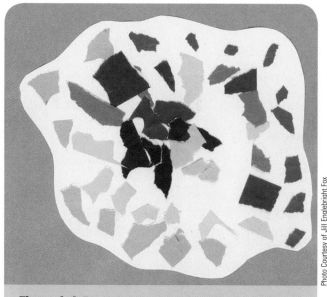

Photo Courtesy of Jill Englebright Fox

Figure 4–4 Tearing paper is an alternative to cutting with scissors.

placed in a box tend to tangle together. Various types of scissors are commercially available. Blunt scissors have rounded ends. Clip-type scissors have one pointed and one rounded end. Sharp scissors have two pointed ends. There are different scissors for different cutting needs and abilities. For example, smaller 4-inch scissors with rounded tips are safe for use by young children. Their blades are fairly dull, but their metal handles may pinch or irritate the skin.

a. Scissors with rubber-coated finger holes are more comfortable and will not hurt.

b. Plastic safety scissors are lightweight, inexpensive, comfortable, and easy to use.

c. Squeeze-type scissors have an easy-grip, continuous-loop handle. A gentle squeeze with two hands, the fingers and palm of one hand, or the thumb and fingers of one hand will cut. The two blades are blunt and fairly small. They are good for snipping and fringing. Extensive cutting will take more squeezing and hand activity than using scissors with longer blades.

2. Cutting thin, pliable play dough is a good introduction to using scissors.

3. Snipping or fringing paper is a beginning step in using scissors with paper. Give children a narrow 1/4- or 1/2-inch-wide paper strip. Show them how to make a single cut or snip into the paper. Children enjoy snipping off small pieces. Small snips into a wider 1-inch strip will produce fringe. With practice, the young child will be able to make repeated snips in a sequence or line. Draw a thick, straight line on paper, and show children how to follow it while cutting. It does not matter if children stray from the line. The aim is to help them coordinate repeated snips into a continuous cutting action.

4. Advanced cutters can practice cutting wavy, bending, or angular lines. Children can also practice cutting out geometric shapes.

5. Cutting along interior lines, such as the eyes in a mask or paper-bag puppet, is difficult. It is also potentially dangerous because children tend to begin the hole by poking with the point of the scissors.

● Rules for the proper use of scissors should be established, discussed, and posted in words or pictures or both. For example: Scissors are used only for cutting paper; walk when carrying scissors; when passing scissors to someone else, hold with the closed points down in your own hand.

6. A scissors rack provides safe storage for scissors and makes scissors easy to get and return to their upright position. Metal stands are commercially available at a modest cost. Scissors that are merely

7. Some young children, including those with special needs and/or poor fine motor coordination, have difficulty learning to cut. Merely observing someone else cutting or trial-and-error practice may not be enough. Try using double-handled training scissors with four rubber-coated finger holes. The teacher and child cut together as one. Over time, these children may graduate to using scissors independently.

8. Both right- and left-handed scissors should be made available. It is difficult and frustrating for a "lefty" to hold and cut with scissors designed for a "righty."

9. Children's 5-inch pointed metal scissors are longer, heavier, and sharper. More-skilled cutters in kindergarten and the primary grades may prefer these.

10. Some young children have difficulty holding scissors in the air and working both blades. Children who find scissors heavy or awkward can rest the bottom blade on the table and let only the top finger do the work.

11. Some paper is easier to cut than others. Very lightweight paper, including tissue and cellophane, are flimsy, difficult to cut, and will tear. Cardboard, poster board, and wallpaper are too thick and resistant for most children's strength and scissors. Manila, butcher paper, newspaper, newsprint, and drawing paper are recommended for beginning cutters. Skilled cutters can move on to construction paper.

Practicing gross and fine motor skills makes art activities valuable for children, including those with physical disabilities. The tactile and visual qualities of art activities make them ideal for visually or hearing-impaired

SOMETHING EXTRA.....

DAP Tailoring Art for Children with Special Needs

Some general guidelines for tailoring art for children with special needs include the following:

Visual

- Verbally describe materials and the ways they may be used.
- Engage in art activities with children while verbally describing your actions.
- Encourage children to manipulate items as you talk. For example, finger paint may feel cold and repulsive if children are not prepared for the experience and have no visual cues.
- Keep art tools within reaching distance.
- Use the buddy system; pair children with special needs with peers who can provide support.

Auditory

- Model the process. Demonstrate precisely, especially if several steps are involved.
- Face the children when speaking, and use facial expressions for emphasis.
- Communicate with children about their art using sign language and other signals and gestures they understand.

- Combine verbal, visual, and physical cues. For example, say, "I'm painting" while moving a brush in an up-and-down motion at the easel.

Physical

- Allow for using materials in different ways, such as lying on the floor over a bolster.
- Tape a group of crayons or markers together for easier grasping.
- Apply nonskid tape, sandpaper, or corrugated cardboard to marking instruments to ensure a better grip.
- Tape children's papers to work surfaces to prevent sliding.
- Encourage paper tearing for children unable to use scissors.
- Provide finger paint and soft play dough for easier manipulation.
- Allow children to hold brushes in their mouths instead of their hands if preferred.
- Model the process for children.
- Gently guide children's hands when manipulating art tools.
- Put children in control by asking how they want tools to move.

children. Through art, children can communicate their ideas to others without being dependent on either oral language or visual symbols. For children with fine or gross motor disabilities, most art activities can be adapted for their full participation.

According to Karnes (1993), the value of art activities for children with special needs cannot be overemphasized. However, because art may be a new experience for some, a good beginning is talking about art media and modeling how to use materials. The goal is to first make children feel comfortable and successful. After this, provide time and space for them to explore, discover, and create. Remain a resource and consultant to them, offering assistance as needed.

Art Safety. No discussion of physical development would be complete without a discussion of health and safety. Growing up healthy and safe is a major component of physical development.

The following information will ensure art experiences that do not compromise a child's physical health and safety.

glitter—Glitter is not recommended. The small pieces are sharp and can easily scratch the eye. Children often have glitter on their fingers and then rub their eyes. If you decide to use glitter, provide ample supervision and use with children aged four and older. Provide shakers for dispensing glitter onto glue rather than using their fingers. Remind children to wash their hands thoroughly when finished using glitter.

knives or sharp objects—Children should not use knives, sharp scissors, or objects such as a compass.

electricity—Young children should not use appliances that are plugged into the wall and generate heat. Examples include a hot plate, electric skillet, or iron. These may be used with older school-age children, provided there is one adult supervisor for each child in the activity.

hot glue gun—Liquid glue is preferred because it is difficult for children visually to determine when a glue gun is hot enough to use. Glue guns can be used with school-age children, provided there is one adult supervisor for each child. Glue guns with a "cool" setting are also recommended but still require supervision.

rubber cement—Rubber cement is often misused as an inhalant and should not be provided for children.

balloons—Balloons are very dangerous for toddlers and young children, who tend to put things in their mouths. Pieces of popped balloon are very inviting and may resemble candy to children with strong oral needs.

powder paints—Paints in powder as opposed to liquid form pose a threat. The fine powder granules may either promote an allergic reaction or trigger a respiratory condition such as asthma. They also pollute the air. Children should neither mix nor directly use powder paints. Adults should use a mask when mixing.

nature items—Some flowers and leaves are poisonous if ingested. Nature items can be used in art projects provided there is ample supervision.

Styrofoam™ trays—Styrofoam trays can be used in many ways in early childhood programs. They can hold collage items or become the background for a collage. They can be used as paint containers if lined with paper towels for a printmaking activity. They also make great frames. However, plastic foam trays that once held any kind of raw meat or fish may carry bacteria that cause illness. Plastic foam meat trays are very porous and hold more bacteria and juices than clear plastic trays. It is strongly suggested that you use only trays that held fruit, vegetables, or baked goods in early childhood classrooms.

crayons—Tests conducted show that three major brands of crayons scribbled with and nibbled on by millions of children worldwide contain asbestos. The asbestos is most likely a contaminant of the talc that most companies use in crayons as a strengthener for the paraffin and coloring agents. Because the dangers of asbestos are well known, parents and teachers were genuinely alarmed about the potential health risks crayons might pose to children. Follow-up studies conducted by the U.S. Consumer Product Safety Commission, however, concluded that the amount of asbestos in crayons is so small it is scientifically insignificant. The risk a child would be exposed to the fibers either through inhalation or ingestion is extremely low.

Art Poisoning. Many art supplies used by young children can be toxic. Examples include rubber cement, permanent felt-tip markers, pottery glazes, enamels, spray paints, lead-based supplies, and wheat wallpaper paste, among others. These toxic materials can be inhaled, ingested, or absorbed through the skin. Young children are at high risk for many reasons:

- They are still growing and have a very rapid metabolic rate. They absorb toxic materials into their bodies more readily than adults.
- Their brain, lungs, and nervous system are still forming and thus are at risk.
- They have lowered body defenses.
- Their lower body weight puts them at high risk, because a given quantity of a toxic material will be more concentrated in their bodies.
- They may be impulsive, engage in thumb sucking and nail biting, have frequent hand-to-mouth contacts, and neither understand nor follow necessary precautions.

SOMETHING EXTRA.....

naea Fat Crayons or Skinny Crayons?

In years past, fat pencils and crayons were standard equipment in early childhood classrooms through the second grade. In modern classrooms, however, these primary-sized writing and drawing tools have virtually disappeared. Many children are struggling to develop control in their handwriting and drawing as a result. Fat pencils and crayons were designed for the developmental needs of young children. Physical development occurs in a proximodistal direction. This means that development begins at the center of the body and proceeds outward. The child first gains control of the trunk of the body and then gradually develops control of the shoulders, arms, wrists, hands, and finally fingers. Larger tools encourage children to make larger marks (Hanline, Milton, & Phelps, 2007) with arm and hand movements, rather than requiring them to use fine muscles in the fingers before they are developmentally ready to do so. Drawing and writing with skinny tools before they have the opportunity to develop fine muscle strength and acuity is fatiguing for young children and will limit their engagement in these activities. For this reason, the authors recommend the use of fat pencils and crayons for children at least through the first grade.

naeyc naea Art Safety Guidelines. Art can be a safe and pleasurable experience if guidelines are established and followed. Suggested guidelines for teachers are on the following page.

1. Use judgment in providing staplers, staples, sharp scissors, tin cans, glitter, spray paint, toothpicks, hot plates, needles, pins, knives, and so on. Some young children are responsible and can be trusted to use these items at an early age with some supervision. Others may be too young (in developmental age or maturity) to understand the need for proper handling.

2. Take the time to discuss any potential hazards and dangers. Be honest and positive without dwelling on all the fatal possibilities. Focus on educating rather than frightening children.

3. Try out the art activity in advance. Is it safe? Can your particular group of children properly use the tools involved?

4. Demonstrate and model the proper ways to use tools: "This is the way to use a hole puncher. Sally, now you show me how to use it."

5. Supervise all art activities. Aides and parent volunteers can assist in supervision. Some activities will require closer and more direct supervision than others. Remember to anticipate the level of supervision needed when planning.

6. The Art and Crafts Materials Institute has developed a voluntary program designed to promote safety in children's art materials. Look for and purchase those art products bearing the institute's labels: AP for Approved Product or CP for Certified Product.

7. The label "nontoxic" is very misleading. According to present criteria, only materials that are acutely toxic merit a label of "toxic." Therefore, "nontoxic" embraces a wide range of dangers from minimally to acutely toxic. Tests to determine toxicity are done on adult animals. A product considered nontoxic when tested on an adult rat may provoke a very different reaction in a young child.

8. Refuse donated art supplies unless the ingredients are known.

9. Do not use old art supplies. Older materials may be highly toxic. They may have been produced when ingredients were not listed on the label and criteria for toxicity were absent.

10. Insist that children clean up and wash their hands after doing art.

11. Food and drinks should remain at the snack table or kitchen area and are not taken to the art center.

12. Children with open cuts, sores, or wounds that are not properly covered should not do art activities that involve potentially toxic supplies.

13. Parents of children with allergies, asthma, and other medical problems should consult their pediatrician regarding any limits on their child's use of art supplies.

14. Post the number of your local or state poison control center. Call your local hospital for the number. Have the product in hand when you dial so that you can quickly read the ingredients from the label and take prompt action.

naeyc naea What Makes an Art Material "Safe"? Knowledge of materials and their proper use makes them safe. Be sure to read labels on all products so you will know they have been evaluated and are nontoxic or need special handling to avoid possible health hazards from misuse. Look for the ACMI seals so you will know the product has been evaluated by a qualified toxicologist for *both acute and chronic* hazards. Or you may see other indications that the product conforms to ASTM D 4236, the chronic hazard labeling standard that is part of the U.S. labeling law. Follow all safe-use instructions. Observe good work habits and teach them to children.

Although the safety precautions noted earlier are not necessary with ACMI-certified nontoxic products, they are good habits to learn and practice with any art material use. Above all, purchase art materials that have been evaluated with children's safety in mind, and read and follow any label directions to safely enjoy rewarding art, craft, and other creative activities.

DAP naeyc 4-1b Social Development

Infants begin life as social, egocentric beings with little regard for the needs of others. Through socialization, they are introduced to a wider arena of family, relatives, and significant others. Individual desires are slowly curbed in response to the needs of others. Young children are egocentric and may need assistance in learning how to share; wait patiently; take turns; listen to others; and respect the property, rights, and ideas of others. They can also express empathy in appreciating the plight of others who are hurt or in trouble.

According to Erikson (1963), it is important for parents and caregivers to help:

- infants develop a sense of trust rather than mistrust
- toddlers develop a sense of autonomy rather than doubt or shame
- preschoolers develop a sense of initiative rather than guilt

At times, young children will be independent and autonomous. At other times they will be dependent and seek comfort, security, and reassurance. Young children are talkers and socializers. They learn language and social skills from interacting with others, observing significant models, and witnessing the effects of their behavior upon others. For example, a young child who constantly snatches toys from others may find that they refuse to include her in their play. Young children are interested in themselves: who they are, what they look like, what they know, and what they can do. Their interest extends to their peers and the immediate community. They enjoy being part of social groups other than their families.

DAP **naeyc** **Art and Social Development.** Our discussion of art thus far has focused primarily on what happens to individual children as they engage in art. We tend to think of art as an independent activity. But learning through art can be a social activity (Mulcahey, 2009). Young children learn about themselves and others. Children validate their uniqueness by making personal statements through art. "This is my chalk mark," says Deidra. It is a part of her, an extension of herself, and unlike the marks of others. Art helps

---

SOMETHING EXTRA.....

naeyc naea Safety Tips: Read the Label!

Always use products appropriate for individual users. Children in grade six and lower and adults who do not read and understand safety labeling should use only nontoxic materials.

- Do not use products that have passed their expiration dates.
- Do not eat, drink, or smoke while using art and craft materials.
- Wash up after use—clean yourself and your supplies.
- Never use products for skin painting or food preparation unless it is indicated on the label that the product is meant to be used in this way.
- Do not transfer art materials to other containers—you will lose valuable safety information on the product package.

Additional procedures to follow when using products with cautionary labeling:

- Keep products out of reach of children.
- Keep your work area clean.
- Vacuum or wet mop dust; do not sweep it.
- Do not put your brush, pen, and so on in your mouth.
- Keep your work area well ventilated; make sure you have an air exchange system.
- Avoid skin contact. Keep materials out of your eyes and mouth.
- Use any and all protective equipment specified on the label, such as gloves, safety glasses, and masks.
- Use a mask or gloves that are impermeable to whatever product you are using; the wrong type of equipment could do as much or more harm than using no equipment at all!
- Protect any cuts or open wounds by using appropriate gloves, and so on.
- Mix and handle certain dry materials in a locally exhausting hood or sealed box.

- Spray certain materials only in a locally exhausting spray booth with filters.
- Do not mix different food-safe glazes together because the balance of ingredients in the mixed glaze will be disrupted, and the resulting mixture may not be dinnerware safe.
- Carefully follow suggested disposal methods.

Procedures to follow when a product has a flammability warning:

- Do not store or use product near heat, sparks, or flame.
- Do not heat above the temperature specified on the label.
- Use explosion-proof switches and an exhaust fan with an explosion-proof motor, if specified on the label.

Products that are hazardous require the following on their labels:

- a conformance statement to ASTM D 4236, unless impractical and then at the point of sale (This requirement also applies to nontoxic products.)
- a signal word, such as "Warning" or "Caution"
- a listing of the ingredients in the product that are at a hazardous level
- a listing of how the product may hurt you if not used properly (may cause lung cancer, may cause harm to the developing fetus, and so on)
- instructions on how to use the product properly and safely (do not eat, drink, or smoke; use a respirator; wear gloves; and so on)
- an appropriate telephone number, usually the telephone number of the manufacturer or importer
- a statement that the product is inappropriate for use by children

(Reprinted with permission: The Art & Creative Materials Institute, Inc. Hanson, MA.)

children become comfortable with themselves, learning what they like and dislike and what they can and cannot do. Missy finds out that she prefers modeling with clay over cutting and pasting paper. She likes to work intently alone, away from noise and social interaction. Missy is independent, yet she rarely has the art center to herself. The classroom is a social setting, and she is learning to interact positively with others. When two or more children engage in social play with art materials, they expand their imaginations, share ideas, and develop social skills (Thompson, 2005). They must negotiate the use of the materials, share and take turns, and provide appropriate feedback to each other (Sautter, 1994). The art center has rules that protect the welfare of both the group and the equipment. In turn, children learn responsibility for cleanup and return of materials to their rightful places. This is difficult for Missy, who is an only child and used to playing by herself. Slowly, she is learning to share materials, take turns, and wait patiently.

Clemens (1991) views art as a form of positive child guidance. She sees artwork as a preventive measure, a benign alternative to letting emotional children express themselves in destructive ways. Art is offered because it makes survival in the classroom more likely. Controlling children is not the issue. If you give children interesting choices, your class will run smoothly. For these reasons, Clemens believes that art should take a prominent place in the daily classroom schedule.

4-1c **Emotional Development**

Most young children like themselves—who they are, what their names are, their appearance, and their abilities. It is our job to help these positive feelings to continue. Self-concept is in a very formative stage during early childhood. Young children need an abundance of opportunities to experience mastery, success, and acceptance and to witness their own competence. Young children may transfer their parental attachment to their teacher or caregiver. They may express love and affection and be overly possessive. They may be jealous of their peers and expect or demand a caregiver's total time, interest, attention, and praise.

Figure 4–5 Through art, children can represent and master unpleasant experiences.

Photo Courtesy of Robert Schirrmacher

 Art and Emotional Development. Art is an emotionally pleasurable experience. Most children express happiness, joy, and pride in their art. This results in positive mental health and an expression of feelings. Young children are emotional beings, and art allows intense involvement. Merely thinking that there may be a connection between art and emotional development, however, is simplistic and intuitive. For more than three decades, Coles (1992) investigated the inner lives of children through their expressive words and pictures in a variety of settings including hospitals, clinics, homes, schools, and places of worship. He concluded that children disclose their deepest convictions, feelings, and dreams with crayon, paint, and pencil. Art helps children nonverbally express objects, ideas, people, places, experiences, events, and feelings that are emotionally significant. Often, a child is unable or unwilling to verbally discuss emotional topics or feelings about self, family, and friends. Art, however, allows these feelings, fantasies, fears, and frustrations to surface and be expressed (see Figure 4–5). It allows children the opportunity to represent in fantasy what cannot happen in reality. Negative feelings and impulses can be released in

Brain Connection 🧠

The brain's emotional center is tied to the ability to learn. Emotions, learning, and memory are closely linked as different parts of the brain are activated in the learning process. Good learning environments build trust, empower students, and encourage children to explore their emotions and ideas (Rushton & Larkin, 2001).

Figure 4–6 Art allows children to express how they feel.

Photo Courtesy of Robert Schirrmacher

important for children because it is a prerequisite to learning. Children who do not feel good about themselves do not learn. Their energy and attention are focused on fear of failure and self-doubt. It is wiser to focus our attention on developing a positive self-concept in the early years as a preventive measure, rather than attempting to remediate a negative self-concept in older children who may have given up on themselves, learning, and life.

Children with attention deficits or behavioral issues often suffer low self-esteem. Their feelings of frustration and insecurity may emerge as negative social interactions with peers or adults. Participation in art activities provides a positive avenue for expressing emotions and gives a low-stress setting in which they can develop positive social skills. Making art is emotionally satisfying because children have control over the materials they use and the images they create (Seefeldt, Castle, & Falconer, 2010).

Teachers can facilitate children's participation in art activities by:

- Providing children with their own materials and ample workspace. Avoid making children wait for a turn to use materials.

- Allowing children to explore properties of the materials and to make multiple products if they choose.

- Providing materials such as play dough that can be actively used to release energy and feelings.

- Providing child-centered, open-ended activities in which children can be successful. Avoid teacher-directed activities that involve following directions or multiple steps.

- Limiting children to a few choices rather than overwhelming them with permission to use anything and everything in the art center.

4-1d **Cognitive Development**

The early years are a time of very rapid cognitive development. By age two, the brain has reached 75 percent of its adult weight. By age five, the brain has attained 90 percent of its adult weight. The early years provide opportunities for mental stimulation and challenge. Young children are self-motivated, curious explorers who are eager to learn about themselves, others, and the world. They need concrete materials to manipulate; problems to solve; people, places, and events to experience; and a time to discuss and ask questions. Books and the media may provide important vicarious information, but they are no substitute for direct experience.

Constructivism. Piaget's (1962, 1971) theory goes by many names, including cognitive-developmental, transactional, interactionist, and constructivist. Let us examine each of these terms.

Piaget's focus is on thinking, and his developmental stages explain how young children's thinking or

a positive, acceptable way through art (Miskimon, 2011). For example, anger against another cannot be physically expressed in the classroom, but it can be portrayed and expressed through art (see Figure 4–6).

Not only do young children learn to express emotion through art, but they also learn to recognize emotions portrayed in the art of others. In their study of children ages three to six years, Misailidi and Bonoti (2008) found that children were increasingly able to recognize and differentiate various emotions expressed in drawings, particularly happiness, sadness, and fear. The children in this study understood that drawings express the emotions of their creators.

Art enhances self-concept. Because art guarantees success, children experience mastery, which further enhances a positive self-concept. Positive self-concept is cognition changes over time. Changes in a child's cognitive development result from interactions with people, places, and objects in the environment. Children are active agents in their own development. They construct knowledge based on their actions on objects and their interactions with others. Children test new information against what they already know. As a result, mental constructs are revisited, reworked, and refined. Therefore, a basic premise of constructivism is that children must actively construct knowledge. It cannot be given to them through direct teaching. The process is similar to constructing a building. Workers lay brick and cement on top of each other. Over time, a building takes shape. Similarly, the child lays brick after brick in constructing a house of knowledge. Some bricks fit; others must be refashioned or discarded. The process takes time (and hard work). Piaget's work leads teachers to critically examine the role of direct instruction in children's learning. According to Piaget, much of what children learn cannot be verbally transmitted through direct teaching, which involves too little work from the child.

DAP naeyc **Types of Knowledge.** According to Piaget, there are three types of knowledge: physical, social-conventional, and logical-mathematical. Each approaches learning and teaching in a different way. Physical knowledge includes discovering the physical properties of objects. This includes external reality and observable properties such as form, weight, and function. Physical knowledge is best acquired through direct interactions and sensory-motor experiences with objects, and reflection on the results. Social-conventional knowledge refers to information about daily living accepted by society. It includes manners, acceptable behaviors, and customs, along with the names of the days of the week, months of the year, numerals, and alphabet letters. Social-conventional knowledge is best learned through social interaction. Logical-mathematical knowledge is constructed around the relationships between objects. Children form mental concepts about these relationships. Logical-mathematical knowledge is actively constructed as children sort, classify, group, seriate, count, compare, and contrast objects.

How do the types of knowledge affect art? Children construct physical knowledge when they discover the properties of art materials and media. For example, they explore the properties of paint and a paintbrush and what they can do with them. You can try to tell a young child that paint is wet and sticky, but most will prefer to learn this through experience.

Adults facilitate a child's social knowledge when, for example, they provide names and labels for art materials such as "paintbrush" and "paint." The same holds for the names of colors. Although children can discover that paint is wet and sticky, they will not "discover" that the color of the paint is "turquoise."

Wet and sticky are physical properties that can be discovered; turquoise is not. It is an arbitrary and abstract term. It is easier and more appropriate to simply tell children the color name. Logical-mathematical knowledge is constructed when a child compares two paint containers and sees, for example, that one is fuller than the other. This relationship is constructed by the child. More full and less full are not inherent in either of the containers. Paint can be wet, sticky, and turquoise, but the child's comparison of the amount of paint in each container constructed this more/less relationship. One container is only *less full* when the child actively (mentally) compares it with another that holds *more* paint.

So, assume a *hands-off* teacher role and a *hands-on* student role when you want children to discover the properties of objects (physical knowledge). Encourage children to reflect on the results of their actions on objects: "What do you see happening?" Teach children in developmentally appropriate ways when they are learning information that is arbitrary, culture-bound, and cannot be discovered (social-conventional knowledge). Provide children with sets of materials and objects, and encourage them to construct relationships between objects such as grouping and classifying (logical-mathematical knowledge).

According to Piaget, young children's thinking is action oriented and largely nonverbal. He believed that thinking precedes the development of language. Language enhances thinking but is not its source. Children understand and know more than they can verbalize. Likewise, what a child can say or discuss may not be an accurate indicator of intelligence. A young child's understanding and representation of the world proceed through stages.

Overview of Piaget's Stages of Development. During Piaget's sensory-motor stage (birth to age two), infant thinking is limited to sensory impressions and motoric behaviors. A toy rattle is something to be held, shaken, dropped, stared at, listened to, smelled, and tasted. There is no thinking about the rattle apart from these sensory and motoric actions.

Toddlers attain significant cognitive achievements as they leave the sensory motor stage and enter the preoperational stage (ages two through seven). Representation frees toddlers from a reliance on action-based thinking. They now form mental images, symbolize, and think about their world in the absence of direct action. Preschoolers in Piaget's preoperational stage are using symbols, including objects, art, and language, to represent their world. They continue to construct and refine concepts of time, space, classification, seriation, and number. Preschoolers in Piaget's preoperational stage think in ways that are qualitatively different from adult logic or reason.

Children in the primary grades have entered Piaget's stage of concrete operations (ages seven through

Art Therapy

When Art Materials Are Used effectively by art therapists, it is because they were trained to understand not only the art process but also the processes of normal and abnormal human development as well as theories of personality. According to Dunn-Snow and D'Amelio (2000), art teachers have access to students' nonverbal communications, and sometimes those graphic expressions speak louder than words. If a child has expressed something disturbing—either verbally or in graphic form—alerting a counselor, teacher, or parent about a child's verbal or graphic depiction may be the first step in helping to solve the problem, or at least in addressing the issue. Art, play, music, dance, literature, drama, and puppetry are vehicles for psychotherapy. Art therapy is the psychotherapeutic use of art for emotional understanding and healing. Although therapy with adults is largely verbal, children benefit from nonverbal forms.

Qualified therapists look for some of the following in art:

- An expressive use of colors—Red, bright orange, or black may be used repeatedly to symbolize objects of emotional importance. Black may be used to represent fear or death, red for rage or love.

- Personal meaning behind the repeated use of a symbol—Art therapists try to "crack the code," or discover links between artistic symbols and the unconscious. What meaning lies behind a child's repeated portrayal of a charging horse or a monster?

- An exaggeration, distortion, or overemphasis of objects reflecting emotional significance—Perhaps this is why young children first draw themselves as a large head with protruding arms, mounted on stick legs. They like their faces and how they look, so they draw them big. Arms and legs help them do things and get around, so they are also emphasized. Refer to the self-portrait (see Figure 4–7) drawn by a four-year-old. Note the "wound" on the face. At the time, she had a bruise from a fall and was excited to point it out, representing and exaggerating it in her self-portrait.

- The omission or underemphasis of objects also provides emotional clues—For example, children with low self-concepts often omit themselves or make themselves tiny by comparison with others. Children with intense sibling rivalry may simply omit that sibling when drawing the family. Art allows children to accomplish in fantasy what they cannot do in reality.

- Placement as clues to emotional significance— Objects drawn large and in the center of the paper are important. Children with low self-concepts may draw themselves in a corner or in the far background. They may also be hidden behind larger objects of emotional

significance placed in the center foreground. Painful, fear-evoking content may also be reduced in size and safely tucked away in a far corner of the picture.

- Defense mechanisms that protect the ego appear in art—Harmful or painful thoughts and experiences that are repressed in reality may be safely uncovered and expressed through art. The child who has been abused may portray herself with unusual colors or designs on her body. Identification may be reflected in a child's repeated use of a symbol with which to identify. The aggressive child identifies with the soldier or the marauding tiger. The fearful child becomes the scary witch on paper.

There are inherent difficulties in the use of art therapy. First, it requires extensive training. Second, one needs many samples of a child's artwork over a long period of time to recognize patterns, rather than make a rash interpretation. For example, it would be naive to assume that a child's preoccupation with the color red indicates a fixation with blood, violence, fire, or rage. There are many possible explanations. Red may simply be the child's favorite color, the nearest color, or the only one available. Even early childhood educators who are untrained in art therapy, however, can use art to help children nonverbally express their feelings and emotions. Our aim is to provide a vehicle for emotional expression and release rather than analysis or interpretation.

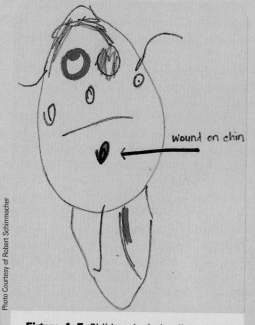

Figure 4–7 Children include, distort, and exaggerate what is personally meaningful to them.

eleven). An operation is an internalized action. Older children have attained several important cognitive operations, including reversibility, conservation, classification, and seriation, as well as addition, subtraction, multiplication, and division, which help them think more logically. Their thinking, however, is still bound to the concrete. They are unable to think abstractly.

DAP naeyc Constructivist Education: Putting Piaget's Theories into Practice. DeVries and Zan (1995), along with Chaillé and Britain (2003), wed Piaget's theory with developmentally appropriate practices, resulting in **constructivist education.** A constructivist approach views young children as theory builders. They focus on physical knowledge and are social beings who need support to develop autonomy. The learner is actively constructing knowledge rather than passively taking in information. Learners do not acquire knowledge that is transmitted to them; rather, they construct knowledge through their cognitive activity. Children take ownership for how and what they learn. Rather than just a set of activities, constructivist education is an approach based on the belief that children construct their own knowledge, intelligence, and personality, as well as social and moral values. A misconception about constructivist education is that, because it values play, it does not include academics. This is not true, for constructivist teachers are serious about children's construction of knowledge about literacy, numeracy, science, social studies, and the fine arts. According to DeVries and Zan (1995), the problem for the constructivist teacher in approaching academics is to distinguish what must be *constructed* from what must be *instructed.* Piaget's differentiation of types of knowledge aids the teacher in making this distinction.

DAP naeyc Vygotsky. Lev Vygotsky was a Soviet developmental psychologist who built his theories on children's learning and development during the early twentieth century. Like Piaget, Vygotsky believed that children actively construct knowledge. He also believed that development cannot be separated from its social context (Vygotsky, 1992). Vygotsky's **sociocultural theory** avowed that learning can lead development. He also believed that *language* plays a central role in cognitive development. Vygotsky's theory is similar to Piaget's in that both believed in the importance of play and that learning is actively constructed. A major difference is Vygotsky's emphasis on the role of language and direct instruction in learning. Also unlike Piaget, he does not propose a universal series of developmental stages. Instead, Vygotsky believes that development and learning are embedded in a child's family and cultural context. Adults teach socially valued skills at an early age. Children's learning is influenced by what their social world values.

Vygotsky's theory challenges Piaget's ideas of language and thought. According to Vygotsky, language plays a critical role in the formation of a child's mind because it is a major vehicle for communication. Language serves as a means by which a child's social experiences are mentally represented. So, language, even its earliest forms, is socially based. Rather than Piaget's concept of young children's speech as egocentric or immature, Vygotsky saw it as connected to what children are thinking. Young children talk aloud, and later this **self-talk** becomes internalized so that children act without having to talk aloud. Vygotsky believed that children speak to themselves for self-guidance and self-direction. The **private speech** that helps children think about their behavior and plan for action is also critical to self-regulation.

Because learning is considered essentially an interpersonal and dynamic process, teachers must develop comfortable and cooperative relationships with children. Children need adults who act as **intellectual mediators** that are readily available to observe, pose questions or problems, challenge, model, give information, or facilitate learning by referring a child to a more knowledgeable or skilled peer. Teachers must know each child's **zone of proximal development (ZPD).** This construct refers to a range of skills, tasks, or abilities that a child cannot yet do alone but can accomplish with adult and peer assistance. **Cooperative learning** and **group projects** are highly recommended. There are upper and lower limits to the ZPD. The lower limit would include those skills, tasks, or abilities that have already been accomplished by the child. The upper range refers to those tasks that are within a child's reach with some degree of assistance. Assistance can range from observing a more skilled peer to direct teaching. **Scaffolding** is an important strategy for teachers working within a child's zone. For example, a young child has been exploring with the three primary colors and is able to accurately name red, blue, and yellow. Let us place this accomplishment at the lower range of color learning. Knowing this, a teacher is able to *scaffold* and help the child to the next step: possibly mixing two primary colors and then naming the resulting color. It appears within the child's zone and is an assisted step that will enhance the child's learning about color.

Art and Cognitive Development. Brooks (2009) makes a strong case for the relationship between art and thought. Creating a drawing or painting involves the child artist's past and present experiences as well as imagination and emergent thinking. Creating art involves memory, experience, imagination, and observation. Children who have directly experienced a wide variety of people, places, and objects will have an array of things to choose from when doing art. Children who have neither been to a zoo nor been exposed to pets will probably not include animals in

Figure 4–8 A field trip to the zoo prompted this six-year-old's painting.

shapes. She discovers that squares combine to form a rectangle. Painting red over yellow makes orange. Lines that intersect form an X or cross shape. White added to blue lightens it and makes it the perfect color for Beth's sky. Difficult spatial concepts, including right, left, up, down, over, beside, through, between, and under, are represented in art. These spatial concepts will be vital to reading comprehension.

Art serves as an index of a child's thinking. We can look at children's artwork, particularly painting and drawing, and find out what they know about their world, what they consider important, and how they choose to represent it. Detailed artwork indicates that a child knows much about that particular subject. Children who can express what they know about their world will be at an advantage later when they are expected to write and read about it. Words, spoken or in print, must have some referent. Art gives children the opportunity to symbolize that referent and serves as a bridge between object and sign (see Figure 4–9). This ability to visualize ideas, concepts, and relationships can help

their art. Children must know about something before they can re-create it in art (see Figure 4–8).

Translating ideas, concepts, and experiences into art involves many thinking skills. Children must decide what to represent and how to execute it. "To make a dinosaur, should I use clay, markers, or paint?" thinks Nate. He must plan, organize, and make choices. Art involves concentration, staying with a task, and seeing it to completion—all important work skills and habits. Nate decides to draw an outline with pencil, trace over it with thick marker pen, cut it out, then paint it at the easel. Art involves problem solving. Nate needs dark paint when only the three primary colors are available. He mixes all three together into a muddy color that he thinks is just right for a "beast." Nate becomes upset when the muddy color runs into the white of the dinosaur's eye. Using too much water has thinned down the paint. Nate has learned about cause and effect. He hypothesizes and gets a crumpled paper towel to gently blot it out. It is impossible to document all the thinking that is going on in Nate's head while he is doing art. By the way, Nate is a bright four-year-old who is largely nonverbal. Art provides an opportunity for him to symbolize what he knows but cannot discuss. Over time, he may choose to explain with words, but for now the artwork communicates his ideas.

Through art, Nate can communicate with himself and others. The thinking cycle moves from planning to implementing, evaluating, and reworking, if necessary. The thinking side of art should not be neglected in favor of identifying physical, social, emotional, and creative ends. The major benefits of art may very well be cognitive in nature.

Through art, children learn about the concepts of color, shape, size, line, texture, and other artistic elements. For example, Beth knows basic geometric

Figure 4–9 Young children are concrete learners. Art helps them symbolize their experiences.

children move to higher levels of thinking (Brooks, 2009). The ability to work at a conceptual level means that children are beyond simply repeating what adults have told them and are truly able to understand links and connections between concepts.

Participation in art activities may be particularly valuable to children with special needs whose patterns of thinking and communicating differ from those of other children. Through art, children with special needs may communicate thoughts and emotions through their own visual symbols. They can participate in art activities with peers to receive positive feedback and practice social skills. Teachers can support participation of children with special cognitive and communications needs by:

- providing verbal directions slowly and clearly, and adding visual cues

- providing close supervision

- providing child-centered, open-ended activities to guarantee success

- breaking multistep activities into small steps

- building various levels of difficulty into activities, for example, allowing children to use precut paper shapes or to cut their own shapes in a collage

- encouraging children to talk about their art, or to dictate words or sentences to accompany their creations

- encouraging children to talk while doing art and to share thoughts and feelings about their artistic experiences

4-1e **Creative Development**

Creativity begins during infancy as babies invent solutions to problems and engage in novel actions. The term "creative" can be used to describe activities that result in something that wasn't there previously. A more appropriate use of the term "creativity," however, would be to describe the mental processes that guide a child's eyes and hands to arrange lines and shapes in a symbolic representation (Di Leo, 2003). Young children are highly imaginative. Imagination is strongly related to creativity.

Art and Creative Development. As seen in Figure 4–10, art allows children to express creativity, originality, and individuality. Children's artistic expressions may be vaguely similar yet still significantly different from all others. Their fantasy can be given form through art. Art is an open-ended activity that encourages discovery, exploration, experimentation, and invention. All of these skills are vital to creativity. Gene thinks about what will happen if he uses two paintbrushes at a time. He tries it out and is pleased with the double-stroked result. He asks his teacher to help him tie a rubber band around three paintbrushes. Through active experimentation, he invents a new way to paint.

Figure 4–10 Art fosters creative expression.

Photo Courtesy of Robert Schirrmacher

Did You Get It?

What describes the concept that parents and/or teachers should devise a model (or use an existing one) for analyzing a child/student's development in a myriad of areas (components), including cognitive, physical, emotional, and creative?

a. Studying development in a vacuum effectively paints a picture of the components of the model.

b. Components of the model are distinct and unrelated.

c. Components of the model are interdependent and interrelated.

d. Activities can easily be devised that fit neatly into only one domain of the model and can isolate the component more deeply.

Take the full quiz on CourseMate.

DAP 4-2 **Considering Individual Children**

Most early childhood teachers work in classroom settings with groups of young children. Classroom space is planned, curriculum is developed, and materials are purchased with the idea that each child will participate in the learning process as part of a larger group. It is important, however, that teachers not lose sight of what children as individuals will need to make their participation meaningful.

DAP naeyc 4-2a Children with Special Needs and Inclusion Classrooms

In the past, educators referred to children with special needs using the terms "handicapped" or "disabled." Both these terms promote negative images and stereotyping. The term "disabled" connotes *not-abled*. The preferred term is "**differently abled**." Other acceptable terms include "exceptional children" and "children with special needs."

Since the passage of the Americans with Disabilities Act (ADA) in 1992, it is against the law for public early childhood programs to refuse to serve a child with special needs. The following terms are often used in discussions about children with special needs in the public schools:

Least-restrictive environment: A setting that is appropriate for the child and provides the most contact possible with children without special needs

Mainstreaming: The placement of children with special needs in programs that have a majority of children who do not have special needs

Full inclusion: An approach in which children with special needs are placed in regular classrooms and receive individualized and appropriate services alongside peers who have no special needs

Full **inclusion** is very important during the preschool and elementary school years. The underlying assumption is that all children belong together, and children with special needs should be served in the same programs they would have attended if they did not have such needs. A single, inclusive system of care, intervention, and education is considered best for all children and their families. Inclusive settings adapt the environment with modifications to welcome children with special needs. Special educators provide services in the regular classroom alongside regular education colleagues. Advocates of full inclusion believe that the pull-out system of serving students with special needs raises issues. Children are labeled and stigmatized, their programming is fragmented, and regular educators assume little or no ownership for children with special needs.

Inclusion is the law. Still, according to Allen and Cowdery (2009), there are a number of concerns about inclusion. One expressed by parents and teachers is that the requirements of children with special needs may not be adequately met in an integrated program. A second concern is that developing children without special needs will receive less than their share of attention. A third concern is that children developing under typical circumstances will learn inappropriate and bizarre behaviors from atypical children. Allen and Cowdery concluded that the advantages of inclusion for both typically developing young children and those with special needs

are numerous and well documented in the research literature. Sharing books is a good way to help young children understand and respect special needs. Check the book's Website for a list of recommended books.

4-2b Individual Differences

A working knowledge of child development is very useful for early childhood teachers. Knowing the needs, interests, and abilities of young children at a given age or stage helps us design developmentally appropriate art activities. Knowledge of child development, however, will give us only a general pattern of what is *normal, typical,* or *average*. Few children conform to the norm or can be considered typical or average. Children are unique individuals. Their physical, social, emotional, cognitive, and creative development will reflect **individual differences** resulting from both heredity and environmental influences. Individual differences make teaching young children fascinating and challenging. Within any age group there will be a wide range of commonalities in terms of physical, social, emotional, cognitive, and creative needs, interests, and abilities. There will also be significant individual differences. Obviously, it would be simpler to work with a group of children with identical developmental characteristics. However, the aim of early childhood education is to foster the development of unique individuals, not to mass-produce automata.

Differences in development and learning that result from heredity or environment or their interaction are expressed in the following ways:

background: race, **culture**, and social class

family: family size, siblings, birth order, divorce and remarriage, parental educational and occupational levels, nutrition, parental teaching style, and child abuse or neglect

individual: gender, personality and temperament, motivation, learning style, and personal interests

Although culture is typically thought of in terms of a group's identity, it is important to note that each of us also develops an individual culture based on our background, family, individual characteristics, and experiences. In this sense, culture can be defined as "the necessarily unique worldview or set of understandings that each of us has no matter what outward similarities align us" (Davis, 2008, p. 22).

DAP 4-2c Cultural Influences

Children's backgrounds are composed of racial, ethnic, and cultural differences. Racial differences are expressed in skin color and other physical characteristics. Cultural differences are expressed not only in foods, celebrations, and dress but also, more importantly, in language, customs, and values. Language, as expressed in both words and art forms, is essential to cultural unity (Cronin and Jones, 1999). Racial and cultural differences extend, enhance, and enrich early childhood classrooms and society in general. Artistic activities will encourage children to appreciate diversity as they experience and appreciate the artwork of others (Miskimon, 2011).

Early childhood teachers have the responsibility of integrating perspectives, activities, traditions, and values from multiple cultures into the curriculum for two reasons. First, it is important that each child recognize that he or she is a valued member of the classroom community; cultural influences on learning must be recognized and honored so that each child learns and develops to his or her full ability. Artwork has the capacity to share and preserve what each child values most (Jalongo & Stamp, 1997). Second, early childhood teachers are models. Children will imitate their teacher's attitudes toward and interactions with other individuals and cultures. The following guidelines help teachers structure learning activities and their interactions with children and families.

1. Accept the child as is, unconditionally, including culture. Treat all children equally. Guidelines, rules, and rewards should apply to all children.

2. Accept, respect, and encourage the child's native language and culture as strengths and expressions of unique individual difference.

3. Help the child feel comfortable in school. Sights, sounds, and surroundings may be unfamiliar and overwhelming to some children who have nothing to compare.

4. Discuss and study similarities and differences among people. It is important for children to focus on human similarities as a framework for individual differences resulting from culture and ethnicity. Some examples include the following.
   What are some things that all people need?
   ● We all need housing and food. Where he came from, Lin lived on a houseboat with his parents and grandparents. What do you think it would be like to live on a boat? Now, Lin lives in an apartment. How many of you have ever lived in an apartment? I did while I was going to school. So even though Lin talks differently from us, he is still a lot like us. He has his own language and a place to live, just as we do. We are going to help Lin learn our language, and he will teach us his.

5. Involve parents. Some immigrant parents may have great reservations about school. Some may be embarrassed about their lack of standard English. Others may be ashamed of their minimal level of education. Some will place great value on their child's education and have unrealistically

high expectations. All will be proud of their culture and willing to share their ethnicity if encouraged and invited. Help them feel comfortable. Let them know that they have something very special that the children and you would like to know more about. For example, Lin's mother was invited to cook a rice dish with the children for a snack. Others could come bring in cultural artifacts. Their presence and participation will make their child feel good about being in school.

6. Help immigrant children be successful and experience mastery. Many are experience *culture shock*. They are aware of language and cultural differences. They need an abundance of things they can do successfully rather than an endless list of things they need to remediate.

7. Understand that cultural differences may underscore a child's reluctance to participate in art activities. Give children time to observe and feel comfortable. Children who have not been encouraged to be independent and autonomous may seek direction and specific assistance during art activities. They may want you to guide their hands or do it for them.

8. Learn key art words in languages your children speak. Ask parents to translate names of colors; words such as "art," "paint," and "play"; and phrases like "Do you want to … ?" and "Do you like that?" in the children's home languages. Use these phrases to talk to children about their art activities. Speaking to children in their native languages helps them to feel included in the classroom (Freshwater et al., 2008) and emphasizes the importance of their engagement in art.

4-2d Art and the Holidays

In early childhood programs, holidays should be observed simply and with sensitivity to children's ethnic and cultural backgrounds. Young children are often overexposed to "mainstream" holiday observances. For children whose families celebrate these holidays, the anticipation and excitement can lead to emotional over-stimulation and even physical exhaustion. For children whose families celebrate other holidays, or none at all, the emphasis on traditional holidays can leave them feeling left out and uncomfortable. In the past, many teachers used traditional "mainstream" holiday motifs, symbols, decorations, and activities while excluding those that were traditional in other cultures. This created bias in children's thinking and view of the world. Cherry and Nielsen (1999) recommend enriching all children's lives by encouraging open-ended, creative art experiences that reflect all cultures present in your classroom and community.

DAP naeyc 4-2e **Food Products in the Creative Process**

In the early childhood classroom, involving children in food preparation or cooking activities in which they will actually consume the healthy snacks they prepare is a valued and developmentally appropriate learning activity. The use of food in the creation of art or craft products which will be displayed or discarded upon completion, however, is not appropriate. Teachers sometimes ask children to string breakfast cereal and macaroni on yarn for necklaces, glue beans and popcorn on paper, or use rice in collage. Younger children enjoy hand painting with pudding or whipped topping. The above activities may be enjoyable and can serve developmental and sensory ends. The authors, however, advise against the use of food in art for several reasons:

1. Food is expensive. If parents want to donate, they can bring in recyclable junk materials, ingredients for cooking, or other more crucial (and perhaps costly) supplies, such as wooden blocks, books, or puzzles.

2. There is such a pressing need for food in developing countries that a casual use of food in art is questionable on moral and ethical grounds.

3. The number of homeless people has increased dramatically in recent years. Families with children represent a large segment of our homeless population. Some areas have a severe shortage of food targeted for the homeless. It is difficult to justify stringing pieces of breakfast cereal when many local children go to bed hungry.

4. The use of food in an art activity may offend some cultural groups who use that food item for religious or ethnic celebration.

5. Adults should never use food in art activities with toddlers because they are developing self-regulatory skills and must learn to distinguish between food and other objects that are not to be eaten (Bredekamp & Copple, 1997).

6. Artwork created with food products cannot be displayed in the classroom or in children's homes as it may attract insects or rodents.

These six points do not negate the value of cooking activities in the early childhood classroom. Classroom cooking activities are very developmentally appropriate and support children's learning in many ways. The difference is that the children will actually eat the food they prepare in cooking activities, while the food products used in sensory and art activities will ultimately be thrown away.

There are many sound alternatives to the use of food in art. Small sections of drinking straws can replace macaroni for stringing. Sand rather than rice can be glued. Styrofoam squiggles can replace beans in

a collage activity. *Early childhood teachers can be creative in identifying alternatives to food in art activities.*

Did You Get It?

Placing a child with special needs into a setting with the most possible contact with children who don't have special needs is callled
- **a.** maximal inclusion.
- **b.** full inclusion.
- **c.** mainstreaming.
- **d.** least-restrictive environment.

Take the full quiz on CourseMate.

4-3 Context: Interaction of Child Development and Environmental Influences

Our developmental profile neatly dissected the whole child for the purpose of analyzing the different aspects of development one at a time. The truth is that children are much more than the sum of their developmental parts: Physical + Social-Emotional + Cognitive + Language = Whole Child. Development is not this simplistic and does not occur in isolation.

Children develop within a context, and this wider setting must be studied to understand its impact upon a developing child. Children's development is influenced by home, community, and environment. Specifically, children will be influenced by family changes, poverty, and socioeconomic variables, including neighborhood crime. The influences are mutual and reciprocal—children also influence their home, community, and environment. For example, children who are under severe stress as a result of divorce may regress and become dependent. In turn, parents may change their parenting techniques, providing extra comfort and reassurance.

Did You Get It?

Young children are strongly influenced by their surroundings, whether peers, family, education, community, or society, and by factors such as socioeconomic, belief-systems, etc. Yet how do children themselves influence these same surroundings? This relationship, comparatively speaking, can most accurately be described as
- **a.** negligible.
- **b.** greater than that exerted upon children themselves.
- **c.** reciprocal and mutual.
- **d.** highly dependent on the individual child.

Take the full quiz on CourseMate.

DAP naeyc naea) 4-4 Processing with Art Materials and Tools

Very young children process with art materials long before they purposely decide to make an art product. They enjoy tearing and taping paper, smearing and spreading paste and glue, and using scissors and staples. It is important to allow children time to explore materials, to develop manual dexterity and skill with the materials before asking them to use the materials creatively. Through this exploration, children discover the potential of the materials and how they might be used (Lasky and Mukerji-Bergeson, 1980; 2003). Some very simple activities include:

- tearing paper
- cutting with scissors
- pasting and gluing
- taping and sticking
- stapling
- punching holes in paper

Each of these is not only enjoyable by itself but also a necessary skill for other art activities.

4-4a Scissors and Cutters

Listed below are several tools for cutting to be used in a classroom for young children. Regardless of the type selected, scissors must cut. Nothing is more frustrating to a young cutter than a pair of scissors that snag, tear, or clog up with paper but do not cut it.

Fiskars®—cut most things. They come with comfort-molded universal ring handles for right or left hand

Krazy Kut® scissors—cut papers in little and big wave, lightning, zigzag, scallop, and zipper patterns

lefty—designed specifically for left-handed children

paper punchers—assorted shapes

safety—lightweight plastic for right- and left-handed cutters

scissors rack—metal or wood for safely and neatly storing scissors

Adhesives, glue, paste, tape, and accessories are also necessary for processing activities. A list of adhesives can be found in the book's Website.

4-4b Personally Expressive Art Activities

Here are some personally expressive art activities for processing with art materials and tools.

Toddler, Preschool, and Kindergarten-Age Activity: Torn-Paper Picture. Torn-paper pieces are arranged and glued onto a piece of paper to form a torn-paper picture. Older children enjoy using construction paper.

Hints

- Mix water, white glue, and food coloring or liquid watercolor for the young paster. Toddlers would also enjoy placing pieces of precut or pre-torn papers onto a piece of construction paper with glue. Glue can be mixed with water to both extend it and eliminate its crusty appearance when dry. Mix water and white glue in equal parts, for example, one cup of white glue to one cup of water.
- Add liquid watercolor to clear glue to get colored glue that is richer in color than colored white glue.
- Tap-N-Glue® cap, has taken the mess and waste out of gluing. Young children can easily turn the bottle upside down and gently tap. The special cap makes the glue come out in small drops. There is no opening and closing of tops and no clogs or leaks. Special caps fit bottles of white glue. Tap-N-Glue® caps are inexpensive and make gluing an economical art activity that can be offered on a daily basis.

Preschool and Kindergarten-Age Activity: Folding and Cutting. Children fold a thin piece of paper and use scissors to snip out a piece. Refold the paper in a different direction and continue snipping. Open the paper, and glue it against a colored piece of construction paper for background. This helps the cutout design stand out.

Kindergarten and School-Age Activity: Rainbow Glue. Add liquid watercolor to clear (not white) glue for brilliant colors. Place in shallow bowls or squeeze bottles. Children can also use their fingers or small brushes to spread rainbow glue on paper.

Kindergarten and School-Age Activity: Starch and Yarn Art. Pour liquid starch into small bowls. Discuss that although starch is a pretty blue color, it is not to be eaten or drunk because it will make you sick. Cut different colors and lengths of yarn. Provide a clean Styrofoam™ tray or sheet of wax paper for each child. Children can dip yarn in the starch and lay it on the surface to create a design. Closely supervise. Provide wet paper towels for children to wipe their fingers before touching their faces.

4-4c Sensory Exploration Activities

Here are some sensory exploration activities for processing with art materials and tools.

Preschool and Kindergarten-Age Activity: Bleeding Art. This is a good outdoor activity. Each child needs a squirt bottle filled with water and a large sheet of white paper. Provide scraps of tissue and crepe paper.

An Opportunity for Teacher Reflection

It Is the First Week of School and Mrs. Denney is getting to know her kindergarteners. She teaches in a rural area, and kindergarten is the first organized group experience for most of her students. Wednesday morning, Mrs. Denney has planned a cut-and-paste activity. Most of the children participate enthusiastically, but Mrs. Denney is concerned to see Kayla sitting quietly at her table, just watching the other children. After a while, Kayla begins her cut-and-paste project, tearing shapes from the paper rather than cutting. Kayla dips a craft stick into the container of glue at her table and carefully dabs glue onto the pieces of paper she has torn. She lays the glue-covered pieces on a larger piece of paper, glue side up, and pats them carefully with her fingers. Kayla appears perplexed that the torn pieces of paper are sticking to her fingers, rather than to the paper. *How can Mrs. Denney best support Kayla in this vignette? Should she intervene, or should she continue to let Kayla experiment and problem solve? What questions might Mrs. Denney ask to scaffold Kayla's experimentation with glue?*

Have children place paper scraps on the white paper in an interesting design and then squirt with water. The colored papers will begin to "bleed," and the colors will run and mix. Wet scraps can be removed and discarded. Place in the sun to dry. If done indoors, place white paper in a large box lid to contain children's squirting. Eliminate squirt bottles by putting papers outside on a rainy day. This combines art and science as children discuss what happened and how.

Toddler and Preschool-Age Activity: Tearing Paper. Very young artists can tear paper. Tearing paper is a good activity for developing and finger muscles. Begin with very thin papers like newspaper, scrap tissue, or old phone directories. Individual pieces can be pasted or glued to each other or onto a piece of paper.

Kindergarten and School-Age Activity: Puffy Paint. Making puffy paint is an economical alternative to buying it. In a bowl, mix equal parts (e.g., one cup each) of flour, salt, and water. Add food coloring or liquid watercolor. Mix thoroughly. Pour into condiment squeeze bottle. Make sure tip has an opening that will allow contents to exit when squeezed by children.

Repeat process if more colors are desired. Experiment by varying the size of the holes in your squeeze bottles. Look for color-coded or clear squeeze bottles so contents are identifiable. Cover small cardboard squares with tinfoil. Puffy paint will squeeze out like toothpaste and sparkle. Spatulas can be provided for smearing the puffy paint. Let dry overnight, and it will harden on the tinfoil in three-dimensional relief. Puffy paint cannot be saved, and containers must be cleaned after use before contents mold or harden.

Toddler, Preschool, Kindergarten, and School-Age Activity: Pasting and Gluing. Very young children enjoy smearing paste or dripping glue for the sheer pleasure of it. They enjoy the smell, cold feel, stickiness, and texture of solid paste. It has a thick, crumbly feel and sticks to the fingers. Liquid white glue has a very different wet feel to it. Children enjoy squeezing glue onto paper. Bottles filled to the brim may be quickly emptied. You may want to add food coloring to your paste and glue to enhance visual appeal for beginning pasters and gluers. Very young children may not be interested in gluing or pasting anything in particular. Older children will combine pasting and gluing with tearing and cutting. Papers that have been cut or torn or both can be pasted or glued onto an art surface.

Paste and glue serve different purposes. Paste will hold lightweight papers together, but glue is needed to bond heavier objects, including boxes and wood.

Kindergarten and School-Age Activity: Stapling. Staplers and stapling fascinate young children. Stapling is more a fine motor skill than an artistic process. A handheld stapler requires a squeezing motion with one

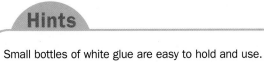
Hints

Small bottles of white glue are easy to hold and use. Because some children feel obligated to use the whole bottle, a smaller bottle may satisfy this need to empty the container without wasting glue. Some teachers prefer to pour small amounts of white glue into a small plastic bowl or lid. This bypasses the use of individual bottles, which dry out quickly because children forget to twist the tops shut. Some children enjoy spreading liquid glue with their fingers. Small sponges can also be used to dab and apply the glue. A special glue stick is easy to make. Wrap a piece of netting twice around a craft stick and secure it with a rubber band at one end. The weave in the netting holds the glue until the child is ready to apply it.

Hints

School Glue Gel is manufactured by the same company that makes white glue. It is less messy than white glue because it will not run or drip.

hand, while a large stapler involves a gentle pounding, or pushing action. Miniature staplers may be too small for children to activate and control. Using a stapler is noisy, but older children enjoy it, and the activity exercises their finger and hand muscles. They will staple just to get a group of staples attached to paper. Sometimes the staples will form a design or pattern on colored paper. At other times, they may use a stapler in place of paste or glue for attaching small pieces of paper, fabric, or collage material to each other or a background.

Preschool, Kindergarten, and School-Age Activity: Sprinkle a Picture. Children can make a design with paste or glue on paper. They can carefully sprinkle:

- confetti
- paper dots (from a hole punch)
- seeds
- pine needles
- sand

Carefully slide the excess off the paper and back into the container.

Toddler, Preschool, and School-Age Activity: Taping and Sticking. Very young children enjoy sticking tape. Teachers can provide plastic or duct tape in varied colors, widths, and lengths. Place cut or torn pieces of tape on a nonstick surface. Children will enjoy lifting them off and placing them on paper. Pieces of torn or cut paper can also be taped onto an art surface.

Toddler, Preschool, and School-Age Activity: Sticker Art. Children enjoy peeling and sticking the colorful labels and stickers available from office supply and stationery stores. Items could include gummed stars and labels, colored dots, or stickers. These can also be licked and placed in a visual arrangement.

Kindergarten and School-Age Activity: Hole and Paper Punch Art. Older children have the muscular strength to work a hole punch using either one or both hands. They seem fascinated with the process. Provide strips of paper from which to punch holes. They may want to save the punched holes. Punched holes can be used for gluing. Children can also make a design outline or picture with punched holes and paste this onto another paper. For example, a design

could be punched out of white paper and glued to a piece of colored construction paper for a greeting card. New versions of hole punches come in smaller squares, which provide a variety of shapes when punched. There is also a Dial-A-Design 6-in-1® paper punch. Simply turn the wheel to choose one of six shapes.

Toddler and Preschool-Age Activity: Stringing Objects. Stringing objects is a good activity for improving eye-hand coordination. Use a shoelace or sturdy yarn with a plastic needle. Knot the far end of the yarn or shoelace to keep the objects from sliding off. Children can string:

- spools
- paper reinforcements
- egg carton cups
- sections of plastic straws
- sections of toilet paper rolls
- buttons
- washers

Items that have been strung can be tied into a necklace, bracelet, or belt and proudly worn.

Toddler and Preschool-Age Activity: Contact Paper Art. Provide various collage materials, including colored tissue paper, yarn, paper scraps, and other flat objects. Cut clear contact paper at least 6 inches in diameter for each child. Remove the backing and place sticky side up on the art table. This eliminates the need for paste or glue. Tape four corners with masking tape to secure. Very young children will enjoy placing objects on contact paper and seeing them magically stick. When done, place a larger sheet of construction paper over the contact paper to frame.

Kindergarten and School-Age Activity: Sand Pendulum. Punch a small hole in the center of the bottom of the inside of a paper cup. Make three evenly spaced holes in the rim of the cup. Cut three pieces of string and run them through the three holes. Tie the three ends into a knot. Set up two matching chairs back to back and about 3 feet apart. Place a pole (e.g.,

Hints

To make colored sand, place sand in a plastic bag. An adult can use a craft stick to scrape colored chalk dust into the bag. Shake well. Some teachers use a few drops of food coloring or liquid watercolor, but this is messier and involves drying overnight.

Did You Get It?

Artistic activities which should be both developmentally appropriate and age appropriate. Creating starch and yarn art is appropriate for which age group?
- **a.** kindergarten and up
- **b.** grades 3 and up
- **c.** preschool
- **d.** toddlers

Take the full quiz on CourseMate.

yardstick, thick dowel rod, or broomstick) between the top of both chair backs. Secure with duct tape. Cut a piece of string long enough to reach from the pole to the floor. Tie one end of this string to the pole and the other end to the knot in the cup's string. Cover the floor with newspaper. Lay black construction paper on top of the newspaper beneath the cup. Cover the hole in the cup with one finger while filling the cup with sand. The child can swing the pendulum while you let go of the cup. As the sand pours from the cup, it will make a design on the black paper. Children can apply glue to their black paper first if they want to save the design. If not, simply refill the cup with the contents on the black paper.

Summary

(4-1) We have moved from an overview of holistic child development to links between art and a child's development. This chapter explained how art fosters a child's physical, social, emotional, cognitive, and creative development. Art was viewed as a developmentally appropriate and important activity. Knowledge of a young child's physical needs and abilities suggested strategies and materials for helping the child learn to cut with scissors. Although art is pleasurable and multisensory, potential art hazards do exist. The relationship between creativity and art has long been recognized, but the link between art and thinking may be as strong. (4-2) It is important that teachers recognize and support children's individual differences as they plan and provide art experiences in the classroom. (4-3) Just as a child's development is influenced by the home, community, and environment, the child in turn influences his or her own environment. (4-4) The chapter concluded with a discussion of art processing and suggested activities for children.

Key Terms

art therapy, 79

concrete operations, 78

constructivism, 77

constructivist education, 80

cooperative learning, 80

culture, 83

differently abled, 82

group projects, 80

holistic model of child
  development, 69

inclusion, 83

individual differences, 83

intellectual mediators, 80

logical-mathematical
  knowledge, 78

physical knowledge, 78

preoperational stage, 78

private speech, 80

process, 85

proximodistal development, 73

scaffolding, 80

self-talk, 80

sensory-motor stage, 78

social-conventional knowledge, 78

sociocultural theory, 80

types of knowledge, 78

zone of proximal development
  (ZPD), 80

✔ Suggested Activities

1. Observe a young child actively involved in an art activity. Record what the child says and does. How did this art experience help the child physically, socially, emotionally, cognitively, and creatively?

2. Observe children aged three, four, and five using scissors. Using the guidelines in this unit, what recommendations can you make for each with respect to tools, paper, activity, or teacher input?

3. Arrange to work with a difficult or troubled young child. Ask the child to draw or paint how he or she is feeling. Encourage the child to talk about the picture. Encourage emotional expression without formally attempting art therapy.

4. Conduct an art safety inspection of an early childhood art center. Identify items that compromise the health and safety of children.

5. Plan and carry out an open-ended art experience in which children process with art materials and tools.

6. In the open-ended art experience you planned and carried out earlier, consider ways you might adapt the experience and/or the materials for children with limited vision or hearing. What

about for children with special cognitive or communicative needs?

7. Visit an early childhood classroom to observe the children. How many expressions of

individual differences do you see and hear? Discuss those differences and the ways in which the teacher meets the needs of individual children.

Review

1. List the five domains of child development.

2. At your midyear open house, a few parents wonder why so much time is devoted to art in your preschool program. Using the holistic model of child development, plan your response to their concerns.

3. A parent is alarmed because her five-year-old is always drawing ghosts and graveyards. She fears that her child is emotionally disturbed. What are some possible explanations for this child's art?

4. Suggest a nonfood art activity for each of the following:

   a. printing with cut vegetables

   b. gluing breakfast cereal on a self-portrait for facial features

   c. sprinkling powdered gelatin over white glue for sparkling lines

   d. making ice cream for a snack and then finger painting with it

5. Identify 10 art materials that are potentially unsafe or unhealthy for children.

6. Explain why fat pencils and crayons encourage young children's fine motor development.

7. Identify and briefly explain three types of knowledge suggested by Piaget.

8. Discuss Vygotsky's sociocultural theory.

9. Visit an early childhood classroom and observe the materials used for art activities. Do the materials follow the safety guidelines outlined in this chapter?

Additional Resources

"Understanding Physical Development in Young Children," by Sean Brotherson (www.ag.ndsu.edu).

Go to Education.com for "Children's Social Development: A Checklist," by Diane McClellan and Lillian Katz.

Go to the Child Development Institute Website for an overview of the developmental tasks involved in the social and emotional development of

children and teenagers based on the work of Erik Erikson.

Go to Slideshare for a discussion on Lev S. Vygotsky.

"Piaget's Theory of Cognitive Development" by W. Huitt and J. Hummel (www.edpsycinteractive.org).

Constructivism as a Paradigm for Teaching and Learning is an online workshop for pre-service teachers (www.thirteen.org).

 Visit CourseMate for this textbook to access the eBook, Did You Get It? quizzes, Digital Downloads, TeachSource Videos, flashcards, and more. Go to CengageBrain.com to log in, register, or purchase access.

Lesson Plan for Kindergarten

Lucy's Picture

GOAL

Scientific investigation and reasoning. The student uses age-appropriate tools and models to investigate the natural world. The student is expected to use senses as a tool of observation to identify properties and patterns of organisms, objects, and events in the environment.

OUTCOMES

The student will:

a. demonstrate how the sense of touch is used by visually impaired individuals.
b. use scissors on a variety of materials to create a collage.

MATERIALS

a. *Lucy's Picture* by Nicola Moon
b. Manila paper, scissors, glue for each child
c. Collage materials: wall paper, ribbon, feathers, wrapping paper, fabric, etc.

INTRODUCTION

Seat the children for story time. Review with the children the five senses. Introduce the story by saying it is about a little girl who thinks the sense of touch is very important. Provide a focus for listening by telling the children that after you finish reading you will ask them to explain why touch was so important to the main character.

DEVELOPMENT

Read the story. Remind the children of the focus for listening and ask for an explanation of why the sense of touch was so important. Review with the children some of the objects and textures that were a part of the story. Write the word *collage* on the board. Tell the children that they will be making their own collage today, just as Lucy did in the book.

Seat the children at their tables/desks. Collage materials should already be on their tables/desks.

Encourage the children to explore the materials and ask them to describe the textures they feel. Distribute Manila paper, scissors and glue and let the children begin.

CONCLUSION

After the glue has dried on the collages, have the children pair and share with a friend. Have each child close his/her eyes and explore the other collage with his/her fingers. The children may try to guess what materials were used on each collage. As a group, discuss their experiences with the children and remind them that people with visual impairments use their fingers to "see" the world around them.

ASSESSMENT

a. Were the children able to identify the collage materials through their sense of touch?
b. Did the children effectively use their scissors to cut paper, fabric, ribbon, and so on?

A full-size version of this lesson plan, and others like it, is available for digital download.

Photo Courtesy of Jill Englebright Fox

What can you tell about the child who created this picture?

How old is this child? How does this piece of art compare with the human figures you have seen children make? Children share many similarities. They all scribble before they engage in controlled drawing. They play with colors before they paint recognizable pictures. Children also draw what is familiar. They use what they know as the basis for their art. This is a self-portrait drawn by a South African boy, age seven.

Learning Outcomes

After reading this chapter, you should be able to:

5-1 Explain the components of children's art.

5-2 Discuss theories of artistic development, including those proposed by Kellogg and by Lowenfeld and Brittain.

5-3 Summarize artistic development from birth through age eight using author Robert Schirrmacher's sequence.

5-4 Provide children with painting experiences.

Standards addressed in this chapter

DAP Criteria

3 Planning curriculum to achieve important goals

4 Assessing children's development and learning

NAEYC Standards

2 Curriculum

4 Assessment

5-1 Explaining Children's Art

Children's art has a mysterious quality to it. The lines, shapes, colors, and overall design may make more sense to the child artist than to the adult observer. Why do children scribble? What does their art mean? Why do they draw stick figures when they know people do not look that way? Theories and stages attempt to provide answers to these questions. This chapter surveys and critiques physical, emotional, perceptual, cognitive, general developmental, and cognitive developmental explanations for children's art. The authors have used stages identified by Kellogg and by Lowenfeld and Brittain in proposing one general sequence to account for children's artistic development.

Appreciating children's art may be easier than understanding or explaining it. Adults have been trying to make sense of it for decades. Researchers, teachers, parents, art educators, and child development specialists are concerned with the content, motive, process, and product. Their interest focuses on the following:

- what children include or represent (content)
- how children create (process)
- why children create (motive)
- what they create as a result (product)

Content refers to the subject matter being represented. This could include a pet, person, feeling, mood, wish, dream, or impulse. The content of children's art is often personal or idiosyncratic. For example, a wide stroke of black paint may represent a tree trunk. On the other hand, it may represent a child's creative exploration with paint and brush and not be intended for public communication. Too often, adults are prone to search for public meaning where there is none. Process refers to the actions and skills involved in creating an art product—cutting and tearing paper, rolling clay, painting, or marking with crayons. Not all art processing results in the creation of a finished product. Many young children process just for the sake of processing. Motive refers to the reasons underlying a child's art. For example, adults may explore why a child filled a paper with wide strokes of black paint. Does the child's preoccupation with the color black signify some underlying emotional problem? Is the mark characteristic of a lack of maturation? Does the solitary mark represent social isolation? Or is the child representing the concept of one? Product refers to the final outcome. Examples include black paint smeared across a paper, a clay dinosaur, a paper-bag puppet, or a geometric design done in watercolor. The finished product may or may not bear any resemblance to the subject matter. In analyzing the what, why, and how of children's art, there is a risk of misinterpreting or reading too much into the art. After studying children and their artwork for an extended period of time, however, trends and patterns do emerge. A skillful observer can note these trends and patterns and begin to make generalizations about what, why, and how children create.

Did You Get It?

Content, process, _____, and product represent the four generally recognized and assessed components of examining children's art.
- **a.** message
- **b.** tools utilized
- **c.** motive
- **d.** cognition

Take the full quiz on CourseMate.

5-2 Theories of Artistic Development

Theories of artistic development attempt to explain what, why, and how children create. The theories are similar yet different. All theories of artistic development attempt to do the same thing—explain a child's artistic development. Each, however, has a different focus. Some theories do a more complete job of explaining than others.

Why is theory of artistic development needed? A theory provides the overall structure or foundation for what we do with children. Different theories suggest different educational practices. For example, there is much debate about the roles of theory and practice in the preparation of early childhood educators. We all want teachers who are competent practitioners. Someone who is long on theory but short on practice would not do well in the classroom. Our aim is to translate theory into practice. A theory is our road map, steering us to developmentally appropriate practice. Theory justifies how, why, and what we do with children.

Theories and explanations that attempt to explain the development of children's art can be grouped into six categories: physical, emotional, perceptual, cognitive, general developmental, and cognitive developmental.

5-2a Physical Explanation for the Development of Child Art

A **physical** explanation for the development of child art holds that the content, process, product, and style of children's art are indicative of their limited physical development. The young child has limited eye-hand coordination, fine motor control, small muscle development, manual dexterity, and visual acuity. Young children mark aimlessly, scribble, and draw unrecognizable shapes because they are physically incapable of anything else. Young children's drawing often appears immature and unintelligible.

It is obvious that the physical development of a young child does affect artistic expression (see Figure 5–1). For example, one cannot expect a toddler to draw a still life in realistic fashion. Yet a child may simply choose to scribble or explore with the medium, just as an adult chooses to doodle. Accomplished artists who have mastered techniques of realism often opt for impressionistic, expressionistic, or abstract styles. Adult primitive art, with its simplistic quality, conveys purposeful intent rather than limited physical development and lack of coordination.

5-2b Emotional Explanation for the Development of Child Art

An **emotional** explanation for the development of child art holds that the content and style of children's art is indicative of their emotional makeup, personality, temperament, and affective state (see Figure 5–2). Objects, emotions, people, and events of significance are often emphasized in children's artwork through an exaggerated, distorted, and expressive use of color,

Figure 5–2 Children explore color and texture in their art.

size, shape, line, texture, and overall treatment. For example, when a child draws her father as a superhero caricature with bulging muscles, a huge red heart, and a wide smile, this may signify love, respect, admiration, and identification rather than distortion due to limited physical development.

5-2c Perceptual Explanation for the Development of Child Art

A **perceptual** explanation for the development of child art holds that the content and style of children's art reflects their perceptual development. Perception is influenced by the neurophysiological structure, personality, and prior learning. The perceptual explanation holds that a child draws what he or she perceives rather than what he or she sees. The task of art is to create the structural equivalent of the perceived three-dimensional object on the two-dimensional canvas. This is a monumental task for the artist, regardless of age.

The development of child art provides support for a perceptual explanation. The young child's first attempts at drawing are **scribbles** with a minimum of line and shape; they gradually increase in complexity and clarity. Some children, however, draw or paint less than they actually see. For example, a child may choose to paint the stripes of a tiger with wide, sweeping strokes and ignore the head or other extremities. It is also possible that the medium can limit expression of the perceptual image. For example, using a wide-bristle brush dipped in watered-down paint might limit the number of details that appear in a painting. The size of the paper also influences what fits into the picture.

Figure 5–1 A child's artistic expression is affected by the child's level of physical development.

An Opportunity for Teacher Reflection

Deborah Teaches First Grade in an urban public school. For the past two weeks, her class has been studying reptiles. Deborah has live snakes and lizards in her science center, and the children have enjoyed observing the animals and drawing and painting them. This morning, the class read a nonfiction book on turtles and then discussed their life cycles, food sources, and habitats. One little girl in the class, Inez, is concerned when she learns that turtles lay their eggs and then walk away. She asks, "But who takes care of the babies?" Inez was horrified at the answer, "Nobody. They are on their own as soon as they hatch." This afternoon, Deborah notices Inez at the easel. As Deborah watches, Inez paints a series of yellow circles on her paper. Each time she pulls the paintbrush around the paper to make the circle, she comments to herself, "Now there goes

a turtle egg. Now there goes a turtle egg." Then, Inez awkwardly picks up two paintbrushes in each hand. Using four colors, she covers the paper in broad up-and-down strokes, saying "Now, cover 'em up, so they'll be safe." When Inez has finished her first picture, she places it in the drying rack and puts a fresh sheet of paper on the easel. She repeats the process of painting yellow circles and covering them with the muddy color. Perplexed, Deborah says to Inez, "Tell me about your picture." Inez is silent for a moment and then responds without looking at Deborah, "The mama turtle lays the eggs for her babies and covers 'em up with dirt. Then she goes away and she never sees her babies again." Deborah realizes Inez is upset about the mother turtle's desertion of her young. *How should Deborah respond to Inez? What might she say to comfort Inez or to build Inez's understanding?*

Brain Connection

Miller and Cummings (2007) have estimated that the number of dendrite connections formed in a child's first five years of life is over 1 billion. It may be that this over-production of neurons enables the child to adapt during these early years. Processing language, adapting to cultural and social norms, and learning to tell right from wrong requires intense neurological growth, strengthening the connections between neurons. This rapid growth encourages discovery, play exploration, and connection with others (Rushton, Juola-Rushton, and Larking, 2010).

DAP naeyc 5-2d Cognitive Explanation for the Development of Child Art

A **cognitive** explanation for the development of child art holds that the content and style of children's art is indicative of general intelligence and a function of conceptualization. According to Coles (1992), a child drawing is a child thinking. Children can draw only what they know. One's concept of an object will determine how that object will be represented. For example, when one draws an apple, one's concept of an apple is determined by one's experiences with its color, taste, size, shape, and smell, and by related experiences in picking apples, polishing apples, planting apple seeds, climbing apple trees, paring apples, bobbing for apples,

mashing apples for cider, and baking and eating an apple pie. Observation of young children involved in art supports a cognitive explanation. Young children rely on memories, images, and experiences when they draw or paint. Detailed drawings will reflect concepts with which the child has had extensive experience. Drawings can also illustrate misunderstandings or gaps in a child's knowledge (Brooks, 2009). For example, it would be expected that an urban child will have a less-developed concept of a silo, tractor, and barn than a child living on a farm. The differences will appear when each child draws a farm scene. The child living on a farm will likely execute a picture with greater detail and elaboration.

Goodenough (1975) developed the Draw-a-Man test, a nonverbal measure of intelligence, now revised as the **Draw-a-Person test**. It is assumed that the child's drawing of the human figure is a reflection of that child's concept of a person. Indices of conceptual maturity include appearance of limbs and location, size, and relationship of body parts (see Figure 5–3). If a child has a well-defined concept of the human figure, reflected in an accurate drawing with properly located body parts, this would indicate a high level of intelligence on the Goodenough measure. The problem with this normative approach is its neglect of individual differences, experiences, and motivational, attitudinal, and environmental factors that can either foster or inhibit concept formation. Ears may be particularly relevant to a child with pierced ears. A child living in an area where both genders sport long hair may be oblivious to ears. A related problem with the human figure

Figure 5–3 Realism is not a concern for this young artist.

Photo Courtesy of Jill Englebright Fox

drawing test is that some children choose to omit body parts out of whim rather than lack of knowledge. The human figure drawn without ears may be simply the result of creative expression and personal preference. It is also possible that the child may have run out of paint, patience, or interest. Test reliability and validity are concerns.

Concept formation and perceptual analysis are reciprocal processes. Knowledge of an object can improve one's ability to accurately observe its details. In turn, careful observation can lead to increased knowledge of the object.

5-2e General Developmental Explanation for Child Art

A fifth explanation for the development of child art is more global. It provides a **general developmental** explanation that incorporates social, cultural, personality, and environmental factors as well as elements of former explanations. General developmental explanations make use of a stage sequence approach in attempting to explain the child's artistic expression in holistic fashion. Theories have given us ages and stages to help understand a child's artistic development. Like

theories, there are many stage sequences for the development of children's art. Knowing stages will help us:

- understand where a child is developmentally.
- set appropriate but flexible expectations.
- plan a developmentally appropriate art program.
- develop a framework for evaluation and for parent conferences.
- appreciate the processes and products of art during the early years.

Kellogg's Theory. Like all development, artistic expression follows a predictable sequence, shifting and changing as children grow. Development, however, is fluid, meaning that children may move back and forth between stages. Development is also individual, and children develop at their own pace. Kellogg (1969) amassed more than a million paintings and drawings of children from the United States and 30 other countries over three decades. Her stages appear in Figure 5–4.

According to Kellogg, some 20 basic scribble patterns make up the first stage of development. These basic scribbles are the foundation for future graphic art, pictorial and non-pictorial. As the child proceeds from scribbling to picture making, he or she passes through stages: placement, shape, design, and pictorial. More specifically, the 20 basic scribbles are subsequently drawn according to some 17 different placement patterns by the age of two. By the age of three, these **diagrams** or *gestalts* contain shapes, including the circle, cross, square, and rectangle. One basic diagram, the **mandala**, dominates the child's visual thinking and serves as a basic artistic referent in future drawing. Children use mandalas to draw people, flowers, and **sun figures** (see Figure 5–5). Gestalt psychology has shown the mandala of a crossed circle to be a universal pattern that the brain is predisposed to utilize in all visual perception.

With the ability to draw diagrams or mandalas, the child moves into the design stage. Two diagrams are put together to make **combines**, or structured designs (see Figure 5–6). Three or more united diagrams constitute an **aggregate**. Between the ages of four and five, most children arrive at the **pictorial stage**, in which their structured designs or aggregates begin to represent objects. Kellogg likens the development of stages in child art with primitive art. Her normative approach supports the position that all children everywhere draw the same things, in the same way, at the same age. They draw what they know how to make and not what they actually see (Beaty, 2002). The development of artistic ability in the individual appears to recapitulate the artistic development of the human species.

Scribble Stage There are 20 basic scribbles

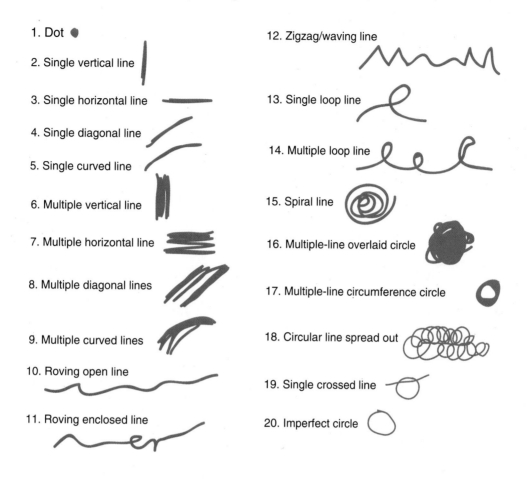

1. Dot
2. Single vertical line
3. Single horizontal line
4. Single diagonal line
5. Single curved line
6. Multiple vertical line
7. Multiple horizontal line
8. Multiple diagonal lines
9. Multiple curved lines
10. Roving open line
11. Roving enclosed line

12. Zigzag/waving line
13. Single loop line
14. Multiple loop line
15. Spiral line
16. Multiple-line overlaid circle
17. Multiple-line circumference circle
18. Circular line spread out
19. Single crossed line
20. Imperfect circle

Placement Stage Two–three-year-olds

Scribbles become more controlled and the child becomes concerned with placement. There are 17 different placements.

Some examples:

All over

Central

Bottom/top

Diagonal

Right/left

Top/bottom quarter

Figure 5–4 Kellogg's stages.

Shape Stage Three-year-olds

Former scribbles drawn at two produce overall gestalts or forms. These gestalts or forms contain the following implicit shapes:

Later, the above implied shapes are drawn as single outline forms called *diagrams*.

The Six Diagrams Three-year-olds

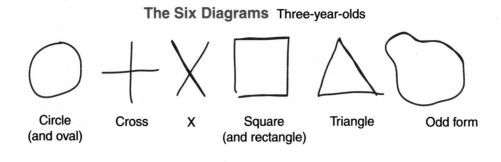

Circle   Cross   X   Square   Triangle   Odd form
(and oval)   (and rectangle)

Design Stage Three–four-year-olds

Two diagrams are united to form a *combine.*

For example:

Examples of *combines:*

Three or more diagrams are united to form an aggregate

For example:

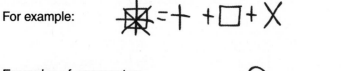

Examples of *aggregates:*

Figure 5–4 *(Continued)*

Pictorial Stage   Four–five-year-olds

Their structured designs begin to look like objects that adults can recognize.

The pictorial stage can be divided into two phases:

1. Early pictorial
2. Later pictorial

Figure 5–4 *(Continued)*

Figure 5–5 An early mandala figure, or mandaloid.

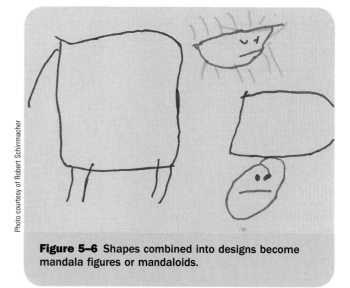

Figure 5–6 Shapes combined into designs become mandala figures or mandaloids.

Kellogg's (1979) stages in drawing a human figure are depicted in Figure 5–7.

Lowenfeld and Brittain's Theory. Lowenfeld and Brittain (1987) were interested in the creative and mental growth of children. Their theory and stages of artistic development are widely recognized and accepted. The ages, stages, and characteristics appear in Table 5–1.

Art Moves from Manipulation to Representation. Children's art does become more realistic over time, and there is a general sequence or progression to their artistic development. Very young children are in a manipulative stage. The younger the child, the greater the reliance on processing, exploring, making, doing, or playing with art materials. During the first year of life, tools are brought to the mouth, rather than placed on the paper. Hand-to-mouth reactions are dominant (Di Leo, 2003). Actions on objects are repeated, and there is little concern for making something. At this point, children are not drawing a picture, but are developing skill in using art tools (Beaty, 2002). For example, a child may simply squeeze and pound play dough without trying to make something from the play dough. Children begin to scribble around 13 months of age. They enjoy watching their own movements leave marks on a surface. They combine their five senses and motor movements to engage in pleasurable activity (Di Leo, 2003). Around age four, children begin to draw tadpole figures which, though lacking in details, still communicate the basic lines of the human figure. Over the next few years, children's drawings are lively and playful with a strong sense of life (Crain, 2000). School-age children become very concerned

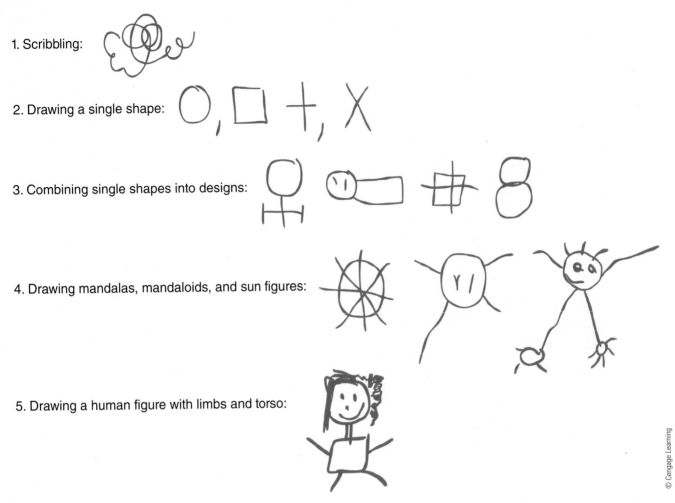

1. Scribbling:

2. Drawing a single shape:

3. Combining single shapes into designs:

4. Drawing mandalas, mandaloids, and sun figures:

5. Drawing a human figure with limbs and torso:

© Cengage Learning

Figure 5–7 Kellogg's stages in drawing a human figure.

Table 5–1 Stages of Artistic Development by Lowenfeld and Brittain

Age (Years)	Stage and Characteristics
1 1/2–4:	**I: SCRIBBLING: THE BEGINNINGS OF SELF-EXPRESSION**
	Scribbling is a developmentally and artistically important kinesthetic, manipulative, and expressive behavior.
1 1/2–2 1/2:	**IA: DISORDERED AND RANDOM SCRIBBLING**
	• large muscle, whole arm movements
	• kinesthetic pleasure, pure processing
	• whole-hand grip on marking tool
	• may not look at paper while marking
	• accidental, random motoric mark making
	• haphazard lines
	• swing of arm coming in contact with paper results in mark
	• uses shoulder motion
	• may scribble beyond confines of paper

Based on Lowenfeld, V., & Brittain, W. L. (1987). Creative and mental growth. New York: Macmillan

(Continued)

Age (Years)	Stage and Characteristics (*continued*)
1 1/2–2 1/2:(*continued*)	**IA: DISORDERED AND RANDOM SCRIBBLING**
	• exploration—what can I do by moving these tools on paper?
	• lines made with simple movements
	• tight grip with rigid wrist position
	• minimal movement with fingers in marking
2, 2 1/2–3:	**IB: CONTROLLED SCRIBBLING**
	• smaller marks, better control and organization
	• marking motions are repeated
	• uses wrist motion with greater control
	• stays within drawing area of paper
	• variety of lines and direction appear
	• better visual and motoric control over where to make lines
	• watches intently while scribbling
	• more intricate loops and swirls appear
	• wider range of scribbles
3, 3 1/2–4:	**IC: NAMED SCRIBBLING**
	• spends more time mark making
	• gives names to scribbles
	• relates scribbles to things in environment
	• name of scribble may change in the process
	• holds marking tools with fingers, better fine motor control
	• greater variety of lines
	• increased concentration
	• more intentional placement of marks
	• awareness and intentional use of empty space
	• scribbles not matching the name or label given except to child artist
	• moving from sheer physical expression to making marks that stand for something else by giving them a name
4–7:	**II: PRESCHEMATIC**
	• A schema is a generalized symbol that represents a specific concept. For example, a child's stick-figure drawing is used to represent all people.
	• child's first representational attempts
	• symbolic representation built up from former scribbles
	• appearance of recognizable geometric shapes
	• placement and size random and out of proportion
	• random floating spatial arrangement
	• may turn or rotate paper while drawing
	• distortion and omission of parts in human figure drawing

(Continued)

Age (Years)	Stage and Characteristics (*continued*)
4–7:(*continued*)	**II: PRESCHEMATIC**
	• head–feet representation of human figure as in Figure 5–8
	• over time, arms, body, fingers, toes, clothes, hair, and other details appearing
	• objects drawn as isolated entities; no relationship
	• art as personal self-expression rather than for public communication
	• very personal idiosyncratic symbols
	• can copy a square at age four, triangle at age five
	• relative size appearing at end of stage
	• child learning that what is known or experienced can be symbolically represented by mark making
	• children drawing how they feel or think about an object, leading to omission, exaggeration, and distortion
	• color used randomly, not realistically
	• schemas or symbols beginning to be recognizable to others
	• children enjoying talking about their art
	• drawing things that are important, relevant, or personally meaningful, such as family, pets, or friends
	• objects drawn facing forward
7–9:	**III: SCHEMATIC: ACHIEVEMENT OF A FORM CONCEPT**
	• form concept developed and repeated
	• drawing reflecting a child's concept, not perception of an object
	• bold, direct flat representation
	• two-dimensional spatial representation
	• baseline appearing to portray space
	• skyline possibly also appearing at top
	• drawing reflecting what a child knows
	• subjective portrayal of space
	• X-ray drawing appearing simultaneously, showing exterior and interior view
	• representation of space showing a frontal and aerial view depicted simultaneously
	• human figure made up of geometric shapes repeated and refined
	• detailed and decorative
	• move to greater conformity or stiffness in drawing things the way they should be
9–12:	**IV: DAWNING REALISM: THE GANG AGE**
	There is a greater awareness of details. Older children are more self-conscious about their art. The plane replaces the baseline. Objects are drawn smaller and less distorted.
12–14:	**V: PSEUDONATURALISTIC/REALISTIC DRAWING**
	Young adolescents are very self-critical of their drawing. Detailed human figures with sexual characteristics appear. Cartoons, caricatures, and action figures are also popular. Depth and proportion appear. End of spontaneous art.
14–17:	**VI: ARTISTIC DECISION: ADOLESCENT ART**
	For some adolescents, natural artistic development does not extend beyond the former stage unless they are given further instruction. Some pursue naturalistic style, while others use art for a personal statement. They may copy an artistic style in forming their own personal style.

that their art achieve photographic realism (Gardner, 1980). They are in the stage of representation and work hard at making their art recognizable to others. It is at this point that many children are frustrated with their inabilities to achieve photographic realism and become reluctant to engage in art.

In sum, developmental explanations, including Kellogg and Lowenfeld and Brittain, use some form of stage sequence to account for the development of child art.

naeyc **Artistic Development and the Environment.** In viewing the child as a whole, developmental explanations also recognize physical, social, emotional, perceptual, and cognitive factors that influence artistic expression. Yet a general developmental explanation must also account for various factors in tracing the development of child art. Culture and religion may affect a child's drawing ability, depending on whether or not the culture values art. A child with an unfulfilled need for acceptance may draw realistic pictures in order to win the praise of a teacher. Environmental factors include home and family who may punish a child for manipulating, experimenting, exploring, and getting messy. A normative comparison could label this child uncreative or developmentally delayed in artistic expression without allowing for environmental effects.

Figure 5–8 Preschematic art: head-feet representation of the human figure, or a sun figure, according to Kellogg.

5-2f Cognitive Developmental Explanation for Child Art

An explanation that incorporates the best of cognitive and general developmental explanations would account comprehensively for the development of child art. Because most early childhood educators have been educated in Piaget's theory, it is practical to examine his theory and its relationship to child art. A comprehensive theory that explains all sectors of child development would be more useful than separate theories that explain different behaviors.

Piaget on Child Art. What can Piaget tell us about children's art? His theory and stages of intellectual development claim to be comprehensive, encompassing, and universal. Artistic expression is, at least in part, a cognitive activity. It follows that a cognitive developmental theory such as Piaget's should explain the development of child art. The task, however, is a difficult one, because Piaget himself believed it is more difficult to establish regular stages of artistic development than of mental functions. He notes that general development is one of progression, whereas artistic development is one of retrogression. The artwork of the young child appears more creative than that of the older child. In reviewing the theories of children's artistic development, it appears that Piaget accounts for physical, emotional, perceptual, cognitive, and individual factors within his cognitive developmental framework.

Piaget's theory is cognitive in that his interest was in how children think. It is developmental in that his focus was on how children's thinking changed over time. He believed all children progress through four major stages of development, which proceed in invariant sequence. Cognitive development proceeds from sensory motor, concrete activity to symbolic, higher-order conceptual functioning.

Piaget holds drawing to be a form of symbolic functions and, as such, a representational activity that is considered to be halfway between symbolic play and the mental image. It is like play in its functional pleasure and autotelism (assimilation), and it is like the mental image in its effort at imitating reality (accommodation). The first spontaneous attempts at artistic expression can be seen as endeavors to reconcile the tendencies inherent in symbolic play and those that characterize adapted behavior. Through drawing, the child attempts to simultaneously satisfy the need for assimilation and to adapt to objects and others through accommodation. According to Piaget and Inhelder (1969), the very first form of drawing does not seem imitative but is more like pure play. It is this play or scribbling that toddlers do when given a pencil, crayon, or marker. Soon, however, the young child recognizes forms in these aimless scribbles and tries to repeat them from memory. There may be little or no likeness between

Table 5–2 Stages of Art Compared with Piaget's Stages of Cognitive Development

Piaget's Stage	Kellogg's Stage	Lowenfeld and Brittain's Stage
Sensory motor (0–2)	**Scribbling (2)**	
Preoperational: (2–7)		
• Preconceptual (2–4)	**Placement (2–3)**	**Scribbling** (2–4):
		• disordered and random
		• controlled
		• named
	Shape (3):	
	• gestalts	
	• diagrams	
	Design (3–4):	
	• combines	
	• aggregates	
• Intuitive (4–7)	**Pictorial (4–5)**	**Preschematic** (4–7)
	• early	
	• late	
Concrete operations (7–11)		**Schematic** (7–9)
		Dawning realism (9–12)
Formal operations (11–adult)		**Pseudorealism** (12–14)
		Artistic decision (14–17)

© Cengage Learning

these scribbles. As soon as this intention exists, Piaget and Inhelder believe, drawing becomes imitation and image.

Lowenfeld and Brittain's stages of artistic development parallel Piaget's stages of cognitive development. A comparison of Piaget with Kellogg and Lowenfeld and Brittain is found in Table 5–2.

Gardner on Child Art. Howard Gardner (1980), an insightful observer of children's creative development, wondered what happens to the spontaneity of early creativity during the elementary years. Further, he asked what would promote continued artistic development. Research convinced him that creativity has distinct forms and different needs during three different developmental phases that extend into adulthood.

In the first stage, preschoolers are instinctively creative, delighted with music, art, drama, and language. Gardner (1980) observed that the expressiveness of their paintings and drawings had much in common with those of talented adults using ideas or images in fresh, unusual ways. A child begins making marks during the second year of life. The child at age two grabs a marker and scribbles enthusiastically on every surface. A three-year-old produces a vast array of geometric forms. The child is establishing a vocabulary of

lines and forms, the basic building blocks of a graphic language. The four- and five-year-old ceaselessly creates and re-creates representations of objects, often recognizable to others. The "tadpole man" appears. The child's drawing of a person is seemingly represented by a tadpole with two legs emanating from a large head. The preschooler evolves fixed patterns, or schemas, for example, house = square with triangle on top. A peak of artistry is achieved at the end of the preschool years. Drawings by preschoolers are characteristically colorful, balanced, rhythmic, and expressive. The drawings of young schoolchildren are often their most striking creations: vibrant, expressive, and exhibiting a strong command of form and considerable beauty. Gardner adds that children's drawings can be said without exaggeration to undergo a complete life cycle of their own.

During the second stage, around age seven, however, the pattern shifts. Children's imaginations appear to get stuck, and they stop engaging in creative processing in favor of a preoccupation with language, games, or peers. Free graphic expression is replaced by a strong determination to achieve photographic realism in drawing. Gardner observed 8- through 10-year-olds searching for literal meanings rather than metaphors. Many prefer to copy or collect pictures rather than create their own.

What has happened in the course of a few years? Some blame schools and families for the strong message children receive to conform and think convergently. There is another explanation. The period of literal thinking with its emphasis on following the rules is also operating at this time. After being so imaginative during the early years, children in this second phase think differently. Because art is a cognitive pursuit, it is not surprising that the nature of their art production also changes.

The third stage, around ages 15 to 25, brings a convergence of abilities to plan a creative project, implement it, and evaluate it. While most people are mastering fixed information or skills in a chosen field, the creative individual stands out as one who continues to take risks, attempt new projects, and preserve individuality. By ages 30 to 35, these patterns are even more evident. Gardner (1980) speaks of a U-shaped curve in artistic development. This means that some important aspects of artistry emerge early in a child's life only to go underground during a period of middle childhood. It is during this period that decisions are made by the individual either to move forward and grow artistically through specialized training or refinement of an individual style, or to forgo art altogether.

5-3 Schirrmacher's Stages: A General Overview of Artistic Development (Birth to Age Eight)

Robert Schirrmacher has attempted to combine the different stages of artistic development suggested by Kellogg, Lowenfeld and Brittain, and others into one workable general sequence. The levels or stages are overlapping, and ages are approximate. Schirrmacher's sequence of early childhood art follows.

5-3a Manipulating the Media: Scribbling and Mark Making (one to two years)

The first art experiences of very young children are purely sensorimotor actions resulting in scribbles. They approach crayons, markers, and play dough with the intent of exploring their properties and discovering what can be done. The very young child lacks fine motor control and eye-hand coordination. Scribbles or vague marks appear random and haphazard to the adult but wonderfully attractive to the young artist who made them. Scribbling is nonverbal self-expression. Scribbling has sensory appeal in that children see the marks they make as they move the tool across the paper. Look what I made happen, thinks the young artist. Toddlers move from random scribbling to making scribbles, which are more controlled, deliberate, and pronounced. Circular strokes are repeated, and crayons are moved horizontally or vertically back and forth, making lines that cross and intersect. Some lines and circles are repeatedly traced over. Scribbles become more purposefully placed rather than extending beyond the paper and onto the table. Scribbles may be named, although there may be no connection between the verbal label and the graphic symbol (see Figure 5–9).

Photo courtesy of Robert Schirrmacher

Figure 5–9 Scribling or mark making produce very personal symbols and designs.

5-3b Making Shapes, Outlines, Designs, and Symbols That Have Personal Meaning (two to four years)

Young preschoolers work at refining their circles, ovals, lines, and attempted geometric shapes. Lines cross or enclose space forming squares, triangles, and rectangles. A cross enclosed by a circle forms a mandala. Children progress from mandalas to suns to stick figures. Single and repeated round and linear marks become a circle that represents the sun. A sun with facial features, including eyes and a mouth, becomes a face. A circle or sun-face with radiating lines develops into a person with arms and legs radiating from the round face. Because infants are intrigued by the human face, it is no surprise that the human figure is first drawn as all face. This stick figure is a schema, a generalized symbol or form concept that will be used to represent any and all human figures, regardless of age, gender, or build. Animals develop from this human figure. They are vertically or horizontally portrayed as the human with a tail or animal ears. A square becomes a schema for any and all buildings. A circle atop a vertical line is the "lollipop" schema used to portray trees and flowers. Eisner (1982) would call these examples of pictographs, or simplified flat, two-dimensional shapes. The child adds, omits, distorts, exaggerates, or streamlines these very personal symbols. The result is an abbreviated form with little concern for actual color, shape, or size. Spatial arrangement is random, and the child may simply rotate the paper to fit objects. The very personal symbol or design may not be recognizable to observers. Children in this stage are still very much process oriented. They delight in playing with colors, shapes, and forms. They enjoy talking about their creations but may walk away from or discard their products, indicating their relative love of processing.

5-3c Pictorial Art That Is Becoming Recognizable to Others (four to six years)

Older preschoolers and young school-age children become concerned with creating art that looks like something. They may plan their art in advance and use details to polish their products. Pictorial art is a stage in the development of children's art when their art is becoming recognizable to others, although color, shape, size, placement, proportion, and perspective are arbitrary. A purple dog may dwarf a green cow, both of which appear to be floating in the sky. Colors are used emotionally, reflecting their relationship to the symbols rendered. Triangles and squares mastered in the prior stage are now combined into houses, which appear to float in space. Later they will rest at the bottom of the paper or on a drawn baseline.

Figure 5–10 An early attempt at representing the human figure.

© Cengage Learning

Over time, houses are decorated with geometric shapes, including a rectangular door, square windows with parted curtains, and a smoking chimney drawn parallel to the roof line, defying gravity. Facial features, body parts, and clothing are added to the human figure. Some personally important parts like the head, eyes, smile, and belly button tend to be exaggerated. If a child's father has a beard, he may be given one in the picture. Figure 5–10 appears distorted as a claw is used to symbolize hands. Some children will choose to simply eliminate body parts such as the neck and shoulders. During this stage, some children become interested and even obsessed with producing multiple products. They will draw a favorite subject over and over again. Their desire to simultaneously portray the inside and outside of objects, for example, the exterior of a plane in a storm and interior with pilot and passengers, leads them to make "X-ray drawings" reflecting what the child knows rather than how it appears in reality. Children in this stage lack the control, coordination, and skill necessary to realistically represent their three-dimensional world on a two-dimensional canvas.

5-3d Realistic (school-age, five to eight years)

School-age children want things to look right—to draw and paint things the way they appear in reality. They strive for photographic realism (see Figure 5–11) and seem dissatisfied making abstract or nonrepresentational art. Nonrealistic art is relegated to younger children who scribble. School-age children work on size, placement, shape, color, perspective, proportion, depth, shading, and the use of details to capture reality. Rather than floating in space, a house rests on a lower baseline, and the sky and sun inhabit a top baseline. Things in the distance are drawn smaller and set back, giving the illusion of depth and perspective. School-age children develop, repeat, and refine symbols that

Figure 5–11 The older artist strives for realism.

Photo Courtesy of Jill Englebright Fox

can often be categorized by gender. Generally, boys draw male superheroes, vehicles, and sports events. Generally, girls draw female superheroes, princesses, horses, and unicorns. With increasing age, children become self-critical and succumb to peer pressure, internalizing hurtful comments that focus on their artistic shortcomings. The few who receive guidance and specific instruction will continue to engage in art. Others pursue impressionistic, expressionist, and nonrealistic art. Unfortunately, too many will close the door on their short-lived artistic and creative career, concluding they are uncreative and untalented in art.

Did You Get It?

According Robert Schirmacher's model of artistic development, the artistic outcome of children up to two years of age is characterized by marking and scribbling, primarily because of

a. undeveloped fine motor control and eye-hand coordination.

b. emotional immaturity.

c. lack of motivation and goals.

d. inability to concentrate on anything more detailed.

Take the full quiz on CourseMate.

DAP naeyc 5-4 **Painting**

Painting is a pleasurable, messy, and creative art activity. It allows children to plan; to make decisions about their subjects, colors, and placement; and to work on their own. Not all children will have had experience painting before coming to school. Painting will be a popular activity. For these reasons, painting should be made available every day. Some children panic when

they see only one or two easels and fear that they will never get a turn if painting is allowed only once a day for a short period of time (see Figure 5–12).

Generally, painting involves the use of tempera or watercolor paints. Tempera paints are opaque and give a smooth, flat covering of intense color. They are water soluble, and adding water will dilute them and dull their intensity. Adding coffee grounds, salt, or sand along with white glue to paint gives it a rough, coarse, gritty texture. Adding sugar will give it a sparkling appearance when dry. Adding sawdust will give it a thick, lumpy texture. Adding white glue to paint thickens it.

Tempera paints come in both liquid and powder form. The liquid form is more expensive but comes ready to use. The powder form is more economical but must be mixed with water. Powdered tempera paints are not recommended for children under the age of 12 (see page 73 and the "warning" on page 109). Powdered tempera creates inhalable dusts, and some colors contain toxic pigments, preservatives, and additives. Wear a mask when preparing the powder, and do not mix it in the presence of children. When your supply of powdered tempera is depleted, switch to liquid tempera for the sake of child safety.

The authors suggest starting beginning painters with the primary colors and buying red, blue, yellow, black, and white paint in bulk. Mixing colors to produce other colors, shades, and tints adds an element

© Cengage Learning

Figure 5–12 Easel painting with a friend.

of science to painting activities. Remember to buy and use only lead-free, nontoxic paint. Adding a little liquid dishwashing detergent to tempera paint will make it bubbly and easier to wash off hands and out of clothes. It will also help paint adhere to slick or glossy surfaces.

Inexpensive plastic paint jars are a good investment for your classroom. Look for resealable lids that open to a second lid with an opening for dipping the paintbrush. The lids will minimize mess and waste from spillage and allow you to store unused paint at the end of an activity. Individual paint jars can be stored in a plastic tub to keep them from tipping over. Make sure the lids are tightly closed, and store them in a cool place.

Watercolor paints are transparent and allow for layering colors. Children should have experience with tempera before graduating to watercolors. Still, children never outgrow their interest in tempera painting. There are many different painting arrangements, including:

standing at an easel—This position allows for whole-arm strokes and total body involvement. It allows for the use of long-handled brushes. Easel painting, however, does have its drawbacks. Given the slant or angle, paint tends to run and drip down. This frustrates some children who expect liquid paint to defy gravity and stay put where they place it. They expect it to act like a marker or crayon. On the positive side, easels encourage verbalization and socialization between painters, especially if the easels are placed side by side.

seated at a table—Children can also paint on a flat surface while seated at a table (see Figure 5–13). This placement keeps paint from dripping and allows layers of paint to be built up. Usually a table can accommodate several painters at one time. Children can use short-handled brushes, as in watercoloring. Paint will be more controllable, but the amount of arm and body movement will be restricted.

Figure 5–13 Two young painters at work.

© Cengage Learning

standing at a table—This position allows for whole-body movements while painting on a flat surface. Whereas four children can sit down and paint at the same time, only one can stand and paint at each end of the table. This position is highly recommended, although standing for a long period of time while painting tires and bores some young children.

on the floor—Painting on the floor provides a flat surface, although this position also restricts whole-body movement. It is hard to involve the bottom torso when one is kneeling. Children, including those who are physically challenged, enjoy sprawling on the floor and may find this position comfortable.

outdoors—Use any of the above arrangements to paint outdoors.

Although painting while standing at a table or easel is highly recommended, it is wise to give children experience painting at a variety of different angles and placements.

WARNING

The reader has been previously warned about using tempera powder with young children. It is important to use up remaining tempera powder and order only liquid paint in the future.

5-4a **Brushes**

There are many different types of brushes recommended for painting. Long-handled brushes with flat bristles are called "flats." They produce wide strokes. Brushes with rounded and pointed bristles are called "rounds." They produce narrow lines and strokes. Long-handled brushes are good for easel painting, when a child stands a short distance from the paper. Short-handled brushes are often used for painting while seated at a table, where the distance between artist and paper is minimal. Children who are exposed to brushes of varied sizes, types, and textures are more likely to experiment with different techniques (Lasky and Mukerji-Bergeson, 2003). Buying flats, rounds, and both short- and long-handled brushes encourages a variety of paint strokes. Brush tips are made of red sable, camel hair, bristle, natural materials, and synthetic materials. A moderately expensive brush with stiff bristles is a good investment. The bristles will hold up to thick paint and will not fall out with the first washing. Never use a brush to mix paint. Instead, use a stick or spoon. Consider the following for painting activities:

bath brush—for easel painting

bowl brush—new, not used, for easel painting

dish pom-pom—for a novel paintbrush (see Figure 5–14)

Figure 5–14 Dish pom-pom painting.

easel—long-handled for painting while standing at the easel

feather duster—for interesting effects while easel painting

foam-head brush—for innovative painting

household brushes—an array of inexpensive household and paintbrushes found at discount stores is also recommended

makeup brushes—provide nice variety for the older artist

nail brush

pastry brush—for painting while seated

scrub brush—for large, vigorous, sweeping strokes

shaving brush—stubby handle is easy to grip

short-handled brush—for painting while seated or close up at easel

silverware sorter or tray—to sort and store brushes

spoon rest—for holding wet brush while painting

stencil brush—short-handled with stiff bristles for dabbing and small strokes when making a stencil

toothbrush—for general painting, stencil, and spatter printing

varnish brush—wide, inexpensive, found at discount stores

watercolor brush—short and thin, with pointed bristles

Brushes can also be homemade. Clamp a small sponge with a pinch-type clothespin and use as a brush. Cotton swabs can be tied with string or yarn and used for dabbing paint.

Brushes need to be washed soon after each use, preferably before the paint becomes dried and crusty. Rinse out excess paint. Add a small drop of liquid detergent and gently wash the bristles. Rinse thoroughly

Hints

- Add a drop or two of oil of cloves or oil of wintergreen to prevent spoilage if you mix paint days in advance.

- Finger paint can be made by:

  ▸ adding liquid laundry starch to tempera or food coloring.

  ▸ mixing wheat paste (wallpaper paste), water, and tempera paint until smooth.

  ▸ mixing liquid starch, soap flakes, and tempera paint.

  ▸ adding small pieces of finely ground colored chalk to paste. Add a few drops of water if too stiff.

- To mix powder paints: Pour powder through a funnel into a paint container. Mix with enough water to form a thick, creamy liquid. Aim for the consistency of yogurt. Test on paper. It should not run. Add more water if too thick, more powder if too thin and runny. A recommended ratio is two parts tempera powder to one part water. Add a few squirts of liquid dishwashing detergent to aid cleanup. Shake or mix well until smooth and creamy.

- To mix liquid paints: Place a spoonful in a container. Slowly add water. Test on paper. Add more water if still too thick, more liquid paint if too thin and runny.

- An extender such as bentonite reduces paint cost and gives the desired consistency. It also can be added to tempera to make finger paint. Other extenders can be made by mixing flour or cornstarch with water; cornmeal will produce a different texture. Soap or detergent powder will also thicken paint.

- Liquid starch makes the paint creamy and results in a glossy finish. Too much starch causes flakiness when the paint dries.

- The following procedure is recommended when children paint at the art table: Place an absorbent paper towel at the bottom of a Styrofoam™ tray and add paint. The towel works as a blotter, absorbing the paint but providing just enough color when touched by a brush. It also facilitates cleanup.

- Make your own no-spill paint containers. Trace the top of a small, empty juice can onto a sponge. Cut out the inside circle. Slide juice can through the sponge. Cut the sponge to snugly fit inside the easel tray. The sponge secures the paint container and catches paint drips.

with warm but never hot water (hot water will melt the glue that holds the bristles in place). Squeeze out excess water. Reshape bristles to their natural shape (e.g., twirl a watercolor brush into a pointed shape). Let air dry. Always store brushes with handles down and bristles up. Tall, thin potato chip cans are ideal for brush storage.

A brush is not the only tool for painting. Also, there is no reason to use only one brush at a time. Children can paint with a brush in each hand or with two brushes tied together. Keep in mind that, although these tools may encourage interesting effects, their use encourages sensory exploration rather than artistic self-expression. Therefore, painting with gadgets should not be a substitute for painting with brushes (Lasky and Mukerji-Bergeson, 2003).

5-4b **Painting Surfaces**

Children do most of their painting on paper. It is important to provide paper in a variety of colors, shapes, sizes, and textures. Children can explore painting on paper that is wet as well as dry. Painting on damp paper will provide an effect similar to that of watercolors. The colors will bleed and blend. The edges will be soft, with many creative accidents as paint runs together to form unusual shapes. Allow time before adding too many colors, which may all run together and form a dark blot.

5-4c **Easel and Art Surfaces**

art storage and easel—a long, double-sided easel with room for four children and shelves for storage; commercially available, but fairly expensive.

chalkboard—for use with chalk.

double- or triple-sided easel—self-standing with paint rack.

easel clips—two clips to hold the upper corners; large paper clips or clothespins will do. Make sure children can work them.

messy tray—a plastic self-contained area for one finger painter. A large cookie sheet will also do.

see-through easel—acrylic, plastic or Plexiglas®, transparent, see-through, wipe-off surface.

wall easel—a board attached to the wall that swings out when in use and stores flat against the wall the rest of the time. A real space saver and a good project for a volunteer parent/grandparent/carpenter.

Easels are an expensive but good investment. Standing easels allow for whole-arm sweeping strokes. Make sure the easel is at the child's height. Paper should be placed in front of the child's chest and within easy

Hints

- Trim the edges of inexpensive foam paintbrushes into shapes and designs.

- Bristles on brushes will split and spread over time. Carefully use a razor blade to trim jagged edges or stray bristles.

- Insert a small paintbrush into a hair roller or ball of clay. This will provide a larger, graspable surface for the child with limited fine motor coordination and control.

reach, neither too high nor too low. Saw off the legs of the easel if necessary. Actually, a minimum of two easels should be provided for a large group of children. Having too few easels makes children anxious and concerned that they will never get a turn.

Remember to use easel clips or clothespins that the children can work by themselves. Some teachers prefer to place several pieces of paper at each easel in the morning. This eliminates continual restocking of paper at the easel. Also, remember to place some form of covering under the easel. Newspaper is easy to come by and recyclable. An old washable throw rug, however, not only protects the floor but also is more attractive and comfortable to stand on.

5-4d **Painting Precautions**

Remember to roll up sleeves, remove sweaters, and use smocks. Provide one brush or painting tool for each color. Do not fill paint jars full. Full jars add to the dripping and mess. Instead, fill jars less than half full and add paint as needed. Try to use clear containers so children can easily see the paint colors. Glass jars are clear but potentially dangerous. Fairly large, see-through plastic cups or containers are ideal. Encourage children to keep paints and brushes to their left and paper to the right. This will reinforce the left-to-right progression so crucial to later reading and writing.

How many colors should be provided? Some believe beginning painters need only one color until they have learned the basic processes involved in holding a brush, dipping for paint, wiping excess, positioning on paper, and making strokes. Others begin with two. The authors recommend providing the three primary colors. Additional colors will appear on the canvas through accidental or purposeful mixing. They can also be mixed using the palette method. Containers of white and black will help children lighten or darken colors. There is no one right answer to the opening question. Those who stress technical skills will recommend only one color. Those who stress the importance of color mixing and creative expression would provide two or more. Five would be the maximum. More is not necessarily better when providing colors of paint. The same holds true for the number of crayons in a box. Children can be as creative with the basic 8 as they can with an overwhelming 64.

Painting is a messy activity. Remind children to scrape the side of the brush on the inside rim of the jar before they remove it from the paint. This will help eliminate dripping of excess paint. Encourage children to replace each brush or painting tool in its designated container. Mistakes will happen. Be sure to rinse brushes thoroughly to avoid unwanted mixing of paints. Children should wash their hands before taking off their smocks. This will avoid smearing of paint on skin, hair, and clothing.

5-4e Paint Palette

Children who have had some experience in color mixing can be introduced to painting with a palette. An aluminum pie plate, frozen dinner tray, or plastic lid is recommended. Children take blobs of mixed paint and mix their own colors, shades, and tints on their palette. Always have the primary colors and white and black available. Children need their own brushes for color mixing on the palette. They also need a cup of water for cleaning the brushes between color mixings.

5-4f Personally Expressive Art Activities

Following are some personally expressive art activities for painting.

Infant, Toddler, Preschool, Kindergarten, and School-Age Activity: Hand Painting. Finger painting is an activity not usually offered at home. *Finger painting* is an inaccurate term. The activity, which involves much more than merely spreading paint with the fingers, should more accurately be called hand painting. The whole hand and arm should be involved. Hand painting is messy but developmentally appropriate. There is no brush to separate the artist from the paint. Children enjoy the cool, slimy texture. It gives them an opportunity to get messy without fear of reprimand. It is an activity that should be provided on an ongoing basis. Some children will be reluctant. They may fear their clothes will get dirty or their parents will be angry about the mess. They will need time. Seeing other children and their teacher engaging in hand painting may reassure them. A child should not be forced to do hand painting against his or her wishes.

When hand painting, children should be encouraged to get fully involved by using the following:

- front or palm of the hand—for wide strokes.
- back of the hand—for wide strokes.
- side of the hand—for long, thin strokes and zigzags.
- fingertips and joints of the fingers—for dabbing marks.
- fingers, front and back—for long marks.
- thumbs—for round marks.
- knuckles—for a series of marks.
- fingernails—for fine lines that etch through the paint.
- fists—for massive marks and round swirls.
- wrists—for massive marks.
- hand with fingers spread wide—for handprints.
- whole arms, toes, and feet—best done outdoors on a warm day.

As with brush painting, sleeves need to be rolled up and sweaters removed to encourage freedom of movement; smocks should be worn. Hand painting while kneeling or sitting on the floor restricts movement. Hand painting while standing at a table is recommended. It allows children to use large arm muscles more freely, reach all over their papers, and have a better view of what they are doing. Standing up also keeps one's smock from dangling in the wet paint. Older infants might be held in an adult's lap or might stand at a very low table. Infants should be monitored carefully to ensure that they don't attempt to taste the paint.

Music sets the mood for finger painting. Slow music encourages lazy, smooth strokes. Fast music encourages rapid, swirling lines.

Shaving cream can be used with older children. It is thicker than most finger paints, and children enjoy the texture. Remind them that it is not whipped cream and is not edible. Squirt a glob for each child and spray water to dilute.

Hand painting should be done on paper with a glossy or glazed surface. Finger-paint paper is commercially available but fairly expensive. Slick cardboard, shiny shelf paper, gift boxes, magazine covers, or a nonstick baking sheet can also be used. Add liquid detergent to the paint and do hand painting directly on a Formica® tabletop. Lay a sheet of paper over the table, rub gently, and take a print of the hand painting. This will please children who want to save what they made. Adding vinegar to the wash water will help clean the tables.

Begin by giving each child a piece of paper. The papers can be laid out glossy side up and sponged down with water first or occasionally squirted with a pump sprayer. Begin with primary colors. Add one teaspoon of paint. Paint that is applied too heavily will crack or chip when dry. It is difficult to manage hand painting with a large group. The first child may finish before you have given paint to the last child. It may be easier and less stressful to do hand painting in small groups. This allows you to observe and interact.

Encourage children to use both hands to spread the paint. Squirt with water if the paint becomes dry. Add a second color. Over time the colors will be thoroughly mixed. Mixing red and blue will make purple. This may be the time to stop. You may want to add yellow or white to lighten it if the children want a third color. Placing the paper flat on newspaper to dry will result in a curled picture. When the picture is thoroughly dry, turn it over and press it flat with a warm iron. Or place the paper on a larger piece of newspaper before painting. Some paint will stick the paper to the newspaper, resulting in less curling when dry. Check the book's Website for a list of recipes for making finger paint.

Preschool, Kindergarten, and School-Age Activity: Whipped Soap Painting. Whipped soap is thick and good for making snow scenes on black construction paper, white hearts on red, or designs on wax paper. Follow the "Whipped Soap Paint" recipe from earlier in this chapter. A few drops of food coloring can also be added.

Kindergarten and School-Age Activity: Etch a Painting. Place tinfoil over a piece of cardboard. Tape it on the back. Children enjoy working with tinfoil. Add Ivory® soap flakes to the paint to help it adhere to the slick surface. Use only one color of paint over the tinfoil background. Let the paint dry. Use a craft stick to carefully etch or scratch a picture through the dried paint. Etching too hard will tear through the tinfoil. The result will be an outline of a picture in shiny silver.

Preschool, Kindergarten, and School-Age Activity: Mirror Painting. Provide handheld or full-length mirrors. Children use tempera paints and brushes to paint facial features and clothing. They could also draw with water-based markers. When done, children wash the mirror, using warm, soapy water, and towel dry for the next person.

Toddler, Preschool, Kindergarten, and School-Age Activity: Mural Painting. This is a good outdoor group activity. Tape a long, wide, heavy length of butcher paper to a fence. Use plenty of masking tape so the paper will not tear or fall down. Place containers of paints and brushes at intervals along the length of the fence. Small tables or sturdy cardboard boxes work well as paint stands. This activity allows for the participation of many children at the same time. A variation of this activity is to provide small paint rollers instead of brushes.

5-4g Sensory Exploration Activities

Following are some sensory exploration activities for painting.

Preschool, Kindergarten, and School-Age Activity: Etched Hand Painting. Objects such as a comb, a paper clip, a fork, a key, or a notched piece of cardboard can be pulled and swirled through the wet hand painting. This will produce an interesting etched design. Still, these are merely accessories and do not replace the active processing with both hands.

Infant, Toddler, Preschool, Kindergarten, and School-Age Activity: Hand Painting Print. Children who are process oriented may not need expensive finger paint paper. They can finger paint directly on a tabletop, tray, or cookie sheet. Older infants (9–12 months) will enjoy tabletop painting but must be closely supervised to make sure they do not put paint in their mouths. If children choose to save what they have created, slowly lay a sheet of paper on top and gently lift up. A print of their finger painting results. This saves on the cost of buying expensive finger paint paper. It also cleans the table. Check the book's Website for directions on doing this activity with shaving cream.

Infant, Toddler, Preschool, Kindergarten, and School-Age Activity: Water Painting: Where Did My Picture Go? Children need something to put on their painting tools, but not necessarily paint. Most young children enjoy painting with water. They may have done it at home in the bathtub, or on the pavement. It is a good introduction to using a brush and is highly recommended as an outdoor art activity. Provide old household brushes and plastic pails of water. Painting caps and old painting clothes (e.g., coveralls) may help ease them into the role of painter. Children can paint cement, brick, trees, outdoor non-rusting equipment, and windows. Food coloring can be added, but it will streak the surface being washed.

Preschool, Kindergarten, and School-Age Activity: Roll a Line Design Painting. Find a lid from a box. Cut paper to fit in. Mix paints. Provide items that roll such as toy cars, small balls, or beads and marbles. Carefully dip them in paint and place them in the box lid. Encourage children to tilt, tip, and move the lid to get the items rolling in different directions. Dip them in more paint if needed. The result will be a criss-crossed linear effect. Using a round frame such as a Frisbee®, pie tin, or cake pan provides a contrast to the linear design of the box lid.

Preschool, Kindergarten, and School-Age Activity: Roll Painting. Children can use a rolling pin or brayer

Hints

- Provide thin, disposable plastic gloves for children with sensitive skin.

- Shaving cream is not recommended for children under the age of three because it can be harmful when ingested or rubbed in the eyes. Only an adult should handle the can of shaving cream. Because children may confuse shaving cream with whipped topping, provide close supervision and discuss safety precautions. Always avoid mentholated shaving cream because its fumes can be harmful if inhaled. Children with skin conditions can wear disposable gloves.

to make their paintings. Use a spoon to add different globs of paint on one half of a large sheet of paper that has been folded and opened. Refold. Roll over it with the rolling pin or brayer. Roll gently from center to sides. This will distribute the paint in different directions. Carefully reopen to reveal mirror design images. Add additional colors if desired.

Kindergarten and School-Age Activity: String Painting. Fold a sheet of paper in half. Open it and spread it flat. Place globs of paint on one half. Place a foot-long piece of string curled up on one inside half before refolding. Make sure one end of the string is sticking out. Gently pull on the string while holding the folded paper in place with the other hand.

Preschool, Kindergarten, and School-Age Activity: Straw Painting: Blow a Blot. Children enjoy blowing through a straw to spread blobs of paint. Young children will need to practice holding and blowing through a straw in preparation for this activity. Perhaps they could blow bubbles for a science exploration. Paint should be fairly thin. Place paint in the middle of the paper with a small spoon. Encourage children to hold their straws close to but not touching the paint. Blow out, not in. Move the paint from the middle to the sides of the paper. Add other colors. Blow the colors into each other. Rotate the paper if necessary. The

Hints

Cut a notch near the top of the straw. If children suck in, the paint will exit the notch rather than entering their mouths. Remind children to use only their own straws.

result will be an interesting design composed of mixed colors, weblike patterns, and intersecting lines.

Preschool, Kindergarten, and School-Age Activity: Special Painting with Special Painters. Children enjoy using sponges and foam as painters. Sponges or foam of various widths can be cut into different shapes and inserted into pinch-type clothespins. A craft stick can also be gently inserted and glued in place. Use a razor blade, X-Acto® knife, or scissors to cut the top edge into a pointed, grooved, forked, notched, or wavy pattern. This will result in a different type of stroke when painting. Encourage children to use the special painters in different ways. They can make dots and dabbing motions, twirls to make circular shapes, and long strokes, either up and down or sideways. Remember to have the painter slightly wet before using special paints.

Toddler, Preschool, and Kindergarten-Age Activity: Squeeze and Dribble Painting. Pour paint into recycled squeeze bottles. Children squeeze and dribble a design on paper. Paint can also be squeezed from a small hole in a thick plastic bag.

Preschool, Kindergarten, and School-Age Activity: Drip Drop a Painting. Children use an eyedropper to make a painting. Paint is squeezed into the eyedropper and slowly dropped in a design on a white paper towel, a coffee filter, or white drawing paper.

Kindergarten and School-Age Activity: Dot Painting. Children dip the end of the paintbrush handle in paint and make a picture composed of circular dots of paint. One finger could also be used to produce the same effect.

Preschool, Kindergarten, and School-Age Activity: Sensory and Texture Painting. Vary the texture of paints you provide at the easel or painting table. Offer thick paint one day and thin and runny the next. Try mixing one or more of the following to your paint:

- sand.
- coffee grounds.
- liquid starch.
- herbs or spices.
- baking soda.
- leaves and flower petals.
- shaved ice.

Encourage children to describe with sensory words.

Toddler, Preschool, Kindergarten, and School-Age Activity: Painting in a Bag. An alternative to the mess (and tactile experience) of hand painting is to paint in a bag. Provide each child with a sturdy zip-lock bag filled with about 4 tablespoons of finger paint or liquid tempera. Glitter could be added for children above the age of four. Shaving cream could also be used. Release extra air and secure with duct tape. Children use their fingers to trace patterns and pictures in the paint through the bag. This is a good alternative for shy children or those with sensitive skin.

Toddler, Preschool, Kindergarten, and School-Age Activity: Vehicle Tracks Painting. Locate cars, trucks, planes, and other toy vehicles with two or more wheels. Provide low but ample containers of paint. Children roll their vehicles in paint and then onto paper. Driving their vehicle creates a design. This activity reinforces discussion on modes of transportation.

Preschool, Kindergarten, and School-Age Activity: Ice-Cube Painting. Fill an ice cube tray with colored water. Use liquid watercolor rather than food coloring. Insert a craft stick in each cube. Sticks do not need to be inserted vertically. Freeze overnight. Children enjoy rubbing their ice cube painters across slick paper. Use finger paint paper. Children love to watch the ice melt, spreading color. This is a good activity to do outdoors on a warm day. This activity extends discussion about the sun or seasons.

As a variation, provide clear ice cubes and tissue paper pieces. Freeze clear water and do not add coloring. Children cut or tear their own pieces of tissue paper. Pieces are laid on a white piece of paper. Children paint over the colored pieces with their ice cube painter. The colors from the tissue paper bleed onto the white paper.

Toddler, Preschool, Kindergarten, and School-Age Activity: Roll a Can Painting. Find coffee cans with lids. Measure the inside circumference and depth. Cut papers accordingly. Provide paint and items that roll, including marbles and golf balls. Curl and position paper inside can. The child places one or more rolling objects dipped in paint into the can. Securely attach lid. Place on the floor and gently roll. Remember to create a path that makes it safe to roll without bumping others.

Kindergarten and School-Age Activity: Oil and Water Painting. Mix one color of paint in a cup until thin and watery. Mix a second color of paint with cooking oil in another cup. Place a sheet of paper in a baking pan or small tray. Children use eyedroppers or spoons to drip spots of thinned paint onto paper, then use different eyedroppers or spoons to drip spots of the oily paint on top of the watery paint. Tip pan back and forth to mix. Observe and discuss what happens. Oil and water do not mix, and the oily paint floats on the water to create unusual effects. Children are both artists and scientists with this activity.

Kindergarten and School-Age Activity: Runaway Paint. This is a good activity for children to observe the effects of their actions on objects. Place a large piece of white paper on a cookie sheet. Secure the corners of the paper with tape. Mix three different colors of liquid paint. Add enough water to get a thin consistency so that the paint will run. Place a spoon in each color and encourage the child to spoon one color onto the paper. Have them tip the cookie sheet to make the color run across the paper. Repeat using different colors. Encourage the child to tip the cookie sheet in different directions. Note how the colors run into each other and mix.

School-Age Activity: Painting with Tissue Paper and Glue. Mix equal amounts of white glue and water. It will look milky but will dry clear and shiny. Each child will need a piece of tinfoil, shiny side up. Children tear colored tissue paper into pieces. Provide brushes, and children paint the glue mixture onto their piece of foil. Encourage them to lay pieces of tissue paper down, then brush more glue over it. The tissue paper will soak up the wet glue and works as the paint. Pieces can be overlapped. Children create new colors where the tissue paper overlaps. Repeat the process by adding layers of tissue and glue.

Did You Get It?

Adults trying to make sense of children's art are concerned with

   a. content, process, product, and materials.
   b. process, product, creativity, and motive.
   c. inspiration, method, material, and creativity.
   d. content, process, motive, and product.

Take the full quiz on CourseMate.

Summary

Children's art has a fresh, spontaneous quality that is easier to appreciate than to explain. (5-1) Adults who view child art may be interested with the content, the motive, process, or the product. Theories attempt to explain what, why, and how children create. Different theories have different explanations for the content, motive, process, and product of children's art. A physical explanation holds that young children scribble and draw unrecognizable marks because they lack motor coordination and control. An emotional explanation states that children distort, add, omit, and exaggerate through art those things that have high emotional value to them. A perceptual explanation holds that children rely on perception when drawing. Young children's perceptions lack clarity and refinement, and their artwork will reflect this. A cognitive explanation holds that children draw what they know. Children who lack experience and sensory involvement with people, places, and things will have little to include in their art. (5-2) A general developmental explanation using a stage sequence approach incorporates the former explanations while addressing the whole child and individual differences. Kellogg's stages move from scribbling to placement, shape, design, and pictorial. Lowenfeld and Brittain's stages include scribbling, preschematic, schematic, dawning realism, pseudonaturalism, and artistic decision. (5-3) Schirrmacher has combined the work of Kellogg, Lowenfeld and Brittain, and others into a workable, general sequence of artistic development. His stages include manipulating the media and making shapes, outlines, designs and symbols, pictorial art, and realistic art. (5-4) Painting as a classroom activity supports children's development and learning in many ways. Teachers add variety to painting activities by providing an assortment of painting tools and surfaces.

Key Terms

aggregate, 96

cognitive, 95

cognitive developmental, 103

combine(s), 96

content, 93

diagrams, 96

Draw-a-Person test, 95

emotional, 94

general developmental, 96

mandala, 96

motive, 93

painting, 115

perceptual, 94

physical, 94

pictorial stage, 96

process, 93

product, 93

scribbles, 94

sun figures, 96

theories of artistic development, 93

U-shaped curve, 105

✔ Suggested Activities

1. Collect several art samples from children (late infancy to age eight). Attempt to sequence them according to Kellogg's, Lowenfeld and Brittain's, and the authors' general sequence. Which system works best? Why?

2. Recall the physical explanation for children's art. Do an internet search on art history. Note the similarities and differences between children's art and adult abstract and "primitive" art.

3. Collect several samples of art from one young child over an extended period of time. Note patterns or growth over time. Attempt to explain the what, why, and how of this child's art using different theories of artistic development.

4. Ask children aged two, three, four, five, and six to draw pictures of themselves using crayons or markers. Ask their permission to keep or borrow the pictures. Try to sequence them according to Kellogg's stages in the development of human figure drawing. Do your data support her stages?

5. Observe a child painting at either an easel or seated at a table. Carefully record how the materials are used and describe the results. Refer to the six theories that explain children's artistic development. Which theory or theories best explain what you observed? Discuss your answer.

6. Develop a response for a parent who questions your decision to include only primary paint colors at the art easel.

7. Review the letter to families included with this section of the text. Pretend you are a third-grade teacher, and rewrite the letter to the families of the children in your class.

Review

1. Match the artistic term on the left with an appropriate example:

   ____ product

   ____ content

   ____ motive

   ____ process

   a. "I get so mad sometimes, and that's why I make scribbles all over my paper."

   b. Jim looks in the mirror and smiles. He runs back to the easel and works on his self-portrait.

   c. Keely paints several lines and shapes. She says, "See my pretty, pretty design."

   d. Amy folds, tears, and staples a sheet of scrap paper. She crumples it up and tosses it in the wastebasket on the way to lunch.

2. Identify the six major theories or explanations for children's art.

3. Match the age range with its appropriate stage according to Lowenfeld and Brittain.

   a. 1 1/2–2, 2 ½   ____ Named scribbling

   b. 2, 2 1/2–3   ____ Schematic

   c. 3, 3 1/2–4   ____ Dawning realism

   d. 4–7   ____ Disordered and random scribbling

   e. 7–9   ____ Preschematic

   f. 9–12   ____ Pseudonaturalistic/realistic

   g. 12–14   ____ Controlled scribbling

4. Identify Schirrmacher's general stages of artistic development:

   1–2 and up   _____

   2–4 and up   _____

   4–6   _____

   5–8, primary grades, and up   _____

5. Discuss Gardner's overview of artistic development. What does he mean by a U-shaped curve in artistic development?

Additional Resources

Art Junction (www.artjunction.org) is a website that provides an illustrated explanation of children's art for teachers and parents.

Creativity Education for Children is a blog on children and the arts, featuring an article on drawing development in children.

Go to YouTube for a video of children's drawing in light of theories of children's drawing, "Drawing Diabetes: Diabetes Through the Eyes of Children."

 Visit CourseMate for this textbook to access the eBook, Did You Get It? quizzes, Digital Downloads, TeachSource Videos, flashcards, and more. Go to CengageBrain.com to log in, register, or purchase access.

Kindergarten Lesson Plan

MATISSE and PATTERNING

GOAL

The children will explore the environment through their senses.

OBJECTIVES

The students will:

a. identify, describe, and extend a repeating relationship (pattern) found in common objects, sounds, and movements.

b. demonstrate comprehension of stories.

c. identify Henri Matisse as an artist who portrayed colorful patterns in his work.

MATERIALS

a. De Paolo, T. (1989). *Bonjour, Mr. Satie*

b. Photos of Picasso and Matisse

c. Reproductions of Matisse's work

d. Wallpaper samples for each child

e. Drawing paper

f. Crayons

g. Paints

INTRODUCTION

Remind the children of the new concept that was introduced yesterday during mathematics: patterning. Review the definition of pattern (something that repeats) and ask children to share examples of patterns that were identified yesterday (hand clapping patterns and patterns in fabric). Tell the children that today we will be reading a book about a famous artist who used many patterns in his paintings. Introduce the book, *Bonjour, Mr. Satie*. Provide a focus for listening by telling children to listen closely and determine if this book is fiction or non-ficition.

DEVELOPMENT

Read the book. Return to the focus for listening. Discuss the children's ideas and help them to see that most parts of this story are make-believe, but that there really were two artists named Pablo and Henri who lived in Paris many years ago and were very competitive in their work.

Write the names *Pablo Picasso* and *Henri Matisse* on the board. Help the children to identify these names as the artists in the story. Show the children photographs of Picasso and Matisse. Share with them the following information about Matisse:

Matisse did not discover that he loved to draw and paint until he was all grown up. When he was sick in bed, his mother brought him a paint set to help him fill the time. Matisse played with the paints and found that he really enjoyed painting. When he was well, he enrolled in art school and studied very hard. Matisse loved to use bright colors in his paintings, and he liked to include patterns. As he grew older, Matisse became sick again, this time losing the use of his legs and eventually his arms. He used a wheel chair to move around. This meant that he couldn't stand and hold a paintbrush. But Matisse loved art so much he couldn't give it up—he just changed his style a little! Instead of painting, Matisse began to express himself through paper cut outs!

Share with the children reproductions of Matisse's work. Ask the children to identify the patterns in each.

CLOSING

Give each child a sample of wallpaper mounted on a larger sheet of paper. Ask them to use crayons to extend the wallpaper pattern.

Circulate around the room. Ask the children to identify the patterns they are making and the name of the artist who used patterns so much in his work.

Have paint and large paper available in the art center during the next few days. Invite the children to design their own wallpaper. When dry, hang the wallpaper in the dramatic play center.

ASSESSMENT

Were the children able to identify patterns in the Matisse reproductions?

Were the children able to identify and extend the wallpaper patterns?

Were the children able to create their own patterns in the art center?

Did the children identify Matisse as the artist who used patterns in his work?

A full-size version of this lesson plan, and others like it, is available for digital download.

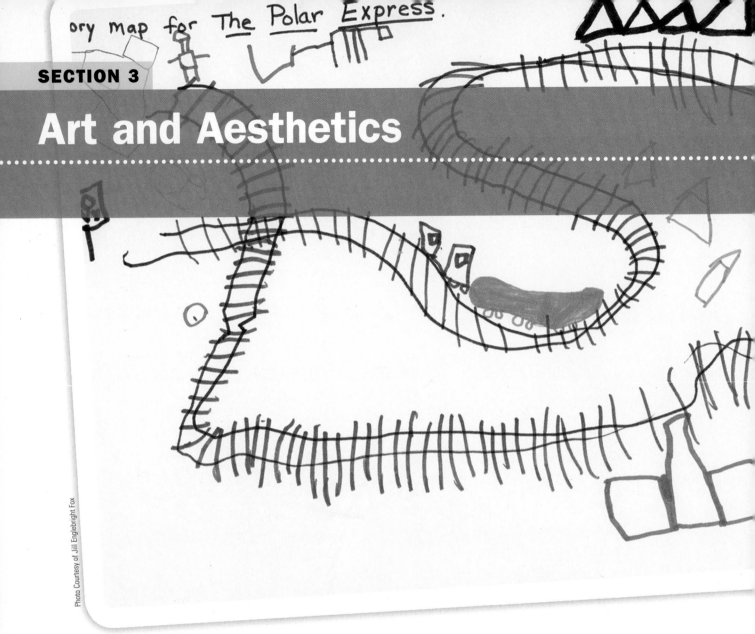

Art and Aesthetics

What do you see in this picture? The child has drawn the story of *The Polar Express.* He made an overhead map of the railroad but has drawn some objects from a frontal perspective. His teacher printed the title across the top of the page. Do you get a sense of how long the railroad is? Can you feel the twists and turns the train will make as it travels along the tracks? Using words and pictures is one way a child can represent understanding of the story.

Chapter 6, The Elements of Art, identifies building blocks that artists use when making art. Artists use line, color, shape or form, mass or volume, design or composition, pattern, space, balance, and texture. Adult artists strive for particular effects by consciously using one or more of these artistic elements. Young children are less deliberate and more spontaneous as they process with media. This does not mean, however, that their artwork lacks artistic elements. A close look at a child's scribbles will reveal a series of colorful lines and shapes in space.

Chapter 7, Aesthetics, focuses on helping children experience and appreciate beauty in their world. Chapter 8, Sensory Experiences, is a resource of activities for the visual, auditory, tactile, olfactory, gustatory, chromatic, thermic, sterognostic, baric, and kinesthetic senses. Providing sensory stimulation helps children have aesthetic experiences. An aesthetically pleasing classroom environment makes good use of all available space.

Is early childhood art ever more than experimentation and exploration? Is there something more to art than scribbling, handling play dough, smearing paint, and gluing things onto a collage?

Chapter 9, The Complete Early Childhood Art Program, provides the bigger picture. A complete art program provides children with time, space, and materials to make art; sensory experiences; an introduction to art, artists, and their styles; and aesthetic involvement.

A LETTER TO FAMILIES

Dear Families,

Art is an important part of your child's learning. While art is an area of study like mathematics or history, art is also a tool through which children can express ideas. Although our school day includes a specific time for art, art is also a part of many other activities.

There are four components to our art program. The first is **Sensing and Experiencing.** Because children learn by taking in information through their senses, learning in our classroom involves seeing, hearing, tasting, touching, smelling, and doing. Hands-on activities throughout the day provide these experiences.

The second part of our art program is **Aesthetics,** the appreciation of beauty. Children have an aesthetic sense that must be cultivated. In our classroom, I include objects like flowers, sculpture, and art prints. I encourage children to look carefully at the objects, talk about them, and decide if they are appealing. My goal is to develop children's aesthetic awareness.

The third part of our program is **Making Art.** Making art allows children to express what they feel and know. Observing children's art helps me to know more about each child and each child's learning.

The fourth part of our program is **Learning about Art, Artists, and Their Styles.** We look at our own artwork and that of others. When we study geometry, we look at Mondrian's paintings. When we study machines, we look at Da Vinci's mechanical drawings. When we study weather, we look at paintings of the seasons by Grandma Moses. We talk about artists' styles and media. Art supports children's learning throughout our curriculum. Because children use art as a communicator of ideas, art knowledge and skills are powerful tools for learning.

Sincerely,

Your Child's Teacher

6 The Elements of Art

© Cengage Learning

Children learn that their world is made up of colors, lines, and shapes.

The boy in this photo sees different colors, lines, and shapes in his birthday cake. The repeating candles and lines of icing form patterns. Later, he will draw pictures of the cake and his birthday celebration. He will include patterns made from the same colors, lines, and shapes.

Learning Outcomes

After reading this chapter, you should be able to:

6-1 List and briefly explain the artistic elements.
6-2 Help children make prints using stamps, stencils, spatter, and screen prints.

Standards addressed in this chapter

DAP Criteria
  3 Planning curriculum to support development and learning.
NAEYC Standards
  2 Curriculum
NAEA Visual Arts Standards
  1 Understanding and applying media, techniques, and processes
  2 Using knowledge of structure and functions

6-1 **Aesthetic Elements**

Some people have difficulty separating whether a work of art is good or bad from how they feel about it. Liking a work of art does not make it good. Although artistic tastes and preferences are personal, we can use accepted criteria to talk about, analyze, and critique art. The **artistic elements** (listed below) are one accepted criterion. A work of art can be critiqued in terms of how the artist has used one or more of the artistic elements. Activities to help children learn about, appreciate, and use the artistic elements will be provided in this chapter.

What does one look for in an aesthetic experience? How does one analyze or critique a dance, a song, or work of art? The various expressive arts have their own criteria. In dance, one could match up an individual dancer's movement with the music. Do the movements flow? Evaluating a song on the basis of rhythm, tempo, and one's emotional response is appropriate when listening to music. The visual arts have their own criteria or artistic elements. These include:

- line
- color
- shape
- mass or volume
- design or composition
- pattern
- space
- balance
- texture

Each of these is explained and illustrated with activities. Some are discussed further in Chapter 8, Sensory Experiences. Please refer to Appendix C for books on the artistic elements—line, color, and shape, in particular.

naea 6-1a **Line**

What is a line? A line:

- is a visible mark made by an artistic tool, such as a crayon, moved across a surface, such as paper.
- is a continuation of a dot.
- usually suggests direction, movement, rhythm, or form.
- does not exist in nature. Nature produces edges. Artists produce lines to represent edges.
- helps the artist define shapes and contours or represent edges.
- is something we use to make letters, words, numbers, symbols, and signs.

Lines can be used in many different ways. Lines have their own dimensions, including size, direction, length, width, and weight. They also have their own personality. Lines can be:

- long or short (length).
- tall or short (height).
- thick, fat, heavy; or thin, skinny, light (weight). Heavy lines may convey a feeling of force, weight, boldness, or strength. Thin lines may add a delicate, light, or timid touch.
- big or little (size).
- horizontal, vertical, or diagonal (direction). Horizontal lines suggest calm, quiet, and a sleeping, restful position. Vertical lines suggest stability and strength. Think of the lighthouse in the middle of the sea, an upright steel girder, or a rocket blasting off. Diagonal lines suggest tension and activity, as in climbing uphill or skiing downhill.
- forward or backward (direction).
- to the right or the left (direction).
- continuous; or broken, dotted.
- open or closed.
- jagged or smooth.
- patterned or irregular.
- straight or curved, zigzag or wiggly. Curved lines suggest graceful movement, as in a dance or in nature. Zigzag lines suggest energy, as in a bolt of lightning.
- controlled, or uncontrolled and spontaneous.
- dark or light.
- parallel or perpendicular, intersecting or crossed.
- fast or slow.
- plain or fancy.
- sharp or soft.

DAP **naeyc** Following are activities to help children learn about lines.

Kindergarten and School-Age Activity: Line Design. Children can make abstract line designs using string and a frame. Secure a wooden picture frame. Hammer small nails a few inches apart around the frame. By pulling the string taut from nail to nail, children create line designs. Different colors of yarn add the element of color to the linear design. A cardboard frame can also be used. Cut 1-inch-long slits on all four sides. Encourage children to connect the slits with yarn. The result will be a line design.

Preschool, Kindergarten, and School-Age Activity: Dancing Lines. This activity is a variation of drawing to music. Play a short passage of music, and ask the children to respond by making a line with a marker, crayon, or paintbrush. For example, a march could suggest a forceful, patterned up-and-down line. A waterfall could suggest thick vertical lines, whereas water dripping from a faucet could suggest a vertical dotted line. What kind of a line is suggested by the following recorded sounds?

- water boiling
- thunder
- rocket blasting off
- hands clapping
- siren blaring
- jumping rope
- sawing wood
- a creaking swing in motion
- music with a good dance beat

Toddler, Preschool, Kindergarten, and School-Age Activity: Line Art. Children make line art by dipping cut pieces of string into a small bowl of white glue. Gluey string is creatively arranged in a linear design on black construction paper. Colored yarn is glued onto white drawing paper. Let dry.

Preschool, Kindergarten, and School-Age Activity: Squeeze and Sprinkle. Children make a linear design using a small bottle of white glue. Before it dries, have them sprinkle sand, glitter, or confetti to highlight their line design. Let dry.

Toddler, Preschool, Kindergarten, and School-Age Activity: Lots of Lines. Children cut line strips from construction paper. Encourage them to make some thick, thin, wide, fat, short, and long. Provide cut strips of paper for very young children who lack scissoring skills. Children arrange their cut-paper lines into a design and glue them onto a piece of colored construction paper.

Toddler, Preschool, Kindergarten, School-Age Activity: Stick Art. Children make line designs using toothpicks, craft sticks, or pipe cleaners. Each of these is spread with glue and pressed onto cardboard or sturdy paper. The arrangement is a linear design with angles. Children bend the pipe cleaners into nonlinear forms.

naea) 6-1b Color

A world ablaze with color provides a beautiful backdrop for our daily lives. What is color? Color:

- is based on the passage of light. It is the visual sensation of light caused by stimulating the cones of the retina. As the light source changes, so does the color. With no light, there is no color.
- comes from the sun. We see colors because of the way certain objects reflect color rays to our eyes. For example, we see a banana as yellow because the banana absorbs all the color rays except yellow and reflects the yellow rays back to our eyes.

makes each of us respond with feeling. Most of us have favorite colors. Children develop color preferences and palettes early in life. Preferences influence the colors used in art and in life.

Colors can be categorized as:

Primary. Red, blue, and yellow are the three **primary** colors. They are called primary because they are used to produce other colors.

Secondary. Mixing two primary colors in equal amounts results in a **secondary** color. For example,

red + yellow = orange

yellow + blue = green

red + blue = purple/violet

Intermediate. Mixing an adjoining primary and secondary color in equal amounts results in an **intermediate** color. For example,

yellow + orange = yellow-orange

red + orange = red-orange

red + violet/purple = red-violet

blue + violet/purple = blue-violet

blue + green = blue-green

yellow + green = yellow-green

Complementary. **Complementary** colors are opposite each other on the color wheel. They provide a dramatic visual contrast. Examples include red and green, yellow and purple, and blue and orange.

Neutral. **Neutral** refers to pigments that do not have a particular color. Black and white are neutrals.

Please refer to the color wheel in Figure 6–1, which identifies colors as primary, secondary, and intermediate.

Colors have recognizable physical properties, including the following.

Hue. **Hue** refers to the color name. Hue is color in its pure, unmixed form. For example, red and blue have different hues.

Value. **Value** refers to the relative lightness or darkness of a hue. It refers to the amount of light that a surface reflects back to the eye. For example, the value of a hue such as yellow is lighter than that of a darker hue such as purple. Red and blue can have the same value (dark) but different hues.

Intensity. **Intensity** refers to the purity of light reflected from a surface. Terms like bright and dull refer to color intensity. Pure colors are most intense or bright, and mixing a color with others dulls its intensity.

Color Wheel

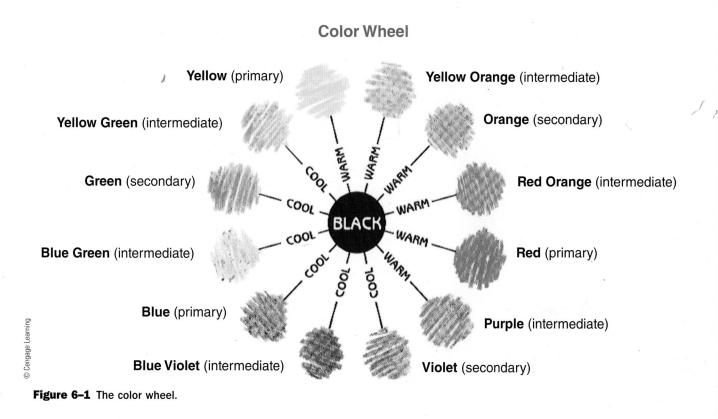

Figure 6–1 The color wheel.

© Cengage Learning

Tint. Adding white to any color lightens its value and results in a **tint**. For example, adding white to red makes pink.

Shade. Adding black to any color darkens its value and results in a **shade**. For example, adding black to red makes maroon.

Colors also have **thermal qualities** which elicit different feelings from the viewer:

- *Warm* colors, including red, yellow, and orange, remind us of hot or warm objects, such as the sun or fire.

- *Cool* colors, including blue, green, and purple/violet, remind us of cold or **cool** objects, such as water, ice, grass, and shade.

- Colors give the illusion of size and space. Light colors make objects appear larger than they actually are. Dark colors make objects appear smaller. For example, painting a room off-white makes it look larger. Painting the same room a dark tan makes it look smaller. Light colors make objects look closer. Dark colors make objects look farther away.

Adult artists are consciously concerned with how the viewer is affected by their color choices. An artist may use red, yellow, and orange to convey the sense of heat in painting a Fourth of July picnic. Blues and greens could be used to paint a ship adrift at sea. Light colors would be used to paint a portrait. Dark colors may be used to hint at the presence of crowds in the far background. Color has many possibilities and personalities. Some of these are:

- light or dark (value)
- bright or dull (intensity)
- warm or cool (thermal quality)
- opaque (oils, acrylics, thick tempera) or transparent (watercolors, thinned tempera)
- primary, secondary, or intermediate
- pure or mixed

DAP **naeyc** Following are activities for color. Others will be presented in sections on the visual and chromatic senses in Chapter 8.

Toddler, Preschool, Kindergarten, and School-Age Activity: Color Sort. Children enjoy sorting different objects by color. Provide a muffin tin or egg carton. Very young children can use only a few openings. Older children can be challenged with a dozen openings. Cut circles of different colors and place one in the bottom of each opening. Use pieces of construction paper, small yarn balls, or pompoms for the children to sort. Children use metal tongs to pick up yarn balls or pom-poms and place them in the matching opening. After sorting objects by color,

Photo Courtesy of Jill Englebright Fox

Figure 6–2 Easel painting provides opportunities for color mixing.

the matching color. Older children may enjoy using a separate set of clothespins that have color names written on them to match with the corresponding colors.

Preschool, Kindergarten, and School-Age Activity: Color Mixing. Children enjoy experimenting with mixing colors. Find six plastic jars. Six sections of a plastic egg carton can also be used. Fill three with several drops of water. Add one of the primary colors of food coloring to each. This leaves three empty for color mixing. An eyedropper can be used to mix equal parts of any two colors. What new colors result? Repeat the process, using two different colors.

A variation on this task includes additional materials. Provide a color-mixing directions card as follows:

red + blue =

blue + yellow =

red + yellow =

Provide a separate eyedropper for each of the primary colors. Label three jars red, blue, and yellow. Label three other jars red + blue, blue + yellow, and red + yellow. Young children need directions using actual color swatches rather than the color words. Older children can do the color mixing by reading the color names.

Infant, Toddler, Preschool, Kindergarten, and School-Age Activity: Hand Painting. Finger or, more appropriately, hand painting is a good opportunity to learn about color mixing. Provide one primary color, and encourage children to use their entire hands in moving the paint about. Next, add a second primary color. What happens when they mix? What color did they make? This may be enough color mixing in one sitting for young children. At a different time, repeat this process using the primary color not originally involved. As stated previously, infants may engage in this activity while sitting in an adult's lap or standing at a low table. Infants should be closely supervised to be sure they do not attempt to taste the paint.

children can include all of those in a color of their choice in a collage (see Figure 6–2).

Preschool, Kindergarten, and School-Age Activity: Wheel of Colors. Use a round, clean pizza cardboard. Glue on pie-shaped wedges of different colors, using the color wheel in Figure 6–1 as your guide. Find as many pinch-type clothespins as you have color wedges. Use markers to color each clothespin a corresponding color. For example, a red pie wedge will have a clothespin marked with red. Encourage children to clip each clothespin to

An Opportunity for Teacher Reflection

The Four-Year-Olds in Mr. Ramon's Class have been creating art with their finger- and handprints. Their paintings are drying on the cabinet in the art center. Mr. Ramon has given Tarik, Esteban, and Germaine magnifying glasses to study the prints in their paintings. Tarik is now carefully inspecting his fingertips with the magnifying glass, comparing what he sees with the prints in his painting. Esteban offers his own hands, palms down, for Tarik's inspection, "Our fingerprints are all the same color, but our hands are different colors." Germaine responds to Esteban, "Me and Tarik are the same color—

we're black. But you're different. You're brown." "You're not the same," argues Esteban. "Tarik's dark brown, and you're light brown, and I'm lightest brown. We're all brown." "Uh-uh, we're black," insists Germaine. Mr. Ramon is listening carefully to the conversation between the boys. He knows that this discussion is typical of four-year-olds as they begin to observe similarities and differences among their classmates. But he sees Germaine is getting upset. *How should he scaffold this discussion to help the children understand the relationships between ethnicity and skin color?*

Preschool, Kindergarten, and School-Age Activity: Color Clay. Teachers can use one of the recipes for homemade clay or play dough listed in Chapter 11. Start with three uncolored balls. Add a few drops of food coloring of one of three primary colors to each ball. Knead. Divide the primary-colored balls in half. Use half to experiment with color mixing. What happens if balls of red and blue, blue and yellow, or red and yellow are mixed together? What new colors of clay result? The result will be different-colored clay balls.

Preschool, Kindergarten, and School-Age Activity: Made in the Shade. Children learn to make tints and shades of a color. Individual finger paint sets or tempera paints are used. Begin with the three primary colors. Add a small dab of white to each. What colors result? Are they lighter or darker than the ones you started with? Mix the three secondary colors and repeat the process. Repeat the process adding a very small dab of black. Adding white will produce tints of red, yellow, blue, and the secondary colors. Adding black will produce shades.

Toddler, Preschool, and Kindergarten-Age Activity: Color Helpers. Discuss with children how community helpers often wear a certain color. Police officers wear blue. Doctors, nurses, veterinarians, ambulance drivers, paramedics, and hospital workers wear white or green (in surgery). Cooks and chefs also wear white.

Toddler, Preschool, and Kindergarten-Age Activity: Color Day. Declare a day of the week to focus on a specific color. For example, every Friday is color day. This Friday's color will be green. Encourage children to wear something green. Activities, songs, stories, and snacks can be focused on the color green.

Color Stories. Please see the Appendix C for a list of art-related books. Adults can read books like *Brown Bear, Brown Bear* or *My Crayons Talk* to infants and toddlers, comparing the colors on each page to objects in the environment. For older children, Slobodkina's *Caps for Sale* is an excellent book to read and act out. Children will enjoy stacking the red, blue, brown, and gray caps and taking turns being the peddler or the monkeys.

6-1c **Shape**

Shape is an appropriate criterion for critiquing two-dimensional art that has length and width. Specifically, what is a shape? Shape:

- refers to the outside form of an object.
- is the edge of an enclosed space.
- is defined by a line or outline, or by contrasting color or texture in the surrounding area.
- represents positive space or figure.
- is created by connecting lines.

Shape has its own qualities and personalities. Some characteristics are:

- simple or complex.
- circular or angular.
- geometrical, including circle, square, rectangle, or triangle; or nongeometrical including irregular, free-form, organic, or amorphic.
- active or quiet.
- clearly defined or vaguely defined.
- tall or short.
- big and large, or small and little.
- open or closed.
- solid, heavy, massive; or open, light.
- proportional or nonproportional.
- concave or convex.
- transparent or opaque.
- hard or soft.
- abstract or realistic.
- symmetrical or asymmetrical.
- precise or vague.

DAP naeyc 6-1d **Shape Activities**

Following are activities to help children learn about shape (see Figure 6–3).

Infant, Toddler, Preschool, Kindergarten, and School-Age Activity: Sandpaper Shapes. Geometric shapes, including circles, squares, triangles, rectangles, and diamonds are cut from pieces of sandpaper and mounted on sturdy cardboard. Children enjoy using their fingers and hands to feel the shapes. Older children progress to feeling only the outlines of shapes done in sandpaper.

© Cengage Learning

Figure 6–3 Children can explore shapes in their artwork.

Toddler, Preschool, Kindergarten, and School-Age Activity: Puzzling Shapes. Geometric shapes can be carefully drawn with a ruler on poster board. Use a different color for each shape for younger children. Older children will not need the color clue. Cut each shape into a number of pieces. Color-code the pieces on the back if necessary. Laminate individual pieces, and trim the excess. Match the number and sizes of the pieces with your age group. For example, a square cut in half diagonally will challenge a toddler but bore a kindergartner.

Preschool, Kindergarten, and School-Age Activity: Sew a Shape. Trim the raised edges off plastic foam trays. Cut each into a different geometric shape. Sturdy cardboard could also be used. Use a hole punch to carefully punch an inner outline of the shape. Encourage children to sew the shape by following the line of holes outlining the shape. They can use a shoelace or thick yarn rather than thread. Use a large plastic needle, or tape the beginning end to get it through the holes. Tie a large knot, button, or bead at the end so that it will not pull through. Some children will sew with an over-under, in-and-out motion as one would do with needle and thread. Others may prefer to loop or lace around the edge.

A piece of pegboard with the outline of a shape drawn through the holes could also be used. The children could use golf tees rather than yarn to complete the shape outline.

Preschool, Kindergarten, and School-Age Activity: Safety Shape. An awareness of shape serves many purposes beyond mere aesthetic beauty. Different shapes are used on signs that help people live, walk, and drive safely. The same is true for colors. Even if one cannot read a sign, the shape and color tell us what to do. Take a short neighborhood walk and look for safety signs, such as STOP. Safety shapes include the octagon, triangle, diamond, and circle. Children may want to make red, green, and yellow circles and paste them in the proper order against a black background to make a traffic light.

Toddler, Preschool, Kindergarten, and School-Age Activity: Shape Stamps. Children enjoy placing objects on an inked stamp pad and stamping that impression on a piece of paper. Find items that have round, square, rectangular, and triangular shapes. The round edge of a plastic hair roller is ideal for a round shape. Find hair rollers in different sizes. Encourage children to creatively combine the shapes into a design or picture.

Preschool, Kindergarten, and School-Age Activity: Shape Spatter Paint. Cut geometric shapes out of sturdy cardboard. Place a sheet of paper into the lid of a box. Place one shape on the paper. Place a thin screen over the top. Dip an old toothbrush in paint. Carefully brush across the screen, making sure that the paint is spattering around the edge of the shape. Remove the screen and carefully lift up the shape. The outline of the shape will appear on the paper. Repeat the process, combining shapes at different sittings as separate activities.

There are many standard activities that are appropriate for learning about color as well as shape. Some are described here.

Infant, Toddler, Preschool, Kindergarten, and School-Age Activity: Signs. Signs or displays of colors and color names as well as shapes and their corresponding names help children learn these concepts. A color caterpillar can have a body made up of different colored sections. Each circular ball of the body is a different color. A shape train can have a regular locomotive but cars of different geometric shapes. The names can be neatly printed above or below the items in each. Remember to post these at children's eye level rather than up high.

Kindergarten and School-Age Activity: Manipulative Games. Traditional games can be specifically designed and adapted to learn about shapes and color. Recommended examples include the following:

- bingo
- lotto
- dominoes
- card games, including old maid, rummy, hearts, and go fish

Browse through a toy store website or catalogue, noting board games and manipulative materials. Then, creatively adapt your own versions.

Preschool, Kindergarten, and School-Age Activity: Match and Memory. Make pairs of colors or shapes on index cards. Encourage children to match pairs. Older children enjoy turning all the color or shape cards face down and trying to find the matches. Players get another turn if two matching cards are turned up.

Kindergarten and School-Age Activity: Classify. Children can be challenged to find different ways to classify an array of cards. Index cards can be grouped on the basis of color, shape, and size. Older children will enjoy playing with a total deck of 12 cards per color. For example,

Red: circle, square, rectangle, triangle; small, medium, large

Using this formula for each of the three primary colors makes a deck of 36 cards.

Preschool, Kindergarten, and School-Age Activity: Gone Fishing. Draw an outline of a fish on a series of index cards. Add a color or shape to each. Staple a paper clip at the mouth of each fish shape. Use a paper towel roll as a fishing rod. Tie a length of string to one end and a small magnet at the other. Spread the fish out on the floor on top of a piece of blue paper for water. Encourage children to catch a fish, and name the color or shape.

Preschool, Kindergarten, and School-Age Activity: Partner Match. This is a good activity for the entire group. Give each child an outline of a geometric shape or color to hold. Older children may enjoy working with shapes of different colors. Gather children in a circle, holding their shapes. Have them carefully look around to find someone who is holding the same shape. Exchange and repeat.

Kindergarten and School-Age Activity: Flip-Flop Books. Find a book of index cards bound with spiral wire. Neatly cut each card in half. Actually, you will have too many cards, so you may want to remove some. Or you can include color, shape, and other concepts in the same book. Open the book to any page. You will have a top and bottom section on the right and left sides, four index-card sections. For example, for the red page in the color book, find or draw something red in the upper half of the right page. Carefully print the word *red* in red marker on the bottom half of the right page. Find or draw something else that is red, but divide it between the top and bottom halves of the left side. Encourage children to flip-flop through the various pages, top and bottom, until they find a match. For example, the red balloon (top right) with the word in red (lower right) matches the completed picture of a red apple on the left.

6-1e **Mass or Volume**

Mass and **volume** are appropriate criteria for critiquing three-dimensional art, which has height, length, and width. What a circle is to two-dimensional shape, a sphere is to three-dimensional mass or volume. What is mass or volume? These are terms that refer to solid bodies. An artist such as a sculptor can portray mass or volume in many different ways. Mass or volume can be portrayed as:

- heavy, bulky, massive; or light, delicate
- solid, impenetrable, block-like; or open, penetrable
- geometric or organic
- static or dynamic
- hard or soft
- large or little, big or small
- stationary or moving

Brain Connection

Since each child's brain thinks, feels, and learns differently, it is important that teachers provide skill-level materials. When learning experiences are tuned to the needs of individual children, all children can celebrate successes, as well as maximize their abilities to move on to more complex tasks (Rushton, 2011).

6-1f **Design or Composition**

Throughout this book, the term *design* has been used to describe anything and everything young children create in art. A scribble of lines, a splash of colors, and an array of shapes have been referred to as designs. Adult artists use design in a different sense, as in overall composition. Design or composition is the overall mark of success and the standard of achievement. Design and composition as artistic criteria attempt to address these questions:

- Did the artist accomplish what he or she originally set out to do? Was the artist successful?
- Do line, shape, color, texture, and form blend and work together as a unified whole? Is the arrangement of these artistic elements pleasing and satisfying?
- Does the finished work impart a sense of overall order, coherence, equilibrium, and organization?
- Did the artist strike a balance between monotony and chaos or unity and variety?
- Is there a focal point, center of interest, or dominant spot that attracts and holds attention? Does it make the viewer want to return and admire again and again?

With a good design or composition, the answers to the above would be yes. Adult artists walk a fine line among unity, variety, and contrast. It is difficult to create a unified work that hangs together while adding novelty, variety, contrast, and an element of surprise to make it interesting. Child artists, who are less concerned with finished products, may have little concern for design and composition. We can, however, use the principles of design and composition to talk about works of art and make children aware of the planning and energy that accompanies the making of art. Overall design and composition, although less directly relevant to early childhood art than other criteria, form a backdrop for other criteria.

6-1g **Pattern**

Pattern surrounds us. Fence posts, steps, ladder rungs, railroad tracks, and spokes on a wheel all suggest a repetitive pattern. Although children can use patterns to enrich their artwork, skills in patterning will also facilitate learning in the curricular areas of math and reading. Pattern:

- suggests flow, rhythm, motion, or movement.
- suggests regularity and repetition.
- can be made with forms, shapes, lines, colors, textures, or symbols that move across a surface in a recurring sequence.

Patterns have their own identity. They can be:

- ornate and fancy, or plain and simple.
- regular or irregular.
- symmetrical or asymmetrical.
- sequenced or alternating.

DAP naeyc 6-1h **Pattern Activities**

Following are activities for learning about pattern.

Kindergarten and School-Age Activity: Sponge Painting. Cut geometric and abstract shapes out of household sponges. Encourage children to identify and repeat a pattern (for example, circle-square-circle) on their paper. The pattern can be arranged in horizontal, vertical, or diagonal fashion (see Figure 6–4).

Kindergarten and School-Age Activity: Pattern Printing. Provide an array of items for printing. Examples include cookie cutters, lids, and corks. Encourage children to verbally identify a pattern and then to come up with different ways to repeat their patterns horizontally, vertically, or diagonally by dipping their items in paint and stamping on paper.

Preschool and Kindergarten-Age Pattern Picture. Shapes cut out of wallpaper, fabric scraps, or gift wrap can be glued in a repetitive sequence. For example, a

pattern could consist of scraps of white burlap, foil, gift wrap, and white burlap glued in a row.

Preschool, Kindergarten, and School-Age Activity: String a Pattern. Children can use wooden beads and a shoelace to create a pattern. They may repeat a pattern that a teacher begins or copy a pattern as it appears on an index card. Remember to tie a large knot at one end. The lacing end should be pointed and reinforced with tape.

Kindergarten and School-Age Activity: Extend a Pattern. Glue small squares of patterned wallpaper or wrapping paper to one end of a sentence strip. Ask children to identify or read the pattern and then use crayons or markers to extend the pattern on the sentence strip.

naea 6-1i **Space**

An artist's ultimate **space** is determined by the size of the canvas, be it paper, cardboard, or wood. Within the overall space, the artist must deal with the problem of arranging elements. How many shapes or symbols will be used? Where will they be placed? How much room will be left? How much blank space will remain? Basically, there are two types of space:

Positive space is the space taken up by lines, colors, shapes, and forms. Subject matter, content, and design occupy **positive space**.

Negative space is the space between or surrounding subject matter, symbols, or shapes.

Positive space refers to the shape, and **negative space** is what is left empty. In Figure 6–5, the white star occupies positive space and the black background represents negative space.

Artists use space in different ways. Some artworks are completely filled with vibrant colors and exciting designs (positive space), with little white paper (negative space) showing. Others may highlight one object or symbol by surrounding it with much negative space.

Figure 6–4 Making shapes with sponges dipped in paint.

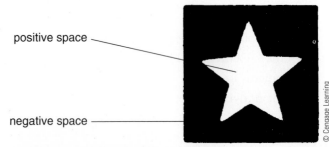

positive space

negative space

Figure 6–5 Example of positive and negative space.

Some of the different ways artists use space include:

- positive or negative.
- unoccupied, empty, sparse; or occupied, filled, dense.
- vertical, horizontal, or diagonal.
- symmetrical or asymmetrical.
- ordered or random.
- balanced or unbalanced.

DAP naeyc 6-1j **Space Activity**

The following activity can help children learn about space.

Kindergarten and School-Age Activity: Stencil. A stencil can be cut out of cardboard. Use an X-Acto® knife or safety razor blade to cut out a simple shape, for example, a star. The cutout star is positive space. The surrounding area is negative. Children can hold the star securely on a piece of paper. They can mark around the star using chalk, crayon, or paint. Chalk is preferred because of its ability to combine with other colors. Also, it does less damage to the stencil than paint. Children can also use the surrounding piece from which the star was cut. Instead of chalking away from the star stencil, they now stroke inward.

naea 6-1k **Balance**

When forms appear to be in proportion to each other, the picture is said to have **balance**, equilibrium, or harmony. Balance involves how an artist uses positive and negative space (see Figure 6–6). Basically, there are two ways of achieving balance.

Symmetrical (formal). With this type of balance, the shapes are evenly or equally balanced around some point, for example, up or down; right or left; or horizontally, vertically, radially, or diagonally. Think of two children of the same weight balanced on the two ends of a seesaw. This is symmetrical or formal balance. Symmetrical balance is often evident in the artwork of children. For example, a house painted on the right side symmetrically balances a large tree on the left. This type of balance is not bad or wrong; it is merely obvious and gets boring with repeated use.

Asymmetrical (informal). With this type of balance, the objects are not evenly or equally balanced from a point. For example, a house painted near the upper-left corner can be asymmetrically balanced with half of a large tree emerging from the right edge of the paper. The balance is unusual and intriguing.

There are many ways to achieve balance. A dark color may balance lighter ones. A massive shape may be balanced with a few smaller ones.

© Cengage Learning

Figure 6–6 An example of positive and negative space is this snowflake cut from folded paper.

An activity to help school-age children to understand balance would be to show children several reproductions of well-known paintings. Have children identify large and small objects portrayed in the paintings. Talk about placement of those objects and how the artist has used the objects to create symmetric or asymmetric balance in the painting.

naea 6-1l **Texture**

Texture refers to the surface quality of a work of art. How does it feel? Layers of paint, heavily applied crayon, and a fabric collage all have texture or a certain feel to them. Texture is a term that is appropriate to discussing and critiquing collage, construction, assemblage, and other three-dimensional art activities. Texture can be actual or implied. Young children work with actual textures. Adult artists use both. Implied texture involves technical proficiency in skillfully using the medium to suggest wood grain or peeling rust that does not actually exist on the canvas.

Some terms that relate to texture in art are:

- rough, bumpy, or smooth
- hard or soft
- coarse or fine

- wet, sticky, or dry
- raised or lowered
- flat
- dull or shiny
- granular
- rubbery, spongy
- slippery
- furry, fuzzy
- sharp

The element of texture will be explored further in Chapter 8.

6-1m **Texture Activities**

Here are two art activities to help children learn about texture.

Toddler and Preschool-Age Activity: Texture Collage. Provide a variety of textured objects. Encourage children to glue an array of textured items onto a piece of sturdy paper. Encourage children to use language to describe the textures they include in their collages.

Preschool, Kindergarten, and School-Age Activity: Texture Rubbings. Go on a texture hunt. Both indoor and outdoor environments offer a wealth of textures. For example, placing a piece of white paper over the bark on a tree and rubbing with the side of a crayon will produce an impression. The same thing will happen if you rub over cement, wood grain, coins, a license plate, corrugated cardboard, or an embossed greeting card. Encourage children to overlap and combine their rubbings. Older children may enjoy sketching a very simple picture containing large objects, such as a house and a tree. Later, they can finish their picture with rubbed areas. For example, rub with a dark crayon over bark in the area drawn for a tree trunk.

DAP naeyc naea 6-2 **Making Prints**

Most young children have experienced making prints at home. Rubbing a food-stained mouth on a napkin leaves a print. Muddy shoes leave prints on the floor, and touching a wall with dirty hands leaves hand prints.

Printing is an extension of painting. Painting involves making movements with a brush or other tool across a surface. Printing involves stamping paper with an object dipped in paint. Printing involves less whole-arm activity and greater concern for placement and overall design. Discuss and show examples of patterns in wallpaper, brick walls, windows, fabric, gift wrap, flowers, and nature when introducing printing. Tempera paints should be fairly thick for the printed impression to show up. A variety of paper can be used.

Children may approach printing activities as extensions of painting. They use printmaking tools as painting tools. In turn, they smear objects over paper, resulting in a paper covered with paint but not clear prints. This tendency reflects a process approach to making art and should not be interpreted as failure in teaching printmaking.

6-2a **Personally Expressive Art Activities**

Following are some personally expressive art activities for making prints.

Preschool, Kindergarten, and School-Age Activity: Monoprint. A pane of glass, a sheet of Plexiglas®, an acrylic cutting board, or any nonporous surface, such as a Formica® tabletop, can be used. Children paint their picture or design right on the surface. Use fairly thick paints. Place a larger piece of paper over the painted area. Rub gently with brayer or fingertips. Carefully lift. As the term *monoprint* suggests, one print is produced off the painted surface. Designs can also be etched into a solid mass of paint before the print is taken.

Kindergarten and School-Age Activity: Plastic Foam Tray Print. Trim the raised edges off small plastic foam trays so that you have a flat piece to work

Hints

- Place a thick stack of newspapers under the printing paper. The thickness will help make a good, clear print.
- To make a print pad, place a few paper towels on a flat plate. Pour on some tempera paint. Press the printing items on the wet pad. This will cover them evenly with paint.

with. Draw or etch a picture or design into the tray, using a craft stick. Press in without breaking through. The incised line will remain white when the tray is covered with ink or paint and printed. Ideally, a brayer is dipped in ink and spread across the tray. Paint can also be brushed on. Paint over the etched surface with a single color of paint. Press a piece of paper over the tray and gently rub with your hand over the entire surface. Carefully lift the paper to see the print. A second print can be taken immediately if paint is left on the tray. Children can make a series of prints this way. Wash the tray before changing colors.

Kindergarten and School-Age Activity: Cardboard Print. Secure sturdy cardboard for the background. Cut smaller pieces of cardboard or thick paper and build a raised picture or design. Glue and let dry. Paint over the design. Press the cardboard on paper, paint side down. Rub gently all over with your hands. Carefully lift the cardboard to reveal your print. Corrugated cardboard is highly recommended for building up interesting line designs that go in different directions.

Kindergarten and School-Age Activity: Crayon Sandpaper Print. Children can draw a picture or design with crayons on a piece of sandpaper. Encourage them to press hard and fill up the sandpaper. An adult can place a piece of white paper over the colored sandpaper and press with a warm iron. The heat will melt the wax from the colored sandpaper and transfer the design or picture to the paper.

Kindergarten and School-Age Activity: Glue Print. Use white liquid glue to draw a design or picture on a piece of cardboard. Make sure the outline or impression is fairly thick. Let the glue dry. Spread the design with ink or paint. Gently press paper on it. The paint or ink will adhere to the raised dried glue outline. Or glue a picture cut from a magazine to your piece of cardboard. Trace the outline with white liquid glue. Repeat the steps involved in making a glue print. This time you will get a print that resembles the picture cut out of the magazine.

6-2b Sensory Exploration Activities

Following are some sensory exploration activities for making prints.

Toddler, Preschool, Kindergarten, and School-Age Activity: Ink-Pad Print. Children enjoy placing their fingers on an ink pad and stamping an impression on paper. Ink pads come in many different colors. What does the fingerprint impression suggest? Children can use fine-point markers to make their basic fingerprints into something else by adding body parts, wheels, and details. Re-ink with liquid ink when the print appears

Figure 6–7 A print designed during a study of insects.

dull. Several thicknesses of heavy paper towels or a washcloth soaked with tempera paint can also serve as a stamp pad.

Toddler, Preschool, Kindergarten, and School-Age Activity: Sponge Printing. Sponges can be creatively cut into an array of shapes and sizes. Encourage children to dip the shapes in paint and make stamped prints (see Figure 6–7). Geometric shapes can be arranged to form a picture. Or children can repeat a sequence or pattern of printed shapes. Provide one or more shapes for each color.

Toddler, Preschool, Kindergarten, and School-Age Activity: Nature Print. Items collected from a nature walk can be inked and printed. Look for leaves, pinecones, and other nature specimens with interesting textures and surfaces.

Kindergarten and School-Age String Printing. Find small blocks of wood or small, sturdy gift boxes. Dip string in white glue and wrap it around the block or box in an interesting design. Or arrange the gluey string in a design on only one side. Let the glue dry. Dip the best side of the block in ink or paint. Place it on paper and gently push down to make an impression. Carefully remove the block to see the print. Repeat and make a continuing series or pattern. Stay with the color chosen rather than trying to wash the printer.

School-Age Activity: Ceramic Tile Print. Roll a layer of ink or paint on a ceramic tile square. Etch a picture or design, using a cotton swab or your finger. Place a small piece of paper over the tile. Rub gently. Carefully remove the paper to reveal your print. A tile with raised or embossed surfaces will have a surface ready for printing.

Kindergarten and School-Age Activity: Bubble Print. Fill a shallow container with water and tempera paint or liquid watercolor to which dishwashing detergent has been added. Two parts tempera paint to one part liquid dishwashing soap is recommended. Stir. Cut out a notch near the top of the straw. Blow bubbles over the rim of the container using a straw. Place white paper on top of the bubbles to get a print. The result will be a print made up of circular designs that can serve as a background for collage, drawing, or other art activity.

Preschool, Kindergarten, and School-Age Activity: Watercolor Tablet Print. Instead of using a paint brush, children wet their fingers with water and press them into the watercolor tablets. Gently press fingers onto paper, making oval designs or a combination of creative shapes.

Toddler, Preschool, Kindergarten, and School-Age Activity: Handprint Mural. Using the hand to make a print is one of the most basic printmaking activities. Children dip their hands in paint and gently press it onto a piece of paper. They can also use a brush to paint one hand before making a print. Prints can be repeated, and children will observe how their handprint fades with repeated prints. For older children, this activity lends itself to a group project. Rather than providing individual pieces, provide a large sheet of paper and encourage each child to add a print. Each child can make a contribution to the handprint mural (see Figure 6–8).

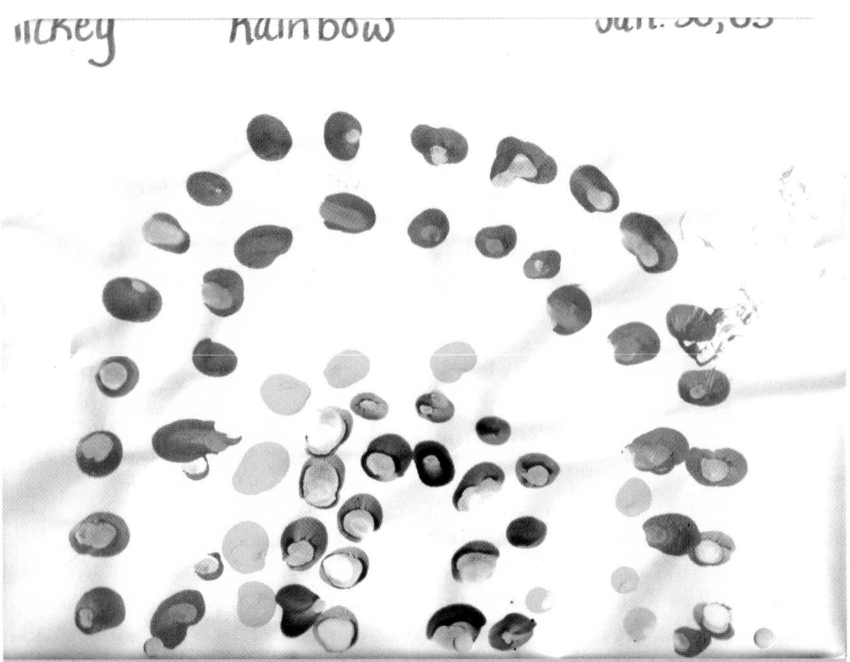

Preschool, Kindergarten, and School-Age Activity: Fold a Print. Encourage children to fold sheets of paper in half. They use a spoon to drop one or more colors of liquid tempera onto one side of their paper. Slowly fold over and press down, using the hand to rub all over. Carefully open to see the mirror-image print. Older children can paint half of their desired image near the fold, but only on one side. For example, a child who paints half a yellow circle near the crease will have a sun emerge when the paper is folded and then opened.

Kindergarten and School-Age Activity: Leaf and Glue Print. Collect an array of leaves and ferns. Children can cover one side of the leaf with glue and press it down on paper, leaving a glue print. Carefully lift off the leaf. Sprinkle small confetti onto the glue print.

Kindergarten and School-Age Activity: Oil Paint Print. Mix tempera paint and cooking oil in a cup until creamy. Set aside. Fill a round cake pan half full with plain water. Spoon a few drops of the oil paint mixture on top of the water. Use a fork to gently swirl. Next, have the child lay a piece of white paper on top of the swirl. Let the paper float for about a minute. Carefully lift the paper out, holding on to two corners. Place the print elsewhere to dry. Use this process to design greeting cards or stationery by first folding white paper in half or quarters.

School-Age Activity: Press and Twist Print. Use a nonporous work surface such as a table or countertop. Fill squeeze bottles with tempera paint and encourage children to gently squeeze one or more small drops of paint onto the work surface. You may want to use masking tape to clearly define children's work area. Place a piece of paper on the drops of paint. Children can gently press down and twist the paper, keeping their fingers stretched wide. Carefully lift the paper to reveal the design. Children can continue experimenting with other colors and different ways of twisting their paper. Keep sponges and soapy water nearby to clean work surfaces between children. For a more sensorial activity, forgo the paper and encourage children to press and twist the paint with their bare hands. Be adventurous, and do the same outdoors with bare feet on a warm day.

Figure 6–8 A fingerprint rainbow.

© Cengage Learning

Preschool, Kindergarten, and School-Age Activity: Simple Sun Print. This activity is best done in the morning of a day that promises to be sunny. A simplified version of this activity is to have children collect small rocks and flat leaves. They can arrange their leaves on a large sheet of construction paper outdoors in the direct sun. Place one rock on each leaf on top of the paper. Rocks secure the leaves and must be smaller than the leaves. Keep in direct sun for at least one hour. Carefully remove items and look for outlines and differences in color. The sun will bleach the surrounding area while the part under the leaf (and hidden from the sun) will remain darker. Experiment with shapes other than nature items. These could include toys, puzzle pieces, stencils, keys, and utensils, as well as alphabet letters and numerals. For example, children can use magnetic letters to make their names.

6-2c **Stencil, Splatter, and Screen Printing**

Stencil, spatter, and screen printing are fairly involved activities that require instruction and special tools. It is unlikely that young children will discover on their own how to make a stencil, spatter, or screen print.

naeyc School-Age Activity: Stencil. A stencil can be cut from sturdy cardboard, tagboard, or poster board. It can also be torn out of construction paper. When you cut a stencil, you actually get two. Recall our discussion of positive and negative space. The shape cut out occupies positive space and is called the positive stencil. The remaining frame or background occupies negative space and is called the negative stencil. Each type of stencil has its own process. Hold the stencil with one hand and use the other hand to stroke from the piece out when using the positive stencil. Hold the background or frame and stroke inward when using the negative stencil.

Stenciling can be done with crayons, paint, or chalk. Chalk dust dabbed on with cotton balls can be blended and does less damage to the stencil than paint. Paint can be gently dabbed on with cotton balls, a sponge, or a brush. Short, stiff-bristle brushes used with an upright, gentle dabbing motion are recommended for the skilled stenciler. Do not saturate the stencil with paint. Be careful that the paint, chalk, or crayon does not get under the stencil, causing smears.

It may be difficult for young children to cut their own stencils out of cardboard. Perhaps the stencil could be drawn by them but cut out by an adult. Encourage children to design simple pictures with minimal details. An X-Acto® knife can be used by an adult to cut out stencils. Remember not to cut through the frame to get to the inside. Very young children can tear out an abstract shape that will work well in a stencil activity.

Stencils can also be painted with spray paint. This method is best done outdoors. Place the paper in the lid of a large box. Tape the back of the stencil in place. Spray with paint. Let dry. Carefully remove the stencil.

Kindergarten and School-Age Activity: Paper Plate Stencil. Put a paper plate down on a piece of thick paper and trace around it. Cut out the circle and fold it into a small wedge. Cut bits out of the folds to make a stencil. Unfold the stencil and put it back on the paper plate. Dip a sponge in tempera paint and gently blot paint on the stencil, transferring the design onto the paper plate.

Kindergarten and School-Age Activity: Spatter Printing. You will need a large but not too deep box, a screen or mesh wire (e.g., a window screen, kitchen grease guard, or metal strainer), and an old toothbrush. Cut or tear a stencil out of paper. Or items with interesting shapes, such as coins, a comb, cookie cutters, keys, and nature specimens, can be used as positive stencils and placed on a sheet of paper inside the box. Dip your toothbrush in paint and gently move it across the screen, releasing a mist of paint. Dark colors will show up best on white paper. The paint will spatter and outline the stencil or objects. The space taken up with the positive stencil or objects will remain white or the color of the background paper. Carefully move the stencil or objects and repeat with a different color. Switch stencils and work with the negative stencil.

Young children will need to use a large box covered with a fairly large spatter screen. Older children may be able to use a small, handheld food strainer and move it around the stencil. They can carefully rub chalk across the food strainer at the same time. A small spatter screen can also be made by carefully cutting the top and bottom off a sturdy, small box. Attach wire or screen to the top. Use with small stencils. Or fasten the plastic mesh or screen into an embroidery hoop. If no screen is available, scrape the bristles of the toothbrush toward you with a stick. If you scrape away from you, the spray will spatter you. The thumb can also be used to scrape bristles.

Kindergarten and School-Age Activity: Printing. Silk-screen printing is actually a stencil method of printing. Paint is forced through a piece of stretched mesh fabric that has been prepared with a design. The paint is printed onto fabric or paper. Silk screen is a way to create several prints of the same image and is therefore recommended for making greeting cards or stationery. First, a screen must be prepared.

An embroidery hoop, a picture frame, or a frame cut from the lid of a shoe box can be used for screen printing. Use an old nylon stocking or a piece of silk or cheesecloth for the silk-screen material. Cut it larger than your frame, pull it tight, and secure it with tacks, tape, or nails. Cut a stencil and place it on paper. Put the silk-screen frame over the stencil. Use a brush, tongue depressor, or cardboard strip to gently spread thick paint on the silk screen, which will cover the stencil. Carefully lift your silk-screen frame. Thoroughly rinse the silk screen after each application of paint. Add different colors if desired. Repeat the pattern while overlapping or creatively combining pieces from different stencils.

Did You Get It?

You take your students outside after it rains and ask each child to put his or her feet in the mud and then place them on a sheet of paper. This concept, printing, is a _____ approach to creating art.

a. goal-oriented
b. product
c. process
d. divergent

Take the full quiz on CourseMate.

Summary

(6-1) Artistic elements are the building blocks of artistic expression. Artists process with line, color, and shape until these elements are successfully combined into a harmonious design or overall composition. Children go through the same steps but on a more informal and often unplanned basis. These elements are the criteria for making, understanding, appreciating, and critiquing art. The categories and physical properties of color make it the first artistic element that most children explore. Children learn about the artistic elements through developmentally appropriate art activities for exploration and personal expression. Our intent is not to turn children into art critics. That would be developmentally inappropriate. Our goal is to use the vocabulary of the artistic elements so that children learn to value and directly participate in the arts. They will come to know good art when they see it and will be able to use the artistic elements in justifying their evaluation. (6-2) Printmaking is an extension of painting and encourages a greater concern for placement and overall design.

Key Terms

artistic elements, 123
asymmetrical (informal), 131
balance, 131
color, 123
complementary, 124
cool, 125
design (composition), 129
hue, 124
intensity, 125
intermediate, 124

line, 123
mass, 129
negative space, 130
neutral, 124
pattern, 129
positive space, 130
primary, 124
prints, 132
secondary, 124
shade, 125

shape, 123
space, 130
symmetrical (formal), 131
texture, 131
thermal qualities, 125
tint, 125
value, 124
volume, 129
warm, 133

✓ Suggested Activities

1. Visit an art museum or an art museum website to look at paintings and prints. Use the artistic elements to analyze a work of art.

2. Working with young children, implement an art activity involving one or more of the artistic elements.

3. Facilitate a printmaking experience with children.

4. Select one of the children's books on artistic elements included in Appendix C. Use that book to develop an instructional activity on one of the artistic elements. Be sure to include opportunities for children to experiment with the artistic element as they create their art.

5. Complete the following color clock activity.

   a. Get white paper.

   b. Use watercolors.

   c. Draw a large circle.
      black-in center
      blob of paint

   d. Fill in (with blob of paint)
      12 = yellow (primary)
       4 = red (primary)
       8 = blue (primary)

   e. Mix (secondary colors)
      12 + 4 = 2 (add blob and name of color to clock)
      4 + 8 = 6 (add blob and name of color to clock)

   f. Mix (intermediate colors)
      8 + 12 = 10 (add blob and name of color to clock)

   f. Mix (intermediate colors)
      12 + 2 = 1 (add blob and name of color to clock)
      2 + 4 = 3 (add blob and name of color to clock)
      4 + 6 = 5 (add blob and name of color to clock) P. S. Mathematically incorrect!
      6 + 8 = 7 (add blob and name of color to clock)
      8 + 10 = 9 (add blob and name of color to clock)
      10 + 12 = 11 (add blob and name of color to clock)

   g. Let dry.

   h. Refer back to Figure 6–1 to verify your color clock is correct.

   i. Turn in to instructor.

Review

1. List the nine major artistic elements discussed in this chapter.

2. Complete the following color equations:

   a. red + _yellow_ = orange

   b. yellow + blue = _Green_

   c. _red_ + _blue_ = purple

3. Put the proper color term in front of each color:

   P for primary
   S for secondary
   I for intermediate
   N for neutral

   _I_ blue-green
   _I_ yellow-orange
   _P_ blue
   _I_ yellow-green
   _S_ orange
   _P_ red
   _S_ green
   _I_ red-violet
   _N_ black
   _P_ yellow
   _N_ white
   _I_ blue-violet
   _I_ purple/violet
   _I_ red-orange

4. Match the following columns related to color.

   a. the colors that are used to produce all other colors

   b. orange, green, and purple

   c. mixing a primary and a secondary color results in this

   d. these colors are opposite each other on the color wheel

   e. black and white are examples

   f. a pure, unmixed color

   g. lightness or darkness of a color

   h. brightness or dullness of a color

   i. adding white will produce this

   j. adding black will produce this

   k. red, yellow, and orange are examples

   l. blue, green, and purple are examples

   _____ neutral colors

   red complementary colors

   _____ hue

   _____ primary colors

   _____ warm colors

   _____ secondary colors

   _____ intensity

   _____ value

   _____ tint

   _____ intermediate colors

   _____ cool colors

   _____ shade

5. Match the following columns related to artistic elements.

a. has hue, value, and intensity   _____ texture

b. can be symmetrical or asymmetrical   _____ balance

c. can be positive or negative   _____ space

d. a recurring, repeated sequence   _____ pattern

e. refers to the integrated whole   _____ mass/volume

f. refers to three-dimensional art   _____ design/composition

g. a visible mark made by moving an artistic tool across a surface   _____ shape/form

h. refers to the surface quality of a work of art   _____ color

i. refers to two-dimensional art   _____ line

Additional Resources

Go to the website, Slideshare, to see *"The Elements of Art,"* a PowerPoint defining and giving examples of the elements of art for pre-service teachers.

Understanding Formal Analysis is a website offered by the J. Paul Getty Museum (www.getty.edu) for educators. It includes downloadable handouts with definitions and activities.

Go to YouTube and view "The Elements of Art" video, designed to explain the elements to elementary students.

Studio Codex is a website that includes guided projects to help visitors understand the elements of art; includes additional resources on visiting museums and developing your own artistic talents.

NGA Classroom: The Elements of Art (www.nga.gov) is an on-line unit of instruction for adult students; includes information and activities.

 Visit CourseMate for this textbook to access the eBook, Did You Get It? quizzes, Digital Downloads, TeachSource Videos, flashcards, and more. Go to CengageBrain.com to log in, register, or purchase access.

Second/Third Grade Lesson Plan

Sequencing with Action Jackson Pollock

GOAL

Students analyze, make inferences, and draw conclusions about and understand expository text and provide evidence from text to support their understanding.

OUTCOMES

Upon completion of this lesson, students will:

a. describe and replicate the order of events or ideas in a text.
b. identify Jackson Pollock as a twentieth century American expressionist artist.
c. create a splatter painting.
d. compare their process to Pollock's process.

MATERIALS

a. Greenberg, J., & Jordan, S. (2002). *Action Jackson.* Brookfield, CT: Roaring Brook Press
b. Large sheet of butcher paper for each child
c. Tempera paint and brushes for each child
d. Paper and pencil for each child

INTRODUCTION

Show the children the picture of Pollock's *Lavender Mist*, found on pages 22 and 23 in the book. Allow the children time to consider it and then ask their opinions. After the children have verbalized, explain that this painting represented a new style of artwork introduced in 1950 by an American artist named Jackson Pollock. Pollock said that his painting were "Energy and motion made visible." Tell the children that you are going to read a story about Jackson Pollock and how he created his artwork. Provide a focus for listening by telling the children that they should pay close attention to the sequence of activities in Pollock's painting.

DEVELOPMENT

Read the story to the children. Ask each child to choose a partner. Have the partners work together to sequence the steps in Pollock's painting process. Allow the children to refer back to the book if needed. Be aware that not each pair of children will identify exactly the same steps. That's fine, as long as the steps identified are in the same sequence. The children should record their steps.

As the pairs finish their steps, they can either check themselves by reviewing the book or the teacher can check their work. Once checked, give the children butcher paper, paint brushes, and paint. Their task now is to follow the steps they identified to complete their own painting of energy and motion. (This is best done outside.) Play jazz music as they work.

CONCLUSION

After the children have finished painting like Jackson Pollock, ask them to write a journal entry on the experience, addressing the following questions:

1. How did your steps differ from what Jackson Pollock did, according to the book?
2. Compare painting energy and motion in this way to painting at the easel or at your desk.
3. What have you learned about Jackson Pollock?

ASSESSMENT

a. Were the children able to identify and replicate the events in Pollock's process of painting?
b. In their journal entries, did they identify Jackson Pollock as a twentieth century American artist?
c. In their journal entries, did they accurately compare Pollock's process to theirs?
d. Did they create a splatter painting?

A full-size version of this lesson plan, and others like it, is available for digital download.

7 Aesthetics

Photo Courtesy of Jill Englebright Fox

Many young children spend much of their waking day in an early childhood facility.

Whether a large center, a small home, or a public school classroom, teachers try to make it a place where children will want to spend time productively. The physical environment should invite children in; it should call out to and engage them. It should also be visually appealing without being over-stimulating. There can be things to stimulate the senses without overloading them—a vase of flowers, a display of artwork, and soothing background music. These aesthetic touches can transform a room into an aesthetically pleasing environment. Wall displays also add aesthetic touches. In the featured photo, a beautiful mural of a Mexican village provides the backdrop for a dramatic play center. The theme of the center is *El Mercado*. Props and activities encourage children to dramatize buying and selling in a Mexican marketplace. The mural adds a visually appealing aesthetic element to the center. Children enjoy looking at it, and the pastoral scene provides a peaceful background for the often busy center. *If you were the teacher, what could you do to modify, improve, or extend this display?*

Learning Outcomes

After reading this chapter, you should be able to:

7-1 Define aesthetics.

7-2 Explain why aesthetics are an important part of children's development.

7-3 Describe how children's understanding of art changes as they mature.

7-4 Discuss the role of the teacher in children's aesthetic development.

7-5 Explain ways to support children's development of art appreciation.

7-6 Provide experiences using watercolors and ink.

Standards addressed in this chapter

DAP Criteria

2 Teaching to enhance development and learning

3 Planning curriculum to achieve important goals

NAEYC Standards

2 Curriculum

3 Teaching

NAEA Visual Arts Standards

2 Using knowledge of structures and functions

3 Choosing and evaluating a range of subject matter, symbols, and ideas

5 Reflecting upon and assessing the characteristics and merits of their work and the work of others

6 Making connections between visual arts and other disciplines

7-1 Defining Aesthetics

Think of a time when you found yourself in a beautiful place. Maybe it was a cathedral or a mountaintop. How did it make you feel? Full of awe and wonder? These positive feelings can also happen in your classroom when you make it an awesome, beautiful place to be. Although taste is individual, both adults and children appreciate beauty and beautiful things. Working in a pleasing environment will accomplish four goals. First, being surrounded by beauty and beautiful experiences will help children's aesthetic development and enrich their lives. Second, it will make the environment a pleasant place for you and the children to be for a large amount of the day. Third, you will feel good about being there and your stress level will be lower. Fourth, it will subtly influence children's behavior in positive ways.

What is **aesthetics**, and why should it be addressed in early childhood? This chapter attempts to answer these basic questions. Our concern for the young child's aesthetic development and education stems from our wider concern for the whole child. Young children are aesthetic experts. They demonstrate aesthetic attitudes in their spontaneity, wonder, and amazement at things that adults often take for granted. What is the teacher's role in aesthetics? Teachers can be aesthetic models in the way they dress, behave, and communicate. The indoor and outdoor environments can also be aesthetically pleasing and stimulating.

Aesthetics is an abstract concept that means "perception" in Greek. Although we may feel it is important that children learn something about aesthetics, we may not be quite sure what the term entails. Aesthetics is not synonymous with art. Aesthetics includes art, and the other expressive arts like music and dance, but it also goes beyond them. Just what is aesthetics? Aesthetics:

- is a nondiscursive and metaphorical way of knowing and experiencing
- involves the love and pursuit of beauty as found in art, movement, music, and life
- is an awareness and appreciation of the natural beauty found in nature and one's surroundings
- means being a beholder of beauty and savoring beautiful things in the world around us
- involves an emotional connection with one's experiences
- links knowing and feeling, the cognitive and affective

For purposes of art education, Lankford (1992) defines aesthetics as a group of concepts for understanding the nature of art. Aesthetic concepts address virtually all aspects of art from process to product to response. Aesthetic inquiry may be defined as the process of clarifying and answering questions about the nature of art. Some examples of aesthetic experiences are the following:

- touching the sparkling design of frost on a window
- viewing the translucent silkiness of a spiderweb
- listening and moving to the beat of an ethnic folk song
- stopping to savor the aroma of freshly baked bread

The type of beauty that aesthetics pursues is the type taken for granted in our everyday lives, rather than the artificial Hollywood definition of beauty.

Did You Get It?

What statement does not describe one of the positive outcomes for teachers, students, and the creative process that can be accomplished by making the classroom a place of beauty?
a. A beautiful, aesthetic environment is proven to lower stress levels of its occupants.
b. The lives of the occupants will be enriched.
c. Grades improve across all subject areas in a beautiful, aesthetic environment.
d. An aesthetic environment makes a classroom a more tolerable place to be for many hours a day.

Take the full quiz on CourseMate.

7-2 Aesthetics and Child Development

Why are aesthetics and aesthetic education important in early childhood? There are five reasons. First, our humanistic concern for the whole child motivates us to provide for all aspects of development. Second, it is our belief that children who marvel at beauty in the world around them will be able to appreciate the beauty of letters, words, numbers, stories, poems, formulas, books, symbols, and other cultures. Third, children with the aesthetic sense will develop into adults who know and value good design and can use this as wise consumers in choosing personal items as well as on a wider level in planning cities, highways, and attempting to solve problems of pollution, war, poverty, and urban blight. Fourth, it is important for children to value the arts and directly participate in a variety of the arts. Fifth, aesthetic experiences foster concept development.

Aesthetics is a branch of philosophy concerned with an individual's pursuit of and response to beauty. Aesthetics involves the following:

- attitude
- process/experience
- response

7-2a Aesthetic Attitude

The **aesthetic attitude** involves:

- openness or childlike freshness
- spontaneity
- intense focusing on the here and now
- a sense of joy, wonder, marvel, or excitement
- willingness to perceive as if experiencing something for the very first time
- commitment or willingness to "stop and smell the roses"

Young children constantly demonstrate aesthetic attitudes. They are sensory gluttons who need to look at, listen to, touch, smell, and taste everything they come in contact with. This may prove embarrassing to some adults: "Nina, please don't touch the daisies." Over time, Nina may decide not to wonder at flowers. She may learn to take them for granted. Or, as her mother told her, "If you've seen one, you've seen them all." Unfortunately, Nina's mother has lost the aesthetic attitude. Author Robert Schirrmacher observed a preschool field trip to the library. The children were stopping to watch and listen to the sights and sounds at a construction site. The teacher was hurrying them along, urging them to walk faster to get to their destination. A rich sensory experience was lost. We live in a fast-paced world. We rush from home to work. In the process, we may ignore rainbows in the sky, colorful patterns in rain puddles, or daisies growing alongside the freeway. Di Leo (2003) suggests that aesthetic attitudes can be encouraged in young children by exposing them to environments rich in opportunities for all kinds of sensory experiences. This exposure, however, must be accompanied by time for children to take advantage of those rich environments, to observe and sense and reflect on the experiences provided.

7-2b Aesthetic Process/Experience

The **aesthetic process/experience** is intrinsically motivating. Children sense and perceive for the sheer joy of it. The aesthetic process involves active engagement rather than passive taking in. It means using all the senses to ravish an object or experience, getting completely lost or totally consumed. Examples of the aesthetic process include:

- listening attentively to music and drawing on images, emotions, and memories, rather than merely hearing a song
- visually exploring or quietly contemplating a work of art, processing the lines, colors, and shapes, rather than just glancing at it
- manipulating and feeling a peacock's feather, considering the colors and textures in light of other tactile experiences, rather than just quickly touching it

Aesthetic processing takes time and a commitment to flow with the experience. Children are more aesthetically proficient than adults. They thoroughly examine their world with all their senses. Adults can learn much about aesthetics from watching children explore the world.

7-2c Aesthetic Response

The aesthetic attitude and process result in an appreciative reaction or **aesthetic response** on many different levels. Our affective response may involve a sense of wonder, appreciation, surprise, a feeling of being moved, awe, exhilaration, or being carried away. We may get lost in the aesthetic experience and totally caught up in the moment. At the physiological level, our response may result in a smile, laugh, perspiration, shiver, sigh, or even goose bumps.

Our reactions will also entail a mental response in the form of a decision, judgment, or evaluation. One may ask these questions:

- Was this personally enjoyable, and why?
- Did the artist, musician, or dancer exhibit skill? What makes me think so?
- Do I like it, and why?

Our intent is to help children apply simple criteria to discuss and critique works of art. They can learn to identify what they like or dislike and why. They can learn that even though a piece of artwork or a performance doesn't appeal to them personally, it still has aesthetic value to others. For example, a child may not like ballet but can still appreciate the beauty and grace of the movements. Over time, children will slowly construct their own personal preferences and tastes. They need not follow the crowd in believing that what is popular or current must be good. They will come to identify with and value the arts. Hopefully, they will grow up reading good literature, listening to a variety of music, and exhibiting tolerance for different artistic styles. Life will offer them more than passive entertainment by technology.

Aesthetic Value. Eaton (1998) believes the difficulty with understanding the very nature of aesthetic activity, experience, and judgment demands explaining how communication is possible when key words such as *beauty* or *art* seem to mean such different things to different people. To our list of the three components of aesthetics, Eaton would add **aesthetic value**. Aesthetic value arises from a positive response of a person or group of people toward something. It is obvious that,

unless someone feels positively inclined toward a thing or event, it cannot have aesthetic value. It is the value a thing or event has because of its capacity to evoke pleasure that is recognized as arising from features in the object traditionally considered worthy of attention and reflection. Aesthetics in art depends on the traditions and culture in which we share beliefs about what is valued.

Did You Get It?

Aesthetics fits most accurately into which domain?
  a. philosophy
  b. art
  c. psychology
  d. sociology

Take the full quiz on CourseMate.

naea 7-3 **Understanding Art**

There are stages in children's artistic development. Are there developmental stages children go through in their understanding of art? Gardner and Winner (1976) conducted interviews with 121 children to identify developmental stages of understanding art. Questions focused on the source of art, the production of art, the medium, style, art and the outside world, formal properties of art, and evaluation. They concluded that children pass through three distinct developmental phases

in their understanding. The ages and characteristics include the following:

4 to 7 years—Young children have a simplistic understanding of art; the making of art is an easy, mechanical activity, and judgments about the artistic quality of a work are all equally acceptable. Some children say that authorities, including parents, determine what is good. Young children emphasize the technical aspects of a work of art, often believing that anyone can make art—including animals. They believe decisions involved in making art are governed by physical limitations rather than aesthetic concerns. For example, they would say the picture is finished when the paper is filled.

10 years—In the middle elementary years, children believe art should be a precise rendering of reality. They believe there are criteria for judging quality in works of art: the more real it looks, the better it is.

Adolescence—Teens are more sophisticated in their understanding of art. They realize one's opinions and values vary; judgments in art are relative and their opinions are valid.

Gardner and Winner (1976) add that children will remain in an arrested state of development in their understanding of art unless their naive opinions are challenged. Perhaps this is the reason so many adults find little value in contemporary art.

Rosenstiel, Morrison, Silverman, and Gardner (1978) sought to identify developmental stages of critical judgment in art. They interviewed children ranging in ages from 6 to 16 with questions related to how judgments are made regarding art. They identified the following developmental characteristics in children's critical judgment:

first graders—Children are limited to identifying subject matter and colors. They use terms such as "good" or "pretty" when critiquing art.

third graders—Along with subject matter and color, children now comment on the details, designs, and shapes in the work. Third graders consider realism "good" because it is difficult to achieve.

sixth graders—Responses parallel those of third graders. Sixth graders tend to use a few more terms from art history in their comments.

tenth graders—Adolescents are far less likely than younger children to make statements without content or substance. They tend to cite a variety of factors when selecting and justifying their responses to works of art. They also tend to mention formal properties, use terminology from art criticism, and mention and recognize work from certain periods in history and specific artists' names.

Rosenstiel and colleagues (1978) concluded that younger children may be able to make finer aesthetic distinctions when viewing works of art but that their verbal responses were restricted by their limited vocabulary.

DAP **naeyc** 7-3a **Expose, Not Impose**

As early childhood educators, our task is to expose rather than impose. Expose children to a wealth of sensory experiences and variety in each of the arts. Encourage them to critique, develop personal preferences, and value art, music, movement, dance, and literature. Children can use accepted criteria, including the artistic elements explored in Chapter 6, as standards in developing their own preferences. Be careful not to impose your own preferences (see Figure 7–1). For example, a teacher may not like abstract art, but that does not mean that it is junk or bad, or that realistic art is better. Help children see that art can be high quality in terms of design or composition even though one may not like it.

Dobbs (1998) views children's understanding of aesthetics as residing along a continuum. For example,

Photo Courtesy of Jill Englebright Fox

Figure 7–1 Exposing children to a variety of art forms and styles.

for young children, a developmentally appropriate activity may be to learn the distinction between expressing preference and making a judgment. They can be assisted in understanding that, although one may like a particular work of art, there are others who do not. Aesthetics is not about uttering subjective preferences, but about the thinking and effort involved in figuring out why we make such choices and how best to support and justify them. Dobbs uses the example of flavors of ice cream, asking children which one they like best. There is no right or wrong answer, nor is it even a question of aesthetics. Instead, it is simply a matter of individual preference. However, to assume that anyone else would value one's choice of ice cream requires a set of reasons supporting a judgment of its goodness. Here one needs to provide a rationale for one's choice, to make a reasoned judgment capable of meeting some external standard or criterion other than one's own preference. This is the idea of objectivity. Aesthetics involves teaching students how to create such argument, how to talk about art in a manner that validates the judgments they have made.

Aesthetic discussion conducted with younger children should be consistent with their level of cognitive and language development. Although younger students may discuss art issues in a less advanced way than older students, and without using technical jargon, they can engage in aesthetic discussion. Simply learning to talk and construct a reasoned argument is an important exercise, not only for aesthetics and art education but also for the general educational goal of schooling.

> ### Did You Get It?
>
> **Howard Gardner and Ellen Winner (1976) emphasize their belief that development ceases ("is arrested") when the child's "_____" opinions are no longer challenged.**
> **a.** rigid
> **b.** impulsive
> **c.** flexible
> **d.** naïve
>
> Take the full quiz on CourseMate.

DAP **naeyc** 7-4 **Teacher's Role in Aesthetics**

What can early childhood educators do to foster aesthetic development? Aesthetics does not come neatly packaged in a set of materials. Still, it is important and within our reach. There are guidelines for making teachers, children, and classrooms aesthetically alive.

7-4a **Teacher as Aesthetic Model**

Becoming aesthetically responsive requires the teacher to invest time and effort. Teachers model their own aesthetic awareness and sensitivity in the way they dress. First and foremost, clothing should be professional, neat, comfortable, and appropriate for stooping, moving, playing, and sitting on the floor. We can reflect an appreciation of color and color harmony in choosing articles of clothing and accessories. For example, a young girl is proudly showing off her new sweater. Her teacher asks her to identify the colors. Nikki replies, "It has red and blue." Her teacher replies, "My dress has red and blue in it, too. And touch of white. My dress has the colors in our flag." Or, "Jim, you mixed blue and yellow in your picture and made green. I wore blue slacks with a yellow blouse and my green belt. We match."

7-4b **Teacher's Relationship with Children**

The teacher's inner beauty can be demonstrated by positively relating to all children and valuing their uniqueness (see Figure 7–2). Find something unique and beautiful in each child, and let that child know. Convey beautiful messages. Children appreciate being talked to in regular tones. There is no need to speak artificially in a high-pitched voice. Refer to oneself as "I" rather than as "Miss Jones" or "Teacher," as in, "Miss Jones doesn't like it when children are not paying attention," or "Teacher will just have to get some more apple juice for snack, won't she?" Talk to children naturally rather than with a condescending tone.

naea 7-4c **Provide for Wide Variety in the Arts**

Children can be exposed to different examples within a variety of the arts. For example, different types of music can be introduced throughout the day: slow lullabies or waltzes during rest, classical as background music during snack, and a march or rock-and-roll during cleanup.

naeyc 7-4d **Aesthetic Classroom**

The physical environment of the classroom significantly influences the attitudes, behaviors, and attention spans of those who spend time in it—both children and adults. A well-planned and aesthetically pleasing classroom encourages a focus on learning and opportunities for positive interaction. Uninspiring environments can negatively affect young children's learning (Danko-McGhee, 2009). A cluttered classroom can provide too much sensory stimulation and make it difficult for children to focus on instructional activities.

The classroom should be an aesthetically pleasing and sensory-rich environment (see Figure 7–3), but the items displayed should have a purpose in the curriculum. Do a check of your room. Are there cartoon characters in bright, competing colors on the bulletin board, motivational posters on the walls at heights children cannot see, or fluorescent alphabet letters on the carpet? How many of these things really have a purpose in your curriculum? How many of these things have really been a topic of discussion between you and the children? These items should be removed and replaced with aesthetically pleasing artwork, wall hangings, posters, stained glass panels, or prints that relate

Figure 7–2 Teachers communicate their inner beauty by building loving relationships with children.

Figure 7–3 An aesthetically pleasing bulletin board display of children's artwork.

to your curriculum. For example, Mondrian prints might be displayed during a study of shapes, stained glass for discussions on light and color, and sculpture during a unit on the human body. Change these elements as the focus of your curriculum changes, bringing back old favorites and introducing new pieces. Most importantly, talk to the children about the aesthetic elements in the classroom. Encourage them to state their opinions and explain what they like and dislike. It is during these conversations that children will come to understand the importance of aesthetics and learn to respect the tastes and opinions of others.

Signs on classroom doors or learning centers should be tastefully constructed, with care taken in the choice of color, material, placement, and printing (see Figure 7–4). Utilize windows and take advantage of natural light. Hang up objects that play with the light, including mobiles made of cellophane and children's art. Items suspended near windows create interesting patterns that move and change throughout the day. Adding mirrors gives a feeling of openness and reflects all the beauty in your room. Mirrors can be placed in different centers and even on the ceiling for interesting perspectives. Have the children grow plants indoors. An outdoor flower garden provides flowers to display throughout the room. Think quality rather than quantity.

Young children can have aesthetic experiences in familiar, ordinary places, including their classrooms, if engaging materials are provided (Danko-McGhee, 2009). Aesthetic centers for experiencing literature, art, music, and movement should be included in the classroom. Aesthetically pleasing displays can be set up with the following:

- beautiful things around a given color, shape, pattern, texture, or design theme, such as things that are square, yellow, checkered, or soft
- flowers, plants, nature specimens, or seasonal fruits and vegetables such as harvest corn
- machine and appliance parts, gears, tools, and mechanical things
- musical instruments
- postcards and souvenirs
- ethnic costumes and artifacts
- antique kitchen gadgets and farm tools
- special collections of cookie cutters, baskets, ceramic or stuffed animals, fans, hats, coins, music boxes, minerals, and rocks
- an array of artwork, including drawings, paintings, pottery, ceramics, sculpture, weaving, stitchery, batik, collages, watercolors, and prints (see Figure 7–5)
- art: books, postcards, prints, posters

Figure 7–4 A welcome sign in a multilingual classroom.

© Cengage Learning

Figure 7–5 An aesthetically pleasing center for literacy.

© Cengage Learning

An Opportunity for Teacher Reflection

Every Year, Before School Begins, the children and their parents are invited to preview the classrooms of which they will be a part during the upcoming year. This year, Ms. Epstein has worked hard to make sure her room is ready for the children's visit. The bulletin boards are covered with bright paper and cartoon figures to welcome the children. Posters with positive captions about being friends and working hard adorn every available wall space. Signs identifying all the learning centers in the classroom hang from the ceiling, and, in one corner, Ms. Epstein has created a large papier-mâché tree from which she has hung apples with children's names on them. Ms. Epstein has used part of her supply budget to purchase a large carpet featuring different-colored blocks with letters of the alphabet and numerals for whole-group activities. She is pleased and excited about the comments she receives from visiting parents. "What a beautiful classroom!" they say. "Ms. Epstein is so creative! The children will be so busy and happy here!" But as Ms. Epstein circulates among the parents and children, she is dismayed to hear seven-year-old Joseph say to his mother, "But where is she going to put our stuff? There's no room for kids in here." Ms. Epstein looks around her classroom, trying to see it through Joseph's eyes. *What is she seeing? What would you do if you were Ms. Epstein?*

Did You Get It?

The foremost and possibly most visible way a teacher can be a model for aesthetic awareness and development is

  a. a constant, unwavering smile.
  b. attire.
  c. a beautiful attitude.
  d. a classroom door that is brightly decorated.

Take the full quiz on CourseMate.

DAP naeyc naea) 7-5 Art Appreciation as an Aesthetic Experience

Mulcahey (2009) points out that although making art is a common activity in most early childhood classrooms, talking about art made by adults is much rarer. Place art reproductions in classroom locations where they relate to the children's interests and activities. For example, hang a painting of mothers and children by Mary Cassatt in the house area. Add one of van Gogh's sunflower paintings in the science center. A three-dimensional, recycled junk sculpture could be placed in the block area. An example of abstract art such as one of Jackson Pollock's drip paintings could be displayed in the art center.

Choose art prints that are high quality but simple for children to understand and relate to. Children tend to pay most attention to the colors and subjects in works of art (Davis, 2008). Yenawine (2003) believes that young children are satisfied with finding, naming, listing, counting, and discussing as well as making up stories about what they see in an art print. Images should be simple and recognizable so as not to overwhelm or confuse. Appropriate content includes children, families, pets, animals, familiar objects, actions, and expressions. As children look at artwork, they will make meaning of what they see based on their personal experiences and their previous exposure to art (Mulcahey, 2009). For example, it would be easier for most young children to relate to a print of a laughing child holding a puppy than a lost herder guiding a camel in a desert storm. Stick with the familiar, and avoid art with hidden meanings or requiring knowledge of history to understand and appreciate.

DAP naeyc 7-5a Art in Picture Book Illustrations

Szekely (1990) views children's picture books as works of art. Illustrators, like artists, use different media to visualize their thoughts and words. A precise sketch in **ink** or a realistic painting may work for one book, while a collage or abstract watercolor may work for another. In sharing a beautifully illustrated book with children, you can treat each picture as an artistic creation. Children can freely explore the works in books, in contrast to works in a museum, perhaps carefully running their clean fingers over interesting details. By commenting on the illustrator's use of color, shape, and other artistic elements, art teachers can use books to enhance children's art appreciation skills.

Children can be introduced to the artistic elements by noting illustrations in picture books. Artists who illustrate their own works are in a special position to find the visual image that best reinforces their words. A list of picture books that can be used to help children notice and understand the artistic elements is included in Appendix C. Visit your local public library and check out books by these and other authors. Share these books with young children. Have children notice the way illustrators use different art media to illustrate their books. Encourage children to use a variety of art media when they illustrate their stories and books. Develop your own list of favorite children's authors to add to the list in Appendix C.

Using Picture Book Illustrations to Support Visual Literacy. Beautifully illustrated children's picture books are works of art. Many emergent readers do not naturally focus their attention on the subtle aspects of illustrations. Visual literacy skills can be developed by prompting emergent readers to carefully examine story book illustrations in the following ways:

1. Encourage children to discuss what they see in the illustrations. Asking "What do you see in the picture?" is a good beginning. Use the artistic elements to frame the discussion. Help children to see how the illustrator used color, shape, and line to make a visual statement.

2. Identify and discuss types of artistic media used. Illustrators use a variety of art media including painting, woodcut, linoleum block printing, collage, photography, and drawing. For example, Eric Carle used cut paper collage to illustrate his classic book *The Very Hungry Caterpillar*. He could have used paint or photographs, but the impact would have been different. Painting was the choice of Huy Voun Lee to illustrate *At the Beach*, while Molly Bang used paper to tell her story of *The Paper Crane*. The illustrator's choice of media is key to understanding and appreciating a story.

3. Identify the genre or artistic style used by the illustrator. Illustrators also use different artistic styles. For example, Robert McCloskey's *Make Way for Ducklings* and Judith Viorst's *Alexander and the Terrible, Horrible, No Good, Very Bad Day* both reflect a realistic style of illustration. In *Anno's Journey* by Anno Mitsumasa and *Mr. Rabbit and the Lovely Present* by Charlotte Zolotow, an impressionistic artistic style is used.

This information is pivotal to understanding stories. Older readers can be guided to compare and contrast illustrations. Show how one illustrator can use the same or different techniques and how a book about families can be illustrated in a variety of ways. Encourage children to illustrate their own stories or books using a variety of media.

Tar Beach by Faith Ringgold (1991) gives us the opportunity to examine the connections between picture book illustrations, literacy, and aesthetic analysis. Ringgold's work is particularly noteworthy because she combines narrative text with fabric to weave a rich story to be read both visually and verbally. Begin by providing a visual reproduction of the artwork. Ask children to describe what they see and how it makes them feel. Help them identify and discuss artistic elements including colors, shapes, borders, textures, and patterns. Next, read the picture book in its entirety. Ask the children to compare the art print with the picture book version. Discuss the author's style of illustration. At the end of the discussion, tell the children about the author and artist. Faith Ringgold grew up in Harlem in the 1930s. She personally experienced the prejudices that existed toward African-Americans during this time. This can generate a discussion of prejudice and exclusion. The author was confined to her home because of childhood asthma. Rather than a hardship, she used this opportunity to spend time with her mother, a fashion designer, who taught her how to sew and to be creative with art and fabrics. The result is a series of story quilts. Each section written on the quilt is a page. In *Tar Beach*, the child in her art symbolizes a little girl's dream of flying and changing circumstances for her family. It is a message of optimism, hope, and love. The children learn that Ringgold is a prominent American artist who creates not only quilts but also murals, paintings, abstract works, masks, and soft sculptures. This personal history prompts the children to reread the book, this time focusing on the interplay of words and art as they reflect the details and meanings of the author's life and work.

7-5b Art Visitors

Invite professional artists, musicians, dancers, craftspeople, volunteers, and parents who have interest and skill in one of the arts. Remember to include this when you survey parents at the beginning of the year concerning any interests and skills that they might volunteer. Get to know the artists, musicians, and dance companies in your area. Remember to provide brief training just as you would with any volunteer. Some may feel more comfortable answering questions or modeling their art or craft. Others may enjoy working directly with the children. Prepare the children for art visitors by providing a little background information. Then, help the children brainstorm a list of questions to ask of the visitor and his or her work. Remember to review with the children the difference between telling a story and asking a question.

7-5c Art Trips

In addition to having visitors come into the classroom, it may be possible to take children on a field trip. Art abounds in nature, and a simple outdoor walk qualifies as a recommended field trip. Most communities have at least one of the following to visit: museum, ballet, art gallery, exhibit, concert, planetarium, artist's studio, children's theater, or arboretum.

Brain Connection

With each new learning experience, a child forms new dendrites. These dendrites branch out to connect with hundreds, even thousands of different regions of the brain (Whalen & Phelps, 2009). The stronger these connections are, the stronger and quicker the child's reactions will be when remembering information (Gallagher, 2005).

Video supplied by the BBC Motion Gallery.

▶❚❚ TeachSource Video

The Reggio Emilia Approach (BBC Motion Gallery Video)

After watching this video, describe what you see as key differences between the Reggio approach and American programs for young children.

Watch on CourseMate.

First attend by yourself to make sure that your particular group will profit from the experience. Field trips involve a great deal of planning, energy, and often expense, and they need to be well thought out. In arranging the field trip, try to match what the experience has to offer with your group's developmental needs, interests, and abilities. For example, most toddlers would not sit still through an hour of chamber music. See if there is someone on the staff who has experience in giving tours to young children. Some museums have special children's rooms and exhibits. Others have education centers that loan collections or specific items for use in classrooms. Many libraries have art prints that may be checked out.

Visiting the Art Museum. While many adults are content to spend an afternoon viewing the various exhibits at an art museum, young children are not likely to be so captivated. An early childhood field trip to the art museum requires considerable teacher planning and preparation. First, make a pre–field trip visit by yourself. Identify the individual works that you want your children to view. These should be pieces that the children have seen and talked about in class or at least pieces by the same artists as they have discussed in class. Also, look for artwork that has specific connections to the current curriculum topics in your class: one of Monet's water lily paintings if you are studying pond habitats, a Grandma Moses primitive to relate to your unit on the farm, or a jungle painting by Henri Rousseau to accent learning about the rain forest. Note where these works are located on a map of the museum, and plan a direct route between the works for you and the children to follow during your visit. For three- and four-year-old children, a 30-minute visit to the museum is long enough. Children ages five to eight years might be able to handle 45 minutes. The objective, however, should be to keep the children interested and to

make them want to return for further experiences in art appreciation.

Before the trip, prepare the children by telling them that museums are for looking at artwork and quietly discussing what they see. Remind them that they will not be able to touch the interesting things in the museum, but they can look, ask questions, and share their observations in quiet voices. Even with a reminder, however, young children are likely to forget and give into the temptation to touch a brightly colored piece of pottery or a sculpture with an interesting texture. Invite other adults on your field trip and ask them to supervise small groups of children as you tour.

7-5d Sensory Literacy

Help children become sensory literate. This can be done in two ways. First, help them to stop, sense, and heighten their awareness of the experience at hand. For example, ask a local veterinarian to visit your class with a dog or a cat. Encourage the children to look closely at the animal, to listen to the sounds it makes, to smell its scent, and, with the veterinarian's permission, to touch its fur. Second, stimulate the senses of the children with appropriate experiences.

In a sense, the teacher and classroom quietly whisper, "Beauty, it is all around you. Together we will take time to explore."

SOMETHING EXTRA.....

The Reggio Emilia Experience

Over the past 20 years, there has been a sustained interest in the Reggio Emilia schools reminiscent of the fervor of open education and the British Infant Schools during the 1970s. In our quest for developmentally appropriate practices, an examination of the Reggio Emilia experience should provide inspiration, insight, and direction.

The Reggio Emilia schools of northern Italy reflect a longstanding commitment (over 60 years) to quality education for children and support for families. Loris Malaguzzi, founder of the Reggio Emilia schools, was influenced by the works of Rousseau, Pestalozzi, Froebel, Dewey, Piaget, and Vygotsky, among others. His philosophy and ideology are shared by contemporary American counterparts. Learning is viewed within an interactive-constructivist framework. It is something that children do, not something done to them. Based on Dewey's concept of progressive education, schools should promote children's natural curiosity and creativity as well as active interaction with their community. Children are active learners—exploring, inquiring, problem solving, and representing their experiences in a number of ways.

Gandini (1993) and Gandini et al. (2005) identified the following points, which capture the Reggio Emilia experience.

1. A positive image portrays children as competent, curious learners with prior knowledge and much potential. This contrasts a negative image viewing the child as deficient, disadvantaged, egocentric, and needy. Bredekamp (1993) makes an interesting point. Viewing children as needy permits adults to do the very least for them, while recognizing children as competent requires that we provide them with the best environments and experiences possible. Children are trusted, and respect is mutual.

2. To understand and work with children, they must be viewed within a social context or system that includes teachers, peers, parents, and the community.

3. Children, parents, and teachers form an important triad. All have needs as well as rights. Children have a right to the best education possible.

4. Parent participation is an essential component. It is an ongoing process taking many forms.

5. The school is viewed as amiable in that it is designed to foster communication and social interaction. Because children learn from their peers, activities are done in small groups. This facilitates problem solving, negotiating, and verbal give-and-take. Each child has a communication box in which letters and notes written by other children are exchanged. This gives new meaning and function to cubbies.

6. Time is fluid, not rigidly set by the clock. Children stay with the same teachers and peers for three-year cycles (infancy to three, and three to six). Each year the group changes environments.

7. Teachers are active partners and co-constructors in the learning process. Their role is to observe, participate, and serve as resources to children.

8. Cooperation and organization form the foundation of the educational system. Teachers work in pairs as equals. Cooperative efforts between staff and families facilitate the attainment of goals set by the Reggio Emilia schools.

9. Rather than being planned in advance, the curriculum is emergent, based on teachers' observations of children at play and at work. Ideas for projects and possible learning experiences emerge from these observations.

10. Children are encouraged to pursue themes and projects. This project method originated with Dewey. Ideas for short- and long-term study originate with the children and not from curriculum idea books, nor from state curriculum standards.

11. The *atelierista*, or artist in residence, operates within an atelier or art studio. (See Chapter 13 for a discussion of art centers.) The art studio is stocked with art materials, in transparent containers on open shelves and in bountiful supply. This enables children to autonomously pursue their interests. Children's two- and three-dimensional art is attractively displayed throughout the school.

12. Teachers take seriously their work as observers and researchers. Documenting what children do is an ongoing process taking many forms. Audio and video recorders are everywhere. This strategy resembles authentic assessment in which teachers assemble individual portfolios.

13. Reggio schools use tools that will keep them current with the communities in which children and families live. Technology, in the form of cameras, audio and video recorders, photocopy machines, and computers, provides tools for children in the atelier.

Two more aspects that can be added to Gandini's (1993) list include aesthetics and the use of space, and the concept of 100 languages, as discussed next.

Reggio Emilia schools believe the arrangement of classroom space influences social interactions and facilitates creative expression. Aesthetically pleasing features include big windows, see-through space with glass walls, portholes, and glass partitions for easy supervision. Inside, there are glassed-in courtyards; outside caves are built into playgrounds. Lofts and tiered risers provide varied spatial viewpoints. There are mirrored structures and fountains. There are tablecloths on the tables in the eating area. Aesthetics is an important part of the classroom.

The metaphor of 100 languages represents the child's ability to symbolize what is being learned in a variety of ways. Multi-symbolic representation includes drawing, painting, clay modeling, talking, using numbers, moving, singing, dramatizing, using puppets, and using technology, among other activities. Absent from the list are paper-and-pencil tests, which are developmentally inappropriate ways of finding out what children know and can do.

The Reggio Emilia experience does not come with a set of tricks or tips to make it happen painlessly overnight. The American school experience operates within a very different social and family structure and its own geopolitical and cultural context. However, reading about, discussing, and observing the Reggio Emilia experience can lead practitioners to reflect upon their own teaching and enhance their classroom settings.

Based on the writings of Malaguzzi (1993); Bredekamp (1993); Gandini (1993); Edwards, Gandini, and Forman (1993); Katz (1990); New (1990, 1993); and Gandini et al. (2005).

Did You Get It?

Christine Mulcahey (2009) considers _____ adult-created art to be lacking in the early-education classroom.
   a. the attempted reproduction of
   b. speaking about
   c. examples of
   d. visiting museums to view

Take the full quiz on CourseMate.

Figure 7–6 Display of tempera paintings.

© Cengage Learning

DAP naeyc 7-6 **Watercolor and Ink**

Tempera painting is a prerequisite to painting with watercolor or ink (see Figure 7–6). Using watercolor and ink requires coordination and fine motor control. These media may frustrate the very young artist because the smaller brushes are harder to manage.

7-6a **Personally Expressive Art Activities**

Following are some personally expressive art activities for watercolor and ink.

Kindergarten and School-Age Activity: Watercolor. **Watercolors** tend to be wet, runny, and transparent. Often, they produce unintended results. The wet colors may bleed when the artist is trying to make facial features. Children should begin using watercolors to make lines, colors, shapes, and abstract designs rather than attempting realistic, detailed art. Watercolors come in their own small sets with individual semimoist cakes. Buy a medium grade. The brushes that come with the cheapest sets have bristles that fall out after the first washing.

Watercolors can be used on either wet or dry paper. Watercolors on wet paper will run and bleed into very interesting patterns and designs. Use a sponge or a pump spray bottle to wet the paper. A sponge allows children to blot up excess water or unwanted runs. Special spots can be saturated with water dropped from an eyedropper to make a bull's-eye effect or rainbow of blended colors.

Because there is only one brush for several colors, it is important that children wash their brushes each time they change colors. They will need individual water containers, which should be emptied whenever they appear muddy. When they are done, excess watercolor paint in the set should be carefully blotted. A careful rinse

Liquid watercolors are nontoxic and less expensive than food coloring. They produce a range of secondary colors and shades that cannot be matched by food coloring. Liquid watercolors wash out of most fabrics. The colors are intense, so they can be used in small amounts or diluted as a liquid dye.

under the sink will remove excess paint. Be careful not to merely rinse away the unused paints. Let the set air dry. Sets that are closed when wet tend to get gummy.

Watercolor paper is expensive if purchased separately by the sheet. Purchased in tablet form, it is still moderately expensive. White drawing paper is acceptable. Onionskin or good stock printer paper have a good texture for watercolor. An office with outdated letterhead stationery may have a surplus of this. You could easily trim off the letterhead.

School-Age Activity: Ink. Even young children appreciate the beauty of Chinese pen and ink drawings that capture nature with a minimum of lines. Ink comes in colors other than black and tends to be fairly expensive. One bottle of black may suffice for use with older children. Ink can be economically used on small sheets of paper with thin brushes. It is appropriate for making linear drawings and designs. Ink can also be used in printing and stencil activities. It is not recommended for use at the easel or for general painting.

7-6b Sensory Exploration Activities

Following are some sensory exploration activities for watercolor and ink.

Kindergarten and School-Age Activity: Tissue Paper Water Coloring. Tear tissue paper into 1-inch squares and separate by color. Fill clear containers with water. Add squares and use a brush to mix. The dye from the paper will bleed into the water. Children discover that adding more squares of the same color strengthens the intensity of that color. Children can also creatively mix colors. You may want to begin by providing the three primary colors. Children can paint with the resulting colored water (see Figure 7–7).

Preschool and Kindergarten Activity: Spray Bottle Watercoloring. Collect child-sized clear spray bottles with a trigger-type release. Fill each with water and add a few drops of liquid watercolor. Show children how to pump the release while aiming at their papers. Provide large pieces of paper and art smocks. This is a good activity to do outdoors. Use clothespins to attach the papers to a fence, or tape them to the cement.

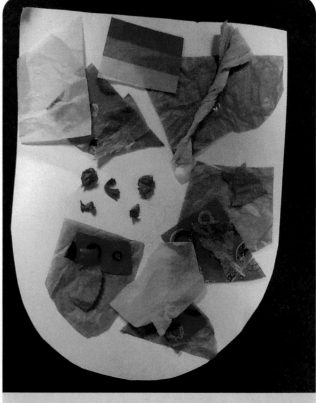

Photo Courtesy of Jill Englebright Fox

Figure 7–7 A tissue paper collage.

Kindergarten and School-Age Activity: Coffee Filter Creations. Provide containers of water to which liquid watercolor has been added. Children can fold a coffee filter and dip it into one color, squeeze, and select other colors if they choose. Open the coffee filter and lay out flat to dry on newspaper (see Figure 7–8). Indicate child's name on masking tape near his or her filter. When dry, provide a pipe cleaner for those children who want to fashion their filters into flowers, butterflies, bows, or creative creations. Vary the activity by providing absorbent paper towels.

School-Age Activity: Dye (Water-Based). Traditionally, dye activities involve the use of food colors, which tend to be expensive, limited in color-range, and stain hands and clothing. Liquid watercolors avoid these pitfalls and can be used as substitutes for food colors.

Kindergarten and School-Age: Dribble Dye. Provide each child with a heavyweight, white paper towel. Encourage him or her to fold it into squares. Provide small bottles of food coloring or liquid watercolor. Children very carefully squeeze small dots or dabs of different colors on the corners, edges, or middle section. Use just enough to bleed through. Open up to reveal a colorful design. Let dry.

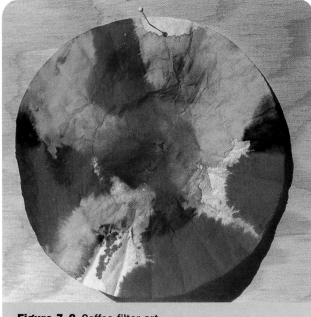

Figure 7–8 Coffee filter art.

Photo Courtesy of Robert Schirrmacher

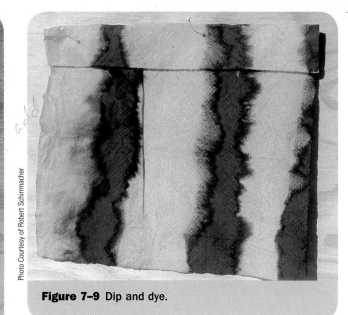

Figure 7–9 Dip and dye.

Photo Courtesy of Robert Schirrmacher

Kindergarten and School-Age: Dip and Dye. Provide a white, heavyweight paper towel for each child. You will also need different colors of dye. Place a few drops of food coloring or liquid watercolor in a small dish or container of water. Adding more drops will make colors darker. Different colors can be poured into the different openings in a muffin tin. Encourage children to fold their paper towels into squares. Different folds (horizontal, vertical, diagonal, and random) will produce different effects. Carefully dip the corner or edge into one color. Gently squeeze out the excess. Dip a second small area into a different color. Colors can also be mixed. For example, dip the towel in yellow and then in red. Orange will result. Dry on layers of newspaper. These can be taped over windows for a colorful effect. They can also be carefully taped together to form a quilt, banner, or backdrop for a bulletin board (see Figure 7–9).

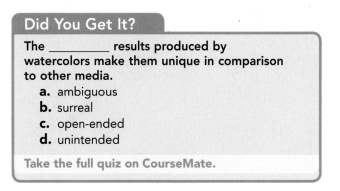

Did You Get It?

The _____ results produced by watercolors make them unique in comparison to other media.

   a. ambiguous

   b. surreal

   c. open-ended

   d. unintended

Take the full quiz on CourseMate.

Summary

(7-1) Aesthetics can be defined as an appreciation or love of beauty. (7-2) Aesthetics and young children go hand in hand. Babies begin by exploring and marveling at their world. Over time, children internalize adult "don'ts" and learn not to look, listen, touch, taste, or smell. They take their senses and the world of lines, shapes, colors, and design for granted. (7-3) Children's understanding of art also changes as they mature. As preschoolers, they believe art is simplistic and focus on colors and subjects. Later, in elementary school, children believe art should be realistic. Teenagers come to understand that judgments in art are relative and that their opinions are valid. (7-4) Our task as early childhood teachers is a multipurpose one. We need to stimulate children's senses; be aesthetic models in dress, behavior, and communication; and set up sensory-rich and appealing learning environments. (7-5) We can support children's development of art appreciation by exposing them to art and encouraging them to form opinions about what they see and feel. (7-6) Art activities with watercolor and ink provide personally expressive and sensory experiences but may be more appropriate for older children.

Key Terms

aesthetic attitude, 142

aesthetic process/experience, 142

aesthetic response, 142

aesthetic value, 142

aesthetics, 141

atelierista, 150

ink, 147

Reggio Emilia, 150

sensory literacy, 149

watercolors, 151

✓ Suggested Activities

1. Reflect on your most recent or vivid aesthetic experience. Sketch it or attempt to put it into words. Describe how you felt and your reaction.

2. Critique the use of indoor classroom space for its aesthetic appeal. Make specific recommendations.

3. Research a local library or museum to discover available resources for teacher use in the classroom. Consider how you might use these resources in your own classroom.

4. Set up an aesthetically pleasing display of objects that have sensory appeal.

5. Arrange an aesthetic experience through a simple field trip such as a nature walk.

6. Begin a collection of photos depicting beautiful learning environments. Note aesthetically pleasing learning centers and displays. This will serve as a resource of ideas when you have your own classroom.

7. Select a children's picture book. Use the three steps discussed earlier in this chapter to engage in a discussion of illustrations.

8. Facilitate a watercolor or ink activity with children.

Review

1. Explain aesthetics as an attitude, process/experience, and a response.

2. List five aspects of the teacher's role as it relates to aesthetics.

3. Briefly discuss the role of art in the Reggio Emilia experience.

4. Identify and describe the developmental stages in children's understanding of art.

5. Identify and describe the developmental stages in how individuals come to make a critical judgment of art.

6. Explain what the authors mean by "expose, not impose" as it relates to children and art.

Additional Resources

Aesthetics Online (www.aesthetics-online.org/) is the official website for the American Society for Aesthetics.

Exploring the meaning of the term "aesthetics" is a lesson on the website "Learning about Art: A Multicultural Approach."

Go to YouTube for a brief video, "Perspectives on Art," from the Aesthetics and Values Film Festival.

Go to Big Think for the blog entry, "The Evolution of Aesthetics: The Origins of Music and Visual Art."

 Visit CourseMate for this textbook to access the eBook, Did You Get It? quizzes, Digital Downloads, TeachSource Videos, flashcards, and more. Go to CengageBrain.com to log in, register, or purchase access.

Pre-Kindergarten Lesson Plan

The Life Cycle in Monet's Pond

GOAL

The student knows that organisms resemble their parents and have structures and processes that help them survive within their environments.

OUTCOMES

The student is expected to:

a. investigate how the external characteristics of an animal are related to where it lives, how it moves, and what it eats.
b. compare ways that young animals resemble their parents.
c. paint a mural of Monet's pond.

MATERIALS

a. *Once Upon a Lily Pad* by Joan Sweeney
b. Photos of the life cycle of a frog
c. Watercolor paints, brushes, and white butcher paper for a mural

INTRODUCTION

Show the cover of the book to the children and ask them to look carefully to see what the book is about. Tell them, today we will be studying the animals that are on the cover (frogs). Provide a focus for listening by telling them that you will ask them to explain how frogs grow and change as they get older.

DEVELOPMENT

Read the book. Ask children to identify characteristics of the pond in which the frogs live: what plants do they see in the illustration? What other animals? What are the frogs eating? And of whom are the frogs afraid and why? Go through the book a second time and ask questions about the illustrations that show the frogs as they grow. Help the children identify the stages as eggs, tadpoles, pollywogs, and adult frogs. Show children photos of the stages of the frog's life cycle. Ask children to put them in the right sequence and to appropriately name each stage.

CONCLUSION

Show the children the painting of Monet's water lilies at the end of the book. Tell them that we will be painting our own version of the Monet's pond. Distribute the watercolors and spread the chart paper. Ask the children paint their versions of the pond. Encourage them to include the frogs from the story. As they finish, ask them to identify the life cycle stage they chose to include in the mural.

ASSESSMENT

a. Did the children identify characteristics of the frogs' habitat?
b. Did the children identify and then sequence the stages of the frog's life cycle?
c. Did the children participate in painting a mural?

A full-size version of this lesson plan, and others like it, is available for digital download.

8 Sensory Experiences

© Cengage Learning

Do these boys seem to be enjoying themselves?

What kinds of experiences are they having? How are they engaged in the activity? How many of their senses are being stimulated? Pretend you are the teacher supervising this activity. Along with providing hay and toy animals, what could you say to help these children reflect on what they are seeing, touching, and hearing? What props could you add to enhance the creative potential of this activity? Would bandanas or wooden blocks be appropriate?

Learning Outcomes

After reading this chapter, you should be able to:

8-1 Discuss the relationship among sensing, perceiving, feeling, thinking, and concept development.

8-2 List and briefly explain the different senses.

8-3 Identify three major learning styles and select the one(s) that best describes the way you learn.

8-4 Develop a multisensory learning activity for young children.

8-5 Provide art activities based on the process called resist.

Standards addressed in this chapter

DAP Criteria

2 Teaching to enhance development and learning

3 Planning to achieve important goals

4 Assessing children's development and learning

NAEYC Standards

2 Curriculum

3 Teaching

4 Assessment

NAEA Visual Arts Standards

1 Understanding and applying media, techniques, and processes

8-1 From Percept to Concept

Young children use their senses to process aesthetic experiences. They are sensory gluttons who are motivated to look, touch, listen to, taste, and smell everything in their environment. They respond on both the affective and cognitive levels. For example, they not only experience pleasure in looking at and smelling flowers but also construct an understanding of what flowers are. We hope young children with well-developed aesthetic senses will grow up to be wise consumers and planners for a better future that includes beauty and peace.

Perception is the ability to receive sensory impressions from the environment and relate them to what is known. Sensing, perceiving, thinking, and developing concepts are closely related. The aesthetic experience merges the cognitive with the affective response. Thinking and feeling come together. For example, when children hear bells chime in a church, they may perceive the sound, smile with amazement, think about it, and relate it to the doorbell at home. The process can be depicted as:

Sense +	Perception +	Feeling +	Thinking =	Concepts
visual	look	enjoy	compare	color
auditory	listens	marvel	contrast	tone
tactile	touch	joy	analyze	texture
oifactory	smell	happy	classify	scent
gustatory	taste	amazed	describe	flavor

A child with a sensory special need or deficit may miss stimuli. Often, such children develop strengths in other areas. For example, a blind child often develops a strong sense of touch or hearing. A child who does not invest time in perceptual activity or who lacks sensory stimulation is also disadvantaged. A child who has never touched, looked at, smelled, or listened to an elephant will be lost when asked to discuss or draw elephants.

Did You Get It?

Perception of stimuli inherent in seeing, feeling, hearing, and smelling involves the reception of information from the environment and relating it to what is
a. real.
b. known.
c. expected.
d. supposed.

Take the full quiz on CourseMate.

8-2 More Than Five Senses

Children use their senses to explore their environment. Traditionally, the five senses are:

1. visual
2. auditory
3. tactile
4. olfactory
5. gustatory

To this list, Montessori (1967) adds the following senses:

6. chromatic
7. thermic
8. sterognostic
9. baric
10. kinesthetic

Each of these senses will be explained and exemplified with activities.

Did You Get It?

The five human senses are formally called olfactory, tactile, visual, auditory, and
a. gustatory.
b. transitory.
c. auricular.
d. redolent.

Take the full quiz on CourseMate.

DAP naeyc 8-3 Children's Learning Styles

Sensory integration, the way we interpret our surroundings through our senses, allows us to organize and explore our environment (Hunter, 2008). Young children use all their senses to discover and make meaning of their world. They also have one or more preferred sensory modalities, favoring their visual, auditory, or tactile-kinesthetic sense. In turn, they are referred to as visual, auditory, or tactile-kinesthetic learners.

Children with **visual** strengths tend to be holistic thinkers. They learn the big picture, not individual pieces. They prefer visual images such as pictures to words. Photos, charts, and graphs give visual clues. They like to read, write, or draw about what they learn and are interested in the finished product.

Children with **auditory** strengths think analytically and are good at speaking and listening. They enjoy discussing what they know and learn from listening to others. They easily follow oral directions and move sequentially from task to task.

An Opportunity for Teacher Reflection

Pat Is Preparing for a Conference with the parents of Andrew, one of her kindergarten students. Although Pat has been teaching for almost 30 years, she finds Andrew be an interesting challenge. Even when he is seated on the floor during group time, Andrew is in constant motion, rising to his knees, leaning back on his elbows, and waving his arms. When the class is working at their tables, Andrew stands beside his chair, frequently darting off to see what other classmates are doing. Pat observes that Andrew's writing and artwork are messy, careless, and don't reflect what he knows and can do. The only time that Andrew is focused and on-task is center time, when Andrew usually chooses to work in either the blocks or the manipulatives center. Pat has several photos of Andrew's block constructions that she believes show his ability to concentrate, plan, and problem-solve much more accurately than does his written or art work. She is concerned about a possible learning disability and has

called this conference to discuss her observations with Andrew's parents.

During the conference, Pat shares photos, other work samples, and her observations that much of Andrew's work does not reflect his knowledge or abilities. Pat and Andrew's mother are sitting at a table where they can examine the work Pat collected. But Andrew's father moves around the room restlessly, stopping to feed carrots to the class pet and to pick up several display items in the science center. He is attentive to what Pat and his wife are saying and asks relevant questions, but he obviously isn't comfortable sitting down for this discussion. As she interacts with Andrew's parents, Pat begins to rethink her concerns about Andrew in light of what she knows about learning styles. *Through this interaction with Andrew's parents, what is Pat learning about Andrew? What questions might she ask Andrew's parents to help her clarify her observations? And, most importantly, how can she best meet Andrew's learning needs in the classroom?*

Children with **tactile-kinesthetic** strengths prefer using their hands and bodies to learn. They are holistic learners who thrive on hands-on activity to get the big picture. They learn by doing and dislike sitting still and listening to someone teaching them verbally. For example, during math they may move around while thinking, relying on their fingers and manipulatives.

DAP naeyc 8-3a **Adult Teaching Styles**

Teachers, in turn, use their own preferred learning styles when teaching. Their individual learning strengths become their **teaching styles**. We teach in ways compatible and consistent with how we learn. For example, a teacher who is a visual learner will use books and printed information to teach. Children will be required to read and write. A teacher who is an auditory learner will rely on teaching verbally and engaging children in discussion. A teacher who is a tactile-kinesthetic learner will use manipulative materials, role playing, creative dramatics, and hands-on activity to facilitate discovery learning.

DAP naeyc 8-3b **Matching Adult Teaching Styles with Children's Learning Styles**

What are the implications? First, recognize that children learn in different ways and discover individual children's preferred learning styles. Are they visual, auditory, tactile-kinesthetic, or a combination of these?

Second, recognize how adults' teaching styles are influenced by their own learning styles. Third, capitalize on how individual children learn and teach to their preferred learning styles. Fourth, teach in ways that honor varied learning styles. For example, teaching children about guinea pigs would include verbal discussions, visual displays, and a real guinea pig for multisensory experiences (see Figure 8–1). Fifth, help children develop competence in weaker sensory modalities. Lasky and Mukerji-Bergeson (2003) caution teachers that bombarding children's sensibilities with various media will do little to build awareness of the differences in what they hear and see. Carefully

Figure 8–1 Learning about a guinea pig.

© Cengage Learning

designed activities that provide intriguing (but not overwhelming) sensory stimuli are needed to help children develop in all learning styles.

8-3c Art and Children's Learning Styles

How does our discussion of learning styles pertain to children's art? Visual learners will be drawn to the visual arts, whereas auditory learners may prefer music. Tactile-kinesthetic learners will enjoy art activities such as finger painting or squishing play dough. Visual learners have no trouble imagining pictures in their heads, which they draw upon as content for their art. They work on the totality of their pictures rather than focusing on component parts. For example, in making a house, they will focus on the entire shape and then add details. These children are interested in their finished artistic products. Auditory learners do not rely on mental pictures. They sequentially make pictures by mastering individual parts and pieces. For example, they make a house by working on parts and details like a door, windows, and chimney. Observing children as they engage in art activities gives teachers valuable information about learning styles. Teachers are able to identify strengths and areas that need to be strengthened by appropriate sensory experiences through such observations (Hunter, 2008).

What can be done for children whose learning strengths do not predispose them to seek out art? When possible, invite these children to participate in activities that are *outside* their sensory strengths. For example, the child with auditory strengths who avoids art could be invited to make a picture related to an audio book or to express visual images related to a favorite song.

Did You Get It?

A young child who is adept at using her visual abilities to see, take in, and make interpretations of the world around her might be considered a _____ thinker.
- **a.** "transfixed"
- **b.** "composite"
- **c.** "holistic"
- **d.** "kinesthetic"

Take the full quiz on CourseMate.

DAP naeyc 8-4 Multisensory Experiences

Most experiences involve more than one sense. Cooking is a good example of a **multisensory experience**. Making popcorn involves looking at and touching the kernels before, during, and after popping; listening to the sound of popcorn popping; smelling the scent of popcorn as it pops; and eating popcorn. Children also enjoy moving like popcorn popping, starting off as small, compact "kernels" that slowly expand and puff up as they heat. A coconut has a distinctive color, shape, covering, texture, and taste. Children look at the outside of a coconut and discuss its color, size, shape, and covering. They open the coconut to examine and taste the meat inside. The same process can be done with many other food experiences.

Field trips are also good opportunities for children to use their senses. For example, pretend it is the end of summer. How could you begin planning for the upcoming change of season and fall holidays? For some, thoughts turn to the harvest, and images of pumpkins come to mind. Wonderful books, songs, flannel board stories, and fingerplays are available. For art, some teachers provide large sheets of pumpkin-shaped paper and have children paint them orange. But are these activities the best introduction to the season? First, the teacher should consider what children really know about pumpkins. Perhaps they have seen pumpkins at the store and think that is where pumpkins "live" or are raised. Children may be able to explain that a jack-o'-lantern is a pumpkin that has been carved. The questions remain: What do children really know about pumpkins, and what is the best way to begin a study of pumpkins? The photo in Figure 8–2 documents a field trip to a pumpkin patch. Here, children got a firsthand look at where pumpkins are grown. Based on the photo, what opportunities might children have for using their visual, auditory, and tactile senses on this field trip?

Photo Courtesy of Jill Englebright Fox

Figure 8–2 A field trip provides multisensory experiences.

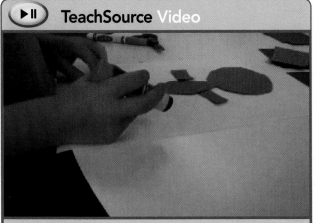

TeachSource Video

Exploring Math Concepts Through Creative Activities

After watching the video, consider the following questions independently or as a group.

a. In this video, children engage in learning activities related to shapes. How many of the activities were multisensory? Which senses were involved?

b. Which learning style do you think was dominant in this classroom—visual, auditory, or tactile-kinesthetic?

c. What shape activities might you include to develop the chromatic sense (discussed in Section 8-4f, The Chromatic Sense) as described by Montessori?

d. What did you see in this classroom that you would like to include in your classroom? Why?

Watch on CourseMate.

Yes, the children got to look at and touch the pumpkins on the vines. The teacher called attention to the sounds of the wind rustling and the smell of the damp soil. Later, in the classroom, the children were involved in carving and cleaning pumpkins, scooping pulp, and seeds. Seeds were baked and tasted along with pumpkin foods including bread and pie. Now, all the books, songs, flannel board stories, fingerplays, and art activities about pumpkins make sense. The multisensory field experience was a concrete and developmentally appropriate starting point for the study of pumpkins.

8-4a Visual Sense

The **visual** sense involves looking and seeing. Ideally, it involves a thorough visual exploration rather than a passing glance. Visual perception and discriminating between letters and words are required for reading and writing.

The indoor classroom should be visually rich and appealing, with nature specimens, artifacts, and objects to visually explore. Samples of children's art as well as art posters are displayed on the walls. A discovery table displays collections of seashells, antique kitchen items, or postcards to visually explore.

DAP **naeyc** Recommended materials to encourage visual exploration include:

- prisms
- magnifying glasses: handheld and three-legged stool or stand
- safety mirrors: handheld and full length
- lenses: concave and convex (making things bigger or smaller)
- microscope and slides (see Figure 8–3)
- telescope
- kaleidoscope
- binoculars
- camera
- cellophane color paddles
- sunglasses
- flashlight

Water play with bubbles is a simple visual activity. Provide a tub of water, liquid dishwashing soap, and rotary

Figure 8–3 A microscope in the science center will encourage children's visual exploration of objects.

eggbeaters. Food coloring is optional. A related activity is blowing bubbles outdoors. Children enjoy trying to catch them. Encourage them to note the transparent quality of bubbles as well as the rainbow of colors.

DAP **naeyc** Following are more visual activities.

Toddler, Preschool, Kindergarten, and School-Age Activity: New View. Encourage children to view indoor and outdoor environments from new perspectives. What do you see when you:

- lie on your back outdoors on the grass? What appears in the sky? What shapes are in the clouds?
- climb to the top of the playscape and look down or up?
- stand on your head?
- are swinging on the swing? What colors and shapes appear?

Infant, Toddler, Preschool, Kindergarten, and School-Age Activity: Nature Walk. Take children on a nature walk. Older children might take magnifying glasses with them, but infants and toddlers will just need you to point out interesting things to see. Look for interesting shapes and designs in nature. Stop to:

- look at moss, berries, insects, mushrooms, nests, tree stumps, shadows, birds, spiderwebs, and ant hills.
- listen to birds chirping, leaves rustling, wind blowing, dogs, cats, squirrels, twigs cracking, and acorns or nuts falling.
- touch tree bark, damp moss, dry leaves, sand, and cold mud.
- smell evergreen trees, pinecones and needles, damp earth, dry leaves, and crisp, cold air.

Collect specimens to bring back to the discovery table. (Some teachers prefer to leave the natural environment intact and not remove bugs, leaves, or twigs.)

Kindergarten and School-Age Activity: Focus Scopes. It is sometimes difficult to notice design and detail in an environment alive with color, shape, sound, and movement. Children may need help focusing. This is why magnifying glasses, cameras, binoculars, and telescopes are recommended. An empty tissue roll makes a good focus scope. Decorate the outside to enhance its appeal. Encourage children to examine indoor and outdoor environments by very slowly exploring with the focus scopes. Pay attention to small things that might be missed by just looking. Focus scopes can also be covered with cellophane at one end and used like color paddles. Children may join their fingers to make a focus frame or use a precut mat for framing a picture.

naeyc **Preschool, Kindergarten, and School-Age Activity: Art Postcards.** Wolf (1988, 1990) applied the skills of matching, pairing, and sorting using postcards showing art masterpieces. The sequence for using art postcards is:

Step 1. Match identical paintings. Children match three identical pairs. Pairs are gradually added until they can match six pairs.

Step 2. Pair similar paintings by an artist. Children pair companion paintings, two paintings by the same artist that are not identical but similar in subject matter and style. An example would be two paintings of birds by Audubon.

Step 3. Group paintings by an artist. Children begin grouping four paintings by each of three different artists. For example, they begin with highly contrasting subjects—four still lifes by Cezanne, four abstract works by Kandinsky, and four paintings of people by Goya.

Step 4. Children refer to control cards to match the last name of artists with their paintings. After repeating the exercise several times, the children attempt to match the name cards to paintings without using the control cards.

Step 5. Control cards are used to learn the names of famous paintings.

Step 6. Children are introduced to paintings grouped according to schools of art.

Step 7. Children put paintings into rows corresponding to the school of art to which they belong.

Step 8. Use of a time line: A large number of paintings of one subject—children, for example—are placed beside a time line according to their dates. When completed, the line graphically illustrates the development of painting through the centuries.

Preschool, Kindergarten, and School-Age Activity: I Spy. This activity involves both looking and listening and can be played with a large group. Focus on an item in the room that has a distinct color or shape. Say, for example, "I spy something bright red. What could it be?" Children may need additional clues. "It is bright red only on the front. The back is white. What could it be?" Or, "I spy something on the wall with a triangle shape. What could it be?" Children enjoy being the leader for this activity. Encourage them to use color or shape clues rather than merely saying, "I spy something on the wall that ticks. What is it?"

8-4b The Auditory Sense

The auditory sense involves hearing and listening, which are two very different processes. Children who hear do not always listen. Children are exposed to much auditory stimulation and learn at an early age to tune much of it out. Casual hearing is appropriate much of the time. Music, literature, or a teacher's directions warrant concentrated listening. Our aim is to help children know when to switch from passive hearing to active listening.

DAP **naeyc** Recommended objects to foster active listening include the following:

- stethoscope
- audio recordings of stories, rhymes, and poems
- CD player with music and story CDs
- rhythm instruments (see Figure 8–4)
- tuning fork
- music boxes
- bells
- metronome

Activities are described in the next sections.

Infant, Toddler, Preschool, Kindergarten, and School-Age Activity: Quiet Time. Quiet time can be a relaxation technique after a noisy activity. Gather children and have them sit quietly. They may giggle at first but will improve with practice. Encourage them to close their eyes and listen. "What do you hear? Think about the sounds but do not talk yet. Let's keep on listening to the noises inside our bodies and around the classroom." Wait a few seconds or minutes, depending on the group. Children may hear their hearts beating, blood flowing, stomachs grumbling, throats swallowing, lungs breathing, or the classroom pet moving about.

Figure 8–4 Playing with rhythm band instruments gives children opportunities for listening and processing.

Toddler, Preschool, Kindergarten, and School-Age Activity: Sounds around Us. Record distinct sounds. Pause between sounds. Play the sounds back, and encourage children to quietly listen (not just hear) and guess what made the sound. Children may want to close their eyes to help focus exclusively on the sounds without distracting visual stimuli. Toddlers, who often know but cannot verbalize, may enjoy hearing sounds and pointing to corresponding pictures.

Kindergarten and School-Age Activity: Water Sounds. Children can listen to sounds and make music in containers filled with one to the top with water, another halfway, and the third a half-inch from the bottom. Different amounts of water will make sounds of different pitch when the bottle is struck with a metal spoon. Practice making sounds that vary in volume (soft and loud) depending on how lightly you strike. Which makes the highest pitch? Which makes the lowest pitch? Encourage children to seriate the sounds from low to high. Children will enjoy playing music. They may want to incorporate their water sounds with music made on rhythm instruments. Additional bottles with different water levels can gradually be added. Close supervision is needed as children experiment with glass containers.

Infant, Toddler, Preschool, Kindergarten, and School-Age Activity: Listen Along. Children enjoy being read to, and this is an important way to encourage their love of literature. Be animated and stress words and phrasing. Encourage children to listen for rhyming words. Storytelling with props, such as puppets or a flannel board, allows you to dramatize the storyline while making continual eye contact. It also encourages children's involvement.

8-4c The Tactile Sense

The **tactile** sense involves feeling and touch. Often, the tactile sense operates in conjunction with the visual sense. Activities that involve touching and feeling textures are categorized as tactile. Those involving touching to identify, recognize, and name an object without looking are categorized as **sterognostic** (they are covered in a later section). A **sensory table** is a great way to support development of children's tactile sense. The table can be filled with items that have tactile and visual appeal and the contents rotated over time. Play at the sensory table encourages children to develop skills through exploration and experimentation. They use their senses to notice similarities and differences between materials and to make connections between new experiences and what they already know. Teachers can use open-ended questions to encourage children's exploration (Hunter, 2008). "What does this feel like? What words can you use to describe what you feel and

Brain Connection

Sensory stimulation, touch, speech, and personal caregiving have been identified as essential needs for children forming attachments to primary caregivers. Lack of such attachment is related to delayed speech and language development during the toddler years (Twardoswz, 2012).

what you see?" Although toddlers enjoy exploring at the sensory table, small items may be problematic because they tend to put everything in their mouths. Provide close supervision, and use only larger items for the very young. An expensive sensory table is not needed. Use a wading pool, baby bathtub, or large basin. Depending on the contents, add small people, vehicles, and animals as well as kitchen utensils and a variety of containers to foster complex sensory play (see Figure 8–5).

Infant and Toddler Activity: Touching Tour. Holding the infant or toddler, walk around the room touching different items. Place the child's fingers on the item. Identify each item and describe how it feels.

Preschool, Kindergarten, and School-Age Activity: Fabric Feel. Children wear blindfolds or close their eyes for this activity. Provide identical swatches of fabrics such as burlap, velvet, terrycloth, vinyl, corduroy, or carpet. Remember to make the size of the swatches the same so that the only clues are tactile. Encourage children to discuss their matched pairs. How do they feel? What word tells us? Are they soft, smooth, rough, wrinkly, or bumpy?

Kindergarten and School-Age Activity: How Does It Feel? Discuss with children how different things feel hard or soft (see Figure 8–6). Encourage them to give examples. Neatly print "hard" and "soft" on separate sheets of paper. Encourage children to say the words after you. Place a picture of something hard and something soft on the corresponding papers. Encourage children to put the following items under the proper headings:

- cotton
- velvet
- stone
- coin
- plush stuffed animal
- wet or dry sponge
- powder puff
- sandpaper
- rubber squeeze toy
- tree bark
- cactus
- yarn ball
- plastic
- emery board
- steel wool

© Cengage Learning

Figure 8–5 A sensory table encourages children to explore with all of their senses.

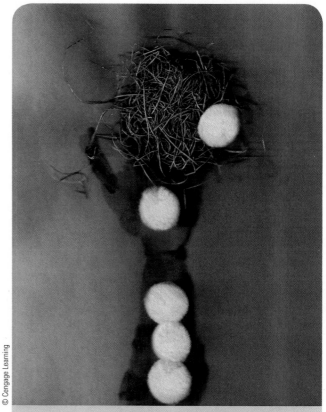

© Cengage Learning

Figure 8–6 Different textures can be part of artwork.

Young children enjoy sorting actual objects. Older children enjoy cutting pictures of hard and soft objects from magazines and pasting them onto the corresponding sheet. They also expand their tactile vocabulary to include rough, smooth, slick, bumpy, prickly, fuzzy, furry, porous, and coarse.

Toddler, Preschool, Kindergarten, and School-Age Activity: Texture Collage. Children enjoy pasting or gluing objects with varied textures into a collage. The group can also work on a thematic collage containing both pictures from magazines and actual objects that are rough, smooth, sharp, fuzzy, or furry. Provide sturdy cardboard for the background when gluing heavy objects.

8-4d The Olfactory Sense

Although animals rely heavily on the sense of smell, people do not. We use our sense of smell on a limited basis, such as to smell food or cologne or to react to unpleasant odors. Children use their sense of smell more than adults (see Figure 8–7). For example, they enjoy scratch-and-sniff stickers. Still, they may refuse to try a food solely on the basis of its smell. Green, yellow, and orange vegetables hold little olfactory appeal for some children. Some activities to stimulate the olfactory sense are:

DAP **naeyc** **Toddler, Preschool, Kindergarten and School-Age Activity: Scent Bottles.** Find a set of identical containers with lids or tops. Empty spice bottles or film containers are ideal. Make four, five, or six pairs. Color code the lids in each set—for example, six green and six orange. Place a ball of cotton in each pair if you are using liquid scents or extracts. Make air holes in the lids if solids are used. Fill each pair with a scented substance such as cinnamon, vanilla, mustard, coffee, or baby powder. Cotton balls soaked in

Figure 8–7 Children use their sense of smell more often than adults.

clear liquids or extracts provide no visual clues. Scents should be fresh and must be replaced periodically. Remind children to replace lids after use. Items like coffee or tea cannot be used in clear containers because the cue will be visual rather than olfactory. Remind children to sniff lightly rather than inhale deeply or taste. Match pairs that smell the same. Use a word to describe how each one smells. Is it sweet, sour, or spicy?

Toddler, Preschool, Kindergarten, and School-Age Activity: It Smells Good Enough to Eat. The olfactory and gustatory senses work together. In general, foods that smell good taste good. Encourage children to close their eyes while you hold a piece of food on a toothpick under their noses. Pause long enough for them to sniff without making skin contact. A piece of banana is one example. Next, hold a different food, such as a pineapple chunk. Do they smell the same or different? Encourage children to match an array of fruits or vegetables on a plate in front of them with your standard. The finale to the activity is eating the samples for snack.

The classroom can also be an olfactory-rich environment. It should be free of stale, musty smells. Spraying with a disinfectant or air freshener may eliminate or mask stale odors. Fresh air and routinely airing out the classroom are essential. Teachers can add scents and aromas. A bowl of rose petals, pine needles, sachet, incense, dried orange rinds, scented soaps, or potpourri provides a lovely fragrance. Flowers such as roses, mums, and carnations, as well as scented candles and perfume samples, also encourage children to stop and smell. The following recipe can be used to produce a cinnamon scent in your room:

> Soak several whole cinnamon sticks in cinnamon oil. Dry. Tie together with dried flowers in a bundle. Add pretty ribbon or lace. The fragrance of cinnamon should last for months.

Children enjoy sticking whole cloves into oranges pierced with holes. Tie with a ribbon and hang. They can be taken home as gifts.

DAP **naeyc** 8-4e The Gustatory Sense

Eating home-cooked meals has become a luxury in many households. Many children never see their parents cook a meal. Meals are now eaten on the run or even skipped. Convenience foods may be bland, precooked, or low in nutritional value. Eating occurs out of habit and routine rather than for gustatory or taste appeal. Eating is something done at different times by each family member, perhaps in front of the television, or merely something children do before going to bed. Perhaps this is why most early childhood educators value snack time and cooking as a time to socialize and share food and experiences (see Figure 8–8). Following are some gustatory activities.

Figure 8–8 Healthy snacks provide enjoyable gustatory experiences.

Figure 8–9 Children's literature can lead to multisensory classroom cooking activities.

Preschool, Kindergarten, and School-Age Activity: Snacks and Cooking. Snacks should be more than crackers and sugary juice. Although they are moderately expensive, nutritious snacks provide their own characteristic look, color, shape, texture, taste, smell, and sound when eaten. Recommended snacks include fresh or dried fruit, raw vegetables, cheese, yogurt, and whole grain crackers.

Cooking experiences using nutritious ingredients and with much child input are highly recommended. For example, children can be actively involved in baking bread, a multisensory cooking activity that involves learning across curricular areas. To bake bread, one must read a recipe and measure ingredients. Children are actively involved in kneading dough. Is it magic or science that makes the dough rise? Bread baking has a wonderful aroma and an equally good taste when eaten with homemade butter. Cooking with apples provides unlimited possibilities for learning and eating. Apples can be cut, peeled, pared, or baked, or the slices can be dipped in melted cheese.

Many early childhood teachers integrate classroom cooking activities into their language arts curriculum (see Figure 8–9). Choosing a book with a cooking theme to read aloud encourages children to develop listening comprehension skills. Following a recipe to create the food item in the book provides opportunities for children to read and comprehend print, sequence activities, and learn new vocabulary. The cooking itself allows children to explore math and science principles with all of their senses. Several books that lend themselves to cooking activities include:

Green Eggs and Ham, by Dr. Seuss

Feast for 10, by Cathryn Falwell

Pancakes, Pancakes!, by Eric Carle

> ▶❚❚ **TeachSource** Video
>
>
>
> **Preschool Cooking**
>
> Using the video as a model, explain how you might organize the activity of preparing a snack to go with a book in cooking stations.
>
> **Watch on CourseMate.**

Stone Soup, by Marcia Brown

Chicken Soup with Rice: A Book of Months, by Maurice Sendak

Toddler, Preschool, Kindergarten, and School-Age Activity: Taste Party. Children can sample an array of foods, classifying them as sweet, sour, hot, cold, or salty. Bitter, bland, and spicy may be difficult for young children. They can be added as children master the basic tastes. Each child will need his or her own spoon. Using an eyedropper, place a drop of a sweet substance (for example, sugar water) onto each child's spoon. Encourage them to think about the taste before guessing. They should wipe their spoon and take a drink of water from their own cups between tastes. Repeat the procedure using salt water. Sample tastes include the following:

- sugar water
- orange juice
- salt water
- lemon juice
- chocolate syrup
- cinnamon
- vinegar water
- maple syrup

Solids can also be introduced at a taste party. Try using these:

- chocolate chips
- cheese chunks
- carrot cubes
- cinnamon candy
- apple squares
- cottage cheese
- banana slices
- melon balls

Remember to check for food allergies before any food experience.

8-4f The Chromatic Sense

The chromatic sense is viewed as a subset of the broader visual sense. The chromatic sense involves the ability to identify, match, and discriminate among colors. Following are activities for the chromatic sense.

naea)Color Seriating. Not all colors are created equal. Colors come in different shades, tints, tones, intensities, and values. Black added to red will turn it into a darker shade, perhaps scarlet. White added to red will turn it into a lighter tint, such as pink. To make a color seriation game, first find color charts or paint strips with variations in tint or shade. Begin with obvious gradations: light green, medium green, and dark green. Glue an identical set to a piece of cardboard or a file folder and let children first match the shapes in order. Later, they can lay them out in a trainlike array from darkest to lightest. Gradually increase the number of colors, or add more difficult gradations in color as children become more proficient. This seriation activity can also be made self-checking. For example, place each of the five shades of red on its own index card. The cards can be coded 1 through 5 in small numbers on the back side. Or a simple picture, such as a caterpillar, can be drawn on the back. When the colors are put in proper sequence, the picture will be complete when the cards are turned over. The caterpillar should appear, whether the cards are seriated from darkest to lightest or lightest to darkest.

Infant, Toddler, Preschool, Kindergarten, and School-Age Activity: Color Our World. Viewing objects through pieces of cellophane distorts their color. Color paddles are sturdy pieces of cellophane or translucent plastic. They are commercially available or can be easily made. Individual sheets of cellophane wrapping paper or term paper covers can be mounted or framed in cardboard to form a sturdy holder. Provide at least the primary colors. Color paddles can be used individually or together. For example, viewing the room through red over blue will make it look purple.

Kindergarten and School-Age Activity: Create Colors. Provide round pieces of tissue paper in the three primary colors for each child. Tissue paper is difficult to cut, and you may have to provide precut pieces for younger children. Cut a large piece of wax paper for each child. Children can arrange any two pieces of tissue paper on the wax paper. Make sure the primary colors have some overlap. Add the third colored circle, making sure it overlaps the other two. Carefully place a second sheet of wax paper on top. Press with a warm iron. Older children should be able to press their own, provided they are supervised. The heat melts the wax and seals the round shapes. Hold the picture up to the light or display it on the window. Notice how purple appears where red and blue overlap, orange where red and yellow overlap, and green where blue and yellow overlap. What color appears in the center, where red, blue, and yellow overlap?

8-4g The Thermic Sense

The thermic sense deals with temperature perception (see Figure 8–10). How do things feel: hot, cold, warm, lukewarm, or tepid? Our thermic sense responds when we touch a hot stove, eat frozen ice cream, or take a cold shower. Recommended materials include a thermometer and barometer. Following are activities for the thermic sense.

Infant, Toddler, Preschool, Kindergarten, and School-Age Activity: Fingers Swim. Fill three shallow bowls with water. One bowl should contain warm water, a second cool or room-temperature water, and a third cold

Figure 8–10 Children can explore their thermic sense through water play.

© Cengage Learning

or melted ice water. The bowls of water should look the same but feel very different. Encourage children to put one or two fingers into one bowl and tell you how it feels. Is the water hot or cold? Pairs of bowls can also be used. Can they find water in another bowl that feels just the same as the water in this one? Because the bowls are open to the air, the hot and cold water will return to room temperature quickly. Encourage children to discuss which one feels like the water they use in the bathtub, to swim in, to water the lawn, to drink on a hot day, or in soup.

Preschool, Kindergarten, and School-Age Activity: Temperature Jars. This activity must be prepared fresh each time. It works best with a small group. Locate three pairs of identical plastic jars. Plastic spice jars are ideal. Fill each pair with equal amounts of one of the following:

- hot (but not scalding) water
- cold or melted ice water
- tepid/lukewarm or room-temperature water

Begin by having children hold one of a pair in one hand. Ask them, "How does it feel? What word describes it? Is it hot, warm, cold, or cool?" Encourage them to use their other hand to find a match that feels the same. This activity must proceed quickly, because the water will quickly return to room temperature. As children master this activity, intermediate temperatures, including finer grades of warm and cool, can be added.

Toddler, Preschool, Kindergarten, and School-Age Activity: How Does It Feel? Encourage children to discuss how they feel when they directly experience some of the following:

- being in snow
- being out in the rain
- standing near the stove or oven
- being near the fireplace
- taking a bath

Encourage children to use thermic terms such as hot, warm, cold, freezing, cool, and burning when discussing their reactions.

Preschool, Kindergarten, and School-Age Activity: Thermic Moves. Encourage children to use their bodies to show what happens to water under different temperature conditions.

- Pretend you are a drop of water in the ocean. Someone picks you up with her shovel and carries you home in her sand pail.
- She leaves you outside, and it is getting colder and colder. Winter is coming, and soon it will snow.

- It is freezing cold, and you turn into an ice cube. Someone picks you up and rolls you in the snow. He keeps rolling you until he gets a big ball of snow. He makes two more big balls and stacks them into a snowman. You are near the snowman's head, and you are very proud.
- The sun starts to shine. It is getting warmer and warmer. You are beginning to melt very slowly.
- All that's left of the snowman is a big puddle of water.
- Someone scoops you into the sand pail and brings you inside. She pours the water into a pot and puts it on the stove. She turns the heat on. It feels good being warm inside. The water comes to a boil, and you start to jump around because it is so hot.
- She pours you into the dishpan, and you help make bubbles and clean the dishes.

Preschool, Kindergarten, and School-Age Activity: Thermic Cooking. There are many simple cooking experiences that include heating or freezing ingredients. Here is a simple one.

Popsicles®

1 cup of hot water
2 cups of lemonade
1 package Jell-O® (any flavor)

Mix and pour into ice-cube trays. Insert a toothpick or Popsicle® stick in each. Freeze. Children and adults enjoy these because the Jell-O® slows down the melting process and eliminates much of the mess.

8-4h **The Sterognostic Sense**

Being able to recognize objects through tactile-muscular exploration without the aid of vision is the sterognostic sense. Touching and feeling a pinecone involve the tactile sense. But closing one's eyes while touching and handling a pinecone to identify it involves the sterognostic sense. Whereas the tactile sense usually involves visual clues, the sterognostic sense does not. Following are activities for the sterognostic sense.

DAP naeyc Toddler, Preschool, Kindergarten, and School-Age Activity: Feely Bag. Place a margarine tub in the toe of an old, large sock. Children enjoy working an arm through the sock to find the object in the tub. Use objects made of wood, metal, paper, plastic, cloth, cork, glass, rubber, and leather. Encourage children verbally to describe:

- how the object feels: Is it rough, smooth, or bumpy?
- the size of the object: Is it big or little?
- the shape of the object: Is it round, square, triangular, flat, or solid?

- what the object is made of: Is it made of wood, paper, rubber, glass, or metal?
- the length of the object: Is it long or short?
- the weight of the object: Is it heavy or light?

Children can also guess the object's

- color
- function or purpose: What is it used for?
- name: What is it called? What do you think it is?

As with all questioning, it is important for children to attempt to justify their answers. Asking them, "How do you know?" or "Why do you think so?" encourages them to go beyond random guessing. For example, "I think it's money cause it's round, small, and feels like a penny." Young children may prefer to match the object they touch with its picture or a sample of the actual object. Toddlers will enjoy merely putting things in and taking them out of the Feely Bag.

Toddler, Preschool, Kindergarten, and School-Age Activity: Blindfold Game. Children can be blindfolded or agree to keep their eyes closed. The child can be given an object—for example, a doll—to thoroughly touch and feel without the aid of vision. The child can use these sterognostic cues to guess what the object is. Young children do tend to peek or tell each other the answer. This is to be expected.

8-4i The Baric Sense

Recognizing objects as heavy or light and gradations in between involves the baric sense. Following is an activity for the baric sense.

DAP naeyc Preschool, Kindergarten, and School-Age Activity: Weight Jars. Find a set of six large plastic spice jars and spray paint the insides the same color or cover them with identical wrap. Separate them into pairs—for example, three brown and three yellow—and fill one of each pair with plaster of paris or some other self-hardening and weighted substance, one to the top, one to the middle, and one a half-inch full.

Encourage children to hold one jar in one hand and find another jar that weighs the same. Children should be encouraged to use both hands like a balance scale, with one jar in each hand. Put the matched pair aside. Keep going until the children have decided that the three pairs weigh the same. Subtly coding each matching pair on the bottom will aid in checking. Encourage children to talk about weight. Which pair is heavy or light? Which pair is the heaviest or lightest? Children can seriate from heaviest to lightest or vice versa. Older children may enjoy using a set of 10 with finer gradations in weight.

8-4j The Kinesthetic Sense

The kinesthetic sense involves a whole-body, sensorimotor muscular response (see Figure 8–11). When we talk about children learning by doing or being actively involved, we are referring to their kinesthetic sense. For example, young children learn about animals by observing, listening, smelling, touching, and using their bodies to act like them. Moving on all fours like a tiger will help the child form a strong concept of that animal, which is necessary for talking about, reading, or making art objects related to tigers. Activities for the kinesthetic sense follow.

DAP naeyc Toddler, Preschool, Kindergarten, and School-Age Activity: Musical Moves. Record or find CDs of different genres of music, including jazz, calypso, lullabies, reggae, classical, and others. Each genre of music has its own characteristic mood, tempo, and rhythm. Therefore, each will suggest a certain type of bodily expression through movement. This activity combines listening with the kinesthetic sense of body movement. Play different samples of music. Hold an infant and move to the music, describing the music and how it makes you want to move. Encourage older children to move the way the music makes them feel. The teacher may want to model and move along with the group. However, encourage children to come up with their own way of moving rather than imitating the teacher's moves. Turning the lights off may help set the tone.

Photo Courtesy of Jill Englebright Fox

Figure 8–11 The kinesthetic sense requires a whole-body sensorimotor response.

Moving with the aid of scarves or pieces of fabric may help some children. Other shy or insecure children may prefer to merely watch, not participate. Reassure them, but also encourage their eventual participation. Over time and with repeated practice, children become more comfortable and confident in their creative movement.

Toddler, Preschool, Kindergarten, and School-Age Activity: Listen and Move. Children can also move in response to recorded sounds. Record some of the following:

- birds chirping, soaring, or flapping their wings
- feet marching
- a jet soaring
- sounds of laughter
- animals growling
- waves pounding against rocks
- popcorn popping
- a chainsaw starting up
- people swimming in a pool

This movement activity is more sophisticated than the former. It takes more thought on the part of older children to translate what they know about a jet airplane into bodily movement.

Toddler, Preschool, Kindergarten, and School-Age Activity: Shapes Movement. Young children will enjoy crawling through openings of different shapes. Find a large cardboard appliance carton. Cut a large geometric shape out of each side. Use a circle, square, triangle, and rectangle. Make sure that each shape is large enough for your biggest child to fit through easily. Mark and reinforce the edges of each cut-out shape with different-colored cloth tape. Children can take turns listening to your directions and crawling through the appropriate shape; for example, "Go in the square and come out the triangle." This activity involves listening, sequencing, shape recognition, and body movement. Make the directions longer and more difficult for older children; for example, "Go in any four-sided figure, come out a red shape (marked with colored cloth tape), and walk around all the shapes two times."

Toddler, Preschool, Kindergarten, and School-Age Activity: Squeeze, Mash, and Taste. Children will enjoy the movement and physical activity needed to:

- squeeze oranges, lemons, limes, or grapefruits on a reamer for juice
- mash apples for cider
- mash strawberries for natural ice cream
- mash bananas for yogurt

The finished products can be sampled for snack. Juices that look the same do not always taste the same. Adding sugar to lemon juice changes it from sour to sweet.

Toddler, Preschool, Kindergarten, and School-Age Activity: Artistic Dramatic Play. Children may enjoy pretending that they are professional artists. Think of what an artist might wear and do. Items to include would be an old white shirt, a beret, an easel, an art supply box (perhaps an old suitcase), a palette, brushes, goggles, and a sketchbook. Place these in the dramatic play center.

Toddler, Preschool, Kindergarten, and School-Age Activity: Keep on Movin'. Find a large, open space and help children locate their own personal space in which they can move without touching another child. "Today, we are going to pretend that our room is filled up with some very different things. Listening and thinking about the different things will help us move. For example, what if the room was filled from the floor to the ceiling with balloons and we had to move? How would we do it? Show me with your body how you would move. How would it feel on your body?" Ask children how they would move to get through these:

Jell-O®	ice
snow	glue
ice cream	water
mashed potatoes	rubber tires
cotton candy	pillows
sand	honey
syrup	jelly beans

Preschool, Kindergarten, and School-Age Activity: Gingerbread Children. Read the children's classic tale about the Gingerbread Boy. Encourage children to take turns acting out different parts. Cooking can also be coordinated. Be sure to check the children's records for food allergies.

Did You Get It?

The activity advocated by Aline Wolf (1988, 1990) using postcards with art masterpieces to create a multisensory experience for young students did not involve
  a. creating.
  b. pairing.
  c. matching.
  d. sorting.

Take the full quiz on CourseMate.

ⒹⒶⓅ ⓝⓐⓔⓨⓒ ⓝⓐⓔⓐ 8-5 Resist Art Activities

A dried design or picture will resist a second liquid put on top. The process of resist is a fascinating one that intrigues children. They do one picture, put a second covering over it, and end up with a totally different effect.

8-5a Personally Expressive Art Activities

Following are some personally expressive art activities for resist.

Preschool, Kindergarten, and School-Age Activity: Crayon Resist. Children can make a picture or design with crayons. It is important to press hard and color fairly dark. Although much of the paper is covered, some empty space should be left. The colored picture can be covered with:

- watercolor
- ink—producing a pitch black, midnight background
- hand painting
- Magic Marker®
- shoe polish
- tempera paint

Whichever is used for the second coating, the crayon wax resists the liquid. The liquid fills in the remaining white negative space. It may also bead up on the colored wax, producing an interesting textured effect.

Kindergarten and School-Age Activity: Paste or Glue Resist. Children paint a picture or design by making thick marks with glue on white paper. Or apply adhesive to paper and fold the paper in half to get a mirror image. Quickly open the paper. Let dry thoroughly. Later, paint over the entire paper with:

- watercolor
- ink
- tempera paint

The glue will resist any of these liquids. The background will fill with color, and the dried adhesive will leave a crackled white picture. Let dry thoroughly.

Kindergarten and School-Age Activity: Ink Resist. Children paint a picture with tempera, leaving some space white. When the paint is dry, they cover the entire sheet of paper with black or colored ink. The effect is striking. Black provides a good background for night scenes or Halloween. Blue ink is effective for underwater or sky scenes.

Kindergarten and School-Age Activity: Wax Paper Resist. Place a piece of wax paper over a sheet of white paper. Secure with tape or paper clips. Use a craft stick to heavily etch a thick line, design, or picture. The pressure will transfer the wax to the paper. Discard the wax paper. Paint over the entire sheet of paper with watercolor or ink. The lines drawn with the craft stick will remain white. This activity takes patience and fine motor control and is recommended for older children.

Kindergarten and School-Age Activity: Black Magic Pictures. The secret of these pictures is using fluorescent crayons that glow brightly through a wash of black paint. Encourage children to press hard with crayons and do thick coloring. Provide black poster or tempera paint. Dilute paint so it is thick enough to color the paper but thin enough to let the colors show through. Have the children brush their pictures using broad, sweeping strokes. The fluorescent crayons resist the paint, so the picture stands out brightly against the black background.

8-5b Sensory Exploration Activities

Following are sensory exploration activities for resist.

Kindergarten and School-Age Activity: Embossed Greeting Card Rubbing. This activity involves families by recycling greeting cards. Remove fronts of cards, saving those with embossed words and pictures. Remove papers from crayons and also provide chalk. Have the child place the card on the table with the embossed side facing up. The child lays thin paper on top and rubs with crayon or chalk. Onionskin paper works well. Remind the child to use the sides of crayon or chalk rather than the tip. Tape the card in place if it moves about. Allow the child to use one card, or mix and match several cards.

Kindergarten and School-Age Activity: Masking Tape Resist. Cut different widths and lengths of masking tape and place on a table with one end unattached for easy removal. Have the child pick off and place masking tape onto white paper, making a design. Some children may want to stop here, and that is okay. Others may want to paint liquid watercolors or tempera over their taped designs. The watercolor will bead on the tape, leaving an interesting effect. When it dries, if children choose to remove the tape, they will see white paper underneath contrasting with their painting.

Toddler, Preschool, Kindergarten, and School-Age Activity: Name Savers. Write the child's name on paper in white wax crayon. Encourage the child to paint over your white marks. Magically, his or her name appears.

Toddler, Preschool, Kindergarten, and School-Age Activity: Spray Bottle Resist. Provide clear child-sized spray bottles with trigger-type handles. Fill each with diluted liquid watercolor. Locate flat objects like keys, combs, craft sticks, and puzzle pieces. This activity is best done outdoors. Roll out a long piece of butcher paper. Have the child choose and arrange shapes on the paper. Teach the child how to use and aim the spray bottles to squirt the objects. The child removes the objects when dry. The shapes resist the watercolor, leaving their impression. Provide a bucket of water and towels so children can wash and dry the objects for the next child.

Toddler, Preschool, Kindergarten, and School-Age Activity: Textured Tabletop Resist. This activity is recommended for three reasons. First, it allows group participation. Second, it can be left up, and children can return to it, thereby continuing and extending their participation. Third, it fosters whole-arm movement and upper body control. Begin by randomly arranging a variety of textured items on a table top. Make sure the items are fairly flat: yarn, cardboard shapes, fabric scraps, craft sticks, and paper clips. Place a large sheet of butcher paper over the table as if it were a tablecloth. Secure the sides and corners of the paper with tape. This will prevent the textured items from sliding around. Peel the paper off several jumbo-size crayons. Encourage children to rub the length of their crayon carefully across the surface while observing the interesting textured shapes that appear. See whether children can guess or match items with their marks.

Did You Get It?

The artistic activity known as "resist" is one which often fascinates and mystifies young children. The initial process involves the creation of a specific picture by your students. By then covering the initial picture with an additional layering of liquid, the resultant outcome is

  a. a mirror-image of the original.
  b. a completely different effect.
  c. indicative of the artistic style termed Surrealism.
  d. an optical illusion.

Take the full quiz on CourseMate.

Summary

Sensory stimulation involves more than the five senses. (8-1) Experiences in sensory stimulation begin in infancy and are the primary way in which young children learn about their world. (8-2) In addition to the senses of sight, hearing, taste, touch, and smell, Montessori identified the chromatic, thermic, sterognostic, baric, and kinesthetic as vital senses. (8-3) As children enter school, one of the senses may emerge as a dominant learning style. Teachers encounter children who are visual, auditory, or tactile-kinesthetic learners in their classrooms. (8-4) Our senses, however, do not operate in isolation, and a multisensory approach is advocated for young children. (8-5) Resist activities provide opportunities for children to engage their visual and tactile-kinesthetic senses.

Key Terms

art postcards, 161
auditory, 157
baric, 168
chromatic, 166
field trips, 159
gustatory, 164

kinesthetic, 168
multisensory experience, 159
olfactory, 164
perception, 157
resist, 170
sensory table, 162

sterognostic, 162
tactile, 162
tactile-kinesthetic, 158
teaching style, 158
thermic, 166
visual, 157

✓ Suggested Activities

1. Select a sensory activity from this unit, and implement it with young children.

2. Plan and implement a multisensory cooking experience.

3. Observe a child engaged in drawing a house as described earlier in this chapter. Does the child focus on the totality of the picture or on the component parts? Is this child a visual, auditory, or kinesthetic learner?

4. Stock a sensory table and use it with young children.

5. Identify three sites in your community that would be good field trip experiences for young children. Put vital information including name, address, phone number, directions, cost, hours of operation, and so forth on an index card. Attach printed information if available. Keep it in your professional portfolio.

6. Provide a resist art activity for one or more young children.

Review

1. Match the sense with its key descriptive terms.

_____ auditory	touch
_____ olfactory	movement
_____ chromatic	weight
_____ visual	color
_____ gustatory	hearing
_____ kinesthetic	temperature
_____ baric	looking
_____ thermic	tactile-muscular
_____ tactile	smell
_____ sterognostic	taste

2. Use the example of a young child eating cotton candy for the first time to explain the following equation:

Senses + Perception + Feeling + Thinking = Concept Formation

3. Identify three major learning styles.

4. Discuss the relationship between learning style and teaching style.

5. Pretend you are teaching kindergarten. You would like to take your children to the local flower and plant nursery sometime in April. You have checked everything out in advance and await your principal's approval. The principal questions your request and asks for verbal justification. How would you convince the principal of the benefits of this field trip?

Additional Resources

The article "Teaching the Five Senses: Tips for Pre-K Teachers" by Shyrelle Eubanks is available on the National Education Association website (www.nea.org).

Read "Learning Styles of Children" by D. H. Sailor on the Education.com website.

Go to the Montessori Teacher Training Blog for "Montessori Education: Sensorial Activities for Sensory Integration."

A list of activities to help young children explore each of their five senses is available from the Neuroscience for Kids website.

 Visit CourseMate for this textbook to access the eBook, Did You Get It? quizzes, Digital Downloads, TeachSource Videos, flashcards, and more. Go to CengageBrain.com to log in, register, or purchase access.

Pre-Kindergarten/Kindergarten Lesson Plan

The Sense of Taste

NOTE
Before using this lesson plan with children, be sure to check the children's records for information on food allergies, and have the children wash their hands.

GOAL
Scientific investigation and reasoning. The student uses age-appropriate tools and models to investigate the natural world. The student is expected to use senses as a tool of observation to identify properties and patterns of organisms, objects, and events in the environment.

LEARNING OUTCOMES
a. The student will identify the five basic senses.
b. The student will match the sensory organs to the corresponding senses.
c. The student will brainstorm descriptive words for the sense of taste.

MATERIALS
a. *Assorted Cakes and Tarts*, a painting by Wayne Thiebaud can be located through an Internet search, printed, or downloaded for display to the children
b. Technology for display of the painting (LCD projector or document camera)
c. Pretzels, unsweetened chocolate, sugar cubes, and dill pickle chips for the children to taste
d. Paper plates
e. Dry erase board and marker
f. Paper and crayons for the children

INTRODUCTION
Seat the children for a whole-group activity. Remind the children of the current science topic: The Five Senses. Use the following to review the five senses:

a. Our five senses help us learn about the world around us. Let's name our five senses.
b. If I had a bottle of perfume here, which one of my senses might I use to learn about it? What part of my body would I use with that sense?
c. If I had a magnifying glass here, which one of my senses would I use to explore the world? What part of my body would I use?
d. If I had a hedgehog here, which one of my senses would I have to be very careful of when I picked it up? What part of my body would I use?

e. When I blow my whistle on the playground, which one of your senses lets you know its time to come inside? And what part of your body do you use?

DEVELOPMENT OF THE CONCEPT
Share with the children that today's focus is on their sense of taste. Use the following to generate a discussion on the sense of taste:

a. What are they exploring when they use their sense of taste?
b. What part(s) of the body do they use to taste?

Ask one or two children to name their favorite things to taste. Respond by describing the taste: "that tastes *sweet*" or "that tastes *salty*." Write *sweet* and *salty* on the whiteboard. Explain that

Pre-Kindergarten/Kindergarten Lesson Plan (*continued*)

almost all of the foods we eat have one of four tastes: sweet, salty, sour, or bitter. Add *sour* and *bitter* to the list on the whiteboard.

Help children explore these four tastes. Distribute to each child a pretzel, a square of unsweetened chocolate, a sugar cube, and a dill pickle chip on a paper plate. Ask the children to identify the foods on their plates. Explain that each of these foods represents one of the four tastes listed on the board. Ask the children to taste the food that they think is *salty*. Discuss what they chose and then identify the pretzel as salty. Ask the children to taste the food they think is *sweet*. Discuss what they chose and identify the sugar cube as sweet. Repeat for *bitter* and *sour*.

Display the painting *Assorted Cakes and Tarts* by Wayne Thiebaud. Give the children a focus question to consider as they first look at the painting: *What story or idea did this artist want you to think about when you look at this painting?*

Ask the children to identify what taste goes with the foods in this painting. Ask them to pretend to eat one of the cakes or tarts in the painting and to describe how it tastes. Write a list of their descriptors on the board. Read the list of descriptors with the children.

Share with children that in his painting, the artist included the sweet cakes and tarts that he enjoyed eating. Ask each child to choose a descriptive word from the list on the board and draw a picture to go along with it.

CONCLUSION

As the children finish their drawings, have them pair and share their drawings with a partner. Ask each child to share the descriptor chosen and explain how that descriptor is illustrated in his/her drawing.

ASSESSMENT

a. Did the children identify the five senses?
b. Did the children identify the corresponding sensory organs?
c. Were the children able to generate vocabulary descriptive of the sense of taste?

VARIATIONS

The following works of art might be used to adapt this lesson for each of the five senses:

- Hearing: *Jitterbugs V* by William Johnson or *Spanish Fountain* by John Singer Sargeant
- Touch: *Miss Ann White's Kitten* by George Stubbs
- Smell: *The Flower Seller* by Diego Rivera
- Sight: The *Domino Players* by Horace Pippin

Go to cengagebrain.com for a full-size version of this lesson plan.

9 The Complete Early Childhood Art Program

© Cengage Learning

Juanita has found that some of her four-year-olds make derogatory comments about each other's art.

They say, "That's dumb" or "It doesn't really look like that!!" How would you respond?

Juanita tries to empower children by encouraging them to talk about how comments hurt their feelings. "I don't like it when you say my picture's ugly." She also reviews her art program regularly to make sure the objectives and activities are appropriate. Is she setting the standards at an appropriate level? Is she expecting symbolic art from children who are still in the exploratory stage? Juanita decides to help her children see that art comes in many forms. She does this by sharing art prints with the children. She helps children see that art can simply be abstract shapes and crossing lines, or it can portray a mother and her baby. Both subjects are valid as art. Does this strategy sound like something you could use with children both to expose them to varied artistic styles and to validate the way they make art?

Learning Outcomes:

After reading this chapter, you should be able to:

9-1 Discuss the importance of art education in the early years.
9-2 Explain how national standards relate to early childhood art education.
9-3 Contrast DBAE with a studio-based approach to early childhood art education.
9-4 Describe and give an example of the four components of a complete early childhood art program.
9-5 Identify and give an example of three artistic styles or movements.
9-6 Use the art critique to discuss a work of art.
9-7 Provide developmentally appropriate collage activities for young children.

Standards addressed in this chapter

DAP Criteria
  3 Planning curriculum to achieve important goals
NAEYC Standards
  2 Curriculum
  8 Community
  9 Physical Environment
NAEA Visual Arts Standards
  1 Understanding and applying media, techniques, and processes
  3 Choosing and evaluating a range of subject matter symbols and ideas
  4 Understanding the visual arts in relation to history and cultures
  5 Reflecting upon and assessing the characteristics and merits of their own work and the work of others

9-1 The Importance of Arts Education

Although making art is a priority, it is only one of four major components of a complete early childhood art program. It is also important for young children to engage in sensory experiences; to learn about art, artists, and their styles; and to pursue beauty through aesthetics. This unit will focus on constructing a complete early childhood art program.

According to the National Standards for Arts Education (Consortium of National Arts Education Associations, 1994), knowing and practicing the arts disciplines are fundamental to healthy development and are a key part of what it means to be "educated." Other reasons to learn about and participate in the arts include:

1. The arts are worth studying simply because of what they are. Their impact cannot be denied. Throughout history, the arts have served to connect human imagination with the deepest question of human existence: Who am I?

2. The arts are used to achieve a multitude of human purposes: to present issues and ideas, to teach or persuade, to entertain, to decorate.

3. The arts are integral to daily life. The arts are all around us from the design of a cereal box to the format of a late-night talk show.

4. The arts offer unique sources of enjoyment and refreshment for the imagination. They explore relationships between ideas and objects and serve as links between thought and action.

5. There is ample evidence that the arts help students develop the attitudes, characteristics, and intellectual skills required to participate effectively in today's society and economy. The arts teach self-discipline, reinforce self-esteem, and foster thinking skills and creativity. They teach the importance of teamwork and cooperation.

6. Arts education cultivates the whole child, gradually building many kinds of literacy while developing intuition, reasoning, imagination, and dexterity into unique forms of expression and communication.

9-2 Art Standards

Children's educational success depends on creating a society that is both literate and imaginative, both competent and creative. The National Standards for Arts Education, published in 1994 by the Consortium of National Arts Education Associations, address competence in the arts as well as provide a foundation for connecting arts-related concepts and facts across the art forms and across the sciences and humanities. The result has been a set of capabilities that help students arrive at their own knowledge, beliefs, and values for making personal and artistic decisions. By the time they complete secondary school, students should be able to do the following:

1. Communicate at a basic level in the four arts disciplines: dance, music, theatre, and the visual arts, including the use of basic vocabularies, materials, tools, techniques, and intellectual methods of each arts discipline.

2. Communicate proficiently in at least one art form, including the ability to define and solve artistic problems with insight, reason, and technical proficiency.

3. Develop and present basic analyses of works of art from structural, historical, and cultural perspectives.

4. Have an informed acquaintance with exemplary works of art from a variety of cultures and historical periods, and a basic understanding of historical development in the arts disciplines, across the arts as a whole, and within cultures.

5. Relate various types of arts knowledge and skills within and across the arts disciplines. This includes mixing and matching competencies and understandings in art making, history and culture, and analysis in arts-related projects.

What does this mean for early childhood education? In kindergarten through grade four, young children should experiment enthusiastically with art materials and investigate ideas presented to them through visual arts instruction. They exhibit a sense of joy and excitement as they make and share their artwork. Creation is at the heart of this instruction. Students learn to work with various tools, processes, and media. They learn to coordinate their hands and minds in visual exploration. They learn to make choices that enhance communication of their ideas. Their natural inquisitiveness is promoted, and they learn the value of perseverance.

Did You Get It?

In evaluating the following statement, "The arts are worth studying simply because of what they are," experts consider this position to be

a. naive and oversimplified.
b. legitimate.
c. anachronistic and better left to a time gone by.
d. fundamentally flawed and potentially leading to wastage in school funding.

Take the full quiz on CourseMate.

SOMETHING EXTRA.....

Art in the First Kindergartens

Friedrich Froebel is known as the "Father of Kindergarten." Although his philosophy was shaped by several of the great thinkers who preceded him, it was his experiences and beliefs that determined the curriculum and the goals of the first kindergartens in Germany and the United States.

Because of early experiences, Froebel felt an affinity with nature and a connection to natural elements. He was fascinated by the concept of unity and studied crystals, physics, natural history, chemistry, Arabic, and Hebrew in order to understand the organic unity of life (Wolfe, 2000). Helping children to understand and achieve unity with nature and with their Creator was a foundational idea in Froebel's kindergarten. He believed that the arts were an important part of education because they were an essential part of the "all-sided nature" of each human being.

"Art and appreciation of art constitute a general capacity or talent of man, and should be cared for early ... A universal ... plan of human education must, therefore, necessarily consider at an early period singing, drawing, painting, and modeling; it will treat them as serious objects of the school. Its intention will not be to make each pupil an artist ..., but to secure each human being full ... development ... and, particularly to enable him to understand and appreciate the products of true art" (Froebel, 1826).

Froebel wanted kindergarten to be a place where children developed fully in all areas (Wolfe, 2000). With this in mind, the curriculum included music, dance, gardening, and nature study but focused on **gifts** and **occupations** to help children build that ultimate understanding of unity.

The gifts developed by Froebel were basically manipulatives designed to decrease in size and increase in intricacy as children developed skills and understanding. The occupations were "planned experiences to train children's eyes, hands, and minds and to allow children to work with malleable materials" (Wolfe, 2000, p. 104).

Although none of the occupations had artistic expression as their primary goal, many were designed to provide children with early experiences with the artistic elements. Very young children were encouraged to draw on frosted window panes to explore lines and shapes or to sort yarn for color discrimination. Experiences like these might lead to the planned occupation of drawing, both on graphing paper and freehand; mat weaving to create patterns; cutting silhouettes from black paper; painting to combine form, color, light and shade; and constructing outlines and surfaces with soft peas and small, round sticks.

Brosterman (1997) believes that experiences with Froebel's gifts and occupations provided inspiration for the work of architect Frank Lloyd Wright and two key figures of Expressionism: Paul Klee and Wassily Kandinsky.

Brain Connection

Each child is unique, growing on his or her own timetable. Teachers need to adjust expectations to age-specific characteristics and unique capabilities of children (Rushton and Larkin, 2001).

Did You Get It?

What is not one of the four disciplines of art recognized by The National Standards for Arts Education, published in 1994?

a. sculpture
b. theatre
c. music
d. visual arts

Take the full quiz on CourseMate.

9-3 Early Childhood Art: Studio Oriented or Discipline Based?

The approach to art advocated in this book is primarily but not exclusively a studio-oriented approach. It holds that young children should be free to experiment with creative materials (see Figure 9–1). The **studio-oriented** approach has dominated teacher training and influences current thinking and practice with respect to early childhood art. Art education theory has shifted from a child-centered, creative self-expression approach to a discipline-based subject approach. It has provided a framework for curriculum development such as in **Discipline-Based Art Education (DBAE)**, an approach advocated by the Getty Center for Education in the Arts. According to Dobbs (1998), DBAE is a comprehensive approach to instruction and learning in art, developed primarily for grades K–12. It is designed to provide exposure to, experience with, and acquire content from

Figure 9–1 In the studio-oriented approach, children are free to explore and experiment with art materials.

several disciplines of knowledge, but especially four fundamental art disciplines: art making, art criticism, art history, and aesthetics. Education in these disciplines contributes to the creation, understanding, and appreciation of art, artists, artistic processes, and the roles and functions of art in cultures and societies. DBAE programs differ in emphasis, but there is a core of basic characteristics they have in common, including a written plan, systematic organization, engagement with artworks, balanced content from the four art disciplines, and developmentally suitable and age-appropriate activities.

The authors' child-centered approach has been somewhat comprehensive in that it stresses a studio approach while going beyond mere art production in building a complete early childhood art program. This complete program also includes aesthetics and learning about art, artists, and their styles. Sensing and experiencing, a foundation in this program, are not included in the Getty Center's components. The authors believe these are vital components for the early years.

Did You Get It?

Art creation, art criticism, art history, and aesthetics of art are components of the _____ approach, a comprehensive approach to art education advocated by the Getty Center for Education in the Arts.

  a. discipline-based
  b. studio-oriented
  c. multi-sensory
  d. holistic

Take the full quiz on CourseMate.

DAP naeyc 9-4 What to Include in an Early Childhood Art Program

It is important children have ample opportunities to make art. However, although it is basic, processing with media to make art is only one of four key components of any complete early childhood art program. A complete program provides:

1. sensory experiences
2. aesthetic experiences
3. time, space, and materials for making art
4. an introduction to art, artists, and a variety of art forms and styles

The four components are interrelated, and the separation exists only for the present analysis. For example, making art is dependent on sensing and experiencing.

naea 9-4a Sensory Experiences

Children do not create in isolation. Their art originates from something personally experienced, an idea, an important object, an event, a feeling, or a person. A child's daily experiences provide a potential bank of things to include in art (see Figure 9–2). For example, Joshua's idea for painting a farm was related to spending the weekend at his grandparents' farm. Class field trips are crucial because they extend a child's personal range of experiences to the wider community and provide new content for art.

In the past, the term "disadvantaged" was used to refer to children who lacked basic environmental experiences. These children may be uncomfortable

Figure 9–2 Hands-on experiences provide a bank from which young children make withdrawls during the creative process.

SOMETHING EXTRA.....

Celebrating Female Artists

According to Lankford (1992), feminist critics, philosophers, and historians have reviled and denounced patriarchal bases of art and culture that have denied women opportunities for participation and recognition in the art world. Historically, women have been poorly represented in the art market, galleries, museums, and art history books. Some notable female African-American artists are listed in the section on non-Western art. Following are a few of the many women who have made significant contributions to the art world:

- Dorothea Lange (photography)
- Margaret Bourke-White (photography)
- Louise Nevelson (sculpture)
- Faith Ringgold (quilting and painting)
- Mary Cassatt (painting)
- Judith Leyster (painting)
- Georgia O'Keeffe (painting)
- Frida Kahlo (painting)
- Joan Mitchell (painting)

- Berthe Morisot (painting)
- Elizabeth Murray (painting)
- Suzanne Valadon (painting)

Art forms traditionally associated with women, such as quilting and weaving, have been devalued as crafts rather than fine art. Countless paintings, prints, and sculptures have portrayed women as primarily sensual in character and as socially subservient. Feminists attempt to correct negative sexist discrimination through positive social action and by raising social consciousness about issues of sexual stereotyping, exploitation, and separatism. Feminist content may reflect feminist concerns, and feminist artists often work collaboratively, promoting a sense of community and interdependence in contrast to the concept of artists as independent.

Add samples, books, and reproductions of works by women to your collection and include them in art teaching and aesthetic displays.

discussing, writing about, or drawing things they have never directly experienced. It is dangerous to assume that all children know about and have experienced libraries, hospitals, airports, skyscrapers, elevators, post offices, seashores, or museums. Encourage parents to take children places and discuss their experiences. In your classroom, provide as many hands-on experiences as possible through field trips, classroom visitors, and real objects for children's exploration and manipulation. This helps children form concepts and serves as a backdrop for future learning. For example, an informal trip to the hardware store can be a simple but sensory-rich experience filled with the sound, smell, and touch of cut wood or tools classified according to form and function.

Young children are sensory gluttons. Infants and toddlers are fascinated by pattern and detail. They will follow a bug crawling across the floor or marvel at water dripping from a melted icicle. Unfortunately, adults take these experiences for granted and need to recapture some of this childlike wonder and awareness. Children need practice to keep it alive.

According to Piaget, children learn about their world through their senses and actions. Our role is to help children note details and use their senses to build rich object concepts. For example, smelling and tasting are appropriate when visiting a bakery, whereas looking and listening are warranted during story time. Nature specimens can be brought in for focused sensory exploration. "Let's look at the empty hornet's nest. Carefully touch the sides. How does it feel? Let's wrap papier-mâché around a balloon and see if we can make our own hornet's nest."

naeyc 9-4b Aesthetic Experiences

Aesthetics is the study of beauty—not the Hollywood view of glamour, but beauty in color, form, and design. In a time of mass production with little concern for effort and quality craftsmanship, the quest for beauty is difficult. Still, there is a human need to make sense of and appreciate self and environment, just as there is a basic need to create.

Beauty is found in nature, in everyday surroundings and objects. Children use their senses and bodies in pursuit of beauty. The eyes visually explore art, and the ears listen to sounds and music. Three-dimensional artworks are touched, scents are smelled, foods are tasted, and the body responds through movement and dance. Young children learn to appreciate beauty through these experiences.

Classrooms or centers can be aesthetically pleasing and models of beauty. The room should be clean, bright, and colorful without being cluttered and gaudy. It should appeal to the senses and have things to look at, listen to, touch, smell, and taste. Flowers, plants, animals, soft pillows, a rocking chair, and a piece of sculpture add aesthetic touches to the room.

Displays are places children visit to refine their senses and build aesthetic appreciation. Aesthetic displays can include nature specimens, items of different textures, collections of postcards, art books, pottery, postage stamps, foreign currency, or items of a given size, shape, or color.

Aesthetics is not confined to the interior environment. Beauty abounds in nature and the community. Children can also visit exhibits of beautiful things in museums, churches, and galleries, and they can attend concerts and performances. Artists, dancers, and musicians can be invited to perform for and work with the children.

Celebrating Non-Western Art. Often, people know more about Western art than non-Western art. When outlining historical styles, periods, and artists in the European tradition, specific dates and names can generally be identified. There are a number of reasons why this may not be the case when examining art from non-European cultures. Many cultures do not view making art as a separate, autonomous activity. Aesthetic products may be intimately tied to ritual objects, dress, and body ornamentation. An artifact may be intended for daily utilitarian use and its maker anonymous, because the product is something that everyone makes and its existence is not considered to be anything special. For example, people make beautiful baskets to carry items to and from the market. Or the culture in question maintains a verbal, rather than a written, record of its history.

It is important to widen one's perspective when learning about art. Take a global perspective and become familiar with art made by Asian, Egyptian, Native American, and African-American artists. Visit museums that specialize in exhibits of non-Western art. Add samples, books, and reproductions to your collection. Include these in your art teaching and aesthetic displays. Enlist the help of parents and community members in your quest to honor non-Western art.

9-4c Time, Space, and Materials for Making Art

Young children need to be personally expressive and creative and to experience success through art. Teachers can help children see relationships between art and experience. For example, a child may say, "Teacher, I don't know what to make." A teacher can help a child refer to significant people, places, and things: "How did you celebrate this past holiday?" or "What do you remember about our story today?" Teachers can encourage children to give artistic form and substance to their ideas, urges, wishes, dreams, fears, or interests. Using the same art processes over time helps children to become secure using materials so that they are able to focus on expressing ideas and feelings (Lasky and Mukerji-Bergeson,

2003). As children have more experiences in creating art in different media, they practice deciding what to create, and learn to focus attention in specific areas of space (Heath and Wolf, 2004b). (See Figures 9–3 and 9–4.)

Figure 9–3 A young artist at work.

Figure 9–4 Making art using scissors and paper.

An Opportunity for Teacher Reflection

The School Year Soon Begins. You've spent the summer planning an aesthetically pleasing classroom and making materials you will use to provide rich multisensory learning experiences for your students. You know that both making art and appreciating the art of others will be important learning activities for your students this year. As you begin planning the curriculum for the first weeks of school, you realize a need to help students construct a definition of art and its purpose in their lives. *How will you do this? What experiences can you plan to help the children understand art as a way of personally communicating thoughts, feelings, and events?*

DAP naeyc naea) 9-4d An Introduction to the World of Art, Artists, and a Variety of Art Forms and Styles

Children may wonder: *What is art? Who are artists? Why do they make art?* Art is a basic human need. People make art to reflect and symbolize their existence. Children's interest in and study of community helpers can extend to artists. Davis (2008) says children, "as active makers of images, feel naturally connected to artists whom they see as trying, as they do, to do a good job" (p. 12). Children learn that some artists make art for a hobby, and others do it as a career. Some work at home, outdoors, or in studios. Some artists exhibit and sell their works in galleries. Famous artists have their works exhibited in museums.

Children can also learn that artists work in different media. Although not all artists paint, all have a desire to communicate. They use media, color, content, form, and the artistic elements to make their points. Helping children accept and value their own art will enable them to appreciate and value the artwork of others.

Our intent is to expose children to their rich artistic heritage rather than teach art history. Children learn that people everywhere and from the beginning of time have made art. It is part of a culture and tells us something about people: who they were, what they looked like, how they lived, what they wore, where they lived, and what they liked to do. A discussion of the major artistic styles and movements follows.

Did You Get It?

A complete art education program includes sensory experiences, aesthetic experiences, an introduction to artists and a broad range of styles, and

  a. a forum for debate.
  b. making art.
  c. proper time, space, and tools.
  d. lectures.

Take the full quiz on CourseMate.

naea) 9-5 Artistic Styles

Different artists use different styles. The same artist may use different styles during different periods. Children also have their own artistic styles. There is no one right or best way. Different styles are appropriate depending on the artist and what is being communicated. Exposing children to major artistic styles or movements serves two purposes. First, it shows children that there are many possible ways to make art. Second, it shows similarities between their own styles and the styles artists have used in the past and continue to use today. For example, children's art resembles both prehistoric art and modern abstract art.

A simplistic breakdown of the major artistic movements includes these:

- realistic or naturalistic
- abstract
- nonobjective

Realistic or **naturalistic art** attempts to represent people, places, and objects as they appear. There is an emphasis on objectivity, detail, and photographic realism. Children who aim for photographic realism in their art will be disappointed because developmentally they lack the necessary perceptual, physical, and cognitive ability. Realism or naturalism is merely one of many styles. Many adult artists are successful and satisfied in spite of their choice not to produce realistic or naturalistic art.

Abstract art bears only a partial resemblance to the object being represented. The object is somehow distorted. An example would be a child's drawing of a box on two wheels to represent a race car.

Nonobjective art involves a creative play with color, shape, line, and design. It is abstract art pushed to the limits. What is produced bears no resemblance to any actual object. For example, a child could paint racing swirls of paint to represent the speed and exhaust fumes associated with a race car rather than abstractly capturing its overall shape.

While these simple descriptions of the artistic movements are likely to meet the needs of most early childhood activities, teachers can and should extend their own knowledge of artistic styles. Familiarity with artistic styles will help teachers in planning appropriate art appreciation activities and in integrating visual art into other curriculum areas. It will also prepare teachers for questions children will ask about artwork they experience. Basic descriptions of specific styles of art are provided in the following section. Names of artists who are known for their work in each style are included, as are children's books and activities to help children identify and understand the essence of each style.

9-5a Prehistoric or Primitive Art

Era: From 25,000 years ago, during the Paleolithic or Old Stone Age, to 10,000–15,000 years later, during the Neolithic or New Stone Age

Artists:

Unknown cave artists

People have been doing art since the beginning of time. Just as we have artists' pictures hanging on our walls today, people decorated the walls of their caves with pictures. Cave artists mixed their own paints out of plants, berries, and other foods as well as earth, mud, and clay, most likely mixed with animal blood. They used sharpened sticks to draw and etch pictures. Cave artists liked to draw simple stick-figure people and animals, including leaping bison and deer, using only a few lines. Outlines were bold, and pictures were decorated with geometric patterns and designs. Proportion was correct. Cave people drew what they knew: themselves, others, and wild animals. That is what their life was about: survival, hunting, food, and safety from wild animals. Primitive people viewed art as magic. To symbolize something meant to somehow capture or control it.

A book to introduce this style to children would be *First Painter*, by Kathryn Lasky. After reading and discussing the book with children, have them paint a person or animal of their choice on a large, smooth stone.

9-5b Naturalistic or Realistic Art

Era: 1700s–1800s (Naturalistic)
Artists:

Honore Daumier

Francisco Goya

Rembrandt

Era: Nineteenth century on (United States) (Realistic)
Artists:

John James Audubon

Georgia O'Keeffe

Norman Rockwell

Charles Russell

Although **Naturalism** and **Realism** are somewhat different terms, we will use them interchangeably. Both terms emphasize the artist's attempt to make art objective and to reflect the actual object. During the 1700s and 1800s, painters attempted to portray life exactly as it was. This was a reaction against a neoclassic and romantic view of the ideal life. Naturalists chose to depict life as it was, often sordid and evil, and people as they were: overweight, ill, and less than beautiful. For example, a still life with flowers and fruit could include bugs and decaying food.

Naturalism and Realism also became popular in the United States in the nineteenth century. Landscapes, birds, farms, the wilderness, and people represented the struggle and simplicity of early American life. Children can examine naturalistic or realistic art and appreciate the time, effort, skills, and talent needed to make a photographic likeness.

An activity for older children could be to set up a very simple arrangement; for example, a stuffed animal and a doll. Encourage children to try to draw or paint the toys just as they are. They will need to examine them repeatedly for color, detail, and shape. This activity may prove frustrating, so it should be offered as an option. Books to introduce Naturalism and Realism to children are *Cowboy Charlie* by Jeanette Winter and *Through Georgia's Eyes* by Rachel Rodriguez.

9-5c Impressionism

Era: late 1800s to early 1900s
Artists:

Mary Cassatt

Edgar Degas

Paul Gauguin

Berthe Morisot

Pierre Auguste Renoir

Henri de Toulouse-Lautrec

Impressionism is an artistic style in which artists paint what they perceive rather than what they know to be there. The first Impressionists were fascinated with color, sunshine, contrasts, light, reflection, and shadow. They were concerned with making only a quick sketch of an object to capture its essence. Later, they rapidly filled in their rough outlines with intense patches of pigment. They used color and light to represent impressions. Impressionists preferred painting outdoors with natural light. Landscapes were popular subject matter. When viewed up close, Impressionist paintings depict a vibrating brilliance of colors, pure and unmixed. When viewed from a distance, however, the eyes fuse these neighboring color patches, constructing form, and perceiving movement.

An activity could be to make an outdoor painting by dabbing paint with an index finger. Encourage children to place separate dabs rather than mixing them. Or children could use bright fluorescent crayons in making their strokes. You can help children learn about Impressionism and Impressionistic artists by reading *Suzette and the Puppy* by Joan Sweeney and *Marie in Fourth Position* by Amy Littlesugar.

9-5d Pointillism

Era: late 1800s to early 1900s

Artist:

Georges Seurat

Pointillism, an offshoot of Impressionism, involved a concern for color and an innovative technique for representing it. Pointillists worked on large canvases, spending as much as a year on one canvas. Small dots or points of pure color were used instead of Impressionist dashes or strokes. Pointillists were concerned with complementary relationships between colors. They did not mix colors but required observers to fuse neighboring colors. For example, pointillists would represent water as composed of neighboring dots or points of green and yellow. When viewed from up close, the observer saw only green and yellow dots. From a distance, however, the eyes blended the yellow and green and perceived blue water.

An activity is to use crayons or markers to make a picture composed entirely of different-colored dots. Encourage children to use dots rather than lines. Or children can make a picture by dipping the eraser end of a pencil into red, blue, and yellow paint and making a print in the shape of dots. This activity is recommended after children have an opportunity to do color mixing. For example, if they want to make a purple car, they can use the pointillist technique of alternating red and blue dots in printing. Dots are placed close together with white space between. Younger children who do not have a command of color mixing should be encouraged to merely make a picture or design with colored dots. Reading *Getting to Know the World's Greatest Artists: Georges Seurat,* by Mike Venezia, will help them understand Pointillism.

9-5e Expressionism

Era: late 1800s to 1900s

Artists:

Paul Gauguin

Henri Matisse

Piet Mondrian

Diego Rivera

Expressionism is an artistic style based on expression of the artist's emotions and feelings. Expressionists, reacting against Impressionism, searched for emotional expression in their artistic statements. Expressionists purposely altered space, form, line, and color to make emotional statements that were expressionistic rather than realistic, naturalistic, or impressionistic. The subject matter was often lost in the colorful and even violent play of color, line, shape, contrast, and movement. Expressionists distorted reality to express their own views and moods. Because this movement was popular at the time of World War I, it is easy to see how the art reflected contemporary culture. Much of the artwork was violent, depressing, and highly emotional.

An activity is to let children finger paint to mood music. Music that conveys sorrow, joy, and anger could be played. Encourage children to paint their feelings. Books to read about Expressionism include *A Bird or Two: A Story about Henri Matisse* by Bijou Le Tord and *The Yellow House* by Susan Goldman Rubin.

9-5f Abstract

Era: late 1940s

Artists:

Elaine de Kooning

Willem de Kooning

Jackson Pollock

Mark Rothko

Abstract artists were intrigued with color and physical qualities of paint: "What can I do with paint on canvas?" Abstract expressionism began after World War II. Jackson Pollock is a good example of an abstract expressionist who practiced action or gesture painting by dripping, dribbling, spraying, pouring, throwing, and splashing paint. Design was often left to chance or accident. These painters worked on large canvases with no concern for capturing reality or for telling a story.

An activity could be to put globs of paint on paper and let children use a soda straw to blow the paint around. The straws should be held close to the paint but not make contact with it. Remind children to exhale or blow out and not inhale. Children may also like to work outdoors on a group mural. Children can take turns dripping paint, using squeeze bottles, or carefully trickling paint from a paper cup. Abstract art is challenging for most adults to understand; children, on the other hand, are much more comfortable with the experimental nature of abstract art. Reading aloud *Action Jackson* by Jan Greenberg and Sandra Jordan and *A Visit to the Art Galaxy* by Anne Reiner may encourage children's exploration even more.

9-5g Fauvism

Era: 1910s

Artists:

André Derain

Raoul Dufy

Amedeo Modigliani

Georges Rouault

Fauvism is an offshoot of Expressionism. Fauvists experimented with pure, bright colors in daring and innovative ways to represent positive emotions, including joy, pleasure, comfort, love, and happiness. Often there was little concern for the naturalistic or realistic use of color. Fauvists were not always concerned with mixing the proper color for skin. Human skin could be painted pink, green, or whatever, depending on the artist's mood. In this way, Fauvists believed that they could use color to make emotional statements. Objects were characterized with bold outlines and abstract lines. An emotional use of color was of primary concern.

An activity could be to make a picture depicting a positive emotion or feeling, such as joy, love, hope, happiness, or caring. Encourage children to select and use the crayons that they believe best capture their feeling, with little or no concern for the naturalistic or realistic use of color. "What does 'happy' mean to you? Let's find a 'happy-colored' crayon to make our happy picture." Books like *That's How It Is When We Draw* by Ruth Lercher Bornstein and *Lily Brown's Paintings* by Angela Johnson and E. B. Lewis will support children in choosing colors and subjects that communicate feelings in their artwork.

9-5h **Cubism**

Era: 1900s

Artists:

Georges Braque

Fernand Léger

Piet Mondrian

Pablo Picasso

Juan Gris

Cubism is the source of all twentieth-century abstract art. It seeks an intellectual conception of form and shape. Cubists attempt to break everything down into component geometric or architectural shapes. How can three-dimensional form—including the back, side, and bottom—be represented on a two-dimensional flat canvas? To do this, Cubists abandoned traditional treatment of space and form and instead focused on the use of the cylinder, sphere, and cube. For example, a Cubist might represent a tree by simultaneously depicting its top, sides, back, insides, and bottom. Intellectually, we are shown the entire tree. There is little concern for color, depth, or proper perspective. Objects appear flat, with little concern for background or foreground. They may be repeated in an overlapping sequence to suggest motion and movement. Cubists introduced the art form of **collage**.

After reading to the children *Picasso and the Girl with a Ponytail* by Laurence Anholt, an activity is to make a collage using only geometric paper shapes, either cut or torn. Because a collage often has letters embedded in it, children could search through magazines and add letters to their own collage.

9-5i **Kinetic Art**

Era: 1920s

Artists:

Alexander Calder

Marcel Duchamp

Why must art be flat and motionless? **Kinetic art** attempts to incorporate physical movement by using levers, gears, and movable parts. Kinetic art invites participation. People interacting with kinetic sculpture cause it to move or change. Wind also causes the hanging objects on a mobile to move.

An activity is to have children make a mobile. Older children could attempt a moving junk sculpture or assemblage. For example, a robot could be constructed using fasteners, yarn, string, wire, nuts and bolts, and rubber bands, which would facilitate movement.

9-5j **Surrealism/Dadaism**

Era: 1900s

Artists:

Marc Chagall

René Magritte

Salvador Dali

Joan Miró

Henri Rousseau

Frida Kahlo

Ben Shahn

Paul Klee

Surrealism means super-realism. It attempts to create a magical, dreamlike world more intense than reality. Dreams, images, fantasies, and the subconscious are the subject matter, portrayed either realistically or abstractly. Objects, space, symbols, size, perspective, and time are distorted, transformed, or superimposed. For example, a fish with a human head may fly through a rock-laden sky. The viewer may appear shocked and ask, "What is it? What is it supposed to be? What does it mean?" The artist has been successful in causing the viewer to stop, observe, and emotionally respond.

Read books like *Dinner at Magritte's* by Michael Garland and *Frida* by Jonah Winter to help children understand the fantasy and imagination in Surrealist art. Then, encourage children to represent their dreams, wishes, fantasies, nightmares, and innermost thoughts and feelings.

9-5k **Pop Art**

Era: 1950s

Artists:

Jasper Johns

Nam June Paik

Roy Lichtenstein

Andy Warhol

Pop art (Popular art) made a social statement or critique of contemporary American culture. Pop artists chose subject matter that was familiar to everyday life—soup cans, soft drink containers, movie stars, cartoons, and other examples of advertising art. The common, taken-for-granted product becomes art. Although obvious in subject matter, these objects were represented, often in repeated fashion, with painstaking, realistic detail. Again, photographic realism was attempted and attained. There was no intent to make an emotional statement beyond the satire of the commercialism of contemporary culture.

The book *Uncle Andy's* by James Warhol shares the perspective of Andy Warhol's nephew on his uncle's art. An activity is to have older children design their own package or wrapper for a candy bar, cereal, or soft drink. Or children draw their own or a group cartoon strip with fine-point markers. Four or five frames may be sufficient.

9-5l **Op Art**

Era: 1960s

Artists:

Frank Stella

Victor Vasarely

Op art (Optical art) was an artistic style that developed in the psychedelic 1960s. Op artists were intrigued with the effects of black and white, color, figure-ground relations, and depth. They used the principles of optics and perception to create optical illusions with shapes, lines, and patterns. Wiggly and concentric lines and patterns suggested movement and form to the beholder. Op art is a style demanding much technical proficiency and does not easily translate into an early childhood art activity. Reading the book *It's Me, Marva: Optical Illusions* by Marjorie Priceman, however, gives children additional experiences with Optical art.

9-5m **The Folk Arts**

Era: late 1700s to 1800s, through contemporary times

Artists:

Grandma Moses

Clementine Hunter

Faith Ringgold

Charles Wysocki

Folklife or folklore is an integral part of social life because it describes the beliefs, customs, values, behaviors, and practices common to a particular cultural group of people. The **folk arts** are the expressions of a cultural group. They are produced by individuals for the use by other members of their group and are made by hand rather than mass-produced. The folk arts are a universal cultural element and a common way for communities to share their experiences. The folk arts encompass all of the arts. They are a tangible way for children to learn about diversity and about commonalities across cultural groups. Examples include handicrafts, dances, music, songs, musical instruments, wood carvings, leather works, metal works, pottery, clothing and accessories, jewelry, weavings, quilts, toys, and cooking utensils, among others. When selecting samples to share with children, remember that items should be authentic to the group. Family and community members are excellent sources of folk arts. Not only do many families have a collection of folk art pieces, but often family members are also good craft makers. They may be pleased to come to your classroom and share their experiences.

More specifically, American folk art refers to a movement of American folk artists who lived in New England, New York, and Pennsylvania in the late 1700s to mid-1800s. American folk artists continue to work at their art form or craft today. American folk art—for example, a painting or quilt—can be identified by its bold, simple designs; vivid colors; and simplistic handling of light, proportion, and perspective. Generally, American folk art makes a social, political, or religious statement. Often, common objects and events such as growing flowers, going to market, or getting married are depicted. It is this "homey" quality that accounts for its appeal. Reading *A Year with Grandma Moses* by W. Nikola-Lisa can introduce children to the folk arts.

Did You Get It?

The three major art movements are realistic, abstract, and _____.

   a. symbolic

   b. aesthetic

   c. surrealistic

   d. nonobjective

Take the full quiz on CourseMate.

naea) 9-6 **Art Critique**

Even young children can be taught to critique a work of art. Merritt (1967) said that "when children look at paintings they like or dislike specific things about them . . . their first reactions are to like paintings because they show puppies or sunsets or other favorite representations" (p. 27).

Langer (1957) wrote that in order for effective art criticism to occur, three components are necessary: a communicator, the artist; a medium, the artwork; and a receiver or viewer who accepts, interprets, and incorporates what the artist has communicated. Cole and Schaefer (1990) add a fourth component, a facilitator. A teacher who guides the encounter between artwork and child by carrying on an art critique is acting as a facilitator. The role of the teacher as facilitator or enabler will be discussed in detail in Chapter 15.

First, a teacher provides background information about the particular piece: who made it, what the artist was like, what the world was like at the time. Young children are egocentric and may be more interested in their own art than in the artwork of others. Cognitively, they will be unable to empathize fully with the lives and historical times of famous artists. Still, an introduction to the foundations of good art and our artistic heritage is warranted.

The **art critique** can focus on the following five points:

1. What is it?

   Is it a painting, drawing, weaving, or print? What are its physical properties? Is it big, small, square, round, solid, moving, or framed? What is it made out of? Did the artist use paper, paint, metal, clay, or yarn?

2. What do you see when you look at this work of art? Encourage children to focus on the artist's use of line, color, shape or form, mass or volume, design, pattern, space, balance, and texture. How are these artistic elements used? What shapes do you see? What colors were used? Can anyone find lines?

3. What is the artist trying to say?

   Try to put the artist's picture into words. What is the message? Pretend that this is a book with pictures. What words go along with the picture the artist has given? Discuss what you see: people, animals, buildings, or events.

4. How does it make you feel?

   Do you feel happy, sad, angry, scared, or funny? What does the artist do to make you feel this way?

5. Do you like it?

   Why or why not? What is it about the work of art that makes you like or dislike it? How would you change it?

Questions 4 and 5 will evoke different responses. Our aim is to help children acquire artistic appreciation and make judgments based on accepted standards, including the artistic elements.

Did You Get It?

The teacher's primary role in teaching students how to critique art is

a. facilitator.

b. communicator.

c. negotiator.

d. bridge builder.

Take the full quiz on CourseMate.

DAP naeyc naea) 9-7 **Collage**

A collage is a picture composed of different shapes or elements. A collage can be two-dimensional and composed of flat pieces of paper, or it can be three-dimensional and made with Styrofoam™ chips and raised layers of fabric. Pieces of paper that are torn, cut, pasted, or taped can be creatively arranged into a collage. Although the activities are listed separately, there is no reason materials used in one activity cannot be included in another. A collage is not limited to paper. There is an infinite supply of collage materials (see Figures 9–5 and 9–6). The key is quality and organization. Not all junk will have artistic potential. Dirty or damaged items hold little aesthetic appeal. A pile of unorganized junk triggers little creative transformation. It is important to organize collage materials according to some scheme—for example, papers in one bin; ribbon, lace, and yarn in another; magazines in a neat stack on the shelf; and so forth. Children need basic order to help them see artistic possibilities.

Photo courtesy of Robert Schirrmacher

Figure 9–5 A valentine collage.

Figure 9–6 Recycled junk collage.

Photo courtesy of Robert Schirrmacher

9-7a **Personally Expressive Art Activities**

Following are some personally expressive art activities for collage.

Toddler, Preschool, Kindergarten, and School-Age Activity: Geometric Shapes Collage. Younger children who lack scissoring skills may enjoy pasting precut geometric shapes into a design or picture. Provide an array of different colors, sizes, and shapes. Older children with scissoring skills can draw and cut their own geometric shapes. Encourage children to place shapes into some arrangement before gluing them. Or a rough sketch or outline can be drawn first and later filled in with geometric shapes.

Kindergarten and School-Age Activity: Corrugated Cardboard Collage. Corrugated cardboard has an interesting texture and linear look. Older children can cut different shapes or pieces from it and make a collage. Encourage them to note how the ridges can go in different directions. This is what gives a corrugated cardboard collage its visual appeal. Corrugated cardboard, with its raised ridges and neutral color, provides a striking contrast when it is used with flat or colorful papers or fabric.

Toddler, Preschool, Kindergarten, and School-Age Activity: Tissue Paper Collage. Colored tissue paper can be torn or cut. Because it is so thin, it may frustrate the young cutter. Provide small bowls of liquid starch and sponges or small brushes for spreading. Encourage children to note the transparent quality of tissue paper and the possibilities for creating new colors by overlapping and building layers.

Or form a tissue paper collage on a piece of wax paper. Lay another piece of wax paper on top. An adult can gently press with a warm iron. The heat will melt the wax and seal the collage.

Or use thinned white glue to paste tissue papers inside the plastic lid of a coffee can. This will provide a ready-made frame. Carefully punch a hole at the top, lace with yarn, and hang.

Kindergarten and School-Age Activity: Montage. *Montage* refers to a collage built around a theme, such as love, friendship, or family. Words and pictures related to the theme can be included. A montage around the theme of vehicles could include pictures of cars, trucks, bikes, airplanes, boats, motorcycles, stop signs, and traffic lights.

Toddler, Preschool, Kindergarten, and School-Age Activity: Collage Mural. A collage can also be a group project correlated with a concept under study. Some examples include colors, shapes, community helpers, farm animals, and ocean life. Children can search magazines looking for examples of the concept. A collage mural can be an extended activity; it need not be completed in a short period of time. It could be set up as a center, with children adding to it from time to time over a period of days.

A collage does not always have to be done on paper. Be creative; provide the following:

- cardboard
- plastic foam
- paper plates
- plastic foam trays
- box lids
- egg cartons
- wood
- containers

Nor does collage entail only the use of paper. Look through your artistic junk for a variety of materials that can be pasted, glued, stapled, or taped.

Toddler, Preschool, Kindergarten, and School-Age Activity: Nature Collage. Nature specimens, such as leaves, petals, grass, and sticks can be carefully glued onto paper or sturdy cardboard (see Figure 9–7).

Other examples of nature items are listed in Appendix A. Some prefer to first press their nature specimens for about a week between layers of newspaper with heavy objects on top to get them flat. Or they can be arranged on wax paper with a second sheet on top and pressed with a warm iron.

Toddler, Preschool, Kindergarten, and School-Age Activity: Fabric, Felt, or Material Collage. Children enjoy using materials other than paper in their collage. Provide small scraps of fabric, felt, or material for children to paste or glue. Older children with fairly sharp scissors and good cutting skills may be able to cut out or tear their own pieces (see Figure 9–8).

Figure 9–7 A nature collage.

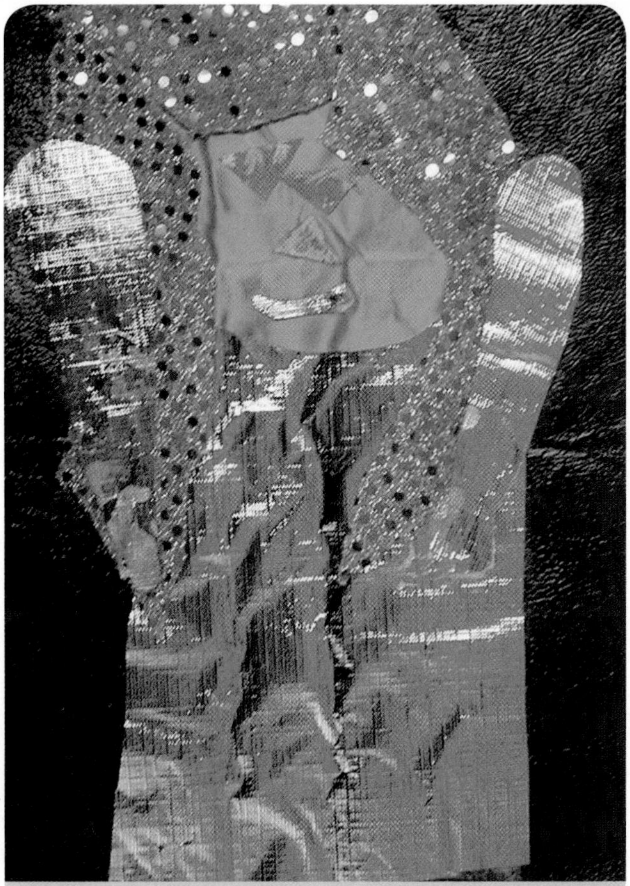

Figure 9–8 Fabric collage with metallic elements.

Preschool, Kindergarten, and School-Age Activity: String or Yarn Collage. A collage can be composed of string or yarn. Each can be dipped in glue and creatively arranged on an art surface. Remind the children to squeeze the excess glue out before placing the string. Other collage material can be incorporated.

Toddler, Preschool, Kindergarten, and School-Age Activity: Texture Collage. Most of the collage activities mentioned involve textures. A collage can also specifically focus on textured papers, including:

- sandpaper
- newspaper
- flocked wallpaper
- magazine pages
- tissue paper

Or you can use a variety of textured fabrics and materials, including:

- wool
- burlap
- cotton
- netting
- velvet
- foam rubber

Textured nature specimens, listed under "Nature Collage," earlier, and in Appendix A, can be included.

9-7b Sensory Exploration Activities

Following are sensory exploration activities for collage.

Toddler, Preschool, Kindergarten, and School-Age Activity: Magazine Picture Collage. Magazines offer a wealth of letters, words, and pictures to be torn or cut out and pasted or taped to paper.

Preschool, Kindergarten, and School-Age Activity: Magazine Mix-Ups. Children make a picture out of unrelated parts—for example, an animal with a human head or the front of a car with the tail of an airplane. Provide part of a picture for each child. The pieces, cut from a magazine, should be different for each child. Examples included a cat's head, a person's body, the trunk of a tree, and a diving board with no steps. Encourage children to look through magazines and find a part to finish their mixed-up picture by adding a silly top, bottom, head, body, or side as needed.

Summary

(9-1) Art education is recognized as making significant contributions to children's learning and development, including helping children develop positive attitudes, characteristics, and intellectual skills. (9-2) The Consortium of National Arts Education Associations (1994) has developed standards describing competencies in the arts and establishing connections between the arts and disciplines such as the sciences and humanities. There are various approaches to art education. (9-3) While the Getty Center for Education in the Arts advocates Discipline-Based Art Education (DBAE), which includes art making, art criticism, art history, and aesthetics, this book focuses on a studio-based approach. (9-4) The studio-based approach is child-centered and includes aesthetics, sensing and experiencing, making art, and learning about art, artists, and their styles. (9-5) A sequential study of art history is not appropriate for young children, but it is helpful for teachers to have knowledge about different artistic styles or movements. This will allow them to answer questions children have or to make curriculum connections. (9-6) Art critique encourages children to look closely at artwork and form opinions. A simple format of art critique can be used to introduce children to the process of art critique. (9-7) Depending on materials used, collage can be an appropriate experience for toddlers as well as older children.

Key Terms

Abstract art, 182

art critique, 187

collage, 185

Cubism, 185

Discipline-Based Art Education (DBAE), 178

Expressionism, 184

Fauvism, 185

folk arts, 186

Impressionism, 183

Kinetic art, 185

National Standards for Arts Education, 177

Naturalism, 183

nonobjective art, 182

non-Western art, 181

Op art (Optical art), 186

Pointillism, 184

Pop art (Popular art), 186

Realism, 183

studio-oriented, 178

Surrealism, 185

✔ Suggested Activities

1. Visit an early childhood classroom. Look carefully to see what aesthetic elements the teacher has included in the classroom. How are these elements related to the curriculum? How were they introduced to the children?

2. Use the art critique to analyze and discuss a work of art. Research the artist and era.

3. Begin a collection of art postcards, photographs, prints, posters, or books. Visit thrift shops, used book stores, and library sales. Look for reproductions of non-Western art and works by female artists.

4. Arrange to accompany a group of young children on an informal field trip to a local art museum, gallery, or artist's studio. Visit in advance to know what is available.

5. Arrange for an artist to come in, model art processing, and informally work with the children.

6. Draft a letter to the families of children in your class asking for recycled items to use in collage activities. How will you explain the value of collage?

7. How will you define art to your students? Develop a definition and consider how you will introduce that definition to the children.

Review

1. List the components of a complete early childhood art program.

2. Identify and briefly explain the three major artistic movements.

3. List the five major points addressed in an art critique.

4. The National Standards for Arts Education lists what six reasons for the importance of arts education?

5. The National Standards for Arts Education identified a set of competencies. How do they relate to early childhood art education?

6. Discuss DBAE.

Resources

Romare Bearden Foundation website (www. beardenfoundation.org), a biography of the artist, an overview of his work and information about exhibits of his art.

Go to YouTube and view "The Dawn of Art" video on Cave Art from Chauvet France.

Go to YouTube and find "Pointillism: Seurat's Grant Jatte and Circus," a webexhibit by Color, Vision, and Art.

American Folk Art Museum (http://folkartmuseum.org), the website for the premier American museum.

Art Criticism is a wiki featuring an art criticism worksheet.

ArtsEdNet is a website originating from the Getty Center for Education in the Arts (www.getty.edu) designed for educators interested in discipline-based art education.

 Visit CourseMate for this textbook to access the eBook, Did You Get It? quizzes, Digital Downloads, TeachSource Videos, flashcards, and more. Go to CengageBrain.com to log in, register, or purchase access.

First/Second Grade Lesson Plan

Recycling with Romare Bearden

GOAL

The student understands his/her role as a steward of the environment.

OUTCOMES

The student is expected to:

a. explain the three Rs of environmental stewardship (reduce, reuse, recycle).
b. identify Romare Bearden as a twentieth century African American artist who reused many materials in making his collage.
c. list ways to reuse resources at home and in the classroom.
d. reuse resources in creating a collage.

MATERIALS

a. Images of Romare Bearden's collages, available online
b. *Me and Uncle Romie* by Claire Hartfield
c. Collage materials, including magazine pictures, wallpaper samples, greeting cards, ribbon, fabric scraps, etc.
d. Manila paper or tagboard, scissors, and glue for each child
e. Chart of the three Rs
f. Towel and paper towel
g. Dry erase board and markers

INTRODUCTION

Remind the children of previous discussions about taking care of the environment and their introduction to the three Rs. Tell them that today we will be learning about the second R—Reuse. Ask them to explain what reusing means. To illustrate their explanation, show the children a terry cloth towel and a paper towel. Ask them which of these represents "Reuse." Have them describe what will eventually happen when we each use a paper towel only one time and what happens when we have a terry cloth towel that we can use more than once.

DEVELOPMENT

Have the children brainstorm items in the classroom and at home that can be reused for the sake of the environment. Record their list on the white board. Introduce the book *Me and Uncle Romie*. Explain that this is a true story of an artist who reused many different materials to tell stories in his artwork. Provide a focus for listening by telling the children you will ask them to name the things the artist reused in his art. Read the story to the children. At the end of the story, go back to the focus for listening and ask the children to name the reused items they identified in the illustrations. Distribute the paper, glue, scissors, and collage materials. Ask the children to reuse collage materials to tell about something important to them.

CONCLUSION

As the children finish their collages, ask them to pair and share with a friend to explain how they reused materials in their collages. Have them compare the items they used to those they saw in Romare Bearden's collages.

ASSESSMENT

a. Did the children recall the three Rs from the previous lesson?
b. Did the children brainstorm reusable items in the classroom and at home?
c. Did the children compare the items they reused with the items Bearden reused?
d. Did the children create collages from reused items?

Go to cengagebrain.com for a full-size version of this lesson plan.

Providing Art Experiences

It is time to translate what you know about art, creativity, and child development into curriculum. What is curriculum? Curriculum is what happens in the classroom—both the planned and unplanned. Our focus will be on planning art activities and turning the unexpected and unplanned into meaningful learning experiences. Chapter 10, Child-Centered Art versus Teacher-Directed Projects, provides guidelines for selecting activities with artistic merit as opposed to nonart activities that rely on adult input. Chapter 11, Planning, Implementing, and Evaluating Art, focuses on the teacher's role as curriculum developer. The chapter also shares different approaches to curriculum development. Chapter 12, Integrating Art across the Early Childhood Curriculum, makes connections between art and the curricular areas. Activities are provided to show how art can support academic learning through integration in mathematics, science, literacy, social studies, and the expressive arts. Chapter 13, The Art Center, provides criteria for creating the classroom art center.

What do you see in this photograph? It appears the teacher has planned an art activity to go along with the class's study of weather. First, the teacher read a story about the wind. She took her class of three-year-olds to the playground, giving each child a long ribbon to tie to the fence. The children watched their ribbons blow in the wind and discussed how the wind blows from different directions, sometimes bringing warm air and sometimes cold. When the children came inside, the teacher gave each a cloud outline drawn on construction paper. The children glued cotton balls on the outline. The teacher applied lines of glue, and the children sprinkled glitter from a shaker. How much of this activity was done by the child? How much by the teacher? How did this activity help children learn about the wind? Did this child do a "good" job? How do you rate the creativity of this activity?

© Cengage Learning

Dear Families,

Your child may have told you about our classroom museum. We've designated a bulletin board to display children's artwork and have placed a table underneath to display sculptures and models. Each child displays one item at a time, but can change the item at any time. Every item must be accompanied by the artist's name, the title, and the completion date of the art. We've added the job of *docent* to our classroom helpers; our docent gives museum tours to visitors. We've used what we learned during our trip to the art museum to create our classroom museum.

The artwork displayed in our museum comes from the children's own ideas and experiences. As their teacher, I might suggest a theme about which the children can draw, but each child chooses what to draw and what materials to use. I also teach children to use tools like scissors and paintbrushes, and then encourage each child to use those tools to express creative ideas.

While child-centered art might appear unorganized or messy, remember that creativity is developing and learning is occurring. Your child develops problem-solving and decision-making skills and gains confidence by expressing original ideas through art.

When your child brings artwork home, please talk to him or her about it. Ask your child about the decisions made during creation: choice of colors, placement of objects, the artist's perspective. Display your child's work and encourage your child to share the display with others. Because the artworks express your child's ideas, please let him or her make the decision about when to take them down or discard them.

We invite you to tour our art museum with our enthusiastic docents. You're sure to enjoy the artwork!

Sincerely,

Your Child's Teacher

10

Child-Centered Art versus Teacher-Directed Projects

© Cengage Learning

What do you see in this photograph?

What does Jacob's face tell you? Does he appear a bit unsure about art?

Jacob has limited experience using paint, crayons, or markers. He watches what other children do and sees that art can be messy. This confuses Jacob because his family expects him to stay clean at school. Jacob's parents also expect him to create beautiful pictures of something recognizable. His family values art. As Jacob's teacher, however, you sense that Jacob is not ready to create realistic art. You want to let Jacob observe and process and explore. You also feel pressure from his parents to teach Jacob how to make art that looks like something they know. What should you do? What art experiences are appropriate for children like Jacob?

Learning Outcomes

After reading this chapter, you should be able to:

10-1 Use the continuum of approaches to describe three different ways to teach art.

10-2 Distinguish child-centered art from teacher-directed projects.

10-3 Explain circumstances in which crafts or teacher-directed projects might be appropriate.

10-4 Plan developmentally appropriate art activities.

10-5 Identify alternatives to activities masquerading as creative art.

10-6 Explain the different viewpoints on teaching art to children.

10-7 Provide art activities using paper.

Standards addressed in this chapter

DAP Criteria
  2 Teaching to enhance development and learning
  3 Planning curriculum to achieve important goals

NAEYC Standards
  2 Curriculum
  3 Teaching

NAEA Visual Arts Standards
  1 Understanding and applying media, techniques, and processes
  4 Understanding the visual arts in relation to history and cultures

DAP naeyc 10-1 A Continuum of Teaching Approaches

There are different ways to approach teaching art. This chapter will identify and critique teacher-directed, guided, and child-centered approaches. What is the teacher's role in children's art? Adults can stimulate children to make art by being models and participants. Adults model creativity in their daily lives and actively participate in art activities themselves. Although it is important to know about art, an adult does not need to be an artist to provide creative art experiences for children.

The different approaches to working with young children reside along a continuum. Teacher-directed and child-centered are two opposite points on the continuum (see Figure 10–1). Both points are valid at certain times for certain children and certain activities. The role of facilitator or guide is a compromise and a midpoint between these two opposite roles.

A facilitator or guide is available without monopolizing the activity, as is the case with direct instruction. A facilitator is a keen observer who knows when to subtly intervene, ask a question, or pose a problem. Children who need assistance know that the teacher is a resource who is available to share knowledge, skills, time, and attention.

Children's art fascinates adults. Although they may not understand it, parents enjoy their children's art. Early childhood educators also value children's art and provide time for it in the daily schedule. Although most young children are neither interested in nor ready for formal academics such as reading, virtually all young children are interested in and ready for art.

Most people agree that early childhood art is important, but not everyone agrees on what it entails. Is scribbling art? Can coloring in a coloring book be considered art? This unit provides guidelines for determining the creative merits of an activity or approach to art. Traditional teacher-directed and product-oriented art activities will be critiqued. Activities masquerading as art are identified and alternatives suggested.

naea What is art? Susanne Langer (1957), the first great female philosopher in America, believed that humans are born with an urgent biological need to create art. Art helps us put our life experiences into symbolic form. We are then able to stand back and clarify, critically examine, and share our experiences. But how is this done? There are many possibilities for artistic self-expression: literature, drama, music, and the visual arts, both visual and plastic. Our focus is on how young children use the visual arts to represent their life experiences.

The plastic, or three-dimensional, arts include sculpture, ceramics, and architecture. The graphic, or two-dimensional, arts include painting, printmaking, and drawing.

Did You Get It?

Which statement about the teacher's role as a facilitator in the creation and critique of art is not true?

a. A facilitator is a guide.

b. A facilitator is aware of the difference between intervention and monopolization.

c. A facilitator always makes him or herself available.

d. A facilitator recognizes that teacher-directed and child-centered activities are essentially one and the same.

Take the full quiz on CourseMate.

DAP naeyc 10-2 Approaches to Teaching Art

The major approaches to teaching are also applicable to teaching art. Some art projects are structured and **teacher-directed**. The teacher has a definite idea of what children will make and how they will go about it. Specific directions are given to ensure recognizable products. There is little input from the children. The teacher may feel that a finished, recognizable product is necessary to provide a tangible representation of what children have learned, for both the children's families and school administrators (Thompson, 2005). For example, a teacher distributes a piece of paper with an outline of a tree. The children are instructed to use black or brown to color the trunk and green for the top. They also cut or tear small circles from red construction paper. These are pasted onto the green top. The completed apple trees look nearly identical. Generally, this approach is used when an art activity accompanies a whole-group lesson plan. These projects are teacher-directed.

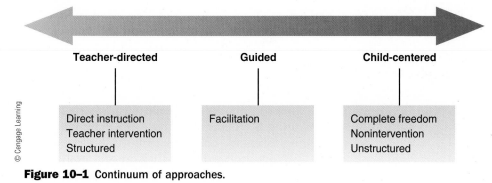

Figure 10–1 Continuum of approaches.

© Cengage Learning

▶❚❚ TeachSource Video

Curriculum Planning: Implementing Developmentally Appropriate Practices in an Early Childhood Classroom

Work with a partner to identify three important characteristics of the developmentally appropriate program portrayed in the video. Discuss how these three characteristics would look in a classroom for school-age children.

Watch on CourseMate.

Seefeldt (1995) critiques teacher-directed art. Asking children to complete patterned artwork or to copy adult models undermines children's sense of psychological safety and demonstrates disrespect for children's ideas, abilities, and creativity. Children who are frequently given patterns to cut out or outlines to color are being told that they, and their art, are inadequate (see Figure 10–2). An opposite approach is to be unstructured and completely **child-centered**. A teacher may distribute paper and encourage children to make whatever they

Figure 10–2 The results of a teacher-directed art activity.

want or encourage them to visit the art center. In this approach, children have much input and choice. There is very little structure. Some children do well with this approach. They may have a bank of ideas to represent through art. They may also see endless artistic possibilities at the easel or art center. Many children, however, are uncomfortable with this approach. It may be too loosely structured. Some children quickly tire of inventing their own daily art program. They look to the teacher for structure, guidance, or possibilities.

According to Wright (2003), unsupported arts learning in the classroom can lead to an "anything goes" type of practice. In this noninterventionist approach, the underlying belief is that whatever children do in the arts is valuable. Teacher interference stifles a child's creativity. This hands-off approach limits the teacher's role to one of organizing the environment and discourages the teacher from suggesting ideas to mediate and scaffold children's learning. With no input from others, children can become bored and even frustrated with experiences that invite only independent experimentation. Children cannot create from nothing. They need background ideas and suggestions. Teacher-directed and child-centered approaches are extremes. Teachers can elect for compromise using support and guidance by becoming a facilitator within a guided approach.

DAP naeyc 10-2a **Children's Drawing: Free Expression or Skill to be Taught?**

In his study of children's use of drawing to explore "big ideas" in science, Brooks (2009) found that drawing plays an essential part in the learning process. For children, drawing can:

- engage their minds.
- bring a concept more clearly into conscious thought.
- focus attention.
- assist with concept formation.
- allow ideas to be revised.
- bridge gaps between perception-bound and abstract thinking.

Brooks sees drawing as an essential activity for young children, and most parents and teachers would agree. Controversy exists, however, around the issue of how children learn to draw. Can young children be taught to draw? More importantly, should they be?

Emberley (1991) views drawing as a skill that can be taught. His series of drawing books, developed for K–3 children, consists of simple, step-by-step instructions using a collection of shapes to draw imaginary creatures, faces, and buildings. Emberley began publishing his books in the 1960s. They are still available in bookstores and online and are often purchased by adults who experienced the books as children and now want them for their own children. Brookes (1986), author of *Drawing with Children*, claims to be able to teach three-year-olds to go beyond stick-figure drawing to make representational and realistic drawings. Her method is based on teaching basic elements of shape: the dot, circle, straight line, curved line, and angle line. These five elements constitute basic visual building blocks that lie at the heart of all other shapes. She encourages children to notice these elements in everyday life and to use them to build their own artistic creations. Students begin by copying simple illustrations, moving on to more complex pictures, and finally drawing from real life.

Johnson's (1990) *Teach Your Child to Draw* is aimed at parents. Her method features learning from what real artists have done. At the heart of each lesson are examples drawn from both old and new masters. Johnson believes that over time, readers begin to see their surroundings with an artist's eye and can break down objects and scenery into lines, patterns, textures, light and dark, shading, negative and positive shapes, proportion, points of view, movement, and distance.

These three authors advocate teacher-directed approaches, according to Figure 10–1. The artistic elements are at the heart of each approach. The authors believe that although artistic elements are the building blocks of art, there is no need to instruct young children in how to make them—just to get them to draw realistically. The artistic elements can be used for analyzing art (Chapter 6) and in responding to children about what they have created (Chapter 15).

Lowenfeld and Brittain (1987) and most contemporary early childhood educators, including the authors, advocate an opposing position that views drawing as free expression. This child-centered position lies at the opposite end of the continuum depicted in Figure 10–1. If children must be taught to draw, they are not developmentally ready. Teaching them how to draw will not enhance their drawing ability but will focus children on pleasing adults rather than expressing their own ideas. It emphasizes product over process.

Edwards's (2012) *Drawing on the Right Side of the Brain: The Definitive* assumes a middle position and compromise. Although she believes older children need to be taught to draw, she does not believe they need a visual symbol system or group of shapes to help them draw effectively. She does not advocate that young children be taught to draw but instead believes that age 10 is a good time to begin formal instruction. By age 10, many preadolescents are frustrated with their own crude attempts and are motivated to learn to draw realistically. Her visual exercises include copying upside-down pictures, drawing a common object such as a stuffed animal without taking one's eyes off it, and paying attention to empty or negative space. Edwards's methods are popular in elementary and secondary art

education programs. Her approach has been successful with adults who claim they could never draw.

DAP naeyc 10-2b **Teacher as Facilitator**

A **teacher-guided** approach offers the best of the two former approaches: subtle structure with much child direction and input (see Figure 10–3). For example:

- A teacher supplies the theme. "Children, it's getting very close to summer. Today, we will make a picture that reminds us of this season." Although the theme is given, there is no specified product. Children are free to use paint, crayons, or markers to make their own versions of what summer means to them. Di Leo (2003), however, reminds teachers that children's favorite subjects in art are most likely to be people—particularly important people in their lives.

- A teacher introduces new materials at the art center. "Today I put some spools and buttons on the art table. Look at them and think how you might use them. Try out different ways of using them." Children are free to use them as brushes, make stamped impressions, or paste them to a collage, as long as the rules for the art center are upheld. Encouraging children to create art related to materials with which they play and learn may "further develop children's development and understanding" (Swann, 2009, p. 231).

- A teacher builds on an existing activity or suggests a new technique. "I've noticed how much we enjoy easel painting with our long-handled brushes. I found these small branches outside and am leaving them at the easels. How might you use them for painting?" Or "Let me show you another way of doing watercolor by first wetting your paper." Or "I see how much you enjoy your paper-bag puppet. If you like, we can sew one out of cloth."

Figure 10–3 A facilitator or guide gives help when needed.

- A teacher poses a problem. "Let's see how many different shapes we can cut out of paper for pasting." Or "How could we use these empty boxes and ribbon?"
- A teacher extends art into other curricular areas. "There seems to be a lot of excitement in your picture. Would you like to share it by telling a story?"

Different approaches may work for certain activities and certain children. Young children will not automatically discover how to use a watercolor set. They need some direction and instruction in its use and care. They need

not, however, be told what to paint or what it should look like. For example, Emily is having difficulty deciding what to include in her summer picture. Her teacher senses her frustration and asks her to name things that remind her of summer. Emily answers, "Sun and swimming." Her teacher further structures the task by asking Emily to choose one. With the teacher's guidance, Emily chooses the sun and now must decide if she should use paints, watercolor, crayons, or markers to represent it. Carefully examine Figures 10–4a–d. Using the continuum of approaches to teaching art (see Figure 10–1 at the beginning of the chapter), do two things. First, decide

Figure 10–4 Where along the continuum of approaches does each photo fit?

where along the continuum each picture best fits. Second, provide a rationale for each answer. Your instructor may use this in a small-group activity and discussion.

DAP naeyc naea) 10-3 Projects and Crafts in the Curriculum

What should be included in an early childhood art program? Mr. Mills has baked cookies, and his toddlers will spread frosting on them for an art activity. Across the hall, kindergartners are neatly coloring a butterfly photocopy as part of their unit on spring. Their teacher reminds them that they have only a few minutes left for art. What can one say about these activities? Which have artistic merit? Do they represent what early childhood art should be? The authors would respond negatively to these questions. Although spreading frosting may be an enjoyable tactile, perceptual-motor, and edible activity, it is not art. Simply coloring a butterfly photocopy may strengthen eye-hand coordination and figure-ground relations, but it offers no opportunity for creativity. A more creative version would be to let the children draw their own butterflies with little concern for realistic rendering.

DAP naeyc 10-3a Child-Centered Art or Teacher-Directed Projects

Arts and crafts are terms that are often viewed as opposite. Hirsch (2004) provides a distinction. The motivation for art comes from within the child. Young children are learning to be autonomous and to take initiative. They are often not interested in teacher-directed experiences.

This is especially true with art. When art is extrinsically motivated, it may lack meaning, expressiveness, or detail. The art may reflect external expectations, or the autonomous child may purposefully create anything but what was requested. The approach is reproductive in that the child merely reproduces the teacher's product. By contrast, when the motivation and purpose for art come from within the child, the artwork reflects personal meaning and purpose. When children have free access

to materials in an art center, they have the opportunity to create meaning and purpose. The approach is productive, not reproductive. In terms of approach, art activities are viewed as **developmentally appropriate** while **crafts** are often teacher-directed, product-oriented, and lacking artistic merit. The term **project** is used in place of *craft*. Although some would refer to teacher-directed activities as crafts, the terms are not interchangeable. Crafts have artistic merit, and craftspeople work hard to produce crafts, many of which reflect their cultures. Crafts may also be functional as with candles, jewelry, or clothing. Therefore, it would not be fair to use crafts in the same sense of teacher-directed art projects. Instead, teacher-directed projects, rather than crafts, are the opposite of child-centered art. Substituting teacher projects for art does children a disservice; it robs them of the opportunity to make self-expressive, self-initiated art.

Is There a Place for Teacher Projects? Although teacher projects should not dominate your art program, they do have a place and are to your art program as spices are to cooking. Some people avoid spices while others use them sparingly to enhance but not dominate the taste of food. When should teacher projects be used? On occasion, they can be used:

- with older children who have a solid foundation in processing and are interested in learning to make art products.

- when children tire of visiting the art center and have run out of ideas for processing. It appears the art center is not being used.

- to introduce children to new cultures by directly experiencing representative crafts. The process involved in making crafts must be tailored to meet the developmental needs of your group.

- while allowing for individual expression, as in the choice of subject or type of decoration added. For example, children can be taught to make a piñata without specifying what it should look like when finished.

DAP naeyc 10-4 Planning Developmentally Appropriate Art Activities

Often it is easy to recognize negative examples of uncreative art. Just what should one look for in planning early childhood art activities?

10-4a Allow Children to Be Personally Expressive

Young children need to express themselves personally with a variety of artistic media. The expression should be personal because individual children approach art in unique ways. Art activities should be planned to allow for a variety of outcomes (Mulcahey, 2009). After visiting the zoo, several children were encouraged to create something related to their experiences. At the easel, Jean painted a caged black bear. Three children headed for the clay table. Jim squeezed a ball of clay and called it a seal. Tam rolled tiny clay ropes to make rays for the hot sun. Kaley cut an outline of an elephant into a slab of clay using a craft stick. Personal choice was reflected in the use of paint or clay. The children at the clay table found different ways to express what was personally meaningful to them.

10-4b Subtly Balance Artistic Process and Product

Art activities provided for young children should subtly balance processing and the making of products. A good art program understands and accepts that individual children can be oriented toward process, product, or both in their approach to art. Art processing includes skills involved in a given art activity. For example, paper work involves tearing, cutting, folding, pasting, stapling, braiding, and weaving. The product refers to the result. Processing with paper may result in a collage, weaving, or sculpture. Young children are process-oriented (see Figure 10–5). They enjoy art for the sake of doing and making, often with little concern for the result. This is why some children fail to claim their finished art products. They forget which one they did or toss it into the wastebasket as they depart. One carpool mother complained that the backseat of her van was strewn with children's art. For these children, the joy was in the process rather than in what resulted, the finished product. Processing is also important for children to develop skills in using art tools (Richardson and Walker, 2011) and their eventual use of those tools in creating expressive art. Older children, however, become product-oriented. They are concerned about size, shape, color, placement, detail, and realism. They are quick to put their names on their art and may become upset when papers tear or paint smears. It may

Figure 10–5 Processing with art media is as important as making a finished product.

be important for these children to take an art product home daily.

Art is dependent on both process and product. Artistic processing is necessary to arrive at a finished product. Elaborating or refining a product involves processing.

10-4c Be Open-Ended, Allowing Children to Be Creative

Early childhood art programs should encourage young children to be creative. They can encourage children to represent their world creatively by allowing them to make choices (Mulcahey, 2009) about:

- what they want to make (content)
- how to go about making it (process)
- what it will end up looking like (product)

In general, loosely structured planned activities set the stage for creative expression. For example, paints, brushes, and paper at the easel may be enough for some children. All they need is time to pursue an idea. Others may need a teacher's subtle guidance. "You told us about the fun time you had with your cousins. Can you paint something that will tell us about what you did? " We rob children of the opportunity for creative artistic expression when we specify what the finished product should be or the process for making it. For example, coloring, cutting out, and correctly pasting together a train does not involve creativity.

Still, creative expression must abide by general rules, guidelines, and limits. Pretend fighting with scissors is dangerous and not creative. Children need to be taught the proper way to handle scissors and all other artistic media, equipment, and supplies. Rules need to be discussed and posted. "Chris, bring me your scissors. They are only for cutting paper."

An Opportunity for Teacher Reflection

Madison, A Six-Year-Old in Your First-Grade Class, is a bright child with strong academic skills. She gets along well with others, has well-developed fine motor abilities, and keen visual perception. Madison is a frequent visitor to the art center, and her artwork reflects her abilities. It is now February, and you have observed a change in the subjects of Madison's artwork. While at the beginning of the year Madison portrayed her family and friends, her dog, and experiences at school, increasingly she has focused on fantasy elements, particularly unicorns. As you review Madison's art portfolio, you note that unicorns are included in every recent entry. Although the artwork isn't particularly dark or frightening, you still see a marked change from the earlier variety of subjects in her artwork. *Should you be concerned about Madison's intense focus on unicorns? How might you follow up on your review of Madison's portfolio? Should you talk to Madison's parents? Should you encourage Madison to branch out in her choice of subjects?*

10-4d Allow for Discovery and Experimentation

Children can arrive at artistic products through discovery and experimentation. For example, explicitly teaching sponge painting or printing may not be necessary.

It is possible to provide paints and an array of sponges and cookie cutters and encourage children to see what they can do with these "painters" and the paint (see Figure 10–6). They experiment by spreading paint with sponges or using sponges in a stamping motion. Either way, they discover for themselves a new technique through their own active experimentation. Art activities should focus on what children learn in the process rather than what they do (Mulcahey, 2009).

Keep in mind, though, that experimentation may mean starting over again. When using new materials, or trying new perspectives, encourage children to begin projects with rough drafts done on scrap paper before initiating the final product. As a classroom teacher, author Jill Fox kept a stack of used computer paper in the art center. Her kindergarteners experimented with art effects on the blank sides of the paper before creating their final versions on more-expensive drawing paper. This practice helped emphasize conservation of resources and provided experience with the steps of drafting and editing the children will use later in the writing process. Exploration, experimentation, discovery, and invention are important elements in art activities for children. A little advance planning can provide the resources children need to fully engage in the artistic process.

10-4e Allow for Active Engagement and Sustained Involvement

Art should actively engage children. They are active physical beings, and their artistic expression should reflect this. They need upright easels to encourage sweeping whole-arm movements while standing. Clay needs to be torn, punched, pulled, rolled, flattened, pinched, and pounded. Art activities will encourage and capitalize on children's needs for sensory-motor

Brain Connection

Hands-on activities stimulate various parts of the brain. Active participation in the learning process helps young children form stronger connections between what they already know and what they are learning (Rushton & Larkin, 2001).

© Cengage Learning

Figure 10–6 Different brushes help children discover and experiment.

exploration and movement. Ample blocks of time are needed to foster sustained involvement. Not all children are able to complete an art activity in a pre-determined block of time. Some will want to continue working later or even the following day. Other children will impulsively finish their art in a few minutes. Obviously, few young children will work for hours at the same art activity. Still, they can be encouraged to examine and extend their art.

10-4f Be Intrinsically Motivating

Art—like music, movement, and play—is intrinsically motivating. Children will engage in art for the pleasure and reward inherent in painting, coloring, working with clay, or making a collage. Young children are internally motivated to learn and to make sense of their world. They manipulate, explore with their senses, and ask endless questions. Although praise and rewards are effective, they are not always needed in art. Author Robert Schirrmacher observed a teacher praising a child's finished art product. "Oh, look how pretty Marla's painting of a house turned out!" Later, several children copied Marla's idea and style to win this teacher's praise. Their motivation for doing art had moved from internal to external. Instead, Marla's teacher could have praised her efforts and involvement. "Maria, you worked so long and hard. You kept going until you got it just as you wanted it!" Research by Lepper and Greene (1975) showed that external motivation and techniques of behavior modification actually decrease a child's intrinsic motivation. Praising preschoolers' use of felt-tip markers actually decreased their interest in using them.

10-4g Be Success Oriented

Early childhood art activities should be success oriented. Choosing art activities that are developmentally appropriate and moderately challenging will ensure a child's success. In turn, feelings of success and mastery foster a child's positive self-concept. A major goal of early childhood education is to help children become competent and confident. Activities that are too difficult or detailed may frustrate children and lead to failure. The danger is that young children may generalize failure at a task to failure as a person. For example, four-year-olds at summer camp were given cardboard insects to trace, cut, and paste. The objects were small and detailed including thin legs and feelers. The cardboard was flimsy, and the scissors dull. The paper tore and insect heads and tails were missing. Few of the children could match the teacher's example hanging overhead. The children became frustrated. The teacher meant well but did not translate the developmental abilities of four-year-olds into a success-oriented art activity.

10-4h Be Available to All Children

Art should be available to all children. Older infants who can hold a nontoxic marker or crayon can be subtly guided to make marks on paper. They can scribble while seated in a high chair or sprawled atop a long sheet of paper on the floor. Toddlers enjoy painting and using markers, crayons, and clay. Preschoolers can be provided with an even wider array of legitimate artistic media. Art is neither masculine nor feminine; both boys and girls should be encouraged to engage in art. If the easels or art center become monopolized by one sex, a teacher may need to do some social engineering. For example, girls in one kindergarten were drawing pictures of food to take to the housekeeping center. The boys avoided both the art and housekeeping centers and concentrated in the block area. After two days of this sex-segregated play, the teacher took action. She suggested the boys work together with the girls in building a restaurant. One boy designed his own play money from scrap construction paper. Another painted a store sign.

Because art fosters feelings of esteem and success, it is vital for children who have special needs. The arts provide opportunities for alternative types of success for children with all kinds of special needs (Davis, 2008). Art gives them the vehicle to make a personal statement: "I am unique, and my art proves it!" Some teachers report using art as a reward for work completed. Good students get to visit the art center or engage in art. Others may be denied art. Although misbehavior and incomplete work cannot be tolerated, the punishment does not fit the crime. The children in question may be those who most need art. Academic deficiencies or behavior problems leave them with few routes for success in school. Success in art may generalize to success in academics. Art can also be used as a springboard to academics. For example, eight-year-old Dusty is a poor reader who draws detailed hot rods. Perhaps his hot rod drawings could be used as a way to help him talk, read, and write about his interests.

10-4i Involve Legitimate Artistic Media

An art program will involve legitimate artistic media. Children work with paint, watercolor, collage, paper, clay, printing, design, resist, and sculpture—the same media that adult artists use. Providing legitimate artistic media tells children, "You are creative artists and can be trusted with appropriate tools and media." The materials, equipment, and supplies related to these media are basic, moderately expensive, and good investments. Paintbrushes, easels, and watercolor sets of good quality will last if given proper care. Generally, buying in advance and in bulk moderates the expense. Expense, however, does not guarantee creative art. For example, one teacher distributed a precut doll shape to a small group of three-, four-, and five-year-old children. The children were instructed to glue on button eyes and precut fur for hair, sprinkle glitter, and to attach a craft stick base. The activity was costly and short-lived, and it involved little artistic processing. The doll puppets looked identical. Creative input from the children was absent. See Appendices A and B for lists of artistic junk and possible sources in your community.

10-4j Be Developmentally Appropriate

What could be an alternative to the cotton ball and glitter activity described in this chapter's opening? A good art activity fosters success by considering children's developmental abilities. For example, the camp teacher, after reading a book on insects and taking a nature walk to collect specimens, could have encouraged the children to draw a favorite bug or create a new one. What might a "butter-squito" or "spider-hopper" look like? There is no right answer; there are many possibilities. Art activities requiring excessive cutting, fine detailing, pasting of small pieces, or precise folding are not developmentally appropriate for young children with limited fine motor control and coordination. Anyone who has felt discouraged and unsuccessful can easily empathize with young children who do not experience success through art.

Developmental Appropriateness. NAEYC published and revised a widely used position statement advocating developmentally appropriate practices for programs serving young children from birth to age eight (Copple and Bredekamp, 2009): The teachers' knowledge of child development and its application in program planning is a key factor in the quality of all early childhood programs.

Developmentally appropriate practices are based on teachers using three knowledge bases to inform decisions about curriculum, assessment, behavior guidance, and interactions with children:

- **Age/Developmental Level:** According to child development knowledge and research, all children grow and develop in a universal, predictable sequence during the early childhood years. An activity must be within a child's developmental ability. Knowledge of the typical development of children within the age span served by a specific program provides a framework from which teachers prepare the learning environment and plan age appropriate activities. However, chronological age can be misleading. For example, a child may have reached his fourth birthday yet exhibit developmental characteristics shared by most three-year-olds. A child's developmental age would be a more useful construct.

- **Individual Child:** Each child has unique patterns of growth, strengths, interests, experiences, temperament, and personality. Because each child is unique, materials and activities must also be individually appropriate and responsive to individual

differences. An activity may be developmentally appropriate for a particular age group yet irrelevant, meaningless, boring, and inappropriate for a particular child. For example, cutting with scissors may be age appropriate for older four-year-olds but individually inappropriate for Lashonda, who lacks fine motor skills and is more interested in tearing paper. Cutting with scissors may be a developmentally appropriate activity for most of your older four-year-olds but would not be a good instructional match, given what you know about Lashonda.

- **Family/Culture:** Children grow, learn, and develop within the context of their families, in which they learn values, beliefs, and ways of behaving. Teachers must recognize and respect each child's social and cultural context. A cultural group may disapprove of an activity that is appropriate in other ways. For example, finger painting may be developmentally and individually appropriate for Xu but disturbing for her parents, who value neatness and cleanliness and warn their child to stay clean at school. Imagine their consternation when they come to pick up their daughter and her hands and clothes are stained with paint.

Did You Get It?

There exists _____ correlation between a child's age and his or her product-oriented approach to art.
- **a.** no apparent
- **b.** a weak positive or negative
- **c.** a negative
- **d.** a positive

Take the full quiz on CourseMate.

DAP naeyc 10-5 Activities Masquerading as Creative Art

Merely labeling an activity as "art" is no guarantee that the activity will have artistic merit. Likewise, uncreative activities are often mistaken as "creative" activities by well-meaning adults. Too many activities masquerade as creative art, including:

- Photocopied sheets
- Cut-and-paste activities
- Tracing patterns
- Coloring book pages
- Dot-to-dot sheets
- Crafts
- Holiday gifts

Although these activities may have merit for skill or concept development, they lack artistic and creative merit. Activities masquerading as creative art share the following criteria:

1. An emphasis on teacher/adult input and direction
2. A high degree of structure
3. A specified product

Bredekamp and Copple (1997) state that workbooks, worksheets, coloring books, and teacher-made models of art products for children to copy are not appropriate for children, especially those younger than age six. Cherry and Nielsen (1999) also recommend avoiding the use of models and patterns. They believe that if art is to be an avenue for creative expression and the development of aesthetic values, children should be allowed to use art materials in their own way, without teacher-made models or patterns. Moyer (1990) identified practices that do not challenge children to grow artistically. These include providing children with premarked papers to fill with specific colors, giving them patterns to produce identifiable products, and expecting them to replicate the teacher's model step by step. Children become dependent on patterns; they learn that their ideas and artistic expressions are not valued by the teacher and therefore are unacceptable. When the emphasis is on the end product rather than on the process, undesirable competition results. Displaying only the "best" artwork, or the products that most nearly meet the teacher's example, discourages individual expression. Moreover, it is difficult, if not impossible, to discuss individual art if all the children have produced identical work.

Victor Lowenfeld (1947), an iconic figure in art education, considered coloring sheets, models, and patterns to be outside influences that would not only negatively impact children's creative output but also cause emotional and mental problems for children. Lowenfeld made the following five claims about coloring books:

- Coloring books limit children's freedom to create.
- Coloring books make children inflexible because they have to follow what is given.
- Coloring books block emotional relief.
- Coloring books do not promote skills and discipline.
- Having to color what an adult has drawn makes children reluctant to draw on their own. (King, 1991)

Lowenfeld's beliefs were based on isolated events within two case studies (King, 1991), but they have influenced generations of early childhood teachers and become a basic tenet of developmentally appropriate practices.

Although some teachers may offer coloring pages to children with the goal of enhancing their fine motor skills and eye-hand coordination or teaching them to use drawing tools (Franklin, 2007), Kellogg (1973) called this practice a "dead end" (p. 9). He believed that only scribbling and drawing develop skills and make connections in children's minds. Mulcahey (2009) observes that children use fewer of the small muscles in their hands and fingers when coloring in coloring books than when they scribble on their own.

Duncum (1995) suggests that coloring books might be beneficial when children are experiencing stress. Because coloring in the outline of a picture requires little thought, coloring books might legitimately be "regarded as a therapeutic strategy for children" who need the comfort provided by a cognitively undemanding activity. Dot-to-dot pages add an element of math to the coloring book page. Connecting the dots in proper numerical sequence results in closure by completing the picture.

An anticipated response in defense of coloring books is that children like them. Children, however, may not be the best judges of what is developmentally appropriate. In an attempt to make coloring books developmentally appropriate, Striker (2003) developed a series of "anti-coloring books," which feature creative activities for problem-solving and drawing rather than pictures to color. Other publishers have developed coloring books that introduce children to artists or genres of art. Activities in the books encourage children to explore color families, extend a theme, or change details in a work of art. While these coloring books are much more cognitively demanding than those of a traditional format, they still do not provide the opportunities for decision-making, problem-solving, visualization, and origination that are inherent in original artwork. Herbert Kohl (1977), well-known author of the classic *Thirty-six Children*, experimented with coloring books and crayons and concluded that, if coloring books are introduced appropriately, they can be very "challenging" (p. 24). The common theme among these enhanced coloring book activities is that they activate children's higher level thinking. However, they are still structured, adult-directed activities that focus on product rather than creative processing.

Sometimes, even in the context of developmentally appropriate creative art activities, teachers display their own finished products as models. Although well intended, this practice frustrates young artists who cannot trace, color, cut, or paste as well as adults. Although the teacher may tell children to "Do your best!" children know their products will never look like their teacher's model.

So-called crafts and holiday gifts are examples of finished products masquerading as creative art. Two small stones glued to a larger stone can be painted to resemble a frog. It looks like something, and it can be used as a paperweight. However, creative art may not

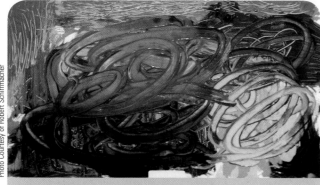

Figure 10–7 Homemade art like this finger painting is the perfect gift for a child to give.

look like anything and may not have any use beyond the initial joy of self-expression.

"Crafts" are often given as holiday gifts. Most parents are delighted to receive a paperweight or pencil holder constructed by their child. Although it is important to please parents, it is equally important to meet the creative needs of children. Providing for child input, planning, decision making, and creative processing guarantees each finished product is as unique and individual as the child who produced it. Gifts need not involve time or expense. A completed finger painting can be ironed flat, framed, wrapped, and presented to parents as a gift. Talking with parents about the nature of children's art will help them appreciate the finger painting for the unique gift it is. See Figure 10–7 for a drawing Mandy made for her mother.

Alternatives to activities that masquerade as art take commitments of time and planning. Art should not be used merely to fill in extra time before lunch or dismissal. Coloring in the figures on a math, phonics, or reading-readiness workbook sheet is not art. Generally, the figures are small, blurred, and drawn by someone other than the child. This is seatwork or busywork, not art. Art is more like turning your finished work over and drawing whatever you want.

See the "How Would You Approach This Art Activity?" feature on page 208.

Did You Get It?

For children/students younger than six years of age, art activities such as tracing and coloring inside pre-drawn lines are

- **a.** too simplistic.
- **b.** entirely inappropriate.
- **c.** less optimal than other activities.
- **d.** the mark of a lazy, inexperienced, and/or incompetent teacher.

Take the full quiz on CourseMate.

Figure 10–8 The artist has been personally expressive in this drawing.

DAP naeyc 10-6 Teaching Art to Children: Different Viewpoints

The authors view art developmentally as a child-centered, open-ended, creative, self-expressive emergent activity discovered by the child. The teacher takes a hands-off approach, being more facilitator than instructor. In

Figure 10–9 This child explores the possibility of using a paint brush.

SOMETHING EXTRA.....

How Would You Approach This Art Activity?

It's Spring and the Flowers are Blooming. Cherry blossoms in shades of pink, red, and white are everywhere. For many children, cherry blossoms are strongly embedded in their culture. There are cherry blossom festivals, and the flowers find their way into many households. Two teachers are planning their upcoming weekly art activities. Both have decided to have the children make cherry blossoms. One teacher provided white sheets of paper upon which were drawn brown branches (see Figure 10–9). Children were given small squares of tissue paper and shown how to twist them into shapes resembling cherry blossoms. They were instructed to glue them onto their branches. Each white paper was mounted onto a black sheet of construction paper and displayed. Some variation appears among the different pieces of artwork.

The second teacher took a different approach. This teacher brought in a vase of cherry blossoms on branches. Children were encouraged to use their senses to look at, gently touch, and smell the flowers. The vase was displayed in the middle of the art table, and children were encouraged to make their own cherry blossom pictures. Paint and papers were provided along with other supplies, including glue. Figures 10–10a and b capture the children hard at work. When completed, the artwork was displayed (see Figures 10–10c and d).

What can you say about either or both of these approaches to art? Compare and contrast the displays in Figures 10-10c and d. How does each relate to the discussion regarding teacher- versus child-centered art?

a

b

c

d

Photo Courtesy of Robert Schirrmacher

Figure 10–10 How does each photo relate to the discussion in this chapter of child- vs. teacher-centered art?

turn, the authors do not directly endorse teaching art to young children in the early years through the K–3 primary grades. Yet it is important to teach skills such as how to hold scissors and how to use glue. The teacher's goal is to teach children how to have enough control over the media to use them creatively. But this is very different from teaching children how to draw a tree with branches. Edwards and Nabors (1993) insist the focus of early childhood art be on the process. They believe it is wonderful when children produce something that is theirs, that they have created and own, but that product must not be the ultimate goal. They go on to add that older children may need specific procedures for completing a project, but for young children techniques should remain closely guarded secrets, revealed only if a child asks. According to Seefeldt (1995), children can be taught to draw in ways that are more mature and complex than is typical for their age. But when they do so to please a teacher, then their drawing is no more self-expression than is coloring in a worksheet or cutting out a pattern.

Older children need instruction in art to advance artistically. Gardner (1980) sees the years of middle childhood as a time when older children develop particular technical skills and become susceptible, if not eager, for specific training. They will not magically discover all there is to know through trial and error processing. Wright (1997) states that it is inappropriate to leave children to their own learning devices in arts education. She believes that children's knowledge of, skill in, and attitudes toward the arts can be enhanced with sensitive guidance. Adults must be present without being intrusive. The teacher must encourage children's response to aesthetic qualities and model interactive dialogue through hands-on and "words-on" approaches.

There are different opinions regarding the teaching of art and the role of the early childhood art educator. For example, teachers in the Reggio Emilia tradition provide opportunities for children to draw from life (see Chapter 7 for a description of Reggio Emilia schools). According to Seefeldt (1995), teachers in Reggio think of children's art as serious work and take very active roles in children's art making, probably more direct when compared with art education in the United States. Strategies used in Reggio include modeling, praising, and showing children how to draw. Based on her visit to Reggio, Hendrick (1997) observed that children are often asked to first draw their ideas, for example, cherry blossoms, and are then taken to visit real cherry blossoms in the garden. There they are encouraged to observe the flowers closely, draw them on the spot, and compare their first drawings with those done after the visit. The process greatly enhances children's powers of observation. It is not intended to promote copying. Edwards et al. (1993) believe that

Reggio children's extensive experience of drawing from observation does not appear to inhibit their desire or ability to draw or paint imaginatively. Contrary to fears, the work of the Reggio Emilia children suggests they are competent in both representational and nonrepresentational art—realistic and abstract visual expression. The visual arts are integrated into the work simply as additional languages available to young children not yet competent in conventional writing and reading. The key for early childhood teachers is taking cues from the children. For example, if a child asks a teacher's assistance in how to draw a cherry blossom, the teacher would not ignore the request. Nor would a teacher simply do the work for the child. He or she would use the Vygotskian (1986, 1987) strategy of scaffolding. Observe what the child can do and match it with an instructional strategy that is optimally challenging. For example, if the child is capable of drawing lines, help the child see how branches can be represented with different types of lines. With the child, carefully examine the bud, breaking down the whole into its smaller shapes.

Did You Get It?

Children in which age group are particularly eager for specific training in the fundamentals of creativity and art?
  a. preschool
  b. early childhood
  c. middle childhood
  d. late childhood to adolescence

Take the full quiz on CourseMate.

10-7 Paper Art

Children have experiences with paper long before they enter school. Some papers are scrap, whereas the pages in books are not to be written on, cut, or torn. Children see their parents handle paper money and read newspapers. Greeting cards and mail are made out of paper. Paper serves many purposes. Art activities dealing with paper are introduced in this section. Instructions for making paper are also provided.

10-7a Processing with Paper

Artists can do many different things to and with paper. As children experiment and explore with paper, they find that it can be any of the following:

- torn
- curled
- cut
- pleated

- glued or pasted
- twisted
- taped
- stapled
- fringed
- folded
- slit
- chained (rings or loops made into a continuous chain)
- hole-punched
- made into a cone or cylinder
- ringed (a strip made into a crown, headband, or bracelet)

10-7b Personally Expressive Art Activities

Following are personally expressive art activities for processing with paper.

Kindergarten and School-Age Activity: Stars and Snowflakes. Round or square paper of thin weight, such as tissue paper or origami paper, can be used. Coffee filters are an ideal size, shape, and thickness. Encourage children to fold paper into quarters (in half and half again). Older children with good scissoring skills can continue folding. The more folds there are, the thicker the paper will be to cut through but the more intricate the design. Encourage children to cut out small snips or to make angular cuts into the folded paper without cutting through or cutting any off. Carefully open. Refold and continue cutting if not satisfied with the star or snowflake. Finished products can be taped over windows for the light to shine through. Or an adult can seal them between two pieces of wax paper using a warm iron.

Preschool, Kindergarten, and School-Age Activity: Paper Weaving. The teacher may need to provide most of the paper for this activity. Fold a 9″×12″ sheet of construction paper in half vertically or horizontally. Cut slits from the folded edge out, stopping about 1 inch from the opposite end. The slits can be evenly or randomly spaced. They can be cut straight, curved, or jagged. Open the paper. Measure how long a strip of paper must be to be woven through the slits from one end to the other. Make several strips. Again, the paper strips can be cut straight, curved, or jagged. Children can weave with the paper strips, using an over-under motion. The next row will necessitate an opposite under-over motion. The ends of the woven paper strips can be secured with a dab of paste or glue. Trim paper strips that extend beyond the edge of the paper.

Cutting the paper and strips straight produces a neat, uniform checkerboard effect. Cutting strips of different widths or angles produces an optical illusion–type design. Try to provide a variety of papers to weave with. Adding strips of wallpaper provides a dramatic touch. Paper weaving is like finger painting, a basic early childhood art activity with many possibilities. Try adding ribbon, lace, yarn, and pipe cleaners along with your paper strips.

Preschool, Kindergarten, and School-Age Activity: Paper Strip Critters. Strips of paper 1/2-inch and wider are formed into three-dimensional characters or animals. Three strips on top of one another form a snowman. An accordion-pleated strip of paper becomes a snake. The possibilities are endless. Try to suggest possibilities without telling children what to make. Encourage them to play around with the paper and see what results.

Preschool, Kindergarten, and School-Age Activity: Paper Mosaic. A mosaic is a design made by placing pieces of tile, stone, glass, or other material very close together. Children can do a mosaic using paper. Begin by drawing a fairly simple large picture on a piece of drawing paper. Cut out small squares of colored paper. Here is where scrap pieces of construction paper that have been saved come in handy. Squares can range from 1/2 to 1-inch square, depending on the children's ages. A teacher may use the paper cutter to cut up squares for young children. Squares can be sorted by color and placed in an egg carton for easy access. Encourage children to paste them inside their sketched picture. Mosaic squares should be close but not touching. A paper mosaic takes much time, planning, and patience. It need not be completed in one sitting and is recommended for older children.

Kindergarten and School-Age Activity: Paper Relief. Relief refers to a raised or three-dimensional effect. One way to get this is to build up layers of paper. Begin with a cardboard base. Use additional cardboard or thick paper to cut out designs or pieces of a picture. Continue building up layers. Cut additional shapes, but make them smaller than the previous ones. Continue to cut and glue smaller pieces until a design or picture with different levels results. This activity takes much time and patience and is recommended for older children.

10-7c Sensory Exploration Activities

Following are some sensory exploration activities for processing with paper.

Preschool, Kindergarten, and School-Age Activity: Magazine Picture Weaving. Children can find a large picture in a magazine that they find interesting. *National Geographic*, with its vivid animal pictures, is highly recommended. Carefully remove the page or cut the picture into a large square or rectangle. Cut the picture into strips. Use the guidelines given in the paper-weaving activity to make a larger slit frame. Weave the magazine picture strips. The result will be a slightly distorted but visually pleasing rearrangement of the selected picture. Or weave the strips in incorrect order for a visually unexpected effect. Or interchange strips from different pictures—for example, an animal head with a child's body.

Preschool, Kindergarten, and School-Age Activity: Paper Making. This activity involves making decorative papers from recycled papers. There are many variations. This multistep process is not difficult but does take much advanced preparation and one-on-one assistance. Try the process yourself first before doing it with children.

Preparation:

1. Collect the following:
   - any nonplastic and nonmetallic papers that easily break down when soaked in water: toilet paper, facial tissue, grocery bags, paper towels, paper napkins, bond paper, newspaper, construction paper, junk mail, computer paper, tissue paper, egg cartons, gift wrap, glossy magazines, old yellow- and white-page phone books
   - one or more kitchen blenders or food processors
   - measuring cup
   - sponges
   - flat tool such as a blunt plastic knife (use with adult supervision)
   - old cloth towels for blotting
   - embroidery hoops (can be shared)
   - mesh window screen (fine), one piece per child
   - tubs or dish pans (at least two)
   - additions to the paper: dryer lint, rose petals, metallic confetti, potpourri, dried flowers, spices like cinnamon, perfume, Easter grass, glitter, small seeds, thread

2. Fill tubs about 6 inches full with water. Cover tables with layers of newspaper. Place tubs on newspaper.

3. Make screen frames by placing the mesh screen inside the two pieces of the embroidery hoop and tighten the screw. Hoops can be shared, but children each need their own piece of mesh screen. Measure size of the hoop and allow extra screen to extend beyond the edge for a tight fit.

Process:

1. Choose your paper and tear into approximately twenty 1- or 2-inch squares. Place in kitchen blender and add 4 cups of water. Add a small amount of food coloring or liquid watercolor to your pulp while it is in the blender, if color is desired. Put on lid and grind at lowest speed for a few seconds or until paper has turned into pulp. Add more water and repeat at high speed. Papermakers call this pulp a "slurry."

2. Pour pulp into another tub half full of water. Mix pulp by hand. Add any of the desired additions listed earlier. Use sparingly, for example, a spoonful of scent.

3. Put screen frame into tub vertically. Slide screen frame on bottom of tub to reach pulp and additions that have sunk to the bottom.

4. Gently stir pulp with one hand while lifting screen to catch pulp and any additions. You want pulp and any additions to float and evenly settle on top of screen. Use both hands to lift screen out, allowing excess water to drain through the screen. Gently blot with a sponge. You should have a thin layer of pulp with no holes or thin spots. If not, turn the screen upside down and lightly tap it in water to remove pulp. Repeat steps.

5. When satisfied with the layer of pulp, remove screen from the frame (hoop) without disturbing the pulp on top. Lay pulp-covered screen on a flat surface and use cloth towels to gently blot. Let thoroughly air dry by placing the screen out in the sun.

6. When dry, run a finger around the bottom edge to lightly lift edge of paper from screen. If necessary, use a flat tool to separate the dried paper from the screen and carefully peel.

Preschool, Kindergarten, and School-Age Activity: Molded Paper. Follow the preceding steps but mold pulp into fancy ice cube trays or candy molds rather than drying flat. Make sure excess water is completely drained. Molded paper can be carefully removed by gently tapping the tray. Given their thickness, allow ample time to dry thoroughly. Molded paper can be used as beads on a necklace or for holiday decorations. It can also be used in collage or glued onto folded paper for a greeting card.

> ### Did You Get It?
> There are so many tools and media available for the creative art process: clay, wood, dioramas, vegetation, and fabric to name but a few. In this regard, experts point to the use of paper as which of the following?
> a. too old-fashioned and boring
> b. flexible and multi-faceted
> c. too limiting for all
> d. too limiting specifically for those students with disabilities
>
> **Take the full quiz on CourseMate.**

Summary

(10-1) Approaches to teaching art range along a continuum of teacher involvement. (10-2) Teacher-directed art usually focuses on a product and requires little input from the child artist. Child-centered art is much more process-oriented and requires the child artist to make decisions about what and how to create. (10-3) Although projects or crafts do not take the place of expressive art activities for young children, they can be used to introduce new techniques or to spur on creative processing. (10-4) Art activities that allow all children to be actively engaged, personally expressive, and creative are recommended. Art should also be success oriented and intrinsically motivating. It should allow for both process and product, be developmentally appropriate, allow for experimentation and discovery, and involve legitimate artistic media. Planning art activities, or any instructional activities, requires teachers to make decisions about what and how to teach. (10-5) Sometimes activities that lack artistic or creative merit masquerade as art. While coloring books and crafts may be entertaining for children, they do not support development and creativity as art does. (10-6) For young children, art instruction should focus on how to use the tools rather than on how to draw. Formal instruction in drawing may be appropriate for older children, but art for young children should be a child-centered, open-ended, creative, self-expressive, emergent activity. (10-7) Many such activities can be planned by using paper as the primary material.

Key Terms

child-centered, 198

crafts, 201

developmentally appropriate, 201

intrinsic motivation, 204

project, 201

relief, 210

teacher-directed, 197

teacher-guided, 199

✓ Suggested Activities

1. Observe children engaged in an art activity. What examples of experimentation and discovery do you see? How does the teacher facilitate their experimentation and discovery? Use the continuum of teaching approaches to plan a single art activity in three different ways:
   - structured and teacher-directed
   - unstructured and child-centered
   - facilitated and teacher-guided

2. Observe an experienced teacher conducting an art activity with a group of young children. Does the activity require the children to be creative? List specific suggestions for making the activity more creative.

3. Observe the children as they participate in an art activity facilitated by an experienced teacher. How do their comments and conversation relate to the themes and subjects about which they have been learning?

4. Visit an early childhood center during art time. Critique the ongoing art activity using our ten-point criteria or guidelines for recommended art activities. Does the activity masquerade as art?

5. Ms. Wilton, a kindergarten teacher, has made sturdy cardboard stencils of a cornucopia and harvest food as a tracing and coloring activity for her unit on fall. Critique this art activity. Suggest an alternative if necessary.

Review

1. What are the three points along a continuum of approaches to teaching?
   1. _____ 2. _____ 3. _____

2. Identify the approach to teaching used in each of the following activities.

   a. The children are free to explore at the art tables or easels.

   b. The teacher encourages children to design their own Valentine's Day cards for their parents. The teacher provides paint and paper.

   c. Children cut out the outline of a heart traced by their teacher. The teacher writes, "I Love You Mom and Dad" across the front.

3. Determine whether each of the following is true or false.

   a. Children should be externally motivated to do art.

   b. Art should always result in something to take home.

   c. Art should allow children to be creative.

   d. Art activities should be planned according to a child's development.

   e. Discovering and experimenting through art are a waste of precious time.

   f. Art activities for young children should take no longer than 8 to 10 minutes to complete.

   g. Art activities should be planned to ensure a child's success.

   h. It is important for children's art to resemble very closely what the teacher had in mind when developing the activity.

   i. The finished art product is more important than the steps leading up to it.

   j. Art is best used as a reward for children who do their work or behave.

4. A teacher has photocopied a bunny pattern for a unit on spring. Children will color, cut, and paste bunnies on egg-shaped pieces of purple construction paper. Critique the creative merits of this activity. Is this an example of child-centered art or a teacher-directed project? Justify your position. Offer specific suggestions for making it more creative. How might you plan a spring art activity without using any patterns?

5. Which of the following activities are masquerading as creative art?

   a. Staying within the lines and neatly coloring in the pages in a holiday coloring book

   b. Coloring in a picture of a rocket ship, using red for all the areas marked 1, yellow for 2, and blue for 3

   c. Using watercolors to paint a picture that shows what each child liked best about a recent field trip

   d. Cutting and pasting a picture of a seal carefully drawn by the teacher

6. Choose the correct term in parentheses within each statement. Recommended early childhood art activities should have:

   a. an emphasis on (teacher/child) input and direction

   b. a (high/low) degree of structure

   c. a(n) (specified/unspecified) product

Additional Resources

"Art in Early Childhood: Curriculum Connections," an article by Jill Englebright Fox and Stacey Berry is available on the Early Childhood News website.

"How to Facilitate the Creative Art Process in Preschool," an article by Deborah Stewart's Making Art with Children blog from the art studio at The Eric Carle Museum (http://www.carlemuseum.org).

Art Lesson Plans Home, a website of the Incredible @rt Department at Princeton University (www.incredibleart.org/index.html).

 Visit CourseMate for this textbook to access the eBook, Did You Get It? quizzes, Digital Downloads, TeachSource Videos, flashcards, and more. Go to CengageBrain.com to log in, register, or purchase access.

First/Second Grade Lesson Plan

Goods and Services in Our Community

GOAL

The student understands the value of work.

OUTCOMES

The student is expected to:

a. give examples of goods and services in our community.
b. describe how specialized jobs contribute to the production of goods and services.
c. create a mural depicting buildings in our community.
d. identify Maurice Utrillo as a cityscape artist.

MATERIALS

a. Images of the artwork of Maurice Utrillo available in the Art Gallery on the www.rosings.com Website
b. Construction paper, scissors, and glue for each child
c. Stapler
d. Bulletin board for displaying the community
e. Photo images of businesses in the community that provide goods and services

INTRODUCTION

Write the word *Jobs* on the board. Ask the children to read it aloud. Have the children brainstorm a list of jobs held by people they know. Then ask the children to explain why people have jobs. Remind the children of the previous lesson on needs and wants.

DEVELOPMENT

Explain to the children that there are two types of jobs: those that provide goods and those that provide services. *Goods* are things that are purchased with the money earned. Some goods are needs, like food and medicine; other goods are wants like toys and candy. *Services* are things we need to have someone else do for us. Some services are needs, like the doctor making you well or the dentist cleaning your teeth; others are wants like getting a manicure or having your picture taken by a photographer.

Show the children the community photos and have them classify them as goods or services, needs or wants. Explain to the children that we will be making a model of community on the bulletin board. Each of them can choose a building representing a good or a service to make. Write the word *cityscape* on the board. Explain that we will be

making a cityscape—a piece of art that portrays a city. Introduce Maurice Utrillo as a cityscape artist and show images of his artwork. Allow time for the children to look closely at each painting. Ask the children to describe what they are seeing. Discuss how they might use some of the features in the buildings they will be making.

Distribute the construction paper, scissors, and glue to the children. Facilitate their work, pointing them back to the Utrillo paintings if they have questions.

CONCLUSION

As each child completes his/her building, encourage him/her to choose the location for displaying it. Ask the child to tell you about the building: does it represent a good or a service, a need or a want?

ASSESSMENT

a. Did the children describe examples of goods and services?
b. Did the children explain relationships between jobs and goods and services?
c. Did the children make buildings to include in a community mural?

Go to cengagebrain.com for a full-size version of this lesson plan.

11

Planning, Implementing, and Evaluating Art

Experienced early childhood teachers know the importance of planning for instruction.

Successful teachers plan the physical environment of their classrooms and their strategies for involving families and guiding children's behavior. Experienced teachers know that *if you fail to plan, you can almost certainly plan to fail.* This maxim certainly applies to curriculum development in early childhood education. Although advanced planning does not guarantee success, it does increase the probability. Even the best-planned activities may not be well received for any number of reasons. For example, a teacher may plan an activity that appeals to him or her rather than one that matches the needs, interests, and abilities of the class.

Examine the opening picture. What do you see? How do you think the teacher planned this activity? What did she provide? The children are using their hands rather than tools. The teacher has covered the table with newspaper to make clean-up easier. She's also given the children plastic smocks to protect their clothes. What else might she have included for this activity? What do you think the children are learning?

Learning Outcomes

After reading this chapter, you should be able to:

11-1 Describe the four types of learning in which children engage.

11-2 Discuss the teacher's role as a planner and deliverer of curriculum.

11-3 Compare and contrast strategies for integrating art into the early childhood curriculum.

11-4 Explain the relationship between intentional teaching and teachable moments.

11-5 Make and use clay and play dough with young children.

Standards addressed in this chapter

DAP Criteria

2 Teaching to enhance development and learning

3 Planning curriculum to achieve important goals

NAEYC Standard

2 Curriculum

3 Teaching

NAEA Visual Arts Standard

1 Understanding and applying media, techniques, and processes

11-1 Knowledge, Skills, Dispositions, and Feelings

How do young children learn? Katz (1987) identified four types of learning: knowledge, skills, dispositions, and feelings. **Knowledge** is information children construct through hands-on, multisensory experiences and exploration. **Skills** are abilities or techniques that build on and apply knowledge. Skills are developed through repetition and practice. **Dispositions** are habits of the mind such as curiosity or flexibility. A disposition is an orientation to the world learned from working with enthusiastic role models. **Feelings** are the emotions associated with learning experiences.

How do these types of learning apply to learning in the arts? Jalongo and Stamp (1997) address this question. Children construct knowledge about **clay** and its properties when they are given opportunities to process with it (see Figure 11–1). They discover that clay is solid yet malleable and can be shaped with hands or tools. They also learn about sculptors and types of clay art. In turn, they build a set of skills, including kneading, rolling, painting, and drawing.

Figure 11–1 What did the children learn when they built this model of a castle?

Photo Courtesy of Jill Englebright Fox

Dispositions are a goal of aesthetic education and experiences in the arts. Children interact with peers and teacher. They learn it is safe to take risks and trust creative impulses, to value their own work and that of others, and to persist at a task. Feelings of success should accompany a child's artistic endeavor. Art should make children feel positive and special rather than inadequate or unhappy.

DAP naeyc 11-2 Teacher as Planner and Curriculum Developer

It is important that teachers keep the four types of learning in mind as they begin to develop curriculum for young children. Teacher **values** and **beliefs** influence the goals and the experiences planned to meet these goals. Our holistic model of child development serves as a framework to ensure that our program is child-centered and developmentally focused. Considering concerns about behavior guidance and classroom management and devising effective procedures help us implement our activity. Evaluation helps us monitor our effectiveness as teachers. Teachers use different strategies in teaching. Four strategies for planning and providing art experiences are portrayed.

All teachers are planners and curriculum developers. Some build their own curriculum; some develop curriculum around state standards; others follow a prescribed curriculum, adapting it to meet the needs of their students. **Curriculum development** involves planning what to teach and how to teach it. A new topic in the curriculum may send the teacher to the library or the Internet for research. **Objectives** must be developed. Learning activities must be organized. Books and software related to the topic must be identified. Centers must be stocked with equipment and supplies relevant to the curricular theme. Teaching without a curriculum is like traveling without a map. It does a disservice to children and hinders the teacher's own professional development. Without curriculum, the teacher operates in a random, disorganized way. Quality teaching requires planning and curriculum development.

One way of planning and developing a curriculum is to ask a series of questions, including the following:

- WHO?
  Who am I as a teacher and what knowledge, talents, and beliefs do I bring to the classroom? Who are my children—ages, needs, interests, abilities, likes, dislikes, family, culture, background?
- WHAT?
  What should my children learn, know, or be able to do?
- WHY?
  Why am I planning this activity? Why should my children know, learn, or be able to do it? Why is this important or relevant?
- HOW?
  How will I carry out this activity? How will I present it? How will I motivate the children or capture their interest? How will I know if I have been successful? How will I know if the children have learned anything? How many children can do this activity at one time? How will it be done—individually or in small groups on a rotating basis?
- WHERE?
  Where will this activity take place? Will the children be sitting on the rug or at their tables?
- WHEN?
  When will this activity take place? How long will it take?

We need to act on what we know about children as we develop curriculum and plan activities. We need to translate theory into practice. How do we begin? Basically, planning is as easy as *PIE*. The three key components of early childhood curriculum development are:

- Planning
- Implementing
- Evaluating

Developing an early childhood curriculum is a lot like taking a trip. *Planning* helps decide where we will go. Do we want to take the fastest or the scenic route? What do we need to take along? These are issues to be considered during planning. *Implementing* is similar to actually taking the trip. We think we have done a good job of planning and now are ready to depart. Implementing our trip involves reading the map, stopping as planned, and allowing for unexpected diversions. Then, we look at how the trip went. Was the trip worth it? Did it cost too much or take too long? Did the benefits make the expense worthwhile? Would you do it again? How could you improve the trip? All of these questions are part of *evaluating* the trip.

Teachers follow the same steps in developing curriculum. **Planning** involves identifying what children are to learn and be able to do. Planning is a continual, ongoing process. It involves acting on what we know about children and their development in setting appropriate goals and objectives. All planning is influenced by the values and beliefs the teacher holds about children and education. **Implementing** involves two major processes. First, classroom management must be considered. Second, effective procedures for carrying out the learning activity must be established. When **evaluating** the learning activity, we assess its effectiveness by answering the following questions: What did the children learn during this activity? What did I learn that will help in planning future activities?

The **PIE** components can be illustrated with the following example. A teacher devises an art activity to help children discover that different types of brushes can be used in painting (planning). Different brushes are located, identified, introduced, labeled, and displayed at the art center (implementing). Evaluation entails observing different ways children use the brushes and their ability to use them, and also considering how these uses might be included in future art activities. The PIE model for planning and curriculum development is depicted in Figure 11–2.

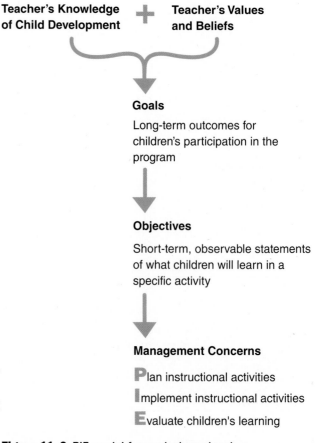

Teacher's Knowledge of Child Development + Teacher's Values and Beliefs

Goals

Long-term outcomes for children's participation in the program

Objectives

Short-term, observable statements of what children will learn in a specific activity

Management Concerns

Plan instructional activities
Implement instructional activities
Evaluate children's learning

© Cengage Learning

Figure 11–2 PIE model for curriculum planning.

11-2a Goals

A goal is a long-range target, a broad description of a desired outcome. Goals give direction or focus to what teachers do with children on a long-term basis. Most early childhood programs have established goals that identify what children will be working toward throughout the school year. In the public schools, goals for learning often come in the form of state-mandated standards for curriculum. These standards outline what is to be taught in each content area at each grade level and are accompanied by a scope and sequence that prescribes the order in which the standards will be presented throughout the year. Student mastery of these standards may be measured through formal, standardized testing. Translating learning goals or standards into more manageable objectives helps teachers plan for the week, day, and hour. Even the most effective planning, however, must sometimes change because of unforeseen events. The relationships between long-term and short-term planning and the relationship between goals and objectives are depicted in Figure 11–3.

The Goals of Early Childhood Education. Although some teachers of young children are required to base curriculum on long-term goals or standards developed by others, all teachers should carefully consider the goals of the field of early childhood education. Our holistic model of child development identifies

learning goals for the children we serve. These may include the following:

1. PHYSICALLY (to develop):
   - large muscle or gross motor coordination
   - small muscle or fine motor coordination
   - perceptual-motor or eye-hand coordination
   - sensory awareness
   - self-care

2. SOCIALLY (to develop):
   - self-understanding and acceptance
   - positive relations with others
   - a positive self-concept

3. EMOTIONALLY (to develop):
   - a positive self-concept
   - positive and appropriate emotional expression
   - self-control

4. COGNITIVELY (to develop):
   - a wide range of thinking skills, including problem-solving and discovery
   - concepts, skills, and learning in the curricular areas
   - language

5. CREATIVELY (to develop):
   - original thinking
   - imagination
   - verbal and nonverbal expression

If these are important developmental indicators, and if our program is child-centered, it follows that these goals influence what we do with the children for whom we are responsible. For example, creative expression, both verbal and nonverbal, is an important aspect of creative development. Art is one way to express one's creativity nonverbally. Art activities help us reach our goals for creative development.

11-2b Values and Beliefs

Goals also reflect our values and beliefs about children—how they develop and learn, what they should know, and the purpose of schooling and life. Teachers who value early academic performance and competition may view early childhood as a time to push children ahead by filling their heads with facts. They set goals that stress competition and early academic accomplishment and select activities in reading, writing, and counting to meet those goals. Teachers who view early childhood as a time for discovery and social interaction set goals for developing curiosity and provide socializing experiences in play to meet those goals. Different values and beliefs lead us to set different goals and activities. There are no right or wrong beliefs. Some values and beliefs may, however, suggest educational practices that conflict with what we know about young children. The key is

Goals

LONG-TERM PLANNING

Year

Term

Half year

Month

Unit

Help us achieve our goals:

Give direction and focus to:

Week

Day

Half day

Hour

Ongoing

Unexpected

SHORT-TERM PLANNING

Objectives

© Cengage Learning

Figure 11–3 Planning cycle.

to consistently match what we value and believe about children and schooling with appropriate curriculum firmly grounded in child development. Although one may value and believe in the formal teaching of reading in the early years, our working knowledge of child development indicates this practice is developmentally inappropriate.

DAP naeyc 11-2c Objectives

Objectives are the bridge between goals and activities. They are specific and short-term intended outcomes. As a result of a given activity, we expect children to be able to say, do, or demonstrate what they have learned. Objectives are worded to describe observable behaviors resulting from learning experiences. Regardless of the wording, teachers need to set objectives and develop activities to meet them. For example, Mr. Thomas wants his four-year-olds to interact positively with others, to think in original ways, and to demonstrate fine motor coordination. These are his instructional goals. His objective is for children to experiment with different tools for painting. He plans to provide a toothbrush and a shaving brush for his proposed art activity.

Referring to Figure 11–2, Mr. Thomas must still address how he will implement and evaluate this proposed activity. He must consider some concerns related to classroom management.

- Where should this activity take place—indoors, outdoors, at the easel, on the floor, or at a table? These are space considerations.

- When will this activity take place—in the morning or afternoon? Will it be offered as an additional free-choice activity, or will it be added to the art center? How much time will be allotted? These are time considerations.

- What is needed? Mr. Thomas has already found two different types of brushes. He will also need to think about paints, paper, and smocks.

- How many children can do this activity at one time? Will everyone get a chance in one session, or will it continue throughout the week? Will children self-select this activity, or will Mr. Thomas systematically rotate them through? These are considerations related to grouping.

- How will this activity be supervised? Will it need the constant supervision of an adult? Probably not.

Mr. Thomas will also need to think through procedures. How will he introduce the activity? Would a story, book, or picture be appropriate? How can he capture children's interest and get them motivated? He chooses to introduce his activity with questions during morning circle time. "Children, today I brought in two things to show you" (holding up a toothbrush and a shaving brush). "Yes, they are both brushes. Each has a special name and use. This one is a toothbrush. How many of you have one and use it? Good. What about the other one?" Jaime says his grandfather has one, but he does not know its name. "Jaime, what does he use it for?" "Yes, for shaving. It's called a shaving brush. You use it to mix shaving soap and water and put it over your whiskers before you shave." The children giggle. "Well, I have a different idea. I wonder if we could use them in our art center?" Children gasp and giggle. "Let's quietly think of how we could use these new brushes to paint." Stephanie says, "You could use the toothbrush to paint up and down just like brushing your teeth." "That's very good thinking. I bet there are many different ways to use them as we paint. Remember to try out some different ways when you get your turn."

Actually, there is no definite teacher-directed procedure, because this is a creative discovery lesson. Mr. Thomas also reminded them to explore creatively while following the rules.

Evaluation was ongoing. Mr. Thomas checked to see whether the brushes were being used in different ways. They were. Children used pulling, pushing, swirling, dotting, and circular motions. The finished products also revealed differences. From this he concluded that the activity was a success. The instructional objectives were met. This activity helped children become more creative and versatile in their painting. As a follow-up activity, Mr. Thomas planned to bring in two additional types of brushes to increase the possibilities. He noted that he should bring in two of each, because it was difficult for children to wait their turn. Also, the child with the brushes was very engrossed and spent more time than he had planned. Even though the activity was successful, he knew it could be improved upon. Mr. Thomas is an experienced preschool teacher for whom planning and curriculum development now come easily. He relies on brief plans that work for him.

That was not always the case. Early in his career, he wrote very detailed plans. He was afraid of leaving something out. He believes that his prior experience in writing detailed lesson plans, although it was time consuming, helped him become the professional early childhood educator he is today.

Did You Get It?

The acronym _____ represents the three-step approach to developing an early childhood art program.
- **a.** PDT
- **b.** RIE
- **c.** PIE
- **d.** FCA

Take the full quiz on CourseMate.

DAP naeyc 11-3 Strategies for Including Art in the Early Childhood Curriculum

Although we have introduced goals, values, and beliefs, we have yet to systematically deal with the nuts and bolts of daily planning and curriculum development. Let us study several general ways to include art in the early childhood curriculum.

11-3a Art as a Separate Activity

A teacher may find, hear about, or read about something that sounds like an enjoyable art activity for children. For example, Mr. Kent was glancing through a magazine in the director's office when he got the idea for printing with sponges of different geometric shapes. The children had not done this activity before. He felt it would encourage creative processing and help his four-year-olds and young five-year-olds with fine motor skills. The activity was developmentally appropriate and sounded enjoyable. He planned to do the activity the next morning. Further, he planned other activities for the morning but did not try to integrate or relate them. His daily lesson plan follows:

DAILY LESSON

TEACHER: Mr. Kent

CLASS: four- and five-year-olds

DATE: Monday

Areas/Activities:

Art—painting and printing with sponges cut into different geometric shapes

Music—sing a "silly song": *I know an old man who had a black dog…*

Movement—alphabet march in a circle

Concept—science (for Monday). Sort and discuss attributes of nature specimens.

Bring in pinecones, leaves, grass, twigs, stones, acorns, and so on.

Group—discuss weekend activities. Encourage Ariel to discuss her hospital stay.

Snack—vegetable slices and cottage cheese dip. Double-check for dairy allergies.

Play—continue work on airport (block corner); restock shelves in grocery store (housekeeping)

Mr. Kent wished he had discovered this art activity last week, when they were studying geometric shapes in concept time. He did not think to find a song or movement activity related to geometric shapes. Mr. Kent's approach is fragmented, with unrelated learning experiences.

11-3b Art Used to Extend or Reinforce Learning in Another Curricular Area

Mrs. Gomez's four-year-old pre-K group had also been studying geometric shapes during math concept time. She tried to find an art activity that would tie in. She cut sponges into geometric shapes and encouraged the children to print with them. During group or circle time, the children had a show-and-tell session in which they discussed the different shapes they invented and named the shapes used. Art extended and reinforced what the children were learning in math. Her lesson plan for the day is found below. The arrows indicate integration between the different activities. Group time and art extended or reinforced the concept of geometric shapes discussed during math concept time.

DAILY LESSON
Mrs. Gomez
four-year-olds
Monday

Welcome:	● do calendar
	● sing good morning song
	● read *Little Red Hen*
Blocks:	● take large hollow blocks outside (with Mrs. Raines) if nice day
Dramatic Play:	● introduce doctors and nurses, tools, careers
	● encourage hospital play
Table Toys:	● put out LEGOs®, new puzzles, flannel boards
Concept Time:	● math (Monday)—discuss geometric shapes
Creative Arts:	● sponge painting with geometric shapes
Group Time:	● show-and-tell with geometric shape pictures

11-3c Art as a Superactivity Integrating Several Curricular Areas

Ms. Lansky's kindergartners were reviewing geometric shapes. She planned to devote Monday to this review. She included the following activities in her superactivity. Note the curricular areas in parentheses, indicating integration.

● Children counted and classified different sponge shapes on the basis of color, shape, and size (math).

● They observed a dry sponge being submerged in water. They noted differences between wet and dry sponges. They put the wet sponge in the sun and predicted and observed what would happen (science).

- They took a field trip outdoors to identify geometric shapes in nature (science).
- They played shape bingo (visual discrimination, pre-reading).
- They discussed things that are hard and soft and the many uses of sponges (speaking, creative thinking).
- They listened to a story on shapes (listening).
- They printed their names or initials with rectangular shapes dipped in paint (prewriting).
- They created their own geometric shape pictures (art).
- They listened to a march and participated in a shapes dance (music and movement).
- They moved like dry stiff sponges, sponges in a bubble bath, sponges being squeezed dry, wet sponges lying in the sun on a beach (movement).
- They discussed diving for sponges and people who dive for a living (social studies).

Ms. Lansky's approach to planning helped children integrate and coordinate all experiences related to learning about geometric shapes, as well as incidental learning about sponges (see Figure 11–4). Ms. Lansky's only objection was that she felt the children's interest and enthusiasm for studying shapes and sponges were more than she had planned for in one day's flow of activities. Chapter 12 continues our discussion of integrating art across the early childhood curriculum.

11-3d Art as an Integrated Part of an Extended Unit of Study

Mr. Fazar enjoys teaching four-year-olds with curriculum units. His units are organized around themes, such as geometric shapes. His units are planned for days and even weeks at a time, depending on children's levels of interest and involvement. He believes a unit approach provides a focus for his planning. Each activity relates to his theme. In turn, everything children experience during the unit is somehow related to the theme under study.

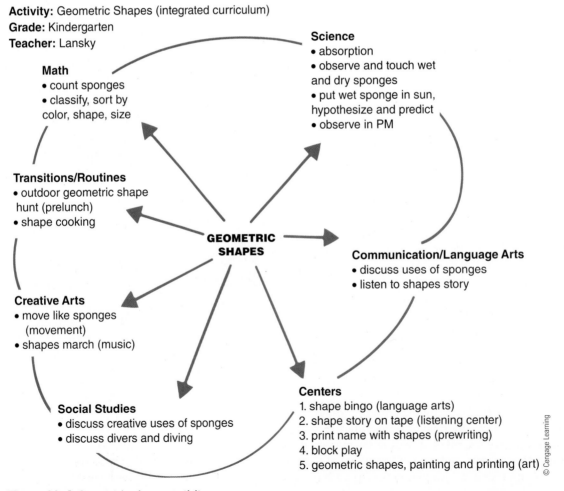

Figure 11–4 Geometric shapes activity.

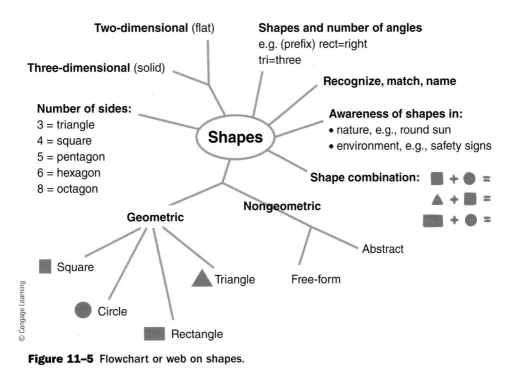

© Cengage Learning

Figure 11–5 Flowchart or web on shapes.

Mr. Fazar begins by sketching a flowchart (see Figure 11–5). He writes his theme of shapes in the center and merely writes in anything and everything related. At this point, he is more concerned with terms, concepts, and understandings than with actual activities. Items on his flowchart will suggest activities. Mr. Fazar brainstorms with his fellow teachers sometimes, using a blackboard to work and rework his flowchart. He may have more on his flowchart than will appear on his plan. Some concepts may be too difficult or may not translate into specific early childhood activities.

The second step is moving from a flowchart to a general plan of activities. Mr. Fazar decides to allow one week for the study of shapes. He bases this decision on the interests of his particular group and his past experiences with teaching this theme. Although he does not teach shapes exactly the same way every year, he does use this flowchart and plans as a general guide. Slowly, he is accumulating a wealth of flowcharts and thematic plans. His weekly plan for shapes is found in Figure 11–6.

Let's compare the four strategies. Mr. Kent taught art and all other areas as separate activities. There was no integration or tie-in. Mrs. Gomez used art and group time to extend and reinforce what children were learning during math concept time. Ms. Lansky planned a superactivity, focusing on geometric shapes and sponges that integrated the day's activities. Mr. Fazar planned for a week around the theme of shapes. Separate activities throughout his day were all related to a study of shapes.

All four of these strategies place the responsibility for curriculum development with the teacher. The problem

© Cengage Learning

Figure 11–6 Clay and play dough provide opportunities for children to use tools and build fine motor skills.

is that curriculum can become overly teacher-directed. What the teacher plans may not be what the children want to do. There may be a mismatch between planned activities and children's interests. A well-planned unit on whales may not work for a group of children who have little interest or need to learn about whales. A good curriculum aims for a balance between the teacher-planned and the spontaneous. This should not be equated with abdicating one's role as planner and curriculum developer. Children cannot plan curriculum. This is not about replacing organization with unplanned chaos. Children do, however, provide cues as to their interests. A skilled observer who watches and listens as children play is privy to a host of cues. Rather than dismissing them as unimportant, seize them as indicators of what children are about. Use them as avenues for high-interest learning. In turn, curriculum organically emerges.

A Time and a Place for Teaching Art. There is a time and place for teaching art. Use direct instruction sparingly. The criterion is whether children could better discover a process on their own. For example, collage need not be taught. Simply laying out an array of collage items along with paper and glue is all most children need. Other activities, however, might never be discovered and therefore should be introduced in unobtrusive ways that allow for individual creativity. For example, some children may never discover the artistic process called *resist*, as discussed in Chapter 8. Introducing children to how to do a resist is very different from specifying what they should make or what their finished product should look like. Art activities can also be informally introduced at times when children appear restless with processing on their own. The following guidelines help you decide when and how to teach art.

1. Practice the activity by yourself. Make sure you have mastered it and it works. Think of the interests and abilities of your children. How could you adapt the activity for a child with special needs or one with limited English?
2. Plan and prepare in advance. Have all materials ready. Waiting is stressful to children, as is having to share one tool among several children.
3. Limit the number of children. The smaller the group, the easier to supervise and give individual assistance. Adjust the number according to children's ages, the complexity of the activity, and the amount of art supplies available.
4. Cover table with newspapers, and drape smocks over chairs. Locate spaces for art activities to dry and to display.
5. Decide on a system—either group or individualized. If group, arrange materials in baskets or trays in the center of the table along with items to be shared, including tape or glue. If individualized, arrange individual setups, with each child receiving a tray of materials needed to complete the activity. This avoids problems with sharing, waiting, and taking turns. It allows children to work at their own pace. When a child is finished, his or her tray is restocked for the next child. Involve children in the cleanup.
6. Build decisions into the activities by providing choices: masking tape or glue? Crayons or markers?
7. Reassure children waiting for a turn that they will get one. Neatly print their names and cross them off as children get their turns. This helps anxious children who worry you will forget that they are next to have a turn. It also becomes a literacy event as children read names.
8. Briefly introduce your activity. Model the process without making and displaying a finished product. Again, your aim is to help children learn a new way of doing art, rather than making art that resembles yours.
9. Allow children to go about the activity in their own ways, as long as health and safety rules are followed. If they choose to ignore your invitation to do resist and want to simply color, that's okay. Allow them to pursue their own creative routes or even leave without finishing. Serve as a resource offering minimal help and only when needed.
10. Talk with children. Focus on what they are doing. Describe colors and efforts while avoiding remarks that judge their products as wonderful or beautiful.

Did You Get It?

Art can be implemented and incorporated into the curriculum in a variety of manners and at a variety of times. With children, even those who are very young (pre-K), art can and should be used to reinforce other (un-related) aspects and principles of the curriculum.

a. This statement is true in all aspects and regards.

b. This statement is untrue as these younger children cannot yet understand the principles inherent in incorporating and reinforcing.

c. This statement is untrue – art should always be studied and created in a vacuum.

d. This might have been true in the past, but with cutbacks in art funding, relying on art as a reinforcer can be risky and perilous.

Take the full quiz on CourseMate.

11-4 Teachable Moments and Intentional Teaching

Teachable moments are those unplanned events that open the door to a high-interest activity and burst of learning. Capitalize on teachable moments for their potential for learning. For example, a group of three-, four-, and five-year-olds found spiders on the playground. They informally organized a spider hunt. They requested bug houses to catch them. The teacher provided plastic cups with clear plastic wrap for lids. She offered magnifying glasses for good measure. One child wanted to kill his spider, which led to a discussion on the value of life. The children compared spiders while focusing on size, shape, color, and markings. Legs were counted. One child expressed dismay at the "poor trapped spiders." The group voted to release the spiders to their natural habitat before coming indoors. The teacher decided to forgo her book on colors to continue the discussion on spiders. She was sure that writing spider stories and making books would dominate the afternoon. Her flexible approach to planning allowed her to capitalize on this teachable moment. This teacher was responsive to possible teachable moments and capitalized on their learning potential.

Although by their nature teachable moments are unplanned, they are actually the result of the teacher making a deliberate decision to pursue an appropriate learning experience for her students. Epstein (2007) calls this **intentional teaching**. According to Epstein, the intentional teacher is one who works toward clearly defined learning outcomes for children, uses instructional strategies appropriate for the children and the outcomes, and continually assesses the children's progress to maximize their learning. The intentional teacher understands how children develop and learn and makes deliberate decisions about curriculum, learning environment, behavior guidance, and feedback based on that understanding.

Melissa is an intentional teacher. She thinks about the art activity in which her children will participate the next day and her goals for the children's learning. She chooses a picture book with which to introduce the learning concept. She develops questions to help focus the children's attention after reading the book. She provides art materials that lend themselves to exploring this concept and time for the children to engage with the materials. As the children work, Melissa observes, occasionally offering a comment or asking a question to support and challenge the children's thinking. Melissa leaves the materials in the art center for the children's continued use and plans subsequent activities to further build the children's understanding over the next few days.

Melissa's practices are based in child development theory, educational research, and the reflections of generations of teachers (Epstein, 2007). They represent intentional decisions to engage in best practices.

11-4a Emergent Curriculum and the Project Approach

Emergent curriculum is not a new approach. There have always been early childhood programs with curricula that emerged day by day, week by week. Emergent curriculum is based on the belief that children's interests and needs should be the foundation of what happens in the classroom (Bredekamp, 2011). Rather than planning out everything months in advance, informed teachers loosely plan curriculum that emerges from children's interests and activities. Jones (1999) is given credit for introducing the term *emergent curriculum* back in the 1970s. Admittedly, the approach may be scary for some teachers, that is, those who have not yet learned how to plan well. For those with some practice in observing and reflecting on child behavior, it can be an enjoyable challenge to take children's interests seriously and become a co-player with them.

There are many ways to develop curriculum. Jones identifies the following: canned, embalmed, accidental/unidentified, and emergent. Canned curriculum comes from the district, state, textbooks, workbooks, and tests. Supposedly, it contains everything children are supposed to know. An added benefit is that it is "teacher-proof." All teachers, even the novice, will experience success. The canned curriculum will always "fit" some children but not others. It is not intended to be changed to meet the needs of individual children or teachers.

Emergent Curriculum

Discuss the role of painting in the example of emergent curriculum given in the video. How can teachers use art activities to assess what their students are learning in emergent curriculum?

Watch on CourseMate.

Brain Connection

When children experience an event for the first time, new dendrites are formed. As more information is gained, the brain works to associate that information to existing dendrites. Curriculum themes help children make connections across the content areas (Rushton, Juola-Rushton, and Larkin, 2010).

The embalmed curriculum is the product of a teacher who has taught for many years. The result is a stack of units, and activities that appear to have worked for many years. For example, every January the children study sea life and engage in a set of sea-life activities. The teacher believes this approach has been successful based on feedback from parents who rave about the wonderful things children bring home.

The accidental/unidentified curriculum just happens. It is full of starting points for an emergent curriculum, but these teachable moments remain missed opportunities, for there is no follow-up by teachers. For example, in group time, one child announces, "My mom's gonna have a baby." The teacher replies, "That's nice," and the potential for extending these comments and translating them into a learning experience is lost. Perhaps the teacher perceives it would take too much work to individualize learning and depart from the pre-set curriculum. In critiquing the first three curriculum approaches, Jones concludes that a preplanned, rational curriculum makes teaching too routine and cannot work because there are too many variables involved.

What about the use of themes and units? Emergent curriculum is different from the typical thematic approach, which is often predetermined and laid out by the teacher months in advance. For example, in February the children learn about the color red, friendship, hearts, and love. The teacher takes pride in the fact that the activities also tie in with Valentine's Day. By contrast, emergent curriculum has no time constraints. The projects evolve on their own organic timetables. In unit work, children are rarely involved in posing questions or taking initiative for investigating the topic.

Do not think of emergent curriculum as an "anything goes" approach. If curriculum planning is to be effective, it must be intentional as well as responsive to children's interests and needs. "In other words, goal-directed curriculum must be flexible and adapt to children's interests and needs and emergent curriculum must use children's interests to help them achieve important learning goals" (Bredekamp, 2011, p. 302). Jones (1999) identifies nine sources for emergent curriculum:

1. Children's interests: Children whose interests are acknowledged and supported do not need to be motivated to learn; their own excitement will keep them engaged. Teacher's interests: Teachers have interests of their own that are worth sharing with children.

2. Developmental tasks: At each developmental stage, there are tasks and skills to be mastered such as walking, skipping, cutting with scissors, and making friends.

3. Things in the physical environment: Children need experience with both manufactured things and natural things such as plants and animals.

4. People in the social environment: Children are interested in all sorts of people—who they are and what they do. Family members and community helpers have roles and experiences to share.

5. Curriculum resource materials: Libraries and resource centers are full of curriculum ideas. Modify and adapt them to fit your setting, teaching style, and children's interests.

6. Serendipity (unexpected events): Become skilled in on-the-spot decision making. Think of how attentive children become at the sight and sound of a fire truck racing by the playground. What about the unexpected hailstorm?

7. Living together—conflict resolution, caregiving, and routines: Cooperation, expressing feelings, problem solving, and conflict resolution are the daily tasks of living together that are potential sources of curriculum.

8. Values held in the school community, family, and culture: If peace is valued, then a learning opportunity arises when children engage in war play. If anti-bias is valued, then a learning opportunity presents itself when children make fun of a child's special needs.

Are all topics equally valuable? Jones (1999) answers no; adult judgment must be used. A good topic is one of interest to adults as well as children. The adult must know enough about the topic or be willing to learn.

The teacher facilitates learning by introducing more ideas and confronting children's misconceptions. A good topic does not promote bias, violence, or commercial exploitation.

Although themes and units have a place in the early childhood and elementary curriculum, Katz (1994) believes they are no substitutes for projects. In the **Project Approach**, children ask questions that guide their investigation and make decisions about the activities to be undertaken. Project topics draw children's attention to questions such as: How do things work? What do people do? According to Katz and Chard (1989), projects are one of the most child-appropriate teaching strategies. They claim the appropriateness of the project approach stems from the opportunities it provides for children to engage in learning that is both personal and meaningful. Open to children's ideas and questions, projects serve to build a flexible curriculum based on children's real-world experiences. Projects respond to the interests of children. Activities can engage a whole group, small group, or individual children. Chard (1997) sees no time constraints with projects. They can range from several days to several weeks. Projects are at the core of Reggio Emilia, which was discussed in Chapter 7.

While engaged in projects, children develop and learn skills as they need them to accomplish specific purposes (Diffily and Sassman, 2002). They learn to use a picture dictionary when they need to write a specific word. Children remember these skills to use again on future projects. They also remember the knowledge gained during their project. Because children chose the project topic, the knowledge and skills have personal meaning and value.

Katz and Chard (1989) see projects developed in three phases. Planning and getting started comprise the initial phase. Teachers do preliminary planning and set the rationale for the upcoming project. Some teachers build a curriculum web during this first phase. A webbing structure records children's ideas, interests, and questions about a topic during brainstorming sessions. The webbing process visually graphs ideas for activities that emerge from the children's knowledge and interests with teacher guidance and input. Projects develop during phase two. Here children are introduced to the topic and engage in project work. Reflections and conclusions characterize the last phase. The objective is to bring closure to the project. According to Katz and Chard, for younger children through age five, culminating experiences include project constructions and role playing. For example, children may conclude a project on veterinarians by constructing their own classroom animal hospital and acting out the different roles (see Figures 11–7 and 11–8).

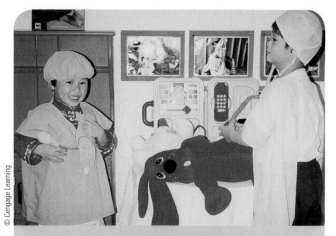

Figure 11–8 Through dramatic play children practice what they've learned about veterinarians.

In summary, there are many approaches to curriculum development. The canned, embalmed, and accidental/unidentified are teacher-directed. The same holds true for the use of units and themes. Children have no input into the topic or the content of their learning. The emergent curriculum and project approach involve children in the process of curriculum development.

11-4b Art as a Child-Centered Pursuit

There is a fifth strategy for curriculum development. Child-centered art is the type that children discover, invent, construct, and create on their own. It empowers

Figure 11–7 The theme of the dramatic play center supports the curriculum theme of "veterinarians."

▶❚❚ **TeachSource** Video

Preschool: Daily Schedules and Program Planning

How will you integrate art throughout your daily schedule? Do you consider art to be an active or quiet part of the day? Explain.

Watch on CourseMate.

them to be autonomous and in control. It may not look like something, but children take great pride in their individual accomplishments. Child-centered art is deceptively simple, but it does not just happen. It occurs when teachers plan and subtly set the stage. Herein lies the balance between teacher-directed art and child-centered art. Provide easy access to a wide variety of art supplies and let children create on their own. Children are motivated indefinitely to pursue this type of art. When they temporarily run out of interest or ideas, supplement by teaching one of the activities listed throughout this book. As always, model the process without specifying the finished product. Chapter 13 continues the discussion of viewing art as a child-directed pursuit by offering guidelines for setting up and maintaining an art center.

11-4c **The 1/3, 1/3, 1/3 Rule**

Regardless of the curriculum source, the *1/3, 1/3, 1/3 Rule* is a general guideline to follow when planning for instruction. Plan for one-third of your instructional time to involve children in **whole-group** activities, another third to engage them in **small-group** activities, and the remaining third for children to pursue **independent** activities. This allotment of time provides for balance in instruction and supports the goals of teaching children to follow adult direction as part of a group, to develop cooperative skills for achieving outcomes in collaboration with others, and to follow their own independent lines of thinking and acting. The 1/3, 1/3, 1/3 Rule also applies to planning for art activities in the early childhood classroom. When planning for art throughout the school year, design roughly one-third of your activities for the whole group, including all children in the classroom. In a whole-group art activity, the teacher sets the topic and provides some general guidelines, but children make their own decisions about how to complete their projects or achieve their goals. For example, during a study of the forest and forest animals, the teacher may ask the children to draw a picture of a forest animal in its home. The children would make decisions about what animal to draw and what the background should be. The children would also make decisions about which media to use. Choices don't need to be endless. Providing the options of crayons, colored pencils, or markers would allow children to follow preferences without overwhelming them with possibilities. A whole-group format complements art activities that support thematic units, as in the above example. A whole-group format might also be used for art appreciation activities. Large-scale posters or electronic images portraying artwork allow careful examination of the art, and the whole-group format encourages sharing reactions and responses. Fiction and nonfiction books about artists and their art can also be shared effectively in whole-group settings.

One-third of the art activities in your curriculum should be designed for small groups. Small-group settings are ideal for engaging children in larger scale projects that they may not be able to achieve independently. For successful small-group activities, teachers must spend some time teaching children to work in that format. Initially, small-group activities should be designed to teach children to share resources, take turns, and make decisions together. After children have built these abilities, teachers may begin to assign projects that children will complete while working collaboratively in a small group. Group sizes may vary according to the nature of the project and the children's experiences, but groups of three to four are usually ideal. Art activities that lend themselves to a small-group format include murals, mobiles and stabiles, and dioramas. Provide children in the group with a general theme and then encourage them to make group decisions about what to include in their art, what materials they will use, and what tasks each group member will complete. Each group may be involved in a totally different project, or each group may have the same project. In either case, the outcomes will be unique as the decisions made by each group will vary. An important part of small-group work is reporting back to the rest of the class. Each group should have an opportunity to share with the rest of the class the processes used and the product completed. Small-group settings are also ideal for introducing new media and techniques to children. Children within the group are able to answer each other's questions and provide feedback for each other.

The remaining one-third of the art activities in your curriculum should be planned to engage individual children. Independent art activities are important opportunities for children to explore their own ideas, abilities, and emotions. Children choose their own topics in independent activities. They determine perspectives and media used, they explore their own abilities, and they make decisions about the time frame in which work will be completed. In independent art activities, children most often choose to use media with which they are familiar but sometimes experiment with using that media in new ways. Masking tape, for example, might be something children have seen their teacher use in practical ways on many occasions. But in an independent art activity, a child may choose to create an intricate patchwork of many pieces of tape in many different sizes. The representative artwork that children produce in their independent activities presents topics of their own choosing. These topics may emerge from the children's past experiences, favorite fantasy stories, or current emotional states. Observant teachers make note of recurring themes as opportunities to learn more about each child. While many children complete independent art activities during one visit to the art center, others may become engrossed in projects they want to return to periodically over several days. Cafeteria trays or cookie sheets can be made available for children to keep their projects and the needed materials organized between work sessions.

Did You Get It?

A teaching curriculum that combines planned activities with room for spontaneity is a(n) _____ curriculum.

a. divergent

b. emergent

c. intentional

d. teachable-moment

Take the full quiz on CourseMate.

DAP **naeyc** **naea** 11-5 **Clay and Play Dough**

Many children have had experiences with commercially available Play-Doh® or the homemade type. They find the look, smell, and feel pleasurable. They approach clay with active processing in mind: "What can I do with clay?" By manipulating and handling it, they discover clay can be pulled, torn, cut, rolled, and so forth. Older children may have a product in mind when they approach the clay table. Often, there is much verbalizing and socializing. "My clay is too hard." "Keep rollin' it till it gets soft." "Can I use the roller when you're done?" Verbal exchange and social skills are demonstrated at the clay table. Children make direct physical contact with clay. There is no brush, scissors, or marker between them and the medium.

Working with clay fosters large muscle and fine motor control. Clay is fairly resistant and must be kneaded and worked to make it pliable. Children can stand or sit while using clay. Standing provides the advantage of a whole-body muscular reaction to the clay (see Figure 11–9).

Hard clay provides solid resistance the child must overcome. This will involve using muscles in the shoulders, arms, hands, and fingers if the child is seated. Slowly, the child gains control over the medium, making it do or become what he or she wants.

Children enjoy working with clay for many reasons. It is a natural material and has the same appeal that water, sand, and wood hold for young children.

As a preferred art form, it allows them to change or undo what they have begun. For example, a snowman can be disassembled, flattened, and transformed

© Cengage Learning

Figure 11–9 Standing while working with clay requires action of all muscles in the body.

into a pizza. This is not always possible with crayons, markers, or paint. It also gives children control over a medium. The snowman's head will stay on top of the body if the two are joined together. The painted outline of a snowman might run or mix with other colors. If the clay head falls off, it can always be put back on. It is more difficult to correct a painting, especially if it has dried.

Working with clay is a multisensory experience. Clay has a distinct texture, temperature, color, and smell. Making homemade **play dough** provides children with learning opportunities in reading a recipe, measuring, and mixing ingredients. It allows children to get dirty and messy. Because of this, some children find clay appealing, while others may find it repulsive. Playing with clay should be an option. Over time and with subtle encouragement, a reluctant child becomes an active participant at the clay table. Seeing that clay can be washed off hands and from under fingernails may be reassuring.

An Opportunity for Teacher Reflection

Ms. Han Teaches a Blended Kindergarten and First-Grade Class in a Midwestern community. This morning, as children gather on the rug for the opening activities, they are filled with stories about the severe thunderstorms and tornado warning the community experienced the evening before. "It was real dark and the wind was blowin' and we heard sirens right by our house!" shares Dani. "Oh, yeah, we heard sirens, too. And my mom made us get in the closet with flashlights when the TV said a tornado was coming," responds Alejandro. "We had to go to my granny's, 'cause she's got a basement. We had to sit like this," Dani models a duck-and-cover position. Wisely, Ms. Han listens patiently as the children share their stories from last night. She knows the children need to talk about the severe weather that was both exciting and frightening for them. She also realizes that a learning opportunity has presented itself. Pretend you are Ms. Han. *How would you build instructional activities for the day around the unexpected severe weather of the evening before? The connections for science are evident. But how might you integrate a language arts experience? What might be an appropriate art activity?*

Working with clay provides opportunities to release feelings in socially acceptable ways. A child may not display aggression against peers but is free to pound on a clay person. Clay has a therapeutic effect. It allows the working through of emotions. A child who is upset by a recent divorce may be unable to express how he or she feels verbally. Clay, however, provides this child with the opportunity to work through feelings by talking to and dramatizing with a family made out of clay.

Children need lots of clay. A grapefruit-sized ball for each sculptor is recommended. Play dough and clay, in particular, will require a lot of kneading to become pliable. Clay must be kept in a sealed container, such as a plastic tub with a snap-on lid. Over time, certain types of clay (earth) washed from hands will clog up the sink. Some teachers prefer that children rinse their hands in a bucket and flush the muddy water down the toilet.

11-5a Types of Clay

Different types of clay let children process in different ways. Below, three major types are described.

Real Clay. Different parts of the country have their own characteristic clays. Many types can be used in the classroom. Soak the clay in a bucket and pour it through a screen to remove sticks and stones. This treatment will make the clay more pliable. Real clay is dug from the earth and can be purchased in art supply stores. Water-based or potter's clay products can be fired and preserved. It is the type of clay with which adult sculptors work. Make sure the brand is nontoxic. It can be bought in a ready-to-mix powder or the more expensive premixed form. Extra time will be needed if you are using a ready-to-mix powder that also needs to set. Real clay is less expensive, messier, but more pliable than Plasticine. Its dull gray or brown color may not be visually appealing, but its cool feel and inviting texture will attract participation. Because it is water based, it will dry out when exposed to air.

Provide a small pan of water and encourage children to wet their fingers and moisten real clay to keep it pliable. This clay will also dry unfired or can be reused by forming it into 4-inch balls and putting it back in the storage container wrapped in a wet paper towel. Poke a hole in each clay ball and fill it with water to further preserve pliability. Check your clay from time to time. If it is too wet, it will get moldy and smell. If it is too dry, it will harden. Add or remove moisture as needed. Real clay is messy and is best suited for outdoor use. Simply hose down the area when you are finished. Products made from real clay can be glazed and fired in a kiln for the beautiful shiny finish that you see on ceramic pieces. Most centers and schools for young children will not have access to a kiln. This is no problem. Finished pieces can also be left to dry on their own; this will take several days. Most young sculptors will be happy returning their mass of clay to its original ball shape for the next clay session.

Koster (1999) discusses the potential for cultural awareness through the use of clay. She recommends bringing in earthenware serving pieces and explaining that, for many years, people have used clay to make eating utensils. Collect and display examples of pottery and clay sculptures from various places and cultures, including Mexican earthenware, Chinese porcelains, Japanese teacups, and Peruvian clay figurines.

Books about clay or people's relation to clay can be shared with young children. Teachers and children also may make their own original big books about clay, illustrated with photographs of the children's clay works along with their dictated captions.

Plasticine. Plasticine is an oil-based clay. It is fairly inexpensive, does not stick to surfaces, and will not dry out if kept covered when not in use. It is fairly solid and requires a good deal of kneading and heat from the hands to become pliable. It is reusable and cannot be fired or painted. It may frustrate the toddler or young preschooler who lacks fine motor strength. Not all children like the smell of Plasticine.

Play-Doh. Play-Doh® is commercially available. It comes in bright colors and is fairly inexpensive. It is also very fragrant and may tempt young sculptors into tasting it. Its major disadvantage is that it tends to crumble and flake, with tiny pieces spreading all over the table and floor. Even in its lidded can, play dough will dry up or mold over time. Try placing the play dough in a sealed sandwich bag before storing it in the container to make it last longer.

Play dough can also be homemade. Children enjoy making and using homemade play dough because it is soft and pliable. It also combines cooking with art. Making this type of clay is fairly inexpensive. Homemade play dough can be baked and preserved. To reuse the homemade play dough, place it in a covered container and store it in the refrigerator. Recipes are provided later in this chapter. Different recipes provide different textures. Be sure to vary colors and scents added.

Very young children will find play dough more appealing and easier to work with than Plasticine. Inhibited children may prefer play dough or Plasticine to real clay. Still, young children should explore a wide variety of clays and play dough.

White Mud is a homemade material for sculpture and tactile exploration. White mud is very malleable and has a smooth, cool texture that might attract children who have not yet developed the fine motor skills for working with Plasticine. While children cannot create lasting products with white mud, it, like snow, provides a wonderful medium for squeezing, molding, constricting, pinching, and pressing. White mud should be stored in a covered container and can last indefinitely.

11-5b **Processing with Clay**

Young children discover there are many different ways to work with clay. Processing with clay may, but need not, result in a finished clay product. Some ways to process with clay include:

- fingering and squeezing the clay
- rolling clay into round balls; coiling, stretching, and lengthening clay into long ropes; patting, flattening, hammering, squashing, or pounding clay into a pancake; pinching off pieces of clay; cutting the clay with blunt scissors; poking holes or openings into clay; tearing or pulling apart; as well as joining pieces of clay
- stamping or imprinting the clay

- twisting or braiding lengths of clay
- molding clay into nests or bowls, squeezing or sculpting clay into a solid three-dimensional, self-standing form, cutting into clay with a plastic knife
- processing with clay and a variety of clay tools and accessories (see Figure 11–10)
- folding or bending clay

11-5c **Stages of Working with Clay**

More has been written about stages of children's drawing and painting than about working with clay. The authors have synthesized research on the child's developmental progression in the use of clay (Brittain, 1979; Golomb, 1974; Hartley, Frank, & Goldenson, 1952) in proposing the following stages.

Stage 1: What Is Clay? In this first stage, two-year-olds experiment with and explore the properties of clay. They use their senses to visually explore, touch, smell, lick and taste, and listen to clay being worked with their hands. They drop it, step on it, throw or try to bounce it, and stick it to their skin. They are not interested in making something out of clay. Their talk will be limited to words related to their sensory experiences with clay, for example, "yucky," "hard," "mushy," or "mmmmmm."

Photo Courtesy of Jill Englebright Fox

Figure 11–10 Processing with play dough, tools, and accessories.

Stage 2: What Can I Do with Clay? The first stage quickly builds into the second. Three-year-olds are more systematic in their attempts at processing with clay. Like scientists, they put clay to a series of tests by rolling, pinching, tearing, pulling, and poking it. By physically acting on clay, they discover its properties. Clay can roll but cannot bounce or pour. The child does not deliberately set out to make something at this stage. By chance and through active manipulation, simple forms such as small balls, patted cakes, or snakes may result. These actions are repeated and become intentional.

Stage 3: Look What I Made! Four-year-olds will creatively combine clay forms and actions performed on them. One clay ball is put on top of another. Flattening and rolling a piece of clay produces a new shape. Openings are pushed into the mass of clay, and pieces are pulled out. There is more labeling and talking about what they are making. For example, while a Stage 2 child may simply poke a hole through a thin sheet of clay, the older Stage 3 sculptor may make a total of three pokes and call it a face. The finished product may be crude and simple. Balls of clay can be added to a coiled snake, with the child saying, "My snake can see you." Children in this stage often dramatize with clay products. The clay snake slithers around the table, hissing and biting the children. Clay products are becoming more complex at this stage. Still, many clay creations are more the accidental result of processing than the result of advanced, systematic planning. Clay creations are idiosyncratic and personal, and others may not recognize the finished products.

Stage 4: I Know What I'm Going to Make Out of My Clay! Five-year-olds approach the clay table knowing what they want to make and announcing this in advance. They have a name and a finished product in mind. They need to find suitable processes or techniques. There is more discussion while processing and about the finished clay product. Products evidence fairly realistic representation and can be recognized by others. Children in this stage know that their clay food is only a symbol and not the actual object itself. They will not try to eat the food as a younger child in Stage 3 might. Five-year-olds enjoy adding details using clay tools and accessories, as well as artistic junk like buttons and toothpicks.

The stages of clay appear to parallel stages of the child's artistic development in painting or mark making. Scribbles come to be named just as children give names to their clay creations. Still, clay is a three-dimensional art form, whereas painting and mark making are two-dimensional. Because children live in a three-dimensional world, it may be easier for them to use clay to represent their world. Putting the three-dimensional world on a flat two-dimensional surface

with paint, crayons, or markers involves abstraction and may be more difficult. Does this mean children should be given clay before other art media? Brittain (1979) conducted a study to determine whether clay would facilitate a more advanced type of representation than drawing. In carefully examining the artwork of 17 preschoolers, he found no superiority of clay over drawing when judging accuracy of representation. A child who is having difficulty drawing a person would have similar difficulties making one of clay. Young children need experience with a variety of artistic media, and no strict order of presentation is supported by research. Still, our knowledge of children and their development tells us that batik is inappropriate for most two- and three-year-olds, whereas play dough is recommended.

11-5d Clay Techniques

Beyond processing with clay, there are specific techniques for making clay products, which older children might enjoy learning. Often, children discover these techniques as they explore the properties and possibilities of clay.

Pinch. Using the pinch method results in a clay bowl or pot. Begin with a clay ball. Stick both thumbs into the center of the ball with the fingers holding the outside. Press the thumbs against the sides while pinching and rotating the clay ball. Continue pinching and pulling the sides upward and out into a pot or bowl.

Coil. The coil method builds on the child's experiences with rolling long clay snakes. A pot or bowl can also be formed with this method. Native Americans made pottery using the coil method over a pinch pot. Begin by wrapping coils of clay over the basic pinch pot or into any shape desired.

Slab. Begin with a slab of clay. Roll it flat with a rolling pin until it is about 1/2-inch thick. Use a plastic knife or other tool to cut out the outline of the desired object. Smooth the cut edges.

Adding Clay. Start with a ball of clay and slowly add parts and details. For example, one child made a horse from a solid mass of clay. A head, legs, and a tail were carefully added. Clay pieces made this way tend to be fragile, and the added parts do not always stay attached. The child was very frustrated because her horse's legs kept breaking under the weight of its heavy body.

Pulling Out Clay. This method will avoid problems associated with adding clay. Start with a fairly large mass of clay. Think of the total object as a solid piece rather than as made up of connected parts. Slowly pull out the parts you need. For example, by molding and carefully pulling out legs, arms, and a head, one child made a person out of clay. It was sturdy and stable because it was an intact mass without added-on parts and pieces.

Taking Clay Away. Start with a fairly large mass of clay. Take away the excess or unwanted pieces of clay, using fingers or clay tools and accessories. For example, one child used a plastic knife to carve her irregularly shaped clay ball into a round jack-o'-lantern, including facial features.

Outlining with Clay. Some children use strips of flattened clay as if they were strokes of paint or lines drawn with pencil, crayons, or markers. They approach clay as if it were a two-dimensional medium and overlook its three-dimensional possibilities. This is to be expected, and for most children it will be a temporary stage. Objects can be outlined in clay rather than represented with a solid mass of clay. Because the object is outlined flat and stationary on the clay board, there is no need to worry about it moving, falling over, or coming apart. This technique allows children to add small details.

Hints

- Remember that clay tools are accessories and not intended to replace manipulative processing with fingers and hands. Do not begin with the tools, but slowly add them as a variation to working clay with the hands.
- Floor tiles, Formica®, and linoleum make good individual clay boards. Some have interesting colors, lines, and designs. Cut into 1-foot squares if they come in a large sheet or roll.
- Add a few drops of perfume, bath oil, or peppermint oil to homemade play dough to keep it sweet-smelling and prevent spoiling.
- Add a few tablespoons of vegetable oil to play dough to make it easier to sculpt.
- Add a tablespoon of powdered alum when making homemade play dough to keep it from molding.

RECIPES FOR CLAY AND PLAY DOUGH

Cooked Play Dough
2 cups flour
1 cup salt
2 cups water
2 tablespoons cooking oil
4 teaspoons cream of tartar
Food coloring (optional)

Mix the flour, salt, and cream of tartar together. Add the water, oil, and food coloring. Cook the mixture over low to medium heat for 3 to 5 minutes. Keep stirring until the mixture forms a solid ball. Cool. Items made can be baked at low heat for 20 to 25 minutes, depending on their thickness.

Uncooked Play Dough
2 ½ cups flour
½ cup salt
1 tablespoon alum
3 tablespoons cooking oil
1 ½ cups hot water
Food coloring

Combine oil, water, and food coloring. Combine dry ingredients. Pour liquid into dry ingredients. Mix thoroughly. Knead.

Peanut Butter Play Dough (edible)
1 cup peanut butter
1 cup honey
1 cup powdered milk
1 cup oatmeal
Food coloring (optional)
Mix thoroughly. Sculpt as if it were clay. Eat!

Goop
2 cups salt
Water
1 cup cornstarch

Mix salt and 2/3 cup water. Heat in a pot for 3 to 4 minutes. Remove from heat and quickly add a mixture of the following:

1 cup cornstarch
½ cup cold water
Stir quickly. Return to heat if too "goopy."

White Mud
3 rolls white toliet paper
1 bar Ivory soap
3/4 cup Borax

Unroll 3 rolls of white bathroom tissue paper into a very large container. Generously add water until covered completely. Grate 1 bar of Ivory soap into mixture, and add 3/4 c. of Borax. Mix well. Store covered.

11-5e **Personally Expressive Art Activities**

Following are some personally expressive art activities for clay.

Preschool, Kindergarten, and School-Age Activity: Clay Creations. Children enjoy decorating their clay creations with recycled junk materials. Some items that go well with clay include the following:

- craft sticks
- pipe cleaners
- paper clips
- nuts and bolts
- acorns
- screws and nails
- seashells
- small sticks and twigs
- buttons
- golf tees
- straws

Preschool and Kindergarten-Age Activity: Baked Ornaments. Check the recipe section for homemade play dough recipes that allow you to paint, bake, and preserve the finished product. Remember to poke a hole in the product before baking it if you want it to hang.

Preschool and Kindergarten-Age Activity: Plasticine Print. Children use clay tools and accessories, such as a plastic knife, to carve designs into a thin slab of Plasticine. Carefully dip the carved piece of Plasticine in paint or press it on a stamp pad. Press it on a piece of paper. Repeat the impression to make a pattern.

Preschool and Kindergarten-Age Activity: Clay Overs. Children enjoy sculpting clay pieces or parts and attaching them to a larger base. For example, a small juice can or box can be decorated with coils and balls of clay.

11-5f Sensory Exploration Activity

Following is a sensory exploration activity for clay.

Toddler, Preschool, and Kindergarten-Age Activity: Clay Numbers and Letters. Young children who are interested in the world of letters and numbers enjoy using magnetic letters and numbers to make clay impressions. Remove the small magnet piece from each. Children use plastic knives, craft sticks, or toothpicks to carve their names, their initials, the alphabet, words, their addresses, or their phone numbers out of clay. These are formed by combining small coils of clay.

Did You Get It?

What statement best describes the use of clay as a medium?

a. Clay should not be used because it can transfer germs and pathogens from one student to another.

b. The use of clay stresses product but leaves little room for process.

c. There is a correlation between students adept at working with clay and those who thrive in mathematics.

d. Clay is an excellent tool for the development of large-muscle and fine-motor skills.

Take the full quiz on CourseMate.

Summary

(11-1) As children grow and development, they learn in different ways. First, they construct knowledge by interacting with the environment. Second, they develop skills to help them apply their knowledge. Third, their dispositions or habits of mind emerge as they work with role models. Finally, feelings are associated with learning experiences. (11-2) Teachers have the responsibility for planning and delivering curriculum to support all types of learning. Teachers use long-term goals and shorter term objectives to plan and implement learning activities and to evaluate children's learning. (11-3) Art may be addressed in early childhood curriculum in several ways: a separate activity, a way to extend or reinforce learning in another curriculum area, a superactivity for integrating several curriculum areas, or an integrated part of an extended unit of study. (11-4) Intentional teaching requires teachers to use their knowledge of children's learning and development to make deliberate and meaningful decisions about curriculum planning, implementation, and evaluation. At times, however, these deliberate decisions involve taking advantage of unexpected events to pursue teachable moments with the children. (11-5) A discussion of clay and play dough, stages of development in children's use of the media, and suggested activities for the early childhood classroom concluded the chapter.

Key Terms

beliefs, 217

clay, 217

curriculum development, 217

dispositions, 217

evaluating, 218

feelings, 217

goal, 217

implementing, 218

independent, 228

knowledge, 217

objectives, 217

PIE, 218

planning, 218

play dough, 229

Project Approach, 226

skills, 217

small-group, 227

values, 217

White Mud, 231

whole-group, 227

✓ Suggested Activities

1. As a group, brainstorm your goals for early childhood education. Are they developmental in focus? Do you agree? How do they reflect different values and beliefs? Can you reach consensus? What could this indicate about the state of early childhood education?

2. Observe in an early childhood classroom. What teachable moments did you see? How did the teacher respond? Would you have responded differently? Divide the class into four groups. Each group is responsible for very general daily planning for teaching the concept of primary colors, using one of the five strategies discussed in this chapter.

3. Interview an early childhood teacher about the goals for learning in his or her program. Have those goals been established by the state or by the program director? Does the teacher develop his or her own goals?

4. Capture a teachable moment during one of your classroom observations. Record the stimulus and how the event transpired. Did you see any learning take place? Were the children involved? What could this tell you about teachable moments?

5. Observe in a classroom where your instructor verifies that one of the following curricular approaches is in place: emergent, Reggio Emilia, or project approach. Write up what you observed and your reactions. Compare this observation with others where approaches such as thematic, academic, or completely teacher-directed were evidenced.

6. Using the 1/3, 1/3, 1/3 Rule, plan a week's worth of art activities for an early childhood classroom.

7. Plan art activities using clay for an early childhood class. Plan a whole-group, a small-group, and an independent activity.

Review

1. Complete the cycle of curriculum and development.

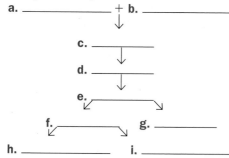

a. _____ + b. _____

c. _____

d. _____

e. _____

f. _____   g. _____

h. _____   i. _____

2. Identify the components of the PIE approach to curriculum development.

P = _____

I = _____

E = _____

3. List strategies for including art in the early childhood curriculum.

4. Identify and briefly explain the four types of learning.

5. Compare and contrast a completely teacher-planned early childhood curriculum with the following: teachable moments, emergent curriculum, and project approach.

6. Explain the 1/3, 1/3, 1/3 Rule. Discuss how you might apply this rule to planning instruction in your class.

Additional Resources

The Project Approach (www.projectapproach.org) is a website that provides resources for experienced and novice teachers implementing projects in their classrooms. It's developed and managed by Project Approach scholar Sylvia Chard.

A Place of Our Own (http://aplaceofourown.org) is an online discussion board for teachers of young children; it focuses on teachable moments.

The Intentional Teacher, a record of an online Q and A with Dr. Ann Epstein, author of *The Intentional Teacher;* sponsored by NAEYC (www.naeyc.org).

"Why Children's Dispositions Should Matter to All Teachers?" is an article by Denise da Ros-Voseles and Sally Fowler-Haughey (www.naeyc.org).

Go to YouTube to view "Hope-abilities with clay," a video of a teacher facilitating a lesson with a child with special needs.

 Visit CourseMate for this textbook to access the eBook, Did You Get It? quizzes, Digital Downloads, TeachSource Videos, flashcards, and more. Go to CengageBrain.com to log in, register, or purchase access.

Second/Third Grade Lesson Plan

Emperor Qin's Army

GOAL

The student understands common characteristics of communities, past, and present.

OBJECTIVE

The student is expected to:

a. identify reasons people have formed communities, including a need for security, religious freedom, law, and material well-being.

MATERIALS

a. Images of Emperor Chin's Terra Cotta Army and the Qin Shi Huang Mausoleum
b. Modeling clay for each child
c. Boxes in graduated sizes, one for every two children
d. Tempera paints and brushes for each child
e. World map

INTRODUCTION

Remind the children of their study of communities. Review the reasons people form communities. Tell the children that today we will be learning about a very different kind of community.

DEVELOPMENT

Have the children identify China on the world map. Explain that China is a very old country and that more than 2,300 years ago it was ruled by an emperor named Qin Shi Huang. At that time in China, people believed that before you died you needed to prepare everything you would need in the afterlife so that you could take it with you.

Emperor Qin worried that armies of other countries wanted to attack China. So he started building his army in real life and for his afterlife. He trained his real soldiers *and* he started building an army of pretend soldiers. Let's look at pictures of the pretend army he built.

Show the children the images of the terra cotta warriors and Emperor Qin's mausoleum.

Share information about the site:

- more than 7,000 soldiers
- life-sized
- each one is unique
- painted life-like colors when they were created, but the paint has worn off
- terra cotta is the same material flower pots are made of

Ask the children to work in pairs to write a paragraph explaining why Emperor Qin developed his community of terra cotta warriors. Each may want to do additional research online. When each pair has finished, ask them to paint one of the boxes as one story of Emperor Qin's palace. Assemble the palace as the boxes dry.

Have each work independently to mold their own terra cotta warriors from Plasticine.

CONCLUSION

After the children finish their soldiers, display them with the assembled palace. With the children, review their written explanations of why Emperor Qin created his community. Compare and contrast these explanations with reasons discussed in previous lessons on communities.

ASSESSMENT

a. Did the children identify Emperor Qin's reasons for creating his community of pretend terra cotta warriors?

Go to cengagebrain.com for a full-size version of this lesson plan.

12 Integrating Art Across the Early Childhood Curriculum

© Cengage Learning

What do you see happening in this picture?

Notice the intent look on this boy's face. He is working on a three-dimensional sculpture or construction. Children are free to add to the sculpture during outdoor play time. The activity was easy to plan—lots of newspaper, glue, and wooden scraps, along with ample time and space. Although teachers are nearby and subtly supervising, there is no need for teacher intervention. Children easily figure out how to adhere objects. If a child were to misuse materials, a teacher would gently intervene and offer guidance. This chapter introduces an array of three-dimensional activities often referred to as *sculpture* or *assemblage*. Just as collage is two-dimensional, or *flat* art, assemblage provides children with a new dimension—depth.

Learning Outcomes

After reading this chapter, you should be able to:

12-1 Compare and contrast two different ways of viewing the early childhood curriculum.

12-2 Provide reasons for integrating art across the early childhood curriculum.

12-3 Discuss how art fosters learning in mathematics, science, language arts, communication and literacy, social studies, and the expressive arts.

12-4 Provide three-dimensional art activities.

Standards addressed in this chapter

DAP Criteria

3 Planning curriculum to achieve important goals

NAEYC Standards

2 Curriculum

NAEA Visual Arts

1 Understanding and applying media, techniques, and processes

2 Using knowledge of structures and functions

6 Making connections between the visual arts and other disciplines

DAP naeyc 12-1 What Is Curriculum?

Curriculum means different things to different people. Two major ways of viewing curriculum are as an overall program or as subject areas. Each is discussed in this chapter. Art is one of many curricular areas. How can art reinforce and extend learning in other curricular areas? Integrating art throughout the early childhood curriculum is the focus of this chapter.

12-1a Integrating Art Across the Early Childhood Curriculum

According to Dever and Jared (1996), integrating art activities into a unit of study benefits learners in at least two ways. First, art gives children opportunities to think about what they are learning as they create representations and products that reflect new understandings. For example, when children make their own farm animals out of clay, they are learning about the animals under study. Second, as children manipulate art materials, they learn about characteristics of materials and what can be done with them. For example, when trying to fashion an animal with head, body, and legs, children are learning about the properties of clay and how they need to work with it to get a creation that somehow represents the animal under study. For those who have yet to try, getting a clay animal to stand on four legs is quite a technical accomplishment.

In another example, a group of older preschoolers has been studying dental health as a follow-up to learning about healthy nutrition. The study was based on a teacher's observation of children's eating habits and dental hygiene. Her informal talks with parents also helped her decide on this topic for study. Integrated learning comes naturally to young children, but it requires conscious planning from adults (Lasky and Mukerji-Bergeson, 2003). Thus, the teacher in question provided an array of activities including books, songs, flannel board stories, media, food activities, a class visit by a parent who was a dental hygienist, a field trip to a dentist's office, and an array of art activities, all of which reinforced learning about eating healthy foods and proper dental care. In one integrated art activity, the teacher encouraged children to think about good health and paint a "healthy" picture (see Figure 12–1). Some children painted themselves smiling, perhaps as the result of what they had learned and would practice.

Photo courtesy of Robert Schirrmacher

Figure 12–1 Healhty pictures from a unit on nutrition and dental hygiene.

Did You Get It?

According to Lila Lasky and Rose Mukerji-Bergeson (2003), integrated learning—a system that demands conscious planning by the instructor—is _____ for/with young children.

  a. extremely difficult and should be used sparingly

  b. a natural style of learning

  c. too difficult and should never be used

  d. appropriate but oftentimes not challenging enough

Take the full quiz on CourseMate.

12-2 Art and the Early Childhood Curriculum

The word **curriculum** is used to refer to an educational program, activity, or set of activities and to guidelines set by a school district, state, corporation, or professional organization. In its widest sense, curriculum refers to what happens in schools or centers. Two major ways of viewing the early childhood curriculum are:

- curriculum as program
- curriculum as subject matter, content, or academic area

12-2a **Curriculum as Program**

To some, curriculum means the total program, such as an infant, toddler, preschool, Montessori, Head Start, or kindergarten program. In this view, curriculum refers to all learning experiences children have in the program. This is a very broad view of curriculum. It includes learning how to wait one's turn, sit in a circle for group time, and share toys, as well as learning about colors and shapes. In this view, children learn through specifically planned learning experiences as well as through incidental experiences. For example, Mel's parents are pleased that he enjoys his child care program and is making friends. However, they are concerned that he has become more verbally and socially aggressive, behaviors they had never observed before he attended child care. Children in groups for long periods of time learn these behaviors as ways to cope and protect themselves. Children learn much more than is planned and intended in any curriculum or program (see Figure 12–2).

12-2b **Curriculum as Subject Matter, Content, or Academic Area**

A second way to look at curriculum is to view it as a separate subject, content, or academic area of study. The present text focuses on art in the early childhood curriculum. Traditionally, the school curriculum has centered around the following curricular areas:

1. math
2. science

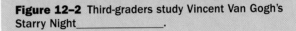

Figure 12–2 Third-graders study Vincent Van Gogh's Starry Night_____.

3. language arts, communication arts, and literacy
   - speaking
   - listening
   - reading
   - writing
4. social studies
5. expressive arts
   - art
   - music
   - movement

See Figure 12–3 for a visual portrayal of this model of the early childhood curriculum.

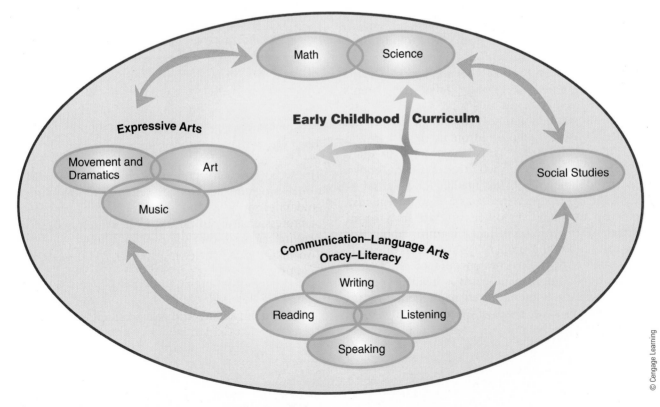

Figure 12–3 Model of integrated early childhood curriculum.

Just as child development cannot be dissected into neat divisions, the curricular areas are not separate entities. The model indicates that the curricular areas interact and influence each other. Children do not "change gears" from mathematical to scientific thinking. Knowledge and skills are not compartmentalized according to subject area. This is why math and science, communication and language arts, and the expressive arts are depicted with overlapping circles. Experiences such as cooking and play are highly recommended because they cut across many curricular areas. Although the separation works for our present analysis, children are holistic individuals who learn holistically. For example, they engage in creative thinking and problem-solving that cut across the areas of math and science, art, and social studies.

▶❚❚ TeachSource Video

© 2015 Cengage Learning.

School Age: Multiple Intelligences

Integrated curriculum provides support for multiple intelligences. The video provides examples of integrated curriculum activities. Brainstorm with a friend on ideas for integrating art appreciation in this thematic study of spiders. Record your ideas.

Watch on CourseMate.

Did You Get It?

Fox's (2010) research on kindergarteners drawing during science observations found that

  a. children were distracted from their observations by the markers they were given to draw with.

  b. children were much more likely to report details and observable facts if they drew their observations.

  c. children used science vocabulary more if they observed without drawing.

  d. the attention spans of kindergarten children are too short for meaningful science observations.

Take the full quiz on CourseMate.

12-3 Art and Learning in Early Childhood Curricular Areas

Both art production and art appreciation activities provide opportunities to make curriculum connections in the early childhood curriculum. Producing a piece of artwork, whether it is a drawing, a sculpture, or a mobile, allows the child artist to share what he or she knows about the subject. Art production gives the teacher a glimpse of children's knowledge and understandings in any curriculum area. Similarly, carefully observing and discussing the objects and ideas presented in a piece of art provide opportunities to introduce new ideas across the curriculum.

12-3a Art and Math

Children quantify as they create. "There, now my bug has six legs, just enough," announces Ty, as he coils a final leg out of clay. Marcy adds a second eye to her self-portrait. She carefully counts fingers and toes as she paints them on one by one. Children use geometric shapes in composing their pictures. "A tall, brown rectangle with a green circle on top. Now, I'll color my tree," announces Tess. A book like *Mathterpieces,* by Greg Tang, provides children with opportunities for mathematical problem-solving within paintings by Cezanne, Degas, Warhol, and Picasso.

12-3b Art and Math Activities

Following are activities that incorporate art with math.

Toddler, Preschool, and Kindergarten-Age Activity: Geometric Shape Picture. Older children cut circles, squares, triangles, and rectangles of different sizes. These can be creatively arranged and pasted to form a picture. Teachers may want to cut geometric shapes for toddlers. Precutting for children is warranted in this activity. Children see how common objects, people, vehicles, and animals are made up of geometric shapes and can be constructed from them.

There are two variations of this activity. Teachers cut shapes from flannel, including circles, squares, triangles, and rectangles that vary in color and size. Children creatively arrange these shapes on a larger piece of flannel that forms the background.

A second variation is to use magnetic tape. Wide strips of magnetic tape can be cut into geometric shapes, or small pieces of magnetic tape can be glued to the back of poster board or cardboard shapes. In turn, these shapes can be creatively arranged on a cookie sheet.

School-Age Activity: Cube Art. Older children enjoy making pictures or designs using graph paper. Graph paper with large squares is recommended. This activity takes time and patience and is not recommended for young children.

School-Age Activity: Lines, Arcs, and Circles. Young children enjoy using the tools of the mathematician: ruler, compass, and protractor. Specific instruction in the proper care and use of these instruments should be given. Model using a ruler, compass, protractor, and pencil to produce interesting designs and patterns. Children may want to color the spaces between or connect forms with thin markers.

Preschool and Kindergarten Activity: Variety of Paper Shapes. Art can be done on round, square, triangular, diagonal, rectangular, and odd-shaped pieces of paper. Each unique shape poses a new challenge to the child artist. Wide, sweeping strokes are appropriate on big rectangular sheets of paper. Smaller, detailed pictures may fit better on smaller six-sided sheets.

Teachers can point out and discuss the different shapes of the paper provided. For example, "I put out some different paper today. What shape could we call it?" (holding up a piece of round paper). Because it is round with a hole cut in the center, the children decide that circle, wheel, and doughnut are appropriate terms.

Teachers can also discuss how a large, square sheet can be cut into smaller, square pieces of paper. Four small squares make one larger square. Cutting the large, diamond-shaped sheet of paper in half makes two tri-angular pieces of paper. In this way, children are intro-duced to fractions through an integrated art activity.

Preschool and Kindergarten Activity: Geoboard. Children practice making geometric shapes with rubber bands on a geoboard (see Figure 12–4 for a geoboard pattern). Find a piece of wood. Carefully hammer in rows of evenly spaced nails.

Use short nails with wide heads. A 1-inch space between rows and columns of nails is recommended. The total number of rows and columns will depend on the size of the board. Eight rows and eight columns are recommended.

Encourage children to answer the following questions:

- How many nails can you fit under just one rubber band?
- How many nails do you need to make a circle (square, rectangle, diamond, triangle, and so on)?
- Does it take more or fewer nails to make a square, triangle, circle, or rectangle?
- How many different shapes can you make using 10 nails?

Kindergarten Activity: String Design. Children make abstract linear designs with string on a wooden frame. Find an old picture frame. Lay the frame down flat and hammer in a row of nails on each of the four upright sides. Encourage children to connect the nails using string or yarn. The result will be a creative linear design. Children can note the designs, patterns, shapes, and angles produced.

Preschool and Kindergarten-Age Activity: Tangram. The tangram is a Chinese puzzle consisting of seven angular shapes that fit together to make a square (see Figure 12–5 for a tangram pattern). The shapes can also be creatively combined to make pictures and designs. You may want to reproduce, cut out, mount on poster board, and laminate the individual pieces to ensure durability. Time invested in protecting the pieces will pay off in the long run. When laminating, remember

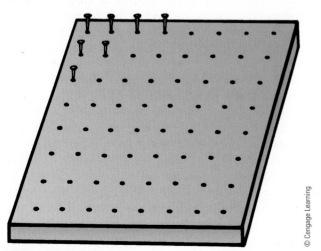

Figure 12–4 Geoboard.

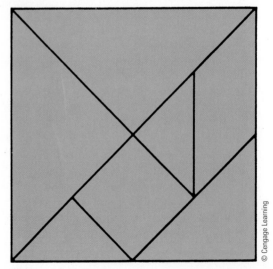

Figure 12–5 Tangram.

Brain Connection 🧠

The human brain is designed to generate and perceive patterns. Finding visual and auditory patterns can be a part of math, language, arts, science, and fine arts activities. (Rushton & Larkin, 2001)

to cut out the individual pieces first, and then laminate them to avoid frayed ends.

Kindergarten-Age Activity: Dominoes Rubbing. Lay a thin sheet of paper over a domino. Encourage children to rub with the side of the crayon or chalk on the paper. Resulting dots can be counted, matched with numerals, added together, used in subtraction, or arranged in a pleasing pattern.

Kindergarten-Age Activity: Seriation Prints. Provide corks in a variety of widths. Children seriate them from smallest to largest. Provide ink pads and paper for them to print their own designs made up of different-sized circular shapes. Encourage children to use comparative words when talking about their picture. For example, "Let's find the biggest shape." A variation of this activity is to provide round lids in a variety of sizes. Children can trace around the lids, creating their own circular designs.

Kindergarten-Age Activity: Math Cards. Children use markers, crayons, or colored pencils to draw sets of objects that match numerals or number words. Separate pages or individual math cards can be bound into group books.

 12-3c Art and Science

Art activities help children discover scientific principles. Adding water to watercolor cakes produces liquid paints. Over time, wet paint dries. Placing wet paintings in the sun hastens the drying process. Clay becomes hard if left unwrapped. Fox (2010) found that the act of drawing helped children to maintain a focus during scientific observations. Kindergarteners in her study were much more likely to report details and observable facts if they drew their observations of animals rather than just by looking. During art activities, children may see that too much water makes paint runny and uncontrollable; little or no water produces a thicker, intense stroke. Pressing hard or lightly produces different effects. Children are learning about force. Children learn about resistance when they discover that they can cut paper but not cardboard with their scissors. A book like Jay Young's *The Art of Science* may provide both adults and children with additional ideas for exploring the connections between visual art and science.

12-3d Art and Science Activities

Following are activities that incorporate art with science.

Preschool and Kindergarten-Age Activity: Food Groups Collage. After studying the major food groups, children are encouraged to find pictures of foods in magazines or supermarket flyers. These are cut and pasted onto poster board sheets, one for each major food group.

Preschool and Kindergarten-Age Activity: Nature Art. Young children and nature go hand in hand. Children enjoy taking short nature walks and collecting nature specimens. These specimens are creatively arranged and glued onto a paper plate, cardboard, or construction paper.

Children also enjoy making nature rubbings. Thin, white paper is placed over leaves, flowers, bark, or stones. Children gently rub one side of an unwrapped crayon over the specimen. The texture and outline leave an impression. Children also take crayons and paper outdoors and make rubbings as they find them. Overlapping produces different, more complex impressions.

Children also make nature prints. Paint can be brushed on leaves, or acorns lightly dipped in paint. The items are then carefully pressed onto white paper. Lifting the items results in prints. Repeated prints result in patterns. Separate prints are creatively combined into new designs.

Preschool and Kindergarten-Age Activity: Color Mixing. Children discover the principles of color mixing. Provide paint and separate brushes and containers for each primary color: red, blue, and yellow. Encourage children to mix any two colors in equal parts and see what happens. What color resulted? What happens if three colors are mixed? This activity can also be done using food coloring, a plastic egg carton, and an eye dropper.

After this tempera paint activity has been completed, white paint can be provided. Say, "What happens if white is mixed with red, blue, or yellow? Let's find out."

Preschool, Kindergarten, and School-Age Activity: Ecology Construction. Scrap paper, boxes, containers, and plastic packaging are recycled into a construction activity. For example, boxes and bottle tops inspired one preschooler to construct a robot. While using these materials, start a discussion about the importance of recycling and avoiding needless waste.

Toddler and Preschool Activity: Colors in a Bag. This no-mess activity helps children discover that two colors produce a third. Give each child a sealable plastic bag. Write the child's name on masking tape and place on the bag. Provide liquid paint in red, blue, and yellow. Ask them to pick any two colors and put a spoonful of each into their bags. Seal securely. Encourage the child to gently squeeze and mix the colors. Discuss what is happening and what results. The child can make a second bag using two different colors, or the activity can continue on another day.

Preschool, Kindergarten, and School-Age Activity: Pet Rock. Take a nature walk and allow children to find an appealing rock or stone. It should be large enough to paint or decorate but small and light enough to fit in a child's hand. The teacher may want to collect a few extras. Upon returning, talk about how the stones and rocks look and feel. Use descriptive words and open-ended prompts like, "Use words to tell me all about your special rock." Provide paint, brushes, and collage trims. Let children personalize their own rocks.

naea 12-3e **Language Arts, Communication Arts, and Literacy**

Art gives children opportunities to represent what they know nonverbally or graphically. With encouragement, they may also talk about what they have created (see Figure 12–6). Children read their artwork just as adults read a book. Any time children's artwork is shared with other children or adults, it is important the child artist have the opportunity to explain the work (Paquette, Fello, & Jalongo, 2007). Allowing others to comment without the artist's explanation may result in misinterpretation and undermine the child's confidence in his or her ability to communicate through art.

Sometimes children enjoy having their titles or storylines printed to accompany their pictures. They can be encouraged to read along with the teacher. Older children may attempt to print their own words as a

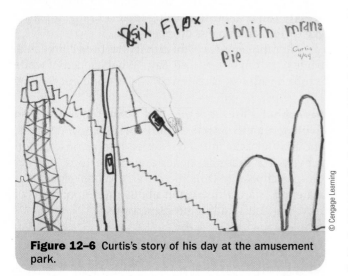

Figure 12–6 Curtis's story of his day at the amusement park.

storyline. They may invent letters and misspell. This is to be expected; it is an important step as children become writers and readers. Scribbling, mark making, and painting strokes are important steps in the development of printing and writing. Although children may choose to include letters, numerals, and/or words in their artwork, it is important that adults demonstrate respect for children and their art by recording text on a separate card or piece of paper. Most children have seen adult art exhibited in their homes, in public places, and (hopefully!) in their classrooms. They know that writing on framed art would damage it. If children have been to a museum, they have seen text explaining art displayed alongside each work. Using this same convention with children communicates that we value and respect their efforts. Because children's art is a product of their cognitive activity and a vehicle for communication, teachers should never discard or destroy it in the children's presence. If a piece of artwork is not to be kept, it should be the child's decision to throw it away (Di Leo, 2003).

Because art is a form of nonverbal expression, there is no language prerequisite and no need to understand verbal directions. Children can discover on their own or observe each other. Art time is a good opportunity for children who do not speak it to hear and informally practice Standard English. The setting for art is usually relaxed, and children feel less inhibited about speaking. Art time is also a good time for children who speak Standard English to hear and practice other languages.

Art gives children opportunities to include art vocabulary in their discussions with peers and adults. Teachers can introduce and model the use of these terms as they talk with children about their art. Children recognize colors, shapes, textures, lines, and movement in their own art and that of others. Lines can be thick, intersecting, crisscrossed, wavy, horizontal, vertical, diagonal, curved, or broken. Paint can be dry, wet, dripping, sticky, tacky, runny, slick, or crackled.

Anne Haas Dyson (1982, 1985, 1986, 1988, 1989, 1990) has studied the links among children's play, pictures, and print. She emphasizes the critical role of art and play in children's growth as symbol makers, particularly as makers of written symbols. Drawing is viewed as a literacy activity, because both drawing and language provide children with opportunities to reflect upon, organize, and share their experiences. When children draw, they are not simply communicating about their experiences; they are also solving visual problems. Discovering solutions to these problems is part of the creative process. Children enjoy resolving issues they encounter in visual representation (Baker et al., 2005). The problems they solve influence the nature of the texts they create. Although children need opportunities to give dictation and have their words written down for them, they also should engage in their own writing. They need to take marker or pencil in hand and explore the connection between meaning and print.

12-3f Art and Language, Communication, and Literacy Activities

Following are activities that incorporate art with language, communication, and literacy.

Toddler, Preschool, and Kindergarten-Age Activity: Art Talk. Encourage children to talk about their art, but do not require art be followed by verbalization: "What would you like to tell me about your picture?" or, "Your colors and shapes make an interesting design; what words could you use to tell about it?" Labels, titles, and storylines can be recorded. For example, Marie asks a parent volunteer, "Can I tell you about my bunny picture?" Marie's words are carefully printed on an index card to be displayed beside her paper on the bulletin board. The parent points to each word as she reads the story back to Marie. She encourages Marie to read along. Marie says she's done for now but will trace over the letters with a pencil tomorrow. Ned prefers to tell his story into the audio recorder. His teacher will listen, transcribe, and read it back to him.

Preschool and Kindergarten-Age Activity: Puppets. Making a puppet is an art activity that can evolve into a speaking activity. For example, Tami, a shy four-year-old, makes an animal puppet out of a folded paper plate. She hides behind a bookshelf and lets her animal speak to and answer questions from two other children. Tami's puppet is a prop that gives her the psychological boost to speak in a group. After all, it is the puppet, not Tami, who is speaking.

Kindergarten-Age Activity: Consonant Collage. One kindergarten class had been studying beginning letter sounds. They practiced beginning sounds at concept time. They hunted through magazines for pictures of things that start with these sounds. The *b* page had pictures of a book, bicycle, bird, boy, Big Bird®, bag, and Band-Aid®. Pictures of a dog, duck, doll, doughnut, dishes, and dancers were pasted on the *d* page. By the end of the year, the children hoped to complete a collage page for each of their sounds.

Preschool and Kindergarten-Age Activity: Art Words. Children at the clay table were trying to think of something new to make. Their teacher suggested they form the letters in their names. Some also made their initials, ABCs, and simple words out of rolled clay.

As a variation, children could finger paint their names or letters of the alphabet. Getting the actual feel and direction of making a *b* and *d* may help some older children who are learning to print and tend to reverse these letters.

Children also enjoy using squirt bottles to paint their names, letters, or words. Find bottles with pointed tips and fairly small openings so paint will not merely run out. Bottles that hold white glue are a recommended size and shape for young hands.

Preschool, Kindergarten, and School Age Art Activity: Listen and Draw. Mrs. Banks enjoys reading books to children. She wants children to listen attentively, appreciate literature, and understand the main idea. She knows how important these skills will be when they learn to read. She often asks her children to draw pictures about the story she has just read. Sometimes she stops short of the ending and asks them to draw how they think the story will end. Their pictures clearly reveal which children were listening and which may need additional practice in this area.

Creative teachers invent many variations on this activity. For example, children can be encouraged to listen and then draw what the teacher requests. For example, "Please draw three cats of any color with long tails sitting by a tree." Children need to listen, remember, and represent. The details requested must be minimal and within the memory range and drawing ability of young children.

Kindergarten-Age Activity: Alphabet Letter Collage. Use stencils or die-cut presses to create precut lowercase letters of the alphabet. Children find and name letters they recognize. Some make their names or simple words; others make creative designs by combining and overlapping letters.

Preschool and Kindergarten-Age Activity: I Can Make My Name. Provide finger paint and encourage children to make their names and other familiar words on glossy paper. You may want to keep their name tags close for reference. Provide craft sticks and have children scrape out their names in paint or shaving cream. Children can also form their names out of play dough or Plasticine.

Preschool and Kindergarten-Age Activity: Personalized Placemat. Provide each child with a large sheet of white paper. Ask the children where they would like you to put their names. Print them neatly in large letters, capitalizing the first letter of their names. Provide crayons and markers and encourage children to decorate the space around their names. For each mat, cut two sheets of contact paper about an inch or two larger than the placemat. Peel off backings and cover both sides of the mat. Trim edges and round off corners. Use at snack or small group time.

naea 12-3g **Art and Social Studies**

Art helps children get in touch with themselves and others. Representing oneself through self-portraits and human figure drawings increases awareness of self, body parts, and others. Through art, one takes on and identifies with the role of artist. A study of artists can be part of a unit on community helpers. Children can visit a museum or gallery. An artist can come in and model artistic processing and work with children. This can also be a brief introduction to history and culture, because artists and their different styles have been around since prehistoric times. Drawings and paintings are often the only visual representations we have to share with children of historical events (Potter, Eder, and Hussey, 2012). Different cultural groups have their own art forms. Sharing with children books like Arline Warner Tinus's *Young Goat's Discovery* and Prestel Verlag's *One Day in Japan with Hokusai* helps them understand that art has been a part of every culture throughout history.

Making art is an element of culture. According to McFee (1993), art, as a form of cultural communication, is one of the basic language skills children need to participate in a multicultural democracy. All cultures have their respective art forms. Experiences in making and appreciating art forms from other cultures help children to understand similarities and differences across cultures.

Multicultural Arts and Crafts. A commitment to cultural diversity includes exposing children to the arts and crafts of various cultures. By looking at and learning through the visual arts, children learn respect for diversity because they see how different artists use the same themes to create different works of art (Mulcahey, 2009). Historically, people everywhere have participated in making arts and crafts characteristic of their cultures. People who have grown up in countries where they learned crafts as children may be comfortable with teaching crafts to children at an early age. *Other teachers might disagree.* Exposing children to cultural artifacts and crafts is one thing; teaching children how to make them raises several issues. First, most crafts are made by adults, and attempts to teach children result in a teacher-directed approach, which is more product-than process-oriented. This raises the issues of developmental appropriateness and creativity. A *teacher's* intentions may be good in teaching children how to do a craft, but what has been gained if children become frustrated and unsuccessful when asked to copy or use skills that are beyond their abilities? Second, some crafts such as tie-dye or batik are not only difficult but also dangerous for children. Third, there is a risk that the craft may not reflect the total cultural group. This would lead to a stereotype and negate efforts to portray the culture with authenticity. Fourth, the study of a group of people and their representative crafts must be done in a way that is holistic and integrated, as opposed to being randomly addressed. The *teacher's* intent should be to help children construct a view of cultural similarities, including the making of arts and crafts, which includes recognizing and valuing differences.

12-3h **Art and Social Studies Activities**

Following are activities that incorporate art and social studies.

Preschool, Kindergarten, and School-Age Activity: "Me" Book. Children illustrate pages of their "All about Me" book. Sample activities include drawing one's face, body, senses, likes, dislikes, house, family, and friends.

Preschool and Kindergarten Activity: My Twin. After learning about "me," children lie down on a long sheet of butcher paper. Encourage children to spread their arms and legs slightly. The teacher carefully traces the outline of each child. Children cut and color their twin, paying attention to color of hair, eyes, and clothing. A full-length mirror should be handy. Do not, however, expect a mirror image or realistic likeness.

Kindergarten and School-Age Activity: Family Flag. Briefly discuss how flags are symbols for countries. In our country, the United States, we use stars and stripes and the colors red, white, and blue. Let children carefully examine the flag. Encourage them to make their own flag for their families. "What can you put on your flag that tells us about you and your family?" Family members and things that remind them of their families can be included.

Preschool, Kindergarten, and School-Age Activity: Murals. Making a mural is a good activity to wrap up or synthesize something. It is an activity to be repeated with different areas or concepts being studied. For example, after studying a unit on the farm, children can represent what they learned about the farm in a mural. If a farm mural does not contain animals, vehicles, and buildings related to the farm theme, the teacher may conclude the children did not learn much about the farm. The teacher may want to review key concepts in discussing the farm mural.

An Opportunity for Teacher Reflection

Mrs. Fox and Her Second Graders have been studying Katsushika Hokusai, an eighteenth-century Japanese artist most famous for his series of paintings, *Thirty-Six Views of Mount Fuji*. The class began by reading *One Day in Japan with Hokusai*, by Prestal Verlag, a fictional story about the artist. Mrs. Fox then asked the children to do research on the Internet and in reference books to determine which events from the fictional story actually occurred in Hokusai's life. On a world map, the children located Mount Fuji and Hokusai's home in Edo, Japan. They observed and reflected on reproductions of *The Thirty-Six Views of Mount Fuji* and written descriptive sentences about the differing perspectives, times of day, seasons, and weather represented in the paintings. This afternoon, Mrs. Fox shared with the children that they were going to be artists who created the works *The Thirty-Six Views of Mary Munford Elementary School*. She gave each child drawing paper, pencils, and a clipboard and took the class to the school yard. The children were instructed to find a spot that would give them a unique perspective for drawing their school. As the children began to work, Mrs. Fox circulated, listening to comments and answering questions. Although most of the children had attended this school since kindergarten, Mrs. Fox recognized that drawing the building was requiring the children to observe the school more closely than ever before. "What's that pipe sticking up from the roof?" one child asked. "How many windows go across this side of the building?" asked another. "The flag's hanging down straight—there's no wind today," observed a third. As the children finished drawing, they went inside with a parent volunteer to fill in their sketches with water colors. Tomorrow, after the paintings are dry, the children will outline their sketches with fine-tipped black markers, similar to the ink outlines in Hokusai's paintings. *How many curriculum areas did Mrs. Fox integrate into this study of Hokusai? Can you think of other activities to extend the integration even further?*

Preschool and Kindergarten-Age Activity: Feelings Puppet. Use group time to discuss different feelings. Label feelings and discuss events that make us feel this way. Make a face and pass around a hand mirror so children can see how a certain feeling makes them look. Discuss how feelings are always good, although the behavior that accompanies them may not be acceptable. For example, it is okay to feel angry and everyone does; it is not okay, however, to hit someone because you are angry. Make a two-sided puppet. Begin a feelings discussion by introducing and comparing feeling happy and sad. A child can make a happy face on one side of the plate and a sad face on another. Discuss what makes each child happy or sad. Attach a craft stick for a handle. Children can turn their puppet to either happy or sad as you discuss specific situations.

Toddler, Preschool, and Kindergarten-Age Activity: "Me" Prints. Children use their fingers, hands, or feet to leave marks that represent who they are. Fingers are pressed on water-soluble ink pads and printed onto paper. Hands and/or feet are painted and printed onto paper. The shapes suggest possible designs, and children combine and customize their body prints.

naea) 12-3i **Art and the Expressive Arts**

Art is one mode of creative expression. Music and movement are two other expressive arts vital to early childhood. Both art and movement involve nonverbal expression. What children represent in art can also be represented through movement. Tracy is fascinated with unicorns and attempted to make one out of clay. Its long horn was prominent. During a "Guess what I am" movement session, Tracy pretended to be a unicorn, moving on all fours while indicating something sticking out of her forehead. Just as music fosters artistic expression through a certain mood, tone, tempo, or beat, it also triggers spontaneous movement.

Following are activities incorporating art with the other expressive arts.

Kindergarten and School-Age Activity: Costumes and Props. Children design, paint, or color masks, costumes, scenery, and props related to a play or movement activity. For example, children design paper-plate masks for the different characters in "The Gingerbread Boy." A mural can be decorated and used as scenery.

Kindergarten and School-Age Activity: Musical Instruments. Children make and play their own musical instruments. There are many possibilities. To make a guitar, for example, children need their own shoe boxes, which can be decorated with paint, crayons, markers, and stickers. The teacher cuts large oval holes in the lids. Cover the boxes, and tape the edges of the lids to the boxes. Wrap four strong rubber bands around the boxes lengthwise. Children can strum their guitars.

Preschool and Kindergarten-Age Activity: Streamers. Children make their own streamers to accompany creative movement and dance activities. Provide small paper plates, which children decorate.

Assist them in attaching lengths of crepe paper by stapling. Turn on music and watch children move creatively indoors while holding their streamers.

 12-4 **Three-Dimensional Art**

Assemblage refers to a three-dimensional collage in which children creatively assemble an array of objects. "Construction" and "sculpture" are similar terms referring to **three-dimensional art**, which may or may not resemble anything. Technically, children can also sculpt with clay; this was discussed in Chapter 11. Our present discussion of sculpture addresses forms other than clay. Even young children are aware that objects are composed of parts and pieces. A table needs a top supported by legs. People have a trunk that supports their head and rests on limbs. Cars have a body supported by a frame on wheels. "How can I make my own three-dimensional model of the things that are important to me?," asks the young sculptor.

12-4a **Fixatives and Fasteners**

Most three-dimensional creations require a fixative or fastener. Some common types include:

- brads
- clothespins—pinch-type
- glue sticks
- metal fasteners
- paper clips
- paper fasteners
- pipe cleaners
- rubber bands
- stapler—and staples
- string
- tape—cellophane, masking, and colored
- twist ties
- white glue
- wire
- yarn

12-4b **Personally Expressive Art Activities**

Following are personally expressive art activities for processing with three-dimensional art.

Kindergarten and School-Age Activity: Container Creations. Shapes of containers suggest shapes of people, animals, vehicles, buildings, machines, and objects. Children enjoy using tape, glue, and staples to hold together an array of boxes, bottles, and cartons. Encourage children to think of something—an animal, a vehicle, or an object—that the containers suggest. For example, square boxes stacked together suggest a robot. A strip of egg cups from an egg carton suggests a caterpillar, snake, or train. A plastic milk container suggests a head if yarn is added for hair. Look for boxes, bottles, and cartons that have unusual shapes. As always, container creations need not resemble anything at all.

Containers can be glued or taped together. Decorate them with bottle caps, lids, ribbon, paper cups, paper scraps, straws, and other small pieces. Creations can be painted, with detergent added to paint to help it adhere.

Preschool and School-Age: Wooden Wonders. Children use liquid white glue to affix small wooden scraps together. A hammer and nails can also be used. The resulting construction represents something or can merely be an assemblage of wood pieces. Creations can also be decorated with trim or nature specimens and painted if the child decides it is necessary. Pieces of string, wire, nuts and bolts, and small machinery parts may be added for decoration (see Figure 12–7).

Kindergarten and School-Age Activity: Tinfoil Treasures. Children glue an array of small objects onto a piece of sturdy cardboard. Recommended three-dimensional items include:

- golf tees
- rubber bands
- paper clips
- buttons
- nuts, bolts, washers, and screws
- small nature specimens
- beads
- cotton swabs
- pieces of yarn, string, or cord

© Cengage Learning

Figure 12–7 Children can explore texture and balance in three-dimensional art.

Use an old brush to paint white liquid glue over the surface. Arrange the items on the gluey cardboard. Carefully place a larger sheet of tinfoil over the raised surface. Very carefully press, wrinkle, and mold the tinfoil around the raised objects to reveal their characteristic shapes. Be careful the embedded objects do not tear through the tinfoil. Fold excess tinfoil under the cardboard and secure it with tape or glue. The result will be an interesting raised effect or relief, done in silver. Thoroughly wash the glue out of the paintbrush before it hardens.

Preschool, Kindergarten, and School-Age Activity: Tinfoil Sculpture. Children enjoy working with tinfoil as the medium for sculpture. For example, tinfoil can be rolled to form an elephant's trunk and wadded to form its head. Individual parts can be taped together or stuck together with straight pins. Or children can form their sculpture out of one piece of tinfoil. For example, the elephant's legs can be carefully pulled, pinched, molded, and rolled out from the body. Remember to start with a fairly large piece of tinfoil—about 12 inches×16 inches. Remind children that, because they are starting with a large, flat sheet, they can expect their finished three-dimensional product to be much smaller.

Preschool and Kindergarten Activity: Plastic Foam and Toothpick Sculpture. Children enjoy sticking toothpicks into plastic foam. An upside-down foam tray or thicker solid piece forms the base. Smaller pieces of plastic foam—chips, squiggles, or egg carton sections—are stuck on toothpicks and inserted into the base. Individual plastic foam pieces can also be connected with toothpicks to add height and a three-dimensional effect. The sculpture can be decorated with paper, ribbon, lace, and other scraps. These sculptures will be very fragile and may not make it home intact. They can be proudly displayed in the classroom art gallery.

Preschool and Kindergarten Activity: Hanger Head. You will need old stockings or pantyhose and coat hangers for this activity. Stretch the hanger out into a fairly round face shape. Cover it with pantyhose or a stocking and tie to secure it. This will form the head. Encourage children to complete the face by adding yarn, felt, fabric scraps, or paper. Leaving the hook on top will allow it to hang. Keeping the hook on the bottom allows it to be held and used as a mask.

School-Age Activity: Paper Strip Sculpture. Strips of construction paper are ideal for making sculpture. Start with a plastic foam tray for a base. Children can secure one end of a paper strip to the base. The balance of the strip can be pleated, folded, or connected to other strips. Continue processing with paper in sculpting a three-dimensional form. Remind children that the result can be an interesting intersection of paper strips and need not look like anything in particular.

Kindergarten and School-Age Activity: Stuffed Newspaper Sculpture. This activity extends beyond a self-portrait. Each child will need four large sheets of newspaper. Older children may want to draw outlines first and then cut them out. For example, a large dinosaur can be sketched. Avoid adding fine details and small parts. Carefully cut out the outline through all four layers of newspaper. Two layers will form the front and two the back. Slowly stuff it with small wads of crumpled newspaper while stapling shut. Use paint, crayons, or markers to decorate.

School-Age Activity: Scene in a Box. Children need their own shoe boxes for this activity, which is also called a *diorama*. This activity takes much time, planning, and patience in positioning smaller items and is recommended for older children. The shoe box becomes the overall three-dimensional frame or stage. Children choose a theme—for example, their family or a favorite story. The inside of the box is decorated like one's house, with family members added. Remember, the internal space is deep, allowing for three-dimensional placement. Objects can be placed in several rows to suggest depth. Items such as fish could be suspended from the inside top with string for an underwater scene. (See Appendix C for a list of art-related books.)

Kindergarten and School-Age Activity: Glue Overs. Each child needs a piece of plastic foam cut from a Styrofoam tray. Encourage them to use markers to make a picture or design. Use varied colors and leave little empty space. Let dry. Use an old paintbrush to paint liquid white glue over the entire surface. Let dry thoroughly. This produces a sealed, slick surface that enhances the colors underneath. These make attractive ornaments or items to hang from a mobile.

Preschool, Kindergarten, and School-Age Activity: Three-Dimensional Junk Collage. A collection of three-dimensional items can be glued to a sturdy cardboard. The result is a three-dimensional collage using recycled or "junk" items including but not limited to corks; craft sticks; Easter grass; and plastic bottle tops from milk, soft drink, and other containers. Notice how some artists use items to extend their art outside the cardboard base. This reflects creativity, because children selected their own materials and arranged them into their own plan for a collage.

12-4c **Sensory Exploration Activities**

Following are sensory exploration activities for processing with three-dimensional materials.

Preschool and Kindergarten-Age Activity: Soap Suds Sculpture. Children enjoy sculpting and molding this white clay substance. To make, pour 1 cup of soap powder and 1 tablespoon of warm water into a mixing bowl. Beat with electric beater to claylike consistency. This will make about 1 cup. Have children sculpt and mold as they would play dough. Items can be decorated with trims. Allow to harden. The clay dries with a permanently hard finish.

Toddler, Preschool, Kindergarten, and School-Age Activity: Ice Sculpture. Making an ice sculpture is a good outdoor activity on a hot day. Freeze water in a large container, such as a plastic mixing bowl, the day before. You can also use a balloon that has been filled with water and left in the freezer for two days. Tear and pull away the balloon. Place the ice chunk in a dish tub or large baking pan. Provide plastic spray bottles. Fill some with clear water and others with water to which you have added liquid watercolor. Provide colors that mix and complement rather than turn muddy when mixed. Also provide shakers of salt and glitter. Set the bottles for *stream*, not *spray*. Encourage children to "mist" the ice with water and observe. What happens when salt is sprinkled on the ice? Shaved ice and ice cubes can also be added and compared. Do some melt faster than others? You can also provide eyedroppers or plastic meat basters, along with containers of warm water. Does water temperature make a difference in the time it takes for the ice to melt?

School-Age Activity: Wire Wonders. Use sturdy but flexible wire for sculpting. Recommended types of wire include copper, brass, steel, florist, aluminum, baling, insulated telephone (in a rainbow of colors), and #19 stovepipe wire. Look for wire in various gauges ranging from 14 to 28. One foot is a good length. Children enjoy twisting and turning the wire into unusual shapes. They may also try to represent something. The wire sculpture can be glued or nailed to a small piece of wood for a sturdy, supportive base.

Kindergarten and School-Age Activity: Salt Sculpture. Children need their own clear glass bottles or jars with lids. You will need several different colors of salt. Salt can be colored by rubbing it with colored chalk. Place one color in each section of a muffin tin or in a paper cup. Gently pour one color into the bottle or jar. Use a small spoon or paper cup, or let it slide in from the fold of a creased paper. Make the layer any height. Add a second color by carefully directing the flow and position as you pour. There is no need to shake or tip the bottle or jar. Each layer will form its own uneven shape. Use a pencil to carefully poke along the sides and through layers for an interesting effect. Add different-colored layers until the jar is full. Let it sit overnight to settle. You may need to add an additional color the next day to get it completely full. Cover the jar tightly with the lid. This makes an excellent gift, especially if the children did most of the work by themselves. Very young children may need to use a fairly small container with a wide top.

Kindergarten and School-Age Activity: Papier-Mâché. Papier-mâché means "chewed paper" in French and refers to the process of building up layers of paper that has been torn, wadded, and molded (although *not* chewed) to make a three-dimensional form. The paper is dipped in an adhesive mixture. Newspaper that has been torn in strips and soaked overnight will be more pliable. Squeeze excess water. Some of the many ways to do papier-mâché that are appropriate for young children are described in the following.

PAPER STRIP METHOD Strips of newspaper or paper towels, about 1/2 to 1 inch wide, are dipped in a mixture of white glue and water or other papier-mâché medium (see recipe). Carefully squeeze out excess liquid between your fingers. Layers too thick with glue or paste will mold when drying. Begin to form your object. The strips should be smooth and overlapping. The layers should go in different directions to provide strength. Remove wrinkles or bubbles by smoothing with the hand. Apply only two or three layers at a time. Let dry. Details can be added to transform the basic shape. Or add additional layers. For example, a wadded ball of newspaper can be added to the top of a jar or bottle to form a head. Secure with masking tape. Let dry thoroughly before adding additional layers. Add a final layer of paper towels to give a clean top surface for painting or final decorating. Set on wax paper to dry thoroughly before painting. An adult can seal tempera paint by spraying with a fixative or cheap hair spray. This activity should be conducted over a series of days. It may prove frustrating for very young children who want projects completed in one short session.

It is recommended that young children do papier-mâché over some solid base or form such as a:

- blown-up balloon: carefully cut finished product in half to get two bowls or two face masks.
- plastic bottle or jar.
- gift box.
- tissue roll.
- container.
- crushed or rolled newspaper.
- plastic milk or detergent bottle.
- light bulb: to make a sound shaker or music maker similar to a maraca. When it is decorated and dry, gently hit it on the floor to break the inside bulb without damaging the exterior papier-mâché shell. Patch if necessary.

Papier-Mâché Paste (cooked)

  3 cups water
  1 1/2 cups flour
  oil of peppermint

  Stir flour into cold water. Cook over low heat until mixture thickens and resembles creamy paste. Add more water if too thick. Cool. Add a few drops of peppermint oil. Use this paste to coat strips of paper.

HANGER OBJECTS The "Hanger Head" activity can also be used with papier-mâché. Stretch a coat hanger into a desired shape or form. Add long strips of newspaper dipped in papier-mâché mixture to form a solid base. Decorate as a face or whatever the shape suggests. For a self-portrait, add yarn for hair and buttons for eyes.

STUFFED BAG A paper bag can be filled with wads of newspaper and shaped into a general form. This can be the base. Strips of newspaper dipped into a papier-mâché mixture can be wrapped around the base and used to form details, such as arms, legs, head, tail, and so forth.

PAPIER-MÂCHÉ RELIEF The older child who is experienced in papier-mâché may like this variation. A piece of card-board is needed for the base. A simple picture or design is sketched in pencil. The picture or design is continued in relief by building it up with strips or small pieces of paper that have been dipped in a papier-mâché mixture. The paper can be twisted, rolled, coiled, or formed into the needed shape. For example, a round, flat mass could be used for the sun, and thin, rolled paper snakes could be the rays. Keep building up additional layers to give the three-dimensional or relief effect.

PIÑATA A blown-up balloon is used as the base for a Mexican piñata. Wrap papier-mâché over the balloon. (Follow the directions for papier-mâché.) Poke the balloon with a needle when finished. Cut open a small hole and fill the piñata with stickers, candy, tokens, or small treats. Cover the hole with additional strips of papier-mâché. Hang it overhead or from a tree limb outdoors. Blindfolded children will enjoy swinging a stick at the piñata. Breaking the piñata results in a shower of goodies and shrieks of excitement.

School-Age Activity: Casting Capers. See the recipe for making plaster. You will also need some damp sand to form the mold for casting with plaster. Line a box or old dishpan with a plastic trash bag or tinfoil and fill it with 4 inches of sand. Make an impression by carefully scooping out the sand. Wiggle your fingers for an interesting effect. Do not scoop down to the bottom of the container. Add nature specimens and small pieces of artistic junk. This will form the front of your cast sculpture and will become your mold. Remember, the casting will be the opposite of the impression you make. For example, holes dug into the sand will be cast as bumps protruding out of your sculpture.

Always add water to powder and mix plaster to a milkshake consistency. Keep stirring and work quickly. Carefully pour plaster into the mold. Add food coloring or tempera if coloring is desired. Gently shake or tap the container to help settle the mixture. Insert a hairpin, paper clip, or bent wire at the surface (which will really be the back side) if you want the sculpture to hang. Or simply insert both hands to cast a hand print. The top will now be your front side. Let the plaster set, and when it is thoroughly dry, gently brush away the sand. Casting is a time-consuming activity that only one child can do at a time, given this setup. It may be easier to do this outside in the sandbox, or ideally at the beach!

Plaster (for molds)

  8 cups patch plaster
  5 cups water

Mix thoroughly. The recipe will make enough for four molds. This recipe can be used in place of plaster of paris, which dries very fast. Patch plaster is inexpensive and takes at least 30 minutes to dry.

Toddler and Preschool-Age Activity: Squeeze a Sculpture. For this activity, simply pour plaster into a small, sturdy, plastic bag. Fill it 3 inches full, squeeze out excess air, and add nature specimens, artistic junk, or coloring. Seal bag securely. Wait several minutes for plaster to thicken. Encourage children to squeeze and manipulate the filled bag into an interesting shape. Hold it in place for a few minutes until it feels warm and begins to harden. Let the plaster dry overnight. Tear away the plastic bag and paint or decorate the sculpture with markers. The result will be a piece of sculpture with an interesting shape that would also make a good paperweight or gift for parents.

Preschool and Kindergarten-Age Activities: Balloon Creatures. Using an old bowl, an adult stirs and mixes plaster of paris until creamy. Pour into an empty balloon using a funnel with a large opening. This takes teamwork involving at least two. Set the plaster-filled balloon on a table, gently molding until it starts to harden. This takes several minutes and may exceed the patience of the very young. Stop handling. Let go and allow it to completely dry for at least 30 minutes. Gently tear off the balloon. Decorate and paint if desired. Disposable kitchen gloves can also be used as the mold. Remember to work quickly, for once mixed the plaster begins to harden. Do not pour excess plaster down the drain for it may harden in the pipes, causing a plumbing problem.

Did You Get It?

A(n) _____ is a three-dimensional collage in which students put together several separate objects into a finished product, usually with a fixative.

- **a.** assemblage
- **b.** diorama
- **c.** conglomeration
- **d.** agglomeration

Take the full quiz on CourseMate.

Summary

(12-1) Curriculum means different things to different people; it can mean the overall program or a particular subject area. In this second view, art is merely one curricular area. (12-2) Integrating art across the curriculum encourages children to create representations of what they are learning and to learn the characteristics of the materials they are using. (12-3) Art has natural connections to the curricular areas addressed in most early childhood programs: math; science; communication arts, language arts, and literacy; social studies; and the other expressive arts. (12-4) Three-dimensional art activities also encourage children to explore concepts and ideas across the curriculum.

Key Terms

assemblage, 248

curriculum, 239

expressive arts, 247

papier-mâché, 250

three-dimensional art, 248

✓ Suggested Activities

1. Interview two teachers regarding their views and definitions of curriculum. Do they agree or disagree? Do their views match those in this chapter?

2. Choose an artist, and research his or her life and work. Devise an activity that integrates appreciation of that artist's work with an art-making activity and with one or more of the early childhood curricular areas.

3. Consider carefully the views outlined in this chapter about including multicultural arts and crafts in early childhood curriculum. What are your views on this issue? Discuss your position with a friend.

4. Consider several different ways that you might record children's text without writing on their artwork. Develop an explanation to share with the families of your students about why it is important not to discard children's artwork in front of them.

5. Facilitate a three-dimensional art activity with children.

Review

1. Identify the two major ways of viewing the early childhood curriculum.

2. List the major early childhood curricular areas.

3. Match each art-related activity with a curricular area that it attempts to incorporate or integrate.

a.	counting the number of children at the art center to see if there are too many	Writing
b.	explaining to another child the steps involved in making a print of one's finger painting	Math
c.	doing a Thanksgiving collage of people and things we are thankful for	Science
d.	Zak painting XZo across his picture for his name	Speaking
e.	Larry finding that quickly stirring water into powder tempera makes colorful bubbles	Social Studies

4. Discuss the benefits of an integrated early childhood curriculum.

5. Develop a lesson plan in which children create a mural to share what they learned during a unit of study.

Additional Resources

Linking Math with Art through the Elements of Design is a presentation given by Renee Goularte to the Asilomar Mathematics Conference.

Read "Curriculum Connections" by Jill Englebright Fox and Stacey Berry and "The Role of Drawing in Kindergarteners' Science Observations" by Jill Englebright Fox on the Art in Early Childhood website (www.artinearlychildhood.org).

Go to YouTube and view a video on children's art called "Drawing the Future: Colors and Music."

"Early Childhood STEM Learning Through the Arts" is available from the Institute for Early Learning Through the Arts on www.wolftrap.org.

 Visit CourseMate for this textbook to access the eBook, Did You Get It? quizzes, Digital Downloads, TeachSource Videos, flashcards, and more. Go to CengageBrain.com to log in, register, or purchase access.

Kindergarten/First Grade Lesson Plan

Young Goat's Discovery

GOAL

The student understands the importance of family customs and traditions.

OBJECTIVE

The student is expected to:

a. describe and explain the importance of family customs and traditions.

b. create a symbol for his/her own family.

MATERIALS

a. *Young Goat's Discovery* by Arline Warner Tinus

b. Brown butcher paper

c. White paint and paintbrushes for each student

INTRODUCTION

Remind the children of their recent study of families and family traditions. Tell them that today we will be reading a story of a boy who learned about the traditions of families long ago. Show the book *Young Goat's Discovery* and provide a focus for listening by telling the children that at the end of the story you will ask them to identify the traditions of long ago.

DEVELOPMENT

Read the book to the children. Return to the focus for listening and ask the children to explain the traditions that the boy learned: The Native Americans of New Mexico left a symbol or sign of their clan on a canyon wall each time they went to the canyon for salt. Discuss as a class the following questions:

a. How do you think each Native American family or clan chose its symbol?

b. Why was it important for families to leave their symbols on the canyon wall?

Tell the children we are going to create a wall in our classroom on which they can leave a symbol of their own families. Show them the bulletin board covered with brown paper. Ask each child to think about activities he/she does with his/her family, things important to his/her family, and to come up with a family symbol. Provide scratch paper on which each child can practice drawing his/her family symbol. After each child completes his/her drawing, invite him/her to paint the symbol on the bulletin board.

CONCLUSION

After each child has painted, ask him/her to explain the symbol and why it is important to his/her family.

ASSESSMENT

a. Did the children describe and explain the importance of traditions for Native American families?

b. Did each child create and explain a family symbol?

Go to cengagebrain.com for a full-size version of this lesson plan.

13 The Art Center

Think of a young child getting ready to engage in art.

There are many decisions to make. The child asks, "What should I make?" "What materials should I use?" What message does the art center in this photo convey to the child? Would you like to have this art center in your classroom? Why or why not? There is room for several children to work at the easel at the same time, and materials for painting appear to be organized and accessible to the children. At another table in this art center, other art materials are available for the children's use. There are several, but not too many, choices. Materials are rotated weekly to sustain children's interest in returning to the center.

Learning Outcomes

After reading this chapter, you should be able to:

13-1 List and discuss the six criteria for setting up an early childhood art center.

13-2 Evaluate the effectiveness of an art center/program.

13-3 Make puppets and masks with young children.

Standards addressed in this chapter

DAP Criteria

3 Planning curriculum to achieve important goals

4 Assessing children's development and learning

NAEYC Standards

1 Relationships

2 Curriculum

4 Assessment

9 Physical Environment

NAEA Visual Art Standard

1 Understanding and applying media, techniques, and processes

DAP naeyc 13-1 The Art Center

Have you ever attended a buffet dinner? Salads were grouped together. Dishes, silverware, and napkins were arranged at the ends of the buffet. Desserts were clustered near the end. Special arrangements were made for keeping certain dishes warm. This kind of logic and organization can be applied to setting up an art center.

Swann (2009) believes that young children are most attracted to classroom learning centers that provide lively social interaction and stimulating construction activities. The art center offers both of these possibilities, as well as encouraging independent and creative expression. Art centers will vary depending on available space, resources, and the individual teacher's style.

The art center will take care of itself most of the time. Many children will be able to make choices, decisions, and see connections between media and materials. Others will process until they tire or until they create a product that pleases them. Some will know what they want to make beforehand. Rotating materials will keep the children returning. Offering new activities will also extend the array of possibilities.

The rationale for setting up your art program around a center format is that this allows for children's discovery, choice, responsibility, and independent activity. The criteria for an art center are explained in this chapter.

The classroom art center is an area where children go to engage in art. Most early childhood programs already have centers set up for manipulatives, table toys, blocks, books, and dramatic play. Others have centers for science, mathematics, and water play. Although space in the classroom is always at a premium, an art center is warranted. Just what is an art center, and how does one go about starting and maintaining it? An art center is:

1. an artist's studio
2. conveniently located and easily accessible
3. well stocked with developmentally appropriate materials
4. orderly and organized
5. a place with rules and limits
6. a setting to display children's work

Each of these six points will be examined in detail.

13-1a An Artist's Studio

An artist's studio should be visually appealing and inviting. By its appearance, it conveys that this is a place where creative art happens. Children need a well-thought-out space where they can explore, not just a table from which the teacher conducts adult-directed projects. An artist's studio is a place to make connections and choices from an array of materials conducive to making two- and three-dimensional art. It is an inviting spot that reflects creative clutter and often some noise, rather than an emphasis on excessive quietness and neatness. It is a place to go, discover, process, experiment, and explore. The art center resembles a workshop where participants engage in maximum effort with some mess. The art center is part of a nurturing classroom climate that vitalizes the artistic process for children (Gelineau, 2004). Artists enjoy visual stimulation and like to see the work of other artists depicted in posters and prints, as well as their own work, displayed at their eye level. Reserve adjacent wall and counter space for displaying children's creations. Be sure to include books about art and artists, thereby connecting your art and literacy programs.

Children should be exposed to a variety of stimulating activities and experiences with legitimate artistic media. These will complement, broaden, and balance self-directed free expression. The activities and experiences you provide depend, in part, on the individual child's developmental level, ability, and interest level. A balance between process and product can be built into the art center. The creative process of painting and exploring visual symbols is as important as the finished product, perhaps a painted picture. Pounding, rolling, pinching, and stretching clay are as important as the aesthetic quality of the finished clay piece.

Art Activities as Suggestions, Not Prescriptions. There is danger in merely listing or prescribing a set of art activities. The following are included merely as suggestions or possibilities, not as a set of activities to fill lesson plans on a daily basis. Teaching them directly as specific activities would negate everything we have discussed about art as a creative discovery process. Instead, encourage children to discover many of these extensions or possibilities on their own. The activities are based on a few media that can be easily and inexpensively included in the art center.

naea **Mixing Media.** Mixing media results in the discovery of new artistic possibilities. For example, let us assume children have worked with crayons at the table and paints at the easel. Ask children, "What would happen if we used them together? Can you paint over your coloring? Have you ever tried to do a collage over your dried hand painting?" The possibilities for creative mixing are endless. Teachers needn't suggest specific combinations but merely reinforce experimenting with and joining different media (see Figure 13–1).

Varying the Tool, Method, and Media. Varying tools will help children discover new artistic possibilities. For example, they have painted with an array of paintbrushes, flat and round. Ask them, "Can we paint

TeachSource Video

Preschool: Appropriate Learning Environments and Room Arrangements

How can you support young children's independence in the art center? Give specific examples.

Watch on CourseMate.

© 2015 Cengage Learning.

with a toothbrush? Is there a brush in your home that could be used for painting? Let's think of things other than brushes that we could use for painting."

Varying the method will also lead to new possibilities (Lasky & Mukerji-Bergeson, 2003). Paint can be spread with a brush to make long, sweeping lines. There are also many other ways to apply paint. It can be dabbed, swirled, sprayed, dripped, and dribbled.

Varying the medium also increases the range of possibilities. Children can paint with water, colored water, transparent watercolors, thick opaque tempera, or tempera to which sand, salt, or sugar has been added.

Figure 13–1 Mixed media with pastels and collage.

© Cengage Learning

Incorporate Both Two- and Three-Dimensional Art Media. Similarly, there should be a balance between two- and three-dimensional art media. Two-dimensional activities involve a flat artistic surface with height and width portrayed. Three-dimensional art activities also portray depth. Some activities, including work with paper, allow for both two- and three-dimensional expression.

13-1b Conveniently Located and Easily Accessible

An art center should be conveniently located and easily accessible. Make sure the center is easy to see and supervise, both up close and from a distance. It should not be placed in the middle of the room, where children will walk through it while visiting other centers. If possible, the art center should be located on tile floor, so that paint spills and crushed crayons can be cleaned up easily. To facilitate cleanup, it is important that the center also be located near the sink. If there is no sink in the classroom, locate the art center near the door, so that a bucket of water can be brought in when needed without having to be carried across the classroom. In either case, paper towels should be provided.

Lighting is also important. If natural light from a window or skylight isn't possible, make sure the center is well lit by artificial lights. A table should be provided with appropriate seating. The tabletop should be easy to clean. Check the height of the table and chairs to make sure that children can work at them comfortably, whether standing or seated. Easels for painting and drawing will encourage gross motor activity during art, and the arrangement of the easels should facilitate social interaction between the artists. Consider including a separate table for clay and sculpting activities. This can prevent the sculptors' rolling and pounding of clay from disturbing other artists. Shelves and cabinets should also be included in the art center for storing materials. The shelves will house supplies that you want children to have access to for the day's activities, while the cabinets house materials that have been put away for future use.

Because different centers have their own noise levels, it is wise to locate the art center near other noisy activities. For example, the art center could be located near the dramatic play center, since both centers encourage children to move, socialize, and be active. This location might also encourage children to make their own props for dramatic play: paper money for shopping or a play dough pizza for dinner. Locating the art center near the book corner or science center will be problematic, as these tend to be quieter, less social centers.

The art center need not be restricted to the indoors. Art can be offered as an activity during outdoor free play. An easel or art cart on wheels can be rolled in and out as needed.

Brain Connection 🧠

Not only is each child's brain unique, but it is also growing on its own time table. Children's ongoing experiences in interactive learning centers help them to develop problem-solving skills and long-term memory. Large blocks of time allow children to assimilate and synthesize both new and known information (Rushton, Juola-Rushton, & Larkin, 2010).

13-1c Well Stocked with Developmentally Appropriate Materials

The art center should be well stocked with developmentally appropriate art media, tools, equipment, accessories, and artistic junk (see Figure 13–2). A common misconception is that children need to have a new type of project or different materials each day. In desperation, teachers resort to patterns and cutouts in the quest for presenting something new and different. Cherry and Nielsen (1999) disagree. They believe that young children like repetition. This is evident in their requests for hearing favorite stories told or read again and again. The same holds true for music and finger plays, as well as dramatic play and block play scenarios. Children enjoy repeatedly processing with basic art media as well as the addition of new and different materials to extend the basic activity. For example, children enjoy painting at the easel on a daily basis. They also appreciate the introduction of new and different colors, paper shapes, and painting tools. Repeated experiences at the easel lead to eventual mastery of the media, but without variation of paper and tools, this repetition might become boring or monotonous. The keys are repetition and variety. Teachers of young children with special needs find that they not only need and enjoy repetition to enhance learning but also welcome elements of novelty and variety.

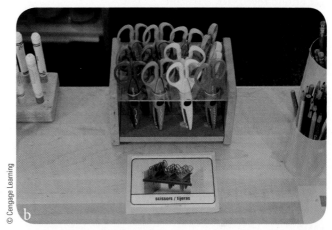

The art center can operate on a modest budget if planning and economical purchasing are involved. Plan with other teachers to order in bulk. Buy high-quality nonconsumable items, such as brushes, that will last. Much of your art budget will go for purchasing consumable items such as paint and paper, which will be used in time and will need to be reordered. Expensive frills like glitter, fur, feathers, sequins, and wiggly eyes are not necessary. Supplement purchased items with things you can recycle. Thrift shops and garage sales are good sources of inexpensive items that can be recycled into art activities. Families are excellent sources for contributions. Send home a list that states specifically what you need. Mom or Dad may be

Figure 13–2 Materials in the art center should be visually organized with labels for easy access and cleanup by the children.

able to donate computer paper from work. Grandma may respond to your request for buttons and fabric by donating the contents of her old sewing box. Donating benefits everyone. The family feels involved, and your art center is well stocked.

What should be on the shelves of your art center? There are at least six basic categories of art materials:

- tools for mark making: crayons, pencils, markers, chalk
- papers in a variety of shapes, sizes, and textures (specific examples to follow)
- modeling and molding materials: clay and play dough, and tools
- items for cutting, fastening, and attaching: scissors, glue, paste, tape, hole punches, staplers and staples, string, pipe cleaners
- items for painting and making prints: paint, brushes, and related tools
- collage items: nature specimens, fabric, old jewelry, wallpaper, yarn, gift wrap

Remember to include materials to provide meaningful experiences for all children in your classroom, including children with special needs. For example, children with low vision and/or poor hearing will enjoy:

- tactile and multisensory experiences with textured and scented paint and play dough
- brightly colored or fluorescent paint that contrasts with the background paper and table top
- reflective safety tape for sticking
- rebus charts with pictures illustrating steps or directions

Papers. There are many different types of paper children can use in their artwork. A list of papers for the art center follows:

brown wrapping paper—for murals, puppets, papier-mâché, paper sculpture, and art activities requiring sturdy paper

butcher paper—a long roll for making murals; good for finger painting

cardboard—flat, corrugated, or tubes for a variety of art activities

catalogues—for paper tearing, cutting, pasting, and collage

construction paper—good for crayons, chalk, and paint but not watercolor; difficult to fold in different directions; will fade over time; buy large sheets in assorted colors and cut down

finger paint paper—glazed surface; buy the largest size!

magazines—for collage and montage

manila paper—a better grade than newsprint: rough surface, cream color, heavier weight; more expensive than newsprint but less expensive than white drawing paper. Manila paper is good for collage, gluing, coloring, painting, and pasting activities. Buy big and cut down.

newsprint—least expensive paper for marking, scribbling, drawing, and coloring. Thick or heavy paint will bleed and soak through. Easy to fold, but tears with pressure. Comes in a variety of sizes. Buy big and cut down.

paper towels—for painting, dyeing, papier-mâché, and cleanup

tissue paper—comes in a variety of colors; buy big and cut down

white drawing paper—a very good grade, heavy and fairly expensive. Good for all art projects, including painting. It looks clean and stands up to erasing; 60-pound weight is recommended. Buy big and cut down.

Tools and Accessories. Accessories for children to use in their artwork are limited only by imagination. Some items to consider:

brayer—for painting and making prints

cookie sheets—as an art surface

cutting board—acrylic, undecorated for monoprints and clay

rubber stamps—for printing

ruler—for making marks with a pencil

sponges—for painting and printing

stamp pad—for printing

To ensure full participation in the art center for children with differing physical abilities, be sure to include the following:

- adaptive art tools such as fat bingo markers, chunky crayons, large markers, and large items for printmaking and collage (Markers are easier to use than crayons.)
- double-handed ambidextrous scissors or spring scissors activated with a squeezing motion
- a cutting wheel and mat to use instead of scissors
- glue sticks rather than bottles of glue
- thickened paint in no-spill paint cups attached to the table with Velcro®
- old knobbed shaving brushes, sponges, foam brushes, or short-handled brushes for easier painting
- foam hair rollers into which paint brushes, markers, or crayons can be inserted for a more secure grip
- a small wall paint roller to paint on paper taped to a wall or easel

Include Culturally Responsive Materials in Your Art Center.

- Avoid presenting only white and black art media for people-making. Few people have pale white skin, and not all dark-skinned people identify with the color black.

- Include multicultural art products (paint, crayons, markers, fabric, felt, and paper). Help children mix paint that matches their skin colors. Keep a mirror handy for close examination. Mix play dough in shades of light, medium, and dark brown, as well as beige, tan, pink, and black. Add cocoa to your basic play dough recipe to make shades of skin color.

- Add fabric scraps representing different cultures to your collage box.

- Provide diverse magazines such as *Ebony, Jade,* and *Latina Style* for children to use in collage or mural-making.

- Include artifacts such as a garlic or tortilla press with clay and play dough tools.

- Provide thick and thin lengths of yarn in shades of yellow, red-orange, brown, black, and gray for making hair.

- Avoid commercial displays and patterns that are stereotypic and give children the mistaken impression that all Hawaiians wear grass skirts or all Africans wear dashikis.

- Look for similarities. Consider common themes that cross cultures: play, family, learning. Choose one theme and share with children examples of art from other cultures that celebrate this theme. Encourage children to record their ideas and experiences through art. For example, show photographs of children playing hopscotch as depicted on the walls of the Egyptian pyramids and share Bruegel's painting *Children's Games,* portraying sixteenth century children at play. Discuss the importance of play in all cultures and throughout time. Ask children to draw, paint, or sculpt their own play activities so that children in other cultures and future times will know and understand how we have fun.

13-1d Orderly and Organized

The art center is orderly and organized to maximize efficiency. Although surplus junk may have creative potential, it is useless until it is organized and attractively displayed. Children do not know where to begin with a box of fabric, ribbon, yarn, and gift wrap all thrown together. Too many items, fostering too many possibilities, overwhelm young children. Similar

Hints

- The larger the paper, the more expensive it will be. Still, large sheets can be used sparingly in their entirety and cut down into smaller sizes and shapes. This will avoid needless waste and be more economical in the long run.

- Try butchers, carpet stores, print shops, and newspaper plants for newsprint, end rolls of paper, and brown wrap. These are good for making murals.

- Use different types of paper, and be sure to include newspaper, paper grocery bags, and cardboard. The want ads make a good backdrop for a painting or collage. The colored comics section makes a good background for linear designs in black. Different surfaces pose a new problem and challenge for the painter. A torn paper collage would work on the colored advertisement section. Provide papers that pose a challenge. For example, cut papers into flag, diamond, rhombus, or amorphous shapes. Cut circles, squares, rectangles, and triangles from the inside of papers. This will force the artist to modify or adapt his or her processing to fit the paper. For example, one cannot merely sweep paint, crayons, or markers across a figure-eight-shaped paper. The curves suggest a different swirling or circular type of arm movement and stroke.

- For children with special physical needs, try using contact paper sticky side up for collage activities. This eliminates the need for glue.

- Formica® and linoleum make good art surfaces for painting with brushes, hand painting, sculpting with clay, or monoprinting. They define the individual artist's space, are easy to obtain, and easy to clean. Old trays or cookie sheets are also recommended.

materials should be grouped together on low, open shelves. Basic tools like crayons, markers, and pencils should be placed next to each other. A second shelf can hold papers grouped by size and shape. Ideally, containers should be clear so contents are clearly visible. If not, add labels. Use a glue gun to affix a sample of the contents to the front of the container. For example, glue a twig and pinecone to the front of the box housing nature items. These tactile labels are especially important for children with low vision. Also, print the words "nature items." Labeling surrounds children with functional print and enhances emergent literacy. Some teachers prefer to stock shelves with activities set up on individual trays. For example, the tray for doing watercolor holds all equipment needed, including the watercolor set, brush, sponge, and water container. Teach children the find-use-return cycle: *every item has a special place where it is found. Use it safely and remember to return it when finished.* This teaches personal responsibility and frees the teacher from sole responsibility for maintaining the art center.

Shelves well stocked with materials, equipment, and supplies provide options from which to select. Start by putting out a limited number from which to choose. Remember the three Rs: replenish, rotate, and renew. Some items such as markers and crayons stay out all the time. Other items such as collage materials are rotated over time. For example, replace the nature specimens with fabric scraps. Initially, take children on a tour of the art center explaining the items, their names and uses, and where to find and return them. Continue to add items and enrich the art center over time as children display ability to handle additional options. New items are introduced during group time. For example, when placing sponges or twigs at the easel say, "Today I replaced the brushes at the easels with twigs. Think of how you might use a twig to paint and see what happens." Aim for balance between new and old. Replenish materials when children become bored but do not feel compelled to present new materials daily. According to Dighe, Calormiri, and Van Zutpen (1998), constantly introducing or changing art materials may actually stand in the way of a child's mastering the material enough to express ideas or feelings.

Encourage children to keep work spaces in the art center organized and orderly as well. This is especially important for children with special needs. Providing a tray will define a specific work space for a child unable to see where others are working and will set boundaries for a child who has not learned to share space with peers.

Consider purchasing an art drying rack for storing children's artwork while paint or glue is drying (see Figure 13–3). Some teachers string a clothesline in the art center for children to attach their work with clothespins. But when artwork is hung vertically, paint drips and glue runs. Artwork is ruined, and a mess is made! Other teachers reserve floor or cabinet space on which drying artwork can be laid flat. This consumes large amounts of space that might be needed for other activities and provides no protection for the artwork as it dries. Although an art drying rack may be expensive, it offers the advantage of keeping artwork flat while it dries and protecting the artwork from spills or careless feet. Countertop and freestanding rolling drying racks are available.

Photo Courtesy of Jill Englebright Fox

Figure 13–3 An art drying rack provides a non-messy and safe way to store children's artwork as the paint and glue dry.

Hints

- Shelving can be made using sturdy lumber, thick and wide, stacked on cement blocks. Boards should be sanded free of splinters or covered with fabric or adhesive-backed paper. Position blocks in a safe way so that young walkers will not bump into or trip over them.

- A pegboard with hooks by the art center is very useful. Smocks can be hung up on hooks. A sign system to indicate the number of people allowed at the art center at any one time can be displayed—for example, four palettes, one per hook, in the top row. Some art accessories can be hung from the hooks. For example, clear plastic or vinyl bags containing ribbon, fabric, and trims can be hung.

- Regardless of the storage facility, make sure all containers are clearly labeled in print. A picture of the box's content is also helpful. Display paper on flat shelves. Put paint and brushes on a plastic-lined shelf. This will stand up to water and drops of wet paint.

13-1e A Place with Rules and Limits

Why rules and limits? Won't rules and limits stifle creativity? Swann (2009) states that children are most attracted to classroom centers that offer opportunities for lively social interaction. The art center should be one in which children share ideas, problem-solve together, and describe and give advice about the processes in their work. Nevertheless, rules and limits are needed for children to work together productively. According to Cherry and Nielsen (1999), by carefully setting limits, teachers can help children make the fullest use, according to their needs and interests, of the art materials provided. Creativity happens within the confines of safety. With a few reasonable and appropriate limits, children have greater freedom for creative self-direction and self-pacing than if there are no guidelines at all or if the limits are too many and too restricting.

Rules and limits should be fairly and equally applied to all children. Young children with special needs may require special assistance and/or additional teacher monitoring. They may need to have directions repeated or broken down into smaller steps. Still, children are children, and all need to follow classroom rules, although different incentives and strategies may be needed by some children to foster compliance. All children want to belong.

An art center provides children with unlimited opportunities for attaining self-responsibility. Children abide by reasonable rules and limits. These rules and limits are verbally discussed in advance, with the reasons for each rule clearly explained. Children need to know both the rules and the reasons behind them. For example, discuss with children the proper use of materials. Paintbrushes are for painting. Waving paintbrushes in the air could either splash paint or hurt someone. Role-playing the rules, showing what happens when the rules are and are not followed, also helps young children to understand rules and the reasons behind them.

Rules are posted in writing and with pictures near the art center for easy reference. Rules and limits need to be discussed, posted, and enforced. Children who break a rule are removed from the art center. When they have time to reflect and agree that they are ready to abide by the rule, they can return.

Rules and limits will vary from teacher to teacher, center to center, classroom to classroom, program to program, and age group to age group. Children's health and safety always come first. Encourage children to wash their hands before and after working with art materials. Children should not eat or drink while engaged in art. Carefully supervise and remind the very young and oral child that art materials are for making art, not tasting. Provide age-appropriate materials. The following is a comprehensive list of guidelines from which you can select those that work best for your class.

Limit the Number of Children at the Center at Any One Time. This number depends on the number and size of tables, floor space, and easels. For example, Mrs. Tull displays four "Art" signs on clothespins at her art center. When all have been removed, children know the center is full. Ms. Valdez allows eight children in her larger art center. Four children can work at the tables, two at the easel, and two on the floor. When children ask if they can do art, she asks them to count the number of children in the center to see if there is a vacant spot.

Use a Smock during Art Activities. Children whose parents warn them about staying clean and avoiding messy activities may be apprehensive about doing art. Teachers can strongly recommend that parents provide "work" or "play" clothes for school. Young children need to dress appropriately for active days at school, and art activities will involve getting dirty. Adding liquid detergent to paint makes the paint easier to wash out in the laundry. Remind children to let their paintings dry thoroughly before moving them or taking them home. This will minimize smudging and smearing of paint onto clothing.

Slightly oversized children's shirts make good smocks. Cut off the sleeves, put them on backwards, and have someone button up the back. Smocks are vital during painting. They also protect clothing when children use glue, paste, and markers. It is a good idea to wear a smock for all art activities (see Figure 13–4). Shirt sleeves should be rolled or pushed up above the elbows. Removing sweaters allows greater freedom of movement and

TeachSource Video

© 2015 Cengage Learning.

5-11 Years: Developmental Disabilities in Middle Childhood

Pretend that Derek and Michaela are in your second grade class. Work with a partner to consider how you might modify activities in the art center to meet their needs. Describe your suggested modifications.

Watch on CourseMate.

An Opportunity for Teacher Reflection

Mr. Jackson Teaches Three- and Four-Year Olds in a Head Start program. The school year is ready to begin, and Mr. Jackson knows that most of the three-year-old children who will be joining his classroom have never been in an organized early childhood program and that their experiences with art have been very limited. He also knows that the returning four-year-olds in his class enjoyed rich art experiences in the program last year and will remember how to use materials in the art center. Mr. Jackson is fortunate to have a well-stocked art center in his classroom. As he surveys the materials available, he sees drawing and construction paper, crayons, markers, finger paints and finger paint paper, easel paints, scissors, glue, tape, and a wonderful collection of recycled three-dimensional objects. *What art activities should Mr. Jackson plan for the first weeks of school? What materials should he provide for children in the art center? How can Mr. Jackson introduce the three-year-olds in his classroom to art experiences, while at the same time building on the art expertise that his four-year-olds will bring to the art center?*

Figure 13–4 Art smocks protect these children's clothes during art activities.

© Cengage Learning

eliminates the possibility of their getting stained with paint. Smocks can also be made from oilcloth or vinyl cut into a large square with a head opening and worn as a poncho. Velcro® or elastic can hold the sides.

Use Art Tools Properly. This is not to suggest that there is only one way to paint or draw. It does mean that brushes are for painting and scissors are for cutting paper. Teachers should discuss and model proper care and use of all art media in advance.

Use Only What You Need. Discuss the economical use of materials and the avoidance of needless waste. Have a variety of paper sizes available. Not all children need or want to work on a large sheet of paper. Some children have a small idea that fits nicely onto smaller paper. Avoid putting too much paper out at any one time. Children may feel obligated to deplete the pile or believe there is an endless supply.

Complete Your Art Activity. Occasionally, a child will deplete a pile of paper by making a series of aimless, quick marks on each sheet. Quality rather than quantity should be the goal. Teachers can encourage children to take their time and finish each picture.

Share Supplies. Items at the art center must be shared. There may not be enough glue or staplers to go around. Children learn that the items belong to the school or center and are available for all children to use. Some children have difficulty following this rule. They become possessive and clutch the newest pair of scissors or the prettiest roll of ribbon.

Respect Others. Children learn to respect and value the ideas, styles, and work of others, just as they come to value their own. Children cannot ridicule or criticize the ideas and work of others. Children's statements may be well intended, but the messages can hurt. Negative messages also hamper creative expression. Teachers can discuss how children can draw, color, or paint anything in any way they want. It is their decision and their rendering, not someone else's, that matters. Perhaps children who receive criticism or correction for their own artwork also become overly critical of others.

Children may also get possessive of available space. They may try to occupy the majority of the table. Young children who are used to having their own way and having one of everything at home will need guidance. Young children who have little space and no toys may also squander and require intervention.

Return Everything to Its Place When Finished. Small paper scraps are thrown in the wastebasket. Larger scraps of construction paper are saved in a scrap paper box for collage. Smocks are hung on a hook.

Clean Up When Done. Remind children to leave their space clean for the next artist to use. Children know they need to wash their hands and clean the space they occupied. They should also check the floor before they leave. In short, children learn the art center is primarily their responsibility, with the teacher playing a minor role through guidance, maintenance, and supervision. To combine art with a literacy experience, post directions cards in your art center. For example, the directions cards for easel painting in Figure 13–5 depict the series or sequence involved in painting a

1. Put on smock

2. Paint picture

3. Place picture in drying rack

4. Wash hands

© Cengage Learning

5. Hang up smock

Figure 13–5 Directions cards for easel painting.

picture. Words and pictures are used to help children learn the following directions for easel painting: put on your smock, paint a picture, place picture on the rack to dry, wash your hands, and hang up your smock.

13-1f **Displaying Children's Art**

The art center should include spaces for displaying children's artwork (Figure 13-6). Displaying their artwork in the classroom is a powerful incentive for children to participate in both art appreciation and art-making activities. As children experience art appreciation in the curriculum, they begin to recognize the conventions associated with displaying adult art in museums and galleries. They see that adult artwork is matted and framed and often accompanied by a separate narrative that includes the artist's name and the date. Providing these same conventions for children and their artwork demonstrates that adults take their efforts seriously and respect the work they produce.

Designating a bulletin board or wall space within or close to the art center will allow children to display their drawings and paintings. Likewise, a table or countertop can be used to display sculptures and constructions. Gitter (1968) encouraged teachers to plan for "quiet" spaces when displaying children's artwork:

> Putting up the children's work indiscriminately served no purpose, for the children did not feel especially proud of pictures jammed in with dozens of others. They were well aware that their work was not truly appreciated but only looked at perfunctorily and hung up because it was the thing to do. (p. 86)

Instead of displaying classwide or whole-group art projects indiscriminately, consider developing classroom routines in which each child makes a thoughtful decision about whether or not to display an individual

Photo Courtesy of Jill Englebright Fox

Figure 13–6 In this art center, children can choose to display their own artwork on mounted magnet boards.

project. That child might then work with the teacher or a parent volunteer to carefully mat the artwork and prepare a card with the date, a title, and the artist's name for display beside the artwork.

While it may be challenging to display all of the artwork in the classroom at children's eye level, it should definitely be shown at a comfortable viewing level for children. Whether on a wall, a bulletin board, or a table surface, artwork should be neatly arranged with minimal distracters. Decorative borders or bulletin board characters will take the viewers' focus away from what should truly be the center of attention: the art!

The role of *docent* may be added to the responsibilities of classroom helpers. Classroom docents can be charged with choosing the arrangement of work on the bulletin board and sharing the display with visitors to the classroom. Children, as the creators of the artwork, are uniquely qualified to tell others about their work and the ideas behind them (Thompson, 1995).

Did You Get It?

Learning activities that stimulate the mind and those that foster _____ should be included in every art center for young learners.
- **a.** social and language interaction
- **b.** debate and discourse
- **c.** a healthy dose of rebelliousness, or "thinking outside the box"
- **d.** work at home

Take the full quiz on CourseMate.

DAP naeyc 13-2 Evaluating An Art Center/Program

Evaluate the effectiveness of your art center by honestly answering the following questions:

1. Is your art center more child-centered than teacher-directed? Do you let children discover, invent, and process with the media as opposed to teaching art?
2. Do you capitalize on the language/literacy potential in art by providing labeled supplies and rebus directions in the art center?
3. Do children have ample time and equal access to an art center on a daily basis? Do all children in your class choose to visit the art center on a regular basis?
4. Do you follow the three R's—replenishing, rotating, and renewing the items in your art center?
5. Do you take activities and materials from the art center outdoors for children to enjoy on a regular basis?

6. Do you provide materials in the art center that encourage children to include people of all races and many cultures in their artwork?
7. Do you facilitate children's artistic development by supervising and offering yourself as a resource? Are you careful not to impose suggestions and solutions?
8. Do you value developmental appropriateness in art and thereby provide multisensory, messy activities involving more processing than the making of a predetermined product? Do you supplement by occasionally teaching children a new art technique?
9. Do you offer space for children to display their artwork if they choose? Do you provide the same conventions for the children's artwork that are provided for adult artwork?

The ideal would be to answer affirmatively to all these questions. This may not always be possible or practical, given individual situations and constraints. The purpose of answering the questions is to assess the effectiveness and appropriateness of your art center and suggest some next steps to take to make your center comprehensive, developmentally appropriate, integrated, and child-centered. It is a process that takes time, commitment, and faith in children's innate capacity to be creative and make art.

Did You Get It?

The authors of your text take which of the following positions as pertains to teachers physically (in writing) labeling art supplies, classroom sections, and activities?
- **a.** Children should not need these visual and language cues as these activities should be spontaneous and relaxed, and far removed from seeming like formal lessons.
- **b.** This practice is useful and highly-recommended.
- **c.** It is simply a matter of personal preference on the part of the teacher as to whether or not to label.
- **d.** The children are attempting to learn and should be expected to navigate an art center without this form of assistance.

Take the full quiz on CourseMate.

DAP naeyc naea 13-3 Puppets and Masks

Puppets and **masks** serve many developmental ends. They are psychological props. They give young children something to hold and hide behind when speaking. After all, if a child makes a mistake or speaks incorrectly, it is the puppet or mask rather than the child who is to blame. Puppets and masks allow children to hide their identity and become someone or something else for a period of time. Children also have a way of sharing emotionally important events through play with puppets and masks, often things they would never say or do without the props.

Young children enjoy making puppets and masks as much as they enjoy dramatizing, verbalizing, and problem-solving with them. Puppets can help children decide how disagreements can be resolved. A teacher can use a puppet to play the part of an imaginary young child who refuses to share. Children can use other puppets to discuss and act out this scenario and possible solutions.

There are many ways to make puppets and masks. Although construction of the puppet may be craftlike, the design of facial features and clothes for the puppet's body allow children to be artistically expressive. Here are some activities for young children.

13-3a Puppets from Paper

Papier-Mâché Puppets

PUPPET HEAD A puppet head is slowly built by draping gluey paper over a crushed ball of newspaper and a tissue paper roll. Refer to the section on papier-mâché in Chapter 12. Begin winding paper around the roll to form a neck and continue to build up a head over the crushed newspaper ball. Paint with tempera when thoroughly dry. Attach fabric for a body.

The papier-mâché can also be made over a clay base. Children use clay to make their puppet head. Next, wind strips of papier-mâché over the form. Make the layers go in different directions for strength. Let dry thoroughly. Carefully cut the head in half with a sharp knife and remove the clay. Use additional papier-mâché to seal the two halves together. Reinforce the neck with additional strips. Smooth rough spots with sandpaper. Paint or decorate with trims. Seal with hair spray if it is painted with tempera. Add a puppet body, following the directions given here.

PUPPET BODY A simple puppet body can be made from a 12-inch-square piece of scrap fabric. Fold in half and cut three small openings along the center fold. The middle opening will be for the index finger, which also supports the puppet head. The two side openings are for the thumb and middle fingers, which serve as hands. Measure children's hand spans before cutting to ensure the openings are neither too close nor too far apart.

Preschool, Kindergarten, and School-Age Activity: Paper Bag Puppet. Provide each child with a lunch-size paper bag, neither too big nor too small for their hand to fit in and grasp. Paper bags are recommended because their construction provides a built-in movable mouth. Children use paint, crayons, markers, and trims to decorate their puppet.

Preschool, Kindergarten, and School-Age Activity: Stuffed Paper Bag Puppet. Stuff a large paper bag with crumpled newspaper. Insert a stick, ruler, or dowel. Make sure the end of the handle is sticking out for a handle. Continue stuffing. Gather the bag and tie securely at the handle with string to form a neck. Decorate the stuffed paper bag head with paint, crayons, or markers. Add paper scraps, yarn, and trims.

Preschool, Kindergarten, and School-Age Activity: Paper Plate Puppet. An easy puppet can be made by decorating a paper plate and attaching it to a handle, such as a stick or ruler. Or paper plates can be folded to make a talking puppet. Each child will need two paper plates. Fold one in half. Cut the other in half. Staple one half to the top and the other half to the under side of the folded paper plate. This allows four fingers to be inserted into the top jaw and the thumb in the lower jaw. The child moves his or her fingers to make the puppet talk. Although a frog readily comes to mind, a folded paper plate puppet can be used to make a variety of animals, people, and objects. Decorate with crayons, markers, paper scraps, and trims. A cloth sleeve on the child's arm creates an added effect.

Preschool, Kindergarten, and School-Age Activity: Cardboard Tissue Tube Puppet. Children use paint, crayons, or markers to decorate a cylindrical puppet. A roll or tube is ideally sized for small hands. Nothing else is needed. A smaller section can be used as the head with a puppet body made from fabric. Place the puppet's cloth body over the fingers and insert the puppet head over the index and middle fingers.

Kindergarten and School-Age Activity: "Me" Puppet. Children enjoy making and using life-sized puppets. These puppets can be decorated to look like their makers. Each child needs two sheets of sturdy butcher paper that matches their height along with one and a half heavyweight paper plates. One plate will be used for the face and the other half for the back. This is where they will insert their hand to walk, dance, and move with their "Me" puppet. This activity is best done in shifts over a period of time. You may want to set up the activity at different stations so long as adults are present to offer assistance when needed. On the floor, an adult traces each child's body onto the double sheets of paper. Children use crayons, markers, or paint to add clothing and details. Another adult provides a mirror, and children carefully note their faces and make them on the paper plates. You may want to provide yarn for hair as well as buttons and trims. Think multiculturally and provide paint, markers, and crayons in varied skin tones. You may need to assist children in stapling their two body outlines together. As you staple, stuff with crumpled newspaper to give a full, three-dimensional effect. An adult can staple the paper plate half onto the back of the puppet's head. Children can slip their hand into the half paper plate. The last step is to attach the head to the body. An adult uses strong glue or a hot glue gun to make sure the head is securely attached to the body.

13-3b Puppets from Wood

Preschool, Kindergarten, and School-Age Activity: Wooden Stick Puppet. Tongue depressors and craft sticks are used and decorated as the puppet itself. They can also be used as the base or handle to which a paper plate, magazine picture, cardboard, poster board, or other type of puppet is attached. Dowel rods or drinking straws can also be used as handles for puppets.

Preschool, Kindergarten, and School-Age Activity: Wooden Block Puppet. A small rectangular piece of scrap wood is fashioned into a puppet. Features are added with paints, crayons, markers, small wood scraps, or trims. Make sure the edges are sanded smooth and free of splinters.

Preschool, Kindergarten & School-Age Activity: Wooden Spoon Puppet. An old, large wooden cooking spoon is turned into a puppet. Decorate with fine markers. A piece of scrap material is tied at the neck of the spoon to add the element of clothing and conceal the stick handle. Add yarn for hair. Children hold the stick handle while working their puppets.

13-3c Puppets from Fabric

Kindergarten and School-Age Activity: Sock Puppet. Find an old sock. Cut a slit across the toe, halfway to the heel, for the puppet's mouth. Cut a piece of felt or material to fit inside the mouth. Fold it in half, position it in place, and glue it on (see Figure 13–7). Four fingers fit into the upper jaw. Glue a piece of cardboard under the lower jaw. This helps the thumb. Add trims: buttons and beads for eyes, yarn for hair, and so on.

Kindergarten and School-Age Activity: Glove Puppet. Old garden, work, utility, driving, dress, or plastic gloves are made into puppets. Encourage the child to put on the glove and think of decorative possibilities.

Small trims—buttons, yarn, and so forth—are sewn or glued on. Or single fingers can be cut off to make

one puppet, which will nicely fit on one or two child-sized fingers.

13-3d Puppets from Containers

Preschool, Kindergarten, and School-Age Activity: Plastic Foam Cup Puppet. Cut one hole into a plastic foam cup. Encourage the child to put one finger through. Does it remind you of anything? It could be an elephant with the finger for a trunk. Or could it be a head, tail, leg, or tongue? Try cutting two holes at opposite sides. Encourage children to put one finger into each hole. What does it remind you of? Could these be arms or legs? Do four holes allow fingers to represent arms and legs or wheels on a vehicle? Or the cup could be decorated with markers without cutting holes and snugly positioned on a toddler's clenched fist or raised fingers.

Preschool, Kindergarten, and School-Age Activity: Container Puppet. Plastic and cardboard containers for holding milk, detergent, shampoo, toothpaste, or bleach have their own characteristic shapes and will suggest vehicle, person, or animal puppets to make. Skinny necks on containers make good handles to hold when using the puppet. Other containers come with built-in handles. Decorate containers with paper and other trims.

Preschool, Kindergarten, and School-Age Activity: Box Puppet. Boxes with interesting shapes, including toothpaste and fast-food boxes, may suggest puppet possibilities. Decorate them with paper and other trims. Add dishwashing detergent to tempera paint to make it stick if the surface is slick. A small milk carton is ideally sized for a fist puppet.

Kindergarten and School-Age Activity: Coat Hanger Puppet. Bend a wire coat hanger into a geometric or abstract shape of a puppet. Keep the hook at the bottom for a handle. Place a nylon stocking or pantyhose over the coat hanger and fasten it with string or a rubber band. Decorate the puppet with fabric scraps, yarn, ribbon, trims, and paper.

13-3e Puppet Stage

There is no need to spend money on a commercially made puppet stage. Children can make, paint, and decorate their own. Find a large appliance box, such

Cut: Sew: Reinforce with cardboard:

Figure 13–7 Sock puppet.

© Cengage Learning

as a refrigerator carton. Remove the back side and cut a window opening in the front panel for the puppets. The opening or window should be placed so that when children are sitting or kneeling behind the screen it is above their heads but within arm's length. Include a window in the stage that opens and closes by folding the cardboard back. Curtains can be hung. To provide a backdrop, hang scenery the children create from a dowel or curtain rod. Make sure the pole fits across the top. Make a small notch in each side panel of the carton in which the scenery hanger can securely rest. Allow room for puppets to move about freely in front of the scenery. One foot from the front is recommended. The puppet stage can be painted and decorated as the children see fit. It should be a project inviting group participation and planning. Children will be proud of their accomplishment and will likely use it as a result.

13-3f **Masks**

Making masks is an ancient art form that is practiced in many cultures. Often, masks have utilitarian value in religious and cultural celebrations. Presently, masks are used in this country for the celebration of Halloween and Mardi Gras. Many children are frightened by masks. Some refuse to put something over their heads or faces. They may fear suffocation or loss of identity. Their wishes should be respected. Others enjoy losing their identity, at least temporarily, by putting on a mask and being someone or something else.

There are many ways to make a mask, but only two ways to wear a mask: putting it over the head or attaching it to the face. Figure 13–8 shows a mask made by a first-grader. Here are some masks appropriate to make with young children.

13-3g **Over-the-Head Masks**

Preschool, Kindergarten, and School-Age Activity: Grocery Bag Mask. Find a paper grocery bag that slips easily over the child's head. Place it over the child's head and use pencil to indicate where the eyes should be placed. Take the bag off and cut eyeholes for the child. Cut additional openings for the nose and mouth to help the child breathe better. Slit the four sides so the bag easily slips over the child's shoulders and stays in place. Encourage the child to use paint, crayons, markers, and trims to decorate.

Preschool, Kindergarten, and School-Age Activity: Cardboard Box Mask. Find a cardboard box that fits easily over a child's head. Place it over the child's head and use pencil to indicate where the eyes should be. Take the box off and cut eyeholes. Add openings for the nose and mouth if needed. Encourage the child to use paint, crayons, markers, and trims to decorate.

13-3h **Face Masks**

Preschool, Kindergarten, and School-Age Activity: Pie Plate Mask. Hold a pie plate over the child's face and indicate where the eyes should be placed. Cut eyeholes. Make sure the cut metal leaves no sharp edges. Add dishwashing liquid to paint so it will adhere to the aluminum pie plate. Trims can also be glued. When the mask is completed, attach a string to each side and tie in back. Children like the slick, shiny metal surface, which suggests robots or superheroes.

Kindergarten and School-Age Activity: Papier-Mâché Mask. mask may be made by draping gluey paper over a large, relatively flat bowl, box or dish. Wind paper carefully around the bowl. Cut holes for eyes, nose, and mouth before the papier-mâché dries. Paint with tempera when thoroughly dry. Papier-mâché masks are likely to be too heavy for children to actually wear, but they might be made as part of learning about another culture.

© Cengage Learning

Figure 13–8 A mask made by a first grader.

Did You Get It?

Masks are recommended artistic props for a myriad of reasons. One psychologically beneficial reason for their use is the fact that they

  a. allow children to repress and hide unhealthy emotions.

  b. allow children to enter a fantasy world in which many problems magically disappear.

  c. allow the child to develop alternate personalities.

  d. create a psychological barrier against risk, fear, and anxiety.

Take the full quiz on CourseMate.

Summary

This chapter focused on setting up an art program in a learning center format. (13-1) By definition, an art center is an artist's studio, conveniently located and easily accessible, well stocked, orderly and organized, with rules and limits and opportunities to display children's artwork. (13-2) Teachers should regularly evaluate the effectiveness of the art center by asking and answering questions about its child-centeredness, language and literacy connections, access, the three R's, and more. (13-3) Making masks and puppets in the art center provides opportunities for children to be creative and explore communicating in another persona.

Key Terms

art center, 257

masks, 266

mixing media, 257

puppets, 266

✔ Suggested Activities

1. Observe a successful art center. Describe the teacher's role.

2. On graph paper, design the art center you would create for your classroom. List the materials with which you would stock your art center.

3. Consider the letter to families at the beginning of this section. How might you change the letter to send to families of children in a third-grade classroom? In a class for three-year-olds?

4. Help a teacher establish a classroom museum for displaying children's artwork. Work with the children to develop the rules for displaying their artwork.

5. Facilitate a puppet- or mask-making activity with children. Integrate it with another curricular area. For example, a puppet- or mask-making activity may extend or grow from reading a book or from a storytelling session. Refer to Chapter 12 for a discussion of integrating art across the early childhood curriculum.

Review

1. List the criteria or guidelines for an early childhood art center.

2. List five major rules for successfully operating an early childhood art center.

3. List any five questions that address the effectiveness of an early childhood art center/program.

4. A recommendation from this chapter is to aim for a balance between old and new. Use a nontext example to explain this quote.

Additional Resources

Preschool Plan-It is a website created by a preschool teacher that provides resources for teachers, such as classroom and learning center designs.

Puppetry Arts (www.puppetryarts.org) is a website on puppetry in education.

ArtsEdge (http://artsedge.kennedy-center.org) communicates the National Standards for Arts Education and lesson plan ideas.

Masks of the World at the University of Missouri Museum of Anthropology (http://anthromuseum .missouri.edu) has a mini-gallery on masks of many cultures (http://anthromuseum.missouri .edu/minigalleries/worldmasks/intro.shtml).

 Visit CourseMate for this textbook to access the eBook, Did You Get It? quizzes, Digital Downloads, TeachSource Videos, flashcards, and more. Go to CengageBrain.com to log in, register, or purchase access.

First/Second Grade Lesson Plan

Veterans' Day Puppets

GOAL

History. The student understands the historical significance of landmarks and celebrations in the community, state, and nation.

OBJECTIVE

The student is expected to:

a. explain the significance of various community, state, and national celebrations such as Veterans Day.
b. make a puppet to honor one branch of the military.

MATERIALS

a. Paper plates, one for each child
b. Tongue depressor for each child
c. Tempera paints and brushes
d. Photos of service men or women from each branch of the service
e. World map
f. Library books on American holidays and Veteran's Day

INTRODUCTION

Share with the children that today we will prepare to celebrate an upcoming holiday: Veteran's Day. Write Veteran's Day on the board. Ask each child to work with a partner to make a list of all they know about Veteran's Day. When the partners have finished their lists, come back together as a whole group and discuss the children's lists. Create a master list on the board.

DEVELOPMENT

Have the children return to their partners and use the library books to identify additional information on Veteran's Day. Return again to whole group and add any new information. Fill in information as needed until the following information on Veteran's Day has been shared:

Back in the early twentieth century, America, France, Great Britain, and Germany fought a war. At the eleventh hour of the eleventh day of the eleventh month, these countries all signed a peace treaty. The next year, the president chose that same day, November 11, to remember and honor all the soldiers who had died for their countries in that war. There were four more wars in the the twentieth century. Gradually, Americans began to see November 11 as the day to honor all of the military who have served our country, in times of war and peace.

Share with the children photos of service men and women who serve in each branch of the military. List the branches on the board and review with the children what each of these branches does.

Share with the children that Veteran's Day is often celebrated with parades and programs: "Our school is having an assembly program and inviting veterans in the community to be recognized. Our class will participate in the assembly by leading a parade of students. We will be making and wearing masks to honor each branch of the military in the parade."

Ask each child to choose a branch of the military and create a mask to portray a member of that branch. Assist the children in cutting out the eyeholes and attaching the tongue depressor. Children can decorate their masks with tempera paint or trim.

CONCLUSION

Have the children share their masks with their partners, sharing what they have learned about Veteran's Day and the branch of the service they chose to represent.

ASSESSMENT

a. Did the children explain the significance of Veteran's Day?
b. Did each child create a mask to honor a branch of the military?

Go to cengagebrain.com for a full-size version of this lesson plan.

Roles and Strategies

© Cengage Learning

What do you see in this picture?

Caitlin is one of the first-graders whose paintings are included in this hall exhibit. Caitlin is fortunate to have a teacher who encourages children's individual expression through art. For example, after reading the book *Blue Dog* and reviewing primary colors on the color wheel, the teacher encouraged the children to draw their own versions of Blue Dog using primary colors. The teacher asked children to share their paintings with each other and then allowed each child to decide if his or her painting would be included in the hall exhibit. Though Caitlin was excited that her work was on display, several other children preferred to take their paintings home to share with their families.

Planning is one of the many things teachers do in providing art experiences. Chapter 14, "Art Experiences through Technology," discusses the impact of technology on children's learning and the teacher's role in providing appropriate, supportive art experiences for young children. Chapter 15, "Roles, Responses, and Strategies to Support Children's Art," concentrates on teacher-child interactions during the artistic process. It also provides ideas for sparking the production of children's art and ways to celebrate it. How do you know how children are progressing in art? Chapter 16, "Art Assessment," focuses on children's artistic development and stresses the importance of observation coupled with art samples as a way of gathering valuable developmental information. The instrument for artistic evaluation, based on the whole child, informally attempts to evaluate children's artistic development.

A LETTER TO FAMILIES

Dear Families,

In our classroom, children use computers as tools to look at and to make art. Over the Internet, children have looked at artwork in the Louvre in Paris and at the Museum of Modern Art in New York City. The children have created their own art using draw and paint programs on classroom computers and tablets. Just like their first efforts with crayons and paper, children began their computer drawings by exploring the possibilities, varying the colors and strokes they made by clicking and dragging the mouse and stylus. As the children learned to make choices and vary the effects, they began to use the computer as just one more tool for creating artwork. In our classroom museum, computer-generated art is displayed along with easel paintings, collages, and sculptures.

The children have also begun to experiment with photography as an art form. We have looked at the work of professional photographers and developed criteria for artistic photographs. We have three digital cameras, and the children experiment with perspective, distance, detail, and focus as they take photographs inside and on the playground.

As your child brings home paintings, computer-generated art, and digital photographs, don't worry if you can't figure them out! The beauty may reside in your child's use of colors and shapes and in the choices your child makes about subject and perspective. Do not ask, "What is it?" Say, "tell me about this," and encourage your child to discuss it if he or she chooses. Compare your child's art with pictures and paintings brought home at the beginning of the year. Consider the growth you see in control of the crayon or paintbrush, changes in objects and themes portrayed, and the increasing details. Looking at your child's artwork is an exciting way to see how he or she is growing and learning!

Sincerely,

Your Child's Teacher

This letter is available for digital download.

14 Art Experiences through Technology

This photograph depicts a kindergarten computer center.

Children visit this center singly and in small groups to play games with numbers and letters, to write stories, and to explore faraway places on the Internet. Children also visit this center to participate in art appreciation and production activities. The computer provides an exciting extension to the early childhood art center. Creating art on the computer requires children to explore many of the same skills and thinking processes used in traditional art activities, as well as abilities unique to the computer as an art medium. The teacher sets the stage for computer use in both art appreciation and production activities. The teacher provides resources and opportunities for young children to engage in art activities in the computer center.

Learning Outcomes

After reading this chapter, you should be able to:

14-1 Discuss relevant research on the impact of technology use on young children's learning and development.

14-2 Discuss and critique the concept of computer art, including both advantages and disadvantages as they pertain to young children.

14-3 Identify four keys to successful integration of computers into the early childhood curriculum.

14-4 Facilitate children's use of the digital camera as an art tool.

Standards addressed in this chapter

DAP CRITERIA
  2 Teaching to enhance development and learning
  3 Planning curriculum to achieve important goals

NAEYC Standards
  1 Relationships
  2 Curriculum
  3 Teaching
  7 Families
  9 Physical Environment

NAEA Visual Arts Standards
  1 Understanding and applying media, techniques, and processes
  4 Understanding the visual arts in relation to history and cultures

DAP naeyc 14-1 Technology in Early Childhood Education

Computers are commonplace in homes, businesses, and classrooms. Tablets are becoming increasingly common as well. We have come to expect the efficiency and convenience that technology contributes to our daily activities in most settings. As we consider the use of technology in early childhood classrooms, however, teachers need to consider issues beyond efficiency and convenience. For example, are computer activities developmentally appropriate for young children? What can computers and other technology contribute to an early childhood art curriculum? How can teachers best support children's interactions with technology? This chapter provides an overview of the role of computers and other technology in an early childhood art curriculum. A discussion of the impact of computers on children's development and learning is presented, along with effective suggestions and strategies for the classroom.

"Screen time" is the term used to describe the collective time children spend engaging with various technology devices, including televisions, computers, DVD players, smartphones, and tablet devices. American children under the age of two have, on average, more than two hours every day of screen time (Ravichandran & de Bravo, 2010). In 2012, the National Association for the Education and Young Children and the Fred Rogers Center for Early Learning and Children's Media at St. Vincent College issued a joint position statement titled "Technology and Interactive Media as Tools in Early Childhood Programs Serving Children from Birth through Age Eight." The statement recommends that children younger than age two should absolutely not engage in passive screen time, and that passive and non-interactive screen time be discouraged for children ages two through five years. This position statement emphasizes that teachers and parents must ensure that technology experiences meet children's needs for physical movement, human interaction, and cognitive stimulation (see Figure 14–1). When used appropriately, technology has the potential to engage children in exploration, experimentation, problem-solving, and creative thinking. In the early childhood classroom, computers in particular can empower children as independent learners. Computer use can be a social activity with children speaking, working, and learning together. Computers provide avenues for children to use their multiple intelligences. Computers are both patient and forgiving in that they allow children to correct or change their responses.

Papert (1993) is a pioneer in the area of children and computers. A student of Piaget, Papert applied Piaget's developmental theory and constructivist point of view to children's use of computers. He created a graphics program named **LOGO**®, which is programmable

Photo Courtesy of Jill Englebright Fox

Figure 14–1 Technology individualizes children's learning.

rather than direct-manipulation software. Rather than manipulating a program designed by someone else, the child assumes full control. Through LOGO®, young children discover fundamental principles of math while learning to write simple computer programs. Also called "turtle geometry," LOGO® invites the child programmer to input commands to a small turtle icon on the screen, which then walks a certain number of steps, drawing a line as it goes. The "turtle" is actually a futuristic-looking object that beeps, walks, and turns on typed commands from the child at the keyboard, thus making the experience appropriate for young programmers. For example, in programming the turtle to draw a square, the child develops his or her own process of walking a straight line, turning 90 degrees, and repeating the movement three more times to complete the shape. Papert viewed computers as a way to revolutionize education. Specifically, he believed that discovery-oriented interactions with computers enhance learning by encouraging children to explore interests in art, music, or engineering through technology and mathematics.

Kinderlogo is one of the newest versions of LOGO. Designed for children in kindergarten through grade 3, Kinderlogo puts children in charge of their computer experience, allowing them to move the turtle around the screen by using easy commands introduced in five levels. They use the turtle to explore patterns and create

© Cengage Learning 2015

Figure 14–2 Teacher as technology facilitator.

original designs as they explore mathematics. Also based on LOGO technology, Bee-bot is a robot designed for young children. Children use directional keys to enter up to 40 different commands which send Bee-Bot forward, back, left and right. The goal is for children to enter increasingly more creative and complex command sequences.

Technology is one of many tools in a developmentally appropriate program. It should neither be a substitute for concrete learning nor replace the human factor, the teacher (see Figure 14–2). It should be used in moderation and integrated into the classroom to enhance learning experiences (NAEYC & the Fred Rogers Center for Early Learning and Children's Media at St. Vincent College, 2012). The appropriate question for early childhood educators is no longer whether computers should be used in the classroom but rather how to use them effectively to support learning and the development of the whole child. As computers are connected with young children and integrated into curriculum, the benefits to children become clear. However, if technology experiences are not developmentally appropriate, children would be better off without them. Before children experience technology, they should have an understanding of real-world relationships. Skeele and Stefankiewicz (2002) say adults should assess this understanding before allowing children to use computers. Generally, children are ready for an introduction to computers at around three years of age (American Academy of Pediatrics, 2001; Haugland, 1999).

The positive impact computers have on young children is dependent on the types of experiences children have with the computer. Seymour Papert (1993) stressed that computers in the classroom should provide concrete experiences for children and that children should have free access to the computer. While working at the computer, children should have control of their learning experiences, making decisions about the purposes of their work and the software they use, and making choices about how to proceed through a specific piece of software. Papert recommended teachers facilitate peer tutoring at the computer, rather than engaging in adult problem-solving, and that teachers take advantage of the computer's capabilities to teach powerful ideas.

When computers are used under these general guidelines, research indicates the positive impact of computers on young children's learning and development is significant across several developmental domains. Young children's socio-emotional development is an important focus in early childhood curriculum and classrooms. While Seo, Chun, Jwa, and Choi (2011) found that extensive and unsupervised computer use, particularly for playing games, could delay young children's socio-emotional development, appropriate use of computers is actually a positive factor in socio-emotional development. Anderson (2000) found children will engage in cooperative play in the computer center and the block center for similar amounts of time. This research suggests that both the computer and the block center can provide a context for beginning and extending social interaction among young children.

Clements (1994) believed computers can be catalysts for social interactions. His research on children's social interactions at the computer showed that children prefer to work with friends rather than alone, and that they displayed more positive emotions and interest in activities when working together. While working at the computer, the children in Clements's study spontaneously provided help and instruction for their peers, and they talked about and built on each other's ideas.

Research on young children with special needs also supports the idea that computers have a positive impact on socio-emotional development. When young children with special needs work on the classroom computer, they have more social interaction with their peers (Spiegel-McGill, Zippiroli, & Mistrett, 1989) and show greater gains in their overall socio-emotional development. Again, however, the types of experiences children have on the compute affect the nature of their interactions.

Open-ended software, such as draw-and-paint programs, encourages children to collaborate. Drill-and-practice programs, however, foster turn-taking and competition among the children. Gaming software may undermine children's socio-emotional development (Seo et al., 2011) and is associated with lower linguistic and literacy abilities (Bittman, Rutherford, Brown, & Unsworth, 2011).

In terms of cognitive development, **drill-and-practice software** has been shown to help children with certain memorized skills, like counting and sorting (Clements and Nastasi, 1995). Open-ended software that encourages children to solve problems, however, enhances children's creativity, logico-mathematical thinking, and critical thinking. For example, Wright

Brain Connection 🧠

Learning doesn't happen as individual, isolated events in the brain. When a child is learning, many areas of the brain are activitated at the same time. Children understand meaning within the context in which it is encountered. Real-life experiences are important for children to interpret and make meaning of as well as to broaden their understandings of the world. Field trips, guest speakers, technology, and multicultural experiences help children learn about society and themselves (Rushton, Juola-Rushton & Larkin, 2010)

(1994) found that software allowing the creation of pictures with geometric shapes helped children understand concepts such as symmetry, patterning, and spatial order. Software that allows children to manipulate objects and shapes has other benefits to cognitive development as well. Such programs allow children to save their work and come back to it for long-term projects. Shapes and objects can be resized or cut, and children's awareness of mathematical operations is raised as they rotate, flip, and rearrange manipulatives (Clements and Sarama, 1998).

Despite the computer's positive impact on children's learning and development, however, teachers must consider carefully how they will integrate the computer into the classroom. Children need time to explore the software and its functions before they are expected use it for a specific purpose. Early childhood teachers should provide children access to technology tools specifically for exploration and experimentation (NAEYC & the Fred Rogers Center for Early Learning at Children's Media at St. Vincent College, 2012).

Lemerise (1993) also believed children's free exploration of software is essential but cautioned that too much free exploration could lead to boredom. Open-ended projects with software encourage children's purposeful engagement and problem-solving. An effective use of technology in the classroom should connect on-screen and off-screen activities and emphasize co-viewing and co-participating between children and adults and children and their peers (Takeuchi, 2011). Haugland (1992) found that children exposed to appropriate software showed gains in intelligence, nonverbal skills, long-term memory, and manual dexterity. However, children who also engaged in related off-computer activities had similar scores in these areas as well as higher scores in verbal problem-solving and conceptual skills. The research supporting the use of computers with young children is powerful. Success, however, is dependent on teacher decisions about how the computer is used in the classroom and the software to be provided.

Skeele and Stefankiewicz (2002) suggest the following to help teachers and parents provide appropriate computer experiences for young children:

- Regulate the amount of time children spend at the computer.
- Stimulate children's senses by providing off-computer experiences that match things being learned on the computer.
- Provide time for children to manipulate real objects in balance with the time they spend on the computer.

Are there critics? Is work on the computer nothing more than an animated workbook? Some early childhood educators question the sedentary nature of two-dimensional computer work that is limited to fine motor movements. This view contrasts with beliefs that young children learn best through concrete, hands-on activities with real objects. Perhaps graphic images on the screen, such as animals, are real to the child, as real as the pictures of animals in books or toy stuffed animals.

Elkind (1996) believed the danger is that young children's proficiency with the computer might tempt us to ignore what we know about cognitive development. Despite their skill with technology, many kindergarten children have yet to attain the concrete operations described by Piaget. Concrete operations enable children to follow rules, for example. Elkind warned that if we forget how time-consuming and effortful the path to these attainments is, and if we rate a child's intellectual competence by his or her performance on a computer, then we lose what we have been working for: a broad appreciation of developmentally appropriate practice.

Morgan and Shade (1994) offered a different view on this criticism. Although Piaget did assert that young children construct much of their knowledge through active manipulation of the environment, they believe this interpretation of his theory is too narrowly literal in two major ways. First, the meaning of active construction and concrete operations may be taken verbatim. For the child, "concrete" refers to what is meaningful and manipulatable to the child. Active mental processing and reflection may be equally important. Children can be active learners with symbols such as a stuffed bear or computer images of a bear. Second, descriptions of Piaget's stages represent milestones along the developmental pathway rather than rigid age-based norms. Perhaps in the last few decades children have become more capable and technologically ready than once thought.

14-1a Young Children with Special Needs

For most children, working on a computer is one of many activity choices available in an early childhood classroom. For other children, however, working on a computer may be the key that makes learning and social interaction possible. Children with special physical needs (including visual and auditory impairments) may use computers as assistive or communication devices to support their learning (Thouvenelle and Bewick, 2002). Voice-to-text software allows children to receive and produce written communication, either with words or symbols. that would be impossible without the computer. Children with special intellectual or learning needs are able to practice concept mastery by repeating material and activities on the computer. The frequent and consistent positive reinforcement that occurs in developmentally appropriate software helps sustain their attention and participation (Parette, Hourcase, & Helple, 2000). Some children with special physical and learning needs are challenged to communicate in writing or in text (Thouvenelle and Bewick, 2002). Adaptive peripherals, usually special switches or hardware that plug into the computer, provide alternatives for children unable to use a mouse or a keyboard. Particularly useful are touch screens that allow children to point and touch, with their fingers, items on the monitor. Touch-screen technology is helpful for three- and four-year-old children who may have difficulty with the indirect cause-and-effect of using a mouse to change things on the screen or with children of any age who have physical difficulties using a mouse or keyboard.

[DAP] [naeyc] 14-1b Age-Appropriate Computer Use and the Teacher's Role

General guidelines for computer use in early childhood classrooms can be established from the existing literature. These guidelines assist teachers in creating a structure for computer use in the classroom and in developing computer activities that support young children's learning and development. Guidelines also outline the role that teachers play as children at each age interact with classroom computers.

For infants and toddlers, responsive interactions with adults and other children are essential to early brain development and to cognitive, social, emotional, physical, and linguistic development. Because of this, most experts agree that children younger than age three years should not use computers at all and that screen time in general be limited to experiences and activities that strengthen adult-child relationships (National Association for the Education of Young Children and the Fred Rogers Center for Early Learning at Children's Media and St. Vincent College, 2012). Between the ages of three and five years, however, computers should be one of many experiences available to children in the classroom. Ideally, children should be working at the computer for short periods of time, about the length of time they would spend working a puzzle or building with blocks, and with a partner or in a small, teacher-led

group. Open-ended software, such as drawing and music-making programs, are most appropriate at this age and allow children to explore and develop awareness of the computer's capabilities. The teacher's role for children ages three to five years is to introduce new software by modeling in small groups. As children begin to explore software independently, the teacher stays nearby to provide prompts or scaffolding as needed.

In kindergarten and the primary grades (five to eight years of age), children can continue working at the computer with a partner, but they should also begin to work independently. Simple word-processing software should be added to the drawing and music-making programs previously available. Word-processing software encourages young children to use and expand the written language skills they are acquiring in other curriculum activities. It also provides an avenue for children to express themselves in written language when their developing fine motor skills limit expression with traditional paper and pencil. The teacher's role in kindergarten and the primary grades is to furnish the computer center with appropriate software that complements curriculum and grade-level objectives. The teacher monitors the children's activities and intervenes when needed to pose questions and provide support.

Did You Get It?

Screen time refers to:
  a. time spent in front of the computer engaged in any activity.
  b. time spent in front of the computer engaged in passive activities only.
  c. all time spent in front of the screen of any device, including computers, televisions, and phones.
  d. time spent in front of the screen of any device engaged in interactive activities only.

Take the full quiz on CourseMate.

[DAP] [naeyc] [naea] 14-2 Computers and Art

How do you feel about the use of computers to make art? Do you see it as uncreative and threatening to the nature of creative art? Do you believe children's time would be better spent working with real art materials? Schwall (2005) recommends teachers and children learn to interweave technology with traditional media in the art center. Try viewing computer art as one component of your art program—a component that is used in combination with, rather than as replacement for, hands-on art experiences in the classroom. The computer becomes another art medium, not a rejection of all other media.

Figure 14–3 Draw and paint artwork by a seven-year-old.

A computer loaded with a simple graphic-painting program is another way to create lines and shapes (see Figure 14–3). The screen is the canvas or paper, and the mouse is the tool for applying lines, shapes, and colors. Although the child manipulates colored light rather than actual media, the artistic decisions and choices are the same.

What are the advantages? In most schools, public and private, curriculum funding for the arts is not a priority. Even including time in the school day for art activities is frowned upon in some settings. Engaging children in activities that promote computer training and literacy, as well as creative thinking and expression, may provide opportunities that would otherwise be denied (Sabbeth, 1998). Because of experiences with computers at home, many young children enter early childhood programs already familiar with computers and excited about their abilities to use them. Including computer art activities and opportunities in the curriculum may very well attract children who would have little interest in traditional art activities (Matthews, 1997). Computer centers are set up to foster peer interaction and communication. A computer artist can easily reverse his or her actions and *unpaint* or remove color if needed. Good painting software provides an unlimited number of colors and trims for embellishing computer art. The computer

fosters an art-language connection, providing opportunity for the artist to type words to accompany the art.

More than half the children in this country have regular access to a mobile technology device in their homes—either a smartphone, a video iPod, an iPad, or other tablet device (Zero to Eight, 2011). Computer tablets offer young children unique opportunities for artistic expression. The stylus tool as an interface with the tablet surface is easier for most children to manipulate than a traditional mouse (Matthews & Seow, 2007). Working with four-year-olds, Couse & Chen (2010) found that with minimal support from adults, children learned quickly how to use a stylus in drawing and writing programs on a computer tablet and that the quality of their drawing and writing was comparable to that done with traditional media.

What are the disadvantages? For some children, using a mouse or stylus is more difficult than using a paintbrush, marker, or crayon. The sensory qualities of the media, including touch and smell, are missing. Moving colored lines on the computer screen is different from smelling and smearing cold paint. Young children are impulsive and may lack the patience needed to print their computer art. Is the drawing in Figure 14–4 just mechanized lines and designs, or is it art? Philosophers have debated the nature of art for centuries. What do you think?

14-2a **Draw and Paint Programs**

Children create images on a computer in two ways: painting programs and drawing programs. Although these two types of software are often discussed interchangeably, there are some basic differences teachers should be aware of before introducing them to the classroom.

Painting programs are based on an older technology and use bitmapping to create images displayed on

Figure 14–4 A collage created on the computer.

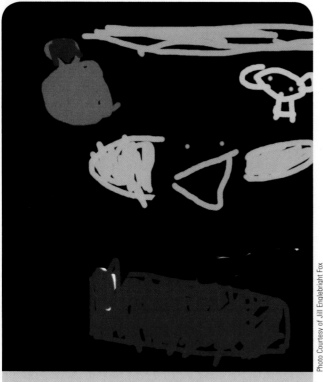

Figure 14–5 Draw and paint artwork by a four-year-old.

the computer screen (see Figure 14–5). Children working in a bitmapping program are able to draw shapes and lines on the screen. They can layer the images they draw and then use the eraser tool to remove any part of their drawing. Erasing a shape or line drawn on top of something else leaves an empty space in the drawing. Adding text to a drawing is very similar to word-processing. The cursor can be inserted for editing or making corrections.

Drawing programs are more challenging. While text is added in much the same way as in painting programs, there is no eraser tool for changing parts of lines and shapes in the drawings. Instead, the entire object (shape or line) is clicked on, highlighted, and deleted so that the artist must begin again (Sabbeth, 1998; Nusayr, 2012). Before purchasing a drawing or painting program for your classroom, consider how the children will use it.

naea) 14-2b **Art Appreciation**

Computers in an early childhood classroom can also be used to provide children with unique experiences in art appreciation. **Simulation software** can take children on a virtual museum tour. Although most of this software is designed for adults or older children, a teacher-directed activity can effectively prepare children for an upcoming field trip or even take the place of a field trip if an art museum is not nearby. The following software

packages can provide such experiences, as well as narratives to give teachers background information:

- *Museums of the World* by Topics Entertainment
- *Virtual Art Museum* by Pearson
- *Meet the Masters Art Program*

Most of the major art museums in this country and abroad have websites that offer art appreciation experiences. The Louvre in Paris provides a virtual tour of its holdings. The Website of the Museum of Fine Arts in Boston has a "My Favorite Art" function that enables visitors to collect artwork from the online collections to save in their own mini-galleries for later viewing. Although most museums have online resources for teachers and parents, some also offer special activities for children related to their collections. The Museum of Modern Art in New York City, for example, features the children's Website *Destination Modern Art* through which children can view artwork by painters Van Gogh and Kahlo and sculptor Boccioni. Age-appropriate activities related to the artwork and the artists encourage children to examine details, look for meaning, and describe what they see.

How Should the Computer Center Be Arranged and Set Up? The work station should be large enough to hold all the computer equipment and accommodate four children. Place two child seats in front of the computer and one or two at the side, which the teacher will often use. Ideally, each computer learning center should house two computers and one printer. Strive for a 10:1 ratio (or better) of children to computers to encourage ample time on the computer, social and language interaction, and equal access for all children. Partner children at the computer, and encourage turn taking and shared problem-solving rather than competition. Include curriculum-integration activities that incorporate learning strategies.

Children in the K–3 grades who are beginning to use the word-processor more extensively, as well as researching with DVD encyclopedias, can benefit from three or four available computers. Adjustable work stations are highly recommended to avoid the strain from a monitor and keyboard or mouse that is either too high or too low. The table should be low enough for children to sit comfortably in chairs with the keyboard at waist level and the monitor at eye level. Provide an adult-sized teacher chair where you can facilitate, engage children in problem-solving, monitor progress, and supervise use of the Internet. The computer table or work station should be placed against a wall with direct access to a power source and surge protector to guard against electrical damage to the computer. The computer should be located away from direct sunlight and foot traffic, as well as any source of water such as a water table. The computer should not be near magnets, paint, chalk dust, and windows that cause a direct glare on the monitor. Heat is another potential hazard both to the disks and the **central processing unit** (CPU). To enhance learning in curricular areas, some teachers place their computer center in close proximity to other centers, such as math manipulatives, a book area, or writing center. Use a sign-up book or clipboard along with timer to manage turn taking.

Computer Center Rules and Limits

1. The computer stays on.
2. Keep food and drink away from the computer center.
3. Use only the controls found on the keyboard or mouse.
4. If you need help, ask a friend or teacher.
5. Wash hands before using the computer and handling software.
6. Use gentle hands and soft touches with the mouse or keyboard.
7. Only the computer operator uses the mouse or keyboard. Help only if you are asked.

Did You Get It?

Sabbeath (1998) describes an unfortunate situation in which financial cutbacks and austerity measures hit the arts more than perhaps any other area in a school's curriculum. That being said, quite unfortunately, proposing hi-tech adjuncts to the art curriculum is often/usually

a. out of the realm of financial possibility.

b. possible, but an ineffective and poor substitute.

c. a means to create opportunity where it might not otherwise exist.

d. a method that only results in passive and passing learning.

Take the full quiz on CourseMate.

DAP naeyc 14-3 How to Best Use Computers in the Classroom

The teacher's choice of software determines the role of software in children's learning. Developmentally inappropriate software cannot foster positive computer experiences for young children. Open-ended programs foster collaboration and creativity, whereas drill-and-practice programs support competition.

Thouvenelle and Bewick (2002) offer advice for choosing developmentally appropriate software. Identify educational goals, what you want children to learn, and specifically how this particular software will get you there. Read reviews of the software you are considering and preview it yourself. Evaluate the software for bias and stereotypes. Healy (1999) recommends looking for software with varying levels of difficulty and understandable graphics enabling children to navigate the program's features. Graphics should have aesthetic merit. Software should be multisensory and interactive and allow children to express creativity. Choosing open-ended software encourages discovery, experimentation, problem-solving, originality, and knowledge construction. Teachers should consider how the computer will interface with curriculum.

There are many ways to use computers to support curricular and program goals. In some classrooms, computers are used mostly for educational games or as rewards for work completed. The purpose is entertainment and "time filling." Computers are treated as video games. In other classrooms, computer activities resemble electronic workbooks reinforcing what was taught with skill-oriented drill-and-practice tasks such as matching shapes, letters, or numbers. This approach is tutorial. Software provides ways for children to work on skills that need to be practiced for mastery. Children are given a certain number of problems, feedback on the correctness of their answers, and a reward for correct answers. Healy (1999) characterized this type of software as "edutainment." Some software programs help children progress independently through levels of ability while others focus on problem-solving and concept-building skills. This approach should be used after children have learned a concept—for example, with manipulatives—and need additional practice for mastery. Both of these approaches free the teacher to work with other children, but the valuable teacher–child interactive feature is missing. Opportunities for mediating and scaffolding are lacking because the teacher is busy doing something else. Adult participation, support, and guidance are critical to children's learning experiences at the computer. Along with questioning the developmental appropriateness of these approaches, the issue of creativity can be raised. Software can be either closed-ended or open-ended, as with some writing and drawing software. Computers can reduce creativity if children's use is restricted to drill-and-practice with closed-ended software in which they merely provide correct answers.

What is the role of the teacher? Because the computer is meant to supplement rather than replace the teacher, there are many roles for teachers to play. Once the computer is set up, the teacher needs to develop expertise with the hardware and the software available in the classroom. Operating systems have varied capabilities and avenues for problem-solving. Because troubleshooting problems while a group of children are waiting can be frustrating for teacher and students alike, teachers should acquaint themselves thoroughly with the operating system before introducing a new computer into the classroom.

Likewise, teachers should familiarize themselves with the software available to children in the computer center. Checking out the activities on a particular piece of software not only can help teachers decide how to use the software, but also equips the teacher to help children solve problems during computer activities. Teachers need to find out about children's computer experience: what they already know and can do on a computer. Computers and software should be introduced to young children in the same way that any other new material or activity would be introduced: individually or in small groups. With a small-group approach, gather several children at a time around the center while two children sit in chairs. Name and point to the parts of the computer the children will need to know: the keyboard, monitor, mouse, and printer. Show children how to turn on the computer.

Start with a simple program and encourage children to figure out how it works. Some teachers prefer to use only one program at a time until everyone in the group understands how to use it. Let this first small group use the computer as soon as it has been introduced. Children need to apply what they have learned immediately. This approach ensures that all children use the computer, including those who are hesitant or reluctant to try new things. Otherwise, children using computers may be only those who are confident and experienced in using a computer. Once computers have been introduced, teachers need to monitor and facilitate children's computer use.

How can teachers match computer to curriculum? Thouvenelle and Bewick (2002) suggest consulting national, state, or district-level curriculum standards for your grade level to identify educational goals for your group. Review assessment and reporting requirements. Then use curriculum strategies such as webs, themes, or projects to create a meaningful framework that connects computer experiences with other hands-on classroom activities. Can computers assist teachers in assessment? According to Thouvenelle and Bewick (2002), one additional benefit of technology is that it can support documenting student progress in meeting curricular goals. Teachers can carefully observe children's computer use and collaboration with others, as well as thinking processes and computer-generated products, such as stories. To successfully use the computer as an assessment tool, teachers must focus on children's processes as well as on their products. Consideration of the computer-generated artwork in Figure 14–6 yields little information of the artist's knowledge or skills. Teacher observation of children in the process of creating the picture, however, revealed multiple layers to the artwork and the children's detailed knowledge of story structure, and their willingness to explore the capabilities of the draw and paint software.

14-3a Technology Tools

Technology tools are computer hardware or software used to create original work. According to Blanckensee (1999), open-ended tools support learning and development when used appropriately. Technology tools available for use with young children include the following:

Cameras and video cameras—cameras allow teachers to record and immediately document children's art activities and help children recall art processes. Photos can be resized by scanning and digitizing pictures. A digital camera allows immediate access to photos, and it also allows photos to be uploaded to the computer and be shared with others via the Internet outside the classroom. Photo Kit Jr.®, a software package published by ATPE, allows children ages three and up to "play" with their digital photos using editing tools and a variety of games. (More on digital photography can be found in this chapter on page 286.)

Printers and scanners—allow for customizing of image size and type font. Because children enjoy taking their original work home, a scanned copy of their artwork can remain in their portfolio.

Drawing tablets—such as Sketchboard Studio® from KB Interactive allow children to draw on a natural, flat surface that can be transferred to the computer screen (see Figure 14–7).

Multimedia or hypermedia authoring tools—combine text, sound, animation, and graphics to create teaching aids, reports, or projects. Even young children can write a story and use computerized drawing tools. The use of multimedia empowers learners by putting them in charge of developing a project and constructing knowledge

Figure 14–6 Creative computer art.

Photo Courtesy of Jill Englebright Fox

Figure 14–7 Even very young children can experiment with "digital" cameras.

using digital photos, videotaping, and recorded sound to create powerful and personally meaningful work.

E-mail—used for writing and receiving communication from families of students or expert sources of information from around the world.

Internet access—for finding information, publishing, and visiting community sites by taking virtual field trips. Find out if your classroom is already networked to the Internet. Children can also publish their own work on the Internet and see other children's work. Precautions must be taken. Because the World Wide Web is unregulated, anyone can place anything on the Internet. Use an Internet filtering software or desktop management program such as Kid Desk: Internet Safe®, Net Nanny®, or Cyber Patrol® to block children's access to inappropriate websites. Although filtering devices are essential in early childhood classrooms, they are not by themselves sufficient to keep children safe on the Internet. Regular monitoring by the classroom teacher is essential.

Video recordings—These are useful for documentation of how individual children process with art materials.

Kids Works Deluxe®—This talking word-processor is available from Great Wave Software.

14-3b **Communicating with Technology**

In twenty-first-century classrooms, teachers regularly use technology to document children's learning, to store and access information, and to communicate with students' families (Schwall, 2005). Previously, teachers relied on telephone calls and notes to inform families of classroom events and children's achievements and difficulties. Because more than 80 percent of Americans now have computers in their homes—and, of these families, almost 92 percent have Internet access (Nielsen, 2009)—many teachers now use classroom websites to keep families current. Classroom websites provide a simple way for busy teachers to keep families abreast of routine information and events in the classroom. Although professional designers may be easily accessed by teachers, these are often expensive. Instead, teachers may use a program such as Microsoft Publisher® to design their own web pages to post on school websites, or take advantage of an online company that designs template web pages for teachers to fill in information pertaining to their own classrooms and post on the school's website. Such companies usually charge a small monthly fee for posting and maintaining a single teacher's website, or schools may pay a larger fee for an entire website on which teachers may post individual web pages.

A variety of information may be included on classroom websites. To begin, the website should obviously include the teacher's name and an e-mail link for communication. The grade or age level of the teacher's class and a room number, as well as the school address and phone number, may also be helpful. Include the class's daily and weekly schedules to assist family members planning to visit or volunteer. Dates and times for which field trips, guest speakers, parent-teacher conferences, parent meetings, school pictures, and health screenings are scheduled can also assist parents in planning and preparing their children for school each day. Primary-grade teachers may also include information on homework assignments, upcoming assessment activities, and lists of spelling or vocabulary words the children are currently studying.

Many teachers also use websites to provide families with information on the children's activities during the school day. Descriptions of learning centers and curriculum topics, illustrated by digital photographs, help families understand learning in an early childhood classroom. A classroom website can also be used as an online museum for children's artwork. Digital photographs displaying children's drawings, paintings, sculptures, and designs may be posted, along with dictated descriptions or explanations. An online museum can be valuable in helping children to see their creative work enjoyed by others and help families see development in children's artwork as the year progresses.

Whatever is included on the classroom website, it is critical that the teacher makes the commitment to update the site regularly. A website is useful only if information is current and accurate. Teachers should also consider that, although most families have Internet access at home, some do not. A survey of families at the beginning of the school year will tell teachers whether more traditional communications will be more appropriate.

An Opportunity for Teacher Reflection

It Is The End of September, and Mrs. Martinez has been getting to know her kindergarteners for almost a month. As she began to assess the children during the first weeks of school, Mrs. Martinez was surprised to find that one of her kindergarteners, Parker, was reading at the third-grade level. She quickly began to develop individualized instructional activities for Parker, with the goal of supporting his emerging literacy skills. She found that Parker enjoyed reading fiction and nonfiction, that he had a strong knowledge of reading and writing conventions and phonemic awareness, and that he was very creative in developing his own stories. Her assessments also revealed that, in spite of his advanced reading level, Parker's fine motor skills were typical of most five-year-olds. While Parker had a large sight word vocabulary and was not afraid to use new words in his stories, his writing skills could not keep up with the thoughts he wanted to capture on paper. Parker often grew frustrated when his hand grew tired, and he had to stop writing. Many of his writings were left unfinished, though Parker had already developed the storyline in his head. How might Mrs. Martinez support Parker's development as a reader and a writer? Can technology provide an answer? What kinds of hardware and software should Mrs. Martinez provide for Parker? What kinds of off-computer activities should she make available?

Did You Get It?

What is not a component of a responsible model for the institution, teacher, or teachers shopping for computer software to integrate into the educational curriculum?

   a. previewing the software through a free trial
   b. choosing software beyond the level that is age appropriate and developmentally appropriate to increase the chances it will challenge students
   c. identifying which software will be an avenue towards goal attainment
   d. weeding out software programs that are biased and/or stereotypical

Take the full quiz on CourseMate.

DAP naeyc naea 14-4 Digital Photography

Since the early twentieth century, photography has been a medium for artistic expression. Previously, the delicacy of equipment and the expense of flash, film, and photo developing limited the use of cameras by young children. Digital photography and digital cameras designed specifically for children have now made this medium available to young children. Manufacturers have designed cameras that can withstand rough handling, occasional drops, and experimental button pushes from child photographers. With these advances, digital cameras have become rather common in classrooms for young children.

Although professional photographers use complicated cameras and software, a digital camera for children need only meet some very basic criteria:

1. A memory card. A memory card allows children to take and store numerous photos over a daylong event or through a class project in which several children are using the same camera.
2. A flash for the many photos that will be taken inside the classroom. A flash will keep photos from being too dark.
3. A USB connection for uploading pictures to the classroom computer.
4. The capability to take photos at more than 1 megapixel. Digital photographs are made of tiny units of color called **pixels**; higher numbers of pixels in photos mean clearer colors and images. Photos taken at less than 1 megapixel will be blurry.

Byrnes and Wasik (2009) recommend a minimum of three digital cameras in the classroom for children's use. This allows children to take photos and then view or print them immediately. It will allow the teacher to immediately incorporate photos into curricular activities. The following digital cameras have been designed specifically for children. Their controls and durability are more suitable for use in early childhood classrooms than digital cameras designed for adults:

- Kid-Tough Digital Camera from Fisher Price
- Polaroid Pixie Kids Digital Camera
- Crayola kids digital camera
- Vivitar Vivicam

While teachers often use cameras to document children's learning and record special events in the life of the classroom, these uses do not necessarily encourage children's artistic expression. If the camera is to be a tool for artistic expression in the classroom, it is important that children make decisions about the photos they will be taking, their subjects, backgrounds, camera angles, and so on. Einarsdottir (2005) found that children unaccompanied by adults were more likely to take photos that capture their own views of and interests in their environment.

Consider setting up a center for digital photography in the classroom or designating a table in the art center for photographers to explore and experiment. Include a computer for uploading and editing photos, a variety of tablecloths or large pieces of fabric that might be used as backdrops, baskets of objects that could be arranged for still lifes, and costumes for children to wear when posing for portraits. Include also books about photography and photographers. Display photographed portraits, landscapes, cityscapes, seascapes, and still lifes. Provide wall space for displaying the children's photographs.

As with any new art tool, children will require basic instruction in using a digital camera. This is most effectively done in a small-group setting. Introduce the camera as a special piece of equipment that needs to be handled with care. Explain how the camera works, and encourage children to practice turning it on and off. Show them how to look through the viewfinder, focus on a specific image, and take a photo. Demonstrate the wide-angle and telephoto functions of the lens and how to review photos that have already been taken. After children have had time to explore, share with them photos taken by professionals and amateurs. Talk about the subjects of the photos and the different angles from which they were taken.

Some children will be imprecise in taking photographs, while others will rapidly learn to take focused and framed photographs. In either case, the experience of taking photos and viewing the images they've recorded will give children a sense of mastery and accomplishment (Byrnes and Wasik, 2009).

14-4a **Personally Expressive Art Activities**

Following are some personally expressive art activities for the digital camera.

Preschool, Kindergarten, and School-Age Activity: What's Different? Have children examine reproductions of still life paintings. Provide objects like flowers, vases, scarves, fruit, feathers, and so on for children to arrange their own still life displays. Ask each child to photograph his or her display, change one item in the display, and then take a second photo. Print the photos or view them on the computer. Have the children examine each other's "before" and "after" photos to find what item has been changed.

Preschool, Kindergarten, and School-Age Activity: Opposites. Ask children to generate a list of opposites like day and night, dark and light, big and little, tall and short. Assign or have children choose partners to work as pairs. Assign one set of opposites to each pair. Each child should design and take a photograph of a scene that illustrates one of the words in the pair's set of opposites. When all of the photos have been taken and printed, children can work together or independently to match the opposites.

Preschool, Kindergarten, and School-Age Activity: Me Albums. Children can create digital albums by taking photographs that answer questions about their personal likes and dislikes, their experiences, friends, and abilities. Ask children questions like, "what's your favorite book?" and "who is your hero?" and encourage them to design and take photographs that will answer those questions. Arrange the photos in an online album. Encourage the children to write or dictate captions.

Kindergarten and School-Age Activity: A Day in the Life. During the school day, ask a child to take photos of his or her favorite events and activities. Later, after reviewing and sequencing the photos, ask the child to write or dictate a story to describe the activities depicted.

Kindergarten & School-Age Activity: School Directory. Make a list of key helpers in your school or center. Have children photograph each individual. Encourage children to pose the helpers in ways that illustrate their jobs. Upload the photos to a classroom computer and let children write or dictate captions for each. Arrange the photos to create a digital directory of the helpers.

Preschool, Kindergarten, and School-Age Activity: Matching Game. Have each child take a photo of an individual object or a part of an object in the classroom. Print the photos and put them in random piles. Divide the children into small groups, and ask each group to search the room for the objects depicted in their pile of photos.

Preschool, Kindergarten, and School-Age Activity: Telling the Story. Encourage a photographer to take photos of classmates during dramatic play. Upload the photos to a computer and have the photographer write or dictate the story of the dramatic play.

14-4b **Sensory Exploration Activities**

Following are some sensory exploration activities for the digital camera.

Preschool, Kindergarten, and School-Age Activity: Documentation. Children can use the digital camera to document the growth of a classroom pet or plant for their science journals. Have children review and compare photos taken over time to identify changes in the plant or animal's size and appearance.

Kindergarten and School-Age Activity: Near and Far. Encourage children to experiment with the telephoto and wide-angle features of the digital camera. Ask individual children to choose an object on the opposite side of the classroom to photograph using first the telephoto and then the wide-angle functions. Print the photos or review them on the computer. Talk with children about the differences.

> **Did You Get It?**
>
> **What is not one of the minimum recommendations for a digital camera for the classroom?**
> **a.** a USB connection
> **b.** a flash
> **c.** an eight megapixel resolution
> **d.** a memory card
>
> **Take the full quiz on CourseMate.**

Summary

This chapter focused on children's use of technology in art production and appreciation activities. (14-1) Although young children's use of computers is questioned by some adults, current research supports the benefits of appropriate computer use for children's cognitive and socio-emotional development. Guidelines have been established on the appropriate age at which to introduce technology to children and the appropriate structure for computer use in the classroom. (14-2) Draw-and-paint software can be one choice of media in a developmentally appropriate art program. (14-3) Teachers should choose developmentally appropriate software and Websites that have meaningful connections to the early childhood curriculum. The classroom computer center should be appropriate to children's physical needs and should be designed to support positive social interaction. (14-4) Digital cameras offer young children developmentally appropriate opportunities to explore photography as an artistic medium.

Key Terms

bitmapping, 281

central processing unit (CPU), 283

drawing programs, 281

drawing tablet, 284

drill-and-practice software, 278

LOGO®, 277

open-ended software, 278

painting programs, 281

pixels, 286

simulation software, 282

telephoto, 287

wide angle, 287

✓ Suggested Activities

1. Your instructor will know teachers who have successfully integrated computers into their program. Arrange to observe these teachers, and focus on management concerns. Who gets a turn and for how long? What software is being used? How was it selected? Record your observations.

2. Compare drawings made by children with traditional media with drawings done with draw and paint software on the computer. Do children include the same amount of detail? Use color in the same way?

3. Preview some of the software suggested in this chapter. Consider how it could relate to curriculum objectives in an early childhood classroom. Think of ways you could use this software in your own classroom.

4. Interview several parents of children at different ages. Ask them to estimate how much screen time their children have each day. Do the times given fit within the guidelines discussed in this chapter?

5. Interview a teacher about strategies for connecting computer and noncomputer activities in the curriculum.

6. Supervise children in one of the activities for digital photography in this chapter.

Review

1. Discuss research findings on the impact of computer use on young children's cognitive development.

2. What are the differences between drawing software and painting software?

3. List the three criteria teachers should use when evaluating software for classroom use.

4. List the rules for children's participation in the classroom computer center.

5. Describe three technology avenues for communicating with the families of the children in your classroom.

Additional Resources

Technology and Interactive Media as Tools in Early Childhood Programs Serving Children from Birth through Age 8, a joint position statement issued by the National Association for the Education of Young Children and the Fred Rogers Center for Early Learning and Children's Media at Saint Vincent College (www.naeyc.org).

"Screen Time and What It Means to Young Children," an editorial by Jill Englebright Fox on VictoriaAdvocate.com.

ECETech Wiki, a project of the National Association for the Education of Young Children Technology and Young Children Interest Forum.

Center for Children and Technology (http://cct .edc.org/), a website that investigates roles that technology can play in improving teaching and learning.

Seymour Papert, a website devoted to the creator of Logo (http://papert.org/).

Logo Foundation, a website that houses information and resources for learning and teaching Logo (http://el.media.mit.edu/logo-foundation/).

 Visit CourseMate for this textbook to access the eBook, Did You Get It? quizzes, Digital Downloads, TeachSource Videos, flashcards, and more. Go to CengageBrain.com to log in, register, or purchase access.

Kindergarten/First Grade Lesson Plan

Making a Classroom Map

GOALS

The student understands the relative location of places; the student understands the purposes of maps and globes.

OUTCOMES

The student is expected to:

a. describe the location of self and objects relative to other locations in the classroom and school.
b. create and use simple maps such as maps of the home, classroom, school, and community.

MATERIALS

a. Digital cameras
b. Slips of paper, each with a location/item in the classroom printed on it (e.g., windows, doors, water fountain, teacher's desk, art center, rocking chair, class pet)
c. Flannel board
d. Printer and paper
e. Tape
f. Travel map

INTRODUCTION

Share the travel map with the children. Ask them to identify it and share experiences of when their families have used maps. Indicate the U.S. map and the globe in the classroom; explain that there are many different kinds of maps and that people use them in many ways. Tell the children that over the next few days they will be learning to use maps to help them locate themselves, objects, and places.

Put all the slips of paper in a bowl or a bag. Ask each child to draw a slip of paper. During center time, have the children take turns using the digital cameras to take photos of whatever was printed on their slip of paper. Work with the children to print the photos in a 3" x 5" format.

DEVELOPMENT

In a whole-group setting, show the children the flannel board and tell them that we are going to use the flannel board and their photos to make a map of our classroom. Explain that the flannel board represents the outline of the classroom. Demonstrate that the left edge of the board represents the left wall of the classroom. Ask the child who photographed the classroom door to come forward and help him/her to place the photo appropriately on the map. Use the door to orient the children and help each to place his/her photo where it belongs.

CONCLUSION

After all the items have been placed on the map, ask each child to walk from one point to another (don't name the points; just indicate with your finger so that the children are required to "read" the map). Use the map over the next few days to give directions in the classroom such as, "Boys and girls, let's gather in this area for story time."

ASSESSMENT

a. Were the children able to locate themselves and objects on the classroom map?
b. Did the children create a simple map of their classroom?

Go to cengagebrain.com for a full-size version of this lesson plan.

15 Roles, Responses, and Strategies to Support Children's Art

Most of us enter the field of early childhood education for the joy of working with young children.

The teacher in the photo clearly enjoys what she is doing. She has just joined a group of children painting a mural. She had been observing from a distance and decided to sit down and talk with them. The children were proud of the plan they had come up with for painting a mural about their study of farm animals. The teacher enjoys hearing their plans. She responds both nonverbally and verbally. What could she be saying? What would you say to acknowledge the children's accomplishments and share their enjoyment of painting?

Learning Outcomes

After reading this chapter, you should be able to:

15-1 Discuss the teacher's role as a model and participator in early childhood art.

15-2 Identify ways in which a teacher can be a creative individual and art specialist in the center or classroom.

15-3 Demonstrate how using the six questions proposed by Engel help teachers observe more effectively.

15-4 Use the artistic elements to analyze and discuss children's art.

15-5 Brainstorm strategies for troubleshooting children's art.

15-6 Provide sewing and weaving activities for young children.

Standards addressed in this chapter

DAP Guidelines
1 Creating a caring community of learners
2 Teaching to enhance development and learning
3 Planning curriculum to achieve important goals

NAEYC Standards
1 Relationships
2 Curriculum
3 Teaching

NAEA Visual Arts Standards
1 Understanding and applying media, techniques, and processes
2 Using knowledge of structures and functions

DAP naeyc 15-1 Teacher as Model and Participator

What is the teacher's role in children's art? Young children stay involved in art activities for longer periods of time when an adult is present and engaged in what they are doing (Brittain, 1979). Adults stimulate children to make art by being models and participants. Adults can model creativity in their daily lives and actively participate in art activities themselves. Although it is important to know about art, an adult does not need to be a talented artist to provide creative art experiences for children.

Children learn in different ways. Some benefit from listening to a teacher. Others learn by observing what a teacher does. For example, it would be more beneficial for a teacher to demonstrate how to sew or weave than verbally to tell children all the steps involved. The teacher serves as a **model** or demonstrator. Modeling a new activity draws a small group of curious observers who can be eased into participating. For example, a teacher who models different ways to work with clay and clay tools will soon find the clay table filled with willing sculptors. One way of learning to be a good teacher is to observe others modeling good teaching.

As a model, never let children hear you say, "I can't draw" or "I'm not a good singer." If children see you are not comfortable with your own adult efforts, they are more likely to be unsatisfied with their childish efforts. Instead, focus on your enjoyment of participating in art and music activities and your willingness to try new experiences.

Children enjoy playing, both by themselves and with other children. They also enjoy an adult's participation in their activities. There are times when a teacher would be most welcome as a **participant** or player in a learning center.

Engage in art with children but be careful not to do art for them. Doing art for children sets them up for disappointment. Inevitably they will try to copy you and end up frustrated and discouraged. Announce that sometimes you do not like what you do on the first try and you simply try again. Share your frustration with trying to get it just the way you want when the paint runs and colors bleed in ways you do not like. Children will welcome your participation, especially if they appear stuck or frustrated. Work along with them but focus on just doing, rather than overwhelming them with your adult products. For example, the play dough table is a great opportunity to work with children. Sit with the children and observe what is happening. If children appear stuck, participate by modeling options. Say, "I think I'll try squeezing and flattening my play dough. Let's see what happens." Children may join in by squeezing and flattening their play dough, which

Figure 15–1 Enabling children to engage in art.

provides them with a new option and opens the door to discussion. Children may talk about their "pancake" shapes. They can also choose not to follow your suggestions.

In Figure 15–1, a child engages in art with the teacher observing and ready to provide support if needed. It is important that children sometimes have a teacher's participation in their activity. The close contact is valuable, especially since the children are being met on their terms. Most of the time, children will welcome participation from adults. At other times, children will not welcome an adult's presence and may even ask him or her to leave. "No grown-ups, just kids!" states a group of block builders. Their wishes should be respected. This stands in opposition to a teacher-directed activity, where children are simply assimilated into the existing activity.

Although the authors recommend taking the role of participator, some early childhood educators may feel that it is intrusive and robs children of the opportunity to discover techniques on their own, for example, squeezing and flattening play dough. Where do you stand on the adult's role as participator in children's art activities?

Did You Get It?

In the role of model, the teacher should never use which phrase?

   a. "I can't…" or "I'm not good at…"
   b. "Don't…"
   c. "This is the correct way…"
   d. "Why…"

Take the full quiz on CourseMate.

DAP naeyc 15-2 Teacher as Creative Individual and Art Specialist

A teacher must also be a creative, unique individual. Creative teachers model and encourage creativity in their students. "I don't have a paper cutter. What else can I use to make paper strips for our weaving?" "We don't have an easel to take outdoors. How else can we have art outside?" Children come to see that creative problem solving is a necessary part of daily living.

The creative teacher develops:

FROM	TO
1. viewing children in terms of groups on the basis of sex, age, or ability	1. viewing children as unique individuals
2. viewing highly creative children as a threat, nuisance, or menace	2. seeing creativity as an asset
3. stressing conformity in thinking and behavior	3. encouraging creative thinking and different ways to do things
4. looking for children to give the one right answer or best idea	4. considering many possible solutions and ideas
5. viewing self as uncreative	5. seeing how all people have the potential to be creative
6. providing a teacher-centered program	6. providing a child-centered program that values child input and decision making
7. providing a structured program, planned in detail	7. offering subtle planning that allows for diversion and sudden twists and turns
8. equating creativity with art, music, and movement	8. seeing creativity as a focus that cuts across the program
9. adding creative activities here and there	9. weaving creativity throughout the entire program
10. confining creativity to a certain day, time slot	10. including creativity throughout the entire day

Creativity is something we strive for. We may not be very creative in our first years of teaching, but we hope to move toward the goal of becoming creative early childhood educators.

It is also important for teachers of young children to be **art specialists**. We need to know about art, artists, artistic elements, and developmentally appropriate art activities. Just as one need not be a hockey player to

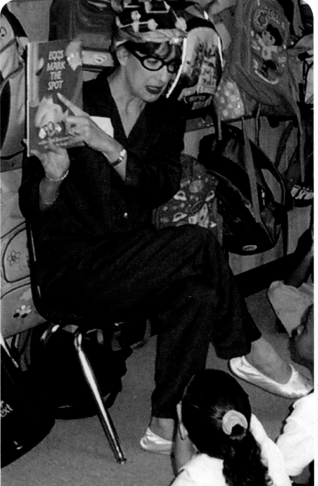

Photo Courtesy of Jill Englebright Fox

Figure 15–2 Author Jill Fox creatively shares a favorite book with a class of second graders.

enjoy viewing a game or be a musician to appreciate a concert, one need not be a gifted artist to provide art experiences for children. It is more important that teachers display artistic knowledge, sensitivity, awareness, and discovery than that they develop an endless list of art activities. In any art activity we plan, it is important to ask children to think like artists (Mulcahey, 2009). Encouraging children to use all their senses to experiment, explore, and represent what they know about the world makes the teacher an art specialist.

Davis (2008) suggests that leaving the teaching of art to art experts would be like limiting the learning of art only to children with talent. When young children *learn* with a teacher of art, they are able to directly learn necessary skills and processes associated with the various artistic media. But young children profit from observing, talking with, and working beside enthusiastic and more experienced peers and adults (see Figure 15–2). It is not necessarily important for an early childhood teacher to excel in any one of the arts, but it is important for teachers to think in artistic ways.

DAP naeyc 15-3 Teacher as Observer

It is important that children's art be appreciated, respected, and taken seriously by adults who view it (Isenberg and Jalongo, 2005). Why? Because a close observation of children's art reveals something about them—what they see as important, how they view their environment, and how they are connected to it. How do adults see these things? By learning to look. Engel (1996) stresses the importance of closely observing the visual art of young children and, as a result, seeing more in it, having more questions to ask, and having more to say about it. Her questions are useful in considering a child's artwork as well as having conversations with artists about their work. Observers can ponder the following questions or pose them to the child artist.

1. What is it made of?
   This refers to materials used, including size, tools, and media.
2. What does the observer see?
   This refers to artistic elements including lines, angles, shapes, colors, and so forth. Refer to Chapter 6 for a more detailed discussion of artistic elements.
3. What does it represent?
   This refers to design, story, scene, or symbol depicted.
4. How is it organized?
   Aspects of meaning include perspective, composition, action, point of view, and completion.
5. What is it about? What is the nature of involvement?
   This refers to the function or intent that might include providing information, explaining, expressing feelings, experimenting, exploring ideas, and so on.
6. Where does the idea come from?
   Source or origin could include the child's imagination, observation, literature, imitation, media, and conversation, as well as "messing about."

© Cengage Learning

Figure 15–3 What do you observe in this child's art?

Ask yourself the preceding six questions while studying the sample of child art seen in Figure 15–3. Possible answers include:

1. The girl is using tempera paint and a brush while painting at the easel on a large sheet of white paper.
2. She uses short vertical and large, circular brush strokes in orange and black.
3. A design is emerging. The observer refrains from trying to guess what it is. Talking with the child may provide verbal cues as to what it's supposed to be. It may be a design of black and orange shapes.
4. The painting appears to border the edges of the paper at this point. Some areas of the paper are as yet unpainted.
5. While observing the child, it appears she is interested in experimenting and exploring with the paint but intent on keeping colors separate. She also enjoyed watching her short, vertical strokes of black paint run off the edge of the paper.
6. The observer would guess that the girl is "messing about" with the media to see what she can make her paintbrush do with these colors on the paper.

Analyzing her art in this way helps the teacher engage in meaningful dialogue with the child.

Brain Connection

Brain research tells us that a spread in differences of up to two and even three years between children is completely normal. Teachers should provide children with classroom choices that meet their levels of development. Multi-age classes or looping, where the teacher stays with the same group of children for more than one year, support this wide spread of normal development (Rushton, Juloa-Rushton, & Larkin, 2010).

Did You Get It?

What is not one of the three fundamental principles that the teacher adheres to concerning children's artwork?

   a. providing unconditional and unwavering approval no matter what

   b. appreciation

   c. taking the creations and process seriously

   d. respect

Take the full quiz on CourseMate.

DAP naeyc 15-4 Teacher as Responder

Adults can respond both verbally and nonverbally to children's art. What should one say to a child artist? Should a teacher praise, judge, question, or correct? **Art dialogue**, a strategy using the artistic elements, is presented as a preferred approach. Although the art program runs smoothly most of the time, individual children may have difficulty on occasion and need direct intervention.

Teachers can respond and react to children's art both nonverbally and verbally. Often, we are unaware of our nonverbal communication. A smile conveys approval, while a frown or puzzled look conveys disapproval. For example, a teacher may verbally say that he or she likes a child's abstract artwork, but a wrinkled forehead and squint convey the opposite. Posture and overall body language also communicate messages. Giving a cold stare to a child who is making a creative mess communicates one's preference for order and neatness. Hands on hips or crossed arms while staring down at a child or a child's artwork convey a cold, aloof message. Stooping to eye level or sitting close to a child conveys warmth, respect, and acceptance. Young children are physical beings who use their bodies to express what they feel. In turn, they are sensitive to nonverbal messages conveyed by adults. One goal for early childhood educators is to develop positive nonverbal communication and establish congruence between nonverbal and verbal messages

to children. Research indicates that between the ages of two and five years, children become aware of gender, race, ethnicity, and disabilities. Because some of the most basic elements of ethnic identity are established before age three, very young children thrive in a setting that is culturally diverse and culturally respectful. Caregivers and teachers must recognize and support what is unique, and possibly culturally inspired, about individual children (Bredekamp and Copple, 1997) and their artwork.

An observant teacher who is attuned to students and their work styles and listens to children's comments can judge when a child is ready to talk about his or her artwork (Merritt, 1967). But according to Engel (1996), even observant teachers who approach children at the appropriate time to talk about their art often resort to positive, appreciative comments like the following:

- "What a nice painting! Let's hang it up where we can enjoy it."
- "I really like your painting. Would you like to have another turn at the easel tomorrow?"
- "You're painting much better now. I can see you wiped off your brush so the paint didn't run down."
- "All done? Do you want to tell me about it?"

Remarks such as these are supportive and encouraging. They are also appropriate at some times for some children. On the positive side, these remarks do not criticize or correct the creative work of young children. But teachers should also learn to discuss children's artwork with them in more serious, constructive ways.

15-4a Art Dictation

As children dialogue with their teacher about their artwork, some provide accompanying titles, labels, or sentences (see Figure 15–4). Some teachers very neatly print the children's words across the picture. The authors, however, recommend using a separate piece

Photo Courtesy of Jill Englebright Fox

Figure 15–4 A teacher can label as a child dictates.

of paper or a notecard for dictation for two reasons. First, adult artists rarely have words written across their canvas. Second, often there is little blank space, and the words have to be written too small or squeezed in. Using a separate piece of paper allows a separate story to be stapled or taped to the bottom and allows you to print in fairly large letters. Therefore, it is easier for the child to see and read back, and having the child read back what was dictated is an important step in the process. It allows room for the child to trace over the letters and words. Leaving blank space between lines provides room for the child to attempt to copy the letters, words, and sentences. Lastly, not inserting print into the art shows respect for the child's artistic efforts.

Why take art dictation? According to Greenburg (1999), there are five reasons. First, it deepens your understanding of each child. Second, it furthers your relationship with each child. Third, each child receives your undivided attention. Fourth, it shows each child that you respect his or her work and ideas. Fifth, it teaches literacy as children learn the connection between spoken and written word.

15-4b Art Dialogue

Talking to children about their artwork communicates subtle messages about the values the teacher places on it (Mulcahey, 2009). Verbal comments that teachers traditionally make concerning children's art take the following approaches:

- complimentary
- judgmental
- valuing
- questioning
- probing
- correcting

The impact of each on the child artist is analyzed in the following paragraphs, and an alternative to the six traditional approaches is presented.

With the complimentary approach, teachers tell children their art is nice, pretty, lovely, super, or beautiful. Specific comments include, "That's a beautiful painting," "Pretty, a very pretty picture," or "Yes, very nice." In turn, the child will often smile, say "thank you," and walk away. Opportunities for rich, verbal dialogue are limited. A second limitation is that these terms become vague and overworked. For example, the term *nice* is used so freely, as in "Have a nice day!" that it conveys little meaning or sincerity. What are the criteria for a "nice" picture? The term *pretty* is another example. Not all children's art is pretty. A solid mass of black paint may be dark, massive, thick, layered, or rectangular, but it is not pretty. The terms "nice" and "pretty" should be replaced with terms that provide specific feedback to the child.

With the judgmental approach, the teacher tells children that their art is good or great. Specific comments include, "Very good" and "That's great work." Because most teachers do not want to judge and rank children's art as good, better, or best, they may simply tell all children that all of their art is good. In turn, these judgmental terms become overworked and meaningless. A teacher loses credibility with the judgmental approach. How can one child's impulsive scribble and another's detailed portrait both be good? Is the teacher not telling the truth? Or could it be the teacher is not really looking but merely rubberstamping them in production-line fashion with the same empty judgment?

With the valuing approach, the teacher tells children he or she likes or even loves their art. Specific comments include, "I like that a lot" and "Oh, I just love it." Obviously, it is important to tell children you recognize all the time and effort they have spent processing with the medium. You can appreciate how hard a child worked to get a clay dinosaur to stand up. Rewarding and encouraging the child for processing, however, is different from putting the teacher's seal of approval on the finished product. Children create to express themselves. They should not make art to please a teacher. Unfortunately, many children create art that is personal and therefore devalued by adults. Stereotypic, impersonal art is often the type valued by adults. A classic example is the square house flanked by trees with a triangle roof and a smoking chimney. Often there are two windows with parted curtains and a smiling sun in the sky. Adults understand and may even encourage the making of stereotypic art. This type of picture gets praised and displayed at home on the refrigerator door. The stereotypic symbols convey public meaning. Although they may reflect a developmental landmark in attaining realism, they are not better than children's abstract art.

With the questioning approach, a teacher directly asks children, "What is it?" or "What is that supposed to be?" An older or very verbal child may answer. Some children may not be able to verbalize what they have represented on a very personal level. It may be difficult for a child to respond, "I just painted how I feel inside when I'm mad." Young children may not know why or what they have painted. In response, they may shrug, cast their eyes downward, say, "I don't know," or walk away. Some teachers continue questioning. "Well, is it a . . ., or is it a . . .?" A child may verbally play along to end the interrogation. Much of young children's art is private, egocentric, and not intended to look like something. According to Smith (1982), it is unwise and even harmful to ask, "What is it?" of a child who is making nonrepresentational art. For young children who engage in nonrepresentational art, art may have primary value as a physical knowledge activity (Kamii and DeVries, 1993; Fox, 2000). Motoric hand and arm movements result in brushing, dabbing, swirling, and smearing paint. The finished product or end result is of no consequence. Other children may be hurt or insulted that their teacher did not immediately recognize their splash of thick blue paint as the ocean. Children with language delays or children just learning English may not yet have the vocabulary to fully describe the idea or experience portrayed in their artwork. For these reasons, the questioning approach will not provide the responsive support and encouragement that young artists need.

With the **probing approach**, the teacher attempts to draw from children some hint, title, or verbal statement about their art. Typical comments include, "Please tell me all about it." This approach is less forward and abrasive than the previous one. It is supported by an integrated approach to curriculum development (Chapter 12) in which children's art is used as a lead-in to other curricular areas. This probing approach has merit, but it should be used sparingly. Children cannot and need not always verbalize, dictate a story, or write about their art. Also, there is a tendency for this approach to grow stale with repeated use. Encouraging but not mandating that children talk about their art is sound practice (see Figure 15–5).

The **correcting approach** attempts to provide children with specific feedback that will enable them to improve their art or make it "better" by more closely approximating reality. For example, a child shows her teacher a drawing of a green spider. The teacher replies, "Very good, but don't forget to draw legs on your spider. Spiders have many legs. And remember when you color that most spiders are black." This teacher's intentions were good but misdirected. Art, and child art in particular, is not a copy of the real world. Photography, not art, copies reality. Instead, the child artist freely chooses to creatively improvise. For example, children know what their faces look like. Still, their self-portraits may reflect faces that lack ears or eyebrows.

Figure 15–5 Children sometimes enjoy inventing their own spelling to provide captions for their drawings.

Eisner (1976, 1982) recommends that teachers shift from searching for representation in child art and focus on abstract, design qualities or *syntax*, such as shape and form. Children's art is related to the work of adult artists in the use of these artistic fundamentals. Discussing the formal elements of the visual arts is vital to the development of aesthetic awareness and potential. Even very young children can understand artistic terms such as shape, pattern, line, design, and color.

However, merely knowing about artistic elements will not suffice. Teachers can use the aesthetic elements of art as a framework for verbally responding to children's art. One need not be an artist to understand and implement this approach. There are different ways of identifying and organizing the artistic elements. Consensus is lacking on the one best approach. Hardiman and Zernich (1981) emphasized the following 10 artistic elements:

- color
- shape
- line
- space
- mass or volume
- texture
- pattern
- balance
- overall design or composition
- time and effort

This list is both manageable and developmentally appropriate for talking with young children about their art. It will serve as the framework for the alternative approach advocated in this section.

Keep three principles in mind when talking with young children about their art. First, consider children's developmental levels. For toddlers and young preschoolers, keep your comments short and to the point. Talk about physical movement, saying, "Look how fast your arm is moving the crayon." Or, "I see thick dots where you pressed hard." Second, relate comments to the artistic elements the child has used in picture making. Say, "Look at all the colors; let's name them—red, blue, and purple." Or, "Big squares that make rectangles are up at the top of your paper." Third, use encouragement rather than praise. Say, "I know you feel proud when you get the scissors to cut all by yourself." This conveys a different message than saying, "Good girl" or "Great job." Saying, "The smiling sun in the sky matches your happy face" conveys your interest and appreciation. Encouraging words help children feel good about their art. Children can get addicted to praise and end up doing art to please adults and get verbal rewards.

When talking to children engaged in art activities, Dodge and Colker (1996) recommended these strategies:

Describe what you see—

"I see you used all the colors at the easel today."

"I see three round, white balls painted on top of each other."

Talk about children's actions—

"You like to roll and pound the play dough."

"You used tape over your glued-down button to make sure it would stick."

Ask children about the process—

"How did you make that new color?"

"Would you like to tell the other children how you got your wood pieces to stay glued together?"

Ask open-ended questions that encourage children to think and respond—

"What might happen if you tried mixing different colors?"

"What might you paint that would be new and different today?"

Use words to encourage and support children's efforts—

"You painted two paintings today. You decide which one we should hang up."

"You have been busy at the play dough table. I see you made three different things."

naea 15-4c Develop an Art Vocabulary Based on the Artistic Elements

Let us match specific comments to the 10 artistic elements listed previously.

color—

"I see bright colors. Here (pointing) are the three primary colors—red, blue, and yellow."

"You made purple on your paper. Do you know how you did that? Yes, you mixed red and blue together."

shape—

"Look at the different shapes you made. Help me name them. Yes, there's a circle and here's a rectangle. And over here? Yes, your square house has a triangle roof."

line—

"So many lines are on your paper. Some are straight up and down; others are curvy. These two lines formed a cross, and here you made an X."

space—

"Your hand painting fills up all of your paper. There is no empty space left."

mass or volume—

"Your clay animal is heavy and solid."

"Let me see what you have put on your Styrofoam. You used toothpicks, yarn, and sticks deep in the back. What a massive piece of art."

texture—

"Thank you for showing me your collage. The shiny metallic paper feels smooth. But over here the dried glue with sand feels bumpy and rough. You have two different textures."

balance—

"Do you know your picture is balanced? What do you think that means? On the left side (pointing) you drew yourself, and over here on the right (pointing) you drew your bunny."

Pattern—

"You've alternated red and blue to make stripes across the bottom of your paper. You've included a pattern in your painting."

overall design or composition—

"You used many different lines and shapes to make your picture. Here they fit into each other like puzzle pieces. You placed them all over your paper. It makes a very interesting design."

time and effort—

"I can tell you worked very long and hard on this picture. You must be very proud of yourself" (encouraging remark).

"I bet you're glad you didn't give up. You finally got the play dough to work so your animal can stand up."

Teachers can also say, "I like the way you . . .

- are working so hard."
- are being so creative."
- are trying to come up with your very own idea."
- are trying new ways."
- are putting things away."
- are sharing at the art center."

Teachers can also verbally reflect the way a piece of art makes them feel. For example, "Robbie, your bright colors make me feel happy." Or, "All those lines racing around your paper make me feel like moving around." Teachers are responsive when they carefully examine children's art and provide rich dialogue emphasizing the artistic elements. No one piece of children's art contains all the artistic elements. Texture is useful in describing collage or painting, where surfaces are rough, smooth, nubby, or layered. Mass or volume in three-dimensional art is a useful term in describing a child's clay work, sculpture, construction, or assemblage.

It is also important to comment on the handling of the materials and media. A child's unsuccessful attempts or disappointments with the media should be discussed. For example, a child tries to paint a rainbow with watercolors, but the colors run together. A teacher could say, "I know you worked hard at trying to keep your colors separate. Watercolors get very wet, and colors sometimes run. What could you do differently next time?" A teacher may want to relate art to life. "You have drawn so many colorful flowers they remind me of my backyard flower garden." Or, "I see so many squares and rectangles in your picture. Remember our field trip downtown when we saw all those tall buildings that looked like squares and rectangles?" Or, "How is your robot like the ones you see on TV?"

Mulcahey (2009) believes children really want adults to pay attention to their artwork, not just compliment it. With this in mind, it may be wise to wait and say nothing. This serves two purposes. First, it gives the teacher time to study the child's art and reflect on the artistic elements evidenced before speaking. This eliminates an impulsive, curt response like, "That's nice." Second, it gives the child an opportunity to talk first if he or she so chooses. This provides a lead-in and agenda for a teacher's comments. It may be difficult to break the habit of immediately responding with words like "good," "wonderful," or "beautiful" when children share their art with you. Post the 10 elements at your eye-level in the art center as a reminder. Practice using them. Add them to your art vocabulary. Do not feel compelled to give an immediate response. Saying, "That's interesting," or "Let me look for a minute" buys you time to think and structure a meaningful comment.

It is also important to help parents respect and encourage their children's artistic processing and production.

Did You Get It?

The system by which a teacher or observer should respond to a child's process and product in the realm of art is

a. art monologue.

b. critique.

c. art dialogue.

d. art repartee.

Take the full quiz on CourseMate.

DAP **naeyc** ## 15-5 Teacher as Troubleshooter

Not all young artists trust their own creative urges and impulses. Some have learned to doubt their own ability or personal worth. Others are frustrated by their inability to meet a standard of realism held by others. From time to time, all children need a teacher's subtle guidance and direction in making art. They may need verbal and nonverbal encouragement

to accept, trust, and act on their creative impulses. Dodge and Colker (1996) offer the following suggestions for when a child

- needs encouragement—

  Try saying, "What do you think you could do with these brushes?"

- ends an activity abruptly—

  Try saying, "Is there anything else you would like to add to your collage?"

- is unsure about the next step—

  Try saying, "Here is some colored chalk. What do you think will happen if you dip it in water before drawing?"

- wants you to make a drawing for him or her—

  Try saying, "Let's think about what you want to make. What's the biggest part of your animal? Try drawing that first."

A teacher can act as a **troubleshooter**, identifying children who are artistically or creatively blocked and use an appropriate intervention strategy. Following are examples of blocked children and intervention strategies.

15-5a Children Who Criticize Another's Art

One child at an easel tells another at the other side, "Your picture is dumb; it doesn't look like nothing!" The second child gets upset and cries. Children need to know that they cannot criticize another's art idea or work. "Tyrone has worked very hard at painting his colorful picture. Remember, pictures can be made of bright colors without looking like anything." Or, "It is Tyrone's picture, and he can paint anything he wants. If he doesn't want it to look like something, that's okay."

15-5b Children Who Copy and Imitate

Although imitation and copying may be forms of flattery to adults, children do not see them that way. "Teddy has spent a lot of time making his picture. Let's all come up with our own ideas." "Remember, it's yours—your idea, your way, and your own picture."

15-5c Children Who Are Not Progressing Artistically

Artists, whether young or old, sometimes get stuck in a rut. They continue to make the same things in the same way. A teacher can help by suggesting a new activity. Try, "Emma, I see how much you enjoy painting houses at the easel. What other kinds of buildings could you paint?"

An Opportunity for Teacher Reflection

Four-Year-Old Talia is the youngest child in a large family. Having worked with two of Talia's older siblings, Ms. Amin, Talia's pre-kindergarten teacher, knows the family is positively interactive, enthusiastic, and involved. Talia is accustomed to positive reinforcement from her parents and siblings for her efforts in any area. Talia is working in the art center today, modeling a figure from clay. When she is finished, Talia brings her figure to show Ms. Amin. Ms. Amin looks at the figure carefully and comments with a smile, "I see you've made a figure that is heavy at the bottom and smaller at the top." Talia frowns and asks Ms. Amin, "Don't you think it's pretty?" Ms. Amin responds, "Artwork doesn't have to be pretty, Talia. Artwork means something special to the artist and I see that your figure is important to you!" Talia looks worriedly up at Ms. Amin, "But don't you like it?" *How should Ms. Amin respond to Talia?*

15-5d Children Who Refuse to Try

Some children will totally avoid involvement in art. They will stand close by but refuse to try. They may need a teacher's subtle prompting, guidance, and guarantee of success. "Here, Nikihl, I'll stay and get you started. I'll dip the brush in the paint. Now you take over. I know you can finish on your own."

15-5e Children Who Do Not Like to Get Dirty or Messy

For some young children, staying neat, clean, poised, compliant, quiet, and obedient reflects cultural values. They will avoid messy art activities. There is a cultural difference because both the school and the teacher value messy art activities. The issue is not who is right or wrong but how to resolve the issue diplomatically. Other children grow up in homes where they are discouraged from getting messy or dirty. They may have been punished for playing with their food, soiling their clothes, or walking in mud. Others will come to school inappropriately dressed in expensive clothes with a warning to "stay clean." Young children get messy and dirty. This is a fact of childhood. Smocks, however, can protect clothing, and hands can be washed (see Figure 15–6). Children need to be reassured that they will not get in trouble for getting dirty or messy. "Your parents know we paint at school and want you to enjoy it. You can wear a smock and clean up afterwards." It is also important to inform parents of the importance of art and that making a mess and getting dirty are part of the process. Encourage parents to send their children appropriately dressed for dirty, messy work.

A child may be repulsed by messy art activities. Allow time for the child to see that others enjoy the activity and that the paint does wash off. Offer activities that use brushes rather than hand painting, or perhaps plastic gloves may be acceptable to the child. Go slowly. Putting one finger in the paint may be the first step. Keep paper towels nearby for a quick cleanup if the child is uncomfortable.

15-5f Children Who Avoid Art

Some children completely avoid the art center. Given the choice, they choose other learning centers. It is like the child who, if given a choice, eats only meat and refuses any vegetables. Occasionally, this may be acceptable. However, over time all children need to participate in all centers. One solution is to rotate children through the centers. "Joey, I know you like to go to the blocks, but there are other things to do. Today, I want you to spend some time in the art center and try at least one activity. Let me know when you are finished so we can talk."

© Cengage Learning

Figure 15–6 A painting smock can be reassuring to a child concerned about being messy during art time.

15-5g **Children Who Do Not Know What to Make**

"Teacher, what should I make?" "I don't know what to paint." Some children say this, hoping someone else will give them an idea. Usually this is the case for a child who has been pampered or parented in an overly permissive style. Try diverting the question back to the child. "Kimiko, that's a good question. What should you make? Since you are the artist, you need to come up with an idea. Try to get a picture in your head. Look around the room, outside, or in our books. There are many things just waiting for you to make in art." A list of books on color, shape, senses, and art, which may also be a stimulus for making art, is found in Appendix C.

15-5h **Children Who Dislike Their Own Art**

Some children are overly critical of their own artwork. They may tear up picture after picture because it does not turn out just right. Sometimes they are frustrated with their childlike results. Others have poor self-concepts and doubt their own abilities. Perhaps their parents hold unreasonably high expectations and will accept only the best. These children need heavy doses of encouragement. "Oh, Todd, please don't throw that picture away. I'd like to add it to my collection of children's art." Or, "I don't think it looks like a dumb giraffe. I see a tall, yellow animal. You worked very hard."

15-5i **Children Who Want an Adult to Do Art for Them**

"Teacher, I can't draw a pig. Make one for me." Adults should not do art for children. It makes them dependent on others and teaches them to distrust their own ability. "Sean, I have difficulty drawing animals, too. Just try and do your best." Or, "Sean, everyone has to do his own work. I can help you in many ways, but I cannot make art for you. I know you are an artist, and artists just keep trying and practicing." For some children, it may help for the teacher to look at a photograph with the child and talk through the shapes that can be drawn to make the object. "Let's look at this photograph of a pig in the barn. What shape do you see in his body? Yes, I see a big oval, too. Why don't you start by drawing an oval and then go on to add the head and the legs?"

Did You Get It?

Most nonverbal interventions by a teacher when a young artist is "stuck" should be in the form of
  a. guidance.
  b. explicit directions.
  c. analogies.
  d. open-ended questions.

Take the full quiz on CourseMate.

TeachSource Video

© 2015 Cengage Learning

School Age: Guidance

Consider the teacher roles described in this chapter. Which of these roles is the teacher in this video assuming? Based on what you have seen in this video, describe how you think this teacher will interact with children in the art center.

Watch on CourseMate.

DAP **naeyc** **naea** 15-6 **Sewing and Weaving**

Sewing, stitchery, appliqué, and weaving are activities that allow both creative expression and practice in eye–hand coordination and fine motor control. They are recommended for both boys and girls. Unfortunately, they are often overlooked when developing an art program for young children. The following books may provide some background information or inspiration for children engaging in sewing or weaving projects:

Sunflower Sal by J. S. Anderson

The Quilt Store by T. Johnston and T. dePaola

Charlie Needs a Cloak by T. dePaola

Tar Beach by F. Ringgold

The Patchwork Path: A Quilt Map to Freedom by B. Stroud

15-6a **Sewing**

Sewing involves little more than painting with needle and thread or yarn (see Figure 15–7). Young children can invent their own simple in-and-out or over-and-under way to sew and need not learn fancy stitches like the French knot.

© Cengage Learning

Figure 15–7 Simple stitching on teacher-made patterns.

15-6b Personally Expressive Art Activities

Following are personally expressive art activities for sewing.

Preschool and Kindergarten-Age Activity: Yarn Picture. This is a pre-sewing activity recommended for young children who are not able to use a needle and yarn. You will need a piece of wood. Sand the edges to remove sharp edges or splinters. Hammer nails in randomly. One-inch round-head brass brads are recommended. Nail them halfway in. Encourage children to take a length of yarn and wrap it around the nails to make a picture or design.

School-Age Activity: Paper Stitchery. Older children with experience in sewing might enjoy making stitches in heavy paper. This will be good preparation for sewing on fabric. Paper has the advantages of being easier to obtain and providing a sturdy surface. A large plastic needle with yarn will tear the paper. Provide a large metal needle and embroidery or sewing thread. A picture can also be drawn in advance. This same activity could be done on a plastic foam tray.

Kindergarten-Age Activity: Mixed Media. Why not encourage children to creatively combine art media that

usually do not go together? For example, they could stitch a frame around their drawing. Or they could use needle and thread to highlight lines in their painting. Or they might enjoy stitching fabric to a paper collage. What are some other creative ways to combine art media?

School-Age Activity: Fabric Stitchery. Older children experienced in sewing enjoy using cloth as the background for their stitchery. Any loosely woven fabric will do. A piece of old sheet can be secured in an embroidery hoop as a preparation for fabric stitchery.

Children draw the outline of an object, such as an animal, on a piece of folded fabric, perhaps an old white sheet. Carefully cut through both pieces of material. Begin to sew the two together while stuffing with small pieces of cotton or stuffing. Continue to sew and stuff. Decorate the pillow with fabric markers when it is completed. Children enjoy making stuffed people pillows by adding yarn for hair and buttons for eyes after the sewing and stuffing is completed.

15-6c Sensory Exploration Activities

Following is a sensory exploration activity for sewing.

Preschool, Kindergarten, and School-Age Activity: Simple Sewing. We can reduce some of the steps and frustration involved in sewing by providing a sewing surface already perforated with holes. Such a surface is similar to commercially available sewing cards, although we need not provide a specific outline to complete. Carefully poke or punch out smooth holes. All the child needs to do is guide a needle and yarn in and out of the holes. Select a fairly sturdy surface (see Figure 15–8). Some recommended sewing surfaces include:

● plastic foam tray
● cardboard shape with holes punched around the edges
● berry basket
● poster board
● mesh hardware cloth (1/4 inch), cut into squares with tin snips
● plastic screen
● paper plate

Flimsy sewing surfaces, such as burlap and other open-weave fabrics or the mesh bags that onions or grapefruit come in, should be secured in an embroidery hoop. Beginning sewers have a tendency to sew over the hoop. This poses no problem, because the stitches can later be cut to provide a fringed effect. Provide a large, blunt plastic needle and yarn. Or use a bobby pin as a needle. Enclose the yarn and wrap the open ends shut with tape. There is no need to even use a needle. Merely dip the sewing end of the yarn into white glue.

Photo Courtesy of Jill Englebright Fox

Figure 15–8 Tagboard is a sturdy material for beginning weavers.

Form the yarn into a point and let it dry. The end can also be wrapped with clear tape and shaped into a point. Tie a knot at the opposite end. Older children with experience in sewing can move on to using a smaller needle with embroidery or sewing thread.

15-6d **Weaving**

Weaving is another art activity often overlooked in early childhood programs. This may be because weaving is a detailed activity, involving much patience, eye–hand coordination, and fine motor control. For very young children or children with limited experience, weaving is an exploratory activity in which they build fine motor dexterity. The paper-weaving activities discussed in Chapter 10 provide a good introduction. Once children have mastered the alternating over–under and under–over movement with paper, they may want to continue by weaving with yarn or other items. At this time, weaving becomes an artistic activity as children focus on the colors and patterns in their creations. Weavers use their own vocabulary.

- The **loom** is the structure you weave on.
- The **warp** is the lengthwise yarn or string that is strung on your loom.
- The **weft** is the yarn that is woven over–under and under–over the warp.

Following are simplified weaving activities for young children.

Kindergarten and School-Age Activity: Twig Weaving. Provide each child with a Y-shaped or forked twig for a loom. Wrap the twig with parallel rows of yarn stretching between the two branches. This will form the warp. Do not pull too tightly or the branches will snap. Weave lengths of yarn (weft) with an alternating over–under, under–over movement, starting from the notch and moving to the top of the "Y" shape. Encourage children to push their rows fairly close together and to alternate colors. Because no two twigs are exactly the same, the finished products will be unique. Older children who are experienced weavers may enjoy weaving on a larger twig with three or more forked branches.

Kindergarten and School-Age Activity: God's Eye Weaving. *Ojo de Dios* means "eye of God" in Spanish. Mexican Indian tribes made these for good luck. They are visually attractive and culturally meaningful. You will need two crossed craft sticks or dowel rods for the base.

Form a cross with the two sticks and tie yarn in a knot around the sticks where they cross. Add a dab of glue to secure. Encourage children to use their over–under and under–over motions. With a length of yarn, weave over one stick and under the next, back over and under again to where you started. Continue this pattern without crossing over previous rows. Each successive layer builds the diamond-shaped pattern, or God's eye. Change colors of yarn often for a multicolored effect. Also, vary the thickness of the yarn. Lengths of yarn can also be twisted before wrapping to provide a different visual effect.

Kindergarten and School-Age Activity: Bag Weaving. Look for mesh bags the next time you go grocery shopping. Check the produce aisles for mesh bags that hold potatoes, onions, and other vegetables. These bags provide a good, flat surface for weaving, and the webbing has spaces large enough for young weavers to use an in-and-out motion. Each side of the bag results in at least one section. Provide strips of ribbon, yarn, fabric, or cord to weave into their mesh section. One foot is a recommended length. Encourage children to weave both horizontally and vertically.

Kindergarten and School-Age Activity: Mixed Media. Sewing and weaving go well together. Experienced weavers may enjoy sewing or stitching onto their weaving. Individual lengths or widths of burlap can be gathered and tied with thread, ribbons, or lace to break the monotonous solid appearance.

School-Age Activity: Soda Straws. You will need four or five plastic straws to make this loom. The straws become the warp and are held in place with the hand. Tape the ends together. You may want to start this weaving for the child. Hold the straws in a spread fan position. Begin with the ends that are held close together in your hand and slowly wrap them with yarn in an over–under motion. When they are fairly secure, let the child take over. Continue weaving to the top of the straws.

Preschool, Kindergarten, and School-Age Activity: Fence Weaving. Think of your outdoor chain-link fence as a loom just waiting for children to weave upon. This is a good activity for working together and practicing social as well as creative skills. Provide strips of fabric, old scarves, crepe paper, as well as lengths of string, rope, ribbon, lace, or yarn. Children can best handle strips that are no longer than 2 to 3 feet. Encourage children to begin weaving materials in and out of the openings in the fence. They will find creative ways to wrap and intertwine the materials they weave.

Preschool, Kindergarten, and School-Age Activity: Weaving a Six-Pack Ring. Children will need their own plastic six-pack ring, which serves as a loom. Provide short strips of paper as well as short lengths

of yarn, ribbon, and lace. Strips should be at least 12 inches long so they do not fall out of the holes when woven. Also provide pipe cleaners, straws, and feathers. Expect creative weaving. Younger children will most likely weave a random design. Older children may be interested in learning the over-and-under then under-and-over pattern. Weavings can be hung from the ceiling. Use string or small twist ties to join individual six-pack weavings to form a larger group weaving.

Did You Get It?

Sewing with needle and thread is, essentially, _____ with a needle and thread.
- **a.** painting
- **b.** drawing
- **c.** sketching
- **d.** conceptualizing

Take the full quiz on CourseMate.

Summary

This chapter focused on the teacher's multifaceted role with respect to children's art. (15-1) A teacher can model and participate in art activities. (15-2) Knowing about art will help the teacher to become an art specialist and to provide creative experiences for children. (15-3) Engel (1996) poses six questions for teachers to consider as they observe children's artwork. These questions will help the teacher to understand the artwork and provide a framework for the teacher's response. The teacher's responses to children's art are a powerful influence on the creative process. Complimentary, judgmental, valuing, questioning, probing, and correcting response approaches were critiqued. (15-4) Art dialogue, a strategy incorporating the artistic elements, was provided as an alternative to saying "pretty," "nice," "good," or "What is it?" (15-5) Teachers also serve as troubleshooters by giving children prompts or suggestions to overcome obstacles to creating art. (15-6) Sewing and weaving are often overlooked in early childhood art programs but can be valuable learning activities for young children.

Key Terms

art dialogue, 296

art dictation, 297

art specialists, 294

complimentary approach, 297

correcting approach, 298

judgmental approach, 297

model, 293

participant, 293

probing approach, 298

questioning approach, 297

sewing, 302

troubleshooter, 300

valuing approach, 297

weaving, 304

✓ Suggested Activities

1. Practice being a model and participator as you interact with children making art. Record what transpired as well as your reactions.

2. Listen to a teacher talking with a child about his or her art. Which approach was used? How did the child respond? If necessary, think of some alternatives that would be more effective.

3. Encourage one child to show you his or her artwork. Use the artistic elements as a framework for your art dialogue. If possible, record your

session. Did you use any of the traditional approaches or remarks? If so, suggest alternative responses.

4. Make a list of the artistic elements to provide reminders for your art conversations with children. Think about where you will post that list in your own classroom.

5. Encourage, but do not demand, that a child talk about his or her art. Conduct art dictation.

6. Identify a child who is having difficulty or who is artistically stuck. Act as a troubleshooter.

7. Ask a teacher's permission to conduct art group time at the end of an art session. Encourage children to talk about their art using the artistic elements. Model the process for them.

8. Ask children's permission to attractively mat, frame, and display their art. Help set up a classroom display of children's art.

Review

1. List five different strategies that foster a child's artistic expression.

2. For each comment, choose the approach to talking with children about their art.

3. What artistic element matches each comment?

_____ "I love it!"	a. Questioning
_____ "I think you left something out."	b. Probing
_____ "That's just wonderful."	c. Correcting
_____ "What is it supposed to be?"	d. Complimenting
_____ "Explain it to me, please."	e. Valuing
_____ "Yes, very, very good."	f. Judging

4. Discuss the importance of art dictation as it relates to a young child's self-esteem and language/literacy development.

_____ "I see red, blue, yellow, and green all over your paper."	a. Shape
_____ "Here your dry paint feels so smooth, but over here, where they mixed, it feels rough."	b. Space
_____ "So many lines—straight, crossing, and swirly."	c. Color
_____ "Your picture fills the entire sheet of paper."	d. Mass/volume
_____ "Your clay elephant is thick and solid and can stand on its own."	e. Balance
_____ "I see rows of circles, squares, and triangles."	f. Texture
_____ "You repeated these trees across the bottom of your paper. What an interesting effect."	g. Line
_____ "Just look at how all the animals fit into your big circle. Yes, I can see how they are all performing in the circus ring."	h. Pattern
_____ "You have spent most of the morning painting at the easel. I can see how hard you have worked to get your painting just the way you want it."	i. Time and effort
_____ "You have drawn a house in the middle of your paper with two tall trees, one on each side."	j. Overall design or composition

5. How could a child's culture influence his or her art production?

6. List guidelines for art group time.

7. Identify and give an example of four roles teachers can play in early childhood art.

Additional Resources

"Redefining the Role of the Teacher: It's a Multifaceted Profession," is an article by Judith Taack Lanier on the Edutopia website (www .edutopia.org).

"U of I Study: Teachers May Need Training to Respond to Children's Emotions," is an article on the College of Agricultural, Consumer and Environmental Sciences (ACES) website at the University of Illinois (www.news.aces.illinois.edu).

The PBS website (www.pbs.org) has a section for parents called Talking with Kids, which provides helpful advice for how to talk to children about various subjects at different ages.

Weaving with Foil Tooled Accent is a lesson plan on weaving in the classroom on the Incredible Art Department website (www.incredibleart.org).

 Visit CourseMate for this textbook to access the eBook, Did You Get It? quizzes, Digital Downloads, TeachSource Videos, flashcards, and more. Go to CengageBrain.com to log in, register, or purchase access.

Kindergarten/First Grade Lesson Plan

Sewing with Betsy Ross

GOAL

Reading/Comprehension of Literary Text/Theme and Genre. Students analyze, make inferences, and draw conclusions about theme and genre in different cultural, historical, and contemporary contexts and provide evidence from the text to support their understanding.

OUTCOMES

Students are expected to:

a. identify elements of a story including setting, character, and key events.
b. discuss the big idea (theme) of a well-known folktale or fable and connect it to personal experience.
c. design and stitch a flag.

MATERIALS

a. *Betsy Ross: The Story of Our Flag* by Pamela Chanko
b. White board and markers
c. 6'×9' square of burlap for each child
d. Plastic needle threaded with red, white, or blue yarn for each child

INTRODUCTION

Remind the children of the class's daily pledge to the flag. Brainstorm with them the reasons for doing this. Tell them that today we are going to learn more about the American flag: who made it and when it was made.

DEVELOPMENT

Introduce the book *Betsy Ross: The Story of Our Flag* as a source of information for learning about the American flag. Write the words *setting, characters,* and *key events* on the board. Review with the children the meaning of each. Provide a focus for listening by telling the children you will be asking questions about these features of the story after you read it.

Read the book to the children. Return to the focus for listening and where the setting for the story was (be sure to show the location of Philadelphia relative to your community on an American map). Ask the children to name each character. Then ask the children to think of one or two words that describe each character. Finally, ask the children to describe the key events in the story. Record all their responses on the white board. Ask the children

to think about how the characters' personalities contributed to the key event in the story.

Distribute the burlap, needles, and yarn to the children. Tell the children that today they are going to design a flag and sew it like Betsy Ross. Model for them the up and down process of making stitches if necessary. Circulate among the children to provide help as needed.

CONCLUSION

As the children finish stitching, return to a whole-group setting and discuss the sewing process. How would they describe it? Having tried to sew, what do they now think of Betsy Ross, who sewed the first American flag? What word would they use to describe her now?

ASSESSMENT

a. Did the children identify elements of the story, specifically, the setting, characters, and key events?
b. Did the children connect ideas from the story to their own personal experiences?
c. Did the children design and stitch a flag?

Go to cengagebrain.com for a full-size version of this lesson plan.

16 Art Assessment

© Cengage Learning

What are the children in this picture doing?

One appears actively engaged in painting while the other is preparing to paint, checking to make sure the paint is the right color or consistency. How does the painter hold the brush? Can you see signs of the two artists working or talking together?

Observing children engaged in art provides opportunities to gather and record valuable information about them and their artistic development. Which of your children enjoys art? Who is reluctant to get dirty? Who is willing to take creative risks? Who is more comfortable watching and copying others? Over time, these recorded observations, supplemented with actual samples of children's work, provide developmental records.

Learning Outcomes

After reading this chapter, you should be able to:

16-1 Discuss the teacher's role as observer, recorder, and assessor and how observational data assist in artistic assessment.

16-2 Explain how children's art files and folders can be used to organize formal and informal assessment information.

16-3 Discuss the role of assessment in art.

16-4 Describe how the holistic model of child development can be used as a framework for assessing children's artistic development.

16-5 Provide mobile and stabile activities for young children.

Standards addressed in this chapter

DAP Guidelines

  2 Teaching to enhance development and learning

  4 Assessing children's development and learning

  5 Establishing reciprocal relationships with families

NAEYC Standards

  3 Teaching

  4 Assessment

  7 Families

NAEA Visual Art Standard

  5 Reflecting upon and assessing the characteristics and merits of their own work and the work of others.

naeyc 16-1 Teacher as Observer, Recorder, and Assessor

Terms like "testing," "evaluation," and "assessment" may elicit negative reactions. Some parents, teachers, and administrators may be suspicious of attempts to evaluate young children at all, let alone in the areas of creativity and art. This chapter adds observer, recorder, and assessor to our list of teacher roles. Being a keen observer of children and an objective recorder of their behavior helps in assessing children in all areas. Observational data is essential in assessing children's artistic development in authentic ways. Actual samples of children's work and performance included in a portfolio provide a comprehensive developmental portrayal. In turn, the portfolio serves as a basis for noting strengths and documenting progress, matching weaknesses with recommendations, individualizing curriculum, and communicating with parents. This chapter outlines strategies for assessing and sharing children's artistic progress.

Observation allows us to witness development and learning in children's progress. Recording helps capture the moments by putting our observations down in text. Recorded observations can be later analyzed and used to informally assess children. Assessment tells us how children are progressing and is useful in our work with parents and in curriculum development.

16-1a The Importance of Systematically Observing and Recording Children's Behavior

Why study children? Studying children and their development provides a working knowledge of children at different ages and stages. Studying individual children helps you apply what you have learned about how they grow, learn, and develop. Following is a discussion of the reasons for studying individual children.

To Understand Children. It is enjoyable and often amusing to watch children at play. Random watching, however, does not enhance our understanding of children. A careful study of children does (see Figure 16–1). Observing a child provides valuable baseline data about what children know and can do. Ongoing observation can be documented and included in a child's file or portfolio. Strengths, weaknesses, and recommendations across developmental areas should be included.

Just as photographs of children tell us much about what children look like on the outside, their artwork reveals what they look like on the inside. Children use art to tell us many things about themselves. Learn to read their pictures. Observing children engaged in art

Figure 16–1 This teacher carefully observes a student engaged in art.

and collecting samples of their artwork over time provides a wealth of information.

WHO THEY ARE Children include themselves, the most important person in their world, in their artwork. They begin drawing themselves resembling large O's or potato-like shapes, balanced on stick legs with arms protruding where ears are usually found.

This is a normal stage in artistic development. Children are learning about themselves and their bodies. Although they can look in a mirror and know what body part goes where, they are physically and cognitively unable to represent it in realistic fashion. It serves no purpose to correct children's artwork. It only erodes self-confidence and destroys creativity.

WHO AND WHAT IS IMPORTANT TO THEM Children live in a family context, and they introduce you to their family through art. Grandpa may suddenly appear in a child's art, announcing he has come to stay with the family. Dad may suddenly disappear after a divorce. Pets are included as valued family members. Children choose as subject matter things important to them. If they have just learned to use in-line skates, there is a good chance they will depict themselves skating in their artwork.

WHAT IS GOING ON IN THEIR LIVES AND WHAT THEY KNOW ABOUT THEIR WORLD Children use art to communicate how they feel about themselves, others, and their world. If they are happy with themselves and their lives, they paint themselves large and grinning from ear to ear. If they're feeling unimportant, they make themselves small or even missing from family portraits. The ways children use color, shape, size, and placement to portray themselves and significant others are valuable clues to how that child feels about self and others. Look for patterns but do not jump to conclusions. Children may draw themselves without facial features for reasons other than low self-esteem. It's when a child repeats an upsetting image that the teacher should become concerned and look beyond the canvas for other cues. At times, a child's artwork may appear to have regressed, to be careless and detached. An observant teacher will focus on issues facing the child rather than what the child is doing with the art materials (Lasky & Mukerji-Bergeson, 2003).

Children share both pleasant and unpleasant experiences. Art helps them celebrate the pleasant and deal with the unpleasant. The content of children's art reflects things about which they have strong feelings. For example, if they love their pets, then these animals are depicted. If they are afraid of monsters, they use art to express, work through, and eventually master that fear. Their art may also reflect feelings of anger, hate, rage, rejection, and despair. An intense scribbling of color may be all the child artist can express. The result may be unrecognizable, but the content and underlying emotion are very real.

To Document a Problem or Concern. When a problem is suspected or a concern arises, it is wise to collect observational data to substantiate your educated guess. You may be concerned about a child who does art to the exclusion of all other activities or one who never approaches the art center. Your observational data helps you decide on a plan for helping the child in question.

To Develop a Comprehensive Overview of Each Child, Including Strengths, Weaknesses, and Recommendations. Because children learn and develop at rapid rates, it is important to celebrate their achievements. The Instrument for Artistic Assessment toward the end of this chapter serves as one framework for informally assessing artistic development. Children who can only scribble in September may be able to make recognizable shapes by spring. Collecting samples of children's art documents this developmental progression. Art samples can be dated and placed in the child's portfolio. When laid out chronologically and carefully examined, the child's progress is evident. Changes in the child's choices of what to draw, increased sophistication in descriptive language, and more controlled fine motor skills can be shared with family as evidence of developmental progress (Hanline, Milton, and Phelps, 2007a). Artistic and creative achievement is documented. A child's concept of body is reflected in the inclusion and spatial arrangement of body parts. Weaknesses are also noted through observation or collection of performance samples. For example, children's involvement at the play dough table can be photographed at regular intervals. The photos can be

dated and arranged in chronological sequence. Over time, the child may move from random processing to making flat pancake shapes, signifying a developmental advancement in the child's perceptual and spatial awareness. The child has moved beyond working in a flat, two-dimensional plane.

To Plan a Program That Is Developmentally and Individually Appropriate. Observing what interests children and what activities attract sustained involvement provides a basis for curriculum development. For example, observing that a theme of dinosaurs permeates the block area could lead you to provide small plastic dinosaurs for making footprints, or to offer children an opportunity to make dinosaur masks. If children are frustrated using scissors, plan art activities involving tearing paper. You may also plan activities involving fine motor and eye–hand control to help prepare children for using scissors. Or it may simply be that children need individualized instruction and guidance in holding and using scissors.

DAP naeyc To Communicate with Families and Other Adults about Each Child's Learning and Development. Observational data collected from studying individual children helps parents better understand their children. Information collected from various child study techniques forms the basis for ongoing communication and conferencing with parents. It is widely accepted that a child may act one way at home but act very differently at school. Although parents need to see the bigger picture, do not be surprised if they deny information that runs counter to what they have experienced or choose to believe. They may say, "That doesn't sound like my child." You must provide evidence and documentation. This is meant to support your views and assessment rather than proving parents wrong. For example, observational notes based on a child's frequent aggressive use of art tools might help parents see the need for family counseling or a parenting course. Remember that communication is an ongoing, two-way process. Parents may be wary of your attempts to communicate if you only seek them out to report problems. Daily, ongoing communication builds relationships in which parents feel comfortable talking about their child and receiving feedback that not only celebrates their child's strengths but also addresses problem areas. Families can provide a wealth of information, including children's play interests and creative pursuits. A child who has no exposure to art materials at home and has been advised to stay clean at school may not approach the art center. Begin conversations with parents by saying, "Tell me about your child at home." Listen actively, attentively, and without judgment. Reassure parents some behaviors are typical of children at certain ages. For example, many children prefer painting their hands rather than applying paint to paper. Others enjoy mixing several colors together until a dark, unrecognizable, thick mass results. First-time parents in particular may not know what to expect of their child at a given age. Solicit their input and offer specific suggestions. Verbalize and restate a mutually agreed-upon plan. Record what transpired after the conference and plan a follow-up meeting to review progress or rework a plan, if warranted.

DAP naeyc 16-1b Observing and Recording

Knowing and understanding children involves two major strategies: observing and recording. Although you may have excellent vision, you may need to develop the ability to observe. Observation is a learned skill that improves with practice. Observation requires time, a focus, an objective attitude, and patience. Observation must also have a focus, such as children's art. An adult observer is unlike a video camera and cannot objectively observe and write for endless periods of time. Observation alone will not suffice. Observation and recording are complementary processes. Recording guarantees your observation will not be forgotten. Observations must be objectively recorded, with subjective impressions and analysis kept separate. Be factual, using specific and descriptive words. Imitate a video camera and/or an audio recorder, documenting what you observe and hear. Later, become a commentator, adding your analysis, interpretation, or inferences.

DAP naeyc Guidelines for Observing and Recording. The following sections address six guidelines for effective observing and recording.

BE PREPARED TO OBSERVE AND RECORD Develop a system that works for you. Some teachers wear a pen or pencil around their necks and carry clipboards with blank, lined paper. Other observers prefer to use index cards. Punch a hole through a small stack of index cards and attach them to a large key ring. This can be carried around your thumb. File individual index cards into a file box with dividers for each child. Still other observers wear an apron with small note pads in the pockets. You may want to use the larger sticky notes or peel-off adhesive labels that can be posted on the child's folder and later transferred into a permanent record. An audio recorder is useful when recording children's conversation. It helps to capture rich, descriptive language that is sometimes lost. A video recorder captures the words and actions of one child or of children in small groups. This provides the advantage of repeated playbacks at a later time. Set a realistic schedule for observing. It is not humanly possible to observe and record the

Brain Connection

Rushton, Juola-Rushton, & Larkin (2010) encourage teachers to be led by what they know about child development and research on the brain and pursue authentic assessment in their classrooms. Observation of children and careful consideration of the products they make provide teachers with the insights they need on children's learning and development.

behaviors of all the children in your care in one sitting. Supervision is always your first priority. One suggestion is to plan on observing four children per day, so that the entire group is observed on a weekly basis. The main point is to be ready to observe and record at all times.

BE UNOBTRUSIVE Maintain a distance, and do not become involved with the child or children you are observing. Avoid talking or interacting with the child or children. If they approach you, redirect them back to what they are doing. Tell them you are just writing notes about what different children say and do at school. You want children to act naturally, talking and behaving as they normally do. When children know they are being observed and that someone is writing down what they say and do, their behavior changes and your data are contaminated. Children may end up performing. What you observe and record may not be indicative of what they normally say and do.

GET A FOCUS AND BE SELECTIVE ABOUT WHAT YOU OBSERVE Know what you are looking for, and observe and record when it happens. If you are interested in a child's artistic development, then observe during art time and at the art center. If you are interested in creative expression, it makes good sense to select art time. Be flexible and spontaneous enough to capture through observation those unplanned moments that hold a wealth of developmental data.

BE OBJECTIVE, IMPARTIAL, AND UNBIASED IN RECORDING Record what the child says and does. Include nonverbal cues such as facial expression, body posture, and gestures. Add the child's name, date, time, and overall setting, such as "at the art center," as well as who else is involved. Develop a shorthand system using abbreviations that work for you. For example, J = Julia or rgu = argue. Observe frequently. Observe the same child in different settings and at different times. Avoid comments like good, bad, nice, or naughty, for two reasons. First, they cannot be directly observed.

SOMETHING EXTRA.....

Fact or Inference?

Good observation is based on what is heard and seen rather than what is inferred. Decide which of the following statements are based on descriptive observation and which rely on inference.

1. Child is out of sorts and in a bad mood today.
2. Child used her fists to flatten the play dough.
3. Obviously, this child woke up on the wrong side of the bed and is having a bad day.
4. Child quickly ate two halves of toast and asked for seconds.
5. This child finally got a taste of his own medicine.
6. Child carefully turned the pages of the book while retelling the story in her own words.

Which are fact, and which are inference? The odd-numbered items are based on inference, while the even-numbered items are based on fact.

Second, they are evaluative rather than descriptive. What is labeled bad behavior by one observer may not be considered bad by another. Be sensitive about using words that stereotype children on the basis of gender, race, culture, ethnicity, social class, or special needs.

SEPARATE OBSERVATION FROM ANALYSIS AND INTERPRETATION Observation is descriptive and based on fact; analysis and interpretation are based on inference. For example, hitting and kicking behaviors can be directly observed, whereas "being aggressive" is a global interpretation, not directly observable. What does it mean to be aggressive? Does it mean swearing, talking back, punching, or shouting? The term is unclear. Some observers choose to add interpretations at the end of their observations or at a later point in time. This allows time for reflection through a careful rereading and insightful analysis, rather than jumping to a quick conclusion. Others record observations down the left half of the paper, leaving the right column blank, where an analysis is later added. A one-time observation will provide little if any significant data from which to draw conclusions. Patterns will emerge over time with ongoing observation. Patterns provide support for your analysis and interpretations.

MATCH A STRATEGY TO YOUR PURPOSE IN OBSERVING There are many child study techniques from which to choose. Some are quick to administer; others take much time and writing. Some must be constructed; others require only paper and pencil. Individual techniques provide different pieces of information necessary to understand the whole child. The more time invested in child study and the more strategies employed, the more complete and thorough your understanding of the child. Strategies include **narratives**, time and event sampling, and checklists and rating scales.

Narratives are records of what the observer sees children do and hears them say. Narratives are conducted in natural settings in which the observer tries to remain unobtrusive. Diaries and anecdotes are forms of narratives.

A **diary**, as its name implies, is a journal or ongoing account. One observes and records what a child says and does in wide blocks of time. The diary is made up of a series of entries over a period of time. Compare it to writing your diary on a daily basis. At the end of the week, you can reflect on the preceding events, analyze and evaluate your week, and make plans for next week. Diary accounts provide a wealth of valuable data but require an investment of time in observation. Over time, the diary shows patterns or trends, which help the observer make interpretations. Students of child development often do child studies, depending heavily on diaries.

An **anecdote** is a shortened and more focused version of the diary. Whereas the diary attempts to capture anything and everything happening, the anecdote attempts to capture a specific event or behavior, including how it begins, evolves, and concludes. An anecdote may focus on the child's use of language or how frustration is handled and expressed. Given its broader scope, a diary may house or frame several anecdotes and therefore provide a bigger picture. The observer begins recording an anecdote when the specified behavior begins and stops recording when the child stops engaging in the behavior under study. For example, Martika's teacher has decided to use anecdotal observation to better understand the child's attitude toward art. She plans to observe Martika's involvement at the art center carefully. On Tuesday afternoon, Martika, age four, enters the art area and the teacher records the following:

It's 2:15 and Martika is standing in the art area. She twists her hair with her fingers while silently watching one girl paint at the easel and one boy play with play dough at the table. The girl asks Martika if she wants to paint with

An Opportunity for Teacher Reflection

Four-Year-Old Leo is a student in Mr. Parks's Head Start classroom. Leo has experienced much trauma in his short life. His mother was killed when he was three years old and his father is now in prison. Leo is being raised by his great-grandmother, an elderly woman with health problems and limited mobility. Given Leo's experiences, it is not difficult for Mr. Parks to understand his volatile behavior in the classroom. Leo is aggressive with other children and often destructive with classroom materials. Mr. Parks has found, though, that easel painting is the one classroom activity that keeps Leo calm and focused. Mr. Parks has added another easel to the art center so that one can be available to Leo whenever he needs to settle himself by painting. Mr. Parks shared this strategy with the social worker who works with Leo and his great-grandmother. The social worker was interested in seeing samples of Leo's artwork. Mr. Parks has collected various paintings over the past few weeks. How might Mr. Parks organize or label the paintings for the social worker? *How might Leo participate in presenting his artwork to the social worker?*

her. Martika does not answer. The girl hands Martika a paint smock, but Martika does not put it on. She sits next to the boy at the play dough table. There are several large pieces of play dough available, but Martika sits with her hands in her pockets. She says something that resembles, "It's yucky," and leaves the art area. Ending time is 2:22.

What, if anything, does this descriptive anecdote tell you about Martika and her behavior in the art area? It is too soon to draw any conclusions based on this limited data, and further observation is clearly warranted.

Sampling observations use time intervals or categories of behavior as their focus. Time sampling measures the frequency of a behavior within a given period of time. With time sampling, the observer specifies the behavior under study and then counts how often it occurs within a stated block of time. For example, Martika's mother complains that Martika never brings any artwork home and questions her level of involvement throughout the day. She claims Martika has always been a watcher rather than a doer. Ultimately, she fears Martika will not be ready for kindergarten. At school, Martika does spend a lot of time by herself merely watching others. The teacher chooses to do a time sampling to study the extent of Martika's lack of engagement at school. The teacher will count the number of times Martika engages at a learning center for five consecutive days. She is time sampling by selecting the first 10 minutes on each hour to observe. An assumption is made that what Martika does within this 10-minute block of time is representative of her behavior throughout the hour. A tally indicates the number of minutes that Martika was engaged in play. The teacher's findings for one week are depicted in Table 16–1.

What do the data tell you? Are there days of the week or times of the day when Martika is more engaged and involved than others? Do you see a pattern emerging? What could account for this? It is difficult and dangerous to generalize from this limited data. Based on the limited information provided, however, one can see how Martika's involvement increases

Table 16–1 Time Sampling: Martika's Engagement in Play

	Monday	Tuesday	Wednesday	Thursday	Friday
8:00–8:10					
9:00–9:10	/	//	//	//	//
10:00–10:10		//	//	///	
11:00–11:10					
12:00–12:10					
1:00–1:10					
2:00–2:10		///	///	////	//
3:00–3:10		/	/	/	
4:00– 4:10		/	//		/
5:00–5:10					

and decreases, although the pattern is fairly consistent across the days, except Monday. What could explain the low level of involvement on Monday? Her teacher notices how Martika needs much time to wake up and face the day. Do the data in Table 16–1 support this hypothesis? Why does her participation drop off before lunch and before going home? Are there questions you could formulate to ask Martika's mother to help you better understand the pattern observed in this time sampling?

The next step is to act on the information in the anecdote and time sampling. The teacher plans to question the mother regarding Martika's sleeping and eating habits. Perhaps she is coming to school tired and without eating breakfast. She will also discuss how Martika spends her weekends to better understand her lower level of involvement on Mondays.

With **event sampling**, the observer specifies the behaviors under study and then notes when it happens. The occurrence of each behavior is indicated with a tally. Martika's teacher has been observing the activity choices of her four-year-olds. She is concerned that Martika spends much of her day being idle, rather than engaged, although she spends more time at the art area than elsewhere. By using event sampling, she hopes to learn which art activities engage Martika. The child's initial, M, appears under the art activity at a specified time. Times with no initial indicate lack of engagement (see Table 16–2).

What does the event sampling indicate? It appears that Martika's engagement in art is limited to drawing and coloring. Could it be that drawing and coloring are less risky and less messy than the other art options? Do the three observational tools work together to advance our understanding of Martika? Her teacher wonders whether Martika is bringing her artwork home to share with her mother. Her teacher is also planning to slowly encourage Martika's participation in other art activities.

CHECKLISTS AND RATING SCALES Although commercially available, many **checklists** and **rating scales** are created by teachers. They take time to develop but less time to complete than a narrative. In a checklist, the items are identified, and the observer merely indicates which items are present or absent. For example, a checklist for art could include the following developmental indicators:

_____ scribbles and makes unrecognizable marks

_____ makes geometric shapes

_____ draws mandalas

_____ draws self as face

_____ draws human figure

_____ enjoys using finger paint

_____ creates two- and three-dimensional forms with play dough

_____ art is rich with details

_____ child relies on own creativity rather than copying

The observer could place a check mark or write "yes" or "no" in front of those items that apply. Checklists may be administered more than once, and some forms provide for multiple observations, documenting progress or change over time.

A rating scale is a second time-saving observational tool. In a rating scale, items are identified and the observer makes a judgment regarding the degree to which the item is observed in the child. For example,

Table 16–2 Event Sampling: Martika's Art Choices

		Easel Painting	Collage	Play Dough	Drawing & Coloring
8:30–8:40	Art center closed				
9:30–9:40					M
10:30–10:40	Outdoors				
11:30–11:40	Lunch				
12:30–12:40	Rest				
1:30–1:40	Rest				
2:30–2:40					M
3:30–3:40	Outdoors				
4:30– 4:40					M
5:30–5:40					

the items in the preceding art checklist could be rated along a continuum of high–medium–low or always–sometimes–never. The rating scale provides for more accurate judgment than a checklist. What the checklist and rating scale share in simplicity, however, they lose in terms of judgment. How would you rate the following observed anecdote using a checklist or rating scale?

Kea (who is three) shares toys but not materials in the art center or food at the snack table. She easily shares with adults and younger children but not with those her age or older.

A judgment must be made. Do you indicate "yes" or "no" for sharing? Actually, it may be easier to use a rating scale and rate Kea as "sometimes" or to use a mid-mark indicating a moderate degree of sharing. While being observed, Kea did not ask to be included in the play of others. What does this mean? Does she lack social skills? Does she not know how to ask to be included? Or did it simply not happen this month? To avoid this problem, many rating scales include a "Not Observed" column.

© Cengage Learning 2015

Figure 16–2 Teacher observation is an important assessment tool.

Did You Get It?

Observational data gleaned from watching and assessing children in a comprehensive and all-encompassing manner leads to an overall picture of the child's progression and development which the author of your text deems

a. "realistic."

b. "accurate."

c. "fair-minded."

d. "authentic."

Take the full quiz on CourseMate.

16-2 Children's Art Files and Folders

Keeping samples of children's artwork is a good way to collect evaluative data. Ask the child's permission to record his or her name and the date on the back of the piece. Try to collect a sample at least once a week. Tell children you are saving pieces for their **art folders**. Encourage their participation in choosing artwork they want included. Honor their requests for pieces they prefer to take home. Encourage them to make both "take-home" and "folder" pieces. Use a large, colored file folder or folded piece of poster board to hold the artwork. Periodically lay the pieces

out in chronological order. Look for development, progression, and mastery in the use of media and materials and in the expression of ideas, concepts, objects, and feelings. Match what is artistically rendered with a particular child's artistic and overall level of development. Use these data in reporting to families and for planning future art experiences (see Figure 16–2).

Art files may also include video recordings. For example, art displays can be video-taped as a way of documenting the quality of the work. Children whose work is depicted in the video can view it and give a written or verbal review of their art-making process, telling what they would like to do better or differently (Wachowaik & Clements, 2006).

16-2a Formal Standardized Testing

Would it not be easier to simply test children? Find a test that is quick to administer and easy to score? Would it not provide the same information? According to Lessen-Firestone (1995), **standardized achievement testing** of young children is often inappropriate and may actually be detrimental to school success. Test results are often unreliable and invalid, influenced more by children's test-taking skills, cultural backgrounds, and stress levels than by what they know. Also, as teachers tend to teach with the test in mind, curriculum narrows, and isolated, low-level, testable concepts and skills are stressed. Further, testing situations can be artificial, contrived, stressful, and intrusive, because they do not take place during children's regular activities. Standardized tests provide a formal, less authentic

TeachSource Video

Observation Module for Early Childhood

Practice your observation skills. Record your observation with factual descriptions of the behaviors you see.

Watch on CourseMate.

way to assess what young children know and can do. Young children are not good test takers, but they are good at revealing what they know and can do through their play and daily activities. Children can and should be assessed in less formal and more authentic ways.

16-2b Informally Assess Young Children in Authentic Ways

Assessment for young children should not and need not take the form of testing. View assessment as an ongoing process of documenting and recording a child's development. According to the National Association for the Education of Young Children (NAEYC) (2003), assessment serves the following purposes: to make appropriate decisions about teaching and learning, to investigate concerns requiring interventions for individual children, and to help programs improve educational and developmental interventions. Assessment should be informal and authentic. It should not disrupt the daily program but should happen naturally as children are engaged in playful pursuits. Observing and recording children's behavior and language are key components of authentic assessment. Authentic assessment also involves the person being assessed in the process. The professional artist's mentor does not assemble the portfolio. Involvement fosters responsibility and ownership. Children can analyze and assess their developmental progress and learning over time. Authentic assessment offers a much more natural, sensitive, and realistic

look at development than any set of standardized tests. Authentic assessment of children relies on observation, recording, and analysis, along with samples of a child's activities and work assembled in a portfolio.

16-2c Portfolio Approach to Authentic Assessment

You may associate the portfolio concept with professional artists and models. Artists assemble collections of their artwork in large folders or portfolios. The collections represent what they can do with different art media. Artists may supplement actual art samples with photos, slides, or video recordings of their larger pieces. They may include pieces done at different times to demonstrate their versatility, style, or professional development. Models do the same. They pour through an array of photos and select those that best capture their looks. These are assembled in a binder and shown to potential agents. The same process holds for young children. They are building portfolios based on what they have learned at school. A portfolio is comprehensive and contains multiple sources of information, including:

- samples of children's work, such as art, stories, writing samples
- writing drafts and revisions
- observational data of physical, social, emotional, cognitive, and creative anecdotes
- photographs of blocks or three-dimensional construction
- audio recordings of language, storytelling, reading, dramatic play episodes
- video recordings of children doing art, moving to music, social interactions, dramatic play themes
- health records
- parent input, such as completed questionnaires, conference notes
- notes forwarded from former teachers
- special items selected by the child

A portfolio, however, is more than a collection of information. According to Martin (1994), it is an attitude and a process. As an attitude, it reflects an ongoing openness and commitment to learning more about each child. As a process, it involves using multiple sources, including teacher, child, and family, to provide valuable developmental data.

16-2d Guidelines for Assembling, Maintaining, and Reviewing a Portfolio

There are five basic guidelines for portfolio assessment:

1. Devise a System. Use large, colored folders or boxes. Locate a storage place for the portfolios. Decide how the content will be organized. Provide one container for each child that he or she can decorate. This begins the process of ownership. Portfolio contents must be respected, and confidentiality is important.

2. Add Entries Regularly. Date each sample included. Provide background information. Arrange the items chronologically. Earliest work samples will appear in the front followed by more recent entries. Adding to portfolios should be an ongoing process. You will be overwhelmed if you add only a few times a year. Develop a schedule so that samples are added on a daily or weekly basis.

3. Focus on the Whole Child. Portfolios should be comprehensive. Remember to address all developmental areas, including entries and observations that reflect a child's physical, social, emotional, cognitive, and creative accomplishments.

4. View the Portfolio as a Collaborative Effort. No one person is responsible for the portfolio. All adults who know and either presently work or have worked with the child can have entries included. Resource people and specialists can also have notes included. The same holds for the child. Empower the child to be an active participant in the portfolio process. Let each child decide which samples to include and which to display or take home. This also promotes responsibility and gives them a feeling of control over their education. Include questionnaires and/or notes from parent and family conferences. Ideally, portfolios can follow children throughout their educational career. An end-of-the-year summary sheet with a dated record of the child's progress goes on to the next year's teacher. All other samples are bound and sent home in the form of a memory book.

Genishi (1993) recommends involving the child in the art portfolio process by asking questions like the following:

- Do you like this piece of artwork? What do you like about it?
- Which is your favorite piece? Why do you like it best?
- What art media do you like the best and why?
- Why did you choose to include this particular piece?
- Explain how you got this special effect (pointing to textured area).

Or ask the child to complete the following sentences.

- This is my favorite piece because . . .
- I want this included in my portfolio because . . .
- What I remember most about doing this is . . .

Record the child's comments on an index card and attach it to the corresponding work.

5. Review Periodically. The aim is not to make comparisons between different children and portfolios but to look for and document individual growth, development, and learning over time within a portfolio. Plan a schedule to periodically review each child's portfolio, for example, two per evening. This is especially important before progress reports are due or to prepare for parent conferences.

naea 16-2e **Art Portfolios**

What is an art portfolio? According to Althouse, Johnson, and Mitchell (2003), it is a purposeful collection of children's artwork. It may include completed work or works in progress. Transcriptions of language used by children in the form of dictation to discuss their artwork may be included.

Genishi (1993) believes children's artistic progress may be documented and saved in portfolios that contain not necessarily the best of children's art, but instead samples indicating children's abilities and preferences at specific points in time (see Figure 16–3). These signed and dated pieces comprise the child's personal art museum.

Did You Get It?

A child creates an outstanding piece of artwork of which he or she is proud beyond words. This is definitely a piece to be placed in his or her portfolio.

a. Always - the portfolio is meant to instill pride and tangibly display achievement.

b. Sometimes - the decision rests with the teacher.

c. Sometimes - the decision to include the piece rests with the student.

d. Sometimes - the decision rests with student, teacher, and parents in unison.

Take the full quiz on CourseMate.

Figure 16–3 A girl's concept and drawing of herself develops over time.

16-3 **Art Assessment**

For many early childhood educators, assessment is a difficult concept to embrace. According to Wright (1994), this is particularly true in the arts, in which symbolism, aesthetics, and personal expression are involved. A liberal view of assessment must be developed in arts education to embrace the child-centered, process-oriented philosophy that reflects developmentally appropriate practices. The emphasis is on meaning making and expression through arts symbol systems. For young children, the processes that closely resemble the artistic interests and abilities of young children also apply to all arts domains: music, dance, play/drama, and the visual arts. Based on the works of Gardner (1990) and others, Wright (1994) identifies the following general artistic processes with some exemplary characteristics:

PROCESS	CHARACTERISTICS
Discovery—	observing, exploring options with a range of materials, comparing, questioning, seeking possibilities, finding alternatives
Pursuit—	engaging in arts activities, focusing on specific ideas, exploring in depth, working hard, carrying out one's plans, being goal directed, and staying on task
Perception—	showing sensory awareness; visualizing; showing care and attention to detail; evidencing sensitivity to a variety of genres, cultures, and historical periods
Communication—	expressing ideas or feelings; using symbols to represent; creating words, labels, captions, or stories to accompany one's art products
Self- and social awareness—	working independently, tapping into personal feelings, being involved in preparation and cleanup, sharing discoveries, tolerating frustration, participation in group activities, cooperating, empathizing, appreciating the work of others
Skill use—	manipulating materials, showing eye–hand coordination and fine motor control, controlling basic techniques, showing aesthetic sensitivity
Creativity—	responding flexibly, seeing afresh, taking risks with a medium, using imagination, showing inventiveness, exploring ideas in a variety of ways, crossing artistic domains, combining media
Analysis—	describing to others what is seen, heard, felt, thought, or imagined; articulating artistic goals; reflecting on process and product; showing an interest in using arts terminology
Critique—	appreciating artistic products; talking about one's own artistry and the works of peers and published artists; describing, interpreting, and judging; using the work of others for ideas and inspiration

The characteristics and processes can be used as a basis for assessment. According to Wright (1994), it is helpful for teachers to understand art processes, to recognize how they are used by young children, to focus on processes that assist children in learning about the arts, and to explain children's art development to parents and others. When used as the basis of assessment, observations made of each of the above processes provide qualitative data about the child that enables a teacher to judge the effectiveness of the arts program.

Observations of each of these processes must be specific and focus on:

- the child's learning experience described through anecdotal information
- artistic elements the child could use during the process
- visual arts principles could be implemented by the child

In turn, the data gathered lead to implications for further planning.

Did You Get It?

Symbolic art. Aesthetic art. Art which includes personal expression. Wright (1994) points to which of the following concepts as pertains to these types of work, both in terms of process and product?
  a. They are very difficult to teach.
  b. They are not at all popular among young children.
  c. They are inherently difficult to assess.
  d. It is difficult to delineate when the child is serious and when he or she is simply "acting out" through art.

Take the full quiz on CourseMate.

16-4 Holistic Model for Artistic Assessment

Our holistic model of child development has served many purposes throughout the book: to understand child development, to plan appropriate experiences, to report to parents, and to justify our programs. We can also use it as a framework, or instrument, for assessing children's artistic development.

16-4a Physical

In using artistic tools, the child demonstrates:

1. large muscle or gross motor control
2. small muscle or fine motor control
3. proper use of the following artistic tools:

_____ scissors   _____ markers

_____ glue   _____ clay tools

_____ brushes   _____ watercolor set

_____ crayons

4. concentration and sustained involvement in art
5. completion of the art activity

16-4b Social

1. Ability to work alone at art
2. Demonstrating self-responsibility:

    _____ in getting and returning art materials

    _____ in cleanup

    _____ in following the rules of the art center

3. Self-direction in using own ideas in art rather than copying others (see Figure 16–3)
4. Ability to work cooperatively with others at the easel, art table, or art center
5. Tolerance of others' art ideas, styles, and products

16-4c Emotional

1. Acceptance of own mistakes, errors, and unsuccessful attempts at art
2. Self-assurance and confidence in art rather than an inhibited, fearful, overly cautious attitude
3. Expression of feelings, moods, emotions, and personality through artwork
4. Enjoyment and pride in own art
5. Addition, omission, distortion, and/or exaggeration of things that are emotionally significant

16-4d Cognitive

1. Understands art and why people have made art in the past and continue to do so
2. Is interested in talking about own art and dictating labels, titles, sentences, or stories
3. Knows and uses art vocabulary
4. Evidences:

    _____ very personal representation

    _____ public representation with subject matter recognizable to others

5. Demonstrates a knowledge of colors and color mixing
6. Reflects a knowledge of shapes, including:

    _____ circle

    _____ square

    _____ triangle

    _____ rectangle

    _____ lines

_____ combinations of above

_____ other nongeometric shapes

7. Reflects knowledge of people, places, objects, experiences, and events of personal importance in the environment
8. Draws human figures

16-4e Creative

1. Demonstrates willingness to discover, experiment, and explore with a variety of media
2. Demonstrates ways of creatively combining media, materials, and artistic junk
3. Uses detail, decoration, and elaboration
4. Reflects originality, imagination, and creativity
5. Makes individual and personally unique artistic statements

16-4f Aesthetic

1. Enjoys:

    _____ processing with the media

    _____ making artistic products

2. Uses a variety of:

    _____ two-dimensional artistic media

    _____ three-dimensional artistic media

3. Demonstrates awareness and sensitivity through:

    _____ looking

    _____ touching

    _____ listening

    _____ smelling

    _____ tasting

4. Demonstrates awareness and sensitivity to:

    immediate surroundings

    nature

    environment

5. Sees similarities and differences in artistic styles
6. Appreciates work of artists encompassing a wide range of styles
7. Knows the following artistic elements:

    _____ color

    _____ shape

    _____ line

    _____ space

    _____ mass or volume

    _____ texture

    _____ pattern

    _____ balance

8. Uses artistic elements to discuss and appreciate:

_____ nature

_____ immediate surroundings

_____ environment

_____ own artwork

_____ artwork of others

16-4g **Personal**

Number the child's favorite choices 1, 2, and 3.

Two-dimensional	Three-dimensional
_____ mark making	_____ sculpture
_____ painting	_____ clay
_____ printing	_____ papier-mâché
_____ watercolor	_____ construction or
_____ resist	assemblage
_____ stencil	_____ mask making
_____ paperwork	_____ mobile
_____ collage	_____ stabile
	_____ weaving
	_____ stitchery

16-4h **Teaching Children to Self-Assess**

In a developmentally appropriate art program, children are encouraged to make artistic decisions. They choose their subjects, tools, materials, and colors to create in pleasing ways. Because artistic preferences are based on personal tastes, it is important that children also learn to assess their own artwork—to set their own standards and then decide if their efforts have lived up to their own expectations. To help children develop standards for self-assessment, share with them in a group setting a series of reproductions of masterpiece drawings and paintings. Have children identify those they like and those they don't. Of those that the children like, ask the question, "what makes this a good painting?" Apply their responses to all of the reproductions and help them to generalize their ideas into assessment questions. Keep in mind that the children may include elements in their assessments that aren't necessarily important to adults. One kindergarten class, working through this process with their teacher, developed the following questions for assessing art:

1. Does it tell a story?
2. Does it cover the whole paper?
3. Does it have details?
4. Does it have a background?
5. Does it use lots of colors?

Once the children have developed their questions, record and post them in the art center. As children

finish their artwork, encourage them to use the questions to assess their own efforts. Teachers should also encourage self-assessment when they see a child isn't engaging in a project or needs support in finishing. Self-assessment is especially important when a child's work is criticized by a peer. Learning to judge oneself by one's own standards, in spite of the criticism of others, is a life skill important for all children to learn.

Did You Get It?

The authors of your text suggests sharing with your students reproductions of paintings and drawings done by The Masters, followed by a question and answer session of what the youngsters liked and didn't like, and why. The purpose of this is

   a. to improve the children's art processes.

   b. to improve the children's art products.

   c. to help the children acquire an artistic "taste."

   d. to teach the children principles of self-assessment.

Take the full quiz on CourseMate.

16-5 **Mobiles and Stabiles**

Mobiles and *stabiles* are three-dimensional works of art consisting of separate parts joined together by thin connectors, usually wire or string.

16-5a **Mobile**

A **mobile** is a hanging sculpture that moves. Generally, its pieces are suspended and free to move about. Wind or movement will activate a mobile. Wind chimes and hanging infant toys suspended over the crib are good examples of mobiles. Mobiles contain at least one level from which items are suspended. A mobile can be suspended from a ceiling or doorway by using string and a thumbtack.

Advanced mobile makers are faced with the problem of balance when they work with more than one level (see Figure 16–4). To start, one must find a sturdy overhead base from which the items will be suspended, using string, rope, yarn, thread, or fishing line. Some recommended supports from which heavy items can be suspended include the following:

- driftwood
- dowel rod
- broom handle
- thick tree branch
- three coat hangers wired together at their hooks
- wood ruler
- pencil
- stick
- yardstick
- single coat hanger

Figure 16–4 A multi-level mobile hangs from the classroom ceiling.

Photo Courtesy of Jill Englebright Fox

Supports from which light objects can be suspended include:

- straws
- tongue depressors
- ice-cream sticks

Smaller supports can be creatively combined with the items previously listed.

Following are personally expressive art activities for making mobiles.

Toddler, Preschool, Kindergarten, and School-Age Activity: Group Nature Mobile. You need a fairly sturdy tree branch for this activity. Look for one that has an interesting branched-out shape. This provides a number of different levels from which items can be suspended. Prop up the branch as it will later be hung (somewhere close to the children's level). They need to be able to reach the branches to attach nature items. Nature items can be collected on a nature walk or brought from home. Encourage children to look for nature specimens that have fallen to the ground. Seashells, feathers, acorns, mushrooms, twigs, leaves, and pinecones are well suited. Attach them with string or yarn, and suspend them from a branch. Nature specimens should be suspended at different lengths rather than in a neat row. Lengths of string can have

more than one item suspended from them. When the mobile is completed, place it near a window or doorway where a breeze will activate it. This is a good multisession activity. Items on the mobile can be continually added to or changed. Group mobile projects need not be restricted to the use of nature items. Include any of the recycled junk items listed in Appendix A.

Preschool, Kindergarten, and School-Age Activity: Yarn Shapes Mobile. Begin with a papier-mâché mixture (see recipes in Chapter 12). Each child will need a piece of wax paper to work on. Take lengths of rug yarn and dip them into the papier-mâché mixture. Squeeze out the excess between your fingers. Arrange the yarn lengths into a shape or object. Be sure to crisscross and overlap the yarn. Let dry thoroughly. Carefully peel off the wax paper. Hang the yarn shape from a mobile.

School-Age Activity: Multilevel Mobile. Advanced mobile makers can make a multilevel mobile. For example, begin with a dowel rod and suspend pencils attached to string of different lengths. Do not worry if the mobile does not balance at this point. Start to suspend items and glue string or yarn in place. Slowly work toward balance. One object on a very short line may balance a much lighter object suspended from a long line. More than one object can be placed on any one line, which will also influence balance. Older children enjoy the challenge presented by this activity.

Kindergarten and School-Age Activity: Picture Parts Mobile. Discuss with children how objects can be cut into parts. For example, a picture of a person could be divided into a head, a body, and legs. Each could be connected separately on a line, with a small space left in between. This will provide a comical effect when the wind moves the cut-up parts about. This same process can be done with animals, vehicles, and many other subjects. Magazine pictures are a good source, or children may want to draw their own pictures. A clown, a rocket ship blasting off, and a Christmas tree are just a few that the authors have seen.

16-5b **Stabile**

A stabile is nothing more than a self-standing, stationary mobile. Whereas a mobile is suspended, a stabile, with one or more arched wire arms, rests on a fixed base. Although it is fairly similar to a mobile, a stabile is more difficult to make. You will need at least one length of fairly sturdy wire attached to a sturdy base. The base must be large and heavy enough to support the wires and suspended items without tipping over. Basically, any of the activities recommended for the mobile apply to the stabile. Suspended items that are too big or heavy will pull down the wire. Also, it will be much more difficult to get several layers hanging from a wire that is bent close toward its base than from a mobile hanging overhead.

Preschool and Kindergarten-Age Activity: Simple Stabile. Provide each child with a drinking-cup lid, pipe cleaners, and play dough or Plasticine, as well as an array of greeting cards, postcards, or magazine pictures. Children can glue or tape their cutout pictures onto one end of a pipe cleaner. A piece of play dough is molded either inside or on top of the cup lid. Children gently push pipe cleaners into the play dough. Pipe cleaners can be creatively twisted and arranged at different heights and positions. Stabiles can complement a holiday theme by using relevant pictures. Children may also enjoy making a stabile titled "me" or "my family."

> ### Did You Get It?
> A mobile, which rather than hanging in a suspended position is fixed to a base with arched wires, is referred to as a
> **a.** stabile.
> **b.** decor.
> **c.** spielzeug.
> **d.** jouet.
>
> **Take the full quiz on CourseMate.**

Summary

(16-1) The roles of observer, recorder, and assessor were added to our list of teacher roles. Observation allows teachers to witness children's development and learning. Effective teachers make records of their observations and use them to share with parents, plan curriculum and identify children's individual needs. (16-2) Art files or folders can be used to organize information gathered through informal authentic assessments. (16-3) In the arts, the focus for assessment should be on meaning making and expression through the arts symbol systems. (16-4) Assessment in the arts should embrace the whole child and include elements from each of the developmental domains. (16-5) Mobiles and stabiles are art products that will engage children in multiple domains of development.

Key Terms

anecdote, 314

art folders, 317

assessment, 311

assessor, 311

checklists, 316

diary, 314

event sampling, 316

mobile, 323

narratives, 314

observer, 311

portfolio, 311

rating scales, 316

recorder, 311

self-assessment, 323

stabile, 324

standardized achievement testing, 317

time sampling, 315

✔ Suggested Activities

1. Working in teams, interview teachers about their views on assessment in early childhood, how they evaluate young children, and what they use to evaluate children's artistic progress.

2. Collect samples of one child's art over an extended period of time. Lay the artwork out in chronological order. Use the instrument for artistic evaluation presented in this chapter to make some statements about this child's artistic development. Can you make any recommendations?

3. Devise your own early childhood–style portfolio documenting what you have learned and can do as a result of teacher education.

4. Lead a group of children through the process of developing questions for the self-assessment of their artwork. What questions do they develop? How do they apply those questions to their own work?

5. Your instructor may have access to examples of standardized tests used with young children. If so, work in small groups and critically examine the test format and content. How do you feel about the use of standardized tests with young children?

6. Facilitate a mobile or stabile activity with school-age children.

Review

1. Identify and briefly discuss three teacher roles identified in this chapter.

2. Provide five reasons for the importance of observing and recording the behavior of young children.

3. Identify a major strategy for collecting and storing children's art.

4. Critique the developmental appropriateness of standardized testing for use with young children.

5. Discuss portfolio assessment as an authentic way to informally assess young children.

6. Identify the five steps in portfolio assessment.

Additional Resources

"Assessing Development and Learning in Young Children" is a position statement from the Southern Early Childhood Association (www.southernearlychildhood.org). Click on Public Policy, then Position Statements.

"Assessing Young Children" is an article by Dr. Cathy Grace available on the earcly childhood section for teachers on the PBS website (www.pbs.org).

Click on Articles and then scroll to the article title.

Assessment in the Early Childhood Classroom is a section of the Utah Education Network website (www.uen.org) that provides an overview for K–2 educators.

Calder Foundation is a website devoted to the life and work of Alexander Calder (www.calder.org).

 Visit CourseMate for this textbook to access the eBook, Did You Get It? quizzes, Digital Downloads, TeachSource Videos, flashcards, and more. Go to CengageBrain.com to log in, register, or purchase access.

Prekindergarten/Kindergarten Lesson Plan

Balance with Alexander Calder

GOAL

Measurement. The student directly compares the attributes of length, area, weight/mass, capacity, and/or relative temperature. The student uses comparative language to solve problems and answer questions.

OBJECTIVE

The student is expected to:

a. compare two objects according to weight/mass (heavier than, lighter than, or equal to).
b. identify Alexander Calder as an artist who created *mobiles* and *stabiles.*
c. create a mobile.

MATERIALS

a. Wire coat hangers, cut into smaller straight sections
b. Construction paper
c. Yarn
d. *Getting to Know the World's Greatest Artists: Alexander Calder* by Mike Venezia
e. Balance scale

INTRODUCTION

Share with the children that today we are going to study an artist who used the mathematical concept of balance to create his work. Show the children the book on Alexander Calder. Provide a focus for listening by telling them that after reading the story, you will ask them what types of art forms Calder created. Read the book to the children.

DEVELOPMENT

Return to the focus for listening and ask the children to identify the art forms created by Calder. Write the words *mobile* and *stabile* on the board. Encourage the children to develop definitions for each. Remind the children of their experiences with the balance scale in the math center. Explain that making a mobile means adding elements to the center piece until balance is achieved. Begin with a dowel rod and suspend lengths of the coat hanger from it. Ask the children to cut shapes from construction paper and start to suspend them from the lengths of wire. Help the children to work toward balance. Have them use the math vocabulary *lighter* and *heavier* to identify where additional shapes should be added to achieve balance.

CONCLUSION

Hang the mobile in the classroom. Have the children use the balance scale to review the terms *heavier* and *lighter*.

ASSESSMENT

a. Did the children compare the weights of the objects added to their mobile?
b. Did the children identify Alexander Calder as an artist known for mobiles and stabiles?
c. Did the children create a mobile?

Go to cengagebrain.com for a full-size version of this lesson plan.

Artistic Junk

Dear Parents,

We need your help! In our daily art program, we use all kinds of creative junk. Our slogan is, "Don't throw it away! Recycle it by sending it along with your child." If you have any of the following objects, please send them along with your child. We also encourage donations of creative junk from your office, business, workplace, or other sources in the community.

Thank you!

A adhesive-backed paper
apple divider
appliances (small, broken—good for parts)
artificial flowers

B bakeware
baking cups
baskets (plastic)
bath brush
beads
berry baskets
blocks (wooden)
bolts
bottle caps and tops
bottles—plastic pump-type, squeeze
bowl brush (new)
bowls (plastic mixing)
boxes (gift)
braiding
brayer
burlap
butter tubs
buttons

C calendars
canceled stamps
candles
carbon paper
cardboard fabric bolts
cardboard sheets and tubes
cards (old greeting)
catalogues
cellophane (colored)
checkers

cheese slicer
clock parts
cloth
clothespins
coat hangers
coffee filters
combs (cleaned)
computer paper
confetti
cookie baking tray
cookie cutters
cord
corks
corrugated cardboard
cosmetic brushes, sponges, and applicators
costume jewelry
costumes
cotton balls, puffs, and swabs
craft sticks
crayons (old, broken)
cupcake liners
cupcake tins
curtain rings
cutting board

D detergent bottles (squeeze-type with lids)
dice
dominoes
dowels

E egg cartons: cardboard and plastic
egg slicer
electronic parts
embroidery hoops and thread

envelopes
excelsior
eyedropper

F fabric scraps
feather duster
feathers
felt
film spools
flannel
floor-length mirror
florist's foil
foam
foam rubber
foil
food grater
food storage containers
fruit trays
funnels

G game pieces
gears
gift boxes
gift wrap
glass beads
grater (metal, food)
greeting cards
grocery bags
gummed labels
gummed paper and stickers

H hair rollers (cleaned)
hairbrushes (cleaned)
hangers
hat boxes
holiday cards and decorations
hot plate
housewares

I ice cream cartons (large, commercial)
ice cube trays
iron (electric, in working order)

J jar lidsjewelry
junk (any and all!)
junk mail

K keys
kitchen gadgets and utensils
kitchen shakers and containers

L lace
leather
lids
linoleum tiles

M machine parts (small)
magazines
magnets
maps
marbles
margarine tubs
material remnants
measuring cups and spoons
meat baller
melon baller/scoop
mesh—potato, onion, grapefruit bags
milk carton plastic tops
mirrors (handheld, full-length)
mosaic tiles
muffin tins
muslin

N nail brush
nails
necklaces
needles and thread
netting
newspaper
newsprint rolls
nuts
nylons and pantyhose (old, clean)

P packing material
pails (plastic)
paint charts
pans (old)
pantyhose
plastic egg containers
plastic jars
paper bags
paper doilies
paper plates
paper reinforcements
paper scraps and tubes
pastry blender/brush
pastry tube
picture frames
pie slice lifter
pie tins
pipe cleaners
pizza cardboards
place mats
plastic containers
plastic foam trays
plastic fruit baskets
plastic pieces and parts
poker chips
polyfiber fill

pom-pom dish scrubber
pot scrubber with knobbed handle
pots
puzzle pieces

Q quilts, quilt scraps

R rhinestones, rhinestone jewelry
ribbon
ribbon rolls
rickrack
rolling pin

S sandpaper
scraper
spatula
screening—plastic and wire seals (holiday)
sequins
sheets (old white)
shoe boxes
shoelaces
shoe polish applicator
shopping bags
sieves
socks
spice bottles (empty)
splatter screen (for catching cooking grease)
sponges (household)
spools
spray paint can lids
sprayers
springs
squeeze bottles
stamps (canceled domestic and foreign)
stationery
stationery boxes
stickers
stockings (old)
straws
string

T telephone wire
thread
tiles
tinfoil
tissue paper
tongue depressors
toothbrushes (old)
toothpicks
towels (old)
tracing paper
travel brochures and posters
trays
trinkets

tubes—toilet paper, paper towel, mailing
tubs (margarine with lids)
twine

U upholstery fabric and stuffing
utensils (old, cooking)

V velvet

W wallpaper sample books and scraps
wax paper
weaving loom
wire (thin)
wire mesh
wire screen
wire whisk/whip (kitchen)
wood scraps
wooden beads
wooden blocks
wrapping paper

Y yarn
Nature Specimens
acorns
bark
corn husks
cornstalks
dried flowers and plants
driftwood
feathers
fossils
gourds
hives
leaves
minerals
moss
natural clay
nests
nuts
pebbles
pinecones
pods
pressed flowers
reeds
sand
sawdust
seed pods
seeds
shells
smooth stones
straw
twigs
wood shavings

Where to Go in Your Local Community for Artistic Junk

The following list is by no means complete. The number and variety of possible sources will vary depending on the size and location of your community. Add, delete, and personalize depending on where you live and work. Please request more than is listed below. Individual sources may have a vast supply of colorful parts and pieces just waiting to be claimed. Most sources will be very willing to save, as long as you provide a prompt pickup. Specifically stating your purpose and suggesting some sample activities may help them identify artistic junk that is not contained on the list. Happy hunting!

Architectural firm
blueprint paper
outdated tools
surplus paper

Art supply store
damaged supplies
surplus stock
used goods

Attic sale
anything and everything reasonably priced!

Builder's supply and contractors
carpeting
Formica®
linoleum
tile
wallpaper samples
wood scraps, trim, and molding

Building site
discarded hardware
wood scraps, shavings, trim, and molding

Carpentry and woodworking shop
sawdust
wood scraps, shavings, molding, and trim

Church sale
anything and everything reasonably priced!

Computerized office
outdated forms
scrap computer papers and forms

Container and packaging companies
boxes
cardboard

Craft and hobby shop
damaged goods

packing
small boxes

Dentist's office
see Hospital/medical

Department store
gift wrap scraps
outdated forms
small boxes
store displays

Doctor's office
see Hospital/medical

Dressmaking and alteration shop
bobbins
buttons
fabric scraps
thread spools
thread
trims

Drugstore and pharmacy
plastic containers
store displays

Electric power company
packing materials
wire

Electronics firm
circuit boards
components
metal parts
pieces
plastic parts
wire

Estate sale
anything and everything reasonably priced!

Flea market or swap meet
anything and everything reasonably priced!

Florist shop
dried flowers
ribbon
surplus nature items

Frame shop
frame scraps
mat board scraps

Furniture showroom
cartons
packing materials

Garage sale
anything and everything reasonably priced!

Garment manufacturer
buttons
empty spools
fabric scraps
trim

General office and small business
envelopes
general supplies
old rubber stamps
outdated business forms
surplus or outdated business machines
surplus paper

Gift shop
boxes
ribbon
spools
tissue paper

Gift wrap service
cardboard rolls
damaged gift boxes
ribbon scrap
tissue paper
wrapping paper

Hardware store
linoleum
spare parts and pieces
tile

Hospital/medical
boxes
containers
plastic parts and pieces
trays
X-rays

Ice cream shop
cardboard packing
commercial drum-shaped ice cream cartons

Interior design studio
boxes
displays
fabric
packing
sample books

Locksmith
keys
padlocks
combination locks

Lumberyard
dowels
molding
sandpaper
sawdust
wood scraps and shavings

Machine shop or small plant
small specialized pieces and parts

Moving and storage company
cardboard cartons
wrapping paper

Nature and outdoors
nature specimens

Newspaper plant
newsprint
paper roll ends
scrap papers

Office supply store
cardboard
damaged goods
packing
small boxes

Paint store
linoleum
paint charts
surplus water-based paint
tile

Photography shop
containers
scrap papers

Plastic company
parts
plastic pieces
Plexiglas®
tubing
wire

Plumbing supply
plastic pipes and pieces

Print shop
cardboard pieces and tubes

heavyweight papers
paper "seconds" and scraps
tickets

Rug store
carpet squares
carpet scraps
samples

Rummage sale
anything and everything reasonably priced!

Stationery store
"as is" papers
paper scraps
small boxes

Supermarket and grocery store
baskets
cardboard
lining and packing
old price stampers
small boxes
store displays
thin tissue paper

Tag sale
anything and everything reasonably priced!

Telephone company
large spools
thin colored wire

Textile and fabric shop
buttons
cardboard
bolts
fabric scraps
material

remnants
spools
yarn cones

Thrift shop
anything and everything reasonably priced!

Tile and ceramic shop
linoleum tile

Travel agency
displays
old posters
outdated forms
surplus brochures
tickets

Upholstery shop
buttons
fabric spools
trims

Wallpaper store
drapery
samples
wallpaper books and scraps

White elephant sale
anything and everything reasonably priced!

Wine and liquor store (cover brand names before using with children)
cartons displays
fancy boxes
gift paper
ribbons
wooden boxes

Yard sale
anything and everything reasonably priced!

Art-Related Books

• •

The following list contains books that focus on the artistic elements, including color, shape, and line, and the five senses, artists, and art in general.

Alcorn, J. (1991). *Rembrandt's Beret*. New York: Tambourine Books.
An old artist reminisces about being trapped in a museum as a boy and conversing with the Old Masters, whose self-portraits had come to life. The Old Masters cast lots to see who could paint the boy in one final portrait. Rembrandt, the winner, not only painted the portrait, but also presented the boy with his own paint brushes and beret.

Appel, J., & Guglielmo, A. (2006). *Feed Matisse's Fish*. New York: Sterling.
Textured inserts encourage children to tactilely interact with great works of art from the twentieth century. A rhyming verse accompanies each painting.

Auch, M. J. (1996). *Eggs Mark the Spot*. New York: Holiday House.
A chicken named Pauline can lay magical eggs. She can copy anything she sees. Her eggs will help solve a mystery at the art gallery.

Beaumont, K. (2005). *I Ain't Gonna Paint No More!* San Diego: Harcourt.
A rhyming song about a little boy in trouble for making a mess with his paints.

Blizzard, G. S. (1991). *Come Look with Me: Enjoying Art with Children*. Charlottesville, VA: Thomasson-Grant.
Presents color reproductions of paintings of children done by artists ranging from Holbein to Picasso. Background information on artists and their paintings as well as questions are included to stimulate discussion. Recommended for older children.

Brown, A. (2003). *The Shape Game*. New York: Farrar Straus Giroux.
During a family visit to the museum, a little boy and his brother imagine the paintings as contemporary events in their own lives.

Carle, E. (1992). *Draw Me a Star*. New York: Penguin Putnam Books for Young Readers.
A young artist draws a star, then the star asks for him to draw a moon, and then the moon asks for him to draw a tree. This continues on throughout his life, and so the artist continues to draw the night sky until he flies away with a star.

Carle, E. (1992). *Let's Paint a Rainbow*. New York: Scholastic.
Carle teaches children about the colors of the rainbow, as well as the order of these colors.

Cressy, J. (2004). *Can You Find It, Too?: Search and Discover More Than 150 Details in 20 Works of Art*. New York: Harry N. Abrams.
Children approach art as detectives, browsing through 20 beautifully reproduced paintings in search of more than 150 details that are fun to find. With works from renowned institutions including The Metropolitan Museum of Art in New York and the National Gallery of Art in Washington, D.C., and featuring art by renowned artists from all over the world.

Dellessert, E. (2008). *Full Color*. Mankato, MN: Creative Editions.
An exploration of colors in paintings of fantasy creatures.

dePaola, T. (1991). *Bonjour, Mr. Satie*. New York: Putnam Publishers.
Two talented Parisian artists end their feud with the help of Uncle Satie.

Diakité, B. W. (1997). *The Hunterman and the Crocodile: A West African Folktale*. New York: Scholastic.
This traditional West African tale is beautifully illustrated with hand-painted ceramic tiles. The book is about a cautious hunter who helps some clever crocodiles and in the process learns a lesson about the relationship between man and nature.

Ehlert, L. (2004). *Hands: Growing up to be an Artist*. Orlando, FL: Harcourt.
A little girl watches her mother and father work with their hands and dreams of using tools in the same way to build, garden, draw, and paint.

Engel, D. (1989). *The Little Lump of Clay*. New York: Morrow Jr. Books.
A little lump of clay that desperately wants to become something has its wish granted.

Gill, B. (2008). *What Color Is Your World?* New York: Phaidon.
The book encourages children to think like artists and use colors in unexpected ways.

Guery, A., & Dussutour, O. (2009). *Alphab'art: Find the Letters Hidden in the Paintings.* London: Frances Lincoln Children's Books.
Letters of the alphabet are hidden in famous classical paintings.

Hartfield, C. (2002). *Me and Uncle Rommie.* New York: Dial Books for Young Readers.
This is the story of a young boy who is sent to Harlem for the summer to stay with his uncle, artist Romare Bearden (Rommie). He learns many things from his Uncle Rommie, including the value of family.

Hillenbrand, W. (2009). *Louie!* New York: Penguin.
A fictionalized account of the life of Ludwig Bemelmans, the author of the *Madeline* books, and how his experiences with art helped him to create the Madeline character.

Ho, M., & Meade, H. (1996). *Hush! A Thai Lullaby.* New York: Orchard Books.
Cut paper collage art beautifully complements the story of a mother who asks nocturnal animals of the Thai countryside to "hush" so baby can sleep.

Hopkins, L. B. (2007). *Behind the Museum Door: Poems to Celebrate the Wonders of Museums.* New York: Abrams.
A collection of poems for children about exhibits in art and science museums.

IllusionWorks. (2004). *Amazing Optical Illusions.* Ontario: Firefly Books.
Visual puzzles and optical illusions to make readers think twice about what they are seeing.

Johnson, C. (1995). *Harold and the Purple Crayon.* New York: Harper & Row.
The story of Harold and his adventures with a purple crayon. Harold goes out for a walk and sketches some adventures. The book is small, compact, and made for small hands. The illustrations are simple, and the purple line is bold. The story resolves itself with Harold falling asleep and dropping his purple crayon.

Lionni, L. (1991). *Matthew's Dream.* New York: Knopf.
An enchanting fable about a mouse who wants to become a painter. Explores the role of art and artist in shaping our vision and expanding our dreams.

Martin, B., Jr. & Carle, E. (1967). *Brown Bear, Brown Bear, What Do You See?* New York: Holt, Rinehart and Winston.
Children see a variety of animals, each one a different color, looking at them. Big, bold, colorful illustrations. Children will enjoy the repetitive, catchy rhyme.

Mayhew, J. (2000). *Katie and the Sunflowers.* New York: Orchard Books.
Katie follows all the paintings that have sunflowers and tries to pick the best ones for her grandmother.

Merberg, J., & Bober, S. (2003). *Dancing with Degas.* San Francisco: Chronicle Books.
Through the use of a playful and rhythmic narrative, Degas's paintings are used to show the life of a dancer.

Metropolitan Museum of Art (2006). *Museum Colors.* New York: Little, Brown, and Company.
A focus on colors in well-known paintings in the Metropolitan Museum of Art.

Metropolitan Museum of Art (2005). *Museum Shapes.* New York: Little, Brown, and Company.
A focus on shapes in well-known paintings of the Metropolitan Museum of Art.

Micklethwait, L. (2004). *Animals: A first Art Book.* London: Francis Lincoln.
This book provides early experiences with visual art for very young children by introducing them to paintings featuring different animals.

Morrison, P. (2005). *Art for Baby.* Somerville, MA: Templar.
A collection of black and white images created by some of the world's leading modern artists. The images are designed to help babies begin to recognize pictures and connect with their environment.

Niepold, M., & Verdu, J. (2009). *Oooh! Picasso.* Berkeley, CA: Tricycle Books.
Provides close-up looks at Picasso's sculptures, encouraging children to consider parts and wholes.

Noyes, D. (2004). *Hana in the Time of Tulips.* Cambridge: Candlewick Press.
Hana lives in Holland in the seventeen century. Her wealthy father's tulips crop, the family's main income, is not having a good season. To try help the family, Hana paints tulips under the encouragement and inspiration of a family friend, the famous painter, Rembrandt.

Obiols, A. (2004). *Dali and the Path of Dreams.* London: Frances Lincoln Children's Books.
As a little boy, artist Salvador Dali finds a key on the seashore. The key opens a drawer of dreams in which little Salvi discovers the symbols he will one day include in his paintings.

Oliver, S. (2005). *Gelbo's World: Remembering Colors.* Canada: Oliver.

A little boy lives in a black and white world until he meets a blind man who shows him how to see colors in his colorless world.

Pavlova, A. (2001). *I Dreamed I Was a Ballerina*. New York: Atheneum.
In a story drawn from Edgar Degas's paintings and Anna Pavlova's memoirs, Anna describes her first visit to the ballet to see Sleeping Beauty. She was inspired to be a ballerina and dreams of performing in that same theater—the Mariinsky in St. Petersburg.

Priceman, M. (2001). *It's Me, Marva! A story about Color and Optical Illusions*. New York: Alfred A. Knopf.
Marva is an inventor down on her luck. Her latest invention blows up and spews ketchup everywhere, which causes a whole string of mishaps throughout the day.

Reynolds, P. H. (2003). *The Dot*. Cambridge, MA: Candlewick Press.
This is a story of Yashti and how drawing a simple dot on a piece of paper can develop a person into an artist.

Rubin, S. (2001). *The Yellow House: Vincent Van Gogh and Paul Gauguin Side by Side*. New York: Harry N. Abrams.
Vincent van Gogh invited Paul Gauguin to come live with him in his Yellow House. For two months, in the fall of 1888, these two famous painters painted side by side. The story revealed how artists generated and shared ideas and work in very different ways.

Ryan, P. (2002). *When Marian Sang*. New York: Scholastic Press.
Marian was a talented vocalist who overcame segregation with the help of her family, church, and her strength of character. In 1939, Marian Anderson sang in front of the Lincoln Memorial, which drew an integrated crowd of 75,000 people in pre-Civil Rights America.

Scanlon, L. G., & Newton, V. B. (2012). *Think Big!* New York: Bloomsbury.
ISBN: 978-1-59990-611-9
A classroom of children explores their creativity in painting, sculpting, cooking, dancing, building, and thinking.

Schaefer, C. L. (1999). *The Squiggle*. New York: Crown Books.
A few spare and colorful lines bring to life a preschool girl and her vivid imagination.

Schulte, J. (2005). *Can You Find It Inside? Metropolitan Museum of Art*. New York: Abrams.
Questions encourage children to look carefully at "inside" paintings from the Metropolitan Museum of Art.

Schulte, J. (2005). *Can You Find It Outside? Metropolitan Museum of Art*. New York: Abrams.
Questions encourage children to look carefully at "outside" paintings from the Metropolitan Museum of Art.

Schwaetz, A. (2005). *Begin at the Beginning: A Little Artist Learns about Life*. New York: Katherine Tegen Books.
Sara is overwhelmed when her teacher asks her to paint a picture for the second grade art show. Many young readers will be able to relate with Sara's frustration as she struggles to overcome her "artist block" and procrastination and Sara's joy as she finally begins to paint.

Shaddox Isom, J. (2001). *The First Starry Night*. Dallas: Whispering Coyote Press.
Jacques encounters and befriends Vincent van Gogh when he comes to stay in the boarding house where he works.

Shaw, C. (1992). *It Looked Like Spilt Milk Big Book*. New York: HarperTrophy.
This creative book keeps the children in suspense as they try to discover if the pictures are truly drawings of rabbits, birds, spilt milk, or something completely different.

Spanyol, J. (2003). *Carlo Likes Colors*. Cambridge, MA: Candlewick Press.
Carlo the giraffe introduces readers to how you can find the main ten colors in everyday life. Each spread shows a picture dedicated to a color in which objects of that color are labeled, as well as unlabeled ones for children to find on their own.

Spiotta-DiMare, L. (2005). *Rockwell: A Boy and His Dog*.
Norman Rockwell has decided to include four paintings of a boy and his dog in his upcoming calendar. He's found the right boy but is still looking for the right dog.

Strom, M. D. (1999). *Rainbow Joe and Me*. New York: Lee and Low.
Eloise describes the colors she paints to her blind friend, Rainbow Joe. Joe sees the colors in his own way, a way that he shares with Eliose in a big surprise.

Tabak, S. (2000). *Joseph Had a Little Overcoat*. New York: Viking.
This is the story of a resourceful and resilient tailor who transforms his worn-out overcoat into smaller and smaller garments. The book is illustrated in a variety of media including watercolor, gouache, pencil, ink, and collage.

Tang, G. (2003). *Math-terpieces: The Art of Problem-solving*. New York: Scholastic.
Children learn math concepts through masterpiece art. Every left-hand page not only

has a work of art with the artist and the year, but also includes information about the painting and how it could be connected to a math concept and tells a little about the painting. It also tells the children which era it came from, such as Impressionist, Post-Impressionist, and Cubism.

Tougas, C. (2008). *Art's Supplies*. Custer, WA: Orca Book Publishers.

Art's art supplies decide to have a party and create mayhem in the art studio.

Tullet, H. (2011). *The Game of Patterns*. New York: Phaidon Press.

Presents a game in which players compete to identify and continue the patterns pictured on each page.

Van Allsburg, C. (1995). *Bad Day at Riverbend*. Boston: Houghton-Mifflin.

A father makes up a story to go with his daughter's scribbles in a cowboy coloring book.

Van Gogh, V. (2005). *Vincent's colors*. San Franscisco: Chronicle Books.

A collection of Vincent van Gogh's paintings, each described with a phrase from Vincent's letters to his brother.

Warhola, J. (2009). *Uncle Andy's Cats*. New York: G. P. Putnam's Sons.

Artist Andy Warhol adopts two cats who have several litters of kittens, all of them named Sam. When there are 25 Sams in Andy's house, he begins to wonder how many cats are too many.

Wehri, U. (2003). *Tidying Up Art*. New York: Prestel Publishing.

The author presents individual pieces of masterpiece art, followed by a version in which the elements are rearranged and all the unwanted things swept away.

Wiesner, D. (1999). *Sector 7*. New York: Clarion Books.

This is the story of a small boy on a class trip to the Empire State Building who is transported by a friendly cloud to Sector 7, a great cloud factory high in the sky. This imaginative story is illustrated with striking and dramatic watercolor illustrations that add to the element of fantasy.

Wei Wei, Y. (2010). *Salted Art*. Singapore: National Art Gallery, Singapore.

A little girl visits the National Art Gallery of Singapore with her stuffed rabbit. They notice the smell of fish coming from one of the paintings. The characters in the painting invite her in and teach her about drying and salting fish.

Winter, J. (2002). *Frida*. New York: Arthur A. Levine Books.

This book is an outstanding introduction to the influential artist Frida Kahlo, Diego Rivera's bride. With a poetic narrative the author tells the life of Frida through this striking picture book biography.

Winter, J. (2003). *Cowboy Charlie: The Story of Charles M. Russell*. New York: Farrar, Harcourt Children's Books.

In the 1880s Charlie was a young man who dreamed of being a cowboy. After his fifteenth birthday, he took a train to the American frontier and settled in the Wild West. He became one of the most famous painters of the American West.

Winter, J. (2003). *My Name Is Georgia*. New York: Farrar, Straus and Giroux.

The book presents, in brief text and illustrations, the life of the painter who drew much of her inspiration from nature.

Yenawine, P. (1991). *Stories; Colors; Lines; Shapes*. New York: Delacorte.

A series of four books on modern art created to help teach the basic vocabulary, including lines, colors, and shapes. Each book ends with brief background information that adults will find useful when talking with children about the paintings and sculptures reproduced in this series.

National Standards for Arts Education

These standards describe what every school-aged child should know and be able to do in the arts. They were developed by the Consortium of National Arts Education Associations, which includes the National Association for Music Education (MENC).

National Standards for Dance/Movement in grades K–4 include:

1. identifying and demonstrating movement elements and skills in performing dance
2. understanding choreographic principles, processes, and structures
3. understanding dance as a way to create and communicate meaning
4. applying and demonstrating critical and creative thinking skills in dance
5. demonstrating and understanding dance in various cultures and historical periods
6. making connections between dance and healthful living
7. making connections between dance and other disciplines

National Standards for Music in grades K–4 include:

1. singing a varied repertoire of music, alone and with others
2. performing a varied repertoire of music on instruments, alone and with others
3. improvising melodies, variations, and accompaniments
4. composing and arranging music with specified guidelines
5. reading and notating music
6. listening to, analyzing, and describing music
7. evaluating music and musical performances
8. understanding relationships between music, the other arts, and disciplines outside the arts
9. understanding music in relation to history and culture

National Standards for Dramatic Arts in grades K–4 include:

1. script writing by planning and recording improvisations based on personal experience and heritage, imagination, literature, and history
2. acting by assuming roles and interacting in improvisations
3. designing by visualizing and arranging environments for classroom dramatizations
4. directing by planning classroom dramatizations
5. researching by finding information to support classroom dramatizations
6. comparing and connecting art forms by describing dramatic arts, dramatic media (film, television, and electronic media), and other art forms
7. analyzing and explaining personal preferences, and constructing meanings from classroom dramatizations and from the dramatic arts, film, television, and electronic media productions
8. understanding context by recognizing the role of the dramatic arts, film, television, and electronic media in daily life

National Standards for Visual Arts in grades K–4 include:

1. understanding and applying media, techniques, and processes
2. using knowledge of structures and functions
3. choosing and evaluating a range of subject matter, symbols, and ideas
4. understanding the visual arts in relation to history and cultures
5. reflecting on and assessing the characteristics and merits of their work and the work of others
6. making connections between visual arts and other disciplines

Visit MENC's Web site at http://www.menc.org.

Multicultural Picture Books

The following is a list of some popular children's picture books that embrace diversity.

Aardema, V. (1983). *Bringing the rain to Kapiti Plain.* (African). New York: Penguin.

Ada, A. (1997). *Gathering the sun: An alphabet in Spanish and English.* (African-American). New York: HarperCollins/Rayo.

Alarcón, F. X., & Gonzalez, M. C. (1998). *From the bellybutton of the moon and other summer poems.* (Hispanic). San Francisco: Children's Book Press.

Allen, D., & Nelson, K. (2003). *Dancing in the wings.* (African-American). New York: Puffin.

Ancona, G. (1994). *The piñata maker.* (Hispanic). Orlando, FL: Harcourt.

Ancona, G. (1994). *Ricardo's day.* (Hispanic). New York: Scholastic.

Ashley, B., & Brazell, D. (1995). *Cleversticks.* (Asian-American). New York: Crown.

Bang, M. (1996). *Ten, nine, eight.* (African-American). New York: Grenwillow.

Barber, T., Barber, R., Burleigh, R., & Root, B. (2005). *By my brother's side.* (African-American). New York: Paula Wiseman Books.

Bridges, R. (1999). *Through my eyes.* (African-American). New York: Scholastic Press.

Brill, M. (1998). *Tooth tales from around the world.* (Multicultural). Watertown, MA: Charlesbridge.

Brown, J. (2009). *Jonathan's thunder.* (African-American). New York: Piraas.

Brown, M. (1989). *Once a mouse...* (2nd ed.). (Indian). New York: Aladdin.

Brown, T., & Ortiz, F. (1992). *Hello, amigos!* (Hispanic). New York: Holt.

Browne, E. (2003). *Handa's surprise.* (African). Cambridge, MA: Candlewick.

Brusca, M. C. (1991). *On the pampas.* (South American, Hispanic). New York: Holt.

Bryan, A. (2003). *Beautiful blackbird.* (African-American). New York: Atheneum Books for Young Readers.

Bunting, E., & Diaz, D. (1998). *Going home.* (Hispanic). New York: HarperCollins.

Bunting, E., & Hewitt, K. (2000). *Flower garden.* (African-American). Orlando, FL: Harcourt.

Bunting, E., & Peck, B. (1990). *How many days to America? A Thanksgiving story.* (Americana). Boston: Houghton Mifflin.

Caines, J., & Cummings, P. (1984). *Just us women.* (African-American). New York: HarperCollins.

Carling, A. (1998). *Mama & papa have a store.* (Hispanic). New York: Dial Books for Young Readers.

Cave, K., & Wulfsohn, G. (2003). *One child, one seed: A South African counting book.* (African). New York: Holt.

Cheltenham Elementary School Kindergarteners. (2003). *We are all alike... We are all different.* (Diversity). New York: Scholastic.

Cheng, A. (2000). *Grandfather counts.* (Asian-American). New York: Lee and Low Books.

Cherry, L. (2000). *The great Kapok tree: A tale of the Amazon rain forest.* (Hispanic). Orlando, FL: Harcourt.

Chin, O. (2008). *The year of the rat: Tales from the Chinese zodiac.* (China). San Francisco: Immedium.

Chio, Y. (2003). *The Name Jar.* (Asian American). New York: Dell Dragonfly Books.

Chocolate, D. M. N. (1996). *A very special Kwanzaa.* (African-American). New York: Scholastic.

Climo, S. (1993). *The Korean Cinderella.* (Korean). New York: HarperCollins.

Coerr, E. (2003). *Mieko and the fifth treasure.* (Japanese). New York: Penguin.

Cohen, C. L., & Begay, S. (1991). *The mud pony.* (Native American). New York: Scholastic.

Cohen, M., & Greenberg, M. H. (2003). *Down in the subway.* (Multicultural). New York: Star Bright Books.

Collier, B. (2000). *Uptown.* (African-American). New York: Henry Holt.

Cowen-Fletcher, J. (1997). *It takes a village.* (African-American). New York: Scholastic.

Crews, D. (1991). *Bigmama's.* (African-American). New York: Greenwillow.

Daly, N. (2007). *Pretty Salma: A Little Red Riding Hood Story from Africa* (African). New York: Clarion Books.

dePaolo, T. (1991). *The legend of the Indian paintbrush.* (Native American). New York: Penguin.

DeRolf, S., & Letzig, M. (1997). *The crayon box that talked.* (Multicultural). New York: Random House.

Dooley, N., & Thornton, P. J. (1992). *Everybody cooks rice.* (Multicultural). Minneapolis: Lerner.

Dorros, A. (1994). *Tonight is carnival.* (Hispanic). New York: Penguin.

Dorros, A., & Grifalconi, A. (2004). *Julio's magic.* (Hispanic). New York: Harper Collins.

Dorros, A., & Kleven, E. (1999). *Isla.* (Hispanic). New York: Penguin.

Dotlich, R. K., & Lyon, T. (2002). *A family like yours.* (Multicultural). Homesdale, PA: Boyds Mill Press.

Edwards, P. D., & Cole, H. (1998). *Barefoot: Escape on the underground railroad.* (African-American). New York: Harper-Collins.

Evans, F. W. (2008). *Hush Harbor: Praying in secret* (African American). Minneapolis: Carolrhoda Books.

Falwell, C. (1995). *Feast for 10.* (African-American). Boston: Houghton Mifflin.

Farris, C. K., & Soentpiet, C. (2005). *My brother Martin: A sister remembers growing up with the Rev. Dr. Martin Luther King.* (African-American). New York: Aladdin.

Fazio, B. L. (1996). *Grandfather's story.* (Asian-American). Seattle: Sasquatch.

Flournoy, V., & Pinkney, J. (1985). *The patchwork quilt.* (African-American). New York: Dial.

Ford, J. G., & Walker, S. (1996). *A kente dress for Kenya.* (African-American). New York: Scholastic.

Fox, M., & Staub, L. (2001). *Whoever you are.* (Multicultural). Orlando, FL: Harcourt.

Goble, P. (2001). *The girl who loved wild horses.* (Native American). New York: Atheneum/Richard Jackson Books.

Gonzalez, L. M., & Delacre, L. (1994). *The bossy gallito.* (Cuban). New York: Scholastic.

Greenfield, E., & Gilchrist, J. S. (1986). *Honey, I love.* (African-American). New York: HarperCollins.

Greenberg, P. (2002). *Oh Lord, I wish I was a buzzard.* (African-American). San Francisco: Chronicle Books.

Grimes, N., & Lewis, E. B. (2002). *Talkin' about Bessie: The story of aviator Elizabeth Coleman.* (African-American). New York: Orchard Books.

Haley, G. E. (1988). *A story, a story.* (African). New York: Aladdin.

Hamanak, S. (1999). *All the colors of the Earth.* (Multicultural). New York: Mulberry Books.

Hartfield, C., & Lagarrigue, J. (2002). *Me and Uncle Romie.* (African-American). New York: Dial.

Havill, J., & O'Brien, A. S. (1987). *Jamaica's find.* (African-American). Boston: Houghton Mifflin.

Herron, C. (1997). *Nappy hair.* (African-American). New York: Random House.

Hoffman, M., & Binch, C. (1991). *Amazing grace.* (African-American). New York: Dial.

Hooks, B., & Evans, S. W. (2002). *Homemade love.* (African-American). New York: Hyperion.

Howard, E. F., & Ransome, J. (1995). *Aunt Flossie's hats (and crab cakes later).* (African-American). Boston: Houghton Mifflin.

Hubbell, P., & Tate, D. (2003). *Black all around!* (African-American). New York: Lee & Low.

Hudson, C. W., & Ford, G. (1997). *Let's count, baby.* (African-American). New York: Cartwheel.

Hurwitz, J., & Pinkney, J. (1993). *New shoes for Silvia.* (Hispanic). New York: William Morrow.

Isadora, R. (1991). *Ben's trumpet.* (African-American). New York: William Morrow.

Isadora, R. (1994). *At the crossroads.* (African). New York: William Morrow.

Johnson, A., & Ransome, J. E. (1993). *Do like Kyla.* (African-American). New York: Scholastic.

Johnson, A., & Peck, B. (2007). *Just like Josh Gibson.* (African-American). New York: Aladdin.

Joosse, B., & Christie, R. G. (2001). *Stars in the darkness.* (African-American). San Francisco: Chronicle Books.

Joosse, B., & Lavallee, B. (1991). *Mama, do you love me?* (Native American/Alaskan). San Francisco: Chronicle Books.

Jordan, D., Jordan, R. M., & Nelson, K. (2000). *Salt in his shoes: Michael Jordan in pursuit of a dream.* (African-American). New York: Simon & Schuster Children's Publishing.

Jordan, D., Jordan, R. M., Jordan, M., & Nelson, K. (2007). *Michael's golden rules.* (African-American). New York: Paula Wiseman Books.

Katz, K. (2002). *The colors of us.* (Multicultural). New York: Henry Holt.

Keats, E. J. (1996). *The snowy day.* (African-American). New York: Viking.

Keegan, M. (1999). *Pueblo girls: Growing up in two worlds.* (Multicultural). Santa Fe, NM: Clear Light Publications.

Kerley, B. (2002). *A cool drink of water.* (Multicultural). New York: National Geographic Society.

Kimmelman, L., & Himmelman, J. (1996). *Hooray! It's Passover!* (Jewish-American). New York: HarperCollins.

King, M. L., Jr. (1999). *I have a dream.* (African-American). New York: Scholastic.

Kleven, E. (1996). *Hooray, a piñata!* (Hispanic). New York: Penguin.

Krebs, L., & Cairns, J. (2003). *We all went on safari: A counting journey through Tanzania.* (African). Cambridge, MA: Barefoot Books.

Krull, K. (2003). *Harvesting hope: The story of Cesar Chavez* (Hispanic). Orlando, FL: Harcourt Brace.

Kuklin, S. (1998). *How my family lives in America.* (Indian). New York: Simon and Schuster.

Lawrence, J. (1995). *The great migration: An American story*. (African-American). New York: HarperCollins.

Lee, S., Lee, T. L., & Nelson, K. (2006). *Please, baby, please*. (African-American). New York: Aladdin.

Leighton, M. R., & Nolan, D. (1992). *An Ellis Island Christmas*. (Immigration, Diversity). New York: Viking.

Levine, E., & Bjorkman, S. (1995). *I hate English!* (Asian-American, General). New York: Scholastic.

Levine, E., & Nelson, K. (2007). *Henry's freedom box*. (African-American). New York: Scholastic Press.

Lin, G. (2003). *Dim Sum for everyone* (Chinese American). Decorah: Dragonfly Publishing.

Manders, J. (2003). *Senor Don Gato*. (Hispanic). Cambridge, MA: Candlewick Press.

McGill, A., & Cummings, M. (2000). *In the hollow of your hand: Slave lullabies*. (African-American). Boston: Houghton Mifflin.

McKissack, P. C., & Pinkney, J. (2001). *Goin'someplace special*. (African-American). New York: Atheneum Books for Young Readers.

Medearis, A. S., & Byrd, S. (1995). *Dancing with the Indians*. (Native American). New York: Holiday House.

Miller, J. P., Greene, S. M., & Meisel, P. (2000). *We all sing with the same voice*. (Multicultural). New York: HarperCollins.

Mitchell, R. (1997). *The talking cloth*. (African-American). New York: Scholastic.

Mora, P., & Lang, C. (1994). *Pablo's tree*. (Hispanic). New York: Simon & Schuster.

Morales, Y. (2003). *Just a minute! A trickster tale and counting book*. (Hispanic). San Francisco: Chronicle Books.

Mosel, A., & Lent, B. (1995). *Tikki, tikki, tembo*. (Chinese). New York: Holt.

Myers, W. D., & Myers, C. (1996). *Harlem*. (African-American). New York: Scholastic.

Napoli, D. J. (2010). *Mama Miti*. (African-Kenyan). New York: Simon and Schuster.

Noguchi, R., Jenks, D., & Kumata, M. R. (2001). *Flowers from Mariko*. (Japanese). New York: Lee & Low.

Nolen, J., & Nelson, K. (2005). *Hewitt Anderson's great big life*. (African-American). New York: Paula Wiseman Books.

Osofsky, A., & Young, E. (1992). *Dreamcatcher*. (Native-American). New York: Scholastic.

Pelligrini, N. (1991). *Families are different*. (Korean, Multicultural). New York: Holiday House.

Pinkney, S. L., & Pinkney, M. (2000). *Shades of black: A celebration of our children*. (African-American). New York: Scholastic.

Polacco, P. (1995). *Babushka's doll*. (Russian). New York: Simon & Schuster.

Polacco, P. (1998). *Chicken Sunday*. (Multicultural). New York: Penguin.

Polacco, P. (2001). *The keeping quilt*. (Jewish-American). New York: Simon & Schuster.

Pomeranc, M. H., & Disalvo-Ryan, D. (1998). *The American wei*. (Multicultural, Immigration). New York: Albert Whitman.

Reich, S., & Colon, R. (2005). *Jose! Born to dance: The story of Jose Limon*. (Hispanic). New York: Paula Wiseman Books.

Riehecky, J., & Stasiak, K. (1994). *Cinco de Mayo*. (Hispanic). New York: Scholastic.

Ringgold, F. (1992). *Aunt Harriet's underground railroad in the sky*. (African-American). New York: Crown.

Ringgold, F. (1996). *Bonjour, Lonnie*. (African-American). New York: Hyperion.

Ringgold, F. (1996). *Tar beach*. (African-American). New York: Dell.

Ringgold, F. (1999). *If a bus could talk: The story of Rosa Parks*. (African-American). New York: Simon & Schuster.

Robbins, R., & Sidjakov, N. (1986). *Baboushka and the Three Kings*. (Russian). Wilmington: Houghton Mifflin.

Robles, A., & Angel, C. (2003). *Lakas and the Manilatown fish*. (Filipino). Berkeley, CA: Children's Book Press.

Rosa-Casanova, S., & Roth, R. (1997). *Mama Provi and the pot of rice*. (Diversity). New York: Simon & Schuster.

Rosen, M. J., & Robinson, A. B. L. (1997). *Elijah's angel: A story for Chanukah and Christmas*. (Jewish, General). Orlando, FL: Harcourt.

Ryan, P. M., & Selznick, B. (2002). *When Marian sang: The true recital of Marian Anderson*. (African-American). New York: Scholastic Press.

Say, A. (1993). *Grandfather's journey* (Asian-American). Boston: Houghton-Mifflin.

Say, A. (1996). *El Chino*. (Hispanic). Boston: Houghton Mifflin.

Seeger, P., & Hays, M. (1994). *Abiyoyo*. (African). New York: Simon & Schuster.

Siegelson, K. L., & Pinkney, B. (1999). *In the time of the drums*. (African). New York: Jump at the Sun/ Hyperion Books for Children.

Simon, N., & Flavin, T. (2003). *All families are special*. (Multicultural). New York: Whitman.

Smalls, I., & Hays, M. (1994). *Jonathan and his mommy.* (African-American). New York: Little, Brown & Company.

Smith, W., & Nelson, K. (2005). *Just the two of us.* (African-American). New York: Scholastic.

Soto, G. (1998). *Snapshots from the wedding.* (Mexican-American, Hispanic). New York: Penguin.

Soto, G., & Guevara, S. (2000). *Chato and the party animals.* (Hispanic). New York: Putnam.

Soto, G., & Martinez, E. (1996). *Too many tamales.* (Hispanic). New York: Penguin.

Starr, M., Hu, Y., & Van Wright, C. (2001). *Alicia's happy day.* (Hispanic). New York: Bright Books.

Steptoe, J. (1987). *Mufaro's beautiful daughters.* (African). New York: William Morrow.

Stutson, C., & Lamb, S. C. (1996). *Prairie primer A to Z.* (Americana). New York: Penguin.

Stuve-Bodeen, S., & Boyd, A. (2003). *Babu's song.* (African). New York: Lee & Low.

Surat, M. M., & Mai, V. D. (1990). *Angel child, dragon child.* (Vietnamese). New York: Scholastic.

Suyenaga, R., & Miyaki, Y. (1993). *Obon.* (Japanese-American). Lebanon, IN: Curriculum Press.

Swamp, Chief Jake, & Printup, E., Jr. (1997). *Giving thanks: A Native American good morning message.* (Native American). New York: Lee & Low.

Swartz, L. A., & Chwast, J. (1994). *A first Passover.* (Jewish-American). New York: Simon & Schuster.

Tarpley, N. A., & Lewis, E. B. (2001). *I love my hair!* (African-American). New York: Little, Brown & Co.

Thomas, S. M., & Futran, E. (2002). *Somewhere today: A book of peace.* (Multicultural, General). New York: Whitman.

Tomioka, C. (1992). *Rise and shine Mariko-Chan!* (Japanese). New York: Scholastic.

Tyler, M. (2005). *The Skin You Live In.* (Multicultural). Chicago: Chicago Children's Museum.

Uchida, U. (1996). *The bracelet.* (Asian-American). New York: Penguin.

Udry, J. M., & Sayles, E. (1991). *What Mary Jo shared.* (African-American). New York: Scholastic.

Wallace, I. (1984). *Chin Chiang and the dragon's dance.* (Chinese). New York: Simon & Schuster.

Wells, R. (1998). *Yoko.* (Japanese). New York: Hyperion.

Williams, K. L., & Cooper, F. (1994). *When Africa was home.* (African-American). New York: Scholastic.

Williams, V. B. (1991). *Cherries and cherry pits.* (African-American). New York: William Morrow & Co.

Williams, V. B. (1996). *"More, more, more," said the baby.* (Multicultural). New York: Willam Morrow & Co.

Winter, J. (2005). *The librarian of Basra: A true story from Iraq.* (Iraqi). Fort Worth: Harcourt Children's Books.

Winter, J., & Juan, A. (2002). *Frida.* (Hispanic). New York: Arthur A. Levine Books.

Wood, D., & Desimini, L. (1996). *Northwoods cradle song: From a Menominee lullaby.* (Native American). New York: Simon & Schuster.

Yarbrough, C., & Byard, C. (1979). *Cornrows.* (African-American). New York: Coward, McCann & Geoghegan.

Young, E. (1996). *Lon Po Po: A Red-Riding Hood story from China.* (Chinese). New York: Putnam Juvenile.

Zamarano, A., & Vivas, J. (1999). *Let's eat!* (Spanish). New York: Scholastic.

Glossary of Key Terms

1/3, 1/3, 1/3 Rule—a general guideline that encourages curriculum development to include equal amounts of large-group, small-group, and independent activities for learning.

Abstract—an artistic style in which artists experiment with color and the physical properties of paint.

aesthetic attitude—an openness or spontaneity to objects and experiences.

aesthetic process/experience—active engagement with all the senses.

aesthetic response—an appreciative reaction.

aesthetic value—the result of a positive response from a person or group of people toward something.

aesthetics—a group of concepts for understanding the nature of art.

aggregate—formed when three or more diagrams are united together.

anecdote—a shortened and more focused version of the diary used in child observation.

antibias—a belief in equality that condemns prejudice, exclusion, discrimination, or preferential treatment.

art center—a classroom area where children go to do art.

art critique—teacher facilitates an aesthetic and verbal encounter between children and a work of art.

art dialogue—verbal interactions that teachers have with children concerning their art.

art dictation—a strategy that involves listening to what children have to say about their art and then neatly printing their words on paper.

art files—a sampling or collection of an individual child's artwork.

art folders—devices for storing a child's file or collection of art.

art group time—large-group time when children come together to show and discuss their artistic accomplishments.

Art Idea Book—a collection of interesting pictures that serves as an inspiration for possible art subject matter.

art kiosk—a self-standing structure with three or more sides that can be used to display art.

art postcards—postcards of art reproductions used in learning games.

art specialists—one who knows about art, artists, artistic elements, and developmentally appropriate art activities.

art standards—a set of art competencies for K–12 students.

art therapy—the psychotherapeutic use of art for emotional understanding and healing.

artistic decision—time during adolescence when natural artistic development ceases unless children are given further instruction.

artistic elements—criteria used to analyze, appreciate, and judge the visual arts. Artistic elements are also the building blocks of art and can be used to talk with children about their art.

arts—literature, drama, music, dance, and the visual arts.

assemblage—three-dimensional collage.

assessment—an ongoing process of documenting and recording a child's development, not to be limited to testing or equated with evaluation.

assessor—one who conducts an assessment, usually a teacher or parent. Assessment is an ongoing process of documenting and recording a child's development, not to be limited to testing or equated with evaluation.

asymmetrical (informal)—informal balance in which the objects are unevenly or unequally balanced.

atelierista—Italian for art teacher.

auditory—the sense involving hearing and listening. Auditory also refers to a learning style in which the learner learns best through speaking and listening.

balance—the result of how space is used.

baric—the sense of weight.

beliefs—principles held to be true.

bias—an attitude, belief, or feeling that results in and helps to justify unfair treatment of one's identity.

bitmapping—a system used to display drawn images on the computer screen in a painting program; a system that allows images to be moved on the screen and/or parts of images to be erased.

bodily-kinesthetic—a way of demonstrating one's intelligence through the use and control of one's bodily movements.

brain research—a line of study documenting that early experiences have a decisive impact on the architecture of the brain and on the nature and extent of adult capacities.

central processing unit (CPU)—the main part of a computer that does all the "thinking" and processes the data and information.

checklists—an observational strategy in which developmental items are identified and the observer merely indicates or checks off which items are present or absent.

child-centered—an approach to art that is unstructured and gives children much input and many choices as to how and what to make.

chromatic—the sense that allows one to identify, match, and discriminate among colors.

clay—natural substance from the earth that can be molded, sculpted, and fired in a kiln.

closed-ended—a term referring to items or questions that are conducive to conformity.

closed-ended question—a type of question in which there is one right answer.

cognitive—an explanation for artistic development that asserts that the content and style of children's art is indicative of their level of intelligence and function of conceptualization.

cognitive developmental—an explanation for child development that incorporates the best of cognitive and general developmental theories.

collage—artwork composed of different shapes or elements.

color—the visual sensation of light caused by stimulating the cones of the retina.

combine(s)—the result of two diagrams united.

complementary—colors opposite each other on the color wheel.

complimentary approach—an approach that praises children's artwork.

composition—the overall mark of success or the standard of achievement in artistic creation.

concrete operations—Piaget's third stage of cognitive development in which thinking is bound to the concrete and cannot engage in abstract thinking.

constructive play—a type of play involving building with blocks.

constructivism—a view of development based on the belief that children construct or build knowledge based on their actions with objects and their interactions with peers and adults.

constructivist education—a model of schooling based on constructivism.

content—the subject matter of a work of art.

convergent (noncreative) thinking—noncreative thinking based on coming up with the one right answer.

convergent production—coming up with the one right answer.

cool—colors including blue, green, and purple/violet, which symbolize cold or cool objects.

cooperative learning—working together when children practice language and social skills while working toward a common end.

correcting approach—an approach that attempts to correct or improve children's art.

crafts—a teacher-directed activity involving the assemblage of materials for a predetermined product.

creative movement—a type of movement that encourages children to move as they see fit, as opposed to following or imitating a teacher.

creativity—the ability to see things in new ways or combine unrelated things into something new.

critical thinking—thinking that requires making decisions and judgments.

Cubism—an artistic style in which artists attempt to break their subject matter down into its component geometric or architectural shapes.

cultural differences—those qualities and practices that people use to define themselves as a cultural group.

cultural diversity—recognizing and accepting the influence of many cultures on society.

cultural elements—language, religion, dress, social customs, and other things that define one's culture.

cultural pluralism—a view that groups should be allowed, even encouraged, to hold on to what gives them their unique identity while maintaining membership in the larger society.

culture—the attitudes, values, beliefs, customs, norms, traditions, and social habits shared by a particular group of people.

curriculum—educational program, activity, set of activities, or guidelines.

curriculum development—the process of planning activities for children on the spontaneous, short-term, and long-term basis.

curriculum standards—an outline of the content that is to be taught in each content area at each grade level.

dawning realism—the age during which young adolescents show a greater awareness of details in their art.

design (composition)—the overall mark of success or the standard of achievement in artistic creation.

developmentally appropriate—an activity that takes into account a child's developmental abilities, background, and individual interests.

diagrams—shapes drawn as single outline forms.

diary—a journal or ongoing account of what a child says and does.

differently abled—having a range of physical and/or cognitive abilities that may differ from the norm.

disability—a loss or reduction of functional ability that results from an impairment.

discipline-based art education (DBAE)—a comprehensive approach to instruction and learning in art developed primarily for K–12 students.

dispositions—inclinations or habits of the mind.

divergent production—the generation of multiple responses.

diversity—an umbrella term for differences that celebrates individual uniqueness.

docent—a knowledgeable individual who shows and provides background information on displays of artwork or artifacts for visitors.

dramatic play—a type of play involving fantasy, imagination, or make-believe.

drawing program—a program that uses an object-oriented system to display drawn images on the computer screen.

Draw-a-Person test—a nonverbal measure of intelligence based on the drawing of a human figure.

drawing tablet—a computer screen on which the user creates bitmapped images using a stylus or mouse.

drill-and-practice software—software that presents the user with an activity or question for which there is only one correct response; if the user does not choose the correct response, the software presents a series of tasks that will teach the user the correct response.

elaboration—a term characterizing thinking that is detailed.

emergent curriculum—activities that spontaneously emerge or arise as a result of children's ongoing interest in and exploration of their world.

emotional—an explanation for the development of child art that stresses that the content and style of children's art is indicative of their emotional makeup, personality, temperament, and affective state.

evaluation—the process of collecting data to make judgments that help determine whether one has successfully met one's goals and objectives.

event sampling—an observational strategy in which the observer specifies the behaviors under study and then notes when it occurs.

Expressionism—an artistic style based on an expression of the artist's emotions and feelings.

expressive arts—art, music, and movement.

Fauvism—an offshoot of Expressionism. Fauvists experimented with pure, bright colors in daring and innovative ways to express emotions.

feelings—emotions associated with a learning experience.

field trips—opportunities for children to use all their senses and gain concrete experience with people, events, and places in their local community.

flexibility—a term characterizing thinking that generates different ideas that cross categories or break boundaries.

fluency—a term characterizing thinking that generates many ideas and solutions.

folk arts—the expressions of members of a cultural group that are produced by individuals for the use of their group members and are made by hand rather than mass produced.

formal operations—Piaget's fourth stage of child development during which adolescents engage in abstract thinking.

formalized standardized testing—paper-and-pencil assessment with individual scores compared to a norm.

framing—providing a frame to "finish" a work of art.

full inclusion—an approach in which children with disabilities are placed in the same programs or classrooms and receive individualized and appropriate services alongside their nondisabled peers.

games—a type of rule-based play engaged in by older children.

general developmental—a global explanation for the development of child art that incorporates social, cultural, personality, and environmental factors as well as elements of other explanations.

gifts—Froebelian manipulatives designed to decrease in size and increase in intricacy as children develop skills and understanding.

gifted/gifted and talented—children of high intelligence who also demonstrate high creativity receive this label.

goal—something to strive for; a long-term aspiration.

group projects—educational activities based on children's common interests in which they can interact, support, assist, and learn from each other.

gustatory—the sense of taste.

handicap—the disadvantage caused by a disability.

holistic model of child development—a model of child development that integrates the physical, social, emotional, cognitive, and creative aspects.

hue—the name of a color.

impairment—an anatomic or functional abnormality or loss that may or may not result in a disability.

implementing—the process of carrying out an idea or putting a plan into action.

Impressionism—an artistic style in which artists painted what they perceived rather than what they knew to be there.

inclusion—services are brought into the regular classroom to support children with special needs so that the children can learn and develop with typically functioning peers and the general education teacher.

independence/independent—a cultural style in which individuality is valued.

independent activities—curriculum activities in which children participate individually, without peers or teachers.

individual differences—background, family, and individual variation.

ink—an opaque liquid medium usually in black with other colors available.

intellectual mediators—adults who are readily available to facilitate a child's learning.

intensity—the purity of light, for example, bright or dull, reflected from a surface.

intentional teacher—a teacher who understands how children develop and learn and uses this knowledge to make deliberate decision about curriculum, learning environment, and behavior guidance.

interdependence/interdependent—a cultural style in which family togetherness and group belongingness are valued.

intermediate—the result of mixing an adjoining primary and secondary color in equal amounts.

interpersonal—intelligence is demonstrated through personal interactions with others.

intrapersonal—intelligence is demonstrated through knowing oneself.

intrinsic motivation—doing something for the sheer pleasure in doing it and in the absence of some extraneous reward.

judgmental approach—an approach that judges children's art.

kinesthetic—the sense involving a whole-body, sensory-motor muscular response.

Kinetic art—an attempt to incorporate physical movement into art by using movable parts.

knowledge—information children construct through hands-on, multisensory experiences and exploration.

large-group activities—curriculum activities designed to include all children in the classroom.

lateral thinking—a way of using one's mind or mental processes that leads to creative thinking or products.

least restrictive environment—a setting that is appropriate for the child and provides the most contact possible with nondisabled children.

left hemisphere—the hemisphere of the brain housing the thinking abilities traditionally associated with school, for example, reading, writing, and math.

line—visible mark made by an artistic tool.

literate—knowing how to read and write (*literacy* is the state of being literate; *literate* means knowing how to read and write).

logical-mathematical—being good at math, logical and abstract thinking, and problem solving characterizes this intelligence.

logical-mathematical knowledge—information that is constructed around the relationship of objects to each other.

LOGO®—a computer programming language designed for functional programming by children and using turtle graphics.

mainstreaming—the placement of children with disabilities in programs having a majority of children who are not disabled.

mandala—a basic diagram and universal symbol consisting of a cross within a circle.

mandaloids—figures and objects drawn using mandalas.

mark making—a term referring to the variety of artistic marks that young children make using crayons, markers, chalk, pencils, and so on.

masks—decorated items worn over or held in front of the face to hide or disguise one's identity.

mass—refers to a solid, three-dimensional body that has height, length, and width.

matting—providing an attractive border for a piece of art.

media literacy—competence in reading, analyzing, evaluating, and producing communications in a variety of media including electronic.

mixing media—combining or using more than one medium when making art.

mobile—hanging sculpture that moves.

model—an older, wiser person from whom a less experienced person learns by watching and imitating.

modes of creative expression—ways of expressing one's creativity including play, language, music, and movement.

motive—the underlying reason or purpose.

multicultural arts and crafts—providing children with activities that attempt to authentically capture the arts and crafts representing a particular culture.

multiple intelligences—a construct reflecting the belief that intelligence is not a single concept but that there are many ways of demonstrating one's intelligence. Gardner has identified eight multiple intelligences to date.

multimedia authoring tools—software used to create interactive multimedia presentations that can include text, graphics, video, audio, and animation.

multiple literacies—many ways of being considered literate and competent.

multisensory experience—an activity or experience involving many of the senses.

musical-rhythmic—demonstrating one's intelligence through singing, dancing, and making music.

narratives—a record of what an observer sees children do and hears them say.

National Standards for the Arts—the standards that address competence in the arts, in addition to providing a firm foundation for connecting arts-related concepts and facts across all art forms as well as across disciplines such as the sciences and humanities.

naturalism—a term that emphasizes the artist's attempt to make art objective and like the actual object.

naturalistic—an understanding of nature and natural phenomena characterizes this intelligence.

negative space—the space left between or surrounding subject matter, symbols, or shapes.

neutral—pigments, including black and white, that do not have a particular color.

nonobjective art—abstract art pushed to the limits with no resemblance to the actual object.

non-Western art—art from non-European cultures.

objectives—the short-term bridge between long-term goals and activities.

observer—one who skillfully and unobtrusively watches children to learn more about them.

occupations—planned experiences in a Froebelian kindergarten designed to help children synthesize manipulative skills and begin to use them for creative expression.

olfactory—the sense of smell.

op art (Optical art)—an artistic style in which artists created "psychedelic" art by playing with the effects of black and white, color, figure-background relations, and depth.

open-ended—a term referring to items or questions that are conducive to creative expression.

open-ended question—a type of question in which there is no one right answer.

open-ended software—software that allows the user to create and respond to open-ended challenges, enhancing knowledge construction.

originality—a term characterizing thinking that is unique and unusual.

painting—the process of applying paint to a surface using a hand, brush, or other tool.

painting programs—uses a bitmapping system to display images on the computer screen; lines and shapes may be edited in part or in total with an eraser tool.

papier-mâché—process of building up layers of paper that has been torn, wadded, and molded to make a three-dimensional form.

participant—the teacher's role as he/she participates in the classroom activities of the children.

participator—one who partakes or becomes involved in the activities of another.

pattern—a mark or design that is repeated in some recurring sequence.

perception—the ability to receive sensory impressions from one's surroundings and relate them to what one knows.

perceptual—an explanation for the development of child art that stresses that the content and style of children's art reflect what they perceive rather than what they see.

physical—an explanation for the development of child art that stresses that the content, process, product, and style of children's art are indicative of their limited physical development.

physical knowledge—information about the physical properties of objects.

physical play—a type of play involving motor activity and movement.

pictorial art—the beginnings of an artistic stage in which objects drawn or painted become visually recognizable to adults.

pictorial stage—when children create objects that adults can recognize.

PIE—the cycle of curriculum development including planning, implementation, and evaluation.

pixels—tiny units of color from which digital photos are composed.

planning—the proactive process of determining what and how to teach.

play—the freely chosen, process-oriented activities of children through which learning occurs most effectively.

play dough—a soft, clay-type molding medium that is commercially available or can be made with common cooking ingredients.

play therapy—a dynamic interpersonal relationship between a child and a counselor who provides selected play materials with which the child can fully express and explore self through play.

play with natural materials—play involving water, sand, or wood.

Pointillism—an artistic style in which artists painted using small dots or points of color.

Pop art (Popular art)—an artistic style in which artists chose subject matters that were part of everyday life.

portfolio—a comprehensive collection of a child's work including samples and observational data.

positive space—the space taken up with lines, colors, shapes, and forms.

pre-operational stage—Piaget's second stage of child development, during which the child attains representation and thinks in ways that are qualitatively different from adult logic or reason.

primary—red, blue, and yellow; the colors used to produce the other colors.

prints—the artistic process of making a print in which paint is applied to an object and then pressed onto paper. When the object is lifted, a print results.

private speech—internalized self-talk that helps with self-guidance and self-direction in Vygotsky's sociocultural theory.

probing approach—an approach that attempts to draw from children information about their art.

process—the act of doing or being involved in an activity.

process vs. product—a comparison of the relative values of the acts associated with artistic creation and the finished products of artistic creation.

processing—discovering the physical properties of art materials and tools.

product—the tangible or finished result of processing.

project—a teacher-directed activity requiring specific steps to yield a predetermined product.

project approach—a curriculum approach in which children are actively involved in developing long-term research-type activities into areas of personal interest.

Project Zero—Gardner's approach to art education in the early years.

proximodistal development—physical development that begins at the center of the body and proceeds outward.

pseudo-naturalistic—the stage when the art of young adolescents becomes realistic.

puppets—often three-dimensional props representing people, animals, or objects.

questioning approach—an approach that questions children about their art.

rating scales—an observational strategy in which developmental items are identified and the observer makes a judgment regarding the degree to which the item is observed in the child.

Realism—a term that emphasizes the artist's attempt to make art objective and like the actual object.

recorder—one who writes down their observations of children.

Reggio Emilia—schools found in Italy with a distinct and creative curriculum.

resist—a type of art activity in which a dried design or picture will resist a second liquid put on top of it.

right hemisphere—the hemisphere of the brain specializing in creative ways of processing information.

scaffolding—a strategy for a teacher working within a child's zone of proximal development to offer the appropriate level of support, assistance, questioning, or challenge.

schematic—the third stage according to Lowenfeld and Brittain when school-aged children achieve a form concept.

screen time—the collective time children spend engaging with various technology devices, including televisions, computers, DVD players, smart phones, and tablet devices.

scribbles—random marks made on paper by a young child using some type of writing instrument that leaves a mark when pressure is applied. In Kellogg's stages of artistic development, there are some 20 basic scribble patterns that comprise the first stage.

secondary—result of mixing two primary colors in equal amounts.

self-assessment—the process through which the child establishes criteria for assessment of a product or a learning process and then judges his/her own efforts.

self-talk—talking aloud, which Vygotsky sees as connected to what children are thinking.

sensory literacy—using all the senses to become aware of one's surroundings and experiences.

sensory-motor stage—Piaget's first stage of child development during which infant thinking is limited to sensory impressions and motoric behavior.

sensory table—a large container filled with sensory-rich objects for children to explore.

serendipity—making unexpected discoveries while searching for something else.

sewing—an art process that uses needle, thread, or yarn.

shade—the result of adding black to any color (refers to the outside form of an object).

shape—refers to the outside form of a two-dimensional object that has length and width.

simulation software—software that allows the user to experience a computer-based model of a real-life situation.

skills—abilities or techniques that build on and apply knowledge.

small-group activities—curriculum activities designed for groups of three to five children to complete cooperatively with minimal teacher intervention.

social-conventional knowledge—information about daily living accepted by society.

sociocultural theory—Vygotsky's theory based on the beliefs that learning can lead development and that language plays a major role in cognitive development.

socio-dramatic play—an advanced form of dramatic play that revolves around a theme with children engaging in theme-based behaviors.

software—educational programs that are run on the computer.

space—the total area defined by the size of the artist's paper or canvas.

special needs—children who are different in one or more of the areas of visual, auditory, physical, emotional, and/or cognitive functioning.

stabile—self-standing, stationary mobile.

standardized achievement testing—the use of tests that compare children's scores and thereby are a formal, less authentic way to assess what children know and can do.

sterognostic—the sense that allows one to recognize objects through tactile-muscular exploration without the aid of vision.

story songs—stories and books based on songs with a strong rhythmic component.

structure of the intellect—a construct viewing the intellect as consisting of three dimensions: contents, products, and operations.

studio-oriented—an approach that holds that young children should be left free to experiment with creative materials.

sun figures—human figures drawn using lines and circles.

Surrealism—or Dadaism, is an artistic style in which artists attempt to create a dreamlike world that is more intense than reality.

symmetrical (formal)—balance in which the shapes are evenly or equally balanced around some point.

synergistic—combining existing elements in new ways to create something greater than the sum of the individual elements.

tactile—the sense involving feeling and touch.

tactile-kinesthetic—a learning style in which learners use their hands and bodies to process and understand.

teachable moments—unplanned events that trigger high-interest activity and learning.

teacher-directed—an approach to art in which projects are structured and specific directions are given to ensure a recognizable product.

teacher-guided—a compromise between a teacher-directed and child-centered approach to art.

teaching style—way of teaching that is influenced by individual learning styles.

telephoto—a camera feature that allows close-up shots of distant objects.

texture—the surface quality of a work of art; how it feels.

theories of artistic development—explanations for what, why, and how children create.

thermal qualities—use of certain colors conveys a sense of warmth, coolness, or the illusion of size and space.

thermic—the sense of temperature.

three-dimensional art—art with height, width, and depth.

time sampling—an observation strategy used to measure the frequency of behavior with a given period of time.

tint—the result of adding white to any color.

tourist curriculum—multicultural experiences that are limited to a celebration of holidays.

troubleshooter—a role in which teachers provide encouragement and assistance to children who are artistically or creatively blocked.

types of knowledge—according to Piaget, there are three different types of knowledge: physical, social-conventional, and logical-mathematical.

types of learning—knowledge, skills, dispositions, and feelings.

U-shaped curve—a graphic representation of Gardner's belief that some important aspects of artistry emerge early in a child's life only to go underground during a period of middle childhood.

value—the relative lightness or darkness of a hue.

values—things that are important, valuable, worthwhile, or significant to an individual.

valuing approach—an approach that offers children value-laden comments.

verbal-linguistic—being skilled in using words defines this intelligence.

vertical thinking—learning more about something or arriving at a conventional, accepted, convergent answer.

visual—the sense involving looking and seeing. Visual also refers to a learning style in which children learn best using pictures and visual images.

visual literacy—the ability to understand and produce visual messages.

visual-spatial—the use of pictures, such as art and maps, characterizes this intelligence.

volume—a term that refers to a solid, three-dimensional body that has height, length, and width.

warm—colors including red, yellow, and orange that symbolize hot or warm objects.

watercolors—transparent color that comes in cake or liquid form.

weaving—a fabric art that involves a patterned in–out or over–under motion, which is repeated in the alternating out–in or under–over pattern.

whole-group activities—learning activities in which all children in the class fully participate.

wide angle—a camera feature that allows distance shots of objects close to the photographer.

zone of proximal development (ZPD)—a range of skills, tasks, or abilities that a child cannot yet do alone but can accomplish with assistance from an adult or skilled peer.

References

Alexander, J. (1995, June 11). We need arts in our schools' lives, says NEA chief. *San Jose Mercury News*, A9.

Allen, K. E., & Cowdery, G. E. (2009). *The exceptional child: Inclusion in early childhood education* (6th ed.). Clifton Park, NY: Thomson Delmar Learning.

Allen, K. E., & Marotz, L. R. (2010). *Developmental profiles* (6th ed.). Belmont, CA: Wadsworth Cengage Learning.

Alliance for Childhood. (2000). *Fool's gold: A critical look at computers in childhood.* College Park, MD: Alliance for Childhood.

Althouse, R., Johnson, M. H., & Mitchell, S. T. (2003). *The colors of learning: Integrating the visual arts into the early childhood curriculum.* New York: Teachers College Press.

American Academy of Pediatrics. (2001). Children, adolescents, and television. *Pediatrics.* (*107*), 423–426.

Ancona, G. (1994a). *The piñata maker.* San Diego: Harcourt Brace.

Ancona, G. (1994b). *Ricardo's day.* (Hispanic). New York: Scholastic.

Anderson, G. T. (2000). *An empirical comparison of the proportion of cooperative play of 4-year-old preschool children observed as they interact in four centers: Block, computer, housekeeping, and manipulative.* Atlanta: National Association for the Education of Young Children.

Anderson, J. S. (1997). *Sunflower Sal.* Morton Grove, IL: Albert Whitman.

Anderson, R., Manoogian, S. T., & Reznick, J. S. (1976). The undermining and enhancing of intrinsic motivation in preschool children. *Journal of Personality and Social Psychology, 34*, 915–922.

Anholt, L. (1998). *Picasso and the girl with a ponytail.* Hauppauge, NY: Barron's Educational Series.

Arnheim, R. (1973). Child art and visual thinking. In H. P. Lewis (Ed.), *Child art: The beginnings of self-affirmation* (pp. 46–72). Berkeley, CA: Diablo Press.

Aramowicz, J. (2008). *Art, Music Stimulates Brain, Helps with Cognitive Development.* Online at www.kstatecollegian.com/opinion/art-music-stimulates-brain-help-withcognitive-development-1.2657973. Accessed on 26 April 2012.

Ashley, B. (1992). *Cleversticks.* New York: Crown.

Association for Play Therapy (1997). Play therapy definition. Retrieved from http://www.a4pt.org/ps.playtherapy.cfm?ID=1653 on July 29, 2012.

Backstein, K. (1992). *The blind men and the elephant.* New York: Scholastic.

Baker, P. M., Hunter-McGrath, P., Topal, C. W., & Monaco, L. (2005). Voices from the studio. In L. Gandini, L. Hill, L. Cadwell, & C. Schwall (Eds.), *In the spirit of the studio: Learning from the Ateliers of Reggio Emilio* (pp. 107–132). New York: Teachers' College Press.

Balke, E. (1997). Play and the arts: The importance of the "unimportant." *Childhood Education, 73*, 355–360.

Bang, M. (1999). *When Sophie gets angry—Really, really angry.* New York: Scholastic.

Bang, M. (1996). *Ten, nine, eight.* (African-American). New York: Grenwillow.

Bang, M. (1993). *Yellow ball.* New York: Penguin.

Baumrind, D. (1966). Effects of authoritative parental control on child behavior. *Child Development, 37*, 887–907.

Berk, L. E. (1994). Vygotsky's theory: The importance of make-believe. *Young Children*, 30–39.

Berk, L. E. (1996). *Infants, children and adolescents* (2nd ed.). Boston: Allyn & Bacon.

Berk, L. E., & Winsler, A. (1995). *Scaffolding children's learning: Vygotsky and early childhood education.* Washington, DC: NAEYC.

Bittman, M., Rutherford, L., Brown, J., & Unsworth, L. (2011). Digital natives? New and old media and children's outcomes. *Australian Journal of Education, 55*(2), 161–175.

Blanckensee, L. V. (1999). *Technology tools for young learners.* Larchmont, NV: Eye on Education, Inc.

Blizzard, G. S. (1991). *Come look with me, enjoying art with children.* Charlottesville, VA: Thomasson-Grant.

Bodrova, E., & Leong, D. J. (1996). *Tools of the mind: The Vygotskian approach to early childhood education.* Columbus, OH: Merrill.

Bornstein, R. L. (1997). *That's how it is when we draw.* New York: Houghton Mifflin.

Boutan, M. (Ed.). (1996). *Art activity packs: Matisse.* San Francisco: Chronicle Books.

Bredekamp, S. (1993). Reflections on Reggio Emilia. *Young Children, 49,* 13–17.

Bredekamp, S. (2011). *Effective practices in early childhood education: Building a foundation.* Boston: Pearson.

Bredekamp, S., & Copple, C. (1997). *Developmentally appropriate practice in early childhood programs* (rev. ed.). Washington, DC: NAEYC.

Brill, M. (1998). *Tooth tales from around the world.* Watertown, MA: Charlesbridge.

Brittain, W. L. (1969). Some exploratory studies of the art of preschool children. *Studies in Art Education, 10,* 14–24.

Brittain, W. L. (1979). *Creativity, art, and the young child.* New York: Macmillan.

Brooks, M. (2009a). Drawing, visualization & young children's explorations of "big idea." *International Journals of Science Education, 31*(3), 319–341.

Brooks, M. (2009b). What Vygotsky can teach us about young children's drawing. *International Art in Early Childhood Research Journal, 1*(1), 1–13.

Brookes, M. (1986). *Drawing with children.* Los Angeles: J. P. Tarcher.

Brosterman, N. (1997). *Inventing kindergarten.* New York: Harry N. Abrams. Brown, M. (1947). *Stone soup.* New York: Aladdin.

Brown, T. (2005). *Someone special, just like you.* New York: Holt.

Brusca, M. (1991). *On the Pampas.* New York: Holt.

Bryan, A. (1995). *What a wonderful world.* New York: Atheneum.

Bunnett, R. (1996). *Friends at school.* New York: Star Bright Books.

Bunting, E. (1998). *How many days to America: A Thanksgiving story.* New York: Clarion.

Burningham, J. (2003). *Colors.* Cambridge, MA: Candlewick.

Burns, M. (1995). *The greedy triangle.* New York: Scholastic.

Buton, L., & Kuroda, K. (1981). *Artsplay.* Reading, MA: Addison-Wesley.

Byrnes, J., & Wasik, B. A. (2009). Picture this: Using photography as a learning tool in early childhood classrooms. *Childhood Education, 85*(4), 243–248.

Cabrera, J. (2000). *Over in the meadow.* New York: Holiday House.

Carle, E. (1973). *I see a song.* New York: Thomas Y. Crowell.

Carle, E. (1982). *Let's paint a rainbow.* New York: Scholastic Books.

Carle, E. (1990). *Pancakes, pancakes.* New York: Aladdin.

Carle, E. (2001). *Hello, red fox.* New York: Simon & Schuster.

Carmichael, K. D. (2006). *Play therapy: An introduction.* Upper Saddle River, NJ: Merrill.

Carmichael, M. (2007). Stronger, faster, smarter. *Newsweek.* Retrieved January 25, 2010, from www.msnbc.msn.com/

Chaille, C., & Britain, L. (2003). *The young child as scientist.* Boston: Allyn & Bacon.

Chapman, L. H. (1978). *Approaches to art in education.* New York: Harcourt Brace Jovanovich.

Chard, S. C. (1997). *The project approach: Making curriculum come alive and managing successful projects.* New York: Scholastic.

Charlesworth, R. (2004) *Understanding child development* (6th ed.). Clifton Park, NY: Thomson Delmar Learning.

Chase, A. E. (1962). *Famous paintings: An introduction to art.* New York: Platt & Monk.

Chenfeld, M. B. (1983). *Creative activities for young children.* New York: Harcourt Brace Jovanovich.

Chernoff, G. T. (1974). *Clay-dough play-dough.* New York: Scholastic Book Services.

Cherry, C. (1990). *Creative art for the developing child* (2nd ed.). Belmont, CA: Fearon.

Cherry, C., & Nielsen, D. M. (Ed.). (1999). *Creative art for the developing child.* New York: McGraw-Hill.

Chocolate, D. M. N. (1996). *A very special Kwanzaa.* New York: Scholastic.

Chocolate, D. M. N. (1997). *Kente colors.* New York: Walker.

Christie, J. F., & Johnson, E. P. (1987). Reconceptualizing constructive play: A review of the empirical literature. *Merrill Palmer Quarterly, 33*(4), 439–452.

Clemens, S. G. (1991). Art in the classroom: Making every day special. *Young Children, 46,* 4–11.

Clements, D. H. (1994). The uniqueness of the computer as a learning tool: Insights from research and practice. In J. L. Wright and D. D. Shade (Eds.), *Young children: Active learners in a technological age.* Washington, DC: National Association for the Education of Young Children.

Clements, D. H., & Nastasi, B. K. (1995). Computers and early childhood education. In M. Gettinger, S. N. Elliott, & T. R. Kratochwill (Eds.), *Advances in school psychology: Preschool and early childhood treatment directions* (pp. 187–246). Hillsdale, NJ: Lawrence Erlbaum Associates.

Clements, D. H., & Sarama, J. (1998). *Building blocks: Foundations for mathematical thinking, pre-kindergarten to Grade 2: Researched based materials development. National Science Foundation, grant number ESI-9730804.* Buffalo, NY: State University of New York at Buffalo. Retrieved from http://www.gse.buffalo.edu/org/buildingblocks/

Clements, D. H., & Sarama, J. (2002). The role of technology in early childhood learning. *Teaching Children Mathematics, 8*(16), 340–343.

Cohen, M. (1980). *No good in art.* New York: Greenwillow.

Colbert, C., & Taunton, M. (1992). *Developmentally appropriate practices for the visual arts education of young children.* (NAEA Briefing Paper). Reston, VA: National Arts Education Association.

Cole, E., & Schaefer, C. (1990). Can young children be art critics? *Young Children, 45,* 33–38.

Coles, R. (1992). *Their eyes meeting the world: The drawings and paintings of children.* Boston: Houghton Mifflin.

Consortium of National Arts Education Associations. (1994). *National standards for arts education. Dance, music, theatre, visual arts: What every young American should know and be able to do in the arts.* Music Educators National Conference, Reston, VA.

Cook, R. E., & Armbruster, V. B. (1983). *Adapting early childhood curriculum.* St. Louis, MO: Mosby.

Cooper, E. (1997). *Country fair.* New York: Greenwillow.

Copple, C., & Bredekamp, S. (Eds). (2009). *Developmentally appropriate practice in early childhood programs serving children from birth through age 8.* (3rd Ed.). Washington, DC: NAEYC.

Couse, L. J., & Chen, D. W. (2010). A tablet computer for young children? Exploring its viability for early childhood education. *Journal of Research on Technology in Education, 43*(1), 75–98.

Cowen-Fletcher, J. (1994). *It takes a village.* New York: Scholastic.

Crain, W. (2000). *Theories of development: Concepts and applications.* Upper Saddle River, NJ: Prentice-Hall.

Crews, D. (1978). *Freight train.* New York: Greenwillow.

Crews, D. (1982). *Carousel.* New York: Greenwillow.

Crews, D. (1991). *Bigmama's.* New York: Greenwillow.

Cromwell, E. S. (2000). *Nurturing readiness in early childhood education: A whole-child curriculum for ages 2–5.* Boston: Allyn & Bacon.

Cronin, S., & Jones, E. (1999, April). Play and cultural differences. *Exchange.* Retrieved June 4, 2010, from http://www.ccie.com/search/?search=Play+and+Cultural+differences

Csikszenthmihalyi, M. (1997, September/October). Happiness and creativity. *The Futurist.*

Cumming, R. (1979). *Just look . . . A book about paintings.* New York: Charles Scribner's Sons.

Danko-McGhee, K. (2009). The environment as third teacher: Pre-service teachers' aesthetic transformation of an art learning environment for young children in a museum setting. *International Art in Early Childhood Research Journal 1*(1), 1–17.

Davis, J. H. (2008). *Why our schools need the arts.* New York: Teachers' College Press.

Davis, M. D., Kilgo, J. L., & Gamel-McCormick, M. (1998). *Young children with special needs: A developmentally appropriate approach.* Boston: Allyn & Bacon.

Davol, M. W. (1997). *The paper dragon.* New York: Atheneum.

Day, M. D. (1985). Evaluating student achievement in discipline-based art programs. *Studies in Art Education, 26,* 232–240.

Day, M. D. (1999). Markers of multicultural/antibias education. *Young Children, 54,* 43–57.

Debelak, M., Herr, J., & Jacobson, M. (1981). *Creating innovative classroom materials for teaching young children.* New York: Harcourt Brace Jovanovich.

DeBell, M., & Chapman, C. (2006). *Computer and Internet use by students in 2003. (NCES 2006-065).* U. S. Department of Education. Washington, DC: NCES.

DeBono, E. (1970). *Lateral thinking: A textbook of creativity.* London: Ward Lock Educational.

Dennis, W. (1966). *Group values through children's drawings.* New York: Wiley.

dePaola, T. (1973). *Charlie needs a cloak.* New York: Scholastic.

dePaola, T. (1991). *The legend of the Indian paintbrush.* New York: Penguin.

dePaola, T., & Lear, E. (1991). *Bonjour, Mr. Satie.* New York: Putnam.

Derman-Sparks, L. (1989). Anti-bias curriculum challenges diversity. *School Safety, 3,* 10–13.

Derman-Sparks, L., & ABC Task Force. (1989). *Anti-bias curriculum: Tools for empowering young children.* Washington, DC: NAEYC.

Derman-Sparks, L., Gutierrez, M., & Phillips, C. B. (n.d.). *Teaching young children to resist bias: What parents can do.* Washington, DC: NAEYC.

DeRolf, S. (1997). *The crayon box that talked.* New York: Random House.

Dever, M. W., & Jared, E. J. (1996). Remember to include art and crafts in your integrated curriculum. *Young Children, 51,* 69–73.

DeVries, R., & Zan, B. (1995). Creating a constructivist classroom atmosphere. *Young Children, 51,* 4–14.

Dewey, J. (1958). *Art as experience.* New York: Capricorn Books.

Diakite, B. W. (1997). *The hunterman and the crocodile: A West African folktale.* New York: Scholastic.

Diffily, D., & Sassman, C. (2002). *Project-based learning with young children.* Portsmouth, NH: Heineman.

Dighe, J., Calormiri, Z., & Van Zutpen, C. (1998). Nurturing the language of art in children. *Young Children*, 53, 4–9.

Di Leo, J. H. (1970). *Young children and their drawings.* New York: Brunner/Mazel.

Di Leo, J. H. (1973). *Children's drawings as diagnostic aids.* New York: Brunner/Mazel.

Di Leo, J. H. (2003). Graphic activity of young children: Development and creativity. In L. Lasky & R. Mukerji-Bergeson (Eds.), *Art: Basic for young children.* Washington, DC: National Association for the Education of Young Children.

Dimondstein, G. (1974). *Exploring the arts of children.* New York: Macmillan.

Dixon, A. (1990). *Clay.* New York: Garnett Educational Company.

Dobbs, S. M. (1998). *Learning in and through art.* Los Angeles: Getty Education Institute for the Arts.

Dodge, D. T., & Colker, L. J. (1996). *The creative curriculum for early childhood.* Washington, DC: Teaching Strategies.

Dorros, A. (1991). *Abuela.* New York: Puffin.

Dorros, A. (1994). *Tonight is carnival.* New York: Puffin.

Dorros, A. (1995). *Isla.* New York: Puffin.

Drew, W. F., Christie, J., Johnson, J. E., Meckley, A. M., & Nell, M. L. (2008). Constructive play: A value-added strategy for meeting early learning standards. *Young Children,* 63(4), 38–44.

Drewes, A. & Schaefer, C. E. (Eds.). (2010). *School-based play therapy.* (2nd ed.). Hoboken, NJ: John Wiley & Sons.

Duggleby, J. (1998). *Story painter: The life of Jacob Lawrence.* San Francisco: Chronicle Books.

Duke, L. L. (1993). Foreword. In L. Duke (Ed.), *Discipline-based art education and cultural diversity* (pp. i–iii). Santa Monica, CA: Getty Center for Education in the Arts.

Duncum, P. (1995). Colouring-in and alternatives in early childhood. *Australian Journal of Early Childhood,* 20(3), 33–38.

Dunn-Snow, P., & D'Amelio, G. (2000). How art teachers can enhance artmaking as a therapeutic experience: Art therapy and art education. *Art Education, 53,* 46–53.

Dyson, A. H. (1982). The emergence of visible language: Interrelationships between drawing and early writing. *Visible Language, 6,* 360–381.

Dyson, A. H. (1985). Puzzles, paints, and pencils: Writing emerges. *Educational Horizons, 64,* 13–16.

Dyson, A. H. (1986). Transitions and tensions: Interrelationships between the drawing, talking, and dictating of young children. *Research in the Teaching of English, 20,* 379–409.

Dyson, A. H. (1988). Appreciate the drawing and dictating of young children. *Young Children, 43,* 25–32.

Dyson, A. H. (1989). *Multiple worlds of child writers: Friends learning to write.* New York: Teachers College Press.

Dyson, A. H. (1990). Symbol makers, symbol weavers: How children link play, pictures, and print. *Young Children, 45,* 50–57.

Early Childhood Music Summit. (2000). *Start the music.* Reston, VA: National Association for Music Education.

Eaton, M. M. (1998). *Basic issues in aesthetics.* Belmont, CA: Wadsworth.

Eberle, R. F. (1971). *Scamper: Games for imagination development.* Buffalo, NY: D.O.K. Publishers.

Edwards, B. (1999). *The new drawing on the right side of the brain.* New York: J. P. Tarcher.

Edwards, C., Gandini, L., & Forman, G. (1993). *The hundred languages of children: The Reggio Emilia approach to early childhood education.* Norwood, NJ: Albex.

Edwards, C. P., & Springate, K. W. (1995). *Encouraging creativity in early childhood classroom*s. Urbana, IL: ERIC Clearinghouse on Elementary and Early Childhood Education.

Edwards, L. C. (2006). *The creative arts: A process approach for teachers and children.* (4th ed.). Columbus, OH: Merrill.

Edwards, L. C., & Nabors, M. L. (1993). The creative arts process: What it is and what it is not. *Young Children,* 77–81.

Eisner, E. W. (1976). What we know about children's art—and what we need to know. In E. W. Eisner (Ed.), *The arts, human development, and education* (pp. 5–18). Berkeley, CA: McCutchan.

Einarsdottir, J. (2005). Playschool in pictures: Children's photography as a research method. *Early Child Development and Care, 175,* 523–541.

Eisner, E. W. (1982). *Cognition and curriculum—A basis for deciding what to teach.* New York: Longman.

Elkind, D. (1996). Young children and technology: A cautionary note. *Young Children, 51,* 22–23.

Elkind, D. (2003). Thanks for the memory: The lasting value of true play. *Young Children, 58,* 46–50.

Emberley, E. (1961). *Wing on a flea: A book about shapes.* Boston: Little, Brown.

Emberley, E. (1968). *Green says go.* Boston: Little, Brown.

Emberley, E. (1972). *Ed Emberley's drawing book: Make a world.* Boston: Little, Brown.

Emberley, E. (1973). *Drawing book of animals.* Boston: Little, Brown.

Emberley, E. (1975). *Ed Emberley's drawing book of faces.* Boston: Little, Brown.

Emberley, E. (1977). *Ed Emberley's great thumbprint drawing book.* Boston: Little, Brown.

Emberley, E. (1979). *Ed Emberley's big green drawing book.* Boston: Little, Brown.

Emberley, E. (1980). *Ed Emberley's big orange drawing book.* Boston: Little, Brown.

Emberley, E. (1981). *Ed Emberley's big purple drawing book.* Boston: Little, Brown.

Emberley, E. (1984). *Ed Emberley's picture pie: A book of circle art.* Boston: Little, Brown.

Emberley, E. (1989). *Ed Emberley's Christmas drawing book.* Boston: Little, Brown.

Emberley, E. (1991). *Ed Emberley's drawing book: Make a world.* Boston: Little, Brown.

Engel, B. S. (1995). *Considering children's art: Why and how to value their works.* Washington, DC: NAEYC.

Engel, B. S. (1996). Learning to look: Appreciating child art. *Young Children, 51,* 74–79.

Engel, D. (1989). *The little lump of clay.* New York: Morrow Jr. Books.

Epstein, A. S. (2001). Thinking about art: Encouraging art appreciation in early childhood settings. *Young Children, 56,* 38–43.

Epstein, A. S. (2007). *The intentional teacher: Choosing the best strategies for young children's learning.* Washington, DC: NAEYC.

Erikson, E. H. (1963). *Childhood and society.* New York: Norton.

Everett, G. (1991). *Li'l sis and Uncle Willie.* New York: Hyperion Books.

Fassler, J. (1991). *Howie helps himself.* New York: Albert Whitman.

Fazio, B. (1996). *Grandfather's story.* Seattle: Sasquatch Books.

Feeney, S., & Moravcik, E. (1987). A thing of beauty: Aesthetic development in young children. *Young Children, 42,* 7–15.

Fiarotta, P., & Fiarotta, N. (1974). *Sticks and stones and ice cream cones.* New York: Workman Publishing Company.

Fisher, E. F. (1978). *Aesthetic awareness and the child.* Itasca, IL: F. E. Peacock.

Fisher, L. E. (1984). *Boxes! Boxes!* New York: Viking.

Florian, D. (1991). *A potter.* New York: Greenwillow.

Flux, P. (2002). *Henri Matisse.* Portsmouth, NH: Heinemann.

Fowler, V. (1982). *Paperworks.* Englewood Cliffs, NJ: Prentice-Hall.

Fox, J. E. (2010). The role of drawing in kindergarteners' science observations. *The International Art in Early Childhood Research Journal, 2*(1).

Fox, J. E. (2000). Constructive play in the art center. *Dimensions of Early Childhood Education, 28*(4), 15–20.

Fox, J. E., & Diffily, D. (2001). Integrating the visual arts: Building young children's knowledge, skills, and confidence. *Dimensions, 20*(1), 3–10.

Fox, M. (1997). *The straight line wonder.* New York: Mondo Publishing.

Fox, M., & Staub, L. (2001). *Whoever you are.* San Diego: Harcourt Brace.

Franklin, R. (2007). Drawing inside the box. *School Arts,* December 2007, p. 12.

Freeman, D. (1976). *Chalk box story.* New York: Lippincott.

Freeman, D. (2008). *Corduroy.* New York: Viking Press.

Freeman, D. (1978). *Bearymore.* New York: Penguin Putnam.

Freshwater, A., Sherwood, E., & Mbuga, E. (2008). Music and physical play. *Childhood Education, 85*(1), 2–5.

Friskey, M. (1973). *What is the color of the wide, wide, world?* Chicago: Children's Press.

Froebel, F. (1974). *The Education of Man* (W.N. Hailmann, translated). Clifton, NJ: A.M. Kelley. (Original work published 1826)

Furrer, P. J. (1982). *Art therapy activities and lesson plans for individuals and groups.* Springfield, IL: Charles C. Thomas.

Galin, D. (1976). Educating both halves of the brain. *Childhood Education, 53,* 17–20.

Galinsky, E. (1997). New research on the brain development of young children: Implications for families, early education and care. *CAEYC Connections,* 117–118.

Gallagher, K. (2005). Brain research and early childhood development: A primer for developmentally appropriate practice. *Young Children, 63*(4), 38–44.

Gandini, L. (1993). Fundamentals of the Reggio Emilia approach to early childhood education. *Young Children, 49,* 4–8.

Gandini, L., Hill, L., Cadwell, L., & Schwall, C. (Eds.). (2005). *In the spirit of the studio: Learning from the Atelier of Reggio Emilio.* New York: Teachers College Press.

Gardner, H. (1970). Children's sensitivity to painting styles. *Child Development, 41,* 813–821.

Gardner, H. (1973). *The arts and human development.* New York: Wiley.

Gardner, H. (1980). *Artful scribbles: The significance of children's drawings.* New York: Basic Books.

Gardner, H. (1990). *Art education and human development.* Los Angeles: Getty Center for Education in the Arts.

Gardner, H. (1991). *The unschooled mind.* New York: Basic Books.

Gardner, H. (1993a). *Frames of mind.* (10th ed.). New York: Basic Books.

Gardner, H. (1993b). *Creating minds.* New York: Basic Books.

Gardner, H. (1998). Are there additional intelligences? The case for naturalist, spiritual, and existential intelligences. In J. Kane (Ed.), *Education, information, and transformation.* Upper Saddle River, NJ: Prentice Hall.

Gardner, H. (1999). *Intelligence reframed: Multiple intelligences for the 21st century.* New York: Basic Books.

Gardner, H. (2006). *Multiple intelligences: New horizons in theory and practice.* New York: Basic Books.

Gardner, H., & Winner, E. (1976). How children learn . . . three stages of understanding art. *Psychology Today, 9,* 42–43.

Gardner, K. G., & Moran, J. D. (1990). Family adaptability, cohesion and creativity. *Creativity Research Journal, 3*(4), 281–286.

Gargiulo, R., & Kilgo, J. L. (2005). *Young children with special needs: An introduction to early childhood special education.* (2nd ed.). Clifton Park, NY: Thomson Delmar Learning.

Garland, M. (1995). *Dinner at Magritte's.* New York: Dutton's Children's Books.

Garvey, C. (1990). *Play.* (Enlarged edition). Cambridge, MA: Harvard University Press.

Gelineau, R. P. (2004). *Integrating the arts across the elementary school curriculum.* Belmont, CA: Wadsworth/Thomson.

Genishi, C. (1993, October). Art, portfolios, and assessment. *Scholastic Early Childhood Today, 67.*

Gerstein, M. (2004). *The man who walked between the towers.* New York: Roaring Brook Press.

Getty Center for Education in the Arts. (1985, April). *Beyond creating: The place for art in America's schools. A report by the Getty Center for Education in the Arts.* Santa Monica, CA.

Getty Center for Education in the Arts. (1989). *Education in art: Future building.* Proceedings of a National Invitational Conference, Los Angeles.

Getz, D. (1997). *Floating home.* New York: Holt.

Getzels, J., & Jackson, P. (1962). *Creativity and intelligence.* New York: Wiley.

Ginsburg, M. (1997). *Clay boy.* New York: Greenwillow.

Gitter, L. (January, 1968). Art and the Montessori approach in a poverty-stricken rural area. *Bulletin of Art Therapy,* 85–93.

Golomb, C. (1974). *Young children's sculpture and drawing—A study in representative development.* Cambridge, MA: Harvard University Press.

Gonzalez-Mena, J. (1993). *The child in the family and community.* Columbus, OH: Merrill.

Gonzalez-Mena, J. (1998). *Foundations: Early childhood education in a diverse society.* Mountain View, CA: Mayfield.

Gonzalez-Mena, J. (2001). *Multicultural issues in child care.* Mountain View, CA: Mayfield.

Goodenough, F. L. (1975). *Measurement of intelligence by drawings.* New York: Arno Press.

Goodhart, P. (1997). *Row, row, row your boat.* New York: Crown.

Goodman, R. F., & Fahnestock, A. H. (2002). *The day our world changed: Children's art of 9/11.* New York: Harry N. Abrams.

Goodnow, J. (1977). *Children drawing.* Cambridge, MA: Harvard University Press.

Gordon, A. M., & Browne, K. W. (2008). *Beginnings and beyond: Foundations in Early Childhood Education* (7th ed.). Clifton Park, NY: Thomson Delmar Learning.

Greenberg, J., & Jordan, S. (2002). *Action Jackson.* Brookfield, CT: Roaring Brook Press.

Greenburg, P. (1999). Listening to children talk while they draw. *Young Children, 54,* 13.

Greene, R. G. (1997). *When a line bends . . . a shape begins.* Boston, MA: Houghton Mifflin.

Grifalconi, A. (1986). *The village of round and square houses.* New York: Little Brown & Company.

Grifalconi, A. (1993). *Kinda' blue.* New York: Little, Brown & Company.

Grover, M. (1996). *Circles and squares everywhere!* Orlando, FL: Harcourt.

Guilford, J. P. (1977). *Way beyond the IQ.* Buffalo, NY: Creative Education Foundation.

Hall, N. S. (1999). *Creative resources for the anti-bias classroom*. Clifton Park, NY: Thomson Delmar Learning.

Hanline, M. F., Milton, S., & Phelps, P. C. (2007a). Influence of disability, gender, and time engaged on the developmental level of children's art work: Findings from three years of observation. *Journal of Early Intervention*, Winter 2007. Retrieved February 24, 2010, from http://findarticles.com/p/articles/mi_7602/is_200701/ai_n32211360/?tag+content;col1

Hanline, M. F., Milton, S., & Phelps, P. C. (2007b). Influence of disability, gender, and time engaged on the development of children's art work: Findings from three years of observation. *Journal of early intervention, 29(2)*, 141–153.

Hardiman, G. W., & Zernich, T. (1981). *Art activities for children*. Englewood Cliffs, NJ: Prentice-Hall.

Harris, D. B. (1963). *Children's drawings as measures of intellectual maturity*. New York: Harcourt, Brace.

Hartfield, C. (2002). *Me and Uncle Romie*. New York: Dial Books.

Hartley, R. E., Frank, L. K., & Goldenson, R. M. (1952). *Understanding children's play*. New York: Columbia University Press.

Haskell, L. L. (1979). *Art in the early childhood years*. Columbus, OH: Charles E. Merrill.

Haugland, S. W. (1992). Effects of computer software on preschool children's developmental gains. *Journal of Computing in Early Childhood, 3*, 15–30.

Haugland, S. W. (1999). What role should technology play in young children's learning? Part 1. *Young Children*, 26–31.

Haugland, S. W. (2000). What role should technology play in young children's learning? Part 2—Early childhood classrooms in the 21st century: Using computers to maximize learning. *Young Children, 55*, 12–18.

Haugland, S. W., & Shade, D. D. (1994). Software evaluation for young children. In J. Wright & D. D. Shade (Eds.), *Young children: Active learners in a technological age* (pp. 63–76). Washington, DC: NAEYC.

Haugland, S. W., & Wright, J. L. (1997). *Young children and technology: A world of discovery*. Boston: Allyn & Bacon.

Hawkinson, J. (1974). *A ball of clay*. Chicago: Whitman.

Hawkinson, J. (1978). *Pat, swish, twist and the story of Patty Swish*. Chicago: Albert Whitman.

Healy, J. M. (1994). *Your child's growing mind*. New York: Doubleday.

Healy, J. M. (1998). Eight ways to keep television from stunting brain's growth. *AAP News, 14*(5), 23.

Healy, J. M. (1999). *Failure to connect: How computers affect our children's minds—and what we can do about it*. New York: Simon & Schuster.

Heath, S. B., & Wolf, S. (2004a). *Art is all about looking*. London: Creative Partnerships.

Heath, S. B., & Wolf, S. (2004b). *Hoping for accidents: Media and technique*. London: Creative Partnerships.

Hellan, J. R. (2000). *Rolling along: The story of Taylor and his wheelchair*. Atlanta: Peachtree.

Heller, R. (1995). *Color*. New York: Puffin Books.

Henderson, D., & Thompson, C. (2011). *Counseling children*. (8th ed.). Belmont, CA: Brooks/Cole.

Hendrick, J. (Ed.). (1997). *First steps toward teaching the Reggio way*. Columbus, OH: Merrill.

Herberholz, B., & Hanson, L. (1990). *Early childhood art*. (4th ed.). Dubuque, IA: Wm. C. Brown.

Hesse, P., & Lane, F. (2003). Media literacy starts young. *Young Children, 58*, 20–26.

Himmelman, K. (1996). *Hooray! It's Passover!* New York: HarperCollins.

Hirsch, R. A. (2004). *Early childhood curriculum*. Boston: Pearson.

Ho, M. (1996). *Hush! A Thai lullaby*. New York: Orchard.

Hoffman, M. (1991). *Amazing grace*. New York: Dial.

Hohmann, M., & Weikart, D. P. (1995). *Educating young children*. Ypsilanti, MI: High/Scope Press.

Hoover, F. L. (1961). *Art activities for the very young*. Worcester, MA: Davis Publishing.

Hopkins, L. B. (2007). *Behind the museum door*. New York: Harry N. Abrams.

Howard, N. S. (1996). *Jacob Lawrence: American scenes, American struggles*. Worcester, MA: Davis Publications.

Hubbard, P. (1996). *My crayons talk*. New York: Henry Holt and Company.

Hughes, S. (1985). *Noisy*. New York: Lothrop, Lee & Shepard.

Humpal, M. E., & Wolf, J. (2003). Music in the inclusive environment. *Young Children, 58*, 103–107.

Hunt, M. (1995). Let there be light! Lighting up the holidays for young children. *Young Children, 51*, 79–81.

Hunter, D. (2008). What happens when a child plays at the sensory table? *Young Children, 63*(6), 77–79.

Hurd, E. T., & Hurd, C. (1971). *Wilson's world*. New York: HarperCollins Children's Books.

Hutchins, P. (1987). *Changes, changes*. New York: Macmillan.

Hyde, M. E. (1996). *Matisse for kids*. New York: Pelican.

Indenbaum, V., & Shapiro, M. (1983). *The everything book for teachers of young children.* Livonia, MI: Partner Press.

Isadore, R. (1998). *Ben's trumpet.* Pine Plains, NY: Live Oak Media.

Isbell, R. T. (2007). *Creativity and the arts with young children.* (2nd ed.). Clifton Park, NY: Thomson Delmar Learning.

Isenberg, J. P., & Jalongo, M. R. (2005). *Creative thinking and arts-based learning: Preschool through 4th grade.* (4th ed.). Columbus, OH: Pearson, Allyn & Bacon/ Merrill.

Jalongo, M. R. (2003). The child's right to creative thought and expression: A position paper of the Association for Childhood Education International. *Childhood Education, 79,* 218–228.

Jalongo, M. R., & Stamp, L. N. (1997). *The arts in children's lives: Aesthetic education in early childhood.* Boston: Allyn & Bacon.

James, B. (1998). *The mud family.* London: Oxford University.

Jameson, K. (1970). *Art and the young child.* New York: Viking.

Janson, H. W., & Janson, D. J. (1984). *Janson's story of painting.* New York: Harrison House/Harry N. Abrams.

Jenkins, S., & Page, R. (2006). *Move!* Boston: Houghton Mifflin.

Jensen, E. (1998). *Teaching with the brain in mind.* Alexandria, VA: Association for Supervision and Curriculum Development.

Johnson, A., & Lewis, E. B. (2007). *Lily Brown's paintings.* New York: Orchard Books.

Johnson, C. (1960). *A picture for Harold's room.* New York: HarperCollins.

Johnson, C. (1981). *Harold and the purple crayon.* New York: HarperCollins.

Johnson, J., Christie, J., & Wardle, F. (2005). *Play, development and early education.* New York: Allyn & Bacon.

Johnson, M. (1990). *Teach your child to draw.* Los Angeles: Lowell House.

Johnston, T., & dePaola, T. (1985). *The quilt story.* New York: Scholastic.

Jonas, A. (1990). *Color dance.* New York: HarperCollins.

Jonas, A. (1997). *Watch William walk.* New York: Greenwillow.

Jones, E. (1993). The play's the thing: Style of playfulness. *Child Care Information Exchange, 18,* 28–30.

Jones, E. (1999). An emergent curriculum expert offers this afterthought. *Young Children, 54,* 16.

Jones, E., & Nimmo, J. (1994). *Emergent curriculum.* Washington, DC: NAEYC.

Jones, S. (1979). *Learning for little kids.* Boston, MA: Houghton Mifflin.

Joose, B. (1991). *Mama, do you love me?* San Francisco: Chronicle Books.

Joose, B. (1996). *I love you the purplest.* San Francisco: Chronicle Books.

Kaagan, S. S. (1990). *Aesthetic persuasion: Pressing the cause of arts education in American schools.* A Monograph for The Getty Center for Education in the Arts. Santa Monica, CA.

Kalman, M. (2002). *Fireboat.* New York: Penguin.

Kamii, C., & DeVries, R. (1993). *Physical knowledge in preschool education: Implications of Piaget's theory.* New York: Teachers College Press.

Kampmann, L. (1971). *The children's book of painting.* New York: Van Nostrand Reinhold.

Karnes, M. (1993). Art for children with special needs. *Scholastic Early Childhood Today, 63.*

Katz, L. (1987). *What should young children be learning?* (ERIC Digest). Urbana, IL: ERIC Clearinghouse on Elementary and Early Childhood Education.

Katz, L. (1990). Impressions of Reggio Emilia preschools. *Young Children, 45,* 11–14.

Katz, L. (1994). *The project approach* (ERIC Digest, ED 368509). Urbana, IL: ERIC Clearinghouse on Elementary and Early Childhood Education.

Katz, L., & Chard, S. C. (1989). *Engaging children's minds: The project approach.* Norwood, NJ: Ablex.

Katz, L. G. (1987). *What should young children be learning?* Champaign, IL: ERIC Clearinghouse on Elementary and Early Childhood Education.

Keats, E. J. (1978). *The trip.* New York: Greenwillow.

Kellogg, R. (1969). *Analyzing children's art.* Palo Alto, CA: Mayfield Publishing.

Kellogg, R. (1973a). Stages of development in preschool art. In H. P. Lewis (Ed.), *Child art: The beginnings of self-affirmation,* Berkeley, CA: Diablo Press.

Kellogg, R. (1973b). Misunderstanding child art. *Art Education, 26*(6), 7–9.

Kellogg, R. (1979). *Children's drawings/children's minds.* New York: Avon Books.

Kellogg, R., & O'Dell, S. (1967). *The psychology of children's art.* San Diego: CRM-Random House.

Kellogg, S. (1976). *Can I keep him?* New York: Penguin Putnam.

Kellogg, S. (1982). *Mystery of the stolen blue paint.* New York: Dial.

Kemple, K. M., & Nissenberg, S. A. (2000). Nurturing creativity in early childhood education: Families are part of it. *Early Childhood Education Journal, 28*(1), 67–71.

Kessler, E., & Kessler, L. (1966). *Are you square?* Garden City, NY: Doubleday.

Kieff, J. E., & Casbergue, R. M. (2000). *Playful teaching and learning: Integrating play into preschool and primary programs.* Boston: Allyn & Bacon.

King, I. L. (1991). In search of Lowenfeld's proof that coloring books are harmful to children. *Studies in Art Education, 33*(1), 36–42.

Kocher, A. (1994). *Ravi's Diwali surprise.* Cleveland, OH: Modern Curriculum Press.

Kohl, H. (1977). Copying and coloring. *Teacher, 95*(4), 23–26.

Kohl, M. A. (1985). *Scribble cookies and other independent creative art experiences for children.* Bellingham, WA: Bright Ring Publishing.

Koster, J. B. (1999). Clay for little fingers. *Young Children, 54,* 18–22.

Kottman, T. (2009). Play therapy in Vernon, A. *Counseling Children & Adolescents,* 4th ed. pp. 123–146. Denver, CO: Love Publishing Company.

Kramer, E. (1974). *Art as therapy with children.* New York: Schocken Books.

Krauss, R. (1956). *I want to paint my bathroom blue.* New York: Harper & Row.

Kristeller, J. (1994, November/December). Creating curriculum as a workshop. *Scholastic Early Childhood Today,* 58–60.

Kunhardt, D. (1962). *Pat the bunny.* New York: Golden Books.

Laden, N. (1998). *When pigasso met mootisee.* San Francisco: Chronicle Books.

Lamorisse, A. (1956). *The red balloon.* Garden City, NY: Doubleday.

Landreth, G. (2012) *Play Therapy: The art of the relationship.* (4th ed.). New York: Taylor & Francis Group.

Langer, S. K. (1957). *Philosophy in a new key.* Cambridge, MA: Harvard University Press.

Lankford, E. L. (1992). *Aesthetics: Issues and inquiry.* Reston, VA: National Art Education Association.

Lansing, K. M. (1969). *Art, artists, and art education.* New York: McGraw-Hill.

Lasky, K. (2000). *First Painter.* New York: Dorling-Kindersley Publishing.

Lasky, L., & Mukerji, R. (1980). *Art: Basic for young children.* Washington, DC: National Association for the Education of Young Children.

Lasky, L., & Mukerji-Bergeson, R. (2003). *Art: Basic for young children.* Washington, DC: National Association for the Education of Young Children.

Lears, L. (2003). *Ian's walk: A story about autism.* New York: Albert Whitman.

Leighton, M. (1994). *An Ellis Island Christmas.* New York: Puffin.

Lemerise, T. (1993). Piaget, Vygotsky and Logo. *The Computing Teacher, 20,* 24–28.

Lepper, M. R., & Greene, D. (1975). Turning play into work: Effects of adult surveillance and extrinsic rewards on children's intrinsic motivation. *Journal of Personality and Social Psychology, 31,* 479–486.

Lessen-Firestone, J. (1995, March). The trials of testing. *Scholastic Early Childhood Today,* 23.

LeTord, B. (1995). *A blue butterfly: A story about Claude Monet.* New York: Doubleday.

LeTord, B. (1999). *A bird or two: A story about Henri Matisse.* Grand Rapids, MI: William B. Eerdmans.

Leuck, L. (1998). *Teeny, tiny mouse: A book about colors.* Bridgewater Books.

Levine, E. (1989). *I hate English.* New York: Scholastic.

Lewis, H. P. (Ed.). (1973). *Child art—the beginnings of self-affirmation.* Berkeley, CA: Diablo.

Linder, T. W. (1983). *Early childhood special education.* Baltimore, MD: Paul H. Brooks.

Linderman, E. W., & Heberholz, D. S. (1974). *Developing artistic and perceptual awareness.* Dubuque, IA: Wm. C. Brown.

Linderman, E. W., & Linderman, M. (1984). *Arts and crafts for the classroom.* New York: Macmillan.

Lionni, L. (1968). *Swimmy.* New York: Alfred A. Knopf.

Lionni, L. (1973). *Frederick.* New York: Alfred A. Knopf.

Lionni, L. (1979). *Little blue and little yellow.* New York: Ivan Obolensky.

Lionni, L. (1985). *Colors to talk about.* New York: Alfred A. Knopf.

Lionni, L. (1991). *Matthew's dream.* New York: Knopf.

Littlesugar, A. (1996). *Marie in fourth position.* New York: Philomel Books.

Lobel, A. (1981). *On Market Street.* New York: Greenwillow.

Logan, C. (1996). *Scruffy's museum adventures.* Boston: Museum of Fine Arts, Boston.

Loss, J. (1974). *What is it? A book of photographic puzzles.* Garden City, NY: Doubleday.

Lowenfeld, V. (1947). *Creative and mental growth.* (1st ed.). New York: MacMillan.

Lowenfeld, V. (1968). On the importance of early art expression. In W. L. Brittain (Ed.), *Viktor Lowenfeld speaks on art and creativity* (pp. 20–27). Washington, DC: National Art Education Association.

Lowenfeld, V., & Brittain, W. L. (1987). *Creative and mental growth.* New York: Macmillan.

MacAgy, D., & MacAgy, E. (1959). *Going for a walk with a line: A step into the world of modern art.* Garden City, NY: Doubleday.

MacKinnon, D. W. (1962). The nature and nurture of creative talent. *American Psychologist, 17*, 484–495.

Maguire, A. (1999). *Special people, special ways.* Santa Monica, CA: Portunus.

Malaguzzi, L. (1993). For an education based on relationships. *Young Children, 49*, 9–12.

Martin, B. (1996). *Brown bear, brown bear.* New York: Henry Holt.

Martin, B. (1997). *Polar bear, polar bear.* New York: Henry Holt.

Martin, S. (1994). *Observation and portfolio assessment in early childhood.* Don Mills, Ontario: Addison-Wesley.

Marzollo, J. (1977). *Supertot—Creative learning activities for children from one to three and sympathetic advice for their parents.* New York: Harper & Row.

Marzollo, J. (1997). *Pretend you're a cat.* New York: Viking Penguin.

Matlock, R., & Hornstein, J. (2004) Sometimes a smudge is just a smudge and sometimes it's a sabertoothed tiger. *Young children on the web, July 2004, 1–6.*

Matthews, J. C. (1997). *Computers and art education.* ERIC digest (ERIC document reproduction no. ED410180). Bloomington, IN: ERIC Clearinghouse for Social Studies/Social Science Education.

Matthews, J., & Seow, P. (2007). Electronic paint: Understanding children's representation through their interactions with digital paint. *Journal of Art Design, 26*(3), 251–263.

Mattil, E. L., & Marzan, B. (1981). *Meaning in children's art.* Englewood Cliffs, NJ: Prentice-Hall.

Mayhew, J. (2000). *Katie and the Sunflowers.* New York: Orchard Books.

McCorminck, L., & Feeney, S. (1995). Modifying and expanding activities for children with disabilities. *Young Children, 50*, 10–18.

McCracken, J. B. (1993). *Valuing diversity: The primary years.* Washington, DC: NAEYC.

McFee, J. K. (1970). *Preparation for art.* Belmont, CA: Wadsworth.

McFee, J. K. (1993). DBAE and cultural diversity: Some perspectives from the social sciences. In *Discipline-based art education and cultural diversity* (pp. 116–135). Santa Monica, CA: Getty Foundation for Education in the Arts.

McNeill, E., Allen, J., & Schmidt, V. (1991). *Cultural awareness for young children.* Reading, MA: Addison-Wesley.

MENC: The National Association for Music Education. (1994). *The school music program: A new vision.* Lanham, MD: Rowman and Littlefield Education.

Merberg, J., & Bober, S. (2002). *Magical day with Matisse.* San Francisco: Chronicle Books.

Merritt, H. (1967). *Guiding free expression in children's art.* New York: Holt, Rinehart and Winston.

Metropolitan Museum of Art, The. (2005). *Vincent's colors.* San Francisco: Chronicle Books.

Meyer, D. J. (1997). *Views from our shoes: Growing up with a brother or sister with special needs.* Las Vegas: Sagebrush.

Michel, M., & Dudek, S. Z. (1991). Mother-child relationships and creativity. *Creativity Research Journal, 43*, 281–286.

Micklethwait, L. (1996). *A child's book of play in art.* New York: DK Publishing, Inc.

Micklethwait, L. (2004). *I spy shapes in art.* Greenwillow Books.

Miller, B., & Cummings, J. (Eds.). (2007). *The human frontal lobes.* New York: Guilford Press.

Miller, L. G. (2008). Dramatic play: A daily requirement for children. *Early Childhood News.* Retrieved January 19, 2010, from http://www.earlychildhoodnews.com/earlychildhood/article_view.aspx?ArticleID=263

Millman, I. (2002). *Moses goes to a concert.* New York: Straus and Giroux.

Misailidi, P., & Bonoti, F. (2008). Emotion in children's art: Do young children understand the emotions expressed in other children's drawings? *Journal of Educational Research, 6*(2), 189–200.

Miskimon, R. (2011). Art Development in Young Children. Online at www.livestrong.com/article/127486-art-development-young-children/. Accessed on 26 April 2012.

Mitchell, R. (1997). *The talking cloth.* New York: Orchard.

Moll, P. B. (1985). *Children and scissors—a developmental approach.* Tampa, FL: Hampton Mae Institute.

Montessori, M. (1967). *The absorbent mind.* New York: Holt, Rinehart & Winston.

Moon, N. (1995). *Lucy's picture.* New York: Dial Books for Young Readers.

Morgan, G. G., & Shade, D. D. (1994). Moving early childhood education into the 21st century. In J. Wright & D. D. Shade (Eds.), *Young children: Active learners in a technological age* (pp. 135–149). Washington, DC: NAEYC.

Moyer, J. (1990). Whose creation is it, anyway? *Childhood Education, 66*, 130–131.

Mulcahey, C. (2009). *The Story in the Picture: Inquiry and art making with younger children*. New York: Teachers College Press.

National Association for the Education of Young Children (NAEYC). (2003). *Early childhood curriculum, assessment, and program evaluation*. A Joint Position Statement with the National Association of Early Childhood Specialists in State Departments of Education. Washington, DC: NAEYC. Retrieved from http://www.naeyc.org /about/positions/pdf

National Association for the Education of Young Children (NAEYC). (1996). NAEYC position statement: Technology and young children—ages three through eight. *Young Children, 51,* 11–16.

Naumberg, M. (1973). *An introduction to art therapy*. New York: Teachers College Press.

Neely, L. P. (2001). Active for life: Developmentally appropriate movement. Practice: Children learn what they live. *Young Children: 56,* 32–37.

Neely, L. P. (2002). Practical ways to improve singing in early childhood classrooms. *Young Children, 57,* 80–85.

Neugebauer, B. (Ed.). (1987). *Alike and different— Exploring our humanity with young children*. Redmond, WA: Exchange Press.

New, R. (1990). Excellent early education: A city in Italy has it. *Young Children, 45,* 4–10.

New, R. (1993). Cultural variations on developmentally appropriate practice: Challenges to theory and practice. In C. Edwards, L. Gandini, & G. Forman (Eds.), *The hundred languages of children: The Reggio Emilia approach to early childhood education* (pp. 215–232). Norwood, NJ: Ablex.

Newcome, Z. (2002). *Head, shoulders, knees and toes and other action rhymes*. Cambridge, MA: Candlewick Press.

Newman, E. (1990, April). Yani: The brush of innocence. *Bay Area Parent,* 24–26.

Nielsen. (2009). *Home technology report*. Retrieved March 10, 2010, from http://www.marketingcharts. com/interactive/home-internet-access-in-us-still -room-for-growth-8280/nielsen-internet-access -household-income-february-2009jpg/

Nieto, S. (1992). *Affirming diversity—The sociopolitical context of multicultural education*. White Plains, NY: Longman.

Novak, M. (1994). *Mouse TV*. New York: Orchard Books.

Nusayr, A. (Personal communication, September 14, 2012).

Obiols, A. (2003). *Dali and the path of dreams*. London: Frances Lincoln Children's Books.

O'Connor, J., & Hartland, J. (2002). *Henri Matisse: Drawing with scissors*. New York: Grosset & Dunlap.

O'Neill, M. (1961). *Hailstones and halibut bones*. Garden City, NY: Doubleday.

Osofsky, A. (1992). *Dreamcatcher*. New York: Orchard.

Papert, S. (1993). *Mindstorms: Children, computers and powerful ideas (2nd ed.)*. New York: Basic Books.

Parks, M. E. (1994). *The art teacher's desktop reference*. Englewood Cliffs, NJ: Prentice-Hall.

Parette, H. P., Hourcase, J. J., & Helple, G. S. (2000). The importance of structured computer experiences for young children with and without disabilities. *Early Childhood Education Journal, 27*(4), 243–250.

Parsons, M. J. (1987). Talk about a painting: A cognitive developmental analysis. *The Journal of Aesthetic Education, 21,* 37–55.

Paquette, K. R., Fello, S. E., & Jalongo, M. R. (2007). The talking drawings strategy: Using primary children's illustrations and oral language to improve comprehension of expository test. *Early Childhood Education Journal, 35*(1), 65–73.

Patel, A. (2002). *On that day*. Berkeley, CA: Ten Speed Press.

Pavlova, A. (2001). *I dreamed I was a ballerina*. New York: The Metropolitan Museum of Art.

Percy, G. (1994). *Art house*. San Francisco: Chronicle Books.

Perrault, C. (1997). *Cinderella*. New York: Simon & Schuster.

Pfleger, S. (1998). *A jungle expedition: Henri Rousseau*. Munich: Prestel-Verlag.

Phillips, R. S. (1978). *The great artists*. New York: Funk & Wagnalls.

Piaget, J. (1953). Art education and child psychology. In E. Ziegfeld (Ed.), *Education and art* (pp. 39–56). Switzerland: UNESCO.

Piaget, J. (1962). *Play, dreams, and imitation in childhood*. New York: Norton.

Piaget, J. (1971). *Mental imagery in the child*. New York: Basic Books.

Piaget, J., & Inhelder, B. (1956). *The child's conception of space*. London: Routledge and Kegan Paul.

Piaget, J., & Inhelder, B. (1969). *The psychology of the child*. (H. Weaver, Trans.) New York: Basic Books.

Pica, R. (2004). *Experiences in movement: Birth to age 8*. (3rd ed.). Clifton Park, NY: Thomson Delmar Learning.

Pico, R. (1994). *The red comb*. New York: BridgeWater.

Pile, N. F. (1973). *Art experiences for young children*. New York: Macmillan.

Pinkwater, D. M. (1977). *The big orange splot.* New York: Scholastic.

Poffenberger, N. (2001). *September 11th, 2001.* Cincinnati, OH: Fun Publishing.

Polacco, P. (1988). *The keeping quilt.* New York: Simon & Schuster.

Pomeranc, M. H. (1998). *The American wei.* Morton Grove, IL: Albert-Whitman & Company.

Position Statement on Early Childhood Education. (1990). National Association of Music Educators. Retrieved from www.menc.org/information/prek12/echild.html

Potter, L. A., Eder, E. K., & Hussey, M. (2012). Letter from Thomas Moran to Ferdinand Hayden and paintings by Thomas Moran. *Social Education, 76*(3), 117–122.

Priceman, M. (2001). *It's me, Marva.* New York: Alfred A. Knopf.

Raboff, E. (1987–1988). *Art for children.* New York: Harper-Collins.

Raboff, E. L. (1991). *Henri Matisse.* New York: Harper Collins.

Ramirez, J. (1998). *Sensory integration and its effects on young children.* Research paper at Lehman College. ERIC Document identification number: ED432071.

Ravichandran, P., & de Bravo, B. F. (2010). *Young children and screen time (television, DVDs, Computer).* National Research Center for Women and Families. Available at http://www.center4research.org/2010/05/young-children-and-screen-time-television-dvds-computer/ Accessed on August 10, 2012.

Reddy, L., Files-Hall, T., & Schaefer, C.E. (Eds.). (2005). *Empirically based play interventions for children.* Washington, DC: American Psychological Association.

Reid, K. (2000). *Magical Mondays at the art museum.* Richmond, VA: Cockadoodledoo Creations.

Reiner, A. (1990). *A visit to the art galaxy.* San Marcos, CA: Green Tiger Press.

Reynolds, P. H. (2003). *The dot.* Cambridge, MA: Candlewick Press.

Richey, D. D., & Wheeler, J. J. (2000). *Inclusive early childhood education.* Clifton Park, NY: Thomson Delmar Learning.

Richardson, J., & Walker, S. (2011). Processing process: The event of making art. *Studies in Art Education, 53*(1), 6–19.

Riehicky, J. (1993). *Cinco de Mayo.* Chicago: Children's Press.

Ringgenberg, S. (2003). Music as a teaching tool: Creating story songs. *Young Children, 58,* 76–79.

Ringgold, F. (1991). *Tar beach.* New York: Crown.

Robertson, J. (2003). *Oscar's spots.* New York: Troll.

Robinson, K. (1999). *All our futures: Creativity culture and education.* National Advisory Committee on Creative and Cultural Education.

Robles de Melendez, W., Beck, V., & Fletcher, M. (2000). *Teaching social studies in early education.* Clifton Park, NY: Thomson Delmar Learning.

Rogers, F. (2000). *Let's talk about it: Extraordinary friends.* New York: Penguin.

Rogriguez, R. (2006). *Through Georgia's eyes.* New York: Henry Holt and Company.

Rosa-Casanova, S. (1997). *Mama Provi and the pot of rice.* New York: Atheneum.

Rosenstiel, A. K., Morrison, P., Silverman, J., & Gardner, H. (1978). Critical judgement: A developmental study. *The Journal of Aesthetic Education, 12,* 95–107.

Rubin, J. A. (1978). *Child art therapy.* New York: Van Nostrand Reinhold.

Rubin, S. G. (2001). *The yellow house: Vincent Van Gogh & Paul Gauguin side by side.* New York: Harry N. Abrams.

Rushton, S., Juola-Rushton, A., & Larkin, E. (2010). Neuroscience, play and early childhood education: Connections, implications and assessment. *Early Childhood Education Journal, 37,* 351–361.

Rushton, S. P., & Larkin, E. (2001). Shaping the learning environment: Connecting developmentally appropriate practices to brain research. *Early Childhood Education Journal, 29*(1), 25–33.

Russell, I., & Waugaman, B. (1952). A study of the effect of workbook copy experiences on the creative concepts of children. Cited in V. Lowenfeld & W. L. Brittain, Creative and mental growth. *Research Bulletin, Eastern Arts Association, 3*(1).

Sabbeth, C. (1998). *Crayons and computers: Computer art activities for kids ages 4 to 8.* Chicago Review Press.

Samton, S. W. (1985). *The world from my window.* New York: Crown.

Sarracho, O. N., & Spodek, B. (Eds.). (1983). *Understanding multicultural experience in early childhood education.* Washington, DC: National Association for the Education of Young Children.

Saunders, S. W. (2002). *Active for life: Developmentally appropriate movement programs for young children.* Washington, DC: National Association for the Education of Young Children.

Sautter, R. C. (1994). An Arts Education Reform Strategy. *Phi Delta Kappan, 75*(6), 433–440.

Say, A. (1990). *El Chino.* Boston: Houghton Mifflin.

Say, A. (1999). *Tea with milk.* Boston: Houghton Mifflin.

Sazer, N. (1976). *What do you think I saw? A nonsense number book.* New York: Pantheon.

Schaefer, C. L. (1996). *The squiggle.* New York: Dragonfly Books.

Schiller, M. (1995). An emergent art curriculum that fosters understanding. *Young Children, 50,* 33–38.

Schirrmacher, R. (1980). Child art. In S. Modgil & C. Modgil (Eds.), *Toward a theory of psychological development* (pp. 733–762). Windsor, England: National Foundation for Educational Research.

Schirrmacher, R. (1986). Talking with young children about their art. *Young Children, 41,* 3–7.

Schwall, C. (2005). The atelier environment and materials. In L. Gandini, L. Hill, L. Caldwell, & C. Schwall (Eds.), *In the spirit of the studio: Learning from the atelier of Reggio Emilio* (pp. 16–31). New York: Teachers College Press.

Schwartz, A. (1983). *Begin at the beginning.* New York: HarperCollins Children's Books.

Scott, L. G., May, M. E., & Shaw, M. S. (1972). *Puppets for all grades.* New York: The Instructor Publications.

Seefeldt, C. (1995). Art—A serious work. *Young Children, 45*(3), 39–45.

Seefeldt, C., Castle, S., & Falconer, R. (2010). *Social Studies for the Preschool/Primary Child* (8th ed.). Princeton, NC: Merrill.

Seminar proceedings. (1993). *Discipline-based art education and cultural diversity.* Santa Monica, CA: J. Paul Getty Trust.

Sendak, M. (1962). *Chicken soup with rice.* Harper Trophy.

Seo, H. A., Chun, H. Y., Jwa, S. H., & Choi, M. H. (2011). Relationship variables between young children's habitual computer use and influencing variables on socio-emotional development. *Early Childhood Development and Care, 181*(2), 245–265.

Seuss, Dr. (1960). *Green eggs and ham.* Random House.

Shade, D. (1996). Software evaluation. *Young Children, 51,* 17–21.

Shallcross, D. J. (1981). *Teaching creative behavior.* Englewood Cliffs, NJ: Prentice-Hall.

Shapur, F. (1972). *Round and round and square.* London: Abelard-Schuman.

Shaw, C. G. (1947). *It looked like spilt milk.* New York: Harper & Row.

Shaw, C. G. (1988) *It looked like spilt milk.* New York: HarperCollins.

Shore, R. (1997). *Rethinking the brain.* New York: Families and Work Institute.

Shriver, M. (2001). *What's wrong with Timmy?* New York: Little, Brown & Company.

Silberstein-Storfer, M., & Jones, M. (1982). *Doing art together.* New York: Simon & Schuster.

Skeele, R., & Stefankiewicz, G. (2002). Blackbox in the sandbox: The decision to use technology with young children w/ annotated bibliography of Internet resources for teachers of young children. *Educational Technology Review* (online serial). *10* (2), 79–95.

Slobodkina, E. (1968). *Caps for sale.* Reading, MA: Addison-Wesley.

Small, D. (1986). *Imogene's antlers.* New York: Crown.

Smilansky, S. (1968). *The effects of sociodramatic play on disadvantaged preschool children.* New York: Wiley.

Smilansky, S (1971). *Can adults facilitate play in children? Theoretical and practical implications.* Washington, DC: National Association for the Education of Young Children.

Smith, N. R. (1982). The visual arts in early childhood education: Development and the creation of meaning. In B. Spodek (Ed.), *Handbook of research in early childhood education* (pp. 295–317). New York: Free Press.

Smith, N., Fucigna, C., Kennedy, M., & Lord, L. (1993). *Experience and art—Teaching children to paint.* (2nd ed.). New York: Teachers College Press.

Smith, R. A. (1993). Introduction to the symposium on aesthetic value and arts education. *Arts Education Policy Review, 95,* 10–12.

Smith, R. A., & Simpson, A. (1991). *Aesthetics and arts education.* Urbana and Chicago: University of Illinois Press.

Snape, M. (1991). *Boy with the square eyes.* New York: Simon Schuster.

Sorgen, M. (1999, June). *Applying brain research to classroom practice.* Materials presented at the University of South Florida Brain/Mind Connections Conference, Sarasota, FL.

Sortland, B., & Elling, L. (1999). *Anna's art adventure.* Minneapolis, MN: Lerner.

Soto, G. (1997) *Snapshots from a wedding.* New York: Putnam.

Spanyol, J. (2003). *Carlo likes colors.* Cambridge, MA: Candlewick Press.

Spiegel-McGill, P., Zippiroli, S., & Mistrett, S. (1989). Microcomputers as social facilitators in integrated preschools. *Journal of Early Intervention, 13*(3), 249–260.

Spier, P. (1977). *Noah's ark.* New York: Random House.

Spinelli, E. (2001). *In my new yellow shirt.* New York: Henry Holt.

Spodek, B. (1982). *Handbook of research in early childhood education.* New York: Free Press.

Spodek, B. (1993). Selecting activities in the arts for early childhood education. *Arts Education Policy Review, 94,* 11–19.

Spodek, B., Saracho, O. N., & Lee, R. C. (1984). *Mainstreaming young children.* Belmont, CA: Wadsworth.

Steig, W. (1982). *Doctor Desoto.* New York: Scholastic.

Sternberg, R. J. (1985). *Beyond IQ.* New York: Cambridge University Press.

Sternberg, R. J. (1997). *Successful intelligence.* New York: Plume.

Sternberg, R. L. (Ed) (2002). Models of intelligence: International perspectives. Washington DC: American Psychological Association.

Sternberg, R. J., & Lubart, T. I. (1995). *Defying the crowd: Cultivating creativity in a culture of conformity.* New York: Free Press.

Stinson, K., & Betteridge, D. (1995). *Those green things.* Toronto, Ontario: Annic Press.

Striker, S. (1986). *Please touch—How to stimulate your child's creative development.* New York: Simon & Schuster.

Striker, S. (2003). Coloring books revisited. *School Arts,* March 2003, p. 52.

Sturm, E., & Hoena, B. (Eds.). (2003). *Matisse (Masterpieces: Artists and their works).* Mankato, MN: Capstone Press.

Stutson, C. (1996). *Prairie primer.* New York: Dutton.

Stuve-Bodeen, S. (1998). *We'll paint the octopus red.* Bethesda, MD: Woodbine House.

Suyenaga, R. (1994). *Obon.* Cleveland, OH: Modern Curriculum Press.

Swann, A. C. (2009). An intriguing link between drawing and play with toys. *Childhood Education, 85*(4), 230–236.

Swamp, Chief Jake. (1995). *Giving thanks: A Native American good morning message.* New York: Lee & Los.

Swartz, L. (1992). *A first Passover.* Cleveland, OH: Modern Curriculum Press.

Sweet, M. (2002). *Fiddle-i-fee: A farmyard song for the very young.* New York: Little, Brown & Company.

Szekely, G. (1990). An introduction to art: Children's books. *Childhood Education, 66,* 132–138.

Taback, S. (2000). *Joseph had a little overcoat.* New York: Penguin.

Takeuchi, L. M. 2011. *Families Matter: Designing Media for a Digital Age.* New York: The Joan Ganz Cooney Center at Sesame Workshop. http:// joan ganzcooneycenter.org/Reports-29.html. Accessed on August 27, 2012.

Tang, G. (2003). *Mathterpieces.* New York: Scholastic.

Taunton, M. (1984). Reflective dialogue in the art classroom: Focusing on the art process. *Art Education, 37,* 15–16.

Taunton, M., & Colbert, C. (1954). Artistic and aesthetic development: Considerations for early childhood educators. *Childhood Education, 61,* 55–63.

Tchaikovsky, P., & Zwerger, L. (2002). *Swan Lake.* New York: North-South Books.

The Dana Foundation (2008). "Three Year Study at Seven Major Universities Finds Strong Links Between Arts Education and Cognitive Development." Online at www.dana.org /media/detail.aspx?id=11240. Accessed on 27 April 2012

Thompson, C. M. (September, 1995). "What should I draw today?" Sketchbooks in early childhood. *Young Children,* 6–11.

Thompson, S. C. (2005). *Children as illustrators.* Washington, DC: National Association for the Education of Young Children.

Thouvenelle, S. & Bewick, C. J. (2002). *Completing the computer puzzle: A guide for early childhood educators.* Boston: Pearson.

Topal, C. W. (1983). *Children, clay and sculpture.* Worcester, MA: Davis Publications.

Torrance, E. P. (1963a). *Creativity.* Washington, DC: National Education Association.

Torrance, E. P. (1963b). *Minnesota tests of creative thinking.* Minneapolis: University of Minnesota Bureau of Educational Research.

Torrance, E. P. (1965). *Rewarding creative behavior: Experiments in classroom creativity.* Englewood Cliffs, NJ: Prentice-Hall.

Torrance, E. P. (1966). *Torrance tests of creative thinking: Technical-norms manual.* Lexington, MA: Personnel Press.

Torrance, E. P. (1979). *The search for satori and creativity.* Buffalo, NY: The Creative Education Foundation.

Torrance, E. P., & Myers, R. E. (1970). *Creative learning and teaching.* New York: Harper & Row.

Twardosz, S. (2012). Effects of experience on the brain: The role of neuroscience in early development and education. *Early Education and Development,* 23: 96–119.

Uchida, Y. (1993). *The bracelet.* New York: Philomel.

Uhlin, D. (1979). *Art for exceptional children.* Dubuque, IA: Wm. C. Brown.

Van Allsburg, C. (1981). *Jumanji.* Boston: Houghton Mifflin.

Van Allsburg, C. (1985). *The polar express.* Boston: Houghton Mifflin.

Van Allsburg, C. (1995). *Bad Day at Riverbend.* Boston: Houghton-Mifflin.

VanHoorn, J. L., Nourot, P. M., & Scales, B. (2003). *Play at the corner of the curriculum.* New York: Prentiss Hall.

Venezia, M. (1997). *Henri Matisse.* New York: Scholastic.

Venezia, M. (2002). *Getting to know the world's greatest artists: Georges Seurat.* Scholastic Books.

Ventura, P. (1984). *Great painters.* New York: G. P. Putnam's Sons.

Vernon, A. (2009). *Counseling Children & Adolescents.* (4th ed.) Denver: Love Publishing Company.

Vygotsky, L. S. (1978) *Mind and society: The development of higher psychological process.* Cambridge, MA: Harvard University Press.

Vygotsky, L. S. (1980). *Mind in society.* Cambridge, MA: Harvard University Press.

Vygotsky, L. S. (1986). *Thought and language.* Cambridge, MA: Harvard University Press.

Vygotsky, L. S. (1987). Thinking and speech. In R. W. Rieber & A. S. Carton (Eds.), N. Minick (Trans.), *The collected works of L. S. Vygotsky* (pp. 136–159). New York: Plenum.

Vygotsky, L. S. (1992). *Thought and language* (A. Kozulin, Trans.). Cambridge, Massachusetts: The MIT Press.

Wachowiak, F. (1985). *Emphasis art.* New York: Harper and Row.

Wachowaik, F., & Clement, R. D. (2006*). Emphasis art: A qualitative art program for elementary and middle schools.* Boston: Pearson.

Walker, G., & Minnerly, D. B. (1998). *Molly meets Mona and friends: A magical day at the museum.* Bridgeport, CT: Greene Bark Press.

Wallach, M. A., & Kogan, N. (1965). *Modes of thinking in young children.* New York: Holt, Rinehart & Winston.

Walsh, E. S. (1995). *Mouse paint.* Orlando, FL: Harcourt.

Walsh, E. S. (2000). *Magic mouse.* Orlando, FL: Harcourt.

Wankelmen, W. F., Wigg, P. R., & Wigg, M. K. (1974). *A handbook of arts and crafts.* Dubuque, IA: Wm. C. Brown.

Warhola, J. (2003). *Uncle Andy's.* New York: G. P. Putnam's Sons.

Watson, E. (1996). *Talking to angels.* Orlando, FL: Harcourt.

Weikart, D. L., Rogers, C., Adcock, C., & McClelland, D. (1971). *The cognitively oriented curriculum: A framework for preschool teachers.* Washington, DC: National Association for the Education of Young Children.

Weisgard, L. (1956*). Treasures to see.* New York: Harcourt, Brace & World.

Weitzman, J. P., & Glasser, R. P. (1998). *You can't take a balloon into the Metropolitan Museum.* New York: Dial Books.

Wellington, M. (2000). *Squeaking of art: The mice go to the museum.* New York: Penguin.

Wescott, N. B. (1991). *Peanut butter & jelly: A play rhyme.* New York: Penguin.

Whalen, P., & Phelps, E. (Eds.). (2009). *The human amygdale.* New York: Guilford.

Wiesner. D. (1999). *Sector 7.* New York: Clarion.

Wien, C. A. (2008). Moving into uncertainty: Sculpture with three- to five-year-olds. *Young Children, 63*(4), 78–86.

Wiggins, K. D., & Smith, N. D. (1900). *Froebel's Occupations.* Boston & New York: Houghton, Mifflin & Co.

Wildsmith, B. (1984). *Fishes.* London: Oxford University Press.

Wilkens, D. K. (1996). *Multiple intelligences activities (Grades K-4).* Westminster, CA: Teacher Created Materials, Inc.

Williams, G. (1969). *The rabbits' wedding.* New York: HarperCollins.

Williams, S. (1996). *I went walking.* Orlando, FL: Harcourt.

Williams, V. B. (1990). *"More, more, more," said the baby.* New York: Greenwillow.

Willis, J. (2000). *Susan laughs.* New York: Henry Holt.

Winn, C. M., & Walsh, D. (1996). *Box-head boy.* Minneapolis, MN: Fairview Press.

Winter, J. (1995). *Cowboy Charlie.* San Diego: Harcourt Brace and Company.

Winter, J. (2002). *Frida.* New York: Scholastic.

Wolf, A. D. (1984). *Mommy, it's a Renoir!* Altoona, PA: Parent-Child Press.

Wolf, A. D. (1986). *Child-size masterpieces.* Altoona, PA: Parent-Child Press.

Wolf, A. D. (1988, May/June). Hands on art. *Montessori Today.*

Wolf, A. D. (1990). Art postcards—another aspect of your aesthetics program? *Young Children, 45,* 39–43.

Wolf, J. (1994). Singing with children is a cinch! *Young Children, 49,* 20–25.

Wolf, J. (2000). Sharing songs with children. *Young Children, 55,* 28–30.

Wolfe, J. (2000). *Learning of the Past: Historical Voices in Early Childhood Education.* Alberta: Piney Branch Press.

Wolff, R. J. (1968). *Feeling blue.* New York: Charles Scribner's Sons.

Wood, A., & Wood, D. (1984). *The napping house.* Orlando, FL: Harcourt.

Wood, D. (1996). *Northwoods cradle song from a Menominee lullaby.* New York: Simon & Schuster.

Wright, C., & Wright, S. (1986). A conceptual framework for examining the family's influence on creativity. *Family Perspective, 20,* 127–136.

Wright, J. L., & Shade, D. D. (Eds.). (1993). *Young children: Active learners in a technological age.* Washington, DC: National Association for the Education of Young Children.

Wright, S. (2003). *The arts, young children, and learning.* Boston: Allyn & Bacon.

Wright, S. K. (1994). Assessment in the arts: Is it appropriate in the early childhood years? *Studies in Art Education, 36,* 28–43.

Wright, S. K. (1997). Learning how to learn: The arts as core in an emergent curriculum. *Childhood Education, 73,* 361–365.

Wyse, L. (1998). *How to take your grandmother to the museum.* New York: Workman.

Yenawine, P. (1991). *Lines.* New York: Random House.

Yenawine, P. (1991). *Stories; colors; lines; shapes.* New York: Delacorte.

Yenawine, P. (2003). Jump starting visual literacy: Thoughts on image selection. *Art Education, 56,* 6–11.

Yolen, J. (1987). *Owl moon.* New York: Penguin.

Young, J. (1999). *The art of science.* Cambridge, MA: Candlewick Press.

Zadrzynska, E. (1990). *The girl with a watering can.* New York: Chameleon Books.

Zelinsky, P. O. (1997). *Rapunzel.* New York: Dutton.

Zero to Eight: Children's media use in America. (2011). *A common sense media research study.* Available at http://www.commonsensemedia.org /research/zero-eight-childrens-media-use-america/ Accessed on April 17, 2012.

Index